Keith Martin's Guide to
CAR COLLECTING

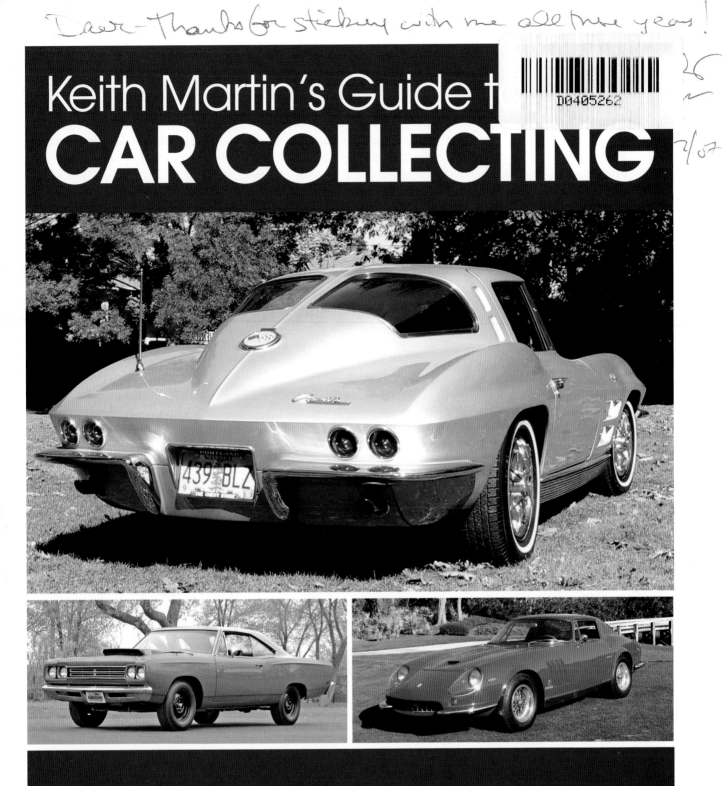

Prepared by the experts at

Sports Car Market

MOTORBOOKS

Thanks

I would like to dedicate this book to my uncle, Virgil McDowell, who, during his long and productive life, was a constant source of encouragement to me, to my first and always best dance teacher, Judy Massee at Reed College, for teaching me that no dream was too big, to my editor at the New York Times, Jim Cobb, who offered me my first insight into the structural mechanics essential to informative writing, and to my daughter Alexandra, for being so full of joy and having such a willingness to embrace a future filled with challenges and excitement.—*Keith Martin*

This edition published in 2006 by Motorbooks, an imprint of MBI Publishing Company, Galtier Plaza, Suite 200, 380 Jackson Street, St. Paul, MN 55101-3885 USA

MBI Publishing Company titles are also available at discounts in bulk quantity for industrial or sales-promotional use. For details write to Special Sales Manager at MBI Publishing Company, Galtier Plaza, Suite 200, 380 Jackson Street, St. Paul, MN 55101-3885 USA

ISBN-13: 978-0-7603-2895-8
ISBN-10: 0-7603-2895-1

Designed by Kirsten Onoday

Printed in China

About the Author

Keith Martin has been involved with the collector car hobby for more than thirty years. As a writer, publisher, television commentator, and enthusiast, he is constantly on the go, meeting collectors and getting involved in their activities throughout the world.

In addition to being the founder and publisher of the monthly Sports Car Market magazine, Martin's columns on collecting and reviews of exotic cars, including the Ford GT and the Bentley Continental GT, have appeared in the New York Times. He also has regular columns on the collector car market in AutoWeek and Automobile.

His Keith Martin on Collecting series, published by Motorbooks International, includes books on Ferrari, Jaguar, Alfa Romeo and Porsche, with another dozen books planned.

The website for his magazine, www.sportscarmarket.com, contains the world's largest and most informative database of collectible cars, with more than 40,000 cars listed with serial numbers, photos, and descriptive and valuation details.

In an effort to foster connoisseurship in the collector car world, Martin has developed a rating system by which his team has rated over 2,000 collectible cars and assigned them a "Martin Rating" on a 100-point scale. He is a commentator on the Speed Channel, has hosted numerous specials on collector cars, and has been co-host of the live coverage of the Barrett-Jackson Scottsdale auction for the past ten years. His new show "What's My Car Worth" can be seen on the Discovery HD Channel.

He is the Chairman of the Meguiar's Collector Car Person of the Year Award Committee, becoming only the second chair in the history of the award. He has also been named to the Board of Trustees of the LeMay Museum and the Hagerty-founded Collectors Foundation.

Martin brings an eclectic background to his passion for cars. His academic background includes the study of Intellectual History at Reed College, in Portland, Oregon, and study as a Dance Major, emphasis in Modern Dance, at the Juilliard School in New York City. He founded the first professional ballet company in Oregon—Ballet Oregon—was its director for over a decade, was awarded an Oregon Art's Commission Individual Artist's Fellowship for new choreography, and was director of dance for the Portland Opera.

Martin and his 15-year-old daughter, Alexandra, live in Portland, Oregon.♦

Table of Contents

INTRODUCTION

Keith Martin 7

What is Car Collecting? 8

Collecting Strategies 10

BY THE NUMBERS

Introduction.. 14

2006

Million-Dollar Sales in 2006 15

Top 1,000 Sales in 2006 by Price 31

Top 1,000 Sales in 2006 by Marque 47

Top 5 Sales in 2005 by Marque 63

2006 Million-Dollar Muscle Cars 74

2006 Auction Company Comparison......... 76

History

All-Time Top 10 Sales 80

Sales Results by Vehicle Era 82

BEST BETS & WORST

Introduction 92

General

Why Buy Collector Cars? 93

Four Great Collector Cars Under $25,000 ... 94

Nine Bargain Exotics 97

The Best Roads, The Best Events 102

Buying Your First Collector Car 108

Italian

Eight Italian Sports Cars for the
First-Time Collector 110

Favorite Ferraris Under $100k 114

Five Best Ferraris Over $1,000,000 117

Ferrari Supercars Through the Ages 120

12-Cylinder Ferraris for the First-Timer 123

Ferrari Movers and Losers 126

Ferraris You're Guaranteed
To Lose Money On 128

New Faces, New Tastes 130

British

Six Solid Roadsters 132

Which XK to Buy? 135

German

Affordability and Collectibility Meet Here ... 137

Five Porsches to Avoid at Any Cost 139

Leading the Porsche Pack 141

American

Best Bets in Cats and Snakes 143

Buying Your First Collectible Muscle Car ... 146

Nine Muscle Car Sleepers 148

BUYING SMART

Introduction 156

What It's Worth

Gee, What Do YOU Think It's Worth? 157

When There's $60,000 Between #1 and #2 ... 159

Why Your Healey 3000 Isn't Worth $143,000 161

Becoming a Muscle Car Detective 163

What to Look For

Buying Online 165

Deferred Maintenance, Deal Killers,
and Diminishing Returns 167

Everything Works, Just Don't Drive It 169

Buying Techniques That Work 170

Choosing Performance Over Originality 173

Five "Must-Checks" When Buying
a Big Healey 175

I'll Trade You My 'Cuda For
Your Four-Cam 177

Finances

Two Words: Agreed Value 179

Exotic Car Leasing 180

I Don't Want It Any More 182

What To Do When It's Time to Pay 184

Automobile Financing 101 185

Will You Take $2,500 for
Your Smashed MG? 186

RESTORATION TIPS

Introduction 192

Restoration to the Highest Level 193

Restoration: Street, Show, or Race? 196

Restoring Your High School Sweetheart 198

The Ins and Outs of Odometer Replacement 200

Leaning Into the Punch of Deferred
Maintenance 202

My 6-Cylinder FrankenPorsche 205

Restoration Escalation 207

Sending the Prince of Darkness
on His Way 209

SELLING

Introduction 216

Is It Legal to Bid on Your Own Car? 217

Tax Consequences of Selling Your Car 219

When the High Bidder Won't Pay Up 221

RESOURCES

Introduction 228

Clubs 229

Restoration Shops 238

Automobilia Websites 243

Vintage Racing Websites 245

Model Car Websites 246

Glossary 250

PRICE GUIDES & RATINGS

Introduction 258

Price Guide 259

Martin Rating: How Does Your Car Rate? 293

Martin Rating: 100 Cars Under $50k 299

Acknowledgments

Contributors

The Sports Car Market magazine gang is a close-knit, hard-working group of enthusiasts. This book is the result of all of them working together for long hours, day and night, to share their insights on collecting with you.

Gary Anderson

Gary Anderson is the co-founder of the Austin-Healey Concours Registry, which created restoration standards and judging guidelines now in use around the world. He is the co-author of the best-selling book *Austin-Healey 100/100-6/3000*. He is the editor and publisher of MC2, the magazine for classic and new Minis, and has recently published the book, *Motoring—Getting the Maximum from Your New MINI*. His "English Patient" column appears monthly in SCM.

Miles C. Collier

Miles Collier is a practicing artist, investor, philanthropist, and noted authority on vintage automobiles. Collier worked for his family's Collier Enterprises until retirement in 1995. He then attended the New York Studio School of Drawing, Painting, and Sculpture, where he studied for three years with the noted Graham Nickson. Collier currently serves as Chairman of the Board of Trustees of Eckerd College.

Colin Comer

Colin Comer estimates he had owned over fifty cars by the age of 20. A career in the automotive world was inevitable, and Comer founded his own business, working out of his garage after hours restoring and selling collector cars. Today, Colin's Classic Automobiles enjoys a loyal following and is regarded as one of the premier classic car dealerships in the nation. His column "Domestic Affairs" appears monthly in SCM.

John Draneas

John Draneas is a Portland, Oregon, attorney who has practiced primarily in the tax and business area since 1977. Draneas is an active SCCA racer, organizes the Sunriver Exotic Car show, served for two years as President of the Oregon Region of the Porsche Club of America, and Chaired PCA's 2006 Parade held in Portland. He drives a 1980 Porsche 911 Targa every day and also owns a 1959 Porsche 356A Coupe, a 1957 Alfa Giulietta Spider, a 1983 Ferrari 308 GTSi, and a Lotus Elise.

David Kinney

David Kinney is an Accredited Senior Appraiser in the American Society of Appraisers, and currently serves as the Personal Property representative on its Board of Governors. Since 1990, David has owned USAppraisal in Great Falls, Virginia, a dedicated automotive-only appraisal firm. Kinney regularly attends nearly every auction on the planet, and his incisive Market Reports have appeared monthly in SCM for several years.

Donald Osborne

Donald Osborne is a native New Yorker, and has contributed to SCM since 1993. Osborne's operatic career as a baritone culminated with his solo debut at the Metropolitan Opera. He is a marketing specialist, and recently started Automotive Valuation Services as a certified auto appraiser. His particular automotive interest lies in Italian cars, but anything strange or bizarre with almost no actual resale value has a way of finding its way into his garage.

Jim Schrager

Jim Schrager writes for SCM as well as the Porsche 356 Registry, and is author of one of the best selling book, *Buying, Driving, and Enjoying the Porsche 356*. In his spare time, he teaches business strategy at the University of Chicago Graduate School of Business. Schrager is married with two sons and works hard to keep his fleet of about 15 vintage Porsches on the road. His monthly column, "Porsche Gesprach," has appeared in SCM for the last decade.

Michael Sheehan

Mike Sheehan has been SCM's featured columnist for all things Ferrari since 1998. He's written hundreds of articles, not only for Sports Car Market, but for Cavallino, the Ferrari Market Letter, and numerous other Ferrari publications. Sheehan bought his first Ferrari, a 250 PF coupe, for $2,000 in 1972. He has raced extensively in several professional series and is currently a Ferrari broker at his business, www.Ferraris-online.com. He is the father of twins Mick and Colleen.

The SCM Team

Editorial: Steve Ahlgrim, John Apen, Carl Bomstead, Diane Brandon, B. Mitchell Carlson, Jennifer Davis, Kathy Donohue, Paul Duchene, Martin Emmison, Dan Grunwald, Kristen Hall-Geisler, Richard Hudson-Evans, Stefan Lombard, John Lucas, Raymond Milo, Norm Mort, Bill Neill, Kirsten Onoday, Jim Pickering, Steve Serio, Joe Severns, David Slama, Thor Thorson

Administration: Cathy Griffis, Nikki Nalum, Rob Sass, Bill Woodard

Internet: Matt Webb, Bryan Wolfe

Sales: Gary Goodrich, Valarie Huston, Cindy Meitle, Ed Prisco◆

Introduction

I was driving home last week and out of the corner of my eye, saw a glint of chrome from deep in an open garage.

I slowed, then stopped. With a little squinting, I determined I was looking at the back of a 1963 Corvette split-window coupe. I couldn't help myself as I dug out a piece of paper, wrote, "If you ever want to sell your Corvette, please call me," and left it at the front door.

Keith Martin's Guide to Car Collecting is dedicated to all of us who are afflicted with an incurable and insatiable passion for cars. If we could, we'd eat our breakfast cereal out of a headlight bucket, use camshafts as chopsticks at lunch, and have dinner served on an engine block. Our idea of a perfect day is one spent at a swap meet, kicking tires and filling a tote wagon with useless bits that will stay in our garage until we sell them at the next swap meet. The very best car in the world is the one we are about to buy, and there is no pain worse than saying goodbye to one that you own.

Photo: John Vincent

With this book, we are creating a one-stop resource directory for the 21st century collector. Through the relentless compilation of data in the Sports Car Market magazine database, we can bring you up-to-date auction results from around the world. By scouring our database, we have come up with the top 1,000 sales of 2006. You'll also find the top sellers by marque, as well as all the cars that sold for over $1,000,000.

You'll get expert advice from leaders in the field, ranging from authority Miles Collier offering a strategy for smart collecting to legal specialist John Draneas explaining what to do if the high bidder at an auction won't pay up.

In the end, reading this book should be like sitting down with a bunch of fellow gearheads, with everyone getting to tell their favorite story. Some will be about muscle cars, others about sports cars. Some will brag about classics like Duesenbergs, others about modern exotics like Lamborghinis.

Just as you would in a clubhouse, you'll find opinions you think are brilliant, and others that you vehemently disagree with. Our goal is that you'll find some new nugget of information on every page of *Keith Martin's Guide to Car Collecting*.

Cars have been good to me, and brought me over forty years of pleasure (and some pain as well). Most importantly, they've been the reason I've met literally thousands of fellow enthusiasts, all of whom have had something to teach me.

With this book, I'm hoping to give back to the car community some of that accumulated wisdom, and offer you new tools that will help you get even more enjoyment out of your own collectible cars in the year ahead.

Keith Martin
Portland, Oregon

What Is Car Collecting?

It's important to understand the difference between a collection of cars and an accumulation of cars

by Donald Osborne

1935 Duesenberg SJ

When many people think of the term "car collecting," they might conjure up an image of celebrities such as Jay Leno, Jerry Seinfeld, Ralph Lauren, or Reggie Jackson. Or perhaps they think of the palatial garages of wealthy owners, where dozens of super-valuable cars—each one more perfect than the next—have been subjected to restorations costing hundreds of thousands, if not millions, of dollars.

While that is certainly a part of the car collecting scene, it is of course far from the mainstream. Thousands of people across the country and indeed around the world are a part of the car collecting hobby in much more modest ways, proof that it's not necessary to own a fleet of cars to be "a collector." You can regard yourself as a collector even if you only have one collectible car, and even if that car doesn't happen to be running at the time. What all car collectors have in common is a passion for the automobiles that interest them and a desire to own, use, and enjoy those cars, and to share that deep feeling with other like-minded souls.

But what is collecting all about? Research, research, and more research. Asking and answering questions is how it begins:

- What is it?
- When was it made?
- How many were made?
- What is the correct equipment for the year and model?
- How much is it worth?
- What are the clubs or groups for my type of car?

Research is a key part of collecting. Finding out all the details about the car in which you have an interest is for some even more of a pleasure than the actual purchase or use of the car.

Whether it consists of a single car, a few, or a hundred, a collection should have a reason for being. Jorge Luis Borges, an Argentine writer, poet, philosopher, and rare book collector, expressed it well, writing *"I believe that collecting books, but, for that matter, collecting anything, begins as an act of love. We collect what we love, but more precisely we collect what we believe represents us. As we collect, we make a statement about ourselves."*

This is why it's important to understand what differentiates a "collection" of cars from an "accumulation" of cars, which could just as easily be found in a dealer's showroom or auction tent. Collections can be made up of cars from a single marque, of a specific body style, from a particular country. They can be comprised of cars that competed with each other when new, of cars of distinctive design, of cars that made engineering breakthroughs, of cars that were complete market failures, or perhaps of cars made the year the collector was born.

Once you've decided on the car or cars of your dreams, done the research to find out more about it, and met and chatted with the folks who already own one, you can begin the process of acquiring the object of your affection. It doesn't matter if you find your car at a leading international auction, an online auction web site, in the small ads in your local paper, or sitting in a driveway around the corner with a sign in the window. What is important is that you buy what you love and what you know about.

For some collectors, the hunt for a car is as thrilling as owning it—perhaps it's looking for the exact make, model, and color you owned when you were 16. Or the car your father or grandfather used for your first driving lesson. Or maybe it's the car the coolest guy or the prettiest girl drove when you were in high school. It could be the last missing piece to complete a list of cars you made 20 years ago. Finding the right car can be the work of a lifetime.

As mentioned earlier, a collection doesn't have to be of many cars. There are plenty of people who are best described as "serial" collectors. Those are people who might make a "wish list" of the cars they want to own eventually and who work their way through that list one car at a time, buying and enjoying a car for a few years then selling it to buy the next. This is also a good way to proceed if you're new to the hobby. Start with a car you know a lot about, which has a good availability of repair and replacement parts, is easily maintained either by yourself or by a good local mechanic, has a strong and active club for support, and of course which fits your budget comfortably. Every one of the big collectors started small. Though it might be tempting to buy a bunch of "restorable" cars to jumpstart a collection, nothing will be more frustrating than to look out at a beautiful day imagining what it would be like to drive an old car while your pile of old cars remains just that, rusting heap of parts in your garage or storage room.

Even if you do want to own every Porsche ever made, but only have a one-car garage and a limited budget, there's another part of car collecting that can help you fulfill your dream. There's no reason why you can't find a single affordable example, and instead of filling a warehouse with the rest, collect scale models instead. It can be just as challenging to find rare and unusual miniatures of the cars you love. But in doing so, you'll be able to assemble a collection that can be housed on shelves in your den or on the walls of your single garage for a fraction of what it would cost to own even two of the real thing.

Another final important part of car collecting is participating in shows, cruise-ins, tours, rallies, and vintage racing. Using your old car rather than locking it away in a garage has become more important than ever to collectors. It also helps to drive the market and determines why many people buy the cars they do. It's useful once again to turn to the words of J.L. Borges to sum it all up: *"Finally, I realize that my collection, and really all collections, are time machines. The books we have are the surest way to travel across time, and to give us a direct image of what the past looked like."*

Every time we sit in our old cars, we share a bit of the lives they've already led and give them another chapter for their future.◆

Collecting Strategies

Intelligence coupled with emotion creates a collection that evokes understanding, appreciation, and delight in others

by Miles Collier

Collier's McLaren

How is it that of two collectors with equal resources and dedication, one becomes a major figure and the other does not? For any given level of resources (income, time, and contacts), a collector is capable of rising to the level that his senses and understanding permit. Sensibility and expertise make the difference between connoisseurship and mere accumulation. The uncanny ability to distinguish the very good from the good, the fine from the ordinary, is a trait of all great collectors.

Beyond even sensibility and taste, good collecting requires establishing criteria that focus the collection and give it intelligible structure. Simultaneously, the collection must be about passion, with a true love for—and understanding of—the object. Similar to much successful creativity elsewhere, the formal, syntactical structure of the collection needs to be counterbalanced by the sheer emotionality of the collector's passion. It is the emotion of the collector that causes him to incorporate the idiosyncratic cars that no expert would dare suggest. It is this willingness to consciously break the formal criteria that gives the collection its savor. Intelligence coupled with emotion is the necessary ingredient required to create a collection that evokes understanding, appreciation, and delight in others. If we are to aspire to significant collections, we must harness our "animal spirits" with understanding and sensibility for the object, and we must have knowledge of basic collecting strategies.

Almost all collections are built with a mixture of strategies, and provided the mix is used consciously, the results can be gratifying. Let us now review the characteristics and properties of six common approaches to collecting.

Nostalgic Collecting Strategy

One common strategy almost universally present in collections is the nostalgic/opportunistic strategy. Despite the title, it is essentially a non-strategy. The nostalgic collecting approach of pure emotionality probably represents the normal starting point for most collectors. It is an "extensive" strategy, being unbounded by any constraint, and usually is without focus. As one collector said, "You kind of just buy."

The nostalgic/opportunist strategy is founded in the hobbyist point of view and takes its direction from areas of deep subjectivity, summed up by the phrase: "I don't know much about cars, but I know what I like." Such collections, while scratching an emotional itch, tend to be excessively repetitive, unfocused, or of very uneven quality. They tend to develop into a hodgepodge of objects that, upon the subsequent development of the collector's taste and experience, require substantial if not total revision. The ultimate size and quality of collections built this way is based on happenstance and the product of the collector's initial obsession. Such collections, being directionless, are limited only by the collector's ambition, appetite, and the capacity to support his activity.

The collector's first great step forward in collecting is the incorporation of cars not directly related to his personal experience. The result of that developmental step is commonly a conversion to a vertical strategy.

Vertical Collecting Strategy

One element of automobile collecting we often take for granted is the extreme complexity of the subject matter, the very complexity that makes the collectible car such a rich and satisfying object. Unfortunately, this complexity also means that the nascent collector must master a great deal of information relating to automotive technology, maintenance, history, original model configuration, subtle variations in specification, etc. that strongly affect value.

As often as not, as the collector's experience grows, the nostalgic/opportunistic strategy, given time to mature, develops a theme either as a primary focus or as a secondary or subsidiary focus by turning from an extensive to an intensive (focused and bounded) strategy. The most logical and simple vertical theme involves a concentration on one marque. Such an approach cuts through time along the production continuum of one maker. Organizing the collection about the chronological sequence of models, vertical strategies are often concerned with "completeness" and the filling out of sets.

Advantages:
• Reduces the collectible universe to a manageable size.
• The collector can master one marque in great detail relatively easily.
• Allows a focus on individual quality, the thing that distinguishes one example of a make/model from another.
• Good strategy for someone who wants to collect definitive examples, therefore good for sharpening the eye and developing connoisseurship skills.
• Easier to know "where the bodies are buried," to get deal flow, and be able to rate the quality of that flow.
• Easier to master the maintenance and restoration technology and sources for research material.

Disadvantages:
• The market for other makes can move away in terms of real dollars, creating a lost opportunity never to be recaptured.
• The marque's collecting scope may be limited with few models and a short history.
• Collection can become self-limiting or hermetic, and the collector parochial in his views.
• After years of collecting, the collector may find his real interest lies elsewhere.

Horizontal Collecting Strategy

Another collecting alternative that can be extensive or intensive in scope is an approach based on collecting within a horizontal slice of time. By limiting the area requiring mastery to a band of time, the collector once more can focus his research to a manageable body of knowledge. For example, he might choose to collect American convertibles of the late 1950s. In so doing, he creates collecting criteria that cut across a series of marques, but is restricted by upper and lower temporal boundaries as well as specific car types.

Advantages

The horizontal strategy enjoys many of the same advantages as the vertical strategy. In addition, however, it opens collectors to:
• Seeing market value changes across a broader spectrum of cars. Seeing the bigger picture reduces the danger of being left out in the cold by rapid market shifts.
• Serendipity. The collector may find he is more interested in cars of type "x" than type "y."

Disadvantages:
Horizontal strategies make it more difficult to connect

to sources, as typically more than one make of automobile is involved. As cars are normally studied, supported, and even sourced by marque, the research, acquisition, and conservation challenges increase. Consequently, to move from Ferrari to Aston Martin is a harder task than shifting from Ferrari road cars to Ferrari Grand Prix cars.

Implied Horizontal Strategy:

As a collection grows and encompasses more than one make, multiple vertical themes may emerge. The accretion of multiple vertical themes can begin to place a number of cars within the same time period. At some point, sufficient contemporaneous cars exist to make the further pursuit of one or more horizontal strategies a practical reality.

Understanding one marque makes cross-correlating to another make via their common world automotive history much easier. This process is analogous to learning a new language. The more languages you already speak, the easier it is to learn the next due to commonalities. A cross-correlating horizontal strategy may have less validity when two marques are wholly unrelated, i.e. Lotus and Duesenberg, as distinct from Duesenberg and Isotta-Fraschini, or more naturally yet, Duesenberg and Packard.

Thematic Collecting Strategy

Thematic approaches, being intensive in nature, are related to vertical strategies, but have a more random pattern to the connections. Thematic collections are not confined to one make or even a few makes or time slices. Consider the high performance sports car as a theme. Such a collection might start at the turn of the century and terminate with, say, the McLaren F1.

Execution of such a theme becomes a function of judgment and taste, open to debate, argument and differences of opinion. For example, is the 540K Mercedes a required element on the continuum of high performance sports cars? Comparing experts' thoughts on the proper constituents of this sports car-themed collection would be instructive, especially if the judgments came from driving experience in addition to research.

Indeed, the Collier Museum, in Naples, FL, exhibits such a theme in the sports cars of Briggs Cunningham. It is one of our four themed collections in the museum. Obviously the particular selection of cars is open to personal idiosyncrasies (the emotional/expressive element referred to earlier). For example, not all would agree with the selection of the Lotus Elite as a worthy addition to the sports car collection. In this type of collecting, the issue turns on finding the "right" object, as identified by the particular collector through thorough research. In the history of the sports car example, the identity of the individual automo-bile, allowing for condition, would be less critical to the quality of the collection than the absolutely right make and model. By contrast, the individual car *is* critical to a racing-based theme, where the history of each individual car chosen becomes significant (e.g. Jorgensen Eagle Indy car).

With the thematic strategy, the requirement for broader expertise becomes more important. This collecting approach requires a large investment in research and analysis. Fortunately, such research elements are logically connected by development of the theme in question. A thematic strategy will push every collector into unknown areas outside his comfort zone, where his intellect must serve as a guide to his emotion. The focus of such a strategy lies in finding the appropriate make, model, and example to do justice to the theme. If the car in question is very rare, such a requirement makes the search an exercise in patience and focus, to say nothing of pocketbook capacity. Consider for example, a collection based on the history of the Grand Prix car, which sooner or later would require an example of a pre-war Mercedes or Auto-Union.

Relational Collecting Strategy

At first this strategy looks like the nostalgic/opportunistic strategy. Similar to that strategy, it is extensive, being neither bounded nor otherwise thematically constrained. However, the relationship between objects is no longer inchoate, arising out of the collector's psychic stew, but explicit and carefully conceived.

Consider the Ford Model T–Rolls-Royce dyad.

FORD	ROLLS-ROYCE
1908–27	1907–26
Mass/quality	Class/quality
12.8 million	7,900
Mass production	Artisanal
Completely integrated manufacturing	Integrated manufacturing
Industry Standard/Paradigm	Industry Standard/Paradigm
Internationally built for a world market	Internationally built for a world market
Declining demand due to obsolescence.	Failure to see the one-model business strategy was no longer working

What car might we add to create a triad? Let's consider the McLaren F1:
- One-model strategy
- About 100 built (class/quality)
- Artisanal but cutting edge technology

- Non-integrated manufacturing
- Industry standard/paradigm
- U.K.-built for a world market
- Not obsolete—production stopped due to declining demand

The connectivity among these cars could be through history, technology, significance, and so on. The linkages may not be obvious to the casual observer unless explained, but the key is that the linkages are made through similarities and not differences. In the Ford–Rolls example above, the Model T becomes a "surprise" object, hardly the thing that would be suggested by a slew of experts for a "Calendar Collection" of great classic automobiles. The relational approach represents a highly intellectualized step in collecting. In relational collecting, to a great extent, the intellect controls the direction in which the collector's emotions run.

The process of connecting emotionally appealing cars is akin to creating a crossword puzzle. The appropriate car linking several others must be found by inference and through relationships to other cars in the collection. It should be apparent that the successful implementation of relational collecting requires an almost encyclopedic knowledge of automotive history and collectible cars.

Because of the cross connections in relational collecting, the problem of filling out a series, or completing a theme, never applies. Right from the beginning, the collection is always "complete." A collection carefully constructed in this way, incorporating both the collector's love of the objects and his consummate research to create a web of connections, would be intensely exciting for connoisseur and casual enthusiast alike.

Before we conclude, we should consider one important dichotomy among car collectors. This particular trait, whether the collector is contemplative or experiential in his collecting nature, determines many characteristics of his collection.

The experiential collector's primary interaction with his collection is through his kinesthetic senses. He drives his cars, and indeed, has little use or regard for cars he cannot use. This is not to say that he doesn't appreciate his car's technology, beauty, and historic importance; indeed he does. But to this collector, use is paramount.

The contemplative collector, by contrast, interacts with his collection through his intellect. As such, while this collector may enjoy driving his cars, operation is not the key requirement to his collecting. Indeed, some of his cars may not even run. This great and fundamental divide has important implications.

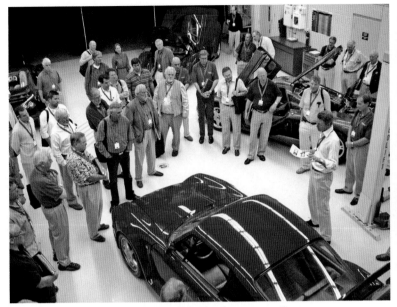
Few modern supercars hold real sway over collectors

The need to drive every car limits the size of the experiential collection. In addition, the variety of cars, their condition, and practicality all need to be limited if the operating constraint is to be fulfilled. For example, highly fragile or delicate cars, whether due to condition or design, are inappropriate and not usually collected. More prone to seeing his collection, not only as a repository of historic objects, but also as an assemblage of sporting or competition equipment, the experiential collector's maintenance and service costs will tend to be much higher per vehicle than the contemplative collector's.

Where a user's collection is limited in size, a contemplative collection is unbounded by practical considerations, and often features "museum type" or other impractical vehicles. Contemplative collectors are much more focused on filling out sets, or collecting according to some idea. In fact, contemplative collectors are probably closer in their sensibilities to collectors in other antiquarian fields.

Conclusion

Human nature being what it is, the strategies discussed above probably have a greater chance of guiding a collection after it has been begun. A strategic collecting plan represents a way to bring structure, editing, and refinement to a group of objects perhaps assembled with a lack of sufficient temperance, but an admirable amount of zeal. The sooner we as collectors can bring focus to our collections, the more we can increase our engagement with these objects in an appropriate way, and the better we can become at preserving our automotive heritage.◆

By The Numbers

Lists tell a story all their own. Without flowery prose or exaggerating adjectives, lists just roll out numbers, one after the next.

And in this case, it is our list of 1,000 Top Sales that heads the list. That's followed by a host of other lists as we examine the results in the Sports Car Market database from a variety of perspectives.

This section is a kind of "Do-it-Yourself" analysis of the market. Look at all the numbers, think about what types of cars are selling for what kinds of dollars, and put together your own picture of what's happening in the collector car market today.—*Keith Martin*

2006 Million-Dollar Sales from the SCM Database

These 45 examples set the standard for rarity, perfection, and extravagance in 2006. Our analysts were there, and, on the pages that follow, we tell you exactly why, in detail, each car made the price it did. *(Sales recorded between 1/1/2006 and 9/30/2006. Complete list of million-dollar sales on page 31.)*

Rank	Year	Car	Sold Price	Lot #	Auction Co.	Location	Date
1	1958	FERRARI 412 S SPORTS RACER	$5,610,000	465	RM	Monterey, CA	8/18/06
2	1953	GM FUTURLINER PARADE OF PROGRESS BUS	$4,320,000	1307	Barrett-Jackson	Scottsdale, AZ	1/14/06
3	1938	TALBOT-LAGO T150C SS TEARDROP COUPE	$3,905,000	29	Gooding & Co.	Palm Beach, FL	1/22/06
4	1928	MERCEDES-BENZ 26/120/180 TYPE S	$3,645,000	52	Christie's	Monterey, CA	8/17/06
5	1934	PACKARD TWELVE RUNABOUT SPEEDSTER	$3,190,000	167	RM	Phoenix, AZ	1/20/06
6	1954	PONTIAC BONNEVILLE SPECIAL	$3,024,000	1304	Barrett-Jackson	Scottsdale, AZ	1/14/06
7	1960	FERRARI 250 GT SWB COMPETITION ALLOY	$2,750,000	142	RM	Amelia Island, FL	3/11/06
8	1927	BUGATTI TYPE 35C GRAND PRIX	$2,585,000	44	Gooding & Co.	Pebble Beach, CA	8/20/06
9	1957	FERRARI 500 TRC SPIDER	$2,282,500	472	RM	Monterey, CA	8/18/06
10	1970	PLYMOUTH HEMI 'CUDA CONVERTIBLE	$2,160,000	1309	Barrett-Jackson	Scottsdale, AZ	1/14/06
11	1938	TALBOT-LAGO T23 TEARDROP COUPE	$2,145,000	155	RM	Amelia Island, FL	3/11/06
12	1956	JAGUAR XKD-TYPE RACER	$2,097,000	521	Bonhams & Butterfields	Carmel, CA	8/18/06
13	1965	ASTON MARTIN DB5 JAMES BOND COUPE	$2,090,000	155	RM	Phoenix, AZ	1/20/06
14	1955	MASERATI 300S RACER	$1,925,000	171	RM	Phoenix, AZ	1/20/06
15	1929	BENTLEY SPEED SIX DUAL COWL TOURER	$1,815,000	454	RM	Monterey, CA	8/18/06
16	1962	SHELBY COBRA 289 RACER	$1,815,000	175	RM	Phoenix, AZ	1/20/06
17	1947	BENTLEY MK VI CONVERTIBLE	$1,728,000	723	Barrett-Jackson	Palm Beach, FL	3/29/06
18	1938	DELAHAYE 135MS COUPE	$1,712,000	527	Bonhams & Butterfields	Carmel, CA	8/18/06
19	1994	MCLAREN F1 COUPE	$1,705,000	471	RM	Monterey, CA	8/18/06
20	1930	DUESENBERG MODEL J SPORT BERLINE	$1,650,000	477	RM	Monterey, CA	8/18/06
21	1967	FERRARI 212 E MONTAGNA RACER	$1,650,000	164	RM	Phoenix, AZ	1/20/06
22	1935	MERCEDES-BENZ 500/540K CABRIOLET	$1,650,000	60	Worldwide Group	Seabrook, TX	5/6/06
23	1963	SHELBY COBRA 289 LE MANS RACER	$1,650,000	164	RM	Amelia Island, FL	3/11/06
24	1952	JAGUAR XKC-TYPE	$1,649,638	86	Christie's	Paris, FR	2/11/06
25	1962	SHELBY COBRA 289 DRAGONSNAKE RACER	$1,601,250	S511	Mecum	Belvidere, IL	5/25/06
26	1958	FERRARI 250 GT TDF	$1,540,000	68	Gooding & Co.	Pebble Beach, CA	8/20/06
27	1953	JAGUAR XKC-TYPE	$1,512,500	150	RM	Phoenix, AZ	1/20/06
28	1931	BENTLEY 8-LITER SPORTSMAN	$1,485,000	153	RM	Amelia Island, FL	3/11/06
29	1938	BUGATTI TYPE 57C ARAVIS DROPHEAD COUPE	$1,375,000	64	Gooding & Co.	Pebble Beach, CA	8/20/06
30	1955	LINCOLN INDIANAPOLIS BOANO COUPE	$1,375,000	57	Gooding & Co.	Pebble Beach, CA	8/20/06
31	1952	FERRARI 225 SPORT SPYDER	$1,280,000	18	Christie's	Monterey, CA	8/17/06
32	1937	BENTLEY 4 1/4-LITER COUPE	$1,265,000	479	RM	Monterey, CA	8/18/06
33	1970	CHEVROLET CHEVELLE SS LS6 CONVERTIBLE	$1,242,000	1287	Barrett-Jackson	Scottsdale, AZ	1/14/06
34	1964	SHELBY COBRA 289 COMPETITION RACER	$1,237,500	159	RM	Monterey, CA	8/18/06
35	1941	CHRYSLER THUNDERBOLT RETRACTABLE HDTOP	$1,210,000	146	RM	Phoenix, AZ	1/20/06
36	1934	DUESENBERG MODEL J RIVIERA PHAETON	$1,210,000	60	Gooding & Co.	Pebble Beach, CA	8/20/06
37	1952	CHRYSLER D'ELEGANCE COUPE	$1,188,000	1306	Barrett-Jackson	Scottsdale, AZ	1/14/06
38	1955	FERRARI 750 MONZA SPIDER	$1,107,000	525	Bonhams & Butterfields	Carmel, CA	8/18/06
39	1939	DELAHAYE 135MS GRAND SPORT CABRIOLET	$1,100,000	52	Gooding & Co.	Pebble Beach, CA	8/20/06
40	1953	CHEVROLET CORVETTE ROADSTER	$1,080,000	1311	Barrett-Jackson	Scottsdale, AZ	1/14/06
41	2004	MASERATI MC12 COUPE	$1,072,500	460	RM	Monterey, CA	8/18/06
42	1911	MERCEDES 37/90HP SKIFF	$1,050,000	63	Worldwide Group	Seabrook, TX	5/6/06
43	1938	BUGATTI TYPE 57C ARAVIS DROPHEAD COUPE	$1,045,000	143	RM	Phoenix, AZ	1/20/06
44	1971	PLYMOUTH HEMI 'CUDA 2-DOOR HARD TOP	$1,045,000	50	Worldwide Group	Seabrook, TX	5/6/06
45	1930	DUESENBERG J DUAL COWL PHAETON	$1,001,000	135	RM	Phoenix, AZ	1/20/06

1 1958 FERRARI 412S SPORTS RACER

Sold at $5,610,000—RM, Monterey, CA, 8/06

Details

#465-S/N 0744. Eng. # 0744. Red/tan fabric. RHD. Current Scaglietti-made aluminum body commissioned to compete with American V8s. Long list of well known owners. Well maintained older restoration, and loaded with documented history. Powered by the engine from the 335S that crashed at the 1957 Mille Miglia, killing 12. It was modifed and fitted in the 375 F1 chassis for the Race of Two Worlds. Driven by Phil Hill, it finished third. Cond: 2.

Comments

This failed to sell at Sotheby's 2005 auction at Maranello at $9.2m. The pre-sale buzz was that this would break the record set a few years back when the Ferrari 330 TRI/LM sold for $6.5 mil. It fell short, but still brought adult money. What's the correct price for a documented car with this provenance? On this day it was $5.6 million—and who's to argue?

2 1953 GM FUTURLINER PARADE OF PROGRESS BUS

Sold at$4,320,000—Barrett-Jackson, Scottsdale, AZ, 1/06

Details

#1307-S/N 011. Red & stainless steel/blue & white vinyl. Odo: 9,549 miles. Built by GM's Yellow Coach Divsion. Beautifully restored to its 1953–56 configuration from a pile of scrap in the late 1990s and used as promo for Canadian cellphone company. Good paint and stainless, with some cracking to paint. Saftey cameras fore and aft. Remote control lights and modern generator for the display compartment. Light wear to the stage. Video monitor, ps, a/c, and air-ride seat added to the cockpit. Powertrain updated to a 401-ci GMC gas V6, in lieu of the original 302-ci I6, and a 4-sp. manual in lieu of the original 4-sp. military-spec HydraMatic with 2-sp. transfer case. Cond: 2+.

Comments

Originally built in 1940 as the 11th of 12 Futurliners, they were mothballed during WWII, then reconfigured in 1950 and 1953 for subsequent Parades of Progress and Motoramas. After its last stint as the Michigan State Police Safety Liner, it was put out to pasture in the Chicago area for several decades before being acquired by "Dream Car" enthusiast Joe Bortz. Rescued by the Canadians who consigned it, it represents the biggest price ever at B-J.

3 1938 TALBOT-LAGO T150C SS COUPE

Sold at $3,905,000—Gooding & Company, Palm Beach, FL, 1/06

Details

#29-S/N 90117. Aubergine/brown leather. RHD. Odo: 508 km. Raced at Le Mans in 1939. The only "Teardrop" coupe built specifically for competition. With the present owner since 1996, and restored for him in 2002, after surviving in original condition. Very nice eggplant paint. Slight surface wear on the pigskin upholstery. Well-presented engine compartment. Wilson Pre-selector gearbox, sunroof, opening rear windshield, fitted luggage. A styling icon. Cond:1-.

Comments

The buyer, an internationally-known collector, was present to stake his claim. The winning bid was a world's record price for a Talbot-Lago T150C, topping two others that sold in August 2005 at Pebble Beach. Though its price was not much more than the others, this car was in far better condition, so we'll call it well-bought by the standards of this rarified class of car.

4 | 1928 MERCEDEZ-BENZ 26/120/180 TORPEDO TYPE S ROADSTER

Sold at $3,645,000—Christie's, Monterey, CA, 8/06

Details

#52-S/N 40156. Eng. # 72151. Cream/tan/red leather. Odo: 31,581 miles. Pleasing, but not perfect. Good paint is to a standard no longer good enough. Some brightwork is dull but still good. Patina is the kind word overall. Interior shows well; good leather and an excellent dash, again showing wear. The driver's seat shows a kind of "booster" seat back with full padding. A stunning car but not a stunning presentation. Cond: 3.

Comments

An incredibly interesting history on this car, it's been owned by one family since new. Beautiful coachwork, the older restoration still looks good, but it is easy to find flaws. Positioned as the last car in the sale, it was also by far the most expensive. Well done all around.

5 | 1934 PACKARD TWELVE RUNABOUT SPEEDSTER

Sold at $3,190,000—RM, Phoenix, AZ, 1/06

Details

#167-S/N 110612. Eng. # 902052. Light blue/blue fabric/black leather. Odo: 67,950 miles. One of four LeBaron Speedsters, with history known since new. Formerly part of the Harrah Collection. The V12 engine features lighter eight-cylinder components, offering more performance than the normal V12. Restored by General Lyons in the early '90s. Flawless everywhere; an icon of American custom coachwork. Cond: 1.

Comments

The big boys were all over this. When the dust settled it was thought to have returned to the General Lyons collection. Arguably THE best American Classic. Expensive but worth every penny.

6 | 1954 PONTIAC BONNEVILLE SPECIAL COUPE

Sold at $3,024,000—Barrett-Jackson, Scottsdale, AZ, 1/06

Details

#1304-Emerald Green/Plexiglas/green leather. 268-ci I8, 4x1-bbl. The bodywork is well-blocked and-prepped, and the paint is excellent. The whole thing looks show-car quality. The brightwork is excellent, and all chrome and stainless are darn near perfect. The interior stainless appears clean and mark-free. Cond: 1-.

Comments

One of two '54 Pontiac Bonneville concept cars. This one has appeared in various states of decay, though the last time at auction was at B-J in January 1999, where this one went unsold for $230k. The condition at the time was rated as #5 . Also seen at Fall Auburn 1998, where it went unsold for $300k. I'm quite sure the restoration was costly, but a ten-fold increase from then to now is not a bad return on an investment.

7 1960 FERRARI 250 GT SWB COMPETITION BERLINETTA

Sold at $2,750,000—RM, Amelia Island, FL, 3/06

Details

#142-S/N 1757 GT. Eng. # 1757 GT. Red/gray leather. Odo: 48,797 km. Excellent paint on alloy panels, with chips to the front end and lots of road wear to the undercarriage. Borranis are caked with dirt and brake dust. No wipers. Excellent crackle finish to dash. Good seats, though the carpet looks out of place in a competition car. Underhood is tidy, but not detailed. Gummy Dunlop non-radials. Looks like it was driven here from the track. Cond: 3+.

Comments

Multiple millions should no longer surprise for any alloy-bodied 250 GT SWB. This example, the cover car for the auction catalog, was presented along with period competition photographs and a race history dating from 1960 through 1962, showing many first-place finishes in both races and hill climbs. Accurately described in the catalog as no "garage queen," this SWB looks and is ready for its next race.

8 1927 BUGATTI TYPE 35C GRAND PRIX RACER

Sold at $2,585,000—Gooding & Company, Pebble Beach, CA, 8/06

Details

#44-S/N 4889. Eng. # 152. Blue/black. RHD. Bugatti factory team car, finished 3rd at San Sebastian GP. Very much an older survivor with a nice patina. Fair paint, fair brightwork. Interior looks to have its original dirt, a very good look. Present with much documentation and several pages in the catalog. Cond: 4.

Comments

Delivered new to Spain, it spent most of its life there until it was brought to the U.S. in 1961. Very complete history to a car with a great look. The catalog states that it's "consistently numbered as constructed by Bugatti in 1927," which is a nice way of saying matching numbers. Sale comes complete with weather equipment including fenders, bracket work, and lights. Expensive, but worth it.

9 1957 FERRARI 500 TRC SPIDER

Sold at $2,285,500—RM, Monterey, CA, 8/06

Details

#472-S/N 0670MDTR. Eng. # 0670MDTR. Red & yellow/red leather. RHD. The first Testa Rossa Ferrari. Targa Florio racing history. Number six of 17 built by Scaglietti. Elegant design. Well-restored and-maintained with a pleasing patina. Verified matching-numbers and history with a Ferrari Heritage Certificate issued in 2004. Complete with 625 TRC spare engine and 500 TR gearbox. Cond: 2.

Comments

Striking design and paint. The last of the four-cylinder Ferraris. Price paid was in line with the estimates, and the car is so rare that no other sales are recorded. Is a 500 TRC with provenance worth a half a million more than a California Spyder? In this case it was, and I doubt the new owner will be disappointed.

10 1970 PLYMOUTH HEMI 'CUDA CONVERTIBLE

Sold at $2,160,000— Barrett-Jackson, Scottsdale, AZ, 1/06

Details

#1309- S/N BS27ROB212172. Vitamin C Orange/black vinyl/black vinyl. Odo: 42,120 miles. 426-ci V8, 4-bbl, auto. Documented with the Broadcast Sheet and a decode, this numbers-matching car was apparently built for a factory executive. Exemplary all around following a full restoration, with excellent paint, chrome, and brightwork, though there is one mismatched, unpolished stainless piece on the driver's door. The interior shows well, though it could use fresh carpets. Cond: 2+.

Comments

So until a 71 comes along, let's call this one the Big Dog. Of the 635 Cuda convertibles built in 1970, this is one of a handful with the equipment everyone's looking for. A Hemi block, a soft top, and Vitamin C brought north of $2m. Imagine this car with a factory 4-speed...

11 1938 TALBOT-LAGO T23 TEARDROP COUPE

Sold at $2,145,000—RM, Amelia Island, FL, 3/06

Details

#155-S/N 93064. Eng. # 23294. Blue/brown leather. RHD. Odo: 56,604 km. Excellent paint-work, with a few light chips present. A dent to the rear passenger side spat. Excellent bright-work, including the beautiful wheel discs. Interior shows a good patina, with some water spots on door cap wood, and very good carpets. Wilson 4-speed pre-selector transmission. Cond: 2-.

Comments

The catalog gave this sensuous car a full 14 pages, plus a foldout to present its rather complete history. Though something in the line of the front fenders appeared a bit off, the presentation in person was every bit as sensational as it was on the pages of the catalog.

12 1956 JAGUAR XK D-TYPE RACER

Sold at $2,097,000—Bonhams & Butterfields, Carmel, CA, 8/06

Details

#521-. S/N XKD553. Eng. # E20469. British Racing Green/green leather. RHD. Odo: 4,154 miles. Excellent panel fit. Very good older paint with a few stress and star cracks, and some fading and polish swirl marks. Interior is nice, with a small hole in the transmission cover panel. Engine compartment looks heavily used, but original. Polished wheels. Cond: 3+.

Comments

Ex-Rosso Bianco collection, Jack Hensley/Pat O'Connor Sebring 12-Hour car. Maintained and lightly restored over many years of various museum displays, it shows a wonderful patina. The price was in the estimate range and spot-on, if not a bit of a deal.

BY THE NUMBERS

13 1965 ASTON MARTIN DB5 JAMES BOND COUPE

Sold at $2,090,000—RM, Phoenix, AZ, 1/06

Details

#155-S/N DB52008R. Silver Birch/blue leather. RHD. Odo: 17,921 miles. One of four James Bond DB5s built for "Goldfinger" and "Thunderball." All kinds of Q-Division spy stuff: functioning revolving license plates and faux Browning machine guns, though the oil slick and nail spreader are disabled. In a museum for 35 years. The paint is worn and blistered, with plenty of chips and scratches. Driver's seat and carpets are tired. Ejector seat has been replaced. As-used condition throughout. Cond: 3.

Comments

One of two "press cars" used for promoting "Thunderball" in the U.S. A piece of motion picture and automotive history, and arguably the "Most Famous Car in the World." Though it would be cool to drive around in a tux and pretend to be Sean Connery, the practical thing would be to return it to a museum for another 35 years. A fun toy, regardless, and well sold.

14 1955 MASERATI 300S RACER

Sold at $1,925,000—RM, Phoenix, AZ, 1/06

Details

#171-S/N 3057. Red/aluminum & black. RHD. One of 30 built. Restored over two years in the early 1990s to factory specs, using many original parts. Very good panels and excellent paint, with polish swirls only. Mark-free Borrani wheels. The spartan interior shows well, with clean aluminum and gauges, and a very nice wood wheel. Fitted with a correct, but non-original 300S engine that shows well. A stunning car inside and out. Five pounds of documentation from 1955 to present. Cond: 2+.

Comments

The mid-1950s were the Trident's golden years, with 150S, 200S, 300S, and 450S sports cars winning all over Europe. Chassis #3057 was raced successfully from new by Belgian privateer Benoit Musy until his death in 1956. After discovery in Angola, where it had been fitted with an American V8, it was overhauled, and is now vintage-raced. Fantastic presentation, romantic history, and plenty of paperwork brought this car correct money, perhaps even a bit light.

15 1929 BENTLEY SPEED SIX SIX DUAL COWL TOURER

Sold at $1,815,000—RM, Phoenix, AZ, 1/06

Details

#454-S/N SB2773. Eng. # NH2731. Green/green fabric/green leather. RHD. Odo: 10,328 km. Coachwork by Cadogan. The Speed Six was an upgraded 6-1/2 Liter with increased horsepower. This is one of three bodied by Cadogan, and the only one as a tourer. Retains original coachwork. Well maintained with little to fault. Driven on many tours but still scores well when judged. Cond: 2.

Comments

A perfect example of a Bentley that was driven and maintained. Price paid was on the low side considering its originality and history.

16 1962 SHELBY COBRA 289 RACER

Sold at $1,815,000—RM, Phoenix, AZ, 1/06

Details

#175-S/N CSX2026. Red/black leather. 260-ci V8, 4x2-bbl, 4-sp. The first Cobra to win in competition, driven by Dave McDonald at Riverside in January 1963. Went on to win the A-Production National Championship that year with Bob Johnson. Restored to high standards to its 1963 Daytona configuration, and using many parts that still retain the initials of Shelby fabricators. Original block and heads. Excellent all around. Cond: 1-.

Comments

Extensive history since new. This one brought adult money, but there is only one "first" and this was it in the Cobra world. Well sold.

17 1947 BENTLEY MK VI CONVERTIBLE

Sold at $1,728,000—Barrett-Jackson, Palm Beach, FL, 3/06

Details

#723-S/N B20BH. Black/red leather. RHD. Bodied by Franay. Not the freshest restoration, but done with lots of flash. Would you have this car any other way? Paint and chrome still show very well, as do wood and leather. Lots of unusual touches, including more chrome than I thought possible, a crank-out windshield, and plenty of custom work to the cockpit-like interior. Cond: 2+.

Comments

Said to be the back-to-back winner of two 1948 European Concours d'Elegances, making this an important post-war effort from the famous coachbuilder, Franay. Not to everyone's taste, this over-the-top effort is all about show. It sold well here, joining what must be a very small list of post-war Bentleys in the million-dollar club.

18 1938 DELAHAYE 135MS COUPE

Sold at $1,712,000—Bonhams & Butterfields, Carmel, CA, 8/06

Details

#527-S/N 60112. Black/tan leather. RHD. Odo: 1,321 km. Excellent panel fit, very good paint with some minor sub-surface imperfections and swirl polish marks. Excellent chrome throughout. Original engine and four-speed transmission. Outstanding interior with excellent wood trim. Upholstery appears as-new, with superb patina. Cond: 1-.

Comments

Ex-Rosso Bianco collection. Beautifully presented, hard to fault. Compared to the teardrop coupes, the proportions of this larger car are a bit iffy, but taken on its own it's still a lovely design. And when compared to the smaller car, a terrific bargain.

BY THE NUMBERS

BY THE NUMBERS

19 1994 MCLAREN F1 COUPE

Sold at $1,705,000—RM, Monterey, CA, 8/06

Details
#471-1994 McLaren F1. S/N SA9AB5AC4R. Yellow/black leather. MHD. Odo: 3,224 miles. Bright yellow paint in near-perfect condition, with no issues. Panel gaps superior, rubber trim perfect. Engine compartment is clean, but minimal use is evident. Nice Interior, with a yellow insert on the driver's seat. Some minor wear to the leather on the passenger seats. Dash, carpet, and dual consoles excellent. As-new throughout. Cond: 2+

Comments
Constructed before the U.S.-mandated OBD-II for vehicles in 1996, this McLaren was 49-state legal. Installing such a system can be an extremely expensive task, and later models require it to be used on the road. Only 107 were built during the entire production span, making the F1 excessively rare and desirable. Prices for these will undoubtedly rise, and this one was well bought at just over the low estimate of $1.7m.

20 1930 DUESENBERG J SPORT BERLINE

Sold at $1,650,000—RM, Monterey, CA, 8/06

Details
#477-S/N 2035. Eng. # J287. Black/tan fabric. Odo: 4,427 miles. Coachwork by Murphy. One-off design by Franklin Hershey with doors going into roof. Original body, chassis, and engine restored to highest standard in 1998 by Chris Charlton. Chrome wheel covers added. Trunk redesigned since belonging to the Harrah Collection. Striking design that has been well maintained. Cond: 2+.

Comments
One of six Duesenbergs ordered by Capt. Geo Whittell Jr. Thought to have been given to his mistress. Interesting history since new. The car was fully priced, but the new owner should have little concern as the car was striking and loaded with history.

21 1967 FERRARI 212 E MONTAGNA RACER

Sold at $1,650,000—RM, Phoenix, AZ, 1/06

Details
#164-S/N 0862. Red & aluminum/black. RHD. A one-off racer, built on a leftover Dino 206 chassis, and originally bodied as a closed 250 P5 for Pininfarina's '68 Geneva show car. Good gaps and panels, with very nice paint. The interior is all business, as is the Tipo 232 engine bay. Body, chassis, and engine are all matching from the 1969 racing season. Cond: 2-.

Comments
Powered by Ferrari's only 2-liter flat twelve, Peter Schelty piloted this car to victory in every race it entered in the 1969 European Mountain Championship, setting records in each. Racers are notoriously tough to value, one-offs perhaps even more so. Offering it up without reserve was wise, as RM allowed the car's fully known and unique history, plus its overall originality, to speak for themselves.

22 1935 MERCEDES-BENZ 500/540K CABRIOLET

Sold at $1,650,000—Worldwide Group, Seabrook, TX, 5/06

Details

#060-S/N 12847. Eng. # U105384. Black/black fabric/red lather. Odo: 1,157 km. Born as a 500K Cabriolet A. Upgraded with a 540K engine in 1938. Restored in 2004. Body fit and finish are excellent, including the paint and brightwork. Interior is finished to the highest standard, with a mother-of-pearl instrument panel. A striking car from every angle. Cond: 1.

Comments

High sale of the auction. Not in the same league as a Special Roadster, but still very desirable. The engine swap was not an issue here, as it was done in the era. I'd go so far as to say this car was well bought.

23 1963 SHELBY COBRA 289 LE MANS RACER

Sold at $1,650,000—RM, Amelia Island, FL, 3/06

Details

#164-S/N CSX2136. Black/black leather. Odo: 211 miles. 289-ci V8, 4x2-bbl, 4-sp. Shelby American team car, as well as Ed Leslie's '64 SCCA A/Production National Champion. Very good paintwork overall, now with some stone chips to the rear fender. Minimal brightwork, but what's there is good. Good leather and carpets. Glovebox vinyl is loose, the only flaw to an otherwise excellent dash. Dunlop racing tires look to be retreads. Cond: 3+.

Comments

$1.65 million and all I got was a lousy set of retreads? The catalog presentation on this car was well done, complete with period racing photographs and a chart showing this chassis's history as a factory team Cobra. A substantial premium was paid for this car's race history, but with this much documentation, it's quite understandable. Not cheap, but possibly a very good buy.

24 1952 JAGUAR XK C-TYPE RACER

Sold at $1,649,638—Christie's, Paris, FR, 2/06

Details

#86-S/N XKC006. Eng. # E10088. Flag Blue Metallic/black leather. RHD. Odo: 17,302 miles. Panel fit is appropriate for a race car. Fair to good paint, with some cracking on the hood, cowl, and rear fender. The race interior shows a good patina. Delamination on tops of the aero screens. Cond: 3.

Comments

Ex-Ecurie Ecosse, it finished first in the 1952 Jersey road race, its first victory. Many podium finishes in the '52–'54 seasons. Largely original, with an excellent look. Christie's tried to unload this Cat in December 2005, a no-sale at $1.9m. Documentation is all in buying a C-type, and despite the lack of a chassis plate, enough people thought this one was right. Market-priced.

BY THE NUMBERS

25 1962 SHELBY COBRA 289 DRAGONSNAKE RACER

Sold at $1,601,250—Mecum, Belvidere, IL, 5/06

Details

#S511-S/N CSX2019. Light blue metalflake/blue metalflake HT/black leather. Odo: 9,106 miles. 289-ci V8, 2x4-bbl, 4-sp. Chips, bubbles, and small cracks in the paint. Hard top paint doesn't match the rest of the car. Windshield is delaminating, and the weatherstripping is cracked. Sun tach screwed onto the dash. Hurst shifter. Turbo headers. Halibrand wheels. Somewhat tattered in this as-raced condition. Cond: 4.

Comments

If you looked closely, you could see remnants of the original red color beneath the metalflake. Designated initially as a Shelby PR car, it was the first of only six Dragonsnakes built, turning the 1/4 mile in 11.73 seconds. Subsequently seen in the movie "Viva Las Vegas," wearing the number 98. Far too important to restore, the battle scars gave it much character. And the sale price gives it a place in history, fully $900k more than the last recorded sale of a Dragonsnake, S/N CSX2472 at RM Boca 2006.

26 1958 FERRARI 250 GT LWB TOUR DE FRANCE BERLINETTA

Sold at $1,540,000—Gooding & Co., Pebble Beach, CA, 8/06

Details

#68-S/N 0933. Gold/red leather. Odo: 48,603 km. Coachwork designed by Pininfarina, constructed by Scaglietti. Great use wear is equal in all places, the car's patina matches from front to rear. Paint quality was excellent, now just good. Plexiglas rear window shows scratches. Decent brightwork. Older leather looks great in the mix, very nice dash. Cond: 3+.

Comments

The patina really added to the appeal of this long wheelbase Tour de France. This car had a great story to tell, which included being abandoned at an airport and later sold by the French tax authorities to pay an outstanding debt. With a well-known provenance and quite stunning coachwork, $1.5 million did not surprise.

27 1953 JAGUAR XK C-TYPE RACER

Sold at $1,512,500—Christie's, Paris, FR, 2/06

Details

#150-S/N XKC014. Eng. # E10148. British Racing Green/black. RHD. Odo: 4,441. One of 53 built. A very original example that retains the factory chassis, body, engine, and majority of important parts. Correct restoration some years ago, though the paint is showing its age now. Part of the Skip Barber collection. Cond: 2.

Comments

Dripping with history. Hit 134 mph on the beach at Daytona. If money was not an issue and you could only have one car then this would be it. Tame enough for the street, strong enough for vintage racing or rallies. Was the price paid too much? Who cares; find another this original for the price.

28 1931 BENTLEY 8-LITER SPORTSMAN FIXED HEAD COUPE

Sold at $1,485,000—RM, Amelia Island, FL, 3/06

Details

#153-S/N YR5088. Eng. # YR5088. Blue & black/black/blue leather. RHD. Odo: 25,703 miles. A stunning example. Paintwork shows only the smallest of flaws, with minor dust and some fade to the outside cowl. Excellent brightwork. Very nice interior shows a light but appropriate patina. Underhood is gorgeous, fully detailed with polish and paint. Unusual and incorrect fans are there for obvious cooling function. Otherwise, the engine bay looks like a museum display. Cond: 2+.

Comments

Not surprising this appealing car busted right through its high estimate of $1.1 million. The automotive version of an art deco steamship or some form of 1930s industrial art, this was a car with massive, masculine presence. The type of car around which you could build an entire collection.

29 1938 BUGATTI TYPE 57C ARAVIS DROPHEAD COUPE

Sold at $1,375,000—Gooding & Company, Pebble Beach, CA, 8/06

Details

#38-S/N 57710. Eng. # 510. Dark blue/black cloth/light blue. RHD. Odo: 130 km. Coachwork by Gangloff of Colmar, designed by Jean Bugatti. Some light scratches to very well done paint; its age is showing in places. Very good brightwork, complete and well done. Very good trim, all the wear and patina are matched. Inside has a good look as well, all leather-trimmed dash looks tres chic; overall a pleasing look to the interior. Cond: 3.

Comments

Well documented ownership history, said to be one of three remaining Aravis cars. A very pleasing body style, very well set up for touring with the dual overhead cam motor. Sold under the estimate, it seemed well priced—but not a bargain.

30 1955 LINCOLN INDIANAPOLIS BOANO COUPE

Sold at $1,375,000—Gooding & Co., Pebble Beach, CA, 8/06

Details

#57-S/N 58WA10902. Orange/white & black leather. Odo: 268 miles. Coachwork by Boano. Geroge Jetson, your car is ready! Very fresh and complete restoration of a totally outragous car you just have to love. Excellent paint and brightwork. Very good glass. Excellent interior. Jim Cox restoration. Cond: 1-.

Comments

Premiered at the 1950 Turin Motor Show, the car was said to have become the property of Henry Ford II at that point, and was rumored to have been owned by Errol Flynn. This car easily surpasses the outrageousness of the Chrysler Ghia concepts of the same era. In comparison, the price seems downright reasonable.

BY THE NUMBERS

31 1952 FERRARI 225 SPORT SPYDER

Sold at $1,280,000—Christie's, Monterey, CA, 8/06

Details

#18-S/N 0160ED. Eng. # 0160ED. Dark red/tan leather. RHD. Odo: 963 km. Another well-presented example with excellent paint and trim. Very good gaps, even the PLEXI windscreen is top notch. Well done interior shows well-fitted leather, beautiful gauges, and an excellent steering wheel. Judges Cup winner at the 1997 Cavallino Classic. Cond: 1-.

Comments

The catalog calls it the most complete, original, correct, and verifiable 225 Sport Spyder in existence. Sold complete with a history folder as well as tools. A little tough to value in this overheated market; somehow the price achieved sounds reasonable.

32 1937 BENTLEY 4 1/4-LITER FIXED HEAD COUPE

Sold at $1,265,000—RM, Monterey, CA, 8/06

Details

#479-S/N B156KT. Eng. # E9BH. Black/saddle leather. RHD. Odo: 35,089 km. Coachwork by Vesters and Neirinck. Stunning design on a Derby Bentley. One owner for the first 37 years. Paint and interior are very original with a nice patina. Large sunroof. Brightwork redone. Engine in original, well-maintained condition. Knock-off style hubcaps. Numerous special features. Cond: 2-.

Comments

Often stated to be the most beautiful Rolls-Bentley in the world. History known since new, and rarely seen in public. Sold at auction in 1989 for a record price. This sale just about doubles the high-water mark for Derby Bentleys. The buzz prior to auction was that the final number here would be seven figures—and how right they were.

33 1970 CHEVROLET CHEVELLE SS LS6 CONVERTIBLE

Sold at $1,242,000—Barrett-Jackson, Scottsdale, AZ, 1/06

Details

#1287-S/N 136670B190703. Blue/white vinyl/black vinyl. Odo: 61 miles. 454-ci V8, 450-hp, auto. Well-documented, with original build sheet, title, and various magazine articles. Recent restoration done to a decent standard. Trunk and right rear quarter gaps are off, with scratches and a small dent on the rear deck. Repro decals. Visible staples in the window felts. Trim tag looks like a repro. Original gauges but no tach. Nothing mentioned about matching numbers. Cond: 2.

Comments

Piloted in 1970 by Ray Allen to victory at the NHRA U.S. Nationals, Super Nationals, World Finals, and more. This was an important piece of U.S. racing history, though certainly most people didn't think it was million-dollar important. Mark this one as a world record price for an LS6 Chevelle.

34 1964 SHELBY COBRA 289 COMPETITION RACER

Sold at $1,237,500—RM, Monterey, CA, 8/06

Details

#159-S/N CSX2473. Guardsman Blue/black & white. Odo: 6,305 miles. 289-ci V8, 4-bbl, 4-sp. The winningest Cobra in history, documented from new. Paint to high standard, with minor swirls and scratches. Driver's seat is two-tone, passenger's black. Engine compartment is clean and tidy. Stated to be in perfect mechanical condition. Cond: 2.

Comments

CSX2473 has won races spanning five different decades. Purchased for $3,778 in '64. Cobra values continue to escalate, and the documented history put this one near the top of the food chain. The condition and race winning history justify the seven figure selling price.

35 1941 CHRYSLER THUNDERBOLT RETRACTABLE HARD TOP CONVERTIBLE

Sold at $1,210,000—RM, Phoenix, AZ, 1/06

Details

#146-S/N 7807976. Eng. # C271552. Red/silver/tan leather. Odo: 81,313 miles. One of five Chrysler concept Thunderbolts produced, with four remaining. Each had subtle differences. This represents the first use of concealed headlight doors and a retractable top, as well as a curved windshield. Fluid Drive transmission. Displayed at major concours, and a Full CCCA Classic. Restored to perfection. Cond: 1.

Comments

Should this be worth more than the two GM Motorama concepts that sold at B-J this year and last? On a relative basis those sales make this one look like a bargain. This could have gone for half a million more without surprise. Under the circumstances, it was well-bought.

36 1934 DUESENBERG MODEL J RIVIERA PHAETON

Sold at $1,210,000—Gooding & Co., Pebble Beach, CA, 8/06

Details

#60-S/N 2550. Eng. # J440. Black & orange/black leather. Odo: 22,883 miles. Coachwork by Brunn and Company. Brian Joseph restoration. Excellent throughout, CCCA Premier Winner. Beautiful paintwork, no visible flaws found. Excellent brightwork, all well done. Interior is well-fitted and done to a jewel-like quality. Sighting down the sides is like looking into a mirror. Cond: 1.

Comments

It's not often you find true #1 cars at auction, but this car met that standard. One of three Brunn Riviera Phaetons, this open 4-door body style looks best in this color combination. Sold within the estimate. Duesenbergs have regained some of their lost value, so this could turn out to be an excellent buy.

BY THE NUMBERS

37 1952 CHRYSLER D'ELEGANCE COUPE

Sold at $1,188,000—Barrett-Jackson, Scottsdale, AZ, 1/06

Details

#1306-S/N 321593. Burgundy/black leather. 354-ci V8, 2x4-bbl, auto. Bodied by Ghia. Fitted in 1954 with a Hemi and Torqueflite automatic. An expert restoration, with flawless paint, chrome, and brightwork. All glass and trim appears new. The handsome interior is well-fitted, with nice custom luggage behind the driver and passenger seats. Excellent in every visible way as far as quality of the restoration. Cond: 1.

Comments

Very appealing presentation of a historically important link between Chrysler and Ghia. A number of Ghia-bodied Chryslers exist. Some have beautiful coach lines; others have not withstood the test of time so well. This is a beautiful example whose lines are appreciated and accepted as automotive art.

38 1955 FERRARI 750 MONZA SPIDER RACER

Sold at $1,107,000—Bonhams & Butterfields, Carmel, CA, 8/06

Details

#525-S/N 0492M. Eng. # 0429M. Red/black vinyl. RHD. Excellent panel fit, very good older paint with a dent in the left rear wheelarch. Minimal brightwork in excellent condition. Dirty interior, with a split side bolster on the driver's seat. Dry, somewhat unused looking engine. Cond: 2-.

Comments

Ex-Rosso Bianco, John von Neumann/Phil Hill car. Great history, connected with two of the leading lights of West Coast Ferrari racing in the '50s. As a bonus, it appeared in the 1959 film "On the Beach." In fine, un-messed-around-with condition, it only needs the recommissioning any museum car requires. Fair deal for both sides.

39 1939 DELAHAYE 135MS GRAND SPORT CABRIOLET

Sold at $1,100,000—Gooding & Co., Pebble Beach, CA, 8/06

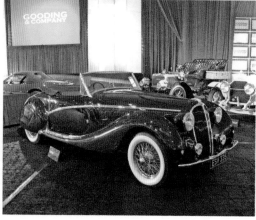

Details

#52-S/N 60158. Eng. # 60158. Black/tan leather. RHD. Odo: 281 km. Coachwork by Figoni and Falaschi. A pleasing restoration, the catalog states that it is fresh, but I would have pegged it for a few years old. Very nice brightwork coupled with good paint. Very good trim outside. Inside is well-fitted and nice, but not fresh. Beautiful dash shows excellent detail. Cond: 2-.

Comments

A beautiful example very nicely commissioned and executed. Very few Delahayes make it into the Million-Dollar Club, but this example undoubtedly deserves to be a member. Coachwork makes all the difference on Delahayes, and this one is falls among the prettiest.

40 1953 CHEVROLET CORVETTE ROADSTER

Sold at $1,080,000—Barrett-Jackson, Scottsdale, AZ, 1/06

Details

#1311-S/N E53F001003. White/black vinyl/red vinyl. Odo: 330 miles. 235-ci I6, 3x1-bbl Carter Type YH, Powerglide auto. This is the oldest surviving production Corvette, the third built. Fit and finish are very much to factory spec, such as it was. Original GM documentation for delivery configuration to the public. Handlaid fiberglass, with expected flaws in the paint. Sold in 1987 at Rick Cole's, Monterey, for $35k, with several problems after unfortunate storage. The restoration aimed to replicate the original build process, and many Corvette theoreticians agree this car is correct. Well-known and documented. The seller wants it to go to a museum. Cond: 1-.

Comments

The seller's hope that it would end up in a museuem likely won't happen. This represents the highest price ever paid for a Corvette at auction. Bought by David Ressler, a North Dakota car dealer who outbid some notable Corvette aficionados to claim this one. Perhaps it will end up as a showroom display in Mandan and add some kick to the ND tourist trade.

41 2004 MASERATI MC12 COUPE

Sold at $1,072,500—RM, Monterey, CA, 8/06

Details

#460-S/N ZAMBDF44BO00012099. Pearl White & blue/blue leather. Odo: 456 miles. One of 50 built in 2004 and 2005. The first example imported into U.S. Built on an Enzo Ferrari platform. List price of $799,000. Naturally aspirated, paddle shifter, carbon fiber body. In as-new condition with little sign of use. Cond: 1-.

Comments

Top end speed of 205 mph. Zero to 60 in 3.8 secconds. MC12Rs have won two of three FIA GT Championship races. If you want a street legal race car, this is it. Rarer than an Enzo, but not legal in California—so you don't have to worry about letting a guy named Dietrich drive it and wreck it.

42 1911 MERCEDES 37/90HP SKIFF

Sold at $1,050,000—Worldwide Group, Seabrook, TX, 5/06

Details

#063-S/N 13504. Wood & black/brown leather. RHD. Yacht-style triple layer wood body, with tiny doors for rigidity. First delivered to hat maker Henry Stetson for $18,000. Original body was recreated utilizing 2,700 brass rivets. Long list of awards from major concours spanning a 10-year period. A work of art, with nothing to fault. Cond: 1.

Comments

Photos do not do this Mercedes justice. It was worth the price of admission to view the car. The price paid seemed in line with a very thin market, and may even have been a bit light. This car has already racked up a long list of hardware, so what will the new owner do with it now? A museum seems like just the place.

BY THE NUMBERS

43 | 1938 BUGATTI TYPE 57C ARAVIS DHC

Sold at $1,045,000—RM, Monterey, CA, 8/06

Details

#143-S/N 57736. Blue/blue leather. RHD. One of four Type 57s bodied by Gangloff, and one of just two supercharged dropheads. Repainted in the 1960s, the paint shows a nice patina overall, with a few scratches and nicks, particularly at panel edges. Some pitting to the chrome, but nothing too distressed. The older leather could be original, and is supple but heavily creased. Very nice wooden dash and wheel. Wilson pre-selector gearbox. Clean engine, but not show. Cond: 2-.

Comments

Truly a lovely car and very well preserved over the years. Ownership history back to new, including a long stint (1952 to 2000) with the Earl of Mourey, who lavished it with regular maintenance. It would be a shame to do anything but continue such maintenance, as this was a pretty piece of history, and any major overhaul would negate that. Fully worth the price.

44 | 1971 PLYMOUTH HEMI 'CUDA 2-DOOR HARD TOP

Sold at $1,045,000—Worldwide Group, Seabrook, TX, 5/06.

Details

#050- S/N BS23R1B405079. Sassy Grass Green/cream vinyl. Odo: 35,782 miles. 426-ci V8, 2x4-bbl, 4-sp. One of 107 built in '71. Long list of awards on this Hemi, which Galen Govier claims as one of five best. Near-perfect eight year restoration to original factory specifications. Fully documented. Correct chalk marks and overspray. Nothing to fault here. Cond: 1.

Comments

It's very difficult to say "a million dollars" and "Plymouth hard top" in the same breath. The seller was actually looking for more. This is likely the only one of its kind in Sassy Grass Green, which is just as well. The seller worked the car prior to the sale and was rewarded with membership in the million-dollar club.

45 | 1930 DUESENBERG J DUAL COWL PHAETON

Sold at $1,001,000—RM, Phoenix, AZ, 1/06

Details

#135-S/N 2336. Eng. # J487. Red & black/black fabric/black leather. Odo: 81,388 miles. The only long wheelbase—153.5"—LeBaron dual cowl built. ACD-certified with original coachwork, though the original engine was J320. Reproduction hood ornament. Body, paint, and interior are flawless. Excellent brightwork. The engine is highly detailed. Magnificent example of America's finest automobile of the era. Cond: 1-.

Comments

Duesenberg prices range from $400k to a couple million, so what makes the difference? Attractive one-off coachwork and restoration quality are major factors. Engine swaps, however, are not such a big deal with Duesenbergs. Here, the ACD Club certification was a plus. All signs indicate this was a fair price. The new owner will come out just fine if he decides to sell in five years or so.

The 1,000 Most Expensive Cars of 2006

$5.6m to $112k, here are the top 1,000 sales of 2006 arranged by price, as reported to SCM by auction companies. *(Sales recorded between 1/1/2006 and 9/30/2006.)*

Rank	Sold Price	Year	Make	Model	Auction Co.	Location	Date	Lot #
1	$5,610,000	1958	Ferrari	412S Sports Racer	RM	Monterey, CA	8/18	465
2	$4,320,000	1950	GM	Futurliner Parade Of Progress Bus	Barrett-Jackson	Scottsdale, AZ	1/14	1307
3	$3,905,000	1938	Talbot-Lago	T150C SS Teardrop Coupe	Gooding	Palm Beach, FL	1/24	29
4	$3,645,000	1928	Mercedes-Benz	26/120/180 Type S Torpedo Roadster	Christie's	Monterey, CA	8/17	52
5	$3,190,000	1934	Packard	LeBaron Twelve Runabout Speedster	RM	Phoenix, AZ	1/20	167
6	$3,024,000	1954	Pontiac	Bonneville Special Motorama Concept Car	Barrett-Jackson	Scottsdale, AZ	1/14	1304
7	$2,750,000	1960	Ferrari	250 GT SWB Alloy Comp Berlinetta	RM	Amelia Island, FL	3/11	142
8	$2,585,000	1927	Bugatti	Type 35C Grand Prix	Gooding	Pebble Beach, CA	8/20	44
9	$2,282,500	1957	Ferrari	500 TRC Spider	RM	Monterey, CA	8/18	472
10	$2,160,000	1970	Plymouth	Hemi 'Cuda Convertible	Barrett-Jackson	Scottsdale, AZ	1/14	1309
11	$2,145,000	1938	Talbot-Lago	T23 Teardrop Coupe	RM	Amelia Island, FL	3/11	155
12	$2,097,000	1956	Jaguar	XK D-Type Racer	Bonhams	Carmel, CA	8/18	521
13	$2,090,000	1965	Aston Martin	DB5	RM	Phoenix, AZ	1/20	155
14	$1,925,000	1955	Maserati	300S Racer	RM	Phoenix, AZ	1/20	171
15	$1,815,000	1929	Bentley	Speed Six Dual Cowl Tourer	RM	Monterey, CA	8/18	454
16	$1,815,000	1962	Shelby	Cobra 289	RM	Phoenix, AZ	1/20	175
17	$1,762,300	1961	Ferrari	250 GT SWB Alloy Comp Berlinetta	Sportscar Auction Co.	Geneva, CH	10/7	42
18	$1,728,000	1947	Bentley	Mk VI Franay	Barrett-Jackson	West Palm Beach, FL	3/29	723
19	$1,712,000	1938	Delahaye	135MS	Bonhams	Carmel, CA	8/18	527
20	$1,705,000	1994	McLaren	F1	RM	Monterey, CA	8/18	471
21	$1,650,000	1930	Duesenberg	Model J Sport Berline	RM	Monterey, CA	8/18	477
22	$1,650,000	1967	Ferrari	212 E Montagna Racer	RM	Phoenix, AZ	1/20	164
23	$1,650,000	1935	Mercedes-Benz	500/540K Cabriolet	Worldwide Group	Seabrook, TX	5/6	60
24	$1,650,000	1963	Shelby	Cobra 289 Le Mans Racer	RM	Amelia Island, FL	3/11	164
25	$1,649,638	1952	Jaguar	XK C-Type Racer	Christie's	Paris, FRA	2/11	86
26	$1,601,250	1962	Shelby	Cobra 289	Mecum	Belvidere, IL	5/25	S511
27	$1,540,000	1958	Ferrari	250 GT LWB Tour De France Berlinetta	Gooding	Pebble Beach, CA	8/20	68
28	$1,512,500	1953	Jaguar	XK C-Type Racer	RM	Phoenix, AZ	1/20	150
29	$1,485,000	1931	Bentley	8-Liter Sportsman Coupe	RM	Amelia Island, FL	3/11	153
30	$1,410,741	1950	Talbot-Lago	T26C	Christie's	Paris, FRA	7/8	125
31	$1,375,000	1938	Bugatti	Type 57C Aravis Drophead Coupe	Gooding	Pebble Beach, CA	8/20	38
32	$1,375,000	1955	Lincoln	Indianapolis Boano	Gooding	Pebble Beach, CA	8/20	57
33	$1,305,970	1959	Ferrari	250 Nembo	Coys	Nuremberg, DE	7/22	233
34	$1,280,000	1952	Ferrari	225 Sport Spyder	Christie's	Monterey, CA	8/17	18
35	$1,265,000	1937	Bentley	4-Liter Fixed Head Coupe	RM	Monterey, CA	8/18	479
36	$1,242,000	1970	Chevrolet	Chevelle SS 454 LS6 Convertible	Barrett-Jackson	Scottsdale, AZ	1/14	1287
37	$1,237,500	1964	Shelby	Cobra 289 Competition	RM	Monterey, CA	8/18	159
38	$1,210,000	1941	Chrysler	Thunderbolt	RM	Phoenix, AZ	1/20	146
39	$1,210,000	1934	Duesenberg	Model J Riviera Phaeton	Gooding	Pebble Beach, CA	8/20	60
40	$1,188,000	1952	Chrysler	D'Elegance	Barrett-Jackson	Scottsdale, AZ	1/14	1306
41	$1,174,354	1936	Mercedes-Benz	540K Cabriolet C	Coys	Monte Carlo, MCO	5/20	240
42	$1,145,804	1956	Maserati	150S Barchetta	Coys	Monte Carlo, MCO	5/20	261
43	$1,107,000	1955	Ferrari	750 Monza Spider	Bonhams	Carmel, CA	8/18	525
44	$1,100,000	1939	Delahaye	135MS Grand Sport Roadster	Gooding	Pebble Beach, CA	8/20	52
45	$1,080,000	1953	Chevrolet	Corvette Roadster	Barrett-Jackson	Scottsdale, AZ	1/14	1311
46	$1,072,500	2004	Maserati	MC12	RM	Monterey, CA	8/18	460
47	$1,050,000	1911	Mercedes	37/90 Skiff	Worldwide Group	Seabrook, TX	5/6	63
48	$1,045,000	1938	Bugatti	T57C Aravis Drophead Coupe	RM	Phoenix, AZ	1/20	143
49	$1,045,000	1971	Plymouth	Hemi 'Cuda	Worldwide Group	Seabrook, TX	5/6	50
50	$1,001,000	1930	Duesenberg	Model J LWB Dual Cowl Phaeton	RM	Phoenix, AZ	1/20	135
51	$990,000	1967	Ferrari	275 GTB/4	RM	Monterey, CA	8/18	462

Rank	Sold Price	Year	Make	Model	Auction Co.	Location	Date	Lot #
52	$990,000	1965	Shelby	GT350 R	RM	Amelia Island, FL	3/11	137
53	$955,500	1965	Shelby	Cobra 289 Competition	Mecum	Belvidere, IL	5/25	S519
54	$942,748	1955	Mercedes-Benz	300SL Alloy	Artcurial	Paris, FRA	2/12	22
55	$935,000	1912	Rolls-Royce	Silver Ghost Touring	RM	Amelia Island, FL	3/11	169
56	$907,500	1929	Duesenberg	Model J Convertible Sedan	RM	Rochester, MI	8/5	237
57	$902,000	1929	Duesenberg	Model J Convertible Coupe	Gooding	Pebble Beach, CA	8/20	71
58	$891,000	1961	Aston Martin	DB4 GT	RM	Monterey, CA	8/18	476
59	$858,000	1911	Rolls-Royce	40/50hp Silver Ghost	RM	Monterey, CA	8/18	447
60	$852,500	1951	Ferrari	340 America	RM	Monterey, CA	8/18	448
61	$845,300	1929	Duesenberg	Model J Murphy Convertible	RM	Boca Raton, FL	2/10	SP48
62	$836,000	1936	Mercedes-Benz	540K Special Roadster	RM	Monterey, CA	8/18	468
63	$819,825	1935	Maserati	4CS-1100/1500	Bonhams	Monte Carlo, MCO	5/20	172
64	$787,500	1971	Plymouth	Hemi 'Cuda	Mecum	Belvidere, IL	5/25	S571.1
65	$781,100	1956	Cadillac	Eldorado Brougham Town Car	RM	Boca Raton, FL	2/10	SP41
66	$781,000	1927	Bentley	Speed Six Fixed Head Coupe	RM	Monterey, CA	8/18	489
67	$776,000	1967	Ferrari	275 GTB/4 NART Conversion Spyder	RM	Phoenix, AZ	1/20	159
68	$748,000	1972	Ferrari	365 GTS/4 Daytona Spyder	Gooding	Pebble Beach, CA	8/20	77
69	$748,000	1965	Shelby	GT350 R	Gooding	Pebble Beach, CA	8/20	80
70	$742,500	1967	Ferrari	275 GTB/4 Berlinetta	RM	Phoenix, AZ	1/20	170
71	$726,000	1937	Maserati	6CM Monoposto Voiturette	Gooding	Pebble Beach, CA	8/20	55
72	$715,000	1952	Chrysler	Thomas Special SWB Prototype	RM	Amelia Island, FL	3/11	162
73	$715,000	1937	Delage	D-8 120 Drophead Coupe	RM	Monterey, CA	8/18	449
74	$715,000	1971	Plymouth	Hemi 'Cuda	Russo and Steele	Scottsdale, AZ	1/20	S222
75	$715,000	1914	Stutz	Bearcat	Gooding	Pebble Beach, CA	8/20	29
76	$715,000	1930	Stutz	Model M Supercharged Coupe	RM	Rochester, MI	8/5	251
77	$704,850	1974	Gulf-Mirage	Cosworth GR8 Endurance Racer	Bonhams	Sussex, U.K.	9/1	222
78	$702,000	1970	Plymouth	Hemi 'Cuda	Barrett-Jackson	Scottsdale, AZ	1/14	1324
79	$695,500	1965	Shelby	Cobra 289 Dragonsnake Racer	RM	Boca Raton, FL	2/10	SP23
80	$694,373	1963	Lola-Chevrolet	Mk 6 GT Endurance Racer	Bonhams	Sussex, U.K.	9/1	211
81	$693,000	1929	Duesenberg	Model J Clear Vision Sedan	RM	Amelia Island, FL	3/11	140
82	$682,000	1938	Bugatti	Type 57 Atalante Coupe	Gooding	Pebble Beach, CA	8/20	64
83	$682,000	1933	Cadillac	V16 Model 452-C Convertible Phaeton	RM	Rochester, MI	8/5	264
84	$671,000	1937	Lagonda	LG45 Rapide	RM	Monterey, CA	8/18	464
85	$662,602	1929	Duesenberg	Model J Convertible Coupe	H&H	London, U.K.	5/24	55
86	$660,000	1980	Ferrari	312 T5 Formula One Racer	Gooding	Palm Beach, FL	1/24	23
87	$660,000	1964	Shelby	Cobra 289 Dragonsnake Racer	RM	Monterey, CA	8/18	181
88	$658,500	1930	Isotta Fraschini	8AS Boattail Convertible	Christie's	Greenwich, CT	6/4	9
89	$649,000	1948	Cadillac	Custom Cabriolet	RM	Monterey, CA	8/18	443
90	$648,000	1971	Plymouth	Hemi 'Cuda	Barrett-Jackson	Scottsdale, AZ	1/14	1319
91	$648,000	2007	Shelby	GT500	Barrett-Jackson	Scottsdale, AZ	1/14	1259.1
92	$643,500	1966	Shelby	Cobra 289 Competition	Russo and Steele	Monterey, CA	8/18	S257
93	$627,000	1931	Chrysler	Imperial Dual Cowl Phaeton AND 1931 Chrysler Imperial Sedan	Gooding	Pebble Beach, CA	8/20	47
94	$621,500	1928	Cadillac	V8 Town Sedan	RM	Phoenix, AZ	1/20	180
95	$621,000	1956	Mercedes-Benz	300SL	Barrett-Jackson	Scottsdale, AZ	1/14	1299.1
96	$616,000	1967	Ferrari	275 GTB/4	RM	Phoenix, AZ	1/20	154
97	$616,000	1914	Marmon	41 Speedster	Gooding	Pebble Beach, CA	8/20	32
98	$614,250	1969	Dodge	Daytona	Mecum	Kissimmee, FL	1/27	X13
99	$605,000	1930	Bentley	Speed Six Le Mans Tourer	RM	Phoenix, AZ	1/20	174
100	$605,000	1968	Chevrolet	Corvette Stingray Racer	RM	Phoenix, AZ	1/20	161
101	$605,000	1957	Mercedes-Benz	300SL Roadster	RM	Monterey, CA	8/18	475
102	$605,000	1967	Shelby	Cobra 427	Russo and Steele	Scottsdale, AZ	1/20	S223
103	$595,425	1963	Ferrari	250 GT Berlinetta Lusso Competizione	Bonhams	Monte Carlo, MCO	5/20	194
104	$594,000	1966	Shelby	Cobra 427	Barrett-Jackson	Scottsdale, AZ	1/14	1291
105	$579,000	1972	Porsche	917/10 Racer	Bonhams	Carmel, CA	8/18	519
106	$577,500	1948	Tucker	48 Torpedo	RM	Monterey, CA	8/18	458
107	$572,400	1932	Auburn	12 Boattail Speedster	Kruse	Auburn, IN	8/30	1047
108	$572,400	2005	Ford	GT	Barrett-Jackson	West Palm Beach, FL	3/29	5001
109	$566,280	1966	Shelby	Cobra 427	Russo and Steele	Scottsdale, AZ	1/20	F227
110	$565,000	1963	Porsche	904	Christie's	Monterey, CA	8/17	26
111	$557,000	1966	Porsche	906 Carrera 6	Bonhams	Carmel, CA	8/18	510
112	$556,200	1960	Lincoln	Continental Mk V Elvis Presley's Limousine	Barrett-Jackson	Scottsdale, AZ	1/14	1316
113	$550,000	1966	Shelby	Cobra 427	RM	Boca Raton, FL	2/10	SP30
114	$543,533	1965	Ferrari	275 GTB/6C Berlinetta	Bonhams	Monte Carlo, MCO	5/20	254

Rank	Sold Price	Year	Make	Model	Auction Co.	Location	Date	Lot #
115	$541,080	1932	Packard	Series 904 Custom Dietrich Convertible Victoria	Leake	Tulsa, OK	6/9	2471
116	$540,750	1964	Shelby	Cobra 289	Mecum	Belvidere, IL	5/25	S530.1
117	$540,000	1963	Dodge	Polara Custom 2-Door	Barrett-Jackson	Scottsdale, AZ	1/14	1292.1
118	$540,000	2005	Lamborghini	Gallardo	Kruse	Auburn, IN	8/30	1449
119	$540,000	1956	Mercedes-Benz	300SL	Barrett-Jackson	Scottsdale, AZ	1/14	1310
120	$533,500	1934	Packard	Twelve Runabout Speedster	RM	Amelia Island, FL	3/11	154
121	$532,090	1935	Mercedes-Benz	500K Kombination Roadster	H&H	London, U.K.	5/24	44
122	$531,744	1964	Porsche	904 GTS	Osenat	Paris, FRA	6/10	566
123	$522,361	1946	Cameron Millar	250F CM4	Artcurial	Paris, FRA	2/12	48
124	$520,349	1966	Shelby	Cobra 427	Coys	Oxfordshire, U.K.	8/26	131
125	$513,000	1970	Chevrolet	Chevelle SS 454 LS6 Convertible	Barrett-Jackson	Scottsdale, AZ	1/14	1320
126	$513,000	1968	Ford	Mustang 428 CJ Fastback	Barrett-Jackson	Scottsdale, AZ	1/14	1274.1
127	$502,000	1929	Duesenberg	Model J Convertible Sedan	Bonhams	Carmel, CA	8/18	548
128	$495,000	1931	Cadillac	V16 Sport Phaeton	RM	Rochester, MI	8/5	229
129	$495,000	1914	Rolls-Royce	40/50hp Silver Ghost	RM	Rochester, MI	8/5	265
130	$489,500	1962	Chevrolet	Corvette	Gooding	Palm Beach, FL	1/24	27
131	$486,000	1969	Chevrolet	Camaro SS Baldwin Motion	Barrett-Jackson	Scottsdale, AZ	1/14	1290
132	$486,000	1969	Chevrolet	Camaro ZL1	Barrett-Jackson	Scottsdale, AZ	1/14	1322
133	$486,000	1970	Plymouth	Hemi 'Cuda	Barrett-Jackson	Scottsdale, AZ	1/14	1274
134	$477,000	1972	Lamborghini	Miura P400 SV	Christie's	Monterey, CA	8/17	11
135	$475,651	1983	Lancia-Martini	LC 2 Endurance Racer	Artcurial	Paris, FRA	2/12	57
136	$474,345	1946	Frazer Nash-BMW	328 Roadster	Bonhams	Sussex, U.K.	9/1	245
137	$473,000	1965	Ferrari	275 GTB/2	Worldwide Group	Seabrook, TX	5/6	85
138	$472,811	1937	Maserati	4CM	Christie's	Paris, FRA	7/8	105
139	$467,747	1947	Alfa Romeo	6C 2500 SS	Coys	Monte Carlo, MCO	5/20	259
140	$467,500	1937	Bugatti	Type 57C Ventoux	RM	Monterey, CA	8/18	473
141	$455,175	1956	Ferrari	250 GT Alloy Berlinetta	Bonhams	Monte Carlo, MCO	5/20	200
142	$455,000	1930	Packard	734 Speedster-Roadster	Christie's	Greenwich, CT	6/4	21
143	$452,800	1953	Fiat	8V Ghia Supersonic	Sportscar Auction Co.	Geneva, CH	10/7	37
144	$449,500	1931	Packard	Deluxe Eight	Christie's	Monterey, CA	8/17	48
145	$445,500	1965	Aston Martin	DB6 Short Chassis Volante	RM	Phoenix, AZ	1/20	166
146	$445,358	1904	CGV	Phaeton Modele H1 6 1/4-Liter	Christie's	Paris, FRA	2/11	73
147	$442,800	1967	Shelby	GT500	Barrett-Jackson	Scottsdale, AZ	1/14	1326
148	$432,000	1935	Auburn	851 Boattail Speedster	Kruse	Scottsdale, AZ	1/26	2750
149	$432,000	1959	Mercedes-Benz	300SL Roadster	Barrett-Jackson	Scottsdale, AZ	1/14	1308
150	$432,000	1968	Shelby	GT500 KR	Barrett-Jackson	Scottsdale, AZ	1/14	1290.1
151	$430,500	1956	Mercedes-Benz	300SL	Bonhams	Carmel, CA	8/18	529
152	$429,000	1952	Ferrari	212 Touring Barchetta	RM	Phoenix, AZ	1/20	179
153	$427,125	1938	Delahaye	135M Cabriolet	Bonhams	Monte Carlo, MCO	5/20	155
154	$426,600	1937	Alfa Romeo	6C 2300 MM	Kruse	Seaside, CA	8/17	410
155	$424,100	1965	Shelby	Cobra 427	Sportscar Auction Co.	Geneva, CH	10/7	36A
156	$423,500	1969	McLaren	M6GT Racer	RM	Phoenix, AZ	1/20	188
157	$420,245	1965	Shelby	Cobra 289	Bonhams	Sussex, U.K.	7/7	560
158	$418,572	1956	Ferrari	250 GT Boano	Coys	Nuremberg, DE	7/22	247
159	$418,000	1957	Mercedes-Benz	300Sc Convertible	Gooding	Pebble Beach, CA	8/20	70
160	$418,000	1956	Mercedes-Benz	300SL	RM	Monterey, CA	8/18	463
161	$418,000	1933	Pierce-Arrow	Twelve Convertible Sedan	RM	Amelia Island, FL	3/11	167
162	$415,596	1964	Ferrari	500 Superfast	Artcurial	Paris, FRA	2/12	46
163	$412,500	1965	Chevrolet	Chevelle Z16	Russo and Steele	Scottsdale, AZ	1/20	S232
164	$412,500	2005	Porsche	Carrera GT	Russo and Steele	Monterey, CA	8/18	S248
165	$412,500	1966	Shelby	Cobra 427	RM	Monterey, CA	8/18	169
166	$410,666	1993	Williams-Renault	FW16C Formula One Racer	Artcurial	Paris, FRA	6/12	29
167	$410,000	1970	Pontiac	GTO Judge Ram Air Iv Convertible	RM	Boca Raton, FL	2/10	SP36
168	$408,923	1964	Ferrari	250 GTL Lusso	Artcurial	Paris, FRA	2/12	51
169	$407,000	1932	Duesenberg	Model J Dual Cowl Phaeton	RM	Amelia Island, FL	3/11	163
170	$407,000	1940	Lincoln-Zephyr	Continental Cabriolet	RM	Hampton, NH	6/10	2186
171	$403,127	1965	Ferrari	275 GTB	Coys	Maastricht, NL	1/14	224
172	$401,003	1931	Bentley	4/8-Liter Four Seater Le Mans Replica	Bonhams	Sussex, U.K.	9/1	215
173	$399,600	1939	Bentley	Royale Custom	Barrett-Jackson	West Palm Beach, FL	3/29	724
174	$396,000	1936	Bugatti	Type 57 Stelvio	RM	Monterey, CA	8/18	481
175	$396,000	1955	Ford	Custom Beatnik Bubbletop	RM	Monterey, CA	8/18	141
176	$396,000	1963	Mercedes-Benz	300SL Roadster	Gooding	Pebble Beach, CA	8/20	87
177	$390,500	1966	Shelby	Cobra 427	RM	Phoenix, AZ	1/20	145

Rank	Sold Price	Year	Make	Model	Auction Co.	Location	Date	Lot #
178	$388,800	1967	Ford	GT40 Mk V	Barrett-Jackson	Scottsdale, AZ	1/14	1314
179	$385,000	1947	Cisitalia	202 Spider Nuvolari	Gooding	Pebble Beach, CA	8/20	73
180	$385,000	1972	Ferrari	365 GTS/4 Michelotti NART Spyder	RM	Monterey, CA	8/18	470
181	$385,000	1964	Shelby	Cobra 289	RM	Phoenix, AZ	1/20	133
182	$385,000	1964	Shelby	Cobra 289	RM	Phoenix, AZ	1/20	158
183	$383,400	1953	Buick	Skylark Convertible	Barrett-Jackson	West Palm Beach, FL	3/29	703.1
184	$381,000	1974	Shadow-AVS	DN4	Bonhams	Carmel, CA	8/18	513
185	$379,500	1970	Plymouth	Superbird	Russo and Steele	Scottsdale, AZ	1/20	F228
186	$378,000	1931	Bentley	Aero Coupe	Barrett-Jackson	West Palm Beach, FL	3/29	723.1
187	$378,000	1967	Chevrolet	Corvette 427/435 Convertible	Barrett-Jackson	Scottsdale, AZ	1/14	1284
188	$378,000	1957	Chrysler	Imperial Convertible	Barrett-Jackson	Scottsdale, AZ	1/14	1278.1
189	$378,000	1953	Ford	Vega "Gardner Special" Roadster	Barrett-Jackson	Scottsdale, AZ	1/14	1276
190	$378,000	1931	Stutz	SV-16 Cabriolet Coupe	Kruse	Scottsdale, AZ	1/26	2749
191	$375,500	1947	Delahaye	135MS Cabriolet	Bonhams	Carmel, CA	8/18	512
192	$375,500	1949	Talbot-Lago	T26 Grand Sport Cabriolet	Bonhams	Carmel, CA	8/18	515
193	$374,000	1953	Cunningham	C-3 Continental	RM	Monterey, CA	8/18	478
194	$372,600	1957	Mercedes-Benz	300SL	Barrett-Jackson	Scottsdale, AZ	1/14	1286
195	$368,500	1963	Shelby	Cobra 289	Russo and Steele	Scottsdale, AZ	1/20	S228
196	$368,500	1915	Stutz	Bearcat	RM	Rochester, MI	8/5	234
197	$367,500	1968	Chevrolet	Yenko Camaro	Mecum	Belvidere, IL	5/25	S514
198	$367,500	1964	Chevrolet	Corvette	Mecum	St. Charles, IL	6/16	S510
199	$367,500	1964	Dodge	Hemi 330	Mecum	Belvidere, IL	5/25	S536
200	$366,560	1954	Mercedes-Benz	300SL	Coys	Maastricht, NL	1/14	215
201	$363,000	1931	Cadillac	V16 Sport Phaeton	RM	Phoenix, AZ	1/20	142
202	$363,000	1954	Packard	Panther-Daytona Roadster Concept Car	RM	Phoenix, AZ	1/20	138
203	$362,250	1969	Dodge	Daytona	Mecum	Belvidere, IL	5/25	S502
204	$361,800	1995	Batmobile	"Batman Forever"	Kruse	Auburn, IN	8/30	8001
205	$357,500	1967	Ferrari	330 GTS	RM	Phoenix, AZ	1/20	134
206	$357,000	1954	Mercedes-Benz	300S Roadster	Coys	Monte Carlo, MCO	5/20	223
207	$348,000	1950	Talbot-Lago	T26 Grand Sport	Bonhams	Carmel, CA	8/18	526
208	$346,500	1955	Chevrolet	Corvette Roadster	Mecum	St. Charles, IL	6/16	S539
209	$346,500	1956	Mercedes-Benz	300SL	Gooding	Pebble Beach, CA	8/20	99
210	$345,600	1939	Lincoln	Lead Zephyr	Barrett-Jackson	Scottsdale, AZ	1/14	1291.1
211	$345,600	1970	Plymouth	Hemi 'Cuda	Leake	Tulsa, OK	6/9	2515
212	$345,000	1967	Ferrari	330 GT 4-Liter Michelotti	Christie's	Monterey, CA	8/17	38
213	$345,000	1959	Porsche	356 Carrera Speedster	Christie's	Monterey, CA	8/17	24
214	$343,750	1956	Mercedes-Benz	300SL	Russo and Steele	Monterey, CA	8/18	S253
215	$342,400	1965	Shelby	Cobra 289	RM	Boca Raton, FL	2/10	NR98
216	$341,585	1967	Chevrolet	Camaro	Silver	Reno, NV	8/6	423
217	$341,250	1970	Plymouth	Hemi 'Cuda	Mecum	Belvidere, IL	5/25	S540
218	$341,000	1971	Dodge	Hemi Challenger R/T	Worldwide Group	Seabrook, TX	5/6	62
219	$341,000	1957	Ferrari	250 GT LWB Berlinetta	RM	Monterey, CA	8/18	461
220	$341,000	1971	Ferrari	365 GTB/4 Daytona "Hot Rod"	Gooding	Pebble Beach, CA	8/20	49
221	$339,040	1970	Dodge	Hemi Challenger	G. Potter King	Atlantic City, NJ	2/23	1024
222	$335,880	1965	Shelby	GT350	Barrett-Jackson	Scottsdale, AZ	1/14	1289
223	$334,800	1969	Chevrolet	Corvette	Barrett-Jackson	Scottsdale, AZ	1/14	1271.1
224	$334,000	1956	Mercedes-Benz	300SL	Christie's	Greenwich, CT	6/4	34
225	$334,000	1972	Porsche	911 RS Prototype	Christie's	Monterey, CA	8/17	29
226	$330,750	1970	Plymouth	Hemi 'Cuda	Mecum	Belvidere, IL	5/25	S524.1
227	$330,000	1970	Mercedes-Benz	600 LWB Landaulet	RM	Phoenix, AZ	1/20	181
228	$330,000	1970	Plymouth	Hemi 'Cuda	RM	Phoenix, AZ	1/20	141
229	$330,000	1968	Shelby	GT500 KR Convertible	Worldwide Group	Seabrook, TX	5/6	31
230	$325,500	1963	Chevrolet	Impala Z11	Mecum	Belvidere, IL	5/25	S518.1
231	$324,500	1970	Chevrolet	Chevelle	Russo and Steele	Scottsdale, AZ	1/20	F226
232	$324,000	1967	Chevrolet	Camaro Z/28 Racer	Barrett-Jackson	West Palm Beach, FL	3/29	733
233	$324,000	1969	Dodge	Daytona Wing Racer	Barrett-Jackson	Scottsdale, AZ	1/14	1335
234	$324,000	1968	Dodge	Hemi Dart	Barrett-Jackson	Scottsdale, AZ	1/14	1232.1
235	$324,000	1963	Mercedes-Benz	300SL Roadster	Barrett-Jackson	Scottsdale, AZ	1/14	1285
236	$323,000	1947	Bugatti	Type 73C Monoposto	Christie's	Monterey, CA	8/17	21
237	$321,237	1957	Mercedes-Benz	300SL	Bonhams & Goodman	Sydney, AU	3/26	11
238	$319,000	1964	Lincoln	Continental Papal Limousine	RM	Monterey, CA	8/18	453
239	$317,183	1964	Cooper-Maserati	Type 61 Mk V Racer	Bonhams	Sussex, U.K.	9/1	224
240	$315,503	1967	Alpine	A210	Artcurial	Paris, FRA	2/12	20
241	$315,000	1971	Dodge	Hemi Charger	Mecum	Belvidere, IL	5/25	S538

Rank	Sold Price	Year	Make	Model	Auction Co.	Location	Date	Lot #
242	$314,868	1963	Aston Martin	DB4 Convertible	Bonhams	Newport Pagnell, U.K.	5/13	132
243	$313,500	1951	Allard	J2X Le Mans Racer	RM	Monterey, CA	8/18	440
244	$313,500	1969	Shelby	GT500	Russo and Steele	Monterey, CA	8/18	S259
245	$310,000	1936	Auburn	852 Supercharged Boattail Speedster	RM	Rochester, MI	8/5	263
246	$308,000	1935	Bentley	3 1/2-Liter Three-Window Coupe	Gooding	Pebble Beach, CA	8/20	41
247	$308,000	1967	Chevrolet	Corvette 427/435	Russo and Steele	Monterey, CA	8/18	S256
248	$308,000	1940	Ford	Deluxe Station Wagon	RM	Hampton, NH	6/10	2184
249	$308,000	1969	Ford	Mustang Boss 429	Russo and Steele	Scottsdale, AZ	1/20	S230
250	$308,000	1965	Shelby	GT350	Russo and Steele	Monterey, CA	8/18	F148
251	$307,800	1965	Shelby	GT350 Custom Fastback	Barrett-Jackson	Scottsdale, AZ	1/14	1302
252	$306,206	1961	Mercedes-Benz	300SL Roadster	Coys	Maastricht, NL	1/14	212
253	$304,973	2006	Ford	GT	Artcurial	Paris, FRA	6/12	35
254	$304,000	1927	Hispano-Suiza	H6B Coupe Chauffeur	Bonhams	Carmel, CA	8/18	553
255	$302,500	1937	Studebaker	Posies Extemeliner Woody	RM	Monterey, CA	8/18	140
256	$302,400	1968	Shelby	GT500 KR Convertible	Barrett-Jackson	Scottsdale, AZ	1/14	1267
257	$300,900	1969	Lamborghini	Miura P400S	Bonhams	Monte Carlo, MCO	5/20	190
258	$299,250	1963	Chevrolet	Impala Z11	Mecum	Kissimmee, FL	1/27	X30
259	$299,000	1937	Horch	853 Cabriolet A	RM	Cortland, NY	6/24	371
260	$297,000	1965	Shelby	GT350	Russo and Steele	Scottsdale, AZ	1/20	F217
261	$296,228	1938	Jaguar	SS100 3 1/2-Liter Tourer	Bonhams	Sussex, U.K.	9/1	244
262	$294,250	1969	Dodge	Hemi Charger 500	RM	Boca Raton, FL	2/10	SP31
263	$291,600	1957	Chevrolet	Corvette ZL1 Convertible	Barrett-Jackson	Scottsdale, AZ	1/14	1295
264	$291,500	1969	Chevrolet	Yenko Camaro	Russo and Steele	Monterey, CA	8/18	S250
265	$290,000	1961	Mercedes-Benz	300SL Roadster	RM	Amelia Island, FL	3/11	136
266	$288,750	1969	Chevrolet	Chevelle SS	Mecum	Belvidere, IL	5/25	S545.1
267	$286,875	1964	Ferrari	250 GTL Lusso	Bonhams	Monte Carlo, MCO	5/20	152
268	$286,785	1992	Ferrari	F40	Coys	Nuremberg, DE	7/22	230
269	$286,000	1988	Porsche	959 Komfort Coupe	RM	Amelia Island, FL	3/11	168
270	$283,500	1941	Packard	Super Eight LeBaron Limousine	Kruse	Auburn, IN	8/30	1058
271	$283,050	1957	Talbot-Lago	Dupont Barquette	Coys	Monte Carlo, MCO	5/20	233
272	$280,500	1933	Chrysler	Imperial Sport Phaeton	RM	Rochester, MI	8/5	259
273	$280,500	1941	Chrysler	Royal Town & Country	RM	Phoenix, AZ	1/20	183
274	$278,369	1955	Bentley	R-Type Continental	Coys	Maastricht, NL	1/14	231
275	$278,250	1964	Chevrolet	Corvette	Mecum	St. Charles, IL	6/16	S507
276	$275,273	1959	Lister-Jaguar	Costin Racer	Bonhams	Sussex, U.K.	9/1	240
277	$275,000	1966	Aston Martin	DBR1 Alloy Replica	RM	Monterey, CA	8/18	467
278	$275,000	1963	Ferrari	250 Drogo Speciale	RM	Monterey, CA	8/18	488
279	$275,000	1934	Ford	Deluxe Station Wagon	RM	Hampton, NH	6/10	2159
280	$275,000	1947	Ford	Super Deluxe Sportsman Convertible	RM	Hampton, NH	6/10	2193
281	$275,000	1956	Mercedes-Benz	300Sc	Gooding	Pebble Beach, CA	8/20	81
282	$275,000	1967	Shelby	Cobra 427	RM	Monterey, CA	8/18	173
283	$275,000	1968	Shelby	GT500 KR	Russo and Steele	Monterey, CA	8/18	F153
284	$275,000	1916	Stutz	Bearcat	RM	Amelia Island, FL	3/11	139
285	$274,459	1971	Ferrari	365 GTB/4 Daytona	Coys	Monte Carlo, MCO	5/20	244
286	$273,264	1960	Aston Martin	DB4 Series 2	Bonhams	Newport Pagnell, U.K.	5/13	125
287	$273,000	1968	Shelby	GT500 KR	Mecum	Belvidere, IL	5/25	S566
288	$272,850	1957	Mercedes-Benz	300Sc Convertible	Bonhams	Monte Carlo, MCO	5/20	177
289	$272,850	1955	Moretti	750S MM Bialbero Spyder Gran Sport	Bonhams	Monte Carlo, MCO	5/20	239
290	$271,082	1973	Ferrari	365 GTB/4 Daytona	Bonhams	Sussex, U.K.	9/1	239
291	$270,000	1935	Auburn	851 Supercharged Cabriolet	Kruse	Scottsdale, AZ	1/26	2748
292	$270,000	1938	Cadillac	90 Series Town Car	Kruse	Auburn, IN	8/30	1057
293	$270,000	1964	Ford	Thunderbolt	Barrett-Jackson	Scottsdale, AZ	1/14	1334.1
294	$270,000	1938	Packard	Custom Limousine	Barrett-Jackson	Scottsdale, AZ	1/14	1553
295	$270,000	1970	Plymouth	Hemi 'Cuda	Barrett-Jackson	Scottsdale, AZ	1/14	1235.2
296	$270,000	1967	Shelby	GT500	Barrett-Jackson	Scottsdale, AZ	1/14	1259
297	$270,000	1964	Shelby	Cobra Daytona Coupe Replica	Barrett-Jackson	West Palm Beach, FL	3/29	720
298	$269,500	1967	Bizzarrini	5300GT Alloy	Worldwide Group	Seabrook, TX	5/6	67
299	$269,500	1960	Jaguar	XK 150S 3.8 Drophead Coupe	Gooding	Pebble Beach, CA	8/20	67
300	$269,500	1917	Packard	2-25 Twin Six Runabout Racer	Worldwide Group	Seabrook, TX	5/6	26
301	$267,750	1954	Mercedes-Benz	300S Cabriolet	Coys	Monte Carlo, MCO	5/20	264
302	$267,585	1928	Bentley	6 1/2-Liter	Bonhams	Hendon, U.K.	4/24	625
303	$267,300	1965	Aston Martin	DB5	RM	Phoenix, AZ	1/20	148
304	$264,600	1967	Dodge	Hemi Coronet R/T Convertible	Barrett-Jackson	Scottsdale, AZ	1/14	1288

Rank	Sold Price	Year	Make	Model	Auction Co.	Location	Date	Lot #
305	$264,000	1964	Ferrari	250 GTO Replica	RM	Monterey, CA	8/18	433
306	$264,000	1968	Howmet	Turbine Racer	RM	Los Angeles, CA	5/13	240
307	$264,000	1938	Lencki	Championship Car	Russo and Steele	Monterey, CA	8/18	S255
308	$264,000	1957	Mercedes-Benz	300SL Roadster	RM	Amelia Island, FL	3/11	185
309	$262,500	1969	Chevrolet	Camaro COPO	Mecum	Belvidere, IL	5/25	S569
310	$262,500	1967	Chevrolet	Corvette	Mecum	St. Charles, IL	6/16	S528
311	$262,098	1955	Bentley	R-Type Continental	Christie's	Paris, FRA	2/11	61
312	$259,200	1931	Cadillac	V12 Convertible Coupe	Kruse	Auburn, IN	5/18	7005
313	$259,200	1969	Chevrolet	Camaro	Barrett-Jackson	Scottsdale, AZ	1/14	1300
314	$259,200	1967	Chevrolet	Corvette 427/435	Barrett-Jackson	West Palm Beach, FL	3/29	659.1
315	$259,200	1953	Mercedes-Benz	300Sc Convertible	Barrett-Jackson	West Palm Beach, FL	3/29	706
316	$258,500	1938	Lincoln-Zephyr	Convertible Coupe	RM	Hampton, NH	6/10	2177
317	$257,722	1938	Jaguar	SS100	Coys	Donington Park, U.K.	4/30	221
318	$257,331	1964	Aston Martin	DB5	Bonhams	Sussex, U.K.	7/7	539
319	$256,413	1939	Talbot-Lago	T150C 4.0-Liter Competition Roadster	Bonhams	Sussex, U.K.	9/1	241
320	$255,000	1989	Ferrari	F40	Bonhams	Monte Carlo, MCO	5/20	192
321	$254,318	1966	Lola-Chevrolet	T70 Group 7 Racer	Bonhams	Sussex, U.K.	9/1	227
322	$253,800	1969	Shelby	GT500 Convertible	Leake	Tulsa, OK	6/9	2529
323	$253,800	1968	Shelby	GT500 KR Convertible	Kruse	Scottsdale, AZ	1/26	2751
324	$253,000	1971	Ferrari	365 GTS/4 Daytona Spyder Alloy Conversion	RM	Monterey, CA	8/18	474
325	$253,000	1966	Lamborghini	GT 400	RM	Monterey, CA	8/18	487
326	$253,000	1933	Lincoln	KB Convertible Coupe	RM	Phoenix, AZ	1/20	184
327	$253,000	1940	Packard	Custom Super Eight One-Eighty Convertible Victoria	Gooding	Palm Beach, FL	1/24	12
328	$253,000	1934	Packard	Model 1104 Super Eight Victoria	Gooding	Pebble Beach, CA	8/20	39
329	$253,000	1937	Rolls-Royce	Phantom III 4-Door Cabriolet	Gooding	Pebble Beach, CA	8/20	76
330	$251,397	1973	Ferrari	365 GTB/4 Daytona	Coys	Nuremberg, DE	7/22	243
331	$251,397	2000	Jaguar	XJR15	Coys	Nuremberg, DE	7/22	241
332	$249,375	1965	Chevrolet	Corvette	Mecum	St. Charles, IL	6/16	S506
333	$248,400	1967	Chevrolet	Corvette 427/435 Convertible	Barrett-Jackson	Scottsdale, AZ	1/14	1298
334	$248,400	1968	Chevrolet	Biscayne	Barrett-Jackson	West Palm Beach, FL	3/29	704
335	$248,400	1939	Lincoln-Zephyr	Custom 2-Door Coupe	Barrett-Jackson	Scottsdale, AZ	1/14	1329
336	$248,400	1968	Plymouth	Hemi Barracuda Factory Racer	Barrett-Jackson	Scottsdale, AZ	1/14	1240
337	$247,500	1939	Alfa Romeo	6C 2500 Sport Cabriolet	Worldwide Group	Seabrook, TX	5/6	39
338	$247,500	1958	Devin	SS Sports Racer	RM	Monterey, CA	8/18	480
339	$245,160	1967	Shelby	GT500	Barrett-Jackson	West Palm Beach, FL	3/29	712
340	$243,840	1965	McLaren	M1A Racer	Bonhams	Sussex, U.K.	9/1	218
341	$243,822	1937	Jaguar	SS100 2 1/2-Liter	H&H	Buxton, U.K.	2/21	65
342	$243,822	1935	MG	R-Type Racer	H&H	Buxton, U.K.	2/21	45
343	$243,000	1995	Lotec	C1000 Racer	Barrett-Jackson	Scottsdale, AZ	1/14	1315
344	$243,000	1999	Mercedes-Benz	300SL Replica	Barrett-Jackson	West Palm Beach, FL	3/29	738
345	$243,000	1953	Oldsmobile	Fiesta Convertible	RM	Novi, MI	9/22	SP05
346	$243,000	1970	Plymouth	Hemi 'Cuda	Barrett-Jackson	Scottsdale, AZ	1/14	1296
347	$242,000	1966	Ferrari	275 GTS	RM	Phoenix, AZ	1/20	144
348	$240,750	1968	Shelby	GT500 KR Convertible	RM	Boca Raton, FL	2/10	SP16
349	$238,000	1983	Jaguar	XJR-5	Bonhams	Carmel, CA	8/18	514
350	$238,000	1930	Rolls-Royce	40/50hp Phantom II Dual Cowl Phaeton	Bonhams	North Brookfield, MA	9/23	1010
351	$238,000	1929	Rolls-Royce	Phantom I Springfield Henley Convertible Coupe	Bonhams	Carmel, CA	8/18	542
352	$237,600	1969	Chevrolet	Corvette	Barrett-Jackson	Scottsdale, AZ	1/14	1325
353	$237,600	1957	Chevrolet	Corvette	Barrett-Jackson	Scottsdale, AZ	1/14	1282.1
354	$237,600	1954	Chevrolet	Corvette Roadster	Barrett-Jackson	West Palm Beach, FL	3/29	652
355	$237,600	1934	Lincoln	KB LeBaron Convertible	Barrett-Jackson	Scottsdale, AZ	1/14	1280.1
356	$237,600	1967	Shelby	GT500	Barrett-Jackson	Scottsdale, AZ	1/14	1297
357	$236,500	1940	Ford	Convertible "Valley" Custom	RM	Monterey, CA	8/18	142
358	$236,500	1967	Shelby	GT500	Russo and Steele	Monterey, CA	8/18	S251
359	$236,250	1969	Mercury	Cougar	Mecum	Belvidere, IL	5/25	S572
360	$236,250	1967	Shelby	GT500	Mecum	Belvidere, IL	5/25	S556
361	$236,071	1961	Jaguar	XKE Competition Roadster	Bonhams	Stoneleigh Park, UK	2/25	347
362	$235,918	1949	Jaguar	XK 120 Alloy Roadster	Christie's	Paris, FRA	2/11	78
363	$235,430	1973	Ferrari	365 GTB/4 Daytona	Artcurial	Paris, FRA	2/12	45
364	$235,000	1931	Packard	845 Deluxe Eight Convertible Coupe	Christie's	Greenwich, CT	6/4	19
365	$234,368	1968	Lamborghini	Miura P400	Coys	London, U.K.	2/28	126

Rank	Sold Price	Year	Make	Model	Auction Co.	Location	Date	Lot #
366	$233,836	1958	Mercedes-Benz	300SL Roadster	Coys	Maastricht, NL	1/14	234
367	$233,363	1969	Lola-Chevrolet	T70GT Mk III Group 4 Racer	Bonhams	Sussex, U.K.	9/1	232
368	$232,200	2003	Aston Martin	DB AR1 Roadster	Barrett-Jackson	Scottsdale, AZ	1/14	1314.1
369	$232,200	1969	Chevrolet	Camaro Z/28 RS	Barrett-Jackson	West Palm Beach, FL	3/29	658
370	$232,200	1970	Shelby	GT500 Convertible	Barrett-Jackson	Scottsdale, AZ	1/14	1244
371	$231,660	1965	Aston Martin	DB5	Bonhams	Newport Pagnell, U.K.	5/13	129
372	$231,000	1938	Cadillac	Series 38-90 V16 Convertible Coupe	RM	Amelia Island, FL	3/11	159
373	$231,000	1963	Chevrolet	Corvette Z06	RM	Monterey, CA	8/18	157
374	$231,000	1951	Ferrari	195 Inter	RM	Monterey, CA	8/18	467A
375	$231,000	1961	Ferrari	250 GT Series II Cabriolet	RM	Phoenix, AZ	1/20	127
376	$231,000	1939	Ford	Deluxe Station Wagon	RM	Hampton, NH	6/10	2180
377	$231,000	1935	Lincoln	Model K Convertible Coupe	RM	Rochester, MI	8/5	249
378	$231,000	1956	Mercedes-Benz	300Sc	Gooding	Palm Beach, FL	1/24	24
379	$231,000	1931	Packard	Deluxe Eight Convertible Victoria	RM	Phoenix, AZ	1/20	173
380	$231,000	1931	Packard	Deluxe Eight Sport Phaeton	RM	Amelia Island, FL	3/11	145
381	$231,000	1930	Packard	Model 745 Convertible Coupe	RM	Amelia Island, FL	3/11	179
382	$231,000	1970	Plymouth	Hemi 'Cuda	Russo and Steele	Monterey, CA	8/18	S254
383	$231,000	1929	Rolls-Royce	Phantom II Imperial Cabriolet	RM	Amelia Island, FL	3/11	149
384	$231,000	1967	Shelby	GT500	Mecum	Belvidere, IL	5/25	S564
385	$230,050	1963	Chevrolet	Corvette Z06	RM	Boca Raton, FL	2/10	SP17
386	$229,500	1938	Packard	1608 Convertible Sedan	Kruse	Auburn, IN	8/30	1034
387	$228,960	1967	Chevrolet	Corvette 427/435 Convertible	Barrett-Jackson	Scottsdale, AZ	1/14	1265
388	$226,800	1967	Chevrolet	Corvette	Mecum	Kissimmee, FL	1/27	X27
389	$226,800	2002	Ferrari	360 Modena Spyder	Barrett-Jackson	West Palm Beach, FL	3/29	649
390	$226,800	1953	Ford	FR100 Pickup	Barrett-Jackson	Scottsdale, AZ	1/14	1236.1
391	$226,800	1970	Plymouth	AAR 'Cuda	Barrett-Jackson	Scottsdale, AZ	1/14	1234
392	$226,800	1967	Shelby	GT500	Barrett-Jackson	West Palm Beach, FL	3/29	656
393	$225,988	1967	Toyota	2000GT	Christie's	Paris, FRA	7/8	124
394	$225,600	1969	Ford	Mustang Boss 429	MidAmerica	Minneapolis, MN	9/22	141
395	$225,500	1950	Jaguar	XK 120 Alloy Roadster	Worldwide Group	Seabrook, TX	5/6	33
396	$225,500	1968	Shelby	GT500 KR	RM	Amelia Island, FL	3/11	160
397	$225,000	1953	Mercedes-Benz	300S Cabriolet	RM	Amelia Island, FL	3/11	193
398	$224,172	1938	Aston Martin	15/98 Short Chassis	Christie's	London, U.K.	6/26	170
399	$222,828	1950	Alfa Romeo	6C 2500 SS "Tubolare"	Christie's	Paris, FRA	2/11	84
400	$222,480	1967	Shelby	GT500	Barrett-Jackson	Scottsdale, AZ	1/14	1250
401	$221,500	1971	Lola-Chevrolet	T260 Racer	Bonhams	Carmel, CA	8/18	517
402	$221,500	1972	Shadow	Chevrolet	Bonhams	Carmel, CA	8/18	516
403	$221,400	1969	Chevrolet	Camaro Z/28	Barrett-Jackson	Scottsdale, AZ	1/14	1030
404	$221,400	1967	Chevrolet	Corvette 427/400 Convertible	Barrett-Jackson	Scottsdale, AZ	1/14	1275
405	$221,400	1967	Chevrolet	Corvette 427/435 Convertible	Barrett-Jackson	Scottsdale, AZ	1/14	1236
406	$221,259	1967	Aston Martin	DB6 Vantage Volante	Bonhams	Newport Pagnell, U.K.	5/13	138
407	$220,500	1963	Chevrolet	Corvette Z06	Mecum	Kissimmee, FL	1/27	X12
408	$220,500	1968	Shelby	GT500 KR	Mecum	Belvidere, IL	5/25	S535.1
409	$220,480	1970	Ford	Mustang	G. Potter King	Atlantic City, NJ	2/23	1784.1
410	$220,000	1933	Ford	Elgin Racer	RM	Hampton, NH	6/10	2158
411	$220,000	1957	Ford	Thunderbird Convertible	RM	Monterey, CA	8/18	466
412	$220,000	1966	Shelby	GT350	Russo and Steele	Scottsdale, AZ	1/20	F224
413	$219,350	1967	Shelby	GT500	RM	Boca Raton, FL	2/10	SP29
414	$216,700	1968	Shelby	GT500 KR	Russo and Steele	Scottsdale, AZ	1/20	S210
415	$216,000	1953	Cadillac	Eldorado Convertible	Barrett-Jackson	Scottsdale, AZ	1/14	1261
416	$216,000	1969	Chevrolet	Chevelle COPO	Barrett-Jackson	Scottsdale, AZ	1/14	1047
417	$216,000	1966	Chevrolet	Corvette 427/425 Convertible	Barrett-Jackson	Scottsdale, AZ	1/14	1263
418	$216,000	1967	Chevrolet	Corvette 427/435 Convertible	Barrett-Jackson	Scottsdale, AZ	1/14	1027
419	$216,000	1967	Chevrolet	Corvette 427/435 Convertible	Barrett-Jackson	Scottsdale, AZ	1/14	1303
420	$216,000	1937	Cord	812 Phaeton Convertible	Barrett-Jackson	Scottsdale, AZ	1/14	1036
421	$216,000	1956	Dodge	Custom Royal Golden Lancer	Barrett-Jackson	Scottsdale, AZ	1/14	1250.1
422	$216,000	1969	Dodge	Super Bee	Barrett-Jackson	Scottsdale, AZ	1/14	1034
423	$216,000	1932	Ford	Custom 5-Window Coupe "The Avenger"	Barrett-Jackson	Scottsdale, AZ	1/14	1327
424	$216,000	1942	Ford	Custom Woody Wagon	Barrett-Jackson	Scottsdale, AZ	1/14	1292
425	$216,000	1939	Ford	Deluxe Custom Convertible "Orange Crush"	Barrett-Jackson	Scottsdale, AZ	1/14	1321
426	$216,000	1932	Lucenti	Special Indy Car	Bonhams	Carmel, CA	8/18	544
427	$215,250	1970	Dodge	Hemi Challenger	Mecum	Kissimmee, FL	1/27	X15
428	$214,500	1907	Ford	Model K Roadster	RM	Phoenix, AZ	1/20	163

Rank	Sold Price	Year	Make	Model	Auction Co.	Location	Date	Lot #
429	$214,500	1970	Ford	Mustang Boss 429	Russo and Steele	Monterey, CA	8/18	S249
430	$214,500	1993	Jaguar	XJ220	RM	Monterey, CA	8/18	457
431	$214,500	1964	Pontiac	Bonneville Convertible "Hank Williams, Jr."	RM	Phoenix, AZ	1/20	153
432	$214,500	1937	Rolls-Royce	Phantom III Sedanca De Ville	RM	Amelia Island, FL	3/11	188
433	$214,500	1966	Shelby	GT350 H	RM	Amelia Island, FL	3/11	135
434	$214,000	1971	Plymouth	Hemi 'Cuda Replica	RM	Boca Raton, FL	2/10	SP26
435	$212,408	1959	Cooper-Climax	Monaco Racer	Bonhams	Sussex, U.K.	9/1	228
436	$212,000	1953	Chevrolet	Corvette Roadster	Branson	Branson, MO	4/21	268
437	$210,600	1955	Chevrolet	Bel Air Custom Convertible	Barrett-Jackson	Scottsdale, AZ	1/14	1293
438	$210,600	1967	Chevrolet	Corvette 427/435 Convertible	Barrett-Jackson	Scottsdale, AZ	1/14	1279
439	$210,600	1938	Packard	V12 Convertible Sedan	Kruse	Auburn, IN	8/30	748
440	$210,600	1964	Pontiac	Banshee XP-833 Prototype	Barrett-Jackson	Scottsdale, AZ	1/14	1312
441	$210,500	1971	Lola-Chevrolet	T222 Racer	Bonhams	Carmel, CA	8/18	524
442	$210,000	1970	Chevrolet	Chevelle SS 454 LS6	Mecum	Belvidere, IL	5/25	F512
443	$210,000	1970	Dodge	Challenger	Mecum	Belvidere, IL	5/25	F555
444	$210,000	1968	Plymouth	Barracuda BO29 Racer	Mecum	Kissimmee, FL	1/27	X16
445	$210,000	1968	Shelby	GT500 KR	Mecum	Belvidere, IL	5/25	F570
446	$209,738	1973	Citroën	DS23 IE Cabriolet	Christie's	Paris, FRA	2/11	74
447	$209,000	1937	Cord	812 Supercharged Phaeton	RM	Amelia Island, FL	3/11	183
448	$209,000	1930	Packard	745 Convertible Sedan	RM	Rochester, MI	8/5	254
449	$209,000	1938	Talbot-Lago	T23 4-Liter Cabriolet	RM	Monterey, CA	8/18	182
450	$208,738	1969	Ferrari	365 GTC	Artcurial	Paris, FRA	2/12	42
451	$208,650	1968	Shelby	GT500 KR Convertible	RM	Boca Raton, FL	2/10	NR22
452	$207,900	1919	American	Lafrance Speedster	Leake	Tulsa, OK	6/9	2476
453	$206,800	1969	Lamborghini	Miura	Russo and Steele	Monterey, CA	8/18	F147
454	$206,326	1936	Bugatti	Type 57	Artcurial	Paris, FRA	6/12	18
455	$205,200	1959	Chevrolet	Bel Air	Barrett-Jackson	Scottsdale, AZ	1/14	1247
456	$205,200	1958	Chevrolet	Corvette	Barrett-Jackson	West Palm Beach, FL	3/29	713
457	$205,200	1929	Ford	Hotrod Pickup "Loaded"	Barrett-Jackson	Scottsdale, AZ	1/14	1323
458	$205,200	1967	Shelby	GT500	Leake	Tulsa, OK	6/9	494
459	$204,600	1965	Shelby	GT350	Russo and Steele	Scottsdale, AZ	1/20	S217
460	$203,661	1948	Delahaye	135M Cabriolet	Coys	Monte Carlo, MCO	5/20	220
461	$203,500	1932	Cadillac	V12 Sport Phaeton	RM	Rochester, MI	8/5	275
462	$203,500	1960	Mercedes-Benz	220SE Cabriolet	RM	Phoenix, AZ	1/20	130
463	$203,500	1968	Shelby	GT500	Russo and Steele	Scottsdale, AZ	1/20	F220
464	$202,725	1981	Lotus-Cosworth	Type (81/3) Formula One Racer	Bonhams	Monte Carlo, MCO	5/20	197
465	$202,125	1965	Chevrolet	Chevelle SS	Mecum	Belvidere, IL	5/25	S601
466	$201,960	2005	Ford	Mustang FR500C #55 Racer	Barrett-Jackson	Scottsdale, AZ	1/14	1281
467	$201,960	2005	Ford	Mustang FR500C Barrett-Jackson Edition	Barrett-Jackson	Scottsdale, AZ	1/14	1245.2
468	$201,930	1965	Lotus-Ford	Type 30 Group 7 Racer	Bonhams	Sussex, U.K.	9/1	238
469	$200,000	1908	Daimler	TC48 Roi-Des-Belges	Worldwide Group	Seabrook, TX	5/6	24
470	$199,800	1961	Chrysler	300G Convertible	Barrett-Jackson	Scottsdale, AZ	1/14	1299
471	$199,800	1970	Pontiac	GTO Judge Convertible	Barrett-Jackson	Scottsdale, AZ	1/14	1025.1
472	$199,500	1967	Chevrolet	Corvette	Mecum	St. Charles, IL	6/16	S521
473	$198,000	1948	Chrysler	Town & Country Convertible	Gooding	Pebble Beach, CA	8/20	35
474	$198,000	1966	Shelby	GT350	Russo and Steele	Scottsdale, AZ	1/20	S215
475	$198,000	1966	Shelby	GT350	Russo and Steele	Monterey, CA	8/18	S261
476	$198,000	1967	Shelby	GT500	Russo and Steele	Monterey, CA	8/18	F154
477	$198,000	1912	Simplex	38hp Double Roadster	RM	Amelia Island, FL	3/11	130
478	$197,640	1963	Chevrolet	Corvette Z06	Barrett-Jackson	Scottsdale, AZ	1/14	1294
479	$197,000	1969	Chevrolet	Camaro COPO	Central PA Auto Auction	Lock Haven, PA	7/22	
480	$196,350	1969	Ford	Mustang Boss 429	Mecum	Belvidere, IL	5/25	S535
481	$195,856	1950	Jaguar	XK 120 Alloy Roadster	Christie's	Paris, FRA	7/8	104
482	$195,800	1967	Ferrari	330 GTC	Russo and Steele	Scottsdale, AZ	1/20	S221
483	$195,713	1949	Alfa Romeo	6C 2500 SS Cabriolet	Bonhams	Monte Carlo, MCO	5/20	169
484	$195,250	1969	Dodge	Hemi Charger 500	Russo and Steele	Scottsdale, AZ	1/20	F225
485	$195,200	1958	Ferrari	250 GT Ellena	Sportscar Auction Co.	Geneva, CH	10/7	40
486	$194,400	1947	Ford	Sportsman Convertible	Barrett-Jackson	Scottsdale, AZ	1/14	1270
487	$194,400	2001	Rolls-Royce	Park Ward Ward Saloon	Barrett-Jackson	West Palm Beach, FL	3/29	728
488	$194,400	1968	Shelby	GT500	Barrett-Jackson	Scottsdale, AZ	1/14	1536
489	$194,250	1967	Chevrolet	Corvette	Mecum	Kissimmee, FL	1/27	X18
490	$194,250	1966	Shelby	GT350	Mecum	Belvidere, IL	5/25	S114
491	$194,000	1947	Delahaye	135M Cabriolet	Bonhams	Carmel, CA	8/18	528

Rank	Sold Price	Year	Make	Model	Auction Co.	Location	Date	Lot #
492	$194,000	1947	Ford	Super Deluxe Sportsman Convertible	Bonhams	Carmel, CA	8/18	533
493	$192,780	1932	Packard	Deluxe Eight 903 Sport Phaeton	Leake	Tulsa, OK	6/9	2497
494	$192,500	1931	Auburn	Boattail Speedster	RM	Phoenix, AZ	1/20	151
495	$192,500	1957	Chevrolet	Corvette	Russo and Steele	Scottsdale, AZ	1/20	S229
496	$192,500	1930	Cord	L29 Convertible Sedan	RM	Rochester, MI	8/5	257
497	$192,500	1997	Dodge	Viper GTS-R Le Mans	Russo and Steele	Monterey, CA	8/18	S252
498	$192,500	1973	Ferrari	365 GTB/4 Daytona	RM	Amelia Island, FL	3/11	173
499	$192,500	1971	Plymouth	Road Runner "Petty"	Russo and Steele	Monterey, CA	8/18	S260
500	$192,150	1967	Chevrolet	Corvette	Mecum	Kissimmee, FL	1/27	S51
501	$191,625	1968	Chevrolet	Nova	Mecum	Belvidere, IL	5/25	S595
502	$191,160	1967	Chevrolet	Corvette 427/400 Convertible	Barrett-Jackson	West Palm Beach, FL	3/29	711
503	$189,200	1938	Lincoln	Lead Zephyr	RM	Monterey, CA	8/18	143
504	$189,000	1970	Chevrolet	Chevelle SS	Mecum	Belvidere, IL	5/25	S557
505	$189,000	1967	Chevrolet	Corvette 427/435 Convertible	Barrett-Jackson	Scottsdale, AZ	1/14	1017
506	$189,000	1967	Chevrolet	Corvette 427/400 Convertible	Barrett-Jackson	West Palm Beach, FL	3/29	653
507	$189,000	1948	Chrysler	Town & Country Convertible	Kruse	Auburn, IN	5/18	1033
508	$189,000	1940	Ford	Woody Wagon	Barrett-Jackson	Scottsdale, AZ	1/14	1338
509	$189,000	1937	Hudson	Terraplane Pickup	Barrett-Jackson	Scottsdale, AZ	1/14	1275.2
510	$189,000	1970	Plymouth	Hemi 'Cuda	Barrett-Jackson	Scottsdale, AZ	1/14	972
511	$188,720	1961	Aston Martin	DB4 Series 3	Artcurial	Paris, FRA	2/12	16
512	$188,700	1970	Ferrari	365 GTB/4 Daytona	Bonhams	Monte Carlo, MCO	5/20	153
513	$187,000	1934	Cadillac	Series 30	RM	Amelia Island, FL	3/11	128
514	$187,000	1969	Chevrolet	Camaro Z/28 RS	Russo and Steele	Monterey, CA	8/18	S244
515	$187,000	1969	Chevrolet	Corvette	Russo and Steele	Scottsdale, AZ	1/20	S208
516	$187,000	1934	Ford	Pickup	RM	Hampton, NH	6/10	2162
517	$186,435	1954	Mercedes-Benz	300S Cabriolet	Coys	Maastricht, NL	1/14	211
518	$185,500	1954	Buick	Skylark Convertible	Silver	Ft. McDowell, AZ	1/23	185
519	$184,275	1968	Shelby	GT500	Mecum	Belvidere, IL	5/25	F591.1
520	$184,250	1962	Chrysler	300G Convertible	Worldwide Group	Seabrook, TX	5/6	42
521	$184,250	1968	Shelby	GT500	Russo and Steele	Scottsdale, AZ	1/20	S233
522	$183,750	1970	Chevrolet	Yenko Deuce Nova	Mecum	Belvidere, IL	5/25	S558
523	$183,600	1970	Plymouth	'Cuda Custom Convertible "Six Shooter"	Barrett-Jackson	Scottsdale, AZ	1/14	1278
524	$183,600	1968	Shelby	GT500	Barrett-Jackson	Scottsdale, AZ	1/14	1342
525	$183,000	1957	Bentley	S1 Continental Saloon	Bonhams	Carmel, CA	8/18	549
526	$182,970	1967	Chevrolet	Corvette 427/435 Convertible	RM	Boca Raton, FL	2/10	SP18
527	$182,249	1932	Alfa Romeo	6C 1750 Grand Sport	Coys	Monte Carlo, MCO	5/20	257
528	$182,249	1959	Cooper	Maserati	Coys	Monte Carlo, MCO	5/20	268
529	$181,900	1911	Stanley	Steamer 10hp Model 63 Toy Tonneau	Bonhams	Brookline, MA	5/6	330
530	$181,500	1954	Buick	Skylark	Russo and Steele	Scottsdale, AZ	1/20	S234
531	$181,500	1912	Columbia	Cavalier 4-Passenger Touring	Gooding	Pebble Beach, CA	8/20	28
532	$181,500	1971	Ferrari	365 GTB/4 Daytona	RM	Monterey, CA	8/18	442
533	$181,500	1934	Ford	Deluxe Roadster	RM	Hampton, NH	6/10	2161
534	$181,500	1965	Ford	GT40 Mk V	RM	Phoenix, AZ	1/20	194
535	$181,500	1935	Packard	Twelve Convertible Sedan	RM	Amelia Island, FL	3/11	192
536	$181,500	1968	Shelby	GT500	Russo and Steele	Monterey, CA	8/18	S246
537	$181,440	2003	Aston Martin	DB AR1 Roadster	Barrett-Jackson	West Palm Beach, FL	3/29	705
538	$181,125	1969	Dodge	Super Bee	Mecum	Belvidere, IL	5/25	S541.1
539	$180,975	1955	Lotus-Bristol	MKX Racer	Bonhams	Sussex, U.K.	9/1	209
540	$180,900	1966	Shelby	GT350 H	Barrett-Jackson	Scottsdale, AZ	1/14	752.1
541	$180,900	1968	Shelby	GT500 Convertible	Barrett-Jackson	Scottsdale, AZ	1/14	1041
542	$180,790	1970	Citroën	DS21 Cabriolet	Christie's	Paris, FRA	7/8	110
543	$180,053	1968	Brabham	BT31 Formula One Racer	H&H	Buxton, U.K.	2/21	29
544	$179,655	1965	Aston Martin	DB5 Vantage	Bonhams	Newport Pagnell, U.K.	5/13	154
545	$179,655	2003	Aston Martin	DB7 Zagato	Bonhams	Newport Pagnell, U.K.	5/13	142
546	$179,280	2006	Ford	GT	Kruse	Scottsdale, AZ	1/26	1048
547	$178,750	1966	Shelby	GT350	Russo and Steele	Scottsdale, AZ	1/20	S219
548	$178,500	1965	Dodge	Coronet A-990	Mecum	Belvidere, IL	5/25	S576
549	$178,200	1969	Chevrolet	Camaro Z/28 RS	Barrett-Jackson	Scottsdale, AZ	1/14	1028.1
550	$178,200	1957	Chevrolet	Corvette	Barrett-Jackson	Scottsdale, AZ	1/14	1017.1
551	$178,200	1962	Dodge	Dart 440 Max Wedge	Barrett-Jackson	Scottsdale, AZ	1/14	1288.1
552	$178,200	1930	Packard	740 Super Eight Deluxe Roadster	Kruse	Auburn, IN	8/30	1064.1
553	$178,200	1970	Porsche	917K Replica	Barrett-Jackson	Scottsdale, AZ	1/14	1328
554	$178,141	1938	BMW	327/328 Cabriolet	Artcurial	Paris, FRA	6/12	17
555	$177,789	1975	Lancia	Stratos Stradale	Coys	Nuremberg, DE	7/22	258

BY THE NUMBERS

Rank	Sold Price	Year	Make	Model	Auction Co.	Location	Date	Lot #
556	$177,620	1958	Cadillac	Eldorado Brougham Town Car	RM	Boca Raton, FL	2/10	SP42
557	$177,600	1962	Lancia	Flaminia Sport Zagato	Sportscar Auction Co.	Geneva, CH	10/7	14
558	$177,550	1968	Shelby	GT500 KR	Silver	Reno, NV	8/6	565
559	$177,100	1969	Pontiac	GTO	Russo and Steele	Scottsdale, AZ	1/20	F216
560	$176,000	1914	Locomobile	48 7-Passanger Touring Car	Gooding	Pebble Beach, CA	8/20	27
561	$176,000	1970	Plymouth	Challenger 440/6	Russo and Steele	Scottsdale, AZ	1/20	F222
562	$176,000	1967	Shelby	GT500	Russo and Steele	Scottsdale, AZ	1/20	F209
563	$176,000	1968	Shelby	GT500 KR	Russo and Steele	Monterey, CA	8/18	F141
564	$174,764	1939	Bentley	4 1/4-Liter Tourer	H&H	Buxton, U.K.	7/25	38
565	$173,250	1965	Chevrolet	Corvette	Mecum	St. Charles, IL	6/16	S524
566	$173,250	1967	Chevrolet	Corvette	Mecum	St. Charles, IL	6/16	S508
567	$173,250	1930	Packard	Deluxe Eight 5-Passenger Phaeton	RM	Rochester, MI	8/5	268
568	$173,073	1971	McLaren	M6B GTR	Coys	London, U.K.	6/24	254
569	$172,800	1931	Auburn	Cabriolet	Barrett-Jackson	Scottsdale, AZ	1/14	1538
570	$172,800	1961	Chevrolet	Corvette	Barrett-Jackson	Scottsdale, AZ	1/14	1252
571	$172,800	1960	Chevrolet	Corvette	Barrett-Jackson	West Palm Beach, FL	3/29	735
572	$172,800	1937	Cord	812 Phaeton Bustleback	Barrett-Jackson	Scottsdale, AZ	1/14	1280
573	$172,800	1969	Dodge	Daytona	Barrett-Jackson	Scottsdale, AZ	1/14	1313
574	$172,800	1932	Ford	Boydster II Fusion	Barrett-Jackson	Scottsdale, AZ	1/14	1271
575	$172,800	2005	Ford	GT40	Barrett-Jackson	Scottsdale, AZ	1/14	1253
576	$172,800	1961	Mercedes-Benz	300D 4-Door Convertible	Kruse	Auburn, IN	8/30	3780
577	$172,800	1999	Mercedes-Benz	300SL Replica	Barrett-Jackson	Scottsdale, AZ	1/14	1272.1
578	$172,800	1970	Plymouth	'Cuda Convertible	Barrett-Jackson	Scottsdale, AZ	1/14	1306.2
579	$172,800	1969	Plymouth	Hemi Road Runner	Barrett-Jackson	Scottsdale, AZ	1/14	1339
580	$172,200	1967	Chevrolet	Corvette	Mecum	Kissimmee, FL	1/27	S68
581	$172,000	1927	Rolls-Royce	40/50hp Phantom I Piccadilly Roadster	Bonhams	North Brookfield, MA	9/23	1007
582	$172,000	1904	Winton	20hp Detachable Rear-Entrance Tonneau	Bonhams	Brookline, MA	5/6	322
583	$170,500	1939	Buick	Century Convertible Coupe	RM	Rochester, MI	8/5	273
584	$170,500	1969	Dodge	Daytona 440	Russo and Steele	Scottsdale, AZ	1/20	F211
585	$170,500	1967	Ferrari	330 GTC	RM	Monterey, CA	8/18	411
586	$170,500	1937	Ford	Deluxe Panel Delivery	RM	Hampton, NH	6/10	2174
587	$170,500	1937	Ford	Deluxe Station Wagon	RM	Hampton, NH	6/10	2175
588	$170,500	1955	Mercedes-Benz	300Sb	RM	Phoenix, AZ	1/20	178
589	$170,500	1941	Mercury	Station Wagon	RM	Hampton, NH	6/10	2187
590	$170,375	1967	Ferrari	330 GTC	Christie's	Monterey, CA	8/17	43
591	$170,100	1966	Chevrolet	Corvette	Mecum	St. Charles, IL	6/16	S552
592	$170,100	1969	Ford	Mustang Boss 429	Mecum	Belvidere, IL	5/25	T12
593	$170,000	1931	Packard	Standard Eight Convertible Sedan	RM	Rochester, MI	8/5	228
594	$168,800	1965	OSCA	1600 GT	Sportscar Auction Co.	Geneva, CH	10/7	29
595	$168,004	1970	Dodge	Challenger R/T Convertible	RM	Toronto, CA	4/7	SP129
596	$168,000	1967	Chevrolet	Corvette	Mecum	St. Charles, IL	6/16	S500
597	$167,990	1957	Chrysler	300C Convertible	RM	Boca Raton, FL	2/10	SP50
598	$167,400	2005	Bentley	Arnage Saloon	Kruse	Auburn, IN	8/30	2720.1
599	$167,400	2001	Bentley	Arnage Saloon	Barrett-Jackson	West Palm Beach, FL	3/29	727
600	$167,400	1957	Chevrolet	Bel Air Convertible	Barrett-Jackson	Scottsdale, AZ	1/14	1241.1
601	$167,400	2006	Ford	Mustang Custom "Stallion"	Barrett-Jackson	Scottsdale, AZ	1/14	1301
602	$167,400	1919	La Bestioni	Firetruck Hot Rod	Barrett-Jackson	West Palm Beach, FL	3/29	724.1
603	$167,200	1970	Oldsmobile	442 W30	Russo and Steele	Monterey, CA	8/18	S262
604	$166,528	1903	Panhard-Levassor	7hp	Christie's	London, U.K.	6/26	181
605	$166,465	1968	Ferrari	330 GTC	Coys	Nuremberg, DE	7/22	244
606	$165,850	1962	Chevrolet	Biscayne Z11	RM	Boca Raton, FL	2/10	SP38
607	$165,850	1969	Shelby	Cobra 427 SC	RM	Boca Raton, FL	2/10	SP106
608	$165,000	2003	Aston Martin	DB AR1 Roadster	Worldwide Group	Seabrook, TX	5/6	88
609	$165,000	1927	Bugatti	Type 44 Roadster	RM	Amelia Island, FL	3/11	138
610	$165,000	1954	Packard	Caribbean Convertible	RM	Monterey, CA	8/18	438
611	$165,000	1968	Plymouth	Road Runner	Russo and Steele	Scottsdale, AZ	1/20	S207
612	$165,000	1957	Pontiac	Bonneville Convertible	RM	Monterey, CA	8/18	500
613	$164,700	1960	Chrysler	300F Convertible	Barrett-Jackson	Scottsdale, AZ	1/14	1340
614	$164,160	1969	Chevrolet	Chevelle COPO	Barrett-Jackson	Scottsdale, AZ	1/14	1013.1
615	$163,080	1966	Chevrolet	Corvette 427/425 Convertible	Barrett-Jackson	West Palm Beach, FL	3/29	707
616	$162,800	1970	Pontiac	GTO Judge	Russo and Steele	Monterey, CA	8/18	S247
617	$162,750	1966	Chevrolet	Corvette 427	Carlisle	Carlisle, PA	4/21	S150

Rank	Sold Price	Year	Make	Model	Auction Co.	Location	Date	Lot #
618	$162,750	1967	Chevrolet	Corvette	Mecum	St. Charles, IL	6/16	S514
619	$162,750	1967	Shelby	GT350	Mecum	Belvidere, IL	5/25	S515
620	$162,000	1936	Auburn	Convertible Replica	Kruse	Auburn, IN	8/30	1070
621	$162,000	1953	Cadillac	Eldorado Convertible	RM	Novi, MI	9/22	SP06
622	$162,000	2001	Cadillac	Northstar Le Mans Endurance Racer	Barrett-Jackson	West Palm Beach, FL	3/29	729
623	$162,000	1967	Chevrolet	Corvette 427/435 Convertible	Barrett-Jackson	Scottsdale, AZ	1/14	1544
624	$162,000	1957	Chevrolet	Corvette	Barrett-Jackson	West Palm Beach, FL	3/29	401
625	$162,000	1911	Daimler	4-Door Touring Phaeton	Kruse	Auburn, IN	5/18	1022
626	$162,000	1964	Ford	Fairlane Racer "Little Georgia Shaker"	Barrett-Jackson	Scottsdale, AZ	1/14	1231.2
627	$162,000	1962	Ford	Galaxie Factory Lightweight	Barrett-Jackson	Scottsdale, AZ	1/14	1334
628	$162,000	1957	Oldsmobile	Starfire 98 Convertible	Kruse	Auburn, IN	5/18	2816
629	$162,000	1936	Packard	Super Eight Convertible Rumble Seat	Kruse	Auburn, IN	5/18	1030
630	$162,000	1969	Plymouth	GTX Convertible	Barrett-Jackson	Scottsdale, AZ	1/14	1545.1
631	$162,000	1960	Rolls-Royce	Phantom Limousine	Kruse	Auburn, IN	5/18	2816
632	$161,000	1951	Bentley	S1 Continental Fastback	Bonhams	North Brookfield, MA	9/23	1000
633	$161,000	1926	Rolls-Royce	40/50hp Silver Ghost London-Edinburgh Torpedo	Bonhams	North Brookfield, MA	9/23	1008
634	$160,650	1992	Jaguar	XJ220	Bonhams	Monte Carlo, MCO	5/20	156
635	$160,619	1969	Toyota	2000GT	Bonhams & Goodman	Sydney, AU	3/26	4
636	$159,840	1969	Chevrolet	Camaro RS/SS	Barrett-Jackson	Scottsdale, AZ	1/14	1064
637	$159,500	1969	Chevrolet	Camaro Z/28	Russo and Steele	Scottsdale, AZ	1/20	S241
638	$159,500	1967	Chevrolet	Corvette 427/435	Russo and Steele	Monterey, CA	8/18	F152
639	$159,500	1941	Ford	Deluxe Station Wagon	RM	Hampton, NH	6/10	2189
640	$159,500	1960	Jaguar	XK 150S 3.8 Drophead Coupe	Gooding	Palm Beach, FL	1/24	18
641	$159,500	1931	Lincoln	Model K Dual Cowl Phaeton	RM	Amelia Island, FL	3/11	133
642	$159,300	2000	Bentley	Azure Convertible	Kruse	Auburn, IN	8/30	787.1
643	$158,852	1989	Aston Martin	V8 Vantage Volante Convertible	Bonhams	Newport Pagnell, U.K.	5/13	126
644	$158,760	2005	Bentley	Continental GT	Leake	Tulsa, OK	6/9	454
645	$158,625	1932	Lincoln	Model KB Convertible Roadster	Christie's	Greenwich, CT	6/4	17
646	$158,360	1967	Chevrolet	Corvette 427/400 Convertible	RM	Boca Raton, FL	2/10	SP115
647	$157,500	1969	Chevrolet	Camaro Z/28	Mecum	Belvidere, IL	5/25	S597
648	$157,500	1971	Chevrolet	Corvette	Mecum	Kissimmee, FL	1/27	X53
649	$157,500	1971	Dodge	Challenger	Mecum	Belvidere, IL	5/25	S582
650	$157,500	1967	Ford	Mustang	Mecum	Belvidere, IL	5/25	F584
651	$156,772	1987	Aston Martin	V8 Vantage Zagato	Bonhams	Newport Pagnell, U.K.	5/13	135
652	$156,600	1966	Chevrolet	Corvette 427/450	Barrett-Jackson	West Palm Beach, FL	3/29	655
653	$156,600	1967	Plymouth	Hemi Satellite Convertible	Barrett-Jackson	Scottsdale, AZ	1/14	1242
654	$156,600	1969	Plymouth	Road Runner	Barrett-Jackson	Scottsdale, AZ	1/14	1339.1
655	$156,000	1969	Chevrolet	Camaro COPO	G. Potter King	Atlantic City, NJ	2/23	1020
656	$155,356	1957	Bentley	S1 Continental Flying Spur	Artcurial	Paris, FRA	2/12	17
657	$155,356	1992	Mercedes-Benz	300SL Replica	Artcurial	Paris, FRA	2/12	28
658	$154,440	1967	Chevrolet	Corvette 427/435	Barrett-Jackson	West Palm Beach, FL	3/29	687
659	$154,000	1959	Aston Martin	DB3 Mk 3 Drophead Coupe	RM	Monterey, CA	8/18	429
660	$154,000	1954	Buick	Skylark	Russo and Steele	Monterey, CA	8/18	S245
661	$154,000	1936	Cord	810 Phaeton Sedan	RM	Rochester, MI	8/5	279
662	$154,000	1969	Dodge	Daytona 440/6	Russo and Steele	Scottsdale, AZ	1/20	S206
663	$154,000	1971	Mercedes-Benz	280SE 3.5 Cabriolet	RM	Phoenix, AZ	1/20	199
664	$154,000	1941	Packard	120 Deluxe Station Wagon	RM	Amelia Island, FL	3/11	158
665	$153,900	1970	Plymouth	Road Runner	Barrett-Jackson	Scottsdale, AZ	1/14	981.1
666	$153,808	1934	Riley	9CV Imp	Christie's	Paris, FRA	2/11	65
667	$153,734	1932	Lagonda	2-Liter Supercharged Tourer	Bonhams	Sussex, U.K.	9/1	223
668	$153,718	1973	BMW	3.0CSL "Batmobile"	Christie's	London, U.K.	6/26	177
669	$153,360	1958	Chevrolet	Corvette	Barrett-Jackson	West Palm Beach, FL	3/29	369
670	$153,300	1958	Retrovette	R-5	Mecum	St. Charles, IL	6/16	S563
671	$152,895	1957	Lotus-Climax	Eleven Racer	Bonhams	Sussex, U.K.	9/1	208
672	$152,820	1996	Lamborghini	Diabolo VT Roadster	Leake	Tulsa, OK	6/9	446
673	$152,750	1962	Bentley	S2 Continental Flying Spur	Christie's	Monterey, CA	8/17	42
674	$152,750	1951	Lancia	Aurelia B50 Convertible	Christie's	Monterey, CA	8/17	44
675	$152,475	1965	Chevrolet	Corvette Convertible	RM	Boca Raton, FL	2/10	SP22
676	$152,250	1967	Shelby	GT500	Mecum	Kansas City, MO	4/28	S519
677	$151,250	1966	Shelby	GT350	Russo and Steele	Scottsdale, AZ	1/20	F230
678	$151,200	1936	Auburn	852 Phaeton	Barrett-Jackson	Scottsdale, AZ	1/14	1330
679	$151,200	1965	Chevrolet	Corvette Convertible	Barrett-Jackson	Scottsdale, AZ	1/14	1245

BY THE NUMBERS

Rank	Sold Price	Year	Make	Model	Auction Co.	Location	Date	Lot #
680	$151,200	1957	Chevrolet	Bel Air Convertible	Barrett-Jackson	West Palm Beach, FL	3/29	708
681	$151,200	1967	Chevrolet	Corvette 427/400	Barrett-Jackson	West Palm Beach, FL	3/29	663
682	$151,200	1939	Lincoln	Lead Zephyr	Barrett-Jackson	Scottsdale, AZ	1/14	1277.1
683	$151,200	1951	Mercury	Convertible	Barrett-Jackson	Scottsdale, AZ	1/14	1231
684	$150,933	1939	Lagonda	V12 Drophead Coupe	H&H	Buxton, U.K.	7/25	91
685	$150,532	1965	Aston Martin	DB5	Bonhams	Newport Pagnell, U.K.	5/13	150
686	$150,150	1967	Chevrolet	Corvette	Mecum	St. Charles, IL	6/16	S34
687	$149,800	1969	Plymouth	Hemi GTX	RM	Boca Raton, FL	2/10	SP33
688	$149,600	1970	Ferrari	365 GT	Russo and Steele	Monterey, CA	8/18	F156
689	$149,040	2000	Bentley	Continental R	Barrett-Jackson	Scottsdale, AZ	1/14	1028
690	$149,040	1967	Chevrolet	Corvette 427/435	Barrett-Jackson	Scottsdale, AZ	1/14	1578
691	$149,040	1967	Chevrolet	Corvette 427/435 Convertible	Barrett-Jackson	Scottsdale, AZ	1/14	1040
692	$149,040	1963	Chevrolet	Impala SS Convertible	Barrett-Jackson	Scottsdale, AZ	1/14	994
693	$148,500	1947	Chrysler	Town & Country Convertible	Barrett-Jackson	Scottsdale, AZ	1/14	1266
694	$148,500	1929	Cord	L29 Convertible Sedan	RM	Phoenix, AZ	1/20	200
695	$148,500	1932	Ford	Custom Speedster	RM	Monterey, CA	8/18	136
696	$148,500	1954	Jaguar	XK 120 Roadster	Gooding	Pebble Beach, CA	8/20	46
697	$148,500	1914	Locomobile	Model 48 Speedster	RM	Monterey, CA	8/18	191
698	$148,500	1950	Mercury	Custom Coupe	RM	Monterey, CA	8/18	146
699	$148,500	1970	Oldsmobile	442 W30	Russo and Steele	Scottsdale, AZ	1/20	F210
700	$148,500	1929	Packard	640 Custom Eight Roadster	RM	Phoenix, AZ	1/20	165
701	$148,500	1936	Packard	Twelve Coupe Roadster	RM	Amelia Island, FL	3/11	196
702	$148,451	1961	Aston Martin	DB4 Series 3	Bonhams	Newport Pagnell, U.K.	5/13	124
703	$148,050	1967	Chevrolet	Corvette	Mecum	St. Charles, IL	6/16	S76
704	$147,960	1957	Chevrolet	Nomad Custom Wagon	Barrett-Jackson	Scottsdale, AZ	1/14	968
705	$147,960	1968	Shelby	GT500 Convertible	Barrett-Jackson	Scottsdale, AZ	1/14	1052
706	$147,125	1968	Shelby	GT500 Convertible	RM	Boca Raton, FL	2/10	177
707	$147,000	1967	Chevrolet	Corvette	Mecum	Belvidere, IL	5/25	S560
708	$146,880	2005	Bentley	Continental GT	Kruse	Auburn, IN	8/30	790.1
709	$146,880	1970	Plymouth	Road Runner Superbird	Leake	Tulsa, OK	6/9	471
710	$146,880	1935	Studebaker	Dictator Custom Sedan	Barrett-Jackson	Scottsdale, AZ	1/14	970
711	$146,625	1948	Alfa Romeo	6C 2500 SS	Bonhams	Monte Carlo, MCO	5/20	160
712	$146,576	1930	Bugatti	Type 44 Roadster	H&H	London, U.K.	5/24	41
713	$146,300	1956	Porsche	356A Speedster	RM	Amelia Island, FL	3/11	151
714	$145,800	1954	Buick	Skylark Convertible	Barrett-Jackson	Scottsdale, AZ	1/14	1273
715	$145,800	1957	Chrysler	New Yorker Convertible	Barrett-Jackson	Scottsdale, AZ	1/14	1555
716	$145,800	1964	Dodge	Hemi Polara 330 Factory Lightweight	Barrett-Jackson	Scottsdale, AZ	1/14	1584
717	$145,800	1959	Jaguar	XK 150 S Roadster	Barrett-Jackson	Scottsdale, AZ	1/14	1331
718	$145,800	1968	Plymouth	Hemi Road Runner	Barrett-Jackson	Scottsdale, AZ	1/14	1360
719	$145,800	1970	Plymouth	Hemi Road Runner	Barrett-Jackson	Scottsdale, AZ	1/14	1029.1
720	$145,800	1968	Shelby	GT350 Convertible	Leake	Tulsa, OK	6/9	474
721	$145,750	1968	Ford	Mustang GT	Russo and Steele	Scottsdale, AZ	1/20	F240
722	$145,750	1958	Porsche	356 Coupe "The Green Hornet"	RM	Amelia Island, FL	3/11	190
723	$145,352	1970	Chevron-Ford	B16 Endurance Racer	Bonhams	Sussex, U.K.	9/1	205
724	$144,720	1970	Plymouth	'Cuda	Barrett-Jackson	Scottsdale, AZ	1/14	1262
725	$144,593	1958	Porsche	356A Speedster	Coys	London, U.K.	6/24	253
726	$144,568	1957	AC	Ace Bristol	H&H	London, U.K.	5/24	54
727	$144,100	1936	Packard	Cabriolet Super Eight	Kruse	Morehead, KY	6/24	3129
728	$143,640	1959	Chevrolet	Corvette	Barrett-Jackson	Scottsdale, AZ	1/14	1046
729	$143,430	1967	Mercedes-Benz	600 Saloon	Coys	London, U.K.	9/30	220
730	$143,100	1967	Austin-Healey	3000 Roadster	Barrett-Jackson	Scottsdale, AZ	1/14	1238
731	$143,100	1982	Duesenberg II	Royalton Replica	Kruse	Auburn, IN	8/30	1056
732	$143,100	2001	Ferrari	360 Modena Spyder	Kruse	Auburn, IN	8/30	3057.1
733	$143,000	1953	Buick	Skylark Convertible	RM	Phoenix, AZ	1/20	121
734	$143,000	1967	Chevrolet	Corvette 427/435 Convertible	RM	Monterey, CA	8/18	434
735	$143,000	1948	Chrysler	Town & Country Convertible	RM	Phoenix, AZ	1/20	172
736	$143,000	1967	Ferrari	330 GTC	Gooding	Palm Beach, FL	1/24	13
737	$143,000	1936	Ford	Deluxe Phaeton	RM	Hampton, NH	6/10	2166
738	$143,000	1936	Ford	Deluxe Roadster	RM	Hampton, NH	6/10	2167
739	$143,000	1962	Jaguar	XKE Series I Convertible	RM	Phoenix, AZ	1/20	129
740	$143,000	1951	Mercury	Custom	Russo and Steele	Scottsdale, AZ	1/20	S245
741	$143,000	1970	Plymouth	'Cuda	Russo and Steele	Scottsdale, AZ	1/20	F214
742	$143,000	1969	Shelby	GT500	Russo and Steele	Monterey, CA	8/18	S242
743	$142,560	2003	Aston Martin	Vanquish V12	Barrett-Jackson	West Palm Beach, FL	3/29	671
744	$142,560	1956	Ford	Thunderbird Convertible	Barrett-Jackson	Scottsdale, AZ	1/14	1022
745	$142,560	1970	Plymouth	'Cuda Custom Convertible	Barrett-Jackson	Scottsdale, AZ	1/14	1558.1

Rank	Sold Price	Year	Make	Model	Auction Co.	Location	Date	Lot #
746	$142,560	1968	Shelby	GT	Kruse	Fredericksburg, TX	3/25	104
747	$141,750	1969	Chevrolet	Camaro Z/28	Mecum	Kissimmee, FL	1/27	S61
748	$141,750	1967	Chevrolet	Corvette	Mecum	Kissimmee, FL	1/27	S10
749	$141,750	1966	Shelby	GT350 H	Mecum	Belvidere, IL	5/25	S580
750	$141,000	1997	Porsche	911 Turbo S	Christie's	Monterey, CA	8/17	31
751	$140,800	1962	Porsche	356B Twin-Grille Roadster	Gooding	Pebble Beach, CA	8/20	58
752	$140,400	1957	Chevrolet	Bel Air Convertible	Barrett-Jackson	Scottsdale, AZ	1/14	1235
753	$140,400	1970	Chevrolet	Chevelle SS 454 LS6	G. Potter King	Atlantic City, NJ	2/23	1001
754	$140,400	1959	Chevrolet	Corvette	Barrett-Jackson	Scottsdale, AZ	1/14	1225
755	$140,400	1966	Chevrolet	Corvette 427/450 Convertible	Barrett-Jackson	West Palm Beach, FL	3/29	714
756	$140,400	1968	Dodge	Charger RT Custom	Barrett-Jackson	Scottsdale, AZ	1/14	1269
757	$140,400	1933	Packard	Standard Eight Coupe Roadster	Kruse	Auburn, IN	8/30	749
758	$140,400	1970	Plymouth	AAR 'Cuda	Barrett-Jackson	Scottsdale, AZ	1/14	990.1
759	$140,400	1970	Plymouth	Superbird	Kruse	Auburn, IN	8/30	2747.1
760	$140,400	1968	Shelby	GT500 Convertible	Barrett-Jackson	Scottsdale, AZ	1/14	1344
761	$140,400	1967	Shelby	GT500 E Eleanor Replica	Barrett-Jackson	Scottsdale, AZ	1/14	1557
762	$140,289	1963	Porsche	356 Carrera 2	Coys	London, U.K.	2/28	127
763	$140,250	1967	Shelby	GT500	Russo and Steele	Scottsdale, AZ	1/20	S244
764	$140,170	1938	Packard	Model 1608 Twelve Conv. Sedan	RM	Boca Raton, FL	2/10	SP98
765	$140,000	1969	Chevrolet	Camaro Z/28	RM	Monterey, CA	8/18	158
766	$139,700	1969	Chevrolet	Camaro COPO RS	Russo and Steele	Monterey, CA	8/18	S258
767	$139,424	1968	Chevrolet	Camaro RS/SS	Coys	Monte Carlo, MCO	5/20	273
768	$139,100	1959	Cadillac	Eldorado Biarritz Convertible	RM	Boca Raton, FL	2/10	NR30
769	$139,000	1924	Rolls-Royce	40/50hp Silver Ghost Landaulette	Bonhams	North Brookfield, MA	9/23	1018
770	$138,600	1968	Shelby	GT500 KR	Russo and Steele	Scottsdale, AZ	1/20	S237
771	$138,050	1965	Aston Martin	DB5	Bonhams	Newport Pagnell, U.K.	5/13	149
772	$137,700	2000	Bentley	Continental R Mulliner Coupe	Barrett-Jackson	Scottsdale, AZ	1/14	1276.1
773	$137,500	1939	Chevrolet	Town Sedan	Russo and Steele	Scottsdale, AZ	1/20	F219
774	$137,500	1948	Ford	Super Deluxe Woody Wagon	RM	Monterey, CA	8/18	426
775	$137,500	1961	Jaguar	XKE Series I Convertible	RM	Amelia Island, FL	3/11	170
776	$137,500	1971	Plymouth	'Cuda 383	Russo and Steele	Scottsdale, AZ	1/20	F243
777	$137,500	1956	Porsche	356A Speedster	RM	Monterey, CA	8/18	486
778	$137,500	1951	Rolls-Royce	Silver Wraith LWB Drophead Coupe	Gooding	Palm Beach, FL	1/24	31
779	$137,160	1967	Chevrolet	Corvette 427/435	Barrett-Jackson	Scottsdale, AZ	1/14	1003
780	$137,160	1962	Chevrolet	Corvette	Barrett-Jackson	West Palm Beach, FL	3/29	719.1
781	$137,160	1969	Dodge	Charger 500	Barrett-Jackson	West Palm Beach, FL	3/29	358
782	$137,160	1937	Packard	115 Convertible	Barrett-Jackson	Scottsdale, AZ	1/14	1015
783	$136,800	1963	Aston Martin	DB4 Vantage Series 5	Bonhams	Carmel, CA	8/18	562
784	$136,500	1963	Chevrolet	Corvette	Mecum	St. Charles, IL	6/16	S519
785	$136,080	2005	Bentley	Continental GT	Kruse	Auburn, IN	8/30	763.2
786	$136,080	1967	Chevrolet	Camaro Z/28	Barrett-Jackson	Scottsdale, AZ	1/14	1008
787	$136,080	1967	Chevrolet	Corvette 427/400 Convertible	Barrett-Jackson	Scottsdale, AZ	1/14	1059
788	$136,080	1957	Chevrolet	Bel Air Convertible	Barrett-Jackson	West Palm Beach, FL	3/29	650
789	$136,000	1965	Plymouth	Belvedere Lightweight	Central PA Auto	Lock Haven, PA	7/22	
790	$135,965	1956	Porsche	356A 1600 S Speedster	Coys	Oxfordshire, U.K.	8/26	118
791	$135,200	1930	Cadillac	Imperial	G. Potter King	Atlantic City, NJ	2/23	1019
792	$135,125	1965	Jaguar	XKE Convertible	Christie's	Monterey, CA	8/17	45
793	$135,000	1960	Austin-Healey	3000 Roadster	Barrett-Jackson	West Palm Beach, FL	3/29	632
794	$135,000	1953	Buick	Skylark Convertible	RM	Novi, MI	9/22	SP04
795	$135,000	1950	Cadillac	Series 62 Convertible	Barrett-Jackson	Scottsdale, AZ	1/14	1317
796	$135,000	1966	Chevrolet	Chevelle SS 396	Barrett-Jackson	Scottsdale, AZ	1/14	731
797	$135,000	1970	Chevrolet	Chevelle SS 454 Convertible	Barrett-Jackson	Scottsdale, AZ	1/14	978
798	$135,000	1962	Chevrolet	Corvette	Barrett-Jackson	Scottsdale, AZ	1/14	745
799	$135,000	1957	Ford	Thunderbird Convertible	Barrett-Jackson	Scottsdale, AZ	1/14	1021
800	$135,000	1970	Plymouth	Road Runner Superbird	Leake	Oklahoma City, OK	2/24	507
801	$135,000	1958	Porsche	356A Cabriolet	Barrett-Jackson	Scottsdale, AZ	1/14	743
802	$134,882	1956	Bentley	S1 Continental Fastback	Bonhams	Northamptonshire, U.K.	6/17	416
803	$134,820	1968	Shelby	GT500 KR	RM	Boca Raton, FL	2/10	SP35
804	$134,750	1938	Ford	Deluxe Station Wagon	RM	Hampton, NH	6/10	2178
805	$134,200	1955	Mercedes-Benz	300Sb	RM	Amelia Island, FL	3/11	161
806	$133,875	1970	Buick	GSX Stage 1	Mecum	Belvidere, IL	5/25	S87
807	$133,778	1995	Bentley	Azure	Coys	Birmingham, UK	1/14	222
808	$133,100	1932	Ford	Deluxe V8 Roadster	RM	Hampton, NH	6/10	2155
809	$133,100	1932	Ford	High Boy Roadster	RM	Hampton, NH	6/10	2156
810	$132,840	1967	Chevrolet	Corvette 427/400 Convertible	Barrett-Jackson	West Palm Beach, FL	3/29	690
811	$132,840	1969	Plymouth	GTX Convertible	Kruse	Auburn, IN	8/30	2759.1

Rank	Sold Price	Year	Make	Model	Auction Co.	Location	Date	Lot #
812	$132,834	1960	Bentley	S2 Continental Drophead Coupe	Christie's	Paris, FRA	2/11	83
813	$132,300	1958	Chevrolet	Corvette "Joie Chitwood" Convertible	Kruse	Auburn, IN	8/30	2760.1
814	$132,300	1957	Chevrolet	Bel Air Custom Convertible	Barrett-Jackson	West Palm Beach, FL	3/29	719
815	$132,000	1954	Buick	Skylark Convertible	RM	Monterey, CA	8/18	174
816	$132,000	1936	Buick/Chrysler	"Topper Car" Mobiloil /Gilmore Special	RM	Los Angeles, CA	5/13	241
817	$132,000	1947	Cadillac	Custom	RM	Phoenix, AZ	1/20	185
818	$132,000	1953	Cadillac	Eldorado Convertible	RM	Amelia Island, FL	3/11	150
819	$132,000	1930	Cadillac	Model 452-A V16	RM	Amelia Island, FL	3/11	152
820	$132,000	1958	Duesenberg	Kollins Le Grande	RM	Phoenix, AZ	1/20	191
821	$132,000	1939	Ford	Deluxe Convertible	RM	Hampton, NH	6/10	2183
822	$132,000	1932	Ford	Speedwagon Phantom Deuce Woody	Gooding	Pebble Beach, CA	8/20	84
823	$132,000	1961	Jaguar	XK 150S Roadster	RM	Monterey, CA	8/18	126
824	$132,000	1936	Packard	Model 120 Club Sedan & Trailer	RM	Monterey, CA	8/18	160
825	$132,000	1957	Pontiac	Bonneville	Russo and Steele	Monterey, CA	8/18	S264
826	$132,000	1904	Searchmont	Rear-Entrance Touring	Gooding	Pebble Beach, CA	8/20	26
827	$132,000	1969	Shelby	GT350	Russo and Steele	Scottsdale, AZ	1/20	S203
828	$132,000	1931	Studebaker	President Four Seasons Roadster	RM	Rochester, MI	8/5	227
829	$131,760	1968	Shelby	GT350	Barrett-Jackson	Scottsdale, AZ	1/14	1548
830	$131,610	1967	Shelby	GT350	RM	Boca Raton, FL	2/10	SP27
831	$131,250	1970	Chevrolet	Chevelle	Mecum	Kansas City, MO	4/28	S568
832	$131,250	1959	Chevrolet	Corvette	Mecum	St. Charles, IL	6/16	S543
833	$131,250	1970	Plymouth	Superbird	Mecum	Belvidere, IL	5/25	F588
834	$131,250	1965	Pontiac	GTO	Mecum	Belvidere, IL	5/25	S516
835	$131,075	1967	Shelby	GT350	RM	Boca Raton, FL	2/10	NR27
836	$131,012	1963	Jaguar	XKE Lightweight Comp. Roadster	Coys	London, U.K.	9/30	236
837	$130,725	1954	Buick	Skylark	Mecum	Belvidere, IL	5/25	F572
838	$130,680	1965	Dodge	Coronet A-990 Replica	Barrett-Jackson	Scottsdale, AZ	1/14	1025
839	$130,680	1971	Mercedes-Benz	280SE 3.5 Convertible	Kruse	Auburn, IN	8/30	1073.1
840	$130,680	1933	Studebaker	82 President Custom Cabriolet	Leake	Tulsa, OK	6/9	462
841	$130,496	1972	Ferrari	Dino 246GT Berlinetta	Bonhams	Monte Carlo, MCO	5/20	191
842	$130,200	1970	Chevrolet	Chevelle SS	Mecum	Belvidere, IL	5/25	S599
843	$129,600	1955	Chevrolet	3100 Custom Pickup	Barrett-Jackson	Scottsdale, AZ	1/14	1272
844	$129,600	2002	Chevrolet	Corvette 427 Stage 4 Lingenfelter	Barrett-Jackson	Scottsdale, AZ	1/14	1335.1
845	$129,600	1958	Devin	Special Roadster	Barrett-Jackson	Scottsdale, AZ	1/14	1227
846	$129,600	1964	Dodge	Coronet 330 Lightweight Max Wedge	Barrett-Jackson	Scottsdale, AZ	1/14	1268
847	$129,600	1969	Plymouth	Hemi Road Runner	Barrett-Jackson	Scottsdale, AZ	1/14	1233.1
848	$129,600	1968	Shelby	GT500 KR	Kruse	Auburn, IN	8/30	747.1
849	$129,250	1969	Chevrolet	Camaro SS 396	Worldwide Group	Seabrook, TX	5/6	46
850	$129,250	1939	Graham	Model 97 Supercharged Convertible Coupe	RM	Rochester, MI	8/5	232
851	$129,250	1934	Packard	1104 Super Eight Phaeton	Christie's	Greenwich, CT	6/4	20
852	$129,150	1970	Chevrolet	Chevelle SS 454 LS6	Mecum	Belvidere, IL	5/25	S574
853	$128,588	1985	Jaguar	XK C-Type Replica	Bonhams	Sussex, U.K.	9/11	220
854	$128,520	1969	Chevrolet	Corvette 427/435 Convertible	Barrett-Jackson	Scottsdale, AZ	1/14	1556.1
855	$128,100	1962	Chevrolet	Corvette	Mecum	St. Charles, IL	6/16	S551
856	$128,099	1958	Rolls-Royce	Silver Wraith Limousine	Christie's	London, U.K.	6/26	182
857	$128,000	1961	Aston Martin	DB4	Bonhams	Carmel, CA	8/18	506A
858	$127,500	1957	Porsche	356A Speedster	Coys	Monte Carlo, MCO	5/20	236
859	$127,440	1970	Ford	Mustang Mach 1 Fastback	Barrett-Jackson	West Palm Beach, FL	3/29	624.1
860	$127,400	1967	Chevrolet	Corvette	G. Potter King	Atlantic City, NJ	2/23	1032
861	$127,200	1966	Shelby	GT350	Silver	Reno, NV	8/6	128
862	$127,050	1970	Chevrolet	Chevelle SS 454 LS6	Mecum	Belvidere, IL	5/25	S554
863	$127,050	1959	Chevrolet	Corvette Custom	Mecum	St. Charles, IL	6/16	F516
864	$126,900	1948	Ford	89-A Woody Wagon	Barrett-Jackson	Scottsdale, AZ	1/14	1037
865	$126,724	1928	Rolls-Royce	Phantom I	Bonhams & Goodman	Sydney, AU	3/26	10
866	$126,500	2005	Apollo	Monza Spider	Russo and Steele	Scottsdale, AZ	1/20	S212
867	$126,500	1941	Cadillac	Series 62 Convertible Coupe	RM	Monterey, CA	8/18	490
868	$126,500	1949	Chrysler	Town & Country Convertible	RM	Phoenix, AZ	1/20	160
869	$126,500	1937	Cord	812 Phaeton	Gooding	Palm Beach, FL	1/24	16
870	$126,500	1961	Ferrari	250 Testa Rossa 59 Replica	Worldwide Group	Seabrook, TX	5/6	25
871	$126,500	1939	Packard	Twelve Town Car	RM	Phoenix, AZ	1/20	192
872	$126,360	1955	Chevrolet	Bel Air Convertible	Barrett-Jackson	Scottsdale, AZ	1/14	1004
873	$126,001	1930	Cord	L29 Cabriolet	Kruse	Verona, NY	7/7	736

Rank	Sold Price	Year	Make	Model	Auction Co.	Location	Date	Lot #
874	$126,000	1957	Chevrolet	Bel Air	Mecum	Belvidere, IL	5/25	S503
875	$126,000	1970	Dodge	Challenger RT/SE	Mecum	Kissimmee, FL	1/27	S21
876	$126,000	1970	Dodge	Charger	Mecum	Kissimmee, FL	1/27	A111
877	$126,000	1970	Dodge	Charger	Mecum	Belvidere, IL	5/25	U552
878	$126,000	2001	Ferrari	360 Modena	Mecum	Belvidere, IL	5/25	U529.1
879	$125,999	1933	Packard	Eight Victoria Cabriolet	Kruse	Verona, NY	7/7	734
880	$125,999	1931	Rolls-Royce	Phantom I Regent Coupe	Kruse	Verona, NY	7/7	727
881	$125,400	1957	Chrysler	300C Convertible	RM	Amelia Island, FL	3/11	178
882	$125,280	1968	Shelby	GT500	Barrett-Jackson	West Palm Beach, FL	3/29	697
883	$125,266	1957	AC	Ace Bristol	Coys	Maastricht, NL	1/14	223
884	$125,080	1970	Dodge	Challenger Convertible	Silver	Ft. McDowell, AZ	1/23	558
885	$125,000	1970	Shelby	GT500	Worldwide Group	Seabrook, TX	5/6	73
886	$124,969	1935	Avions Voisin	C 25 "Clairière"	Artcurial	Paris, FRA	2/12	2
887	$124,963	1937	Lagonda	LG6 Drophead Coupe	Bonhams	Sussex, U.K.	7/7	565
888	$124,950	1958	Chevrolet	Corvette	Mecum	St. Charles, IL	6/16	S568
889	$124,200	1964	Amphicar	770 Convertible	Barrett-Jackson	Scottsdale, AZ	1/14	423
890	$124,200	1956	Chevrolet	Bel Air Convertible	Barrett-Jackson	Scottsdale, AZ	1/14	1045
891	$124,200	1969	Chevrolet	Camaro Z/28	Barrett-Jackson	Scottsdale, AZ	1/14	1233
892	$124,200	1962	Chevrolet	Corvette 327	Barrett-Jackson	Scottsdale, AZ	1/14	1062
893	$124,200	1969	Chevrolet	Camaro	Barrett-Jackson	West Palm Beach, FL	3/29	715
894	$124,200	1967	Chevrolet	Corvette 427/390 Convertible	Barrett-Jackson	West Palm Beach, FL	3/29	704.1
895	$124,200	1948	Chrysler	Town & Country Convertible	Kruse	Auburn, IN	5/18	1034
896	$124,200	1935	Ford	Custom Woody Wagon	Barrett-Jackson	Scottsdale, AZ	1/14	1336
897	$124,200	1966	Plymouth	Hemi Satellite	Barrett-Jackson	Scottsdale, AZ	1/14	1053.1
898	$124,200	1939	Studebaker	Express Pickup	Kruse	Auburn, IN	8/30	1025
899	$123,750	1957	Desoto	Adventurer Convertible	RM	Monterey, CA	8/18	428
900	$123,750	1932	Ford	B400 Convertible Sedan	RM	Hampton, NH	6/10	2157
901	$123,750	1936	Ford	Deluxe Station Wagon	RM	Hampton, NH	6/10	2168
902	$123,200	1974	Ferrari	365 GT4 BB	Gooding	Pebble Beach, CA	8/20	40
903	$123,129	1998	Aston Martin	V8 Vantage	H&H	Buxton, U.K.	7/25	36
904	$122,850	1967	Chevrolet	Corvette	Mecum	Kissimmee, FL	1/27	C61
905	$122,515	1952	Jaguar	XK 120 Roadster	Coys	London, U.K.	9/30	250
906	$122,500	1949	Talbot-Lago	T26 Record Cabriolet	Bonhams	Carmel, CA	8/18	520
907	$122,325	1967	Chevrolet	Corvette	Mecum	Carlisle, PA	8/25	S507
908	$122,129	1971	Lancia	Fulvia 1.6 HF Group 4	Artcurial	Paris, FRA	2/12	53
909	$122,100	1955	Chevrolet	Bel Air Convertible	Worldwide Group	Seabrook, TX	5/6	44
910	$121,500	1967	Chevrolet	Corvette 427/435 Convertible	Barrett-Jackson	Scottsdale, AZ	1/14	419.1
911	$121,500	1962	Facel Vega	2+2	Kruse	Auburn, IN	8/30	746.1
912	$121,500	1970	Plymouth	Hemi 'Cuda Replica	Barrett-Jackson	Scottsdale, AZ	1/14	1243
913	$121,199	1928	Rolls-Royce	Phantom I Open Tourer	Coys	London, U.K.	6/24	214
914	$121,000	1974	Chevrolet	Camaro IROC Racer	RM	Monterey, CA	8/18	165
915	$121,000	1958	Chevrolet	Impala Convertible	Worldwide Group	Seabrook, TX	5/6	48
916	$121,000	1990	Ferrari	308 IMSA GTU	Worldwide Group	Seabrook, TX	5/6	51
917	$121,000	1961	Jaguar	XK 150 3.8 Drophead Coupe	RM	Phoenix, AZ	1/20	187
918	$121,000	1965	Jaguar	XKE Series I 4.2 Convertible	RM	Monterey, CA	8/18	452
919	$121,000	1963	Jaguar	XKE Series I Convertible	RM	Phoenix, AZ	1/20	190
920	$121,000	1996	Lamborghini	Diablo SV-R	RM	Monterey, CA	8/18	459
921	$121,000	1960	Mercedes-Benz	220SE	RM	Phoenix, AZ	1/20	131
922	$121,000	1951	Oldsmobile	98 Convertible	RM	Amelia Island, FL	3/11	129
923	$121,000	1958	Porsche	356A 1600 S Speedster	RM	Amelia Island, FL	3/11	127
924	$121,000	1927	Rolls-Royce	Phantom I Pall Mall Tourer	RM	Rochester, MI	8/5	261
925	$121,000	1969	Shelby	GT500	Russo and Steele	Scottsdale, AZ	1/20	F233
926	$121,000	1959	Stanguellini	Formula Junior Racer	Russo and Steele	Monterey, CA	8/18	S239
927	$120,960	1936	Ford	Street Rod Roadster	Barrett-Jackson	Scottsdale, AZ	1/14	1292.2
928	$120,960	1941	Willys	Americar Coupe	Barrett-Jackson	Scottsdale, AZ	1/14	1567.1
929	$120,750	1967	Chevrolet	Corvette	Mecum	Kissimmee, FL	1/27	S43
930	$120,750	1963	Chevrolet	Impala	Mecum	Belvidere, IL	5/25	S554.1
931	$120,750	1970	Plymouth	Superbird	Mecum	Belvidere, IL	5/25	T26
932	$120,750	1966	Shelby	GT350 H	Mecum	Kissimmee, FL	1/27	C74
933	$120,750	1999	Shelby	Series 1	Mecum	Belvidere, IL	5/25	F607
934	$120,655	1929	Rolls-Royce	Phantom I Tourer	Bonhams	Northamptonshire, U.K.	6/17	415
935	$120,375	1968	Shelby	GT500 KR	RM	Boca Raton, FL	2/10	NR103
936	$120,000	1960	AC	Ace	Gooding	Palm Beach, FL	1/24	33
937	$119,880	1970	Chevrolet	Chevelle SS 454	Kruse	Auburn, IN	5/18	2487
938	$119,328	1954	Aston Martin	DB2/4 Drophead Coupe	Bonhams	Newport Pagnell, U.K.	5/13	140
939	$119,175	1969	Chevrolet	Camaro Z/28 RS	Mecum	Kissimmee, FL	1/27	C45

Rank	Sold Price	Year	Make	Model	Auction Co.	Location	Date	Lot #
940	$118,853	1973	Ferrari	Dino 246GT Berlinetta	Bonhams	Sussex, U.K.	7/7	530
941	$118,800	1931	Auburn	8-98A Phaeton	Kruse	Auburn, IN	5/18	735
942	$118,800	1963	Chevrolet	Corvette Custom	Barrett-Jackson	Scottsdale, AZ	1/14	1237
943	$118,800	1937	Cord	812 Westchester Sedan	Barrett-Jackson	Scottsdale, AZ	1/14	453
944	$118,800	1998	Lamborghini	Diablo/Monterey SV Edition	Kruse	Seaside, CA	8/17	430
945	$118,800	1967	Plymouth	Hemi Belvedere GTX Replica	Barrett-Jackson	Scottsdale, AZ	1/14	59.1
946	$118,800	1970	Plymouth	'Cuda	Barrett-Jackson	West Palm Beach, FL	3/29	659
947	$118,800	1965	Pontiac	GTO Convertible	Barrett-Jackson	Scottsdale, AZ	1/14	957
948	$118,800	1968	Shelby	GT500 KR	Barrett-Jackson	West Palm Beach, FL	3/29	734.1
949	$118,770	1968	Dodge	Dart 440 GSS 2D	RM	Boca Raton, FL	2/10	SP34
950	$118,650	1970	Chevrolet	Chevelle SS 454 LS6	Carlisle	Carlisle, PA	4/21	S156
951	$118,650	1963	Chevrolet	Corvette	Mecum	St. Charles, IL	6/16	S515
952	$118,250	1956	Rolls-Royce	Silver Wraith Express Limousine	RM	Rochester, MI	8/5	236
953	$118,125	1957	Chevrolet	Corvette	Mecum	Carlisle, PA	8/25	S33
954	$117,600	1967	Chevrolet	Corvette	Mecum	Kissimmee, FL	1/27	F17
955	$117,500	1956	Chevrolet	Corvette Roadster	Christie's	Monterey, CA	8/17	47
956	$117,500	1957	Lancia	Aurelia B24S Convertible	Christie's	Greenwich, CT	6/4	7
957	$117,500	1927	Rolls-Royce	Springfield Phantom I	Christie's	Greenwich, CT	6/4	6
958	$117,424	1998	Aston Martin	V8 Volante	Christie's	London, U.K.	6/26	180
959	$117,141	1931	Lorraine Dietrich	B3/6 Labourdette	Osenat	Paris, FRA	6/18	517
960	$117,000	1970	Ferrari	365 GT 2+2	Bonhams	Carmel, CA	8/18	552
961	$116,817	1922	Alfa Romeo	RL Sport Special	Bonhams	Sussex, U.K.	7/7	556
962	$116,640	1933	Ford	Custom 3-Window Coupe	Barrett-Jackson	Scottsdale, AZ	1/14	1282
963	$116,640	1957	Ford	Thunderbird Convertible	Barrett-Jackson	Scottsdale, AZ	1/14	1005
964	$116,214	1934	Bentley	3 1/2-Liter Open Tourer	Coys	Donington Park, U.K.	4/30	245
965	$116,100	1969	Chevrolet	Camaro	Barrett-Jackson	Scottsdale, AZ	1/14	1552.1
966	$116,100	1969	Chevrolet	Corvette 427/435	Barrett-Jackson	Scottsdale, AZ	1/14	975.1
967	$116,025	1958	Chevrolet	Corvette	Mecum	St. Charles, IL	6/16	S533
968	$116,000	1961	Chevrolet	Corvette	Central PA Auto	Lock Haven, PA	7/22	
969	$115,560	1969	Chevrolet	Camaro ZL1	Kruse	Auburn, IN	5/18	7012
970	$115,560	1958	Chevrolet	Impala 2-Door Hard Top	Barrett-Jackson	West Palm Beach, FL	3/29	105
971	$115,500	1967	Aston Martin	DB6	RM	Monterey, CA	8/18	450
972	$115,500	1931	Cadillac	355-A V8 Roadster	RM	Amelia Island, FL	3/11	121
973	$115,500	1970	Chevrolet	Chevelle SS 454 LS6	Mecum	Kissimmee, FL	1/27	S37
974	$115,500	1966	Chevrolet	Corvette	Russo and Steele	Scottsdale, AZ	1/20	F239
975	$115,500	1967	Chevrolet	Corvette	Russo and Steele	Scottsdale, AZ	1/20	S243
976	$115,500	1967	Chevrolet	Corvette	Mecum	Belvidere, IL	5/25	F532
977	$115,500	1954	Chevrolet	Corvette Roadster	Mecum	Kissimmee, FL	1/27	S29
978	$115,500	1956	Chevrolet	Corvette Roadster	Mecum	St. Charles, IL	6/16	S67
979	$115,500	1957	Ford	Thunderbird Convertible	RM	Hampton, NH	6/10	2194
980	$115,500	1955	Mercury	Monterey Woody Wagon	Gooding	Pebble Beach, CA	8/20	50
981	$115,500	1957	Pontiac	Bonneville Convertible	RM	Rochester, MI	8/5	242
982	$114,660	1953	Aston Martin	DB2 Drophead Coupe	Bonhams	Brookline, MA	5/6	325A
983	$114,480	1936	Ford	Street Rod Woody Wagon	Barrett-Jackson	Scottsdale, AZ	1/14	982
984	$114,400	1934	Ford	Coupe	G. Potter King	Atlantic City, NJ	2/23	2018A
985	$113,940	2003	Aston Martin	Vanquish	Kruse	Auburn, IN	8/30	757.1
986	$113,850	1967	Chevrolet	Corvette 427	Russo and Steele	Scottsdale, AZ	1/20	F212
987	$113,400	1932	Auburn	8-100A Custom Phaeton	Leake	Tulsa, OK	6/9	2464
988	$113,400	1957	Chevrolet	Bel Air Convertible	Barrett-Jackson	Scottsdale, AZ	1/14	750
989	$113,400	1961	Chevrolet	Corvette	Barrett-Jackson	Scottsdale, AZ	1/14	963
990	$113,400	1966	Chevrolet	Corvette 427/425 Convertible	Barrett-Jackson	Scottsdale, AZ	1/14	1565
991	$113,400	1967	Chevrolet	Corvette 427/435 Convertible	Barrett-Jackson	West Palm Beach, FL	3/29	717
992	$113,400	1966	Chevrolet	Impala SS Convertible	Barrett-Jackson	West Palm Beach, FL	3/29	641.1
993	$113,400	1970	Dodge	Challenger R/T Replica Convertible	Kruse	Scottsdale, AZ	1/26	783
994	$113,400	1969	Dodge	Charger Daytona	Kruse	Scottsdale, AZ	1/26	783
995	$113,400	1969	Pontiac	GTO Judge	Barrett-Jackson	Scottsdale, AZ	1/14	1228
996	$113,400	1969	Pontiac	Trans Am	Barrett-Jackson	Scottsdale, AZ	1/14	1023.1
997	$113,304	1970	Porsche	914/6 Group 4 Competition	Coys	Oxfordshire, U.K.	8/26	116
998	$112,350	1941	Cadillac	Series 62 Convertible	RM	Boca Raton, FL	2/10	SP104
999	$112,350	1967	Chevrolet	Corvette	Mecum	Kissimmee, FL	1/27	X24
1000	$112,350	1958	Chevrolet	Corvette	Mecum	St. Charles, IL	6/16	S564 ◆

Once Again, Now By Marque

How did ACs do? Or Coopers. Chevrolets or Stanguellinis? Find out here.
(Sales recorded between 1/1/2006 and 9/30/2006.)

Year	Make	Model	Sold Price	Rank	Auction Co.	Location	Date	Lot #
1960	AC	Ace	$120,000	936	Gooding	Palm Beach, FL	1/24	33
1957	AC	Ace Bristol	$144,568	726	H&H	London, U.K.	5/24	54
1957	AC	Ace Bristol	$125,266	883	Coys	Maastricht, NL	1/14	223
1932	Alfa Romeo	6C 1750 Grand Sport	$182,249	527	Coys	Monte Carlo, MCO	5/20	257
1937	Alfa Romeo	6C 2300 MM	$426,600	154	Kruse	Seaside, CA	8/17	410
1947	Alfa Romeo	6C 2500 SS	$467,747	139	Coys	Monte Carlo, MCO	5/20	259
1948	Alfa Romeo	6C 2500 SS	$146,625	711	Bonhams	Monte Carlo, MCO	5/20	160
1950	Alfa Romeo	6C 2500 SS "Tubolare"	$222,828	399	Christie's	Paris, FRA	2/11	84
1949	Alfa Romeo	6C 2500 SS Cabriolet	$195,713	483	Bonhams	Monte Carlo, MCO	5/20	169
1922	Alfa Romeo	RL Sport Special	$116,817	961	Bonhams	Sussex, U.K.	7/7	556
1939	Alfa Romeo	6C 2500 Sport Cabriolet	$247,500	337	Worldwide Group	Seabrook, TX	5/6	39
1951	Allard	J2X Le Mans Racer	$313,500	243	RM	Monterey, CA	8/18	440
1967	Alpine	A210	$315,503	240	Artcurial	Paris, FRA	2/12	20
1919	American	Lafrance Speedster	$207,900	452	Leake	Tulsa, OK	6/9	2476
1964	Amphicar	770 Convertible	$124,200	889	Barrett-Jackson	Scottsdale, AZ	1/14	423
2005	Apollo	Monza Spider	$126,500	866	Russo and Steele	Scottsdale, AZ	1/20	S212
1938	Aston Martin	15/98 Short Chassis	$224,172	398	Christie's	London, U.K.	6/26	170
2003	Aston Martin	DB AR1 Roadster	$232,200	368	Barrett-Jackson	Scottsdale, AZ	1/14	1314.1
2003	Aston Martin	DB AR1 Roadster	$181,440	537	Barrett-Jackson	West Palm Beach, FL	3/29	705
1953	Aston Martin	DB2 Drophead Coupe	$114,660	982	Bonhams	Brookline, MA	5/6	325A
1954	Aston Martin	DB2/4 Drophead Coupe	$119,328	938	Bonhams	Newport Pagnell, U.K.	5/13	140
1959	Aston Martin	DB3 Mk 3 Drophead Coupe	$154,000	659	RM	Monterey, CA	8/18	429
1961	Aston Martin	DB4	$128,000	857	Bonhams	Carmel, CA	8/18	506A
1963	Aston Martin	DB4 Convertible	$314,868	242	Bonhams	Newport Pagnell, U.K.	5/13	132
1961	Aston Martin	DB4 GT	$891,000	58	RM	Monterey, CA	8/18	476
1960	Aston Martin	DB4 Series 2	$273,264	286	Bonhams	Newport Pagnell, U.K.	5/13	125
1961	Aston Martin	DB4 Series 3	$148,451	702	Bonhams	Newport Pagnell, U.K.	5/13	124
1963	Aston Martin	DB4 Vantage Series 5	$136,800	783	Bonhams	Carmel, CA	8/18	562
1964	Aston Martin	DB5	$257,331	318	Bonhams	Sussex, U.K.	7/7	539
1965	Aston Martin	DB5	$267,300	303	RM	Phoenix, AZ	1/20	148
1965	Aston Martin	DB5	$231,660	371	Bonhams	Newport Pagnell, U.K.	5/13	129
1965	Aston Martin	DB5	$150,532	685	Bonhams	Newport Pagnell, U.K.	5/13	150
1965	Aston Martin	DB5	$138,050	771	Bonhams	Newport Pagnell, U.K.	5/13	149
1965	Aston Martin	DB5	$2,090,000	13	RM	Phoenix, AZ	1/20	155
1965	Aston Martin	DB5 Vantage	$179,655	544	Bonhams	Newport Pagnell, U.K.	5/13	154
1967	Aston Martin	DB6	$115,500	971	RM	Monterey, CA	8/18	450
1965	Aston Martin	DB6 Short Chassis Volante	$445,500	145	RM	Phoenix, AZ	1/20	166
1967	Aston Martin	DB6 Vantage Volante	$221,259	406	Bonhams	Newport Pagnell, U.K.	5/13	138
2003	Aston Martin	DB7 Zagato	$179,655	545	Bonhams	Newport Pagnell, U.K.	5/13	142
1966	Aston Martin	DBR1 Alloy Replica	$275,000	277	RM	Monterey, CA	8/18	467
1998	Aston Martin	V8 Vantage	$123,129	903	H&H	Buxton, U.K.	7/25	36
1989	Aston Martin	V8 Vantage Volante	$158,852	643	Bonhams	Newport Pagnell, U.K.	5/13	126
1987	Aston Martin	V8 Vantage Zagato	$156,772	651	Bonhams	Newport Pagnell, U.K.	5/13	135
1998	Aston Martin	V8 Volante	$117,424	958	Christie's	London, U.K.	6/26	180
2003	Aston Martin	Vanquish	$113,940	985	Kruse	Auburn, IN	8/30	757.1
2003	Aston Martin	Vanquish V12	$142,560	743	Barrett-Jackson	West Palm Beach, FL	3/29	671
2003	Aston Martin	DB AR1 Roadster	$165,000	608	Worldwide Group	Seabrook, TX	5/6	88
1961	Aston Martin	DB4 Series 3	$188,720	511	Artcurial	Paris, FRA	2/12	16
1932	Auburn	12 Boattail Speedster	$572,400	107	Kruse	Auburn, IN	8/30	1047
1932	Auburn	8-100A Custom Phaeton	$113,400	987	Leake	Tulsa, OK	6/9	2464
1935	Auburn	851 Boattail Speedster	$432,000	148	Kruse	Scottsdale, AZ	1/26	2750
1935	Auburn	851 Supercharged Cabriolet	$270,000	291	Kruse	Scottsdale, AZ	1/26	2748
1936	Auburn	852 Phaeton	$151,200	678	Barrett-Jackson	Scottsdale, AZ	1/14	1330
1936	Auburn	852 SC Boattail Speedster	$310,000	245	RM	Rochester, MI	8/5	263
1931	Auburn	8-98A Phaeton	$118,800	941	Kruse	Auburn, IN	5/18	735
1931	Auburn	Boattail Speedster	$192,500	494	RM	Phoenix, AZ	1/20	151

BY THE NUMBERS

47

Year	Make	Model	Sold Price	Rank	Auction Co.	Location	Date	Lot #
1931	Auburn	Cabriolet	$172,800	569	Barrett-Jackson	Scottsdale, AZ	1/14	1538
1936	Auburn	Convertible Replica	$162,000	620	Kruse	Auburn, IN	8/30	1070
1967	Austin-Healey	3000 Roadster	$143,100	730	Barrett-Jackson	Scottsdale, AZ	1/14	1238
1960	Austin-Healey	3000 Roadster	$135,000	793	Barrett-Jackson	West Palm Beach, FL	3/29	632
1935	Avions Voisin	C 25 "Clairière"	$124,969	886	Artcurial	Paris, FRA	2/12	2
1995	Batmobile	"Batman Forever"	$361,800	204	Kruse	Auburn, IN	8/30	8001
1934	Bentley	3 1/2-Liter Open Tourer	$116,214	964	Coys	Donington Park, U.K.	4/30	245
1935	Bentley	3 1/2-Liter Three-Window Coupe	$308,000	246	Gooding	Pebble Beach, CA	8/20	41
1939	Bentley	4 1/4-Liter Tourer	$174,764	564	H&H	Buxton, U.K.	7/25	38
1931	Bentley	4/8-Liter Four Seater Le Mans Replica	$401,003	172	Bonhams	Sussex, U.K.	9/1	215
1937	Bentley	4-Liter Fixed Head Coupe	$1,265,000	35	RM	Monterey, CA	8/18	479
1928	Bentley	6 1/2-Liter	$267,585	302	Bonhams	Hendon, U.K.	4/24	625
1931	Bentley	8-Liter Sportsman Coupe	$1,485,000	29	RM	Amelia Island, FL	3/11	153
2005	Bentley	Arnage Saloon	$167,400	598	Kruse	Auburn, IN	8/30	2720.1
1995	Bentley	Azure	$133,778	807	Coys	Birmingham, UK	1/14	222
2000	Bentley	Azure Convertible	$159,300	642	Kruse	Auburn, IN	8/30	787.1
2005	Bentley	Continental GT	$158,760	644	Leake	Tulsa, OK	6/9	454
2005	Bentley	Continental GT	$146,880	708	Kruse	Auburn, IN	8/30	790.1
2005	Bentley	Continental GT	$136,080	785	Kruse	Auburn, IN	8/30	763.2
2000	Bentley	Continental R	$149,040	689	Barrett-Jackson	Scottsdale, AZ	1/14	1028
2000	Bentley	Continental R Mulliner Coupe	$137,700	772	Barrett-Jackson	Scottsdale, AZ	1/14	1276.1
1955	Bentley	R-Type Continental	$262,098	311	Christie's	Paris, FRA	2/11	61
1955	Bentley	R-Type Continental	$278,369	274	Coys	Maastricht, NL	1/14	231
1951	Bentley	S1 Continental Fastback	$161,000	632	Bonhams	North Brookfield, MA	9/23	1000
1956	Bentley	S1 Continental Fastback	$134,882	802	Bonhams	Northamptonshire, U.K.	6/17	416
1957	Bentley	S1 Continental Saloon	$183,000	525	Bonhams	Carmel, CA	8/18	549
1960	Bentley	S2 Continental DHC	$132,834	812	Christie's	Paris, FRA	2/11	83
1962	Bentley	S2 Continental Flying Spur	$152,750	673	Christie's	Monterey, CA	8/17	42
1929	Bentley	Speed Six Dual Cowl Tourer	$1,815,000	15	RM	Monterey, CA	8/18	454
1927	Bentley	Speed Six Fixed Head Coupe	$781,000	66	RM	Monterey, CA	8/18	489
1930	Bentley	Speed Six Le Mans Tourer	$605,000	99	RM	Phoenix, AZ	1/20	174
1957	Bentley	S1 Continental Flying Spur	$155,356	656	Artcurial	Paris, FRA	2/12	17
1931	Bentley	Aero Coupe	$378,000	186	Barrett-Jackson	West Palm Beach, FL	3/29	723.1
2001	Bentley	Arnage Saloon	$167,400	599	Barrett-Jackson	West Palm Beach, FL	3/29	727
1947	Bentley	Mk VI Franay	$1,728,000	18	Barrett-Jackson	West Palm Beach, FL	3/29	723
1939	Bentley	Royale Custom	$399,600	173	Barrett-Jackson	West Palm Beach, FL	3/29	724
1967	Bizzarrini	5300GT Alloy	$269,500	298	Worldwide Group	Seabrook, TX	5/6	67
1973	BMW	3.0CSL "Batmobile"	$153,718	668	Christie's	London, U.K.	6/26	177
1938	BMW	327/328 Cabriolet	$178,141	554	Artcurial	Paris, FRA	6/12	17
1968	Brabham	BT31 Formula One Racer	$180,053	543	H&H	Buxton, U.K.	2/21	29
1938	Bugatti	T57C Aravis Drophead Coupe	$1,045,000	48	RM	Phoenix, AZ	1/20	143
1927	Bugatti	Type 35C Grand Prix	$2,585,000	8	Gooding	Pebble Beach, CA	8/20	44
1927	Bugatti	Type 44 Roadster	$165,000	609	RM	Amelia Island, FL	3/11	138
1930	Bugatti	Type 44 Roadster	$146,576	712	H&H	London, U.K.	5/24	41
1936	Bugatti	Type 57	$206,326	454	Artcurial	Paris, FRA	6/12	18
1938	Bugatti	Type 57 Atalante Coupe	$682,000	82	Gooding	Pebble Beach, CA	8/20	64
1936	Bugatti	Type 57 Stelvio	$396,000	174	RM	Monterey, CA	8/18	481
1938	Bugatti	Type 57C Aravis DHC	$1,375,000	31	Gooding	Pebble Beach, CA	8/20	38
1937	Bugatti	Type 57C Ventoux	$467,500	140	RM	Monterey, CA	8/18	473
1947	Bugatti	Type 73C Monoposto	$323,000	236	Christie's	Monterey, CA	8/17	21
1939	Buick	Century Convertible Coupe	$170,500	583	RM	Rochester, MI	8/5	273
1970	Buick	Gsx Stage 1	$133,875	806	Mecum	Belvidere, IL	5/25	S87
1954	Buick	Skylark	$181,500	530	Russo and Steele	Scottsdale, AZ	1/20	S234
1954	Buick	Skylark	$154,000	660	Russo and Steele	Monterey, CA	8/18	S245
1954	Buick	Skylark	$130,725	837	Mecum	Belvidere, IL	5/25	F572
1953	Buick	Skylark Convertible	$143,000	733	RM	Phoenix, AZ	1/20	121
1953	Buick	Skylark Convertible	$135,000	794	RM	Novi, MI	9/22	SP04
1954	Buick	Skylark Convertible	$185,500	518	Silver	Ft. McDowell, AZ	1/23	185
1954	Buick	Skylark Convertible	$145,800	714	Barrett-Jackson	Scottsdale, AZ	1/14	1273
1954	Buick	Skylark Convertible	$132,000	815	RM	Monterey, CA	8/18	174
1953	Buick	Skylark Convertible	$383,400	183	Barrett-Jackson	West Palm Beach, FL	3/29	703.1
1936	Buick/Chrysler	Mobiloil /Gilmore Special	$132,000	816	RM	Los Angeles, CA	5/13	241
1931	Cadillac	355-A V8 Roadster	$115,500	972	RM	Amelia Island, FL	3/11	121
1938	Cadillac	90 Series Town Car	$270,000	292	Kruse	Auburn, IN	8/30	1057
1947	Cadillac	Custom	$132,000	817	RM	Phoenix, AZ	1/20	185

Year	Make	Model	Sold Price	Rank	Auction Co.	Location	Date	Lot #
1948	Cadillac	Custom Cabriolet	$649,000	89	RM	Monterey, CA	8/18	443
1959	Cadillac	Eldorado Biarritz Convertible	$139,100	768	RM	Boca Raton, FL	2/10	NR30
1956	Cadillac	Eldorado Brougham Town Car	$781,100	65	RM	Boca Raton, FL	2/10	SP41
1958	Cadillac	Eldorado Brougham Town Car	$177,620	556	RM	Boca Raton, FL	2/10	SP42
1953	Cadillac	Eldorado Convertible	$216,000	415	Barrett-Jackson	Scottsdale, AZ	1/14	1261
1953	Cadillac	Eldorado Convertible	$162,000	621	RM	Novi, MI	9/22	SP06
1953	Cadillac	Eldorado Convertible	$132,000	818	RM	Amelia Island, FL	3/11	150
1930	Cadillac	Imperial	$135,200	791	G. Potter King	Atlantic City, NJ	2/23	1019
1930	Cadillac	Model 452-A V16	$132,000	819	RM	Amelia Island, FL	3/11	152
1934	Cadillac	Series 30	$187,000	513	RM	Amelia Island, FL	3/11	128
1938	Cadillac	Series 38-90 V16 Conv. Coupe	$231,000	372	RM	Amelia Island, FL	3/11	159
1941	Cadillac	Series 62 Convertible	$112,350	998	RM	Boca Raton, FL	2/10	SP104
1950	Cadillac	Series 62 Convertible	$135,000	795	Barrett-Jackson	Scottsdale, AZ	1/14	1317
1941	Cadillac	Series 62 Convertible Coupe	$126,500	867	RM	Monterey, CA	8/18	490
1931	Cadillac	V12 Convertible Coupe	$259,200	312	Kruse	Auburn, IN	5/18	7005
1932	Cadillac	V12 Sport Phaeton	$203,500	461	RM	Rochester, MI	8/5	275
1933	Cadillac	V16 Model 452-C Convertible Phaeton	$682,000	83	RM	Rochester, MI	8/5	264
1931	Cadillac	V16 Sport Phaeton	$495,000	128	RM	Rochester, MI	8/5	229
1931	Cadillac	V16 Sport Phaeton	$363,000	201	RM	Phoenix, AZ	1/20	142
1928	Cadillac	V8 Town Sedan	$621,500	94	RM	Phoenix, AZ	1/20	180
2001	Cadillac	Northstar Le Mans Endurance Racer	$162,000	622	Barrett-Jackson	West Palm Beach, FL	3/29	729
1946	Cameron Millar	250F CM4	$522,361	123	Artcurial	Paris, FRA	2/12	48
1904	CGV	Phaeton Modele H1 6 1/4-Liter	$445,358	146	Christie's	Paris, FRA	2/11	73
1955	Chevrolet	3100 Custom Pickup	$129,600	843	Barrett-Jackson	Scottsdale, AZ	1/14	1272
1957	Chevrolet	Bel Air	$126,000	874	Mecum	Belvidere, IL	5/25	S503
1959	Chevrolet	Bel Air	$205,200	455	Barrett-Jackson	Scottsdale, AZ	1/14	1247
1955	Chevrolet	Bel Air Convertible	$126,360	872	Barrett-Jackson	Scottsdale, AZ	1/14	1004
1956	Chevrolet	Bel Air Convertible	$124,200	890	Barrett-Jackson	Scottsdale, AZ	1/14	1045
1957	Chevrolet	Bel Air Convertible	$167,400	600	Barrett-Jackson	Scottsdale, AZ	1/14	1241.1
1957	Chevrolet	Bel Air Convertible	$140,400	752	Barrett-Jackson	Scottsdale, AZ	1/14	1235
1957	Chevrolet	Bel Air Convertible	$113,400	988	Barrett-Jackson	Scottsdale, AZ	1/14	750
1955	Chevrolet	Bel Air Custom Convertible	$210,600	437	Barrett-Jackson	Scottsdale, AZ	1/14	1293
1962	Chevrolet	Biscayne Z11	$165,850	606	RM	Boca Raton, FL	2/10	SP38
1969	Chevrolet	Camaro	$259,200	313	Barrett-Jackson	Scottsdale, AZ	1/14	1300
1969	Chevrolet	Camaro	$116,100	965	Barrett-Jackson	Scottsdale, AZ	1/14	1552.1
1967	Chevrolet	Camaro	$341,585	216	Silver	Reno, NV	8/6	423
1969	Chevrolet	Camaro COPO	$262,500	309	Mecum	Belvidere, IL	5/25	S569
1969	Chevrolet	Camaro COPO	$197,000	479	Central PA Auto	Lock Haven, PA	7/22	
1969	Chevrolet	Camaro COPO	$156,000	655	G. Potter King	Atlantic City, NJ	2/23	1020
1969	Chevrolet	Camaro COPO RS	$139,700	766	Russo and Steele	Monterey, CA	8/18	S258
1974	Chevrolet	Camaro IROC Racer	$121,000	914	RM	Monterey, CA	8/18	165
1968	Chevrolet	Camaro RS/SS	$139,424	767	Coys	Monte Carlo, MCO	5/20	273
1969	Chevrolet	Camaro RS/SS	$159,840	636	Barrett-Jackson	Scottsdale, AZ	1/14	1064
1969	Chevrolet	Camaro SS Baldwin Motion	$486,000	131	Barrett-Jackson	Scottsdale, AZ	1/14	1290
1969	Chevrolet	Camaro Z/28	$159,500	637	Russo and Steele	Scottsdale, AZ	1/20	S241
1969	Chevrolet	Camaro Z/28	$157,500	647	Mecum	Belvidere, IL	5/25	S597
1969	Chevrolet	Camaro Z/28	$141,750	747	Mecum	Kissimmee, FL	1/27	S61
1967	Chevrolet	Camaro Z/28	$136,080	786	Barrett-Jackson	Scottsdale, AZ	1/14	1008
1969	Chevrolet	Camaro Z/28	$221,400	403	Barrett-Jackson	Scottsdale, AZ	1/14	1030
1969	Chevrolet	Camaro Z/28	$140,000	765	RM	Monterey, CA	8/18	158
1969	Chevrolet	Camaro Z/28	$124,200	891	Barrett-Jackson	Scottsdale, AZ	1/14	1233
1969	Chevrolet	Camaro Z/28 RS	$187,000	514	Russo and Steele	Monterey, CA	8/18	S244
1969	Chevrolet	Camaro Z/28 RS	$178,200	549	Barrett-Jackson	Scottsdale, AZ	1/14	1028.1
1969	Chevrolet	Camaro Z/28 RS	$119,175	939	Mecum	Kissimmee, FL	1/27	C45
1969	Chevrolet	Camaro ZL1	$486,000	132	Barrett-Jackson	Scottsdale, AZ	1/14	1322
1969	Chevrolet	Camaro ZL1	$115,560	969	Kruse	Auburn, IN	5/18	7012
1970	Chevrolet	Chevelle	$324,500	231	Russo and Steele	Scottsdale, AZ	1/20	F226
1970	Chevrolet	Chevelle	$131,250	831	Mecum	Kansas City, MO	4/28	S568
1969	Chevrolet	Chevelle COPO	$216,000	416	Barrett-Jackson	Scottsdale, AZ	1/14	1047
1969	Chevrolet	Chevelle COPO	$164,160	614	Barrett-Jackson	Scottsdale, AZ	1/14	1013.1
1965	Chevrolet	Chevelle SS	$202,125	465	Mecum	Belvidere, IL	5/25	S601
1969	Chevrolet	Chevelle SS	$288,750	266	Mecum	Belvidere, IL	5/25	S545.1
1970	Chevrolet	Chevelle SS	$189,000	504	Mecum	Belvidere, IL	5/25	S557
1970	Chevrolet	Chevelle SS	$130,200	842	Mecum	Belvidere, IL	5/25	S599

Year	Make	Model	Sold Price	Rank	Auction Co.	Location	Date	Lot #
1966	Chevrolet	Chevelle SS 396	$135,000	796	Barrett-Jackson	Scottsdale, AZ	1/14	731
1970	Chevrolet	Chevelle SS 454	$119,880	937	Kruse	Auburn, IN	5/18	2487
1970	Chevrolet	Chevelle SS 454 Convertible	$135,000	797	Barrett-Jackson	Scottsdale, AZ	1/14	978
1970	Chevrolet	Chevelle SS 454 LS6	$210,000	442	Mecum	Belvidere, IL	5/25	F512
1970	Chevrolet	Chevelle SS 454 LS6	$129,150	852	Mecum	Belvidere, IL	5/25	S574
1970	Chevrolet	Chevelle SS 454 LS6	$127,050	862	Mecum	Belvidere, IL	5/25	S554
1970	Chevrolet	Chevelle SS 454 LS6	$118,650	950	Carlisle	Carlisle, PA	4/21	S156
1970	Chevrolet	Chevelle SS 454 LS6	$115,500	973	Mecum	Kissimmee, FL	1/27	S37
1970	Chevrolet	Chevelle SS 454 LS6	$140,400	753	G. Potter King	Atlantic City, NJ	2/23	1001
1970	Chevrolet	Chevelle SS 454 LS6 Convertible	$1,242,000	36	Barrett-Jackson	Scottsdale, AZ	1/14	1287
1970	Chevrolet	Chevelle SS 454 LS6 Convertible	$513,000	125	Barrett-Jackson	Scottsdale, AZ	1/14	1320
1965	Chevrolet	Chevelle Z16	$412,500	163	Russo and Steele	Scottsdale, AZ	1/20	S232
1957	Chevrolet	Corvette	$192,500	495	Russo and Steele	Scottsdale, AZ	1/20	S229
1957	Chevrolet	Corvette	$118,125	953	Mecum	Carlisle, PA	8/25	S33
1961	Chevrolet	Corvette	$116,000	968	Central PA Auto	Lock Haven, PA	7/22	
1966	Chevrolet	Corvette	$115,500	974	Russo and Steele	Scottsdale, AZ	1/20	F239
1967	Chevrolet	Corvette	$226,800	388	Mecum	Kissimmee, FL	1/27	X27
1967	Chevrolet	Corvette	$194,250	489	Mecum	Kissimmee, FL	1/27	X18
1967	Chevrolet	Corvette	$192,150	500	Mecum	Kissimmee, FL	1/27	S51
1967	Chevrolet	Corvette	$172,200	580	Mecum	Kissimmee, FL	1/27	S68
1967	Chevrolet	Corvette	$147,000	707	Mecum	Belvidere, IL	5/25	S560
1967	Chevrolet	Corvette	$141,750	748	Mecum	Kissimmee, FL	1/27	S10
1967	Chevrolet	Corvette	$122,850	904	Mecum	Kissimmee, FL	1/27	C61
1967	Chevrolet	Corvette	$122,325	907	Mecum	Carlisle, PA	8/25	S507
1967	Chevrolet	Corvette	$120,750	929	Mecum	Kissimmee, FL	1/27	S43
1967	Chevrolet	Corvette	$117,600	954	Mecum	Kissimmee, FL	1/27	F17
1967	Chevrolet	Corvette	$115,500	975	Russo and Steele	Scottsdale, AZ	1/20	S243
1967	Chevrolet	Corvette	$115,500	976	Mecum	Belvidere, IL	5/25	F532
1967	Chevrolet	Corvette	$112,350	999	Mecum	Kissimmee, FL	1/27	X24
1969	Chevrolet	Corvette	$334,800	223	Barrett-Jackson	Scottsdale, AZ	1/14	1271.1
1969	Chevrolet	Corvette	$237,600	352	Barrett-Jackson	Scottsdale, AZ	1/14	1325
1969	Chevrolet	Corvette	$187,000	515	Russo and Steele	Scottsdale, AZ	1/20	S208
1971	Chevrolet	Corvette	$157,500	648	Mecum	Kissimmee, FL	1/27	X53
1967	Chevrolet	Corvette	$127,400	860	G. Potter King	Atlantic City, NJ	2/23	1032
1957	Chevrolet	Corvette	$237,600	353	Barrett-Jackson	Scottsdale, AZ	1/14	1282.1
1957	Chevrolet	Corvette	$178,200	550	Barrett-Jackson	Scottsdale, AZ	1/14	1017.1
1959	Chevrolet	Corvette	$143,640	728	Barrett-Jackson	Scottsdale, AZ	1/14	1046
1959	Chevrolet	Corvette	$140,400	754	Barrett-Jackson	Scottsdale, AZ	1/14	1225
1961	Chevrolet	Corvette	$172,800	570	Barrett-Jackson	Scottsdale, AZ	1/14	1252
1961	Chevrolet	Corvette	$113,400	989	Barrett-Jackson	Scottsdale, AZ	1/14	963
1962	Chevrolet	Corvette	$489,500	130	Gooding	Palm Beach, FL	1/24	27
1962	Chevrolet	Corvette	$135,000	798	Barrett-Jackson	Scottsdale, AZ	1/14	745
1958	Chevrolet	Corvette "Joie Chitwood" Conv.	$132,300	813	Kruse	Auburn, IN	8/30	2760.1
1962	Chevrolet	Corvette 327	$124,200	892	Barrett-Jackson	Scottsdale, AZ	1/14	1062
1966	Chevrolet	Corvette 427	$162,750	617	Carlisle	Carlisle, PA	4/21	S150
1967	Chevrolet	Corvette 427	$113,850	986	Russo and Steele	Scottsdale, AZ	1/20	F212
2002	Chevrolet	Corvette 427 Stage 4 Lingenfelter	$129,600	844	Barrett-Jackson	Scottsdale, AZ	1/14	1335.1
1967	Chevrolet	Corvette 427/400 Convertible	$221,400	404	Barrett-Jackson	Scottsdale, AZ	1/14	1275
1967	Chevrolet	Corvette 427/400 Convertible	$158,360	646	RM	Boca Raton, FL	2/10	SP115
1967	Chevrolet	Corvette 427/400 Convertible	$136,080	787	Barrett-Jackson	Scottsdale, AZ	1/14	1059
1966	Chevrolet	Corvette 427/425 Convertible	$216,000	417	Barrett-Jackson	Scottsdale, AZ	1/14	1263
1966	Chevrolet	Corvette 427/425 Convertible	$113,400	990	Barrett-Jackson	Scottsdale, AZ	1/14	1565
1967	Chevrolet	Corvette 427/435	$308,000	247	Russo and Steele	Monterey, CA	8/18	S256
1967	Chevrolet	Corvette 427/435	$159,500	638	Russo and Steele	Monterey, CA	8/18	F152
1967	Chevrolet	Corvette 427/435	$149,040	690	Barrett-Jackson	Scottsdale, AZ	1/14	1578
1967	Chevrolet	Corvette 427/435	$137,160	779	Barrett-Jackson	Scottsdale, AZ	1/14	1003
1969	Chevrolet	Corvette 427/435	$116,100	966	Barrett-Jackson	Scottsdale, AZ	1/14	975.1
1967	Chevrolet	Corvette 427/435 Convertible	$378,000	187	Barrett-Jackson	Scottsdale, AZ	1/14	1284
1967	Chevrolet	Corvette 427/435 Convertible	$248,400	333	Barrett-Jackson	Scottsdale, AZ	1/14	1298
1967	Chevrolet	Corvette 427/435 Convertible	$228,960	387	Barrett-Jackson	Scottsdale, AZ	1/14	1265
1967	Chevrolet	Corvette 427/435 Convertible	$221,400	405	Barrett-Jackson	Scottsdale, AZ	1/14	1236
1967	Chevrolet	Corvette 427/435 Convertible	$216,000	418	Barrett-Jackson	Scottsdale, AZ	1/14	1027
1967	Chevrolet	Corvette 427/435 Convertible	$216,000	419	Barrett-Jackson	Scottsdale, AZ	1/14	1303
1967	Chevrolet	Corvette 427/435 Convertible	$210,600	438	Barrett-Jackson	Scottsdale, AZ	1/14	1279
1967	Chevrolet	Corvette 427/435 Convertible	$189,000	505	Barrett-Jackson	Scottsdale, AZ	1/14	1017
1967	Chevrolet	Corvette 427/435 Marquive	$182,970	526	RM	Boca Raton, FL	2/10	SP18

Year	Make	Model	Sold Price	Rank	Auction Co.	Location	Date	Lot #
1967	Chevrolet	Corvette 427/435 Convertible	$162,000	623	Barrett-Jackson	Scottsdale, AZ	1/14	1544
1967	Chevrolet	Corvette 427/435 Convertible	$149,040	691	Barrett-Jackson	Scottsdale, AZ	1/14	1040
1967	Chevrolet	Corvette 427/435 Convertible	$143,000	734	RM	Monterey, CA	8/18	434
1967	Chevrolet	Corvette 427/435 Convertible	$121,500	910	Barrett-Jackson	Scottsdale, AZ	1/14	419.1
1969	Chevrolet	Corvette 427/435 Convertible	$128,520	854	Barrett-Jackson	Scottsdale, AZ	1/14	1556.1
1965	Chevrolet	Corvette Convertible	$152,475	675	RM	Boca Raton, FL	2/10	SP22
1965	Chevrolet	Corvette Convertible	$151,200	679	Barrett-Jackson	Scottsdale, AZ	1/14	1245
1963	Chevrolet	Corvette Custom	$118,800	942	Barrett-Jackson	Scottsdale, AZ	1/14	1237
1953	Chevrolet	Corvette Roadster	$1,080,000	45	Barrett-Jackson	Scottsdale, AZ	1/14	1311
1953	Chevrolet	Corvette Roadster	$212,000	436	Branson	Branson, MO	4/21	268
1954	Chevrolet	Corvette Roadster	$115,500	977	Mecum	Kissimmee, FL	1/27	S29
1956	Chevrolet	Corvette Roadster	$117,500	955	Christie's	Monterey, CA	8/17	47
1968	Chevrolet	Corvette Stingray Racer	$605,000	100	RM	Phoenix, AZ	1/20	161
1963	Chevrolet	Corvette Z06	$230,050	385	RM	Boca Raton, FL	2/10	SP17
1963	Chevrolet	Corvette Z06	$220,500	407	Mecum	Kissimmee, FL	1/27	X12
1963	Chevrolet	Corvette Z06	$197,640	478	Barrett-Jackson	Scottsdale, AZ	1/14	1294
1963	Chevrolet	Corvette Z06	$231,000	373	RM	Monterey, CA	8/18	157
1957	Chevrolet	Corvette ZL1 Convertible	$291,600	263	Barrett-Jackson	Scottsdale, AZ	1/14	1295
1963	Chevrolet	Impala	$120,750	930	Mecum	Belvidere, IL	5/25	S554.1
1963	Chevrolet	Impala SS Convertible	$149,040	692	Barrett-Jackson	Scottsdale, AZ	1/14	994
1963	Chevrolet	Impala Z11	$325,500	230	Mecum	Belvidere, IL	5/25	S518.1
1963	Chevrolet	Impala Z11	$299,250	258	Mecum	Kissimmee, FL	1/27	X30
1957	Chevrolet	Nomad Custom Wagon	$147,960	704	Barrett-Jackson	Scottsdale, AZ	1/14	968
1968	Chevrolet	Nova	$191,625	501	Mecum	Belvidere, IL	5/25	S595
1939	Chevrolet	Town Sedan	$137,500	773	Russo and Steele	Scottsdale, AZ	1/20	F219
1968	Chevrolet	Yenko Camaro	$367,500	197	Mecum	Belvidere, IL	5/25	S514
1969	Chevrolet	Yenko Camaro	$291,500	264	Russo and Steele	Monterey, CA	8/18	S250
1970	Chevrolet	Yenko Deuce Nova	$183,750	522	Mecum	Belvidere, IL	5/25	S558
1955	Chevrolet	Bel Air Convertible	$122,100	909	Worldwide Group	Seabrook, TX	5/6	44
1969	Chevrolet	Camaro SS 396	$129,250	849	Worldwide Group	Seabrook, TX	5/6	46
1958	Chevrolet	Corvette	$124,950	888	Mecum	St. Charles, IL	6/16	S568
1958	Chevrolet	Corvette	$112,350	1000	Mecum	St. Charles, IL	6/16	S564
1967	Chevrolet	Corvette	$199,500	472	Mecum	St. Charles, IL	6/16	S521
1958	Chevrolet	Corvette	$116,025	967	Mecum	St. Charles, IL	6/16	S533
1959	Chevrolet	Corvette	$131,250	832	Mecum	St. Charles, IL	6/16	S543
1962	Chevrolet	Corvette	$128,100	855	Mecum	St. Charles, IL	6/16	S551
1963	Chevrolet	Corvette	$136,500	784	Mecum	St. Charles, IL	6/16	S519
1963	Chevrolet	Corvette	$118,650	951	Mecum	St. Charles, IL	6/16	S515
1964	Chevrolet	Corvette	$367,500	198	Mecum	St. Charles, IL	6/16	S510
1964	Chevrolet	Corvette	$278,250	275	Mecum	St. Charles, IL	6/16	S507
1965	Chevrolet	Corvette	$249,375	332	Mecum	St. Charles, IL	6/16	S506
1965	Chevrolet	Corvette	$173,250	565	Mecum	St. Charles, IL	6/16	S524
1966	Chevrolet	Corvette	$170,100	591	Mecum	St. Charles, IL	6/16	S552
1967	Chevrolet	Corvette	$262,500	310	Mecum	St. Charles, IL	6/16	S528
1967	Chevrolet	Corvette	$173,250	566	Mecum	St. Charles, IL	6/16	S508
1967	Chevrolet	Corvette	$168,000	596	Mecum	St. Charles, IL	6/16	S500
1967	Chevrolet	Corvette	$162,750	618	Mecum	St. Charles, IL	6/16	S514
1967	Chevrolet	Corvette	$150,150	686	Mecum	St. Charles, IL	6/16	S34
1967	Chevrolet	Corvette	$148,050	703	Mecum	St. Charles, IL	6/16	S76
1959	Chevrolet	Corvette Custom	$127,050	863	Mecum	St. Charles, IL	6/16	F516
1955	Chevrolet	Corvette Roadster	$346,500	208	Mecum	St. Charles, IL	6/16	S539
1956	Chevrolet	Corvette Roadster	$115,500	978	Mecum	St. Charles, IL	6/16	S67
1958	Chevrolet	Impala Convertible	$121,000	915	Worldwide Group	Seabrook, TX	5/6	48
1957	Chevrolet	Bel Air Convertible	$151,200	680	Barrett-Jackson	West Palm Beach, FL	3/29	708
1957	Chevrolet	Bel Air Convertible	$136,080	788	Barrett-Jackson	West Palm Beach, FL	3/29	650
1957	Chevrolet	Bel Air Custom Convertible	$132,300	814	Barrett-Jackson	West Palm Beach, FL	3/29	719
1968	Chevrolet	Biscayne	$248,400	334	Barrett-Jackson	West Palm Beach, FL	3/29	704
1969	Chevrolet	Camaro	$124,200	893	Barrett-Jackson	West Palm Beach, FL	3/29	715
1969	Chevrolet	Camaro Z/28 RS	$232,200	369	Barrett-Jackson	West Palm Beach, FL	3/29	658
1967	Chevrolet	Camaro Z/28 Racer	$324,000	232	Barrett-Jackson	West Palm Beach, FL	3/29	733
1957	Chevrolet	Corvette	$162,000	624	Barrett-Jackson	West Palm Beach, FL	3/29	401
1958	Chevrolet	Corvette	$205,200	456	Barrett-Jackson	West Palm Beach, FL	3/29	713
1960	Chevrolet	Corvette	$172,800	571	Barrett-Jackson	West Palm Beach, FL	3/29	735
1962	Chevrolet	Corvette	$137,160	780	Barrett-Jackson	West Palm Beach, FL	3/29	719.1
1967	Chevrolet	Corvette 427/390 Convertible	$124,200	894	Barrett-Jackson	West Palm Beach, FL	3/29	704.1
1967	Chevrolet	Corvette 427/400	$151,200	681	Barrett-Jackson	West Palm Beach, FL	3/29	663

Top 1,000 Sales of 2006 by Marque

Year	Make	Model	Sold Price	Rank	Auction Co.	Location	Date	Lot #
1967	Chevrolet	Corvette 427/400 Convertible	$191,160	502	Barrett-Jackson	West Palm Beach, FL	3/29	711
1967	Chevrolet	Corvette 427/400 Convertible	$189,000	506	Barrett-Jackson	West Palm Beach, FL	3/29	653
1967	Chevrolet	Corvette 427/400 Convertible	$132,840	810	Barrett-Jackson	West Palm Beach, FL	3/29	690
1966	Chevrolet	Corvette 427/425 Convertible	$163,080	615	Barrett-Jackson	West Palm Beach, FL	3/29	707
1967	Chevrolet	Corvette 427/435	$259,200	314	Barrett-Jackson	West Palm Beach, FL	3/29	659.1
1967	Chevrolet	Corvette 427/435	$154,440	658	Barrett-Jackson	West Palm Beach, FL	3/29	687
1967	Chevrolet	Corvette 427/435 Convertible	$113,400	991	Barrett-Jackson	West Palm Beach, FL	3/29	717
1966	Chevrolet	Corvette 427/450	$156,600	652	Barrett-Jackson	West Palm Beach, FL	3/29	655
1966	Chevrolet	Corvette 427/450 Convertible	$140,400	755	Barrett-Jackson	West Palm Beach, FL	3/29	714
1958	Chevrolet	Corvette	$153,360	669	Barrett-Jackson	West Palm Beach, FL	3/29	369
1954	Chevrolet	Corvette Roadster	$237,600	354	Barrett-Jackson	West Palm Beach, FL	3/29	652
1966	Chevrolet	Impala SS Convertible	$113,400	992	Barrett-Jackson	West Palm Beach, FL	3/29	641.1
1958	Chevrolet	Impala 2-Door Hard Top	$115,560	970	Barrett-Jackson	West Palm Beach, FL	3/29	105
1970	Chevron-Ford	B16 Endurance Racer	$145,352	723	Bonhams	Sussex, U.K.	9/1	205
1957	Chrysler	300C Convertible	$167,990	597	RM	Boca Raton, FL	2/10	SP50
1957	Chrysler	300C Convertible	$125,400	881	RM	Amelia Island, FL	3/11	178
1960	Chrysler	300F Convertible	$164,700	613	Barrett-Jackson	Scottsdale, AZ	1/14	1340
1961	Chrysler	300G Convertible	$199,800	470	Barrett-Jackson	Scottsdale, AZ	1/14	1299
1952	Chrysler	D'Elegance	$1,188,000	40	Barrett-Jackson	Scottsdale, AZ	1/14	1306
1957	Chrysler	Imperial Convertible	$378,000	188	Barrett-Jackson	Scottsdale, AZ	1/14	1278.1
1931	Chrysler	Imperial Dual Cowl Phaeton AND 1931 Chrysler Imperial Sedan	$627,000	93	Gooding	Pebble Beach, CA	8/20	47
1933	Chrysler	Imperial Sport Phaeton	$280,500	272	RM	Rochester, MI	8/5	259
1957	Chrysler	New Yorker Convertible	$145,800	715	Barrett-Jackson	Scottsdale, AZ	1/14	1555
1941	Chrysler	Royal Town & Country	$280,500	273	RM	Phoenix, AZ	1/20	183
1952	Chrysler	Thomas Special SWB Prototype	$715,000	72	RM	Amelia Island, FL	3/11	162
1941	Chrysler	Thunderbolt	$1,210,000	38	RM	Phoenix, AZ	1/20	146
1947	Chrysler	Town & Country Convertible	$148,500	693	Barrett-Jackson	Scottsdale, AZ	1/14	1266
1948	Chrysler	Town & Country Convertible	$198,000	473	Gooding	Pebble Beach, CA	8/20	35
1948	Chrysler	Town & Country Convertible	$189,000	507	Kruse	Auburn, IN	5/18	1033
1948	Chrysler	Town & Country Convertible	$143,000	735	RM	Phoenix, AZ	1/20	172
1948	Chrysler	Town & Country Convertible	$124,200	895	Kruse	Auburn, IN	5/18	1034
1949	Chrysler	Town & Country Convertible	$126,500	868	RM	Phoenix, AZ	1/20	160
1962	Chrysler	300G Convertible	$184,250	520	Worldwide Group	Seabrook, TX	5/6	42
1947	Cisitalia	202 Spider Nuvolari	$385,000	179	Gooding	Pebble Beach, CA	8/20	73
1970	Citroën	DS21 Cabriolet	$180,790	542	Christie's	Paris, FRA	7/8	110
1973	Citroën	DS23 IE Cabriolet	$209,738	446	Christie's	Paris, FRA	2/11	74
1912	Columbia	Cavalier 4-Passenger Touring	$181,500	531	Gooding	Pebble Beach, CA	8/20	28
1959	Cooper	Maserati	$182,249	528	Coys	Monte Carlo, MCO	5/20	268
1959	Cooper-Climax	Monaco Racer	$212,408	435	Bonhams	Sussex, U.K.	9/1	228
1964	Cooper-Maserati	Type 61 Mk V Racer	$317,183	239	Bonhams	Sussex, U.K.	9/1	224
1936	Cord	810 Phaeton Sedan	$154,000	661	RM	Rochester, MI	8/5	279
1937	Cord	812 Phaeton	$126,500	869	Gooding	Palm Beach, FL	1/24	16
1937	Cord	812 Phaeton Bustleback	$172,800	572	Barrett-Jackson	Scottsdale, AZ	1/14	1280
1937	Cord	812 Phaeton Convertible	$216,000	420	Barrett-Jackson	Scottsdale, AZ	1/14	1036
1937	Cord	812 Supercharged Phaeton	$209,000	447	RM	Amelia Island, FL	3/11	183
1937	Cord	812 Westchester Sedan	$118,800	943	Barrett-Jackson	Scottsdale, AZ	1/14	453
1930	Cord	L29 Cabriolet	$126,001	873	Kruse	Verona, NY	7/7	736
1929	Cord	L29 Convertible Sedan	$148,500	694	RM	Phoenix, AZ	1/20	200
1930	Cord	L29 Convertible Sedan	$192,500	496	RM	Rochester, MI	8/5	257
1953	Cunningham	C-3 Continental	$374,000	193	RM	Monterey, CA	8/18	478
1911	Daimler	4-Door Touring Phaeton	$162,000	625	Kruse	Auburn, IN	5/18	1022
1908	Daimler	TC48 Roi-Des-Belges	$200,000	469	Worldwide Group	Seabrook, TX	5/6	24
1937	Delage	D-8 120 Drophead Coupe	$715,000	73	RM	Monterey, CA	8/18	449
1938	Delahaye	135M Cabriolet	$427,125	153	Bonhams	Monte Carlo, MCO	5/20	155
1947	Delahaye	135M Cabriolet	$194,000	491	Bonhams	Carmel, CA	8/18	528
1948	Delahaye	135M Cabriolet	$203,661	460	Coys	Monte Carlo, MCO	5/20	220
1938	Delahaye	135MS	$1,712,000	19	Bonhams	Carmel, CA	8/18	527
1947	Delahaye	135MS Cabriolet	$375,500	191	Bonhams	Carmel, CA	8/18	512
1939	Delahaye	135MS Grand Sport Roadster	$1,100,000	44	Gooding	Pebble Beach, CA	8/20	52
1957	Desoto	Adventurer Convertible	$123,750	899	RM	Monterey, CA	8/18	428
1958	Devin	Special Roadster	$129,600	845	Barrett-Jackson	Scottsdale, AZ	1/14	1227
1958	Devin	SS Sports Racer	$247,500	338	RM	Monterey, CA	8/18	480
1970	Dodge	Challenger	$210,000	443	Mecum	Belvidere, IL	5/25	F555
1971	Dodge	Challenger	$157,500	649	Mecum	Belvidere, IL	5/25	S582

Year	Make	Model	Sold Price	Rank	Auction Co.	Location	Date	Lot #
1970	Dodge	Challenger Convertible	$125,080	884	Silver	Ft. McDowell, AZ	1/23	558
1970	Dodge	Challenger R/T Convertible	$168,004	595	RM	Toronto, CA	4/7	SP129
1970	Dodge	Challenger R/T Replica Convertible	$113,400	993	Kruse	Scottsdale, AZ	1/26	783
1970	Dodge	Challenger RT/SE	$126,000	875	Mecum	Kissimmee, FL	1/27	S21
1970	Dodge	Charger	$126,000	876	Mecum	Kissimmee, FL	1/27	A111
1970	Dodge	Charger	$126,000	877	Mecum	Belvidere, IL	5/25	U552
1969	Dodge	Charger Daytona	$113,400	994	Kruse	Scottsdale, AZ	1/26	783
1968	Dodge	Charger RT Custom	$140,400	756	Barrett-Jackson	Scottsdale, AZ	1/14	1269
1964	Dodge	Coronet 330 Lightweight Max Wedge	$129,600	846	Barrett-Jackson	Scottsdale, AZ	1/14	1268
1965	Dodge	Coronet A-990	$178,500	548	Mecum	Belvidere, IL	5/25	S576
1965	Dodge	Coronet A-990 Replica	$130,680	838	Barrett-Jackson	Scottsdale, AZ	1/14	1025
1956	Dodge	Custom Royal Golden Lancer	$216,000	421	Barrett-Jackson	Scottsdale, AZ	1/14	1250.1
1968	Dodge	Dart 440 GSS 2D	$118,770	949	RM	Boca Raton, FL	2/10	SP34
1962	Dodge	Dart 440 Max Wedge	$178,200	551	Barrett-Jackson	Scottsdale, AZ	1/14	1288.1
1969	Dodge	Daytona	$614,250	98	Mecum	Kissimmee, FL	1/27	X13
1969	Dodge	Daytona	$362,250	203	Mecum	Belvidere, IL	5/25	S502
1969	Dodge	Daytona	$172,800	573	Barrett-Jackson	Scottsdale, AZ	1/14	1313
1969	Dodge	Daytona 440	$170,500	584	Russo and Steele	Scottsdale, AZ	1/20	F211
1969	Dodge	Daytona 440/6	$154,000	662	Russo and Steele	Scottsdale, AZ	1/20	S206
1969	Dodge	Daytona Wing Racer	$324,000	233	Barrett-Jackson	Scottsdale, AZ	1/14	1335
1964	Dodge	Hemi 330	$367,500	199	Mecum	Belvidere, IL	5/25	S536
1970	Dodge	Hemi Challenger	$215,250	427	Mecum	Kissimmee, FL	1/27	X15
1970	Dodge	Hemi Challenger	$339,040	221	G. Potter King	Atlantic City, NJ	2/23	1024
1971	Dodge	Hemi Charger	$315,000	241	Mecum	Belvidere, IL	5/25	S538
1969	Dodge	Hemi Charger 500	$294,250	262	RM	Boca Raton, FL	2/10	SP31
1969	Dodge	Hemi Charger 500	$195,250	484	Russo and Steele	Scottsdale, AZ	1/20	F225
1967	Dodge	Hemi Coronet R/T Convertible	$264,600	304	Barrett-Jackson	Scottsdale, AZ	1/14	1288
1968	Dodge	Hemi Dart	$324,000	234	Barrett-Jackson	Scottsdale, AZ	1/14	1232.1
1964	Dodge	Hemi Polara 330 Factory Lightweight	$145,800	716	Barrett-Jackson	Scottsdale, AZ	1/14	1584
1963	Dodge	Polara Custom 2-Door	$540,000	117	Barrett-Jackson	Scottsdale, AZ	1/14	1292.1
1969	Dodge	Super Bee	$181,125	538	Mecum	Belvidere, IL	5/25	S541.1
1969	Dodge	Super Bee	$216,000	422	Barrett-Jackson	Scottsdale, AZ	1/14	1034
1997	Dodge	Viper GTS-R Le Mans	$192,500	497	Russo and Steele	Monterey, CA	8/18	S252
1971	Dodge	Hemi Challenger R/T	$341,000	218	Worldwide Group	Seabrook, TX	5/6	62
1969	Dodge	Charger 500	$137,160	781	Barrett-Jackson	West Palm Beach, FL	3/29	358
1958	Duesenberg	Kollins Le Grande	$132,000	820	RM	Phoenix, AZ	1/20	191
1929	Duesenberg	Model J Clear Vision Sedan	$693,000	81	RM	Amelia Island, FL	3/11	140
1929	Duesenberg	Model J Convertible Coupe	$902,000	57	Gooding	Pebble Beach, CA	8/20	71
1929	Duesenberg	Model J Convertible Coupe	$662,602	85	H&H	London, U.K.	5/24	55
1929	Duesenberg	Model J Convertible Sedan	$907,500	56	RM	Rochester, MI	8/5	237
1929	Duesenberg	Model J Convertible Sedan	$502,000	127	Bonhams	Carmel, CA	8/18	548
1932	Duesenberg	Model J Dual Cowl Phaeton	$407,000	169	RM	Amelia Island, FL	3/11	163
1930	Duesenberg	Model J LWB Dual Cowl Phaeton	$1,001,000	50	RM	Phoenix, AZ	1/20	135
1929	Duesenberg	Model J Murphy Convertible	$845,300	61	RM	Boca Raton, FL	2/10	SP48
1934	Duesenberg	Model J Riviera Phaeton	$1,210,000	39	Gooding	Pebble Beach, CA	8/20	60
1930	Duesenberg	Model J Sport Berline	$1,650,000	21	RM	Monterey, CA	8/18	477
1982	Duesenberg II	Royalton Replica	$143,100	731	Kruse	Auburn, IN	8/30	1056
1962	Facel Vega	2+2	$121,500	911	Kruse	Auburn, IN	8/30	746.1
1951	Ferrari	195 Inter	$231,000	374	RM	Monterey, CA	8/18	467A
1967	Ferrari	212 E Montagna Racer	$1,650,000	22	RM	Phoenix, AZ	1/20	164
1952	Ferrari	212 Touring Barchetta	$429,000	152	RM	Phoenix, AZ	1/20	179
1952	Ferrari	225 Sport Spyder	$1,280,000	34	Christie's	Monterey, CA	8/17	18
1963	Ferrari	250 Drogo Speciale	$275,000	278	RM	Monterey, CA	8/18	488
1956	Ferrari	250 GT Alloy Berlinetta	$455,175	141	Bonhams	Monte Carlo, MCO	5/20	200
1963	Ferrari	250 GTL Lusso Comp Berlinetta	$595,425	103	Bonhams	Monte Carlo, MCO	5/20	194
1956	Ferrari	250 GT Boano	$418,572	158	Coys	Nuremberg, DE	7/22	247
1958	Ferrari	250 GT Ellena	$195,200	485	Sportscar Auction Co.	Geneva, CH	10/7	40
1957	Ferrari	250 GT LWB Berlinetta	$341,000	219	RM	Monterey, CA	8/18	461
1958	Ferrari	250 GT LWB Berlinetta TdF	$1,540,000	27	Gooding	Pebble Beach, CA	8/20	68
1961	Ferrari	250 GT Series II Cabriolet	$231,000	375	RM	Phoenix, AZ	1/20	127
1960	Ferrari	250 GT SWB Alloy Comp Berlinetta	$2,750,000	7	RM	Amelia Island, FL	3/11	142
1961	Ferrari	250 GT SWB Alloy Comp Berlinetta	$1,762,300	17	Sportscar Auction Co.	Geneva, CH	10/7	42

Year	Make	Model	Sold Price	Rank	Auction Co.	Location	Date	Lot #
1964	Ferrari	250 GTL Lusso	$286,875	267	Bonhams	Monte Carlo, MCO	5/20	152
1964	Ferrari	250 GTO Replica	$264,000	305	RM	Monterey, CA	8/18	433
1959	Ferrari	250 Nembo	$1,305,970	33	Coys	Nuremberg, DE	7/22	233
1965	Ferrari	275 GTB	$403,127	171	Coys	Maastricht, NL	1/14	224
1967	Ferrari	275 GTB/4	$990,000	51	RM	Monterey, CA	8/18	462
1967	Ferrari	275 GTB/4	$616,000	96	RM	Phoenix, AZ	1/20	154
1967	Ferrari	275 GTB/4 Berlinetta	$742,500	70	RM	Phoenix, AZ	1/20	170
1967	Ferrari	275 GTB/4 NART Conversion Spyder	$776,000	67	RM	Phoenix, AZ	1/20	159
1965	Ferrari	275 GTB/6C Berlinetta	$543,533	114	Bonhams	Monte Carlo, MCO	5/20	254
1966	Ferrari	275 GTS	$242,000	347	RM	Phoenix, AZ	1/20	144
1980	Ferrari	312 T5 Formula One Racer	$660,000	86	Gooding	Palm Beach, FL	1/24	23
1967	Ferrari	330 GT 4-Liter Michelotti	$345,000	212	Christie's	Monterey, CA	8/17	38
1967	Ferrari	330 GTC	$195,800	482	Russo and Steele	Scottsdale, AZ	1/20	S221
1967	Ferrari	330 GTC	$170,500	585	RM	Monterey, CA	8/18	411
1967	Ferrari	330 GTC	$170,375	590	Christie's	Monterey, CA	8/17	43
1967	Ferrari	330 GTC	$143,000	736	Gooding	Palm Beach, FL	1/24	13
1968	Ferrari	330 GTC	$166,465	605	Coys	Nuremberg, DE	7/22	244
1967	Ferrari	330 GTS	$357,500	205	RM	Phoenix, AZ	1/20	134
1951	Ferrari	340 America	$852,500	60	RM	Monterey, CA	8/18	448
2001	Ferrari	360 Modena	$126,000	878	Mecum	Belvidere, IL	5/25	
2001	Ferrari	360 Modena Spyder	$143,100	732	Kruse	Auburn, IN	8/30	3057.1
1970	Ferrari	365 GT	$149,600	688	Russo and Steele	Monterey, CA	8/18	F156
1970	Ferrari	365 GT 2+2	$117,000	960	Bonhams	Carmel, CA	8/18	552
1974	Ferrari	365 GT4 BB	$123,200	902	Gooding	Pebble Beach, CA	8/20	40
1970	Ferrari	365 GTB/4 Daytona	$188,700	512	Bonhams	Monte Carlo, MCO	5/20	153
1971	Ferrari	365 GTB/4 Daytona	$274,459	285	Coys	Monte Carlo, MCO	5/20	244
1971	Ferrari	365 GTB/4 Daytona	$181,500	532	RM	Monterey, CA	8/18	442
1973	Ferrari	365 GTB/4 Daytona	$271,082	290	Bonhams	Sussex, U.K.	9/1	239
1973	Ferrari	365 GTB/4 Daytona	$251,397	330	Coys	Nuremberg, DE	7/22	243
1973	Ferrari	365 GTB/4 Daytona	$192,500	498	RM	Amelia Island, FL	3/11	173
1971	Ferrari	365 GTB/4 Daytona "Hot Rod"	$341,000	220	Gooding	Pebble Beach, CA	8/20	49
1972	Ferrari	365 GTS/4 Daytona Spyder	$748,000	68	Gooding	Pebble Beach, CA	8/20	77
1971	Ferrari	365 GTS/4 Daytona Spyder Alloy Conversion	$253,000	324	RM	Monterey, CA	8/18	474
1972	Ferrari	365 GTS/4 Michelotti NART Spyder	$385,000	180	RM	Monterey, CA	8/18	470
1958	Ferrari	412 S Sports Racer	$5,610,000	1	RM	Monterey, CA	8/18	465
1957	Ferrari	500 TRC Spider	$2,282,500	9	RM	Monterey, CA	8/18	472
1955	Ferrari	750 Monza Spider	$1,107,000	43	Bonhams	Carmel, CA	8/18	525
1972	Ferrari	Dino 246GT Berlinetta	$130,496	841	Bonhams	Monte Carlo, MCO	5/20	191
1973	Ferrari	Dino 246GT Berlinetta	$118,853	940	Bonhams	Sussex, U.K.	7/7	530
1989	Ferrari	F40	$255,000	320	Bonhams	Monte Carlo, MCO	5/20	192
1992	Ferrari	F40	$286,785	268	Coys	Nuremberg, DE	7/22	230
1964	Ferrari	250 GTL Lusso	$408,923	168	Artcurial	Paris, FRA	2/12	51
1961	Ferrari	250 Testa Rossa 59 Replica	$126,500	870	Worldwide Group	Seabrook, TX	5/6	25
1965	Ferrari	275 GTB/2	$473,000	137	Worldwide Group	Seabrook, TX	5/6	85
1990	Ferrari	308 IMSA GTU	$121,000	916	Worldwide Group	Seabrook, TX	5/6	51
1973	Ferrari	365 GTB/4 Daytona	$235,430	363	Artcurial	Paris, FRA	2/12	45
1969	Ferrari	365 GTC	$208,738	450	Artcurial	Paris, FRA	2/12	42
1964	Ferrari	500 Superfast	$415,596	162	Artcurial	Paris, FRA	2/12	46
2002	Ferrari	360 Modena Spyder	$226,800	389	Barrett-Jackson	West Palm Beach, FL	3/29	649
1953	Fiat	8V Ghia Supersonic	$452,800	143	Sportscar Auction Co.	Geneva, CH	10/7	37
1948	Ford	89-A Woody Wagon	$126,900	864	Barrett-Jackson	Scottsdale, AZ	1/14	1037
1932	Ford	B400 Convertible Sedan	$123,750	900	RM	Hampton, NH	6/10	2157
1932	Ford	Boydster II Fusion	$172,800	574	Barrett-Jackson	Scottsdale, AZ	1/14	1271
1940	Ford	Convertible "Valley" Custom	$236,500	357	RM	Monterey, CA	8/18	142
1934	Ford	Coupe	$114,400	984	G. Potter King	Atlantic City, NJ	2/23	2018A
1933	Ford	Custom 3-Window Coupe	$116,640	962	Barrett-Jackson	Scottsdale, AZ	1/14	1282
1932	Ford	Custom 5-Window Coupe	$216,000	423	Barrett-Jackson	Scottsdale, AZ	1/14	1327
1955	Ford	Custom Beatnik Bubbletop	$396,000	175	RM	Monterey, CA	8/18	141
1932	Ford	Custom Speedster	$148,500	695	RM	Monterey, CA	8/18	136
1935	Ford	Custom Woody Wagon	$124,200	896	Barrett-Jackson	Scottsdale, AZ	1/14	1336
1942	Ford	Custom Woody Wagon	$216,000	424	Barrett-Jackson	Scottsdale, AZ	1/14	1292
1939	Ford	Deluxe Convertible	$132,000	821	RM	Hampton, NH	6/10	2183
1939	Ford	Deluxe Custom Convertible	$216,000	425	Barrett-Jackson	Scottsdale, AZ	1/14	1321
1937	Ford	Deluxe Panel Delivery	$170,500	586	RM	Hampton, NH	6/10	2174

Year	Make	Model	Sold Price	Rank	Auction Co.	Location	Date	Lot #
1936	Ford	Deluxe Phaeton	$143,000	737	RM	Hampton, NH	6/10	2166
1934	Ford	Deluxe Roadster	$181,500	533	RM	Hampton, NH	6/10	2161
1936	Ford	Deluxe Roadster	$143,000	738	RM	Hampton, NH	6/10	2167
1934	Ford	Deluxe Station Wagon	$275,000	279	RM	Hampton, NH	6/10	2159
1936	Ford	Deluxe Station Wagon	$123,750	901	RM	Hampton, NH	6/10	2168
1937	Ford	Deluxe Station Wagon	$170,500	587	RM	Hampton, NH	6/10	2175
1938	Ford	Deluxe Station Wagon	$134,750	804	RM	Hampton, NH	6/10	2178
1939	Ford	Deluxe Station Wagon	$231,000	376	RM	Hampton, NH	6/10	2180
1940	Ford	Deluxe Station Wagon	$308,000	248	RM	Hampton, NH	6/10	2184
1941	Ford	Deluxe Station Wagon	$159,500	639	RM	Hampton, NH	6/10	2189
1932	Ford	Deluxe V8 Roadster	$133,100	808	RM	Hampton, NH	6/10	2155
1933	Ford	Elgin Racer	$220,000	410	RM	Hampton, NH	6/10	2158
1964	Ford	Fairlane Racer	$162,000	626	Barrett-Jackson	Scottsdale, AZ	1/14	1231.2
1953	Ford	FR100 Pickup	$226,800	390	Barrett-Jackson	Scottsdale, AZ	1/14	1236.1
1962	Ford	Galaxie Factory Lightweight	$162,000	627	Barrett-Jackson	Scottsdale, AZ	1/14	1334
2006	Ford	GT	$304,973	253	Artcurial	Paris, FRA	6/12	35
2006	Ford	GT	$179,280	546	Kruse	Scottsdale, AZ	1/26	1048
2005	Ford	GT40	$172,800	575	Barrett-Jackson	Scottsdale, AZ	1/14	1253
1965	Ford	GT40 Mk V	$181,500	534	RM	Phoenix, AZ	1/20	194
1967	Ford	GT40 Mk V	$388,800	178	Barrett-Jackson	Scottsdale, AZ	1/14	1314
1932	Ford	High Boy Roadster	$133,100	809	RM	Hampton, NH	6/10	2156
1929	Ford	Hotrod Pickup "Loaded"	$205,200	457	Barrett-Jackson	Scottsdale, AZ	1/14	1323
1907	Ford	Model K Roadster	$214,500	428	RM	Phoenix, AZ	1/20	163
1967	Ford	Mustang	$157,500	650	Mecum	Belvidere, IL	5/25	F584
1970	Ford	Mustang	$220,480	409	G. Potter King	Atlantic City, NJ	2/23	1784.1
1968	Ford	Mustang 428 CJ Fastback	$513,000	126	Barrett-Jackson	Scottsdale, AZ	1/14	1274.1
1969	Ford	Mustang Boss 429	$308,000	249	Russo and Steele	Scottsdale, AZ	1/20	S230
1969	Ford	Mustang Boss 429	$225,600	394	MidAmerica	Minneapolis, MN	9/22	141
1969	Ford	Mustang Boss 429	$196,350	480	Mecum	Belvidere, IL	5/25	S535
1969	Ford	Mustang Boss 429	$170,100	592	Mecum	Belvidere, IL	5/25	T12
1970	Ford	Mustang Boss 429	$214,500	429	Russo and Steele	Monterey, CA	8/18	S249
2006	Ford	Mustang Custom "Stallion"	$167,400	601	Barrett-Jackson	Scottsdale, AZ	1/14	1301
2005	Ford	Mustang FR500C #55 Racer	$201,960	466	Barrett-Jackson	Scottsdale, AZ	1/14	1281
2005	Ford	Mustang FR500C Barrett-Jackson Edition	$201,960	467	Barrett-Jackson	Scottsdale, AZ	1/14	1245.2
1968	Ford	Mustang GT	$145,750	721	Russo and Steele	Scottsdale, AZ	1/20	F240
1934	Ford	Pickup	$187,000	516	RM	Hampton, NH	6/10	2162
1932	Ford	Speedwagon Phantom Deuce Woody	$132,000	822	Gooding	Pebble Beach, CA	8/20	84
1947	Ford	Sportsman Convertible	$194,400	486	Barrett-Jackson	Scottsdale, AZ	1/14	1270
1936	Ford	Street Rod Roadster	$120,960	927	Barrett-Jackson	Scottsdale, AZ	1/14	1292.2
1936	Ford	Street Rod Woody Wagon	$114,480	983	Barrett-Jackson	Scottsdale, AZ	1/14	982
1947	Ford	Super Deluxe Sportsman Conv.	$275,000	280	RM	Hampton, NH	6/10	2193
1947	Ford	Super Deluxe Sportsman Conv.	$194,000	492	Bonhams	Carmel, CA	8/18	533
1948	Ford	Super Deluxe Woody Wagon	$137,500	774	RM	Monterey, CA	8/18	426
1956	Ford	Thunderbird Convertible	$142,560	744	Barrett-Jackson	Scottsdale, AZ	1/14	1022
1957	Ford	Thunderbird Convertible	$220,000	411	RM	Monterey, CA	8/18	466
1957	Ford	Thunderbird Convertible	$135,000	799	Barrett-Jackson	Scottsdale, AZ	1/14	1021
1957	Ford	Thunderbird Convertible	$116,640	963	Barrett-Jackson	Scottsdale, AZ	1/14	1005
1957	Ford	Thunderbird Convertible	$115,500	979	RM	Hampton, NH	6/10	2194
1964	Ford	Thunderbolt	$270,000	293	Barrett-Jackson	Scottsdale, AZ	1/14	1334.1
1953	Ford	Vega "Gardner Special" Roadster	$378,000	189	Barrett-Jackson	Scottsdale, AZ	1/14	1276
1940	Ford	Woody Wagon	$189,000	508	Barrett-Jackson	Scottsdale, AZ	1/14	1338
2005	Ford	GT	$572,400	108	Barrett-Jackson	West Palm Beach, FL	3/29	5001
1970	Ford	Mustang Mach 1 Fastback	$127,440	859	Barrett-Jackson	West Palm Beach, FL	3/29	624.1
1946	Frazer Nash-BMW	328 Roadster	$474,345	136	Bonhams	Sussex, U.K.	9/1	245
1950	GM	Futurliner Parade Of Progress Bus	$4,320,000	2	Barrett-Jackson	Scottsdale, AZ	1/14	1307
1939	Graham	Model 97 Supercharged Convertible Coupe	$129,250	850	RM	Rochester, MI	8/5	232
1974	Gulf-Mirage	Cosworth GR8 Endurance Racer	$704,850	77	Bonhams	Sussex, U.K.	9/1	222
1927	Hispano-Suiza	H6B Coupe Chauffeur	$304,000	254	Bonhams	Carmel, CA	8/18	553
1937	Horch	853 Cabriolet A	$299,000	259	RM	Cortland, NY	6/24	371
1968	Howmet	Turbine Racer	$264,000	306	RM	Los Angeles, CA	5/13	240
1937	Hudson	Terraplane Pickup	$189,000	509	Barrett-Jackson	Scottsdale, AZ	1/14	1275.2
1930	Isotta Fraschini	8AS Boattail Convertible	$658,500	88	Christie's	Greenwich, CT	6/4	9
1938	Jaguar	SS100	$257,722	317	Coys	Donington Park, U.K.	4/30	221
1937	Jaguar	SS100 2 1/2-Liter	$243,822	341	H&H	Buxton, U.K.	2/21	65

BY THE NUMBERS

Year	Make	Model	Sold Price	Rank	Auction Co.	Location	Date	Lot #
1938	Jaguar	SS100 3 1/2-Liter Tourer	$296,228	261	Bonhams	Sussex, U.K.	9/1	244
1992	Jaguar	XJ220	$160,650	634	Bonhams	Monte Carlo, MCO	5/20	156
1993	Jaguar	XJ220	$214,500	430	RM	Monterey, CA	8/18	457
2000	Jaguar	XJR15	$251,397	331	Coys	Nuremberg, DE	7/22	241
1983	Jaguar	XJR-5	$238,000	349	Bonhams	Carmel, CA	8/18	514
1949	Jaguar	XK 120 Alloy Roadster	$235,918	362	Christie's	Paris, FRA	2/11	78
1950	Jaguar	XK 120 Alloy Roadster	$195,856	481	Christie's	Paris, FRA	7/8	104
1952	Jaguar	XK 120 Roadster	$122,515	905	Coys	London, U.K.	9/30	250
1954	Jaguar	XK 120 Roadster	$148,500	696	Gooding	Pebble Beach, CA	8/20	46
1961	Jaguar	XK 150 3.8 Drophead Coupe	$121,000	917	RM	Phoenix, AZ	1/20	187
1959	Jaguar	XK 150 S Roadster	$145,800	717	Barrett-Jackson	Scottsdale, AZ	1/14	1331
1960	Jaguar	XK 150S 3.8 Drophead Coupe	$269,500	299	Gooding	Pebble Beach, CA	8/20	67
1960	Jaguar	XK 150S 3.8 Drophead Coupe	$159,500	640	Gooding	Palm Beach, FL	1/24	18
1961	Jaguar	XK 150S Roadster	$132,000	823	RM	Monterey, CA	8/18	126
1952	Jaguar	XK C-Type	$1,649,638	25	Christie's	Paris, FRA	2/11	86
1985	Jaguar	XK C-Type Replica	$128,588	853	Bonhams	Sussex, U.K.	9/1	220
1953	Jaguar	XK C-Type Sports Racer	$1,512,500	28	RM	Phoenix, AZ	1/20	150
1956	Jaguar	XK D-Type Racer	$2,097,000	12	Bonhams	Carmel, CA	8/18	521
1961	Jaguar	XKE Competition Roadster	$236,071	361	Bonhams	Stoneleigh Park, UK	2/25	347
1965	Jaguar	XKE Convertible	$135,125	792	Christie's	Monterey, CA	8/17	45
1963	Jaguar	XKE Lightweight Comp. Roadster	$131,012	836	Coys	London, U.K.	9/30	236
1965	Jaguar	XKE Series I 4.2 Convertible	$121,000	918	RM	Monterey, CA	8/18	452
1961	Jaguar	XKE Series I Convertible	$137,500	775	RM	Amelia Island, FL	3/11	170
1962	Jaguar	XKE Series I Convertible	$143,000	739	RM	Phoenix, AZ	1/20	129
1963	Jaguar	XKE Series I Convertible	$121,000	919	RM	Phoenix, AZ	1/20	190
1950	Jaguar	XK 120 Alloy Roadster	$225,500	395	Worldwide Group	Seabrook, TX	5/6	33
1919	La Bestioni	Firetruck Hot Rod	$167,400	602	Barrett-Jackson	West Palm Beach, FL	3/29	724.1
1932	Lagonda	2-Liter Supercharged Tourer	$153,734	667	Bonhams	Sussex, U.K.	9/1	223
1937	Lagonda	LG45 Rapide	$671,000	84	RM	Monterey, CA	8/18	464
1937	Lagonda	LG6 Drophead Coupe	$124,963	887	Bonhams	Sussex, U.K.	7/7	565
1939	Lagonda	V12 Drophead Coupe	$150,933	684	H&H	Buxton, U.K.	7/25	91
1996	Lamborghini	Diabalo VT Roadster	$152,820	672	Leake	Tulsa, OK	6/9	446
1996	Lamborghini	Diablo SV-R	$121,000	920	RM	Monterey, CA	8/18	459
1998	Lamborghini	Diablo/Monterey SV Edition	$118,800	944	Kruse	Seaside, CA	8/17	430
2005	Lamborghini	Gallardo	$540,000	118	Kruse	Auburn, IN	8/30	1449
1966	Lamborghini	GT 400	$253,000	325	RM	Monterey, CA	8/18	487
1969	Lamborghini	Miura	$206,800	453	Russo and Steele	Monterey, CA	8/18	F147
1968	Lamborghini	Miura P400	$234,368	365	Coys	London, U.K.	2/28	126
1972	Lamborghini	Miura P400 SV	$477,000	134	Christie's	Monterey, CA	8/17	11
1969	Lamborghini	Miura P400S	$300,900	257	Bonhams	Monte Carlo, MCO	5/20	190
1957	Lancia	Aurelia B24S Convertible	$117,500	956	Christie's	Greenwich, CT	6/4	7
1951	Lancia	Aurelia B50 Convertible	$152,750	674	Christie's	Monterey, CA	8/17	44
1962	Lancia	Flaminia Sport Zagato	$177,600	557	Sportscar Auction Co.	Geneva, CH	10/7	14
1975	Lancia	Stratos Stradale	$177,789	555	Coys	Nuremberg, DE	7/22	258
1971	Lancia	Fulvia 1.6 HF Group 4	$122,129	908	Artcurial	Paris, FRA	2/12	53
1983	Lancia-Martini	LC 2 Endurance Racer	$475,651	135	Artcurial	Paris, FRA	2/12	57
1938	Lencki	Championship Car	$264,000	307	Russo and Steele	Monterey, CA	8/18	S255
1960	Lincoln	Continental Mk V Elvis Presley'S Limousine	$556,200	112	Barrett-Jackson	Scottsdale, AZ	1/14	1316
1964	Lincoln	Continental Papal Limousine	$319,000	238	RM	Monterey, CA	8/18	453
1955	Lincoln	Indianapolis Boano	$1,375,000	32	Gooding	Pebble Beach, CA	8/20	57
1933	Lincoln	KB Convertible Coupe	$253,000	326	RM	Phoenix, AZ	1/20	184
1934	Lincoln	KB LeBaron Convertible	$237,600	355	Barrett-Jackson	Scottsdale, AZ	1/14	1280.1
1938	Lincoln	Lead Zephyr	$189,200	503	RM	Monterey, CA	8/18	143
1939	Lincoln	Lead Zephyr	$345,600	210	Barrett-Jackson	Scottsdale, AZ	1/14	1291.1
1939	Lincoln	Lead Zephyr	$151,200	682	Barrett-Jackson	Scottsdale, AZ	1/14	1277.1
1935	Lincoln	Model K Convertible Coupe	$231,000	377	RM	Rochester, MI	8/5	249
1931	Lincoln	Model K Dual Cowl Phaeton	$159,500	641	RM	Amelia Island, FL	3/11	133
1932	Lincoln	Model KB Convertible Roadster	$158,625	645	Christie's	Greenwich, CT	6/4	17
1940	Lincoln-Zephyr	Continental Cabriolet	$407,000	170	RM	Hampton, NH	6/10	2186
1938	Lincoln-Zephyr	Convertible Coupe	$258,500	316	RM	Hampton, NH	6/10	2177
1939	Lincoln-Zephyr	Custom 2-Door Coupe	$248,400	335	Barrett-Jackson	Scottsdale, AZ	1/14	1329
1959	Lister-Jaguar	Costin Racer	$275,273	276	Bonhams	Sussex, U.K.	9/1	240
1914	Locomobile	48 7-Passanger Touring Car	$176,000	560	Gooding	Pebble Beach, CA	8/20	27
1914	Locomobile	Model 48 Speedster	$148,500	697	RM	Monterey, CA	8/18	191
1963	Lola-Chevrolet	Mk 6 GT Endurance Marcer	$694,373	80	Bonhams	Sussex, U.K.	9/1	211

Year	Make	Model	Sold Price	Rank	Auction Co.	Location	Date	Lot #
1971	Lola-Chevrolet	T222	$210,500	441	Bonhams	Carmel, CA	8/18	524
1971	Lola-Chevrolet	T260	$221,500	401	Bonhams	Carmel, CA	8/18	517
1966	Lola-Chevrolet	T70 Group 7 Racer	$254,318	321	Bonhams	Sussex, U.K.	9/1	227
1969	Lola-Chevrolet	T70GT Mk III Group 4 Racer	$233,363	367	Bonhams	Sussex, U.K.	9/1	232
1931	Lorraine Dietrich	B3/6 Labourdette	$117,141	959	Osenat	Paris, FRA	6/18	517
1995	Lotec	C1000 Racer	$243,000	343	Barrett-Jackson	Scottsdale, AZ	1/14	1315
1955	Lotus-Bristol	MKX Racer	$180,975	539	Bonhams	Sussex, U.K.	9/1	209
1957	Lotus-Climax	Eleven Racer	$152,895	671	Bonhams	Sussex, U.K.	9/1	208
1981	Lotus-Cosworth	Type (81/3) Formula One Racer	$202,725	464	Bonhams	Monte Carlo, MCO	5/20	197
1965	Lotus-Ford	Type 30 Group 7 Racer	$201,930	468	Bonhams	Sussex, U.K.	9/1	238
1932	Lucenti	Special Indy Car	$216,000	426	Bonhams	Carmel, CA	8/18	544
1914	Marmon	41 Speedster	$616,000	97	Gooding	Pebble Beach, CA	8/20	32
1956	Maserati	150S Barchetta	$1,145,804	42	Coys	Monte Carlo, MCO	5/20	261
1955	Maserati	300S Racer	$1,925,000	14	RM	Phoenix, AZ	1/20	171
1935	Maserati	4CS-1100/1500	$819,825	63	Bonhams	Monte Carlo, MCO	5/20	172
1937	Maserati	6CM Monoposto Voiturette	$726,000	71	Gooding	Pebble Beach, CA	8/20	55
2004	Maserati	MC12	$1,072,500	46	RM	Monterey, CA	8/18	460
1937	Maserati	4CM	$472,811	138	Christie's	Paris, FRA	7/8	105
1994	McLaren	F1	$1,705,000	20	RM	Monterey, CA	8/18	471
1965	McLaren	M1A Racer	$243,840	340	Bonhams	Sussex, U.K.	9/1	218
1971	McLaren	M6B GTR	$173,073	568	Coys	London, U.K.	6/24	254
1969	McLaren	M6GT Racer	$423,500	156	RM	Phoenix, AZ	1/20	188
1911	Mercedes	37/90 Skiff	$1,050,000	47	Worldwide Group	Seabrook, TX	5/6	63
1960	Mercedes-Benz	220SE	$121,000	921	RM	Phoenix, AZ	1/20	131
1960	Mercedes-Benz	220SE Cabriolet	$203,500	462	RM	Phoenix, AZ	1/20	130
1928	Mercedes-Benz	26/120/180 Type S Torpedo Roadster	$3,645,000	4	Christie's	Monterey, CA	8/17	52
1971	Mercedes-Benz	280SE 3.5 Cabriolet	$154,000	663	RM	Phoenix, AZ	1/20	199
1971	Mercedes-Benz	280SE 3.5 Convertible	$130,680	839	Kruse	Auburn, IN	8/30	1073.1
1961	Mercedes-Benz	300d 4-Door Convertible	$172,800	576	Kruse	Auburn, IN	8/30	3780
1953	Mercedes-Benz	300S Cabriolet	$225,000	397	RM	Amelia Island, FL	3/11	193
1954	Mercedes-Benz	300S Cabriolet	$267,750	301	Coys	Monte Carlo, MCO	5/20	264
1954	Mercedes-Benz	300S Cabriolet	$186,435	517	Coys	Maastricht, NL	1/14	211
1954	Mercedes-Benz	300S Roadster	$357,000	206	Coys	Monte Carlo, MCO	5/20	223
1955	Mercedes-Benz	300Sb	$170,500	588	RM	Phoenix, AZ	1/20	178
1955	Mercedes-Benz	300Sb	$134,200	805	RM	Amelia Island, FL	3/11	161
1956	Mercedes-Benz	300Sc	$275,000	281	Gooding	Pebble Beach, CA	8/20	81
1956	Mercedes-Benz	300Sc	$231,000	378	Gooding	Palm Beach, FL	1/24	24
1957	Mercedes-Benz	300Sc Convertible	$418,000	159	Gooding	Pebble Beach, CA	8/20	70
1957	Mercedes-Benz	300Sc Convertible	$272,850	288	Bonhams	Monte Carlo, MCO	5/20	177
1956	Mercedes-Benz	300SL	$418,000	160	RM	Monterey, CA	8/18	463
1957	Mercedes-Benz	300SL	$321,237	237	Bonhams & Goodman	Sydney, AU	3/26	11
1954	Mercedes-Benz	300SL	$366,560	200	Coys	Maastricht, NL	1/14	215
1956	Mercedes-Benz	300SL	$621,000	95	Barrett-Jackson	Scottsdale, AZ	1/14	1299.1
1956	Mercedes-Benz	300SL	$540,000	119	Barrett-Jackson	Scottsdale, AZ	1/14	1310
1956	Mercedes-Benz	300SL	$430,500	151	Bonhams	Carmel, CA	8/18	529
1956	Mercedes-Benz	300SL	$346,500	209	Gooding	Pebble Beach, CA	8/20	99
1956	Mercedes-Benz	300SL	$343,750	214	Russo and Steele	Monterey, CA	8/18	S253
1956	Mercedes-Benz	300SL	$334,000	224	Christie's	Greenwich, CT	6/4	34
1957	Mercedes-Benz	300SL	$372,600	194	Barrett-Jackson	Scottsdale, AZ	1/14	1286
1955	Mercedes-Benz	300SL Alloy	$942,748	54	Artcurial	Paris, FRA	2/12	22
1992	Mercedes-Benz	300SL Replica	$155,356	657	Artcurial	Paris, FRA	2/12	28
1999	Mercedes-Benz	300SL Replica	$172,800	577	Barrett-Jackson	Scottsdale, AZ	1/14	1272.1
1958	Mercedes-Benz	300SL Roadster	$233,836	366	Coys	Maastricht, NL	1/14	234
1957	Mercedes-Benz	300SL Roadster	$605,000	101	RM	Monterey, CA	8/18	475
1957	Mercedes-Benz	300SL Roadster	$264,000	308	RM	Amelia Island, FL	3/11	185
1959	Mercedes-Benz	300SL Roadster	$432,000	149	Barrett-Jackson	Scottsdale, AZ	1/14	1308
1961	Mercedes-Benz	300SL Roadster	$306,206	252	Coys	Maastricht, NL	1/14	212
1961	Mercedes-Benz	300SL Roadster	$290,000	265	RM	Amelia Island, FL	3/11	136
1963	Mercedes-Benz	300SL Roadster	$396,000	176	Gooding	Pebble Beach, CA	8/20	87
1963	Mercedes-Benz	300SL Roadster	$324,000	235	Barrett-Jackson	Scottsdale, AZ	1/14	1285
1935	Mercedes-Benz	500K Kombination Roadster	$532,090	121	H&H	London, U.K.	5/24	44
1936	Mercedes-Benz	540K Cabriolet C	$1,174,354	41	Coys	Monte Carlo, MCO	5/20	240
1936	Mercedes-Benz	540K Special Roadster	$836,000	62	RM	Monterey, CA	8/18	468
1970	Mercedes-Benz	600 LWB Landaulet	$330,000	227	RM	Phoenix, AZ	1/20	181

Year	Make	Model	Sold Price	Rank	Auction Co.	Location	Date	Lot #
1967	Mercedes-Benz	600 Saloon	$143,430	729	Coys	London, U.K.	9/30	220
1935	Mercedes-Benz	500/540K	$1,650,000	23	Worldwide Group	Seabrook, TX	5/6	60
1953	Mercedes-Benz	300Sc Convertible	$259,200	315	Barrett-Jackson	West Palm Beach, FL	3/29	706
1999	Mercedes-Benz	300SL Replica	$243,000	344	Barrett-Jackson	West Palm Beach, FL	3/29	738
1951	Mercury	Convertible	$151,200	683	Barrett-Jackson	Scottsdale, AZ	1/14	1231
1969	Mercury	Cougar	$236,250	359	Mecum	Belvidere, IL	5/25	S572
1951	Mercury	Custom	$143,000	740	Russo and Steele	Scottsdale, AZ	1/20	S245
1950	Mercury	Custom Coupe	$148,500	698	RM	Monterey, CA	8/18	146
1955	Mercury	Monterey Woody Wagon	$115,500	980	Gooding	Pebble Beach, CA	8/20	50
1941	Mercury	Station Wagon	$170,500	589	RM	Hampton, NH	6/10	2187
1935	MG	R-Type Racer	$243,822	342	H&H	Buxton, U.K.	2/21	45
1955	Moretti	750S MM Bialbero Spyder GS	$272,850	289	Bonhams	Monte Carlo, MCO	5/20	239
1970	Oldsmobile	442 W30	$167,200	603	Russo and Steele	Monterey, CA	8/18	S262
1970	Oldsmobile	442 W30	$148,500	699	Russo and Steele	Scottsdale, AZ	1/20	F210
1951	Oldsmobile	98 Convertible	$121,000	922	RM	Amelia Island, FL	3/11	129
1953	Oldsmobile	Fiesta Convertible	$243,000	345	RM	Novi, MI	9/22	SP05
1957	Oldsmobile	Starfire 98 Convertible	$162,000	628	Kruse	Auburn, IN	5/18	2816
1965	OSCA	1600 GT	$168,800	594	Sportscar Auction Co.	Geneva, CH	10/7	29
1934	Packard	1104 Super Eight Phaeton	$129,250	851	Christie's	Greenwich, CT	6/4	20
1937	Packard	115 Convertible	$137,160	782	Barrett-Jackson	Scottsdale, AZ	1/14	1015
1941	Packard	120 Deluxe Station Wagon	$154,000	664	RM	Amelia Island, FL	3/11	158
1938	Packard	1608 Convertible Sedan	$229,500	386	Kruse	Auburn, IN	8/30	1034
1929	Packard	640 Custom Eight Roadster	$148,500	700	RM	Phoenix, AZ	1/20	165
1930	Packard	734 Speedster-Roadster	$455,000	142	Christie's	Greenwich, CT	6/4	21
1930	Packard	740 Super Eight Deluxe Roadster	$178,200	552	Kruse	Auburn, IN	8/30	1064.1
1930	Packard	745 Convertible Sedan	$209,000	448	RM	Rochester, MI	8/5	254
1931	Packard	845 Deluxe Eight Convertible Coupe	$235,000	364	Christie's	Greenwich, CT	6/4	19
1936	Packard	Cabriolet Super Eight	$144,100	727	Kruse	Morehead, KY	6/24	3129
1954	Packard	Caribbean Convertible	$165,000	610	RM	Monterey, CA	8/18	438
1938	Packard	Custom Limousine	$270,000	294	Barrett-Jackson	Scottsdale, AZ	1/14	1553
1940	Packard	Custom Super Eight One-Eighty Convertible Victoria	$253,000	327	Gooding	Palm Beach, FL	1/24	12
1931	Packard	Deluxe Eight	$449,500	144	Christie's	Monterey, CA	8/17	48
1930	Packard	Deluxe Eight 5-Passenger Phaeton	$173,250	567	RM	Rochester, MI	8/5	268
1932	Packard	Deluxe Eight 903 Sport Phaeton	$192,780	493	Leake	Tulsa, OK	6/9	2497
1931	Packard	Deluxe Eight Convertible Victoria	$231,000	379	RM	Phoenix, AZ	1/20	173
1931	Packard	Deluxe Eight Sport Phaeton	$231,000	380	RM	Amelia Island, FL	3/11	145
1933	Packard	Eight Victoria Cabriolet	$125,999	879	Kruse	Verona, NY	7/7	734
1934	Packard	LeBaron Twelve Runabout Speedster	$3,190,000	5	RM	Phoenix, AZ	1/20	167
1934	Packard	Model 1104 Super Eight Victoria	$253,000	328	Gooding	Pebble Beach, CA	8/20	39
1936	Packard	Model 120 Club Sedan & Trailer	$132,000	824	RM	Monterey, CA	8/18	160
1938	Packard	Model 1608 Twelve Convertible Sedan	$140,170	764	RM	Boca Raton, FL	2/10	SP98
1930	Packard	Model 745 Convertible Coupe	$231,000	381	RM	Amelia Island, FL	3/11	179
1954	Packard	Panther-Daytona Roadster Concept Car	$363,000	202	RM	Phoenix, AZ	1/20	138
1932	Packard	Series 904 Custom Dietrich Convertible Victoria	$541,080	115	Leake	Tulsa, OK	6/9	2471
1931	Packard	Standard Eight Convertible Sedan	$170,000	593	RM	Rochester, MI	8/5	228
1933	Packard	Standard Eight Coupe Roadster	$140,400	757	Kruse	Auburn, IN	8/30	749
1936	Packard	Super Eight Conv. Rumble Seat	$162,000	629	Kruse	Auburn, IN	5/18	1030
1941	Packard	Super Eight LeBaron Limousine	$283,500	270	Kruse	Auburn, IN	8/30	1058
1935	Packard	Twelve Convertible Sedan	$181,500	535	RM	Amelia Island, FL	3/11	192
1936	Packard	Twelve Coupe Roadster	$148,500	701	RM	Amelia Island, FL	3/11	196
1934	Packard	Twelve Runabout Speedster	$533,500	120	RM	Amelia Island, FL	3/11	154
1939	Packard	Twelve Town Car	$126,500	871	RM	Phoenix, AZ	1/20	192
1938	Packard	V12 Convertible Sedan	$210,600	439	Kruse	Auburn, IN	8/30	748
1917	Packard	2-25 Twin Six Runabout Racer	$269,500	300	Worldwide Group	Seabrook, TX	5/6	26
1903	Panhard-Levassor	7hp	$166,528	604	Christie's	London, U.K.	6/26	181
1933	Pierce-Arrow	Twelve Convertible Sedan	$418,000	161	RM	Amelia Island, FL	3/11	167
1970	Plymouth	'Cuda	$143,000	741	Russo and Steele	Scottsdale, AZ	1/20	F214
1971	Plymouth	Hemi 'Cuda	$787,500	64	Mecum	Belvidere, IL	5/25	S571.1

Year	Make	Model	Sold Price	Rank	Auction Co.	Location	Date	Lot #
1971	Plymouth	Hemi 'Cuda	$715,000	74	Russo and Steele	Scottsdale, AZ	1/20	S222
1970	Plymouth	'Cuda	$144,720	724	Barrett-Jackson	Scottsdale, AZ	1/14	1262
1971	Plymouth	'Cuda 383	$137,500	776	Russo and Steele	Scottsdale, AZ	1/20	F243
1970	Plymouth	'Cuda Convertible	$172,800	578	Barrett-Jackson	Scottsdale, AZ	1/14	1306.2
1970	Plymouth	'Cuda Custom Convertible "Six Shooter"	$183,600	523	Barrett-Jackson	Scottsdale, AZ	1/14	1278
1970	Plymouth	'Cuda Custom Convertible "Six Shooter"	$142,560	745	Barrett-Jackson	Scottsdale, AZ	1/14	1558.1
1970	Plymouth	AAR 'Cuda	$226,800	391	Barrett-Jackson	Scottsdale, AZ	1/14	1234
1970	Plymouth	AAR 'Cuda	$140,400	758	Barrett-Jackson	Scottsdale, AZ	1/14	990.1
1968	Plymouth	Barracuda BO29 Racer	$210,000	444	Mecum	Kissimmee, FL	1/27	X16
1965	Plymouth	Belvedere Lightweight	$136,000	789	Central PA Auto Auction	Lock Haven, PA	7/22	
1970	Plymouth	Challenger 440/6	$176,000	561	Russo and Steele	Scottsdale, AZ	1/20	F222
1969	Plymouth	GTX Convertible	$162,000	630	Barrett-Jackson	Scottsdale, AZ	1/14	1545.1
1969	Plymouth	GTX Convertible	$132,840	811	Kruse	Auburn, IN	8/30	2759.1
1970	Plymouth	Hemi 'Cuda	$702,000	78	Barrett-Jackson	Scottsdale, AZ	1/14	1324
1970	Plymouth	Hemi 'Cuda	$486,000	133	Barrett-Jackson	Scottsdale, AZ	1/14	1274
1970	Plymouth	Hemi 'Cuda	$345,600	211	Leake	Tulsa, OK	6/9	2515
1970	Plymouth	Hemi 'Cuda	$341,250	217	Mecum	Belvidere, IL	5/25	S540
1970	Plymouth	Hemi 'Cuda	$330,750	226	Mecum	Belvidere, IL	5/25	S524.1
1970	Plymouth	Hemi 'Cuda	$330,000	228	RM	Phoenix, AZ	1/20	141
1970	Plymouth	Hemi 'Cuda	$270,000	295	Barrett-Jackson	Scottsdale, AZ	1/14	1235.2
1970	Plymouth	Hemi 'Cuda	$243,000	346	Barrett-Jackson	Scottsdale, AZ	1/14	1296
1970	Plymouth	Hemi 'Cuda	$231,000	382	Russo and Steele	Monterey, CA	8/18	S254
1970	Plymouth	Hemi 'Cuda	$189,000	510	Barrett-Jackson	Scottsdale, AZ	1/14	972
1971	Plymouth	Hemi 'Cuda	$648,000	90	Barrett-Jackson	Scottsdale, AZ	1/14	1319
1970	Plymouth	Hemi 'Cuda Convertible	$2,160,000	10	Barrett-Jackson	Scottsdale, AZ	1/14	1309
1970	Plymouth	Hemi 'Cuda Replica	$121,500	912	Barrett-Jackson	Scottsdale, AZ	1/14	1243
1971	Plymouth	Hemi 'Cuda Replica	$214,000	434	RM	Boca Raton, FL	2/10	SP26
1968	Plymouth	Hemi Barracuda Factory Racer	$248,400	336	Barrett-Jackson	Scottsdale, AZ	1/14	1240
1967	Plymouth	Hemi Belvedere GTX Replica	$118,800	945	Barrett-Jackson	Scottsdale, AZ	1/14	59.1
1969	Plymouth	Hemi GTX	$149,800	687	RM	Boca Raton, FL	2/10	SP33
1968	Plymouth	Hemi Road Runner	$145,800	718	Barrett-Jackson	Scottsdale, AZ	1/14	1360
1969	Plymouth	Hemi Road Runner	$129,600	847	Barrett-Jackson	Scottsdale, AZ	1/14	1233.1
1970	Plymouth	Hemi Road Runner	$145,800	719	Barrett-Jackson	Scottsdale, AZ	1/14	1029.1
1969	Plymouth	Hemi Road Runner	$172,800	579	Barrett-Jackson	Scottsdale, AZ	1/14	1339
1966	Plymouth	Hemi Satellite	$124,200	897	Barrett-Jackson	Scottsdale, AZ	1/14	1053.1
1967	Plymouth	Hemi Satellite Convertible	$156,600	653	Barrett-Jackson	Scottsdale, AZ	1/14	1242
1968	Plymouth	Road Runner	$165,000	611	Russo and Steele	Scottsdale, AZ	1/20	S207
1969	Plymouth	Road Runner	$156,600	654	Barrett-Jackson	Scottsdale, AZ	1/14	1339.1
1970	Plymouth	Road Runner	$153,900	665	Barrett-Jackson	Scottsdale, AZ	1/14	981.1
1971	Plymouth	Road Runner "Petty"	$192,500	499	Russo and Steele	Monterey, CA	8/18	S260
1970	Plymouth	Road Runner Superbird	$146,880	709	Leake	Tulsa, OK	6/9	471
1970	Plymouth	Road Runner Superbird	$135,000	800	Leake	Oklahoma City, OK	2/24	507
1970	Plymouth	Superbird	$379,500	185	Russo and Steele	Scottsdale, AZ	1/20	F228
1970	Plymouth	Superbird	$131,250	833	Mecum	Belvidere, IL	5/25	F588
1970	Plymouth	Superbird	$120,750	931	Mecum	Belvidere, IL	5/25	T26
1970	Plymouth	Superbird	$140,400	759	Kruse	Auburn, IN	8/30	2747.1
1971	Plymouth	Hemi 'Cuda	$1,045,000	49	Worldwide Group	Seabrook, TX	5/6	50
1970	Plymouth	'Cuda	$118,800	946	Barrett-Jackson	West Palm Beach, FL	3/29	659
1964	Pontiac	Banshee XP-833 Prototype	$210,600	440	Barrett-Jackson	Scottsdale, AZ	1/14	1312
1957	Pontiac	Bonneville	$132,000	825	Russo and Steele	Monterey, CA	8/18	S264
1957	Pontiac	Bonneville Convertible	$165,000	612	RM	Monterey, CA	8/18	500
1957	Pontiac	Bonneville Convertible	$115,500	981	RM	Rochester, MI	8/5	242
1964	Pontiac	Bonneville Convertible "Hank Williams, Jr."	$214,500	431	RM	Phoenix, AZ	1/20	153
1954	Pontiac	Bonneville Special Motorama Concept Car	$3,024,000	6	Barrett-Jackson	Scottsdale, AZ	1/14	1304
1965	Pontiac	GTO	$131,250	834	Mecum	Belvidere, IL	5/25	S516
1969	Pontiac	GTO	$177,100	559	Russo and Steele	Scottsdale, AZ	1/20	F216
1965	Pontiac	GTO Convertible	$118,800	947	Barrett-Jackson	Scottsdale, AZ	1/14	957
1970	Pontiac	GTO Judge	$162,800	616	Russo and Steele	Monterey, CA	8/18	S247
1969	Pontiac	GTO Judge	$113,400	995	Barrett-Jackson	Scottsdale, AZ	1/14	1228
1970	Pontiac	GTO Judge Convertible	$199,800	471	Barrett-Jackson	Scottsdale, AZ	1/14	1025.1
1970	Pontiac	GTO Judge Ram Air Iv Convertible	$410,000	167	RM	Boca Raton, FL	2/10	SP36

BY THE NUMBERS

Year	Make	Model	Sold Price	Rank	Auction Co.	Location	Date	Lot #
1969	Pontiac	Trans Am	$113,400	996	Barrett-Jackson	Scottsdale, AZ	1/14	1023.1
1963	Porsche	356 Carrera 2	$140,289	762	Coys	London, U.K.	2/28	127
1959	Porsche	356 Carrera Speedster	$345,000	213	Christie's	Monterey, CA	8/17	24
1958	Porsche	356 Coupe "The Green Hornet"	$145,750	722	RM	Amelia Island, FL	3/11	190
1956	Porsche	356A 1600 S Speedster	$135,965	790	Coys	Oxfordshire, U.K.	8/26	118
1958	Porsche	356A 1600 S Speedster	$121,000	923	RM	Amelia Island, FL	3/11	127
1958	Porsche	356A Cabriolet	$135,000	801	Barrett-Jackson	Scottsdale, AZ	1/14	743
1958	Porsche	356A Speedster	$144,593	725	Coys	London, U.K.	6/24	253
1956	Porsche	356A Speedster	$146,300	713	RM	Amelia Island, FL	3/11	151
1956	Porsche	356A Speedster	$137,500	777	RM	Monterey, CA	8/18	486
1957	Porsche	356A Speedster	$127,500	858	Coys	Monte Carlo, MCO	5/20	236
1962	Porsche	356B Twin-Grille Roadster	$140,800	751	Gooding	Pebble Beach, CA	8/20	58
1963	Porsche	904	$565,000	110	Christie's	Monterey, CA	8/17	26
1964	Porsche	904 GTS	$531,744	122	Osenat	Paris, FRA	6/18	566
1966	Porsche	906 Carrera 6	$557,000	111	Bonhams	Carmel, CA	8/18	510
1972	Porsche	911 RS Prototype	$334,000	225	Christie's	Monterey, CA	8/17	29
1997	Porsche	911 Turbo S	$141,000	750	Christie's	Monterey, CA	8/17	31
1970	Porsche	914/6 Group 4 Competition	$113,304	997	Coys	Oxfordshire, U.K.	8/26	116
1972	Porsche	917/10	$579,000	105	Bonhams	Carmel, CA	8/18	519
1970	Porsche	917K Replica	$178,200	553	Barrett-Jackson	Scottsdale, AZ	1/14	1328
1988	Porsche	959 Komfort Coupe	$286,000	269	RM	Amelia Island, FL	3/11	168
2005	Porsche	Carrera GT	$412,500	164	Russo and Steele	Monterey, CA	8/18	S248
1958	Retrovette	R-5	$153,300	670	Mecum	St. Charles, IL	6/16	S563
1934	Riley	9CV Imp	$153,808	666	Christie's	Paris, FRA	2/11	65
1927	Rolls-Royce	40/50hp Phantom I Piccadilly Roadster	$172,000	581	Bonhams	North Brookfield, MA	9/23	1007
1930	Rolls-Royce	40/50hp Phantom II Dual Cowl Phaeton	$238,000	350	Bonhams	North Brookfield, MA	9/23	1010
1911	Rolls-Royce	40/50hp Silver Ghost	$858,000	59	RM	Monterey, CA	8/18	447
1914	Rolls-Royce	40/50hp Silver Ghost	$495,000	129	RM	Rochester, MI	8/5	265
1924	Rolls-Royce	40/50hp Silver Ghost Brewster Landaulette	$139,000	769	Bonhams	North Brookfield, MA	9/23	1018
1926	Rolls-Royce	40/50hp Silver Ghost London-Edinburgh Torpedo	$161,000	633	Bonhams	North Brookfield, MA	9/23	1008
2001	Rolls-Royce	Park Ward Ward Saloon	$194,400	487	Barrett-Jackson	West Palm Beach, FL	3/29	728
1928	Rolls-Royce	Phantom I	$126,724	865	Bonhams & Goodman	Sydney, AU	3/26	10
1928	Rolls-Royce	Phantom I Open Tourer	$121,199	913	Coys	London, U.K.	6/24	214
1927	Rolls-Royce	Phantom I Pall Mall Tourer	$121,000	924	RM	Rochester, MI	8/5	261
1931	Rolls-Royce	Phantom I Regent Coupe	$125,999	880	Kruse	Verona, NY	7/7	727
1929	Rolls-Royce	Phantom I Springfield Henley Convertible Coupe	$238,000	351	Bonhams	Carmel, CA	8/18	542
1929	Rolls-Royce	Phantom I Tourer	$120,655	934	Bonhams	Northamptonshire, U.K.	6/17	415
1929	Rolls-Royce	Phantom II Imperial Cabriolet	$231,000	383	RM	Amelia Island, FL	3/11	149
1937	Rolls-Royce	Phantom III 4-Door Cabriolet	$253,000	329	Gooding	Pebble Beach, CA	8/20	76
1937	Rolls-Royce	Phantom III Sedanca De Ville	$214,500	432	RM	Amelia Island, FL	3/11	188
1960	Rolls-Royce	Phantom Limousine	$162,000	631	Kruse	Auburn, IN	5/18	2816
1912	Rolls-Royce	Silver Ghost Touring	$935,000	55	RM	Amelia Island, FL	3/11	169
1956	Rolls-Royce	Silver Wraith Express Limousine	$118,250	952	RM	Rochester, MI	8/5	236
1958	Rolls-Royce	Silver Wraith Limousine	$128,099	856	Christie's	London, U.K.	6/26	182
1951	Rolls-Royce	Silver Wraith LWB Drophead Coupe	$137,500	778	Gooding	Palm Beach, FL	1/24	31
1927	Rolls-Royce	Sprignfield Phantom I	$117,500	957	Christie's	Greenwich, CT	6/4	6
1904	Searchmont	Rear-Entrance Touring	$132,000	826	Gooding	Pebble Beach, CA	8/20	26
1972	Shadow	Chevrolet	$221,500	402	Bonhams	Carmel, CA	8/18	516
1974	Shadow-AVS	DN4	$381,000	184	Bonhams	Carmel, CA	8/18	513
1962	Shelby	Cobra 289	$1,815,000	16	RM	Phoenix, AZ	1/20	175
1962	Shelby	Cobra 289	$1,601,250	26	Mecum	Belvidere, IL	5/25	S511
1963	Shelby	Cobra 289	$368,500	195	Russo and Steele	Scottsdale, AZ	1/20	S228
1964	Shelby	Cobra 289	$540,750	116	Mecum	Belvidere, IL	5/25	S530.1
1964	Shelby	Cobra 289	$385,000	181	RM	Phoenix, AZ	1/20	133
1965	Shelby	Cobra 289	$420,245	157	Bonhams	Sussex, U.K.	7/7	560
1965	Shelby	Cobra 289	$342,400	215	RM	Boca Raton, FL	2/10	NR98
1964	Shelby	Cobra 289	$385,000	182	RM	Phoenix, AZ	1/20	158
1964	Shelby	Cobra 289 Competition	$1,237,500	37	RM	Monterey, CA	8/18	159
1966	Shelby	Cobra 289 Competition	$643,500	92	Russo and Steele	Monterey, CA	8/18	S257
1964	Shelby	Cobra 289 Dragonsnake Racer	$660,000	87	RM	Monterey, CA	8/18	181

Year	Make	Model	Sold Price	Rank	Auction Co.	Location	Date	Lot #
1963	Shelby	Cobra 289 Le Mans Racer	$1,650,000	24	RM	Amelia Island, FL	3/11	164
1966	Shelby	Cobra 427	$594,000	104	Barrett-Jackson	Scottsdale, AZ	1/14	1291
1966	Shelby	Cobra 427	$566,280	109	Russo and Steele	Scottsdale, AZ	1/20	F227
1966	Shelby	Cobra 427	$550,000	113	RM	Boca Raton, FL	2/10	SP30
1966	Shelby	Cobra 427	$412,500	165	RM	Monterey, CA	8/18	169
1966	Shelby	Cobra 427	$390,500	177	RM	Phoenix, AZ	1/20	145
1967	Shelby	Cobra 427	$605,000	102	Russo and Steele	Scottsdale, AZ	1/20	S223
1967	Shelby	Cobra 427	$275,000	282	RM	Monterey, CA	8/18	173
1965	Shelby	Cobra 427	$424,100	155	Sportscar Auction Co.	Geneva, CH	10/7	36A
1966	Shelby	Cobra 427	$520,349	124	Coys	Oxfordshire, U.K.	8/26	131
1969	Shelby	Cobra 427 SC	$165,850	607	RM	Boca Raton, FL	2/10	SP106
1965	Shelby	Cobra 427 Competition	$955,500	53	Mecum	Belvidere, IL	5/25	S519
1965	Shelby	Cobra 289 Dragonsnake Racer	$695,500	79	RM	Boca Raton, FL	2/10	SP23
1965	Shelby	GT350	$335,880	222	Barrett-Jackson	Scottsdale, AZ	1/14	1289
1965	Shelby	GT350	$308,000	250	Russo and Steele	Monterey, CA	8/18	F148
1965	Shelby	GT350	$297,000	260	Russo and Steele	Scottsdale, AZ	1/20	F217
1965	Shelby	GT350	$204,600	459	Russo and Steele	Scottsdale, AZ	1/20	S217
1966	Shelby	GT350	$220,000	412	Russo and Steele	Scottsdale, AZ	1/20	F224
1966	Shelby	GT350	$198,000	474	Russo and Steele	Scottsdale, AZ	1/20	S215
1966	Shelby	GT350	$198,000	475	Russo and Steele	Monterey, CA	8/18	S261
1966	Shelby	GT350	$194,250	490	Mecum	Belvidere, IL	5/25	S114
1966	Shelby	GT350	$178,750	547	Russo and Steele	Scottsdale, AZ	1/20	S219
1966	Shelby	GT350	$151,250	677	Russo and Steele	Scottsdale, AZ	1/20	F230
1966	Shelby	GT350	$127,200	861	Silver	Reno, NV	8/6	128
1967	Shelby	GT350	$162,750	619	Mecum	Belvidere, IL	5/25	S515
1967	Shelby	GT350	$131,610	830	RM	Boca Raton, FL	2/10	SP27
1967	Shelby	GT350	$131,075	835	RM	Boca Raton, FL	2/10	NR27
1968	Shelby	GT350	$131,760	829	Barrett-Jackson	Scottsdale, AZ	1/14	1548
1969	Shelby	GT350	$132,000	827	Russo and Steele	Scottsdale, AZ	1/20	S203
1968	Shelby	GT350 Convertible	$145,800	720	Leake	Tulsa, OK	6/9	474
1965	Shelby	GT350 Custom Fastback	$307,800	251	Barrett-Jackson	Scottsdale, AZ	1/14	1302
1966	Shelby	GT350 H	$214,500	433	RM	Amelia Island, FL	3/11	135
1966	Shelby	GT350 H	$180,900	540	Barrett-Jackson	Scottsdale, AZ	1/14	752.1
1966	Shelby	GT350 H	$141,750	749	Mecum	Belvidere, IL	5/25	S580
1966	Shelby	GT350 H	$120,750	932	Mecum	Kissimmee, FL	1/27	C74
1965	Shelby	GT350 R	$990,000	52	RM	Amelia Island, FL	3/11	137
1965	Shelby	GT350 R	$748,000	69	Gooding	Pebble Beach, CA	8/20	80
1967	Shelby	GT500	$442,800	147	Barrett-Jackson	Scottsdale, AZ	1/14	1326
1967	Shelby	GT500	$270,000	296	Barrett-Jackson	Scottsdale, AZ	1/14	1259
1967	Shelby	GT500	$237,600	356	Barrett-Jackson	Scottsdale, AZ	1/14	1297
1967	Shelby	GT500	$236,500	358	Russo and Steele	Monterey, CA	8/18	S251
1967	Shelby	GT500	$236,250	360	Mecum	Belvidere, IL	5/25	S556
1967	Shelby	GT500	$231,000	384	Mecum	Belvidere, IL	5/25	S564
1967	Shelby	GT500	$222,480	400	Barrett-Jackson	Scottsdale, AZ	1/14	1250
1967	Shelby	GT500	$219,350	413	RM	Boca Raton, FL	2/10	SP29
1967	Shelby	GT500	$205,200	458	Leake	Tulsa, OK	6/9	494
1967	Shelby	GT500	$198,000	476	Russo and Steele	Monterey, CA	8/18	F154
1967	Shelby	GT500	$176,000	562	Russo and Steele	Scottsdale, AZ	1/20	F209
1967	Shelby	GT500	$152,250	676	Mecum	Kansas City, MO	4/28	S519
1967	Shelby	GT500	$140,250	763	Russo and Steele	Scottsdale, AZ	1/20	S244
1968	Shelby	GT500	$203,500	463	Russo and Steele	Scottsdale, AZ	1/20	F220
1968	Shelby	GT500	$194,400	488	Barrett-Jackson	Scottsdale, AZ	1/14	1536
1968	Shelby	GT500	$184,275	519	Mecum	Belvidere, IL	5/25	F591.1
1968	Shelby	GT500	$184,250	521	Russo and Steele	Scottsdale, AZ	1/20	S233
1968	Shelby	GT500	$183,600	524	Barrett-Jackson	Scottsdale, AZ	1/14	1342
1968	Shelby	GT500	$181,500	536	Russo and Steele	Monterey, CA	8/18	S246
1969	Shelby	GT500	$313,500	244	Russo and Steele	Monterey, CA	8/18	S259
1969	Shelby	GT500	$143,000	742	Russo and Steele	Monterey, CA	8/18	S242
1969	Shelby	GT500	$121,000	925	Russo and Steele	Scottsdale, AZ	1/20	F233
2007	Shelby	GT500	$648,000	91	Barrett-Jackson	Scottsdale, AZ	1/14	1259.1
1968	Shelby	GT500 Convertible	$180,900	541	Barrett-Jackson	Scottsdale, AZ	1/14	1041
1968	Shelby	GT500 Convertible	$147,960	705	Barrett-Jackson	Scottsdale, AZ	1/14	1052
1968	Shelby	GT500 Convertible	$147,125	706	RM	Boca Raton, FL	2/10	177
1968	Shelby	GT500 Convertible	$140,400	760	Barrett-Jackson	Scottsdale, AZ	1/14	1344
1969	Shelby	GT500 Convertible	$253,800	322	Leake	Tulsa, OK	6/9	2529

BY THE NUMBERS

Year	Make	Model	Sold Price	Rank	Auction Co.	Location	Date	Lot #
1970	Shelby	GT500 Convertible	$232,200	370	Barrett-Jackson	Scottsdale, AZ	1/14	1244
1967	Shelby	GT500 E Eleanor Replica	$140,400	761	Barrett-Jackson	Scottsdale, AZ	1/14	1557
1968	Shelby	GT500 KR	$432,000	150	Barrett-Jackson	Scottsdale, AZ	1/14	1290.1
1968	Shelby	GT500 KR	$275,000	283	Russo and Steele	Monterey, CA	8/18	F153
1968	Shelby	GT500 KR	$273,000	287	Mecum	Belvidere, IL	5/25	S566
1968	Shelby	GT500 KR	$225,500	396	RM	Amelia Island, FL	3/11	160
1968	Shelby	GT500 KR	$220,500	408	Mecum	Belvidere, IL	5/25	S535.1
1968	Shelby	GT500 KR	$216,700	414	Russo and Steele	Scottsdale, AZ	1/20	S210
1968	Shelby	GT500 KR	$210,000	445	Mecum	Belvidere, IL	5/25	F570
1968	Shelby	GT500 KR	$177,550	558	Silver	Reno, NV	8/6	565
1968	Shelby	GT500 KR	$176,000	563	Russo and Steele	Monterey, CA	8/18	F141
1968	Shelby	GT500 KR	$138,600	770	Russo and Steele	Scottsdale, AZ	1/20	S237
1968	Shelby	GT500 KR	$134,820	803	RM	Boca Raton, FL	2/10	SP35
1968	Shelby	GT500 KR	$129,600	848	Kruse	Auburn, IN	8/30	747.1
1968	Shelby	GT500 KR	$120,375	935	RM	Boca Raton, FL	2/10	NR103
1968	Shelby	GT500 KR Convertible	$302,400	256	Barrett-Jackson	Scottsdale, AZ	1/14	1267
1968	Shelby	GT500 KR Convertible	$253,800	323	Kruse	Scottsdale, AZ	1/26	2751
1968	Shelby	GT500 KR Convertible	$240,750	348	RM	Boca Raton, FL	2/10	SP16
1968	Shelby	GT500 KR Convertible	$208,650	451	RM	Boca Raton, FL	2/10	NR22
1999	Shelby	Series 1	$120,750	933	Mecum	Belvidere, IL	5/25	F607
1968	Shelby	GT	$142,560	746	Kruse	Fredericksburg, TX	3/25	104
1970	Shelby	GT500	$125,000	885	Worldwide Group	Seabrook, TX	5/6	73
1968	Shelby	GT500 KR Convertible	$330,000	229	Worldwide Group	Seabrook, TX	5/6	31
1964	Shelby	Cobra Daytona Coupe Replica	$270,000	297	Barrett-Jackson	West Palm Beach, FL	3/29	720
1967	Shelby	GT500	$245,160	339	Barrett-Jackson	West Palm Beach, FL	3/29	712
1967	Shelby	GT500	$226,800	392	Barrett-Jackson	West Palm Beach, FL	3/29	656
1968	Shelby	GT500	$125,280	882	Barrett-Jackson	West Palm Beach, FL	3/29	697
1968	Shelby	GT500 KR	$118,800	948	Barrett-Jackson	West Palm Beach, FL	3/29	734.1
1912	Simplex	38hp Double Roadster	$198,000	477	RM	Amelia Island, FL	3/11	130
1959	Stanguellini	Formula Junior Racer	$121,000	926	Russo and Steele	Monterey, CA	8/18	S239
1911	Stanley	Steamer 10Hp Model 63 Toy Tonneau	$181,900	529	Bonhams	Brookline, MA	5/6	330
1933	Studebaker	82 President Custom Cabriolet	$130,680	840	Leake	Tulsa, OK	6/9	462
1935	Studebaker	Dictator Custom Sedan	$146,880	710	Barrett-Jackson	Scottsdale, AZ	1/14	970
1939	Studebaker	Express Pickup	$124,200	898	Kruse	Auburn, IN	8/30	1025
1937	Studebaker	Posies Extemeliner Woody	$302,500	255	RM	Monterey, CA	8/18	140
1931	Studebaker	President Four Seasons Roadster	$132,000	828	RM	Rochester, MI	8/5	227
1914	Stutz	Bearcat	$715,000	75	Gooding	Pebble Beach, CA	8/20	29
1915	Stutz	Bearcat	$368,500	196	RM	Rochester, MI	8/5	234
1916	Stutz	Bearcat	$275,000	284	RM	Amelia Island, FL	3/11	139
1930	Stutz	Model M Supercharged Coupe	$715,000	76	RM	Rochester, MI	8/5	251
1931	Stutz	SV-16 Cabriolet Coupe	$378,000	190	Kruse	Scottsdale, AZ	1/26	2749
1957	Talbot-Lago	Dupont Barquette	$283,050	271	Coys	Monte Carlo, MCO	5/20	233
1939	Talbot-Lago	T150C 4.0-Liter Competition Roadster	$256,413	319	Bonhams	Sussex, U.K.	9/1	241
1938	Talbot-Lago	T150C SS Teardrop Coupe	$3,905,000	3	Gooding	Palm Beach, FL	1/24	29
1938	Talbot-Lago	T23 4-Liter Cabriolet	$209,000	449	RM	Monterey, CA	8/18	182
1938	Talbot-Lago	T23 Teardrop Coupe	$2,145,000	11	RM	Amelia Island, FL	3/11	155
1950	Talbot-Lago	T26 Grand Sport	$348,000	207	Bonhams	Carmel, CA	8/18	526
1949	Talbot-Lago	T26 Grand Sport Cabriolet	$375,500	192	Bonhams	Carmel, CA	8/18	515
1949	Talbot-Lago	T26 Record Cabriolet	$122,500	906	Bonhams	Carmel, CA	8/18	520
1950	Talbot-Lago	T26C	$1,410,741	30	Christie's	Paris, FRA	7/8	125
1967	Toyota	2000GT	$225,988	393	Christie's	Paris, FRA	7/8	124
1969	Toyota	2000GT	$160,619	635	Bonhams & Goodman	Sydney, AU	3/26	4
1948	Tucker	48 Torpedo	$577,500	106	RM	Monterey, CA	8/18	458
1993	Williams-Renault	FW16C Formula One Racer	$410,666	166	Artcurial	Paris, FRA	6/12	29
1941	Willys	Americar Coupe	$120,960	928	Barrett-Jackson	Scottsdale, AZ	1/14	1567.1
1904	Winton	20hp Detachable Rear-Entrance Tonneau	$172,000	582	Bonhams	Brookline, MA	5/6	322 ◆

High Five

A quick glance at how the cream of the crop, of each marque, did.
(Sales recorded between 1/1/2006 and 9/30/2006.)

Year	Model	Sold Price	Auction Co.	Location	Date	Lot #
AC						
1957	Ace Bristol	$144,568	H&H	London, U.K.	May 24	54
1957	Ace Bristol	$125,266	Coys	Maastricht, NL	January 14	223
1960	Ace	$120,000	Gooding	Palm Beach, FL	January 24	33
1936	16/80hp Sport Special	$110,874	Coys	Monte Carlo, MCO	May 20	262
1936	16/70hp March Special	$83,216	Bonhams	Sussex, U.K.	July 7	523
Alfa Romeo						
1947	6C 2500 SS	$467,747	Coys	Monte Carlo, MCO	May 20	259
1937	6C 2300 MM	$426,600	Kruse	Seaside, CA	August 17	410
1950	6C 2500 SS "Tubolare"	$222,828	Christie's	Paris, FRA	February 11	84
1949	6C2500 SS Cabriolet	$195,713	Bonhams	Monte Carlo, MCO	May 20	169
1932	6C 1750 Grand Sport	$182,249	Coys	Monte Carlo, MCO	May 20	257
Allard						
1951	J2X Le Mans Racer	$313,500	RM	Monterey, CA	August 18	440
1951	K2 Roadster	$107,250	RM	Monterey, CA	August 18	148
1948	Ml Drophead Coupe	$72,360	Kruse	Auburn, IN	August 30	808
1948	M1	$43,838	Mecum	Belvidere, IL	May 25	U543
1956	K3 Roadster	$39,858	RM	Boca Raton, FL	February 10	NR108
Alvis						
1938	Speed 25 open oourer	$92,857	Coys	Nuremberg, DE	July 22	221
1937	Speed 25 open Tourer by Vanden Plas	$92,649	Coys	Donington Park, U.K.	April 30	218
1932	Speed Twenty SA Tourer	$50,261	Bonhams	Hendon, U.K.	April 24	629
1931	Beetleback sports Tourer	$41,314	H&H	Buxton, U.K.	September 13	46
1934	Silver Eagle S.F. Special	$40,158	H&H	London, U.K.	May 24	26
AMC						
1969	AMX	$55,125	Mecum	Belvidere, IL	May 25	S611
1969	AMX California 500 Special	$54,000	Barrett-Jackson	Scottsdale, AZ	January 14	975
1970	AMX	$43,200	Barrett-Jackson	Scottsdale, AZ	January 14	411
1974	AMX	$37,400	Russo and Steele	Monterey, CA	August 18	S203
1970	Javelin	$36,300	Russo and Steele	Scottsdale, AZ	January 20	S181
Amphicar						
1964	770 Convertible	$124,200	Barrett-Jackson	Scottsdale, AZ	January 14	423
1967	770 Convertible	$68,200	RM	Hampton, NH	June 10	2203
1962	770 Convertible	$57,750	RM	Monterey, CA	August 18	419
1964	770 Convertible	$56,710	RM	Boca Raton, FL	February 10	NR91
1966	770 Convertible	$46,200	Mecum	Kissimmee, FL	January 27	D52
Apollo						
2005	Monza Spyder	$126,500	Russo and Steele	Scottsdale, AZ	January 20	S212
2005	Monza Spyder Prototype	$110,000	RM	Monterey, CA	August 18	147
ASA						
1967	1000 GT	$81,400	RM	Monterey, CA	August 18	118
1965	1000 GT	$56,000	Sportscar Auction Co.	Geneva, CH	October 7	35
Aston Martin						
1965	DB5 "James Bond" Coupe	$2,090,000	RM	Phoenix, AZ	January 20	155
1961	DB4 GT	$891,000	RM	Monterey, CA	August 18	476

Top 5 Sales of 2006 by Marque

Year	Model	Sold Price	Auction Co.	Location	Date	Lot #
1965	DB6 Short Chassis Volante	$445,500	RM	Phoenix, AZ	January 20	166
1963	DB4 Convertible	$314,868	Bonhams	Newport Pagnell, U.K.	May 13	132
1966	DBR1 Alloy Replica	$275,000	RM	Monterey, CA	August 18	467
Auburn						
1932	12 Boattail Speedster	$572,400	Kruse	Auburn, IN	August 30	1047
1935	851 Boattail Speedster	$432,000	Kruse	Scottsdale, AZ	January 26	2750
1936	852 Super charged Boattail Speedster	$310,000	RM	Rochester, MI	August 5	263
1935	851 Supercharged Cabriolet	$270,000	Kruse	Scottsdale, AZ	January 26	2748
1931	Model 36008 Boattail Speedster	$192,500	RM	Phoenix, AZ	January 20	151
Austin-Healey						
1967	3000 Mk III	$143,100	Barrett-Jackson	Scottsdale, AZ	January 14	1238
1967	3000 Mk III	$99,875	Christie's	Greenwich, CT	June 4	23
1967	3000 Mk III	$85,320	Barrett-Jackson	Scottsdale, AZ	January 14	992
1956	100 M	$85,100	Sportscar Auction Co.	Geneva, CH	October 7	24
1966	3000 Mk III	$83,160	Barrett-Jackson	Scottsdale, AZ	January 14	974
Bentley						
1929	Speed Six Dual Cowl Tourer	$1,815,000	RM	Monterey, CA	August 18	454
1931	8-Liter Sportsman Coupe	$1,485,000	RM	Amelia Island, FL	March 11	153
1937	4-Liter Fixed Head Coupe	$1,265,000	RM	Monterey, CA	August 18	479
1927	Speed Six Fixed Head Coupe	$781,000	RM	Monterey, CA	August 18	489
1930	Speed Six Le Mans Tourer	$605,000	RM	Phoenix, AZ	January 20	174
Bitter						
1982	SC	$11,714	Osenat	Paris, FRA	June 18	525
Bizarrini						
1967	5300GT Alloy	$269,500	Worldwide Group	Seabrook, TX	May 6	67
BMW						
1938	327/328 Cabriolet	$178,141	Artcurial	Paris, FRA	June 12	17
1973	3CSL "Batmobile"	$153,718	Christie's	London, U.K.	June 26	177
1980	M1 Coupe	$104,104	Bonhams	Monte Carlo, MCO	May 20	157
1970	Von Dutch 600 Toad	$99,000	RM	Los Angeles, CA	May 13	129
1981	M1	$91,000	Bonhams	Carmel, CA	August 18	555
Bristol						
1954	404	$68,402	Coys	London, U.K.	February 28	120
1948	400/85B	$53,700	Sportscar Auction	Geneva, CH	October 7	38
1948	400	$31,798	Bonhams	Hendon, U.K.	April 24	624
1977	412 Convertible	$14,067	H&H	Buxton, UK	February 21	70
1985	Bristol Brigand Saloon	$12,440	Bonhams	Stoneleigh Park, UK	February 25	360A
Bugatti						
1927	Type 35C Grand Prix	$2,585,000	Gooding	Pebble Beach, CA	August 20	44
1938	Type 57C Aravis Drophead Coupe	$1,375,000	Gooding	Pebble Beach, CA	August 20	38
1938	T57C Aravis Drophead Coupe	$1,045,000	RM	Phoenix, AZ	January 20	143
1938	Type 57 Atalante Coupe	$682,000	Gooding	Pebble Beach, CA	August 20	64
1937	Type 57C Ventoux	$467,500	RM	Monterey, CA	August 18	473
Buick						
1954	Skylark Convertible	$185,500	Silver	Ft. McDowell, AZ	January 23	185
1954	Skylark	$181,500	Russo and Steele	Scottsdale, AZ	January 20	S234
1939	Century Convertible Coupe	$170,500	RM	Rochester, MI	August 5	273
1954	Skylark	$154,000	Russo and Steele	Monterey, CA	August 18	S245
1954	Skylark Convertible	$145,800	Barrett-Jackson	Scottsdale, AZ	January 14	1273
Cadillac						
1956	Eldorado Brougham Town Car	$781,100	RM	Boca Raton, FL	February 10	SP41
1933	V16 Model 452-C Conv. Phaeton	$682,000	RM	Rochester, MI	August 5	264
1948	Custom 4-seat Cabriolet	$649,000	RM	Monterey, CA	August 18	443

Year	Model	Sold Price	Auction Co.	Location	Date	Lot #
1928	V8 Town Sedan	$621,500	RM	Phoenix, AZ	January 20	180
1931	V16 Sport Phaeton	$495,000	RM	Rochester, MI	August 5	229

Chevrolet

Bel Air

Year	Model	Sold Price	Auction Co.	Location	Date	Lot #
1955	Bel Air Custom Convertible	$210,600	Barrett-Jackson	Scottsdale, AZ	January 14	1293
1959	Bel Air	$205,200	Barrett-Jackson	Scottsdale, AZ	January 14	1247
1957	Bel Air fi Convertible	$167,400	Barrett-Jackson	Scottsdale, AZ	January 14	1241.1
1957	Bel Air Convertible	$151,200	Barrett-Jackson	West Palm Beach, FL	March 29	708
1957	Bel Air Convertible	$140,400	Barrett-Jackson	Scottsdale, AZ	January 14	1235

Camaro

Year	Model	Sold Price	Auction Co.	Location	Date	Lot #
1969	Camaro	$486,000	Barrett-Jackson	Scottsdale, AZ	January 14	1322
1969	Camaro SS Baldwin Motion	$486,000	Barrett-Jackson	Scottsdale, AZ	January 14	1290
1968	Yenko Camaro	$367,500	Mecum	Belvidere, IL	May 25	S514
1967	Camaro	$341,585	Silver	Reno, NV	August 6	423
1967	Camaro Z/28 Racer	$324,000	Barrett-Jackson	West Palm Beach, FL	March 29	733

Chevelle

Year	Model	Sold Price	Auction Co.	Location	Date	Lot #
1970	Chevelle LS6 Convertible	$1,242,000	Barrett-Jackson	Scottsdale, AZ	January 14	1287
1970	Chevelle 454 LS6 Convertible	$513,000	Barrett-Jackson	Scottsdale, AZ	January 14	1320
1965	Chevelle Z16	$412,500	Russo and Steele	Scottsdale, AZ	January 20	S232
1970	Chevelle	$324,500	Russo and Steele	Scottsdale, AZ	January 20	F226
1969	Chevelle SS	$288,750	Mecum	Belvidere, IL	May 25	S545.1

Corvette

Year	Model	Sold Price	Auction Co.	Location	Date	Lot #
1953	Corvette Roadster	$1,080,000	Barrett-Jackson	Scottsdale, AZ	January 14	1311
1968	Corvette Stingray Race Car	$605,000	RM	Phoenix, AZ	January 20	161
1962	Corvette Convertible	$489,500	Gooding	Palm Beach, FL	January 24	27
1967	Corvette 427/435 Convertible	$378,000	Barrett-Jackson	Scottsdale, AZ	January 14	1284
1964	Corvette	$367,500	Mecum	St. Charles, IL	June 16	S510

Impala

Year	Model	Sold Price	Auction Co.	Location	Date	Lot #
1963	Impala Z11	$325,500	Mecum	Belvidere, IL	May 25	S518.1
1963	Impala Z11	$299,250	Mecum	Kissimmee, FL	January 27	X30
1963	Impala SS Convertible	$149,040	Barrett-Jackson	Scottsdale, AZ	January 14	994
1963	Impala	$120,750	Mecum	Belvidere, IL	May 25	S554.1
1958	Impala	$115,560	Barrett-Jackson	West Palm Beach, FL	March 29	105

Nomad

Year	Model	Sold Price	Auction Co.	Location	Date	Lot #
1957	Nomad Custom	$147,960	Barrett-Jackson	Scottsdale, AZ	January 14	968
1955	Nomad Custom	$100,440	Barrett-Jackson	West Palm Beach, FL	March 29	384
1955	Nomad Custom	$99,900	Barrett-Jackson	Scottsdale, AZ	January 14	1042.1
1955	Nomad	$89,250	Mecum	Belvidere, IL	May 25	S600.1
1955	Nomad Custom	$86,670	RM	Boca Raton, FL	February 10	SP44

Nova

Year	Model	Sold Price	Auction Co.	Location	Date	Lot #
1970	Yenko Nova Deuce	$183,750	Mecum	Belvidere, IL	May 25	S558
1968	Nova	$191,625	Mecum	Belvidere, IL	May 25	S595
1967	Nova SS Custom	$77,760	Barrett-Jackson	Scottsdale, AZ	January 14	723
1970	Nova SS Custom	$73,440	Barrett-Jackson	Scottsdale, AZ	January 14	967.1
1969	Yenko Nova Replica	$72,600	Russo and Steele	Scottsdale, AZ	January 20	F169

Chrysler

Year	Model	Sold Price	Auction Co.	Location	Date	Lot #
1961	300G Convertible	$199,800	Barrett-Jackson	Scottsdale, AZ	January 14	1299
1962	300G Convertible	$184,250	Worldwide Group	Seabrook, TX	May 6	42
1957	300G Convertible	$167,990	RM	Boca Raton, FL	February 10	SP50
1960	300F Convertible	$164,700	Barrett-Jackson	Scottsdale, AZ	January 14	1340
1957	300C Convertible	$125,400	RM	Amelia Island, FL	March 11	178

Cisitalia

Year	Model	Sold Price	Auction Co.	Location	Date	Lot #
1947	202 Spider Nuvolari	$385,000	Gooding	Pebble Beach, CA	August 20	73

Year	Model	Sold Price	Auction Co.	Location	Date	Lot #
1947	202 Cabriolet	$96,773	Bonhams	Monte Carlo, MCO	May 20	250
1947	202 Replica	$26,325	Bonhams	Carmel, CA	August 18	500
Citroën						
1973	DS23 IE Cabriolet	$209,738	Christie's	Paris, FRA	February 11	74
1970	DS21 Cabriolet	$180,790	Christie's	Paris, FRA	July 8	110
1963	2 CV Sahara	$55,483	Artcurial	Paris, FRA	June 12	3
1969	DS21 Berline Pallas	$26,992	Artcurial	Paris, FRA	June 12	4
1970	DS23 Convertible Conversion	$21,541	Bonhams	Hendon, U.K.	April 24	627
Cord						
1937	812 Phaeton Convertible	$216,000	Barrett-Jackson	Scottsdale, AZ	January 14	1036
1937	812 Supercharged Phaeton	$209,000	RM	Amelia Island, FL	March 11	183
1930	L29 Convertible Sedan	$192,500	RM	Rochester, MI	August 5	257
1937	812 Phaeton Bustleback	$172,800	Barrett-Jackson	Scottsdale, AZ	January 14	1280
1936	810 Phaeton Sedan	$154,000	RM	Rochester, MI	August 5	279
Daimler						
1908	TC48 Roi-des-Belges	$200,000	Worldwide Group	Seabrook, TX	May 6	24
1911	4-door Touring Phaeton	$162,000	Kruse	Auburn, IN	May 18	1022
1964	2.5 V8 Saloon	$22,185	Barons	Esher, UK	June 11	211
1964	2.5 V8 Saloon	$16,243	Barons	Esher, UK	June 11	218
1985	Double Six Saloon	$14,989	Coys	London, U.K.	June 24	236
De Tomaso						
1967	Mangusta	$58,650	Bonhams	Monte Carlo, MCO	May 20	165
1974	Pantera	$49,500	RM	Monterey, CA	August 18	416
1973	Pantera	$32,760	Bonhams	Brookline, MA	May 6	319
1974	Pantera	$39,323	RM	Boca Raton, FL	February 10	NR107
1973	Pantera	$30,800	Russo and Steele	Scottsdale, AZ	January 20	F145
Delage						
1937	D-8 120 Drophead Coupe	$715,000	RM	Monterey, CA	August 18	449
1934	D-6 11 Cabriolet	$102,479	Christie's	London, U.K.	June 26	184
1923	DE Tourer	$76,050	Bonhams	Carmel, CA	August 18	559
1933	D-8 15	$44,170	Bonhams & Goodman	Sydney, NSW, Australia	March 26	16
1954	D-6 3 L	$21,964	Osenat	Paris, FRA	June 18	508
Delahaye						
1938	135MS Coupe	$1,712,000	Bonhams	Carmel, CA	August 18	527
1939	135MS Grand Sport	$1,100,000	Gooding	Pebble Beach, CA	August 20	52
1938	135M Cabriolet	$427,125	Bonhams	Monte Carlo, MCO	May 20	155
1947	135MS Cabriolet	$375,500	Bonhams	Carmel, CA	August 18	512
1948	135M Cabriolet	$203,661	Coys	Monte Carlo, MCO	May 20	220
DeLorean						
1983	DMC-12	$29,150	Russo and Steele	Scottsdale, AZ	January 20	SN173
1981	DMC-12	$21,600	Kruse	Turlock, CA	August 12	146
1983	DMC-12	$18,200	RM	Toronto, Canada	April 7	SP07
1982	DMC-12	$17,280	Kruse	Ft. Lauderdale, FL	January 6	1031
1981	DMC-12	$600	MidAmerica	Minneapolis, MN	September 22	143
DeSoto						
1957	Adventurer Convertible	$123,750	RM	Monterey, CA	August 18	428
1936	Airflow Sedan	$38,500	RM	Rochester, MI	August 5	270
1955	Fire Flight 4-door	$37,800	Kruse	Auburn, IN	August 30	856
1951	Coupe	$34,450	Silver	Reno, NV	August 6	564
1955	Firedome	$29,700	Kruse	Auburn, IN	August 30	446
Devin						
1958	SS Sports Racer	$247,500	RM	Monterey, CA	August 18	480

Year	Model	Sold Price	Auction Co.	Location	Date	Lot #
1958	Special Roadster	$129,600	Barrett-Jackson	Scottsdale, AZ	January 14	1227
1954	Racer	$22,680	Kruse	Las Vegas, NV	April 7	704
1954	Racer	$21,060	Kruse	Auburn, IN	August 30	756

Dodge

Challenger

Year	Model	Sold Price	Auction Co.	Location	Date	Lot #
1970	Hemi Challenger	$339,040	G. Potter King	Atlantic City, NJ	February 23	1024
1970	Hemi Challenger	$215,250	Mecum	Kissimmee, FL	January 27	X15
1970	Challenger	$210,000	Mecum	Belvidere, IL	May 25	F555
1971	Hemi Challenger R/T	$341,000	Worldwide Group	Seabrook, TX	May 6	62
1970	Challenger R/T Convertible	$168,004	RM	Toronto, Canada	April 7	SP129

Charger

Year	Model	Sold Price	Auction Co.	Location	Date	Lot #
1971	Hemi Charger	$315,000	Mecum	Belvidere, IL	May 25	S538
1969	Hemi Charger 500	$294,250	RM	Boca Raton, FL	February 10	SP31
1969	Hemi Charger 500	$195,250	Russo and Steele	Scottsdale, AZ	January 20	F225
1968	Charger RT Custom	$140,400	Barrett-Jackson	Scottsdale, AZ	January 14	1269
1969	Charger 500	$137,160	Barrett-Jackson	West Palm Beach, FL	March 29	358

Coronet

Year	Model	Sold Price	Auction Co.	Location	Date	Lot #
1967	Hemi Coronet R/T Convertible	$264,600	Barrett-Jackson	Scottsdale, AZ	January 14	1288
1965	Coronet	$178,500	Mecum	Belvidere, IL	May 25	S576
1965	Hemi Coronet Replica Racer	$130,680	Barrett-Jackson	Scottsdale, AZ	January 14	1025
1964	Coronet 330 Lightweight Max Wedge	$129,600	Barrett-Jackson	Scottsdale, AZ	January 14	1268
1965	Hemi Coronet AFX Replica Racer	$108,000	Barrett-Jackson	Scottsdale, AZ	January 14	1013

Super Bee

Year	Model	Sold Price	Auction Co.	Location	Date	Lot #
1969	Super Bee	$216,000	Barrett-Jackson	Scottsdale, AZ	January 14	1034
1969	Super Bee	$181,125	Mecum	Belvidere, IL	May 25	S541.1
1971	Super Bee	$84,700	Russo and Steele	Scottsdale, AZ	January 20	S183
1970	Super Bee	$84,000	Mecum	Belvidere, IL	May 25	S143
1970	Super Bee	$72,360	Barrett-Jackson	Scottsdale, AZ	January 14	1560

Duesenberg

Year	Model	Sold Price	Auction Co.	Location	Date	Lot #
1930	Model J Sport Berline	$1,650,000	RM	Monterey, CA	August 18	477
1934	Model J Riviera Phaeton	$1,210,000	Gooding	Pebble Beach, CA	August 20	60
1930	Model J LWB Dual Cowl Phaeton	$1,001,000	RM	Phoenix, AZ	January 20	135
1929	Model J Convertible Sedan	$907,500	RM	Rochester, MI	August 5	237
1929	Model J Convertible Coupe	$902,000	Gooding	Pebble Beach, CA	August 20	71

Edsel

Year	Model	Sold Price	Auction Co.	Location	Date	Lot #
1958	Citation Convertible	$54,000	Kruse	Auburn, IN	May 18	828
1958	Citation Convertible	$53,500	RM	Boca Raton, FL	February 10	SP52
1958	Pacer	$45,580	Silver	Reno, NV	August 6	450
1958	Pacer Convertible	$44,280	Barrett-Jackson	Scottsdale, AZ	January 14	741.1
1958	Station Wagon	$32,400	Barrett-Jackson	Scottsdale, AZ	January 14	62

Excaliber

Year	Model	Sold Price	Auction Co.	Location	Date	Lot #
1980	Phaeton SIV	$20,412	Kruse	Ft. Lauderdale, FL	January 6	2755
1981	Phaeton SIV	$60,500	Worldwide Group	Seabrook, TX	May 6	111
1986	Phaeton SV	$68,584	Shannons	Melbourne, Australia	September 4	16
1982	Phaeton SIV	$33,912	Kruse	Auburn, IN	August 30	3063
1990	Phantom	$16,740	RM	Novi, MI	September 22	604

Facel Vega

Year	Model	Sold Price	Auction Co.	Location	Date	Lot #
1962	2 + 2	$121,500	Kruse	Auburn, IN	August 30	746.1
1964	Facel III Cabriolet	$44,237	Artcurial	Paris, FRA	June 12	15

Ferrari

Year	Model	Sold Price	Auction Co.	Location	Date	Lot #
1958	412S Sports Racer	$5,610,000	RM	Monterey, CA	August 18	465
1960	250 GT SWB Alloy Comp Berlinetta	$2,750,000	RM	Amelia Island, FL	March 11	142
1957	500 TRC Spider	$2,282,500	RM	Monterey, CA	August 18	472

BY THE NUMBERS

Top 5 Sales of 2006 by Marque

Year	Model	Sold Price	Auction Co.	Location	Date	Lot #
1961	250 GT SWB Alloy Comp Berlinetta	$1,762,300	Sportscar Auction Co.	Geneva, CH	October 7	42
1967	212 E Montagna Racer	$1,650,000	RM	Phoenix, AZ	January 20	164
Fiat						
1953	8V Ghia Supersonic	$452,800	Sportscar Auction	Geneva, CH	October 7	37
1952	110 Boat Car	$61,583	Bonhams	Monte Carlo, MCO	May 20	251A
1952	1900 "Kontiki"	$58,727	Christie's	Paris, FRA	February 11	80
1957	Abarth 750/850 Zagato	$55,179	Bonhams	Stoneleigh Park, UK	February 25	335
1959	500 Jolly Beach Car	$48,386	Bonhams	Monte Carlo, MCO	May 20	179
Ford						
Mustang						
1968	Mustang 428 CJ Fastback	$513,000	Barrett-Jackson	Scottsdale, AZ	January 14	1274.1
1969	Mustang Boss 429	$225,600	MidAmerica	Minneapolis, MN	September 22	141
1970	Mustang	$220,480	G. Potter King	Atlantic City, NJ	February 23	1784.1
1970	Mustang Boss 429	$214,500	Russo and Steele	Monterey, CA	August 18	S249
2005	Mustang FR500C #55 race car	$201,960	Barrett-Jackson	Scottsdale, AZ	January 14	1281
Thunderbird						
1957	Thunderbird	$220,000	RM	Monterey, CA	August 18	466
1956	Thunderbird Convertible	$142,560	Barrett-Jackson	Scottsdale, AZ	January 14	1022
1957	Thunderbird Convertible	$135,000	Barrett-Jackson	Scottsdale, AZ	January 14	1021
1957	Thunderbird Convertible	$116,640	Barrett-Jackson	Scottsdale, AZ	January 14	1005
1957	Thunderbird Convertible	$115,500	RM	Hampton, NH	June 10	2194
Giannini						
1970	Fiat 500	$23,100	RM	Monterey, CA	August 18	201
1970	Monza Spyder	$16,500	RM	Monterey, CA	August 18	170
Ginetta						
1964	G4	$26,400	Russo and Steele	Monterey, CA	August 18	F117
1990	G32	$5,561	H&H	Buxton, U.K.	July 25	32
Hispano-Suiza						
1927	H6B Coupe Chauffeur	$304,000	Bonhams	Carmel, CA	August 18	553
Horch						
1937	853 Cabriolet A	$299,000	RM	Cortland, NY	June 24	371
Hudson						
1937	Terraplane Pickup	$189,000	Barrett-Jackson	Scottsdale, AZ	January 14	1275.2
1953	Hornet Twin H-Power Sedan	$110,000	RM	Amelia Island, FL	March 11	171
1937	Deluxe Eight Convertible	$72,600	RM	Rochester, MI	August 5	248
1951	Pacemaker Convertible	$47,520	Kruse	Auburn, IN	August 30	2791
1942	Commodore Eight Sedan	$43,870	RM	Boca Raton, FL	February 10	631
Intermeccanica						
1966	Vetta Ventura GT	$84,700	Russo and Steele	Monterey, CA	August 18	F160
Isotta Fraschini						
1930	8AS Boattail Convertible	$658,500	Christie's	Greenwich, CT	June 4	9
Italia						
1912	14/18 CV Deux Places Roadster	$69,913	Christie's	Paris, FRA	February 11	66
1969	Roadster	$48,600	Barrett-Jackson	Scottsdale, AZ	January 14	960.2
Jaguar						
1956	XK D-Type Racer	$2,097,000	Bonhams	Carmel, CA	August 18	521
1952	XK C-Type Racer	$1,649,638	Christie's	Paris, FRA	February 11	86
1953	XK C-Type Racer	$1,512,500	RM	Phoenix, AZ	January 20	150
1938	SS100 3 1/2-Liter	$296,228	Bonhams	Sussex, U.K.	September 1	244
1960	XK 150 S 3.8 Drophead Coupe	$269,500	Gooding	Pebble Beach, CA	August 20	67
Jensen						
2001	S-V8 Roadster	$46,838	Bonhams	Sussex, U.K.	July 7	545

Year	Model	Sold Price	Auction Co.	Location	Date	Lot #
1974	Interceptor III Convertible	$36,740	H&H	Buxton, U.K.	July 25	46
1953	541 Prototype	$33,878	H&H	Buxton, U.K.	April 12	51
1964	CV8 Mk II	$25,315	Brightwells	Herefordshire, U.K.	October 4	48
1966	CV8 Mk III	$22,672	H&H	Buxton, U.K.	September 13	9
1972	Interceptor III	$17,388	Kruse	Auburn, IN	August 30	3777
Lagonda						
1937	LG45 Rapide	$671,000	RM	Monterey, CA	August 18	464
1932	2-Liter Supercharged Tourer	$153,734	Bonhams	Sussex, U.K.	September 1	223
1939	V12 Drophead Coupe	$150,933	H&H	Buxton, U.K.	July 25	91
1937	LG6 Drophead Coupe	$124,963	Bonhams	Sussex, U.K.	July 7	565
1931	2-Liter Low Chassis Supercharged	$100,693	H&H	Buxton, U.K.	April 12	50
Lamborghini						
2005	Gallardo	$540,000	Kruse	Auburn, IN	August 30	1449
1972	Miura P400 SV	$477,000	Christie's	Monterey, CA	August 17	11
1969	Miura P400S	$300,900	Bonhams	Monte Carlo, MCO	May 20	190
1966	GT 400	$253,000	RM	Monterey, CA	August 18	487
1968	Miura P400	$234,368	Coys	London, U.K.	February 28	126
Lancia						
1983	Martini LC 2 Endurance Racer	$475,651	Artcurial	Paris, FRA	February 12	57
1975	Stratos Stradale	$177,789	Coys	Nuremberg, DE	July 22	258
1962	Flaminia Sport Zagato	$177,600	Sportscar Auction Co.	Geneva, CH	October 7	14
1951	Aurelia B50 PF Convertible	$152,750	Christie's	Monterey, CA	August 17	44
1971	Fulvia 1.6 HF	$122,129	Artcurial	Paris, FRA	February 12	53
LaSalle						
1935	Replica	$103,740	G. Potter King	Atlantic City, NJ	February 23	1041
1928	Model 303 Convertible Coupe	$66,000	RM	Rochester, MI	August 5	290
1940	Series 40-52 Convertible Sedan	$60,500	RM	Amelia Island, FL	March 11	175
1928	Rumble Seat Convertible	$50,868	Kruse	Auburn, IN	August 30	1052
1940	Series 40-52 Convertible Sedan	$33,000	RM	Rochester, MI	August 5	208
Lincoln						
1955	Indianapolis Boano	$1,375,000	Gooding	Pebble Beach, CA	August 20	57
1960	Continental Elvis Presley Limousine	$556,200	Barrett-Jackson	Scottsdale, AZ	January 14	1316
1939	Zephyr Custom	$345,600	Barrett-Jackson	Scottsdale, AZ	January 14	1291.1
1964	Continental Papal Limousine	$319,000	RM	Monterey, CA	August 18	453
1940	Continental Cabriolet	$407,000	RM	Hampton, NH	June 10	2186
Lotus						
1955	Mk X Racer	$180,975	Bonhams	Sussex, U.K.	September 1	209
	Eleven Racer	$152,895	Bonhams	Sussex, U.K.	September 1	208
1981	Type (81/3) Formula One Racer	$202,725	Bonhams	Monte Carlo, MCO	May 20	197
1965	Type 30 Group 7 Racer	$201,930	Bonhams	Sussex, U.K.	September 1	238
1963	23B Racer	$78,296	Bonhams	Sussex, U.K.	September 1	212
Maserati						
1955	300S Racer	$1,925,000	RM	Phoenix, AZ	January 20	171
1956	150S Racer	$1,145,804	Coys	Monte Carlo, MCO	May 20	261
2004	MC12	$1,072,500	RM	Monterey, CA	August 18	460
1935	4CS-1100/1500	$819,825	Bonhams	Monte Carlo, MCO	May 20	172
1937	6CM Monoposto Voiturette	$726,000	Gooding	Pebble Beach, CA	August 20	55
Mercedes-Benz						
1911	Mercedes 37/90 Skiff	$1,050,000	Worldwide Group	Seabrook, TX	May 6	63
1928	26/120/180 Type S	$3,645,000	Christie's	Monterey, CA	August 17	52
1936	540K Cabriolet C	$1,174,354	Coys	Monte Carlo, MCO	May 20	240
1955	300SL Alloy	$942,748	Artcurial	Paris, FRA	February 12	22
1935	500/540K Cabriolet	$1,650,000	Worldwide Group	Seabrook, TX	May 6	60

Year	Model	Sold Price	Auction Co.	Location	Date	Lot #
Mercury						
Cougar						
1969	Cougar	$236,250	Mecum	Belvidere, IL	May 25	S572
1968	Cougar GT	$89,775	Mecum	Kissimmee, FL	January 27	A96
1968	Cougar SMC Custom	$41,250	Russo and Steele	Monterey, CA	August 18	S215
1973	Cougar XR7	$46,200	Worldwide Group	Seabrook, TX	May 6	37
1969	Cougar XR7	$43,200	Barrett-Jackson	Scottsdale, AZ	January 14	945.1
Cyclone						
1971	Cyclone Spoiler	$64,050	Mecum	Belvidere, IL	May 25	S581.1
1970	Cyclone Spoiler	$50,925	Mecum	Belvidere, IL	May 25	S94
1970	Cyclone	$48,600	Barrett-Jackson	West Palm Beach, FL	March 29	759
MG						
1935	R-Type Racer	$243,822	H&H	Buxton, UK	February 21	45
1939	WA Tickford	$104,500	Russo and Steele	Monterey, CA	August 18	S238
1964	Lightweight Competition Roadster	$78,125	Bonhams	Sussex, U.K.	July 7	544
1986	Metro 6R4 Group B Rally Car	$67,873	Bonhams	Stoneleigh Park, UK	February 25	345
1948	TC	$55,000	Kensington	Bridgehampton, NY	June 10	1
Moretti						
1955	750S MM Bialbero Spyder GS	$272,850	Bonhams	Monte Carlo, MCO	May 20	239
1968	500	$7,150	RM	Monterey, CA	August 18	103
Morgan						
1948	Roadster	$39,600	RM	Phoenix, AZ	January 20	115
1933	Super Sports Roadster	$33,130	H&H	London, U.K.	May 24	30
1934	Super Sports Roadster	$31,935	Bonhams	Sussex, U.K.	July 7	555
1962	Plus 4	$30,800	RM	Monterey, CA	August 18	184
2002	4/4 Le Mans 62	$42,184	Christie's	Paris, FRA	July 8	95
Nash						
1948	Ambassador Convertible	$104,500	RM	Rochester, MI	August 5	262
1952	Healey Le Mans Roadster	$74,250	RM	Monterey, CA	August 18	501
1953	Healey Roadster	$46,440	Kruse	Turlock, CA	August 12	150
1937	Ambassador	$37,100	Silver	Portland, OR	October 7	102
1940	Ambassador Convertible	$30,240	Kruse	Auburn, IN	August 30	2851
Oldsmobile						
1970	442 W30	$167,200	Russo and Steele	Monterey, CA	August 18	S262
1970	442 W30	$148,500	Russo and Steele	Scottsdale, AZ	January 20	F210
1970	442 W30	$105,000	Mecum	Belvidere, IL	May 25	F564
1966	442 Convertible	$93,500	Worldwide Group	Seabrook, TX	May 6	92
1970	442	$89,250	Mecum	Belvidere, IL	May 25	F567
Packard						
1934	Twelve LeBaron Runabout Speedster	$3,190,000	RM	Phoenix, AZ	January 20	167
1932	Series 904 Custom Dietrich Convertible Victoria	$541,080	Leake	Tulsa, OK	June 9	2471
1934	Twelve Runabout Speedster	$533,500	RM	Amelia Island, FL	March 11	154
1930	734 Speedster Roadster	$455,000	Christie's	Greenwich, CT	June 4	21
1931	Series 840 Deluxe Eight	$449,500	Christie's	Monterey, CA	August 17	48
Pierce-Arrow						
1935	Model 840 Coupe	$86,900	RM	Rochester, MI	August 5	230
1937	Open Town Car	$81,000	Kruse	Auburn, IN	May 18	7010
1933	Twelve Convertible Sedan	$418,000	RM	Amelia Island, FL	March 11	167
1934	840-A Silver Arrow	$98,975	RM	Boca Raton, FL	February 10	SP108
1932	Model 54 Club Brougham	$57,200	RM	Rochester, MI	August 5	280
Plymouth						
'Cuda						
1970	Hemi 'Cuda Convertible	$2,160,000	Barrett-Jackson	Scottsdale, AZ	January 14	1309

Year	Model	Sold Price	Auction Co.	Location	Date	Lot #
1971	Hemi 'Cuda	$1,045,000	Worldwide Group	Seabrook, TX	May 6	50
1971	Hemi 'Cuda	$787,500	Mecum	Belvidere, IL	May 25	S571.1
1971	Hemi 'Cuda	$715,000	Russo and Steele	Scottsdale, AZ	January 20	S222
1970	Hemi 'Cuda	$702,000	Barrett-Jackson	Scottsdale, AZ	January 14	1324
Satellite						
1966	Hemi Satellite	$124,200	Barrett-Jackson	Scottsdale, AZ	January 14	1053.1
1966	Hemi Satellite	$102,600	Barrett-Jackson	Scottsdale, AZ	January 14	1232
1967	Hemi Satellite	$91,800	Barrett-Jackson	Scottsdale, AZ	January 14	1032
1967	Hemi Satellite Convertible	$156,600	Barrett-Jackson	Scottsdale, AZ	January 14	1242
1966	Hemi Satellite	$71,280	Barrett-Jackson	West Palm Beach, FL	March 29	702
Roadrunner						
1971	Road Runner "Richard Petty" NASCAR	$192,500	Russo and Steele	Monterey, CA	August 18	S260
1969	Hemi Road Runner NASCAR	$172,800	Barrett-Jackson	Scottsdale, AZ	January 14	1339
1968	Road Runner	$165,000	Russo and Steele	Scottsdale, AZ	January 20	S207
1969	Road Runner	$156,600	Barrett-Jackson	Scottsdale, AZ	January 14	1339.1
1970	Road Runner	$153,900	Barrett-Jackson	Scottsdale, AZ	January 14	981.1
Superbird						
1970	Superbird	$379,500	Russo and Steele	Scottsdale, AZ	January 20	F228
1970	Superbird	$131,250	Mecum	Belvidere, IL	May 25	F588
1970	Superbird	$120,750	Mecum	Belvidere, IL	May 25	T26
1970	Superbird	$100,440	Kruse	Ft. Lauderdale, FL	January 6	769
1970	Superbird	$140,400	Kruse	Auburn, IN	August 30	2747.1
Firebird						
1969	Firebird	$89,100	Worldwide Group	Seabrook, TX	May 6	32
1969	Firebird Convertible	$71,280	Kruse	Ft. Lauderdale, FL	January 6	765
1968	Firebird Custom	$62,640	Barrett-Jackson	Scottsdale, AZ	January 14	465
1976	Firebird Trans Am	$48,600	Barrett-Jackson	Scottsdale, AZ	January 14	426.1
1970	Firebird Formula 400	$35,100	Barrett-Jackson	West Palm Beach, FL	March 29	329.1
GTO						
1970	GTO Judge Ram Air IV Convertible	$410,000	RM	Boca Raton, FL	February 10	SP36
1970	GTO Judge Convertible	$199,800	Barrett-Jackson	Scottsdale, AZ	January 14	1025.1
1969	GTO	$177,100	Russo and Steele	Scottsdale, AZ	January 20	F216
1970	GTO Judge	$162,800	Russo and Steele	Monterey, CA	August 18	S247
1965	GTO	$131,250	Mecum	Belvidere, IL	May 25	S516
Trans Am						
1969	Trans Am	$113,400	Barrett-Jackson	Scottsdale, AZ	January 14	1023.1
1969	Trans Am	$106,920	Barrett-Jackson	Scottsdale, AZ	January 14	395
1969	Trans Am	$77,000	Worldwide Group	Seabrook, TX	May 6	66
1970	Trans Am	$52,800	Russo and Steele	Scottsdale, AZ	January 20	S141
1970	Trans Am	$47,250	Mecum	Belvidere, IL	May 25	T32
Porsche						
1972	917/10 Racer	$579,000	Bonhams	Carmel, CA	August 18	519
1963	904	$565,000	Christie's	Monterey, CA	August 17	26
1966	906 Carrera	$557,000	Bonhams	Carmel, CA	August 18	510
1964	904 GTS	$531,744	Osenat	Paris, FRA	June 18	566
2005	Carrera GT	$412,500	Russo and Steele	Monterey, CA	August 18	S248
Renault						
1913	Type DQ 8 1/2-liter 45hp	$82,862	Christie's	Paris, FRA	July 8	94
1972	Alpine A110 1600	$44,800	Sportscar Auction Co.	Geneva, CH	October 7	44
1978	Alpine A310	$27,500	RM	Monterey, CA	August 18	154
1922	Type NN Town Car	$21,150	Christie's	Greenwich, CT	June 4	40
1965	Dauphine Gordini FIA Competition Touring Car	$15,773	Bonhams	Sussex, U.K.	September 1	201

Year	Model	Sold Price	Auction Co.	Location	Date	Lot #
Riley						
1934	9CV Imp	$153,808	Christie's	Paris, FRA	February 11	65
1929	9hp Brooklands Special	$48,967	Bonhams	Sussex, U.K.	July 7	542
1937	1½-Liter Kestrel/Sprite Special	$47,197	Bonhams	Beaulieu, U.K.	September 9	444
1950	RMC 2½-Liter	$28,702	H&H	Buxton, U.K.	April 12	9
1952	Convertible	$28,620	Kruse	Denver, CO	July 21	746
Rolls-Royce						
1912	Silver Ghost Touring	$935,000	RM	Amelia Island, FL	March 11	169
1911	40/50hp Silver Ghost	$858,000	RM	Monterey, CA	August 18	447
1914	40/50hp Silver Ghost	$495,000	RM	Rochester, MI	August 5	265
1937	Phantom III 4-Door Cabriolet	$253,000	Gooding	Pebble Beach, CA	August 20	76
1930	40/50hp Phantom II Dual Cowl Phaeton	$238,000	Bonhams	North Brookfield, MA	September 23	1010
1929	Phantom I Springfield Convertible Coupe	$238,000	Bonhams	Carmel, CA	August 18	542
Rover						
1911	12hp Tourer	$51,488	Bonhams	Beaulieu, U.K.	September 9	467
1921	12/14hp Tourer	$21,453	Bonhams	Beaulieu, U.K.	September 9	470
1939	14hp Drophead Coupe	$15,317	Bonhams	Gaydon, U.K.	May 28	38
1927	16/50hp Doctor's Coupe	$13,887	Bonhams	Gaydon, U.K.	May 28	11
1938	12 6-Light Saloon	$11,139	Brightwells	Herefordshire, U.K.	October 4	62
Saab						
2003	93E Convertible	$18,360	Leake	Tulsa, OK	June 9	1168
2002	93 Turbo	$13,133	Mecum	Belvidere, IL	May 25	T67
2003	95 ARC	$12,360	Mecum	Belvidere, IL	May 25	T33
2003	95 Wagon	$11,588	Mecum	Belvidere, IL	May 25	T31
2002	95 ARC	$11,330	Mecum	Belvidere, IL	May 25	T24
Shelby						
1962	Cobra 289 Roadster	$1,815,000	RM	Phoenix, AZ	January 20	175
1963	Cobra 289 Le Mans Racer	$1,650,000	RM	Amelia Island, FL	March 11	164
1962	Cobra 289 Racer	$1,601,250	Mecum	Belvidere, IL	May 25	S511
1964	Cobra 289 Competition Racer	$1,237,500	RM	Monterey, CA	August 18	159
1965	GT350 R Fastback	$990,000	RM	Amelia Island, FL	March 11	137
Stanguellini						
1959	Formula Junior Monoposto	$121,000	Russo and Steele	Monterey, CA	August 18	S239
1959	Formula Junior Monoposto	$61,583	Bonhams	Monte Carlo, MCO	May 20	206
Stanley						
1911	Steamer 10hp Model 63 Toy Tonneau	$181,900	Bonhams	Brookline, MA	May 6	330
1910	Steamer 10hp Model 60 Runabout	$93,600	Bonhams	North Brookfield, MA	September 23	1006
1922	Steamer Model 740 Touring	$61,600	RM	Amelia Island, FL	March 11	110
Studebaker						
1937	Posies Extemeliner Woody	$302,500	RM	Monterey, CA	August 18	140
1935	Dictator Custom 4-door	$146,880	Barrett-Jackson	Scottsdale, AZ	January 14	970
1931	President Four Seasons Roadster	$132,000	RM	Rochester, MI	August 5	227
1933	82 President Cabriolet Custom	$130,680	Leake	Tulsa, OK	June 9	462
1939	Express Pickup	$124,200	Kruse	Auburn, IN	August 30	1025
Stutz						
1914	Bearcat	$715,000	Gooding	Pebble Beach, CA	August 20	29
1930	Model M Supercharged Coupe	$715,000	RM	Rochester, MI	August 5	251
1931	SV-16 Cabriolet Coupe	$378,000	Kruse	Scottsdale, AZ	January 26	2749
1915	Bearcat	$368,500	RM	Rochester, MI	August 5	234
1916	Bearcat	$275,000	RM	Amelia Island, FL	March 11	139

BY THE NUMBERS

Year	Model	Sold Price	Auction Co.	Location	Date	Lot #
Sunbeam						
1926	3-Liter	$105,205	Bonhams and Goodman	Sydney, NSW, Australia	March 26	15
1927	20.9hp Tourer	$59,612	Bonhams	Sussex, U.K.	July 7	518
1964	Tiger Prototype Roadster	$46,750	RM	Monterey, CA	August 18	421
1954	Alpine Roadster	$37,243	Bonhams	Sussex, U.K.	September 1	237
1962	Harrington Le Mans	$30,250	RM	Monterey, CA	August 18	128
Talbot-Lago						
1938	T150C SS Teardrop Coupe	$3,905,000	Gooding	Palm Beach, FL	January 24	29
1938	T23 Teardrop Coupe	$2,145,000	RM	Amelia Island, FL	March 11	155
1950	T26C	$1,410,741	Christie's	Paris, FRA	July 8	125
1949	T26 Grand Sport Cabriolet	$375,500	Bonhams	Carmel, CA	August 18	515
1950	T26 Grand Sport GS Coupe	$348,000	Bonhams	Carmel, CA	August 18	526
Toyota						
1967	2000 GT	$225,988	Christie's	Paris, FRA	July 8	124
1969	2000GT	$160,619	Bonhams and Goodman	Sydney, NSW, Australia	March 26	4
1969	Landcruiser SUV	$62,000	Central PA Auto Auction	Lock Haven, PA	July 22	
1994	Supra "The Fast & The Furious"	$43,200	Kruse	Auburn, IN	August 30	8005
2001	MR2 Convertible	$28,188	Kruse	Auburn, IN	August 30	1466
Triumph						
1963	TR4	$97,200	Barrett-Jackson	West Palm Beach, FL	March 29	312
1973	TR6	$28,620	Barrett-Jackson	West Palm Beach, FL	March 29	310
1960	TR3A	$26,103	H&H	London, U.K.	May 24	45
1947	1800	$25,110	Kruse	Seaside, CA	August 17	454
1968	TR5	$23,664	Barons	Esher, U.K.	September 10	218
Tucker						
1948	48 Torpedo	$577,500	RM	Monterey, CA	August 18	458
TVR						
1965	Griffith Competition	$64,224	Coys	London, U.K.	June 24	216
1965	Griffith Competition	$55,530	Coys	Oxfordshire, U.K.	August 26	162
1999	Chimaera	$19,051	Barons	Esher, U.K.	September 10	231
1996	Cerbera	$14,539	Barons	Esher, U.K.	September 10	242
1992	Griffith 4.3	$11,722	H&H	Buxton, UK	February 21	20
Volkswagen						
1963	MicroBus	$58,300	Russo and Steele	Scottsdale, AZ	January 20	S255
1956	Beetle Cabriolet	$50,760	Barrett-Jackson	Scottsdale, AZ	January 14	48.1
1956	23-Window Microbus	$50,000	RM	Boca Raton, FL	February 10	SP19
1967	Westfalia Camper	$49,500	Gooding	Pebble Beach, CA	August 20	78
1966	21-Window Microbus	$48,600	Barrett-Jackson	Scottsdale, AZ	January 14	636
Volvo						
1968	P1800 Coupe	$7,560	Kruse	Auburn, IN	August 30	1734
1970	121	$6,951	H&H	Buxton, U.K.	July 25	27
1972	P1800ES	$6,046	H&H	Buxton, U.K.	September 13	75
1998	V70 Station Wagon	$4,024	Silver	Spokane, WA	April 8	12
1972	144 Deluxe	$3,972	H&H	Buxton, U.K.	July 25	24
Zimmer						
1984	Golden Spirit	$27,600	RM	Cortland, NY	June 24	374
1981	Golden Spirit	$25,817	H&H	Buxton, U.K.	July 25	23
1985	Golden Spirit	$25,200	Mecum	Kissimmee, FL	January 27	A76
1986	Golden Spirit	$17,430	Mecum	Kansas City, MO	April 28	S113
1984	Golden Spirit	$16,200	Kruse	Las Vegas, NV	April 7	411 ◆

BY THE NUMBERS

Million-Dollar Muscle

Recent sales have proven that America's supercars have aged gracefully and expensively

by Jim Pickering

U ntil 2000, it may have been laughable to think that any American production car could sell for dollar figures comparable to European exotics. However, recent sales have proven that America's supercars have aged just as gracefully. Four models accounted for the eight examples that sold for over $1m in 2006. *(Sales recorded between 1/1/2006 and 9/30/2006.)*

Muscle Car Rank	Overall Rank	Year	Car	Sold Price	Lot #	Auction Co.	Location	Date
1	10	1970	Plymouth Hemi 'Cuda	$2,160,000	1309	Barrett-Jackson	Scottsdale, AZ	1/14/06
2	16	1962	Shelby Cobra	$1,815,000	175	RM	Phoenix, AZ	1/20/06
3	23	1963	Shelby Cobra 289 Le Mans	$1,650,000	164	RM	Amelia Island, FL	3/11/06
4	25	1962	Shelby Cobra Dragonsnake	$1,601,250	S511	Mecum	Belvidere, IL	5/25/06
5	33	1970	Chevrolet Chevelle SS LS6	$1,242,000	1287	Barrett-Jackson	Scottsdale, AZ	1/14/06
6	34	1964	Shelby Cobra 289 Comp.	$1,237,500	159	RM	Monterey, CA	8/18/06
7	40	1953	Chevrolet Corvette	$1,080,000	1311	Barrett-Jackson	Scottsdale, AZ	1/14/06
8	44	1971	Plymouth 'Cuda Hemi	$1,045,000	50	Worldwide Group	Seabrook, TX	5/6/06

Plymouth Hemi 'Cuda

Built in limited numbers for only two model years, the Hemi 'Cuda is the top dog in American muscle. The 'Cuda was initially positioned to grab a share of the popular muscle car market dominated by the Camaro, Chevelle, Mustang, and GTO. It was available with several different engines, with the 335-hp 383 as standard equipment. The 426 Hemi was developed on the NASCAR circuit, and was conservatively rated for the street at 425 hp. With over 490 ft-lbs of torque, the engine consisted of hemispherical cylinder heads with big valves, a hydraulic-lifter cam, and a 10.25:1 compression ratio. Bright factory paint schemes and a Hemi-standard Shaker hood mounted to the dual fours rounded out the package. Due to poor sales, high insurance costs, and rising gasoline prices, the Hemi option was dropped in 1972. All Hemi 'Cudas are rare, and the recent high sales reflect how few were made and how desirable they have become.

Engine: 426-ci V8, 2x4-bbl, 425 hp

Transmission: 4-speed manual or 727 TorqueFlite automatic

Number built: 781 total

1970: 652 hard tops, 14 convertibles

1971: 107 hard tops, 7 convertibles

Lot 1309, $2,160,000

Lot 50, $1,045,000

Shelby Cobra

The Shelby Cobra is an icon of performance. Built with the backing of Ford, the basic Cobra was aimed squarely at the sophisticated European exotics that were then dominating racetracks worldwide. Shelby's recipe was the quintessential definition of muscle: a lightweight body and chassis fitted with the largest engine possible. Production started using Ford's 260-ci V8, but soon moved to the 271-hp 289. Later coil-spring-chassis cars were available with the 425-hp 427, which dropped quarter mile performance into the low 12 second range. Several Cobras were built with automatic transmissions, but most were delivered as four-speeds. Limited numbers were built for the street to help finance Shelby's racing program, and originals are rare and expensive in any form. However, the most valued examples have traditionally been ex-race winners with documented histories.

Engines: 260-ci V8, 289-ci V8, 427-ci V8

Transmission: 4-speed manual or C6 automatic

Number built: 1,003

Lot 164, $1,650,000   Lot 159, $1,237,500   Lot S511, $1,601,250   Lot 175, $1,815,000

1953 Chevrolet Corvette

The 1953 Corvette was Chevrolet's first attempt at a sports car. It was based on the 1952 EX-122 from GM's Motorama, and went into production largely unchanged from the show car. The internals were sourced directly from Chevrolet's other models, and performance did not match the styling. Extremely limited numbers were built, and Polo White was the only color available. All 1953s came with a standard triple-carbureted 150-hp 235-ci six-cylinder and a two-speed Powerglide transmission. All interiors were red, all soft tops black. Each one was a true roadster, with no roll-up windows or hard tops available. Prices in the $1m range may seem outrageous to some, but these first-year cars are rare, and they are early examples of what has become an American legacy.

Engine: 235-ci straight 6, 150 hp

Transmission: Powerglide automatic

Number built: 300

Lot 1311, $1,080,000

1970 Chevrolet Chevelle SS 454 LS6

The '70 SS 454 LS6 was Chevrolet's highest achievement in muscle cars. The LS6 consisted of a 4-bolt main 454 block, a steel crankshaft, and heavy-duty connecting rods. Forged pistons and cast iron rectangular-port cylinder heads yielded an 11.25:1 compression ratio. A solid-lifter cam, Holley 4-bbl carburetor, and aluminum dual-plane intake manifold rounded out the package. At 450 hp, it had the highest gross output rating of any of Chevrolet's V8s, and was capable of 0–60 times of just over five seconds. An optional vacuum-controlled cowl induction intake, and was available with the Turbo-Hydra-matic 400 automatic transmission or one of three Muncie four-speeds. The F41 heavy duty suspension was standard with the SS 454, and included boxed rear control arms and front and rear sway bars. These cars are not as rare as Hemi 'Cudas, but their performance is undeniable and their styling is arguably some of the best from GM.◆

Engine: 454-ci V8, 4-bbl, 450 hp

Transmission: Muncie 4-speed, Turbo 400 automatic

Number built: 3,733

Lot 1287, $1,242,000

Auction Company Comparison

It was a banner year for the collector car industry, as the results below bear out.
(Sales recorded between 1/1/2006 and 9/30/2006.)

Barrett-Jackson sold $98,116,434 in Scottsdale, AZ.

Auction Co.	Location	Date	Total Sales	Sold	Offered	Sales Rate
Artcurial	Paris, France	12-Feb-06	$5,039,968	28	64	44%
Artcurial	Paris, France	12-Jun-06	$1,921,116	23	44	52%
Barons	Esher, U.K.	07-Feb-06	$455,014	37	n/a	n/a
Barons	Esher, U.K.	24-Apr-06	$1,354,574	40	55	73%
Barons	Esher, U.K.	11-Jun-06	$286,819	27	n/a	n/a
Barons	Esher, U.K.	31-Jul-06	$587,566	45	n/a	n/a
Barons	Esher, U.K.	10-Sep-06	$3,529	36	n/a	n/a
Barons	Surrey, U.K.	13-Mar-06	$186,474	22	n/a	n/a
Barrett-Jackson	Scottsdale, AZ ,USA	14-Jan-06	$98,116,434	1063	1063	100%
Barrett-Jackson	West Palm Beach, FL ,USA	29-Mar-06	$33,898,770	563	563	100%
Bonhams	Beaulieu, U.K.	09-Sep-06	$1,144,139	47	59	80%
Bonhams & Butterfields	Brookline, MA ,USA	06-May-06	$1,252,168	23	42	55%
Bonhams & Butterfields	Carmel, CA ,USA	18-Aug-06	$12,444,099	56	69	81%
Bonhams	Chichester, U.K.	07-Jul-06	$2,431,155	43	66	65%
Bonhams	Chichester, U.K.	01-Sep-06	$6,618,719	38	47	81%
Bonhams	Gaydon, U.K.	28-May-06	$301,866	43	n/a	n/a
Bonhams	Hendon, U.K.	24-Apr-06	$1,354,574	40	55	73%
Bonhams	Monte Carlo, Monaco	20-May-06	$7,485,368	61	135	45%
Bonhams	Newport Pagnell, U.K.	13-May-06	$3,513,333	31	37	84%

Auction Co.	Location	Date	Total Sales	Sold	Offered	Sales Rate
Bonhams	Northamptonshire, U.K.	17-Jun-06	$1,104,121	22	32	69%
Bonhams	Stoneleigh Park, UK	25-Feb-06	$928,447	23	46	50%
Bonhams & Butterfields	North Brookfield, MA ,USA	23-Sep-06	$1,764,763	29	29	100%
Bonhams & Goodman	Melbourne, Australia	23-Apr-06	$1,102,500	258	261	99%
Bonhams & Goodman	Sydney, NSW ,Australia	26-Mar-06	$861,459	10	16	63%
Boyd Coddington's	Springfield, MO ,USA	13-Jul-06	$2,112,791	103	272	38%
Branson	Branson, MO ,USA	21-Apr-06	$2,810,330	128	232	55%
Brightwells	Herefordshire, U.K.	10-May-06	$693,973	53	84	63%
Brightwells	Herefordshire, U.K.	04-Oct-06	$672,161	55	95	58%
Carlisle	Carlisle, PA ,USA	21-Apr-06	$2,986,778	114	252	45%
Carlisle	Carlisle, PA ,USA	29-Sep-06	$1,680,641	87	248	35%
Central PA	Lockhaven, PA ,USA	22-Jul-06	$3,722,250	161	n/a	n/a
Christie's	Greenwich, CT ,USA	04-Jun-06	$3,147,138	31	40	78%
Christie's	London, U.K.	26-Jun-06	$1,412,815	22	31	71%
Christie's	Monterey, CA ,USA	17-Aug-06	$9,613,538	34	50	68%
Christie's	Paris, France	11-Feb-06	$4,155,641	22	34	65%
Christie's	Paris, France	08-Jul-06	$2,889,951	12	39	31%
Coys	Birmingham, UK	14-Jan-06	$738,861	25	51	49%
Coys	Donington Park, U.K.	30-Apr-06	$1,203,748	29	49	59%
Coys	London, U.K.	28-Feb-06	$1,066,389	25	47	53%
Coys	London, U.K.	24-Jun-06	$1,625,044	37	71	52%
Coys	London, U.K.	30-Sep-06	$1,204,988	29	59	49%
Coys	Maastricht, Netherlands	14-Jan-06	$3,306,894	21	53	40%
Coys	Monte Carlo, Monaco	20-May-06	$6,179,574	36	79	46%
Coys	Nuremberg, Germany	22-Jul-06	$3,930,385	28	64	44%
Coys	Oxfordshire, U.K.	27-Aug-06	$1,682,275	26	64	41%
G. Potter King	Atlantic City, NJ ,USA	23-Feb-06	$8,086,260	256	654	39%
Gooding	Palm Beach, FL ,USA	24-Jan-06	$7,106,100	28	52	54%
Gooding	Pebble Beach, CA ,USA	20-Aug-06	$21,168,400	62	78	79%
H&H	Buxton, U.K.	21-Feb-06	$2,225,818	46	68	68%
H&H	Buxton, U.K.	12-Apr-06	$1,018,615	72	85	85%
H&H	Buxton, U.K.	25-Jul-06	$1,767,599	73	94	78%
H&H	Buxton, U.K.	13-Sep-06	$942,456	49	89	55%
H&H	London, U.K.	24-May-06	$2,667,576	42	75	56%
Kensington	Bridgehampton, NY ,USA	10-Jun-06	$581,185	27	68	40%
Kruse	Auburn, IN ,USA	18-May-06	$6,622,506	227	517	44%
Kruse	Auburn, IN ,USA	30-Aug-06	$21,062,257	747	1655	45%
Kruse	Avondale, AZ ,USA	26-Jan-06	$5,960,196	179	515	35%
Kruse	Billings, MT ,USA	17-Jun-06	$68,418	9	42	21%
Kruse	Corona, CA ,USA	30-Sep-06	$320,112	13	65	20%
Kruse	Denver, CO ,USA	21-Jul-06	$983,178	64	152	42%
Kruse	Fredericksburg, TX ,USA	25-Mar-06	$1,312,840	65	133	49%
Kruse	Ft. Lauderdale, FL ,USA	06-Jan-06	$4,533,192	148	232	64%
Kruse	Hot Springs , AR ,USA	10-Mar-06	$435,294	40	98	41%
Kruse	Las Vegas, NV ,USA	07-Apr-06	$1,861,256	84	193	44%

Auction Co. Comparison

Auction Co.	Location	Date	Total Sales	Sold	Offered	Sales Rate
Kruse	Miami, FL ,USA	11-Mar-06	$1,474,632	62	234	26%
Kruse	Morehead, KY ,USA	24-Jun-06	$1,837,165	210	254	83%
Kruse	Nashville, TN ,USA	05-Aug-06	$108,756	11	51	22%
Kruse	Salt Lake City, UT ,USA	05-May-06	$426,222	27	134	20%
Kruse	Sarasota, FL ,USA	03-Feb-06	$385,506	21	116	18%
Kruse	Seaside, CA ,USA	17-Aug-06	$1,064,556	18	57	32%
Kruse	Topsfield, MA ,USA	24-Jun-06	$290,574	27	92	29%
Kruse	Turlock, CA ,USA	12-Aug-06	$1,963,440	68	68	100%
Kruse	Verona, NY ,USA	07-Jul-06	$1,086,912	46	106	43%
Leake	Oklahoma City, OK ,USA	24-Feb-06	$135,000	140	252	56%
Leake	Tulsa, OK ,USA	09-Jun-06	$12,286,487	415	658	63%
Mecum	Belvidere, IL ,USA	25-May-06	$28,995,821	571	979	58%
Mecum	Carlisle, PA ,USA	25-Aug-06	$3,084,422	82	154	53%
Mecum	Des Moines, IA ,USA	22-Jul-06	$1,010,781	86	153	56%
Mecum	Kansas City, MO ,USA	28-Apr-06	$3,310,738	155	243	64%
Mecum	Kissimmee, FL ,USA	27-Jan-06	$13,779,197	297	432	69%
Mecum	St. Charles, IL ,USA	16-Jun-06	$10,391,009	192	344	56%
Mecum	St. Charles, IL ,USA	06-Oct-06	$20,706,251	411	797	52%
Mecum	St. Paul, MN ,USA	24-Jun-06	$2,270,805	121	226	54%
MidAmerica	Maplewood, MN ,USA	01-Apr-06	$437,151	109	150	73%
MidAmerica	Minneapolis, MN ,USA	12-May-06	$1,236,929	95	160	59%
MidAmerica	Minneapolis, MN ,USA	22-Sep-06	$700,008	59	154	38%
Osenat	Paris, France	18-Jun-06	$1,558,489	33	67	49%
Palm Springs Auction	Palm Springs, CA ,USA	02-Feb-06	$4,677,750	247	392	63%
Petersen	Roseburg, OR ,USA	08-Jul-06	$222,653	23	67	34%
Potts	Dalton, GA ,USA	25-Mar-06	$436,667	28	63	44%
Potts	Dalton, GA ,USA	26-Aug-06	$271,198	20	50	40%
RM	Amelia Island, FL ,USA	11-Mar-06	$21,811,000	102	105	97%
RM	Boca Raton, FL ,USA	10-Feb-06	$18,045,821	308	418	74%
RM	Cortland, NY ,USA	24-Jun-06	$1,098,509	83	83	100%
RM	Los Angeles, CA ,USA	13-May-06	$727,150	12	12	100%
RM	Monterey, CA ,USA	18-Aug-06	$42,862,850	188	206	91%
RM	Novi, MI ,USA	28-Apr-06	$1,252,168	106	233	45%
RM	Novi, MI ,USA	22-Sep-06	$1,687,775	88	218	40%
RM	Phoenix, AZ ,USA	20-Jan-06	$31,293,300	106	110	96%
RM	Rochester, MI ,USA	05-Aug-06	$9,259,900	83	94	88%
RM	Toronto, Canada	07-Apr-06	$3,704,198	195	336	58%
Russo and Steele	Monterey, CA ,USA	18-Aug-06	$13,153,690	156	156	100%
Russo and Steele	Scottsdale, AZ ,USA	20-Jan-06	$19,829,178	299	396	75%
Shannons	Melbourne, Australia	05-Jun-06	$457,539	35	46	76%
Shannons	Melbourne, Australia	04-Sep-06	$456,332	28	38	74%
Shannons	Sydney, Australia	15-May-06	$385,980	16	26	62%
Shannons	Sydney, Australia	24-Jul-06	$370,169	16	26	62%

Auction Co.	Location	Date	Total Sales	Sold	Offered	Sales Rate
Silver	Coeur d'Alene, ID ,USA	17-Jun-06	$773,270	61	117	52%
Silver	Ft. McDowell, AZ ,USA	23-Jan-06	$5,718,170	233	376	62%
Silver	Jackson Hole, WY ,USA	02-Jul-06	$971,040	56	118	47%
Silver	Portland, OR ,USA	25-Mar-06	$509,860	49	98	50%
Silver	Portland, OR ,USA	07-Oct-06	$552,684	56	137	41%
Silver	Puyallup, WA ,USA	11-Feb-06	$410,061	39	125	31%
Silver	Puyallup, WA ,USA	13-May-06	$403,436	27	60	45%
Silver	Reno, NV ,USA	06-May-06	$501,327	34	79	43%
Silver	Reno, NV ,USA	06-Aug-06	$14,470,731	568	803	71%
Silver	Spokane, WA ,USA	08-Apr-06	$435,196	46	72	64%
Silver	Spokane, WA ,USA	24-May-06	$706,550	70	n/a	n/a
Silver	Sun Valley, ID ,USA	02-Sep-06	$1,484,106	86	192	45%
Sportscar	Geneva, Switzerland	07-Oct-06	$4,305,200	30	57	53%
Worldwide Group	Seabrook, TX ,USA	06-May-06	$11,085,010	99	110	90%

RM sold $21,811,000 at Amelia Island, FL

And the Winners Are...

From November, 1983 to September, 2006, here are the overall top 10 sales at public auction.

1931 Bugatti Type 41
$8,700,000—Christie's, UK, 11/17/83

1929 Mercedes-Benz 38/250 SSK
$7,443,070—Bonhams, Sussex, UK, 9/3/04

1931 Bugatti Type 41
$6,500,000—Kruse, Reno, NV, 6/15/86

1962 Ferrari 330 TRI/LM
$6,490,000–RM Auctions, Monterey, CA, 8/16/02

1966 Ferrari 330 P3
$5,616,000—Christie's, Pebble Beach, CA, 8/19/00

6

1958 Ferrari 412S
$5,610,000—RM Auctions, Monterey, CA, 8/18/06

7

1930 Bentley Speed Six
$5,109,665—Christie's, Le Mans, FR, 7/23/04

8

1964 Shelby Cobra Daytona Coupe
$4,400,000—RM Auctions, Monterey, CA, 8/19/00

9

1935 Duesenberg SJ
$4,455,000—Gooding & Co., Pebble Beach, CA, 8/15/04

10

1953 GM Futurliner
$4,320,000—Barrett-Jackson, Scottsdale, AZ, 1/14/06

BY THE NUMBERS

Sales Results by Vehicle Era

We have divided the collectible automobiles into seven chronological eras. And for each, we offer an analysis by number of cars sold, total sales per year, and average dollar per car sold.

Categories

Antique, Pre-1905

Veteran, 1905–18

Vintage, 1919–30

Post-Vintage, 1931–45

Classic, 1946–64

Post-Classic, 1965–74

Modern, Post-1974

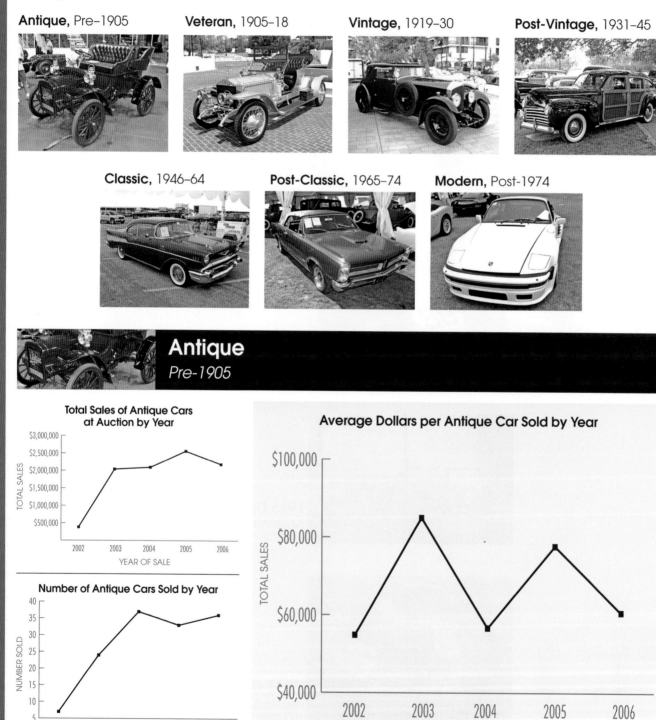

Antique
Pre-1905

Total Sales of Antique Cars at Auction by Year

TOTAL SALES — YEAR OF SALE

Average Dollars per Antique Car Sold by Year

TOTAL SALES — YEAR OF SALE

Number of Antique Cars Sold by Year

NUMBER SOLD — YEAR OF SALE

Veteran
1905–18

Total Sales of Veteran Cars at Auction by Year

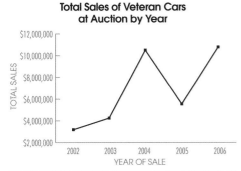

Number of Veteran Cars Sold by Year

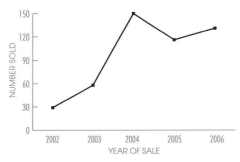

Average Dollars per Veteran Car Sold by Year

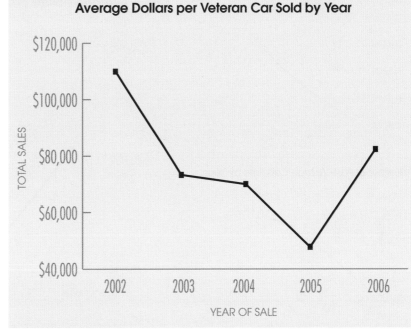

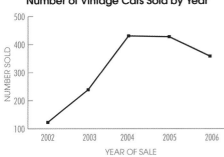

Vintage
1919–30

Total Sales of Vintage Cars at Auction by Year

Number of Vintage Cars Sold by Year

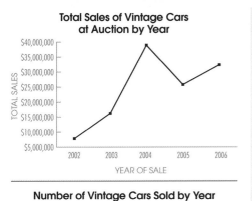

Average Dollars per Vintage Car Sold by Year

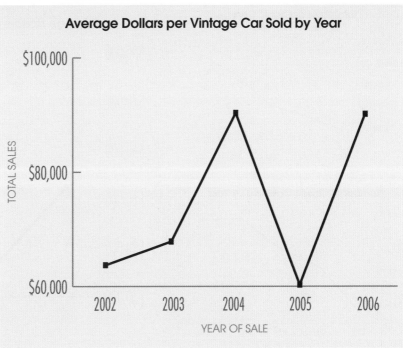

BY THE NUMBERS

BY THE NUMBERS

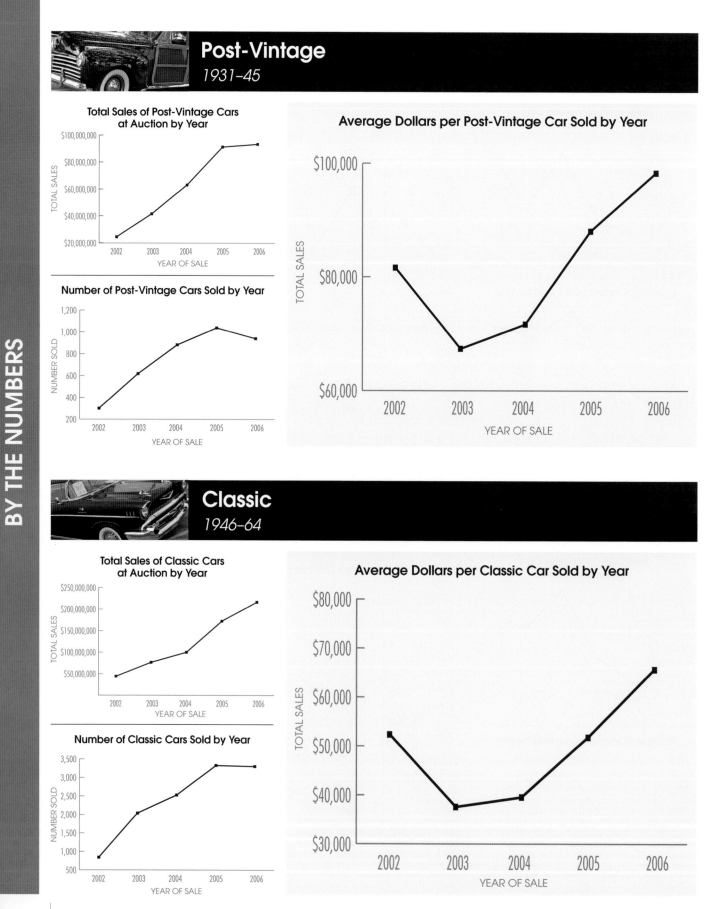

Post-Vintage
1931–45

Total Sales of Post-Vintage Cars at Auction by Year

TOTAL SALES
YEAR OF SALE

Number of Post-Vintage Cars Sold by Year

NUMBER SOLD
YEAR OF SALE

Average Dollars per Post-Vintage Car Sold by Year

TOTAL SALES
YEAR OF SALE

Classic
1946–64

Total Sales of Classic Cars at Auction by Year

TOTAL SALES
YEAR OF SALE

Number of Classic Cars Sold by Year

NUMBER SOLD
YEAR OF SALE

Average Dollars per Classic Car Sold by Year

TOTAL SALES
YEAR OF SALE

Post-Classic
1965–74

Total Sales of Post-Classic Cars at Auction by Year

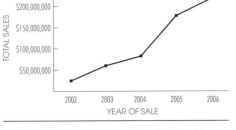

Number of Post-Classic Cars Sold by Year

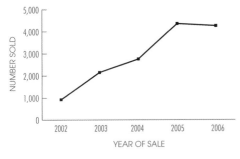

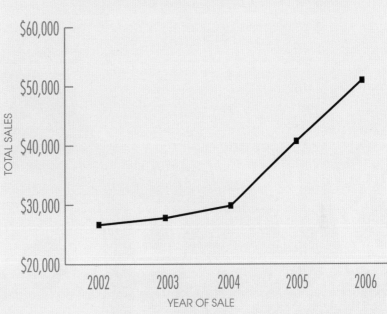

Average Dollars per Post-Classic Car Sold by Year

Modern
Post-1974

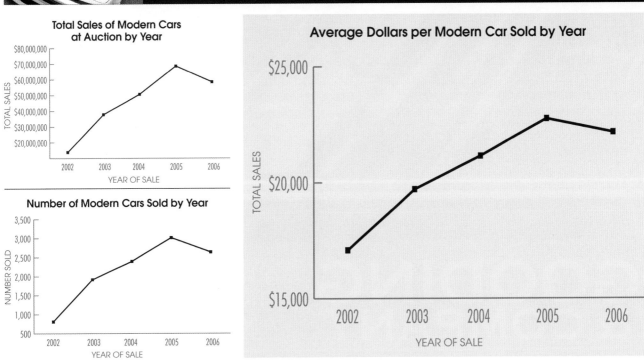

Total Sales of Modern Cars at Auction by Year

Number of Modern Cars Sold by Year

Average Dollars per Modern Car Sold by Year

BY THE NUMBERS

VINTAGE MOTOR CARS IN ARIZONA
January 19, 2007
Arizona Biltmore and Spa
Phoenix, Arizona

THE FLORIDA COLLECTOR CAR AUCTION
February 9-11, 2007
Greater Fort Lauderdale - Broward County Convention Center
Fort Lauderdale, Florida

VINTAGE MOTOR CARS AT AMELIA ISLAND
March 10, 2007
The Ritz Carlton
Amelia Island, Florida

TORONTO INTERNATIONAL SPRING CLASSIC CAR AUCTION
April 13-15, 2007
International Centre
Mississauga, Ontario

THE FERRARI AUCTION, LEGGENDA E PASSIONE
May 20, 2007
Ferrari Spa
Maranello, Italy

VINTAGE MOTOR CARS AT MEADOW BROOK HALL
August 4, 2007
Meadow Brook Hall
Rochester, Michigan

MONTEREY SPORTS & CLASSIC CAR AUCTION
August 17-18, 2007
Portola Plaza Hotel and the Monterey Conference Center
Monterey, California

TORONTO INTERNATIONAL FALL CLASSIC CAR AUCTION
October, 2007
International Centre
Mississauga, Ontario

SWIGART COLLECTION
October, 2007
Hershey, Pennsylvania
Over 60 outstanding barn find motor cars offered at auction for the first time.

WHEN YOU THINK SILVER...
A LOT COMES TO MIND

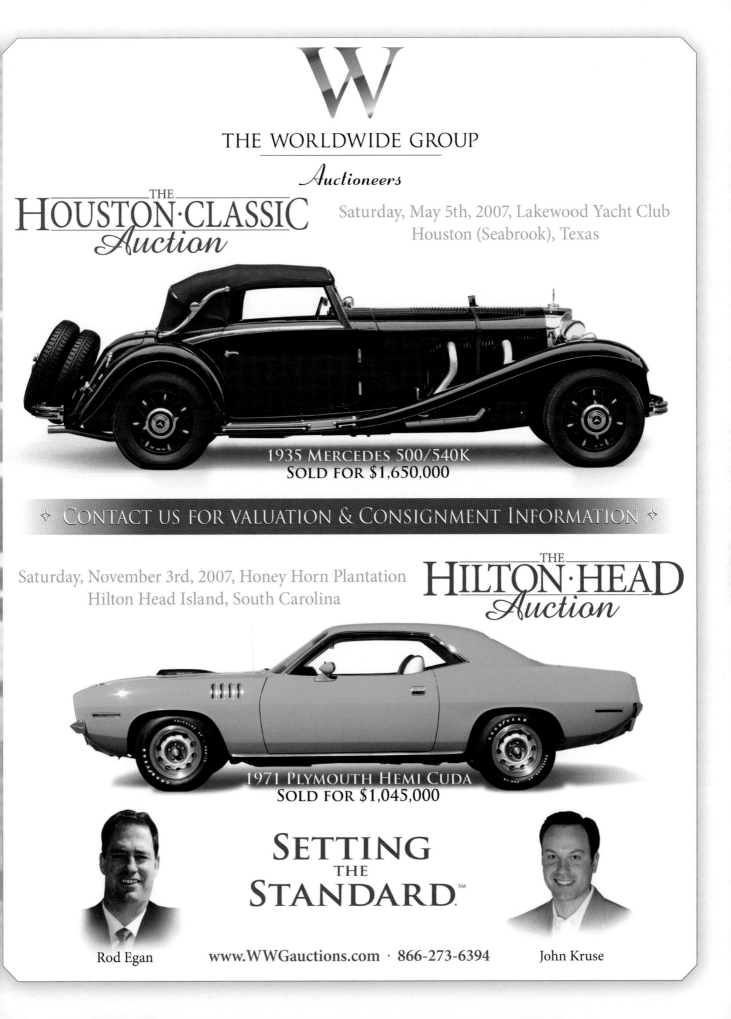

Best Bets & Worst

This section of *Keith Martin's Guide to Car Collecting* is straightforward. We've got experts from Sports Car Market who are simply telling you, straight out with no beating around the bush, exactly which cars are good buys and which ones are not.

You'll find everything from the Five Best Ferraris Over $1m to Nine Muscle Car Sleepers. From Bargain Exotics to Solid English Roadsters. You'll also find thoughtful advice on how to go about building a collection, and why buying something because "it's red and I saw one like it on TV" may not be the way out want to fill your garage.

If you're in the mood to purchase a collector car, this is the one section of the book you simply have to read, as it will help you narrow your choices down from a bewildering array of marques to just a handful, thoughtfully picked and presented.—*Keith Martin*

Why Buy Collector Cars?

You can be fascinated by the sight, sounds, and smell of a particular car

by Donald Osborne

The reasons people become collectors of anything should be obvious. An enthusiasm, born of curiosity, leads to desire and acquisition. Whether it's vintage watches, rare books, baseball memorabilia, cut glass, or beanie babies, it is passion that drives the collecting. It's the same for collector cars.

There's an axiom in the hobby which holds that interest in cars and sometimes the prices they bring is based on a rolling curve. As financially secure adults, people seek those cars they coveted as impressionable teenagers but couldn't afford. So the group that grew up during the Depression, riding bicycles while seeing photos and film of Hollywood stars and wealthy industrialists driving Duesenbergs and Packards, made those cars the object of their affection in the 1960s. Kids who watched Armstrong walk on the moon in that same decade are the ones who are now making Detroit's muscle cars the top of the market today.

Exceptions exist of course—there are certainly not many alive today who were teens when what we today call "brass-era" cars first hit the primitive roads in the early years of the 20th century. Yet today these cars are enjoying a much-deserved revival of interest. Why? Because of the basics of collecting—there are people today who see them as a remarkable expression of mechanical invention, ingenuity, and craftsmanship in steel, wood, brass, and leather. They are machines as art, and it doesn't matter that these collectors never knew them as new cars.

The cars people collect should be a reflection of who they are and what they love. Car collecting is sensuous. You can be fascinated by the sight of a car, by the sound of the engine's pull from idle to redline, by running your hand along a well-shaped fender, or by smelling hot oil, warm brakes, and a well-worn leather interior. It can be an incredibly stimulating experience.

There are also some people for whom the restoration process is the thrill. Finding a derelict car and using your own sweat and effort to return it to life is the most important thing for these folks. In fact, once the car is done, they will more

Osborne with his Crosley (l) and Lancia

often than not sell it, ready to attack their next project. For others, it's all about using their collector car. Whether it's in a national concours d'elegance, local "show-n-shine," or just parked in a lot at the local drive-in, polishing their pride and joy and showing it off to as many people as possible is why they collect.

Some couldn't imagine sitting next to their car on a lawn chair, but would rather be sitting behind the wheel. Vintage rallies, tours, and racing are where these collectors play. They will choose their cars based on the rules of the series or events they most want to run so they can have as much fun as possible.

While some people do collect cars for investment, it should never be the overriding factor in choosing a car. Unless you are very experienced in buying and selling cars, it can be difficult to predict what cars will appreciate most quickly, especially those not at the very top end of the market. It is also important to consider the costs of maintenance, repair, insurance, and storage when thinking about the possible financial return on a collector car. It's much better to buy a car you love, enjoy it in the way you like best, maintain it well, and take your profit in pleasure.◆

Four Great Collector Cars Under $25k

A vintage engine will likely show some signs of oil leakage—but not in the Exxon Valdez range

by Donald Osborne

Multi-million dollar "Pebble Beach" restorations, race cars with Mille Miglia provenance, ex-Reggie Jackson muscle cars—there are plenty of ways to blow your wad if you're a super-rich collector. But what about the regular guy? Yes, you too can find something to put in your garage other than a lawn mower and all those cases of California Cabernet on which you got a great deal at Costco.

There are terrific cars in every price bracket, including many under $25,000. Some have a reasonable chance of appreciating, a few are even rare, and plenty can be more fun to own and drive than cars that cost ten times as much.

One of the most important things to consider when buying a collector car, regardless of price, is how it will be used. There's no point in "saving money" by purchasing a car that doesn't meet your needs or will present such a burden of ownership that the experience turns sour. If you stretch your budget to buy a car that has high maintenance costs, you may not be able to afford to own it. Keep in mind too, that someone is going to need to service the vehicle; get acquainted with a local mechanic before you buy a car that no one in your area can or will work on.

What follows is a list of five popular cars that are all fun to drive, offer few challenges in acquiring parts or service, and are relatively easy to sell when you want to "move up" in the collector car chain.

1966–69 Alfa Duetto, $15,000–$20,000

The Duetto debuted in the U.S. in 1967, with a radical "round tail" rear end that not everyone appreciated at first. Alfa heard the criticism and in 1970 the Spider (as it had since been rechristened) got a more conventional squared-off "Kamm tail." This change of heart means that 1966–1969 models were forever set apart from the many Spiders that followed through the end of production in 1993.

1966 Alfa Duetto

Immortalized in "The Graduate," the Duetto is what many people imagine when you say "Italian sports car," and the reality lives up to the hype. It is great fun to drive, with a free-revving 1,600-cc DOHC four and a slick five-speed transmission. The 1969 model (there was no 1968 U.S. model) received a bigger, 1,779-cc engine with a troublesome fuel injection system, making the 1967 model year the more desirable.

The biggest challenge to buying an old Alfa is a period of deferred maintenance that many went through when they were just cheap used cars. A weak second-gear synchro and head gasket are the chief areas of concern. Any sort of service history is a great bonus, although mechanicals in these cars tend to be robust and the cost of rebuilding an engine, which maxes out at around $4,000, is comparatively low compared to other Italian exotics.

The body, however, needs to be carefully maintained, as old Alfas rust with a vengeance. In addition, the pointed ends that make the car look so great tend to lose out in encounters with the "park by touch" crowd, and inevitably many hoods and trunk lids will have been repaired. Look carefully for a little

1965 MGB GT

1965 Ford Mustang

raised ridge above the center of the grill; if it's not there, the car has been hit and ineptly repaired.

Alfa Spiders are as common as roaches, but the round-tail Duetto is a true classic, one of Alfa Romeo and Pininfarina's greatest accomplishments.

Pros: Sharp-edged, dramatic design; the top goes down; responsive, free-revving engine; slick transmission; great club support; easy parts availability.

Cons: Very vulnerable to parking dings and dents; deferred-maintenance issues; rust problems everywhere.

Bottom line: A famous open Italian sports car, a true classic for a very low price.

1965–67 MGB-GT, $7,500–$11,000

Following the successful introduction of the MGB roadster in 1962, a coupe version was planned. The Pininfarina design would share the roadster's front fenders and hood, but have a slightly taller windshield to allow more room inside. Thus, the well-proportioned MGB-GT was born in 1965, with a folding rear seat and a practical hatchback rear door.

The added weight of the roof somewhat compromised acceleration, but this was mitigated by enhanced aerodynamics and improved handling thanks to shifting more of the weight over the rear wheels. With genuine leather seats, wire wheels, and good build quality, the MGB-GT was sort of a poor man's Aston Martin.

Not surprisingly, when looking for a GT, rust is an important consideration. Due to the high quality of the original paint, MGBs usually rust from the inside out, caused by leaks and corrosion on the floors. Check to see that the seam between the front fenders and the footwells is solid, that the doors don't sag when opened, and check the condition of the rear spring hang-

ers. A rust hole in the rocker panels is generally a terminal sign. Dented fenders, doors, and hatches, however, can be replaced with new items quite easily.

The optional overdrive is a real plus. Avoid cars from 1968 on, as the interior suffered from DOT "safety-itis," and the engine began to be smog strangled.

The engine, like that of most English cars, will likely show some signs of oil leakage—but not in the Exxon Valdez range. The B's 1,789-cc inline four is inexpensive to rebuild, less than $3,000 generally, and parts support for these cars is amazing.

For a true British grand touring experience at a fraction of the cost of a Jaguar, the MGB-GT is a great choice.

Pros: Fun to drive with an elegant style; practical coupe body; great parts availability and club support.

Cons: The top doesn't go down; more expensive to restore than a roadster, but worth less.

Bottom line: A real GT car with a pedigree, wire wheels, leather, and protection from the weather.

1965–66 Ford Mustang Coupe, $15,500–$22,000

The first-generation Mustang was enormously successful, with over 400,000 sold in its first year. Not only did the 'Stang go on to become one of the most beloved nameplates, but it spawned an entire segment, the "pony car."

In today's terms, Mustangs look sportier than they feel, but in period, the Ford Falcon-based sports car was certainly among the most fun-to-drive American cars on the road. Mustangs had vast options lists, allowing for everything from a quasi-economy car with a 120-hp six-cylinder, to a high-performance muscle car with a 271-hp, 289-ci V8, a four-speed manual transmission, and front disc brakes.

The most valuable Mustangs are original factory-built GT models, but as most of the package was available as dealer-installed pieces, it takes original build records to confirm a "real" GT. Cars that have such documentation, as well as convertible V8s, sell for well over $30,000, but the prices of coupes (and some fastbacks) are still hovering below the $25k mark, even with V8s.

If you just want to cruise down to the local ice cream parlor on a Sunday afternoon, a six-cylinder Mustang may suffice, but the V8 is far more desirable, even with the three-speed automatic transmission. Early Mustangs have great style, can be serviced at practically any gas station, and are supported by the hands-down largest network of parts suppliers in the country. These cars are easy to find, inexpensive to own and restore, and are not likely to depreciate.

1973 BMW 2002

There is no more iconic American car than the first-generation Mustang, a perfect first-time collector car.

> **Pros:** Classic design; superb parts availability and ease of service; great club support; tremendous following.
>
> **Cons:** Fairly common; coupes worth considerably less than convertibles; "fake" GT models abound; varying quality of many amateur restorations.
>
> **Bottom Line:** A legend, practically as easy to own and drive as a new car.

1972–74 BMW 2002 tii, $10,500–$16,500

Although it was the homely Isetta bubblecar that saved BMW from almost certain extinction in the 1950s, it was the 2002 that put the automaker back on the map. Fitted with a 100-hp, 2-liter engine (from the 2000 sedan) and independent rear suspension, the two-door 2002 was the antithesis of the American idiom of big, brute power.

It was an instant hit in the U.S. market, causing David E. Davis to write in Car and Driver, "To my way of thinking, the 2002 is one of modern civilization's all-time best ways to get somewhere sitting down."

The ultimate 2002 variant was the Turbo of 1974, which was never officially imported to the U.S. But second in the pecking order is the tii (standing for Touring International Injection), introduced in 1972. The tii boasted higher compression, larger intake valves and brakes, wider wheels, and of course, a Kugelfischer mechanical fuel injection system. It had 25 more horsepower than the standard model, along with a much wider power band.

Mechanically, 2002s are very sturdy, but like most cars of the era the real concern is in the body, which can, and does, rust. The key spots to check are the rear shock towers in the trunk, the spare tire well, the frame supporting the fuel tank, and the rocker panels (which are structural). Parts are readily available through an active network of suppliers and a large club.

A properly set-up 2002 tii provides a very modern driving experience with just enough vintage spirit.

> **Pros:** Great to drive; outstanding original build quality; good parts availability.
>
> **Cons:** Watch out for rust; needs high-octane fuel; '74 and later cars carry big federalized bumpers.
>
> **Bottom Line:** The BMW reputation for performance, without the yuppie image.◆

Nine Bargain Exotics

It is never cheaper to buy a nasty exotic and try to make it nice than it is to buy a nice one

by Rob Sass

The term "bargain exotics" seems like an oxymoron, since there is nothing cheap about these cars in the normal sense of car operative costs. However, the entry fee for a nice example of our picks is generally less than the cost of a loaded new Ford Explorer.

But here's the key: regardless of whether it's a quad-cam V12 under the hood or a pushrod Detroit V8, if you buy a fixer-upper, any of the cars on this list will cost the equivalent of several years of Ivy League tuition to put right. Repeat after me: It is never cheaper to buy a nasty exotic and try to make it nice than it is to buy a nice one.

The key to a happy life with any of these cars is to have your prospective car thoroughly inspected by someone who specializes in the marque and buy the best one you can find.

1967–72 Aston Martin DBS

Aston designed the DBS to take its new four-cam V8. The engine wasn't ready in time for production, so most DBSs made do with the straight-six from the outgoing DB6. Still, in Vantage tune, the DBS is no sloth. While not as famous a James Bond ride as the silver DB5 that 007 drove in "Goldfinger" and "Thunderball," Bond did drive a DBS in the 1969 film "On Her Majesty's Secret Service." Although overshadowed by the earlier DB6 and later V8, the DBS is nonetheless handsome. It makes an

1968 Aston Martin DBS

ideal introduction to the marque, and to the very helpful and well-organized Aston Martin Owners Club. As with any Aston, poorly repaired accident damage and deferred maintenance are the major issues, especially in light of the fact that these expensive-to-maintain cars haven't been worth enough to justify top-flight care, at least on an economic basis. Buying one from an enthusiastic club member is the best bet.

SCM Price Guide: $35,000–$55,000

1968–78 Lamborghini Espada

Penned by Marcello Gandini, whose later efforts included the Countach and Diablo, the Espada was the fastest four-seater around at the time of its introduc-tion. It was named after the small sword used by bullfighters to dispatch the animal after ritually torturing it in the name of sport. There is no truth, though, to the rumor that Espada tool kits contain actual espadas for owners to dispatch themselves after being ritually tortured by their cars. This Lambo has a dramatic presence, but its broad, flat styling either appeals to you or it doesn't. Either way, this is a full four-seater car that goes like stink while making all of the appropriate Italian supercar noises. Aside from a Ferrari 400/412 and the Espada's stable mate, the Jarama, the Espada is the only Italian V12 that can be had for $45,000 or less.

SCM Price Guide: $25,000–$45,000

1971 Lamborghini Espada

1968–76 Jensen Interceptor

The Interceptor is a combination of Italian styling, courtesy of Vignale, British coachwork, and American Chrysler V8 power. This Anglo-Italo-American hybrid is similar in concept to the Aston Martin DBS, but free of the potentially ruinous drivetrain-related repair bills. Most are 2+2 coupes with the controversial fishbowl rear hatch; however, large auctions seem to have at least one of the undeniably handsome '74–'76 convertibles. Most Interceptors come fitted with every possible luxury item, some of which can even be found in working order. With the exception of the grievously rust-prone body panels, most parts are reasonably easy to source; you need look no further than your local NAPA for drivetrain items. Given the recent spike in anything Mopar, the notion of an Interceptor SP with a 440 Six Pack selling in the high teens, compared to a Coronet R/T with the same motor selling in the fifties, is downright absurd. I think there may be an upside for the Interceptor as the last of the cheap Mopar muscle.

SCM Price Guide: coupe $12,000–$20,000; convertible $17,000–$23,000.

1971–73 Maserati Indy

Maserati's answer to the Espada is slightly less roomy and more conventionally styled. With a V8 instead of a

1973 Jensen Interceptor

V12, the Indy is also a slightly less potent performer than the Espada. Nevertheless, it's extremely handsome in person, and Maserati nuts claim that these cars, once properly set up, are quite unfussy for an Italian exotic. Exercise extreme caution in selecting an example, as their values inspire maintenance and repair shortcuts; most four-seater Maseratis don't seem to have been loved by their owners. Like the Ghibli, its two-seat counterpart, the Indy is hideously rust-prone and parts are frighteningly expensive.

SCM Price Guide: $16,000–$24,000

1976–79 Porsche 930

The 911 Turbo stretches the definition of exotic, in that basic service can be had at a Porsche dealer in almost any sizable town, and people drive these cars every day. Also, its styling is not terribly dramatic since, aside from the wide hips and famous whale-tail spoiler, the looks were similar to the "safety" 911 that Porsche introduced in 1974. Drama is, however, evident in the dynamics of

1972 Maserati Indy

these early Turbos. The first ones rode on relatively skinny tires mounted on 15" Fuchs wheels. The added power and wicked turbo lag accentuated the car's diabolical tail-wagging tendencies. Mastering one is an accomplishment. Brakes on the earliest cars, known as "Turbo Carreras," were also not up to the performance of the car. More than

any other car on this list, the Turbo is an icon, and bad to the bone. A word to the wise: Be careful of gray-market cars without proper EPA/DOT paperwork, or with ill-advised "performance" add-ons. Stock really is best here.

SCM Price Guide: $18,000–$23,000

1971–74 Citroën SM

If you subscribe to the definition of "exotic" as being something that is strange or striking in a way that is truly fascinating, this French oddity is the only true exotic on the list. A person who buys a less-than-mechanically-right example may think that "SM" stands for "sadomasochist;" it actually stands for *Systeme Maserati,* as the car shared the same V6 that powered the Maserati Merak. The engine, however, is probably the most mundane aspect of the SM. You want different? How about hydraulics that can raise a tire off of the ground *without a jack,* steering so ultra-quick that a sneeze can cause an unintended lane change, and brakes

1979 Porsche 930

operated by a round, pressure-sensitive button on the floor. Some might argue that these features are just unnecessary complications, but that misses the point, which is simply that SMs are wildly different. Just make sure that the hydraulics, which power virtually everything on the car, have been attended to.

SCM Price Guide: $10,000–$15,000

1971–74 De Tomaso Pantera

The Pantera came to market so underdeveloped that a series of facilities had to be set up around the country to correct production and design flaws. In one legendary incident, Elvis pumped several .38 slugs into his when it let him down. The good news is that 30 years on, most cars have been sorted out and are now capable of driving down the road without overheating on a 60-degree day, spontaneously combusting,

1972 Citroën SM

or provoking an owner into discharging a firearm into it. A 351 Ford Cleveland V8 and a ZF five-speed transaxle sit behind the driver, and the noises coming through the dual ANSA exhausts will leave few people wanting anything

1972 De Tomaso Pantera

more exotic. For those who aspire to a new Ford GT or an original GT40, but come up short in the fundage department, I have one piece of advice: Don't fool around with a GT40 repli-doodad. Buy a Pantera. You'll love it, and you'll have something of real value. Although official Pantera imports stopped in 1974, the car was actually produced for many years after that. Again, beware of gray-market imports without EPA/DOT papers, as well as those with extensive "boy-racer" modifications.

SCM Price Guide: $35,000–$75,000

1976–89 Ferrari 400/412

No list of purported exotics would be complete without the obligatory Ferrari. My feeling is that if you're going to include one, make it a real one with a V12 in front, as God and Enzo intended. The 2+2s always bring up the rear in values, with the 400/412 as the current loss leader. I'm baffled as to the derision these cars take, as there is a lot to like here. With low beltline styling, five-spoke Cromodoras, and the classic Ferrari four-taillight rear treatment, these

1980 Ferrari 400i

are fairly handsome cars in any color other than red or white. There's good headroom, a comfortable driving position, and some room in the rear. On the minus side, automatics outnumber five-speeds, and all are gray-market cars, often with bodged home-boy emission add-ons or non-existent federalization paperwork. Finally, these are tremendously expensive cars to maintain, with little potential for anything other than modest appreciation.

SCM Price Guide: $17,000–$35,000

1966–82 Avanti II

Easily the most practical car of the bunch, Avanti IIs were hand-made cars that were put together much better than the more collectible Studebaker-built cars. Early cars are best, with a Chevy 327 engine that was lighter than the Studebaker 289 lump it replaced. You could have an Avanti II in literally any color combination, which means that there are numerous cars running around that are legacies to their taste-challenged original owners. I personally witnessed, circa 1977, a metallic lime green car with silver leather being completed at the factory while my dad made his more subdued choices. No Avanti can be expected to handle like the European cars on this list, and they are particularly treacherous in the wet. However, their fiberglass bodies will never rust (frames are another story) and parts and service are a breeze. Try to hold out for a '66–'69 with a four-speed. They're rare, but they're out there.

SCM Price Guide: $12,000–$16,000◆

1980 Avanti II

The Best Roads, The Best Events

There's nothing better than a true TSD rally, no modern electronics allowed. Slide rule and Halda Speedpilot fanatics rejoice!

by Kristen Hall-Geisler

(All events listed occur annually. Always check the organizer's website for the most current information.)

Copperstate 1000

No-Frills Iron Bottom Motoring Tour

Location: Begins and ends at The Rose Bowl in Pasadena, CA
Organizers: Ed Pasini and Jack Brown
Email: nfibmt@aol.com
Web: www.bench-racing.com
Dates: April 12–14, 2007
Application deadline: None
Year Founded: 1999
Theme: Drive your own car on public roads for free (a revolutionary concept)
Number of cars accepted: Everyone who shows up. It's a free country
Eligibility: Pre-1976 vehicles: automobiles, trucks, motorcycles
Level of preparation of car: Should not have to be towed to the starting line
Dress code: Clothing-optional
Route: 1,000 miles of Southern California back roads, with two overnights in Paso Robles, CA

Scenery: Ask anyone who has participated, or send an email and ask to see online photos
Gendarme affiliation: Not unless we get caught
Road Rules: Refer to the California Motor Vehicle Code
Included: Not one Gawdamned thing. Make your own room reservations, buy your own food
Cost: Nothing, so long as you don't count the thousands of dollars you will spend getting your crappy old car to run right, and then fixing all the stuff that breaks after the event. But no gearhead ever counts that as a real expense anyway
Major sponsors: None, but we will consider applications as long as they don't offer money
How to get there: Buy a road map. If you can't find it, we can't help you
Intensity Level: We have fun, fun, fun. None of that TSD crap
Quote: "Non Cranius Invertus Rectumus"

Copperstate 1000

Location: Arizona
Organizers: John Leshinski, Patrick Feltes, chairmen
Phone: 602.307.2060
Web: www.mensartscouncil.com
Dates: April 14–18, 2007
Application deadline: December 31, 2006
Year founded: 1990
Number of cars accepted: 60
Eligibility: Pre-1973
Dress code: Business casual
Route: A northerly route this year from Phoenix to the Grand Canyon and Zion National Park, then back
Scenery: Lots of sand and cacti, but snow storms are possible in the mountains
Gendarme affiliation: They're probably not going to bust you for 75 in a 65, but don't try 90
Road rules: Obey all signs, especially in towns
Included: Entry fee, lodging, and all meals
Cost: $4,750
Major sponsors: Bell Lexus, Van Horssen Group, AAA Arizona, Meguiar's, E.D. Marshall Jewelers, U-haul, Car Man's Garage
How to get there: Fly into Phoenix, AZ
Intensity level: No competition, just good-time cruising and great food at the end of the day
Quote: "I've entered rallies all over the country, but I always come back to the Copperstate because of the other participants and how well it's organized"

Tour Auto

Location: France, and possibly neighboring countries
Organizers: Patrick and Sylviane Peter
Phone: glemetayer@peter.fr
Email: info@tourauto.com
Web: www.tourauto.com
Dates: April 23-28, 2007
Application deadline: November 15, 2006
Year founded: 1889, as the Tour de France; current retrospective founded in 1992 by Patrick Peter
Theme: A historic rally race that recreates the spirit and parts of the route of the original
Number of cars accepted: 200
Eligibility: Cars that would have entered the event (and been built) between 1951 and 1973; some exceptions might be made for older cars. The event publishes a list of accepted cars. Any alteration of bodywork or engine makes the car ineligible

Level of preparation of car: For competition section, must be fully race-prepared, present a historic technical passport (HTP), and pass inspection. Driving suits/helmets/competition license required. Regularity section (TSD), car must be licensed and insured and present an FIA or FIVA form
Dress code: Very casual (on extra long days, you'll see participants show up for dinner in their driving suits). Last day dinner and awards ceremony: sport coat and tie or suit
Route: A different route each year. This year the race starts in Paris and ends in Evian, with stops in Vichy, Sarlat, Le Mans, and Albi
Scenery: Historic French secondary roads, race tracks, and hillclimbs
Gendarme affiliation: The French aren't as supportive as the Italians, but they won't write you up unless you really deserve it
Road rules: Respect the rules in towns. Bend them judiciously in the open country
Included: Accommodations and catering, average to good quality
Cost: Approximately $7,000
Major sponsors: Longtime sponsors include Automobiles Classiques, and l'Automobile Club de France
How to get there: Fly into Paris. Organizers will advise on car transport
Intensity Level: There are two sections: Competition and Sport (TSD). The event includes race circuits and special stages (hillclimbs). Competition section has full-bore, flat-out racing. Not for the faint of heart
Quote: "More racing in five days than in a whole season of U.S. competition. This event is all about winning. Organizers are terrific, and the entire field knows that it is there to play hard and go home with a smile"

California Mille Miglia

Location: California
Organizers: Martin Swig, director; Dan Radowicz, administrator
Phone: 415.479.9940
Email: info@californiamille.com
Web: www.californiamille.com
Dates: April 29–May 4, 2007
Application deadline: January 15, 2007
Year founded: 1991
Theme: An American Mille Miglia
Number of cars accepted: 60
Eligibility: Vintage and American cars 1957 and older

Level of preparation of car: No inspection required; must provide proof of vehicle registration and insurance

Dress code: Casual dressy at the opening night dinner, road clothes after that

Route: The route is never the same, but organizers say it will head north this year from San Francisco to Eureka

Scenery: Martin Swig's favorite spot is the undeveloped Lost Coast region, in Northern California near Ferndale

Gendarme affiliation: None. You're on your own

Road Rules: Drive smart. Obey all posted limits, especially in towns. Stupid, unsafe driving will result in getting your number pulled

Included: Accommodations, meals, and the "finest wines"

Cost: $4,800

Major sponsors: Fairmont Hotels and Resorts, Chrysler Corporation

How to get there: Get to San Francisco by car, or fly into one of the Bay Area's three major airports

Intensity level: Not competitive, but participants can drive vigorously, as these are some of the best traffic-free driver's roads in the world. Long straights are perfect for Ferraris and American muscle; the Giuliettas and 356s will catch up on the hill-and-dale twisting coastal sections

Quote: "A tasteful orgy of historic motoring"

Mille Miglia

Location: Italy

Organizers: Giuseppe Lucchini, president; Bruce Male, U.S. rep

Phone: +39.03.028.0036

Email: bruce@myitg.net

Web: www.millemiglia.it

Dates: May 15-19, 2007

Application deadline: Dec. 31, 2006

Year founded: 1927 (original), 1982 (modern recreation)

Theme: A 1,000-mile tour around Italy in historic touring and sports cars

Number of cars accepted: 375

Eligibility: Only actual cars, or types of cars, run in the original Mille Miglia, 1927–1957, preserved or restored to period spec; a few exceptions made for significant cars from that period

Level of preparation of car: Cars must comply with all FIA regulations, and have a FIVA passport and all necessary international documentation, including carnet. Be sure car is properly prepared and sorted before the event

Dress code: Extremely casual except for final awards brunch on last day—sport coat and tie there. For open cars, bring monsoon and snow outfits, as going over the Alps in May can mean driving through snowstorms. Vintage helmets with face shields a must

Route: Roughly a loop starting and ending in Brescia, via Ferrara, Rome, Firenze, and Bologna, with overnight stops in Ferrara, Rome, and Brescia

Scenery: Excellent driving roads and beautiful Italian countryside

Gendarme affiliation: The Italian carabinieri love the Mille Miglia, and will escort you at high speed through traffic. But do something out of the spirit of the event, and they'll pull your license right then

Road rules: Mille Miglia participants own the roads, to the pleasure of the Italians. Be clever, be daring, and always be smart

Included: Accommodation, meals, and entertainment. Note: accommodations are not very good, but you don't go on this event for the rooms

Cost: Approx. $5,250 per vehicle

Major sponsors: Include Mercedes-Benz, Bipop-Carire Bank, Chopard Watches

How to get there: Fly into Brescia, where the race starts and ends

Intensity level: Run as a precision time-check rally, and quite competitive for those who care about that kind of thing. For most of the participants, it's a pleasant but long cruise through the countryside. Cars run in one of three different classes—C, D, or E

Quote: "The world of classic cars come to life, and parading before you at speed"

New England 1000

Location: New England

Organizers: Rich and Jean Taylor

Phone: Vintage Rallies, 800.645.6069

Email: rich@vintagerallies.com

Web: www.vintagerallies.com/newEngland (be sure to capitalize the "E" when entering the URL)

Dates: May 20–25, 2007

Application deadline: May 1, 2007

Year founded: 1993

Theme: A "rally tour" through picturesque New England—a mix of relaxed touring and optional competitive elements—with absolutely everything taken care of along the way. All proceeds go to local charities

Number of cars accepted: 50

Eligibility: 1975 or earlier sports or GT cars; any exotic sports car of any year

Level of preparation of car: Needs to be road-legal and capable of going 1,000 miles

Modena Cento Ore

Dress code: Resort casual for the most part (after all, this is New England)

Route: Not finalized, but entirely within New England

Scenery: Awesome

Gendarme affiliation: None. You're on your own

Road rules: Enjoy yourself within the bounds of reason

Included: All-inclusive at "Grand Luxe" hotels and resorts

Cost: $4,995

Major sponsors: Porsche Cars North America

How to get there: Fly into Burlington, VT.

Intensity level: A mix of competitive and noncompetitive people. The event can be run as a casual tour or as a time-speed-distance rally measured to the second. About two-thirds are relatively serious about the timing

Quote: "The Taylors really know how to take care of you. First-class resorts, excellent meals, wonderful route, fantastic camaraderie. Enjoy the ride"

Modena Cento Ore

Location: Italy

Organizer: Mauro Bompani

Phone: Eventiclassic, +39.0522.849968

Email: info@modenacentooreclassic.it

Web: www.modenacentooreclassic.it

Dates: May or June, 2007

Application deadline: February 2007

Year founded: 2000

Theme: 1,000-km road rally with track events and hillclimbs

Number of cars accepted: About 100

Eligibility: Vintage sports cars. Flexible, but most are 1960s-era

Level of preparation of car: Competition—The car must pass technical inspection at the event and have FIA and FIVA papers. Regularity (TSD)—Must be roadworthy and insured

Dress code: Social events are casual (slacks and open neck shirt) each evening. Sport coat and tie or suit for final awards dinner. Competition events require approved driving suits and helmets, racing harnesses, and current competition licenses

Route: 1,000 kilometers beginning and ending in Modena, with track events at venues such as Mugello, Fiorano, and Misano, and special stages (hillclimbs) through the countryside

Scenery: Italian countryside, and exotic cars on famous racetracks

Gendarme affiliation: The Italian cops like to have you rev your engine as you go by. Be careful and thoughtful through towns

Road Rules: Use the tracks and special stages to be a boy racer, control yourself on the open roads. Organizers will pull your number if you misbehave badly

Included: Accommodations in a double room, hospitality, and meals

Cost: Approx. $4,200 for Competition; approx. $3,800 for Regularity

Major sponsors: Include the Province of Modena.

How to get there: Guglielmo Marconi International Airport in Bologna is probably the best to fly into; event organizers will advise on car transport.

Intensity level: Competitive. Cars run in several different classes, with track events and special "time stages" all part of the scoring

Quote: "Castles to the left, race tracks to the right, GT40s, GTOs, and Lola T70s running on the street, and going at it hammers and tongs on the track. Top it all off with predictably terrific food and wine. What's not to like?"

Monte Shelton Northwest Classic

Location: Portland, OR

Organizer: Jim Gunter

Phone: Jim Gunter, 503.698.8090 or 503.382.4503

Email: nwrally@comcast.net

Web: www.alfaclub.org/msnwc.htm

Dates: August, 2007

Application deadline: May 1, 2007

Year founded: 1988

Theme: "A true TSD rally for vintage cars"

Number of cars accepted: around 80

Eligibility: pre-1974 ("pre-catalyst") sports-type vehicles

Level of preparation of car: Vintage sports cars in good running shape; no projects or conversions. Vehicles must pass an inspection for safety and reliability

Dress code: Casual from start to finish (after all, this is the Pacific Northwest)

Route: Varies, but explores great driving roads throughout Oregon and Washington

Scenery: Challenging roads through both lush and rugged terrain

Gendarme affiliation: None. Bring a radar detector. Locals enjoy using cell phones to call police to report, "them sporty

car types are at it again"

Road rules: Stealth is best. State troopers are few and far between outside cities

Included: Meals for two; apparel; dash plaque; participants pay for own accommodations at hotels reserved by organizers

Cost: $550

Major sponsors: Monte Shelton Motors, Alfa Romeo Owners of Oregon

How to get there: Fly into Portland International Airport.

Intensity level: About ten teams each year really care about winning. Nine of them end up disappointed. The other 65 view the event as a pleasant tour and have a great time

Quote: "The event is a true TSD rally, with no modern electronics allowed. Slide rule and Halda Speedpilot fanatics rejoice! The route allows the opportunity to exercise your classic car, in the manner it was built for, on Oregon and Washington's finest back roads"

Colorado Grand

Location: Vail, CO

Organizer: Steve Meyer, chairman

Contact: Leslie Mangan, 720.733.6776

Email: tcg@themeyerco.com

Web: www.coloradogrand.org

Dates: Late September, 2007

Application deadline: May 1, 2007

Year founded: 1989, by Robert Sutherland

Theme: A friendly, informal event geared toward vintage racers and sports cars, with proceeds going to charity

Number of cars accepted: 75

Eligibility: Sports and racing cars of distinction built prior to 1961

Level of preparation of car: No vehicle inspection or specific driver equipment required. All driving takes place during daylight

Dress code: Sport coats without ties opening night; absolutely casual otherwise

Route: Start and finish in Vail

Scenery: Rocky Mountain scenery, mostly first-class resort properties that are easy to enjoy in the off-season

Gendarme affiliation: Colorado Highway Patrol provides officers on motorcycles (the "Motors") to escort the participants during select, carefully chosen, high-speed test opportunities

Road rules: Pass a Motor, Go Directly to Jail

Included: Accommodation at luxury resort properties and all meals

Cost: About $4,500 per car
Major sponsors: Girard-Perregaux, Mercedes-Benz Classic Center U.S.A., Premier Financial Services, Hagerty Collector Car Insurance
How to get there: Fly into Denver International Airport, then rent a car, or take a shuttle to Vail
Intensity level: A non-competitive event meant for drivers to enjoy their cars and the company of others. The majority of entrants have a fairly significant racing history
Quote: "The most select group of important cars at any U.S. event"

The Double 500

Location: Sausalito, CA, start and finish
Organizers: Martin Swig, Jay Lamm
Phone: 415.479.9950
Web: www.californiamille.com
Email: info@californiamille.com
Dates: September 29–30, 2007

Application Deadline: September 1, 2007
Year Founded: 1998
Theme: 500 km in a $500 car; wacky car decorations earn prizes at the end
Number of cars: Unlimited
Eligibility: $500 purchase price for car
Level of prep: Owner's discretion
Dress code: Dress appropriately for your car, penalty points if your outfit costs more than your car did
Route: 250 km north, then 250 km back the next day
Scenery: Northern California's best
Gendarme affiliation: None
Rules: Try to observe them. Get up to the speed limit if you can!
Cost: $50
Major sponsors: None yet
How to get there: Consult your map
Intensity level: Low, except for mechanical issues
Quote: From last year's Double 500, "I'll give you the car if you drive us to the nearest car rental"◆

Colorado Grand

Buying Your First Collector Car

Think carefully about what kind of car is really best for you and you'll be better prepared to find a good one

by Jim Schrager

Remember your first date? Buying your first collector car can be just as intimidating—and turn out just as poorly—as that initial encounter with the opposite sex. But with a collector car, you have plenty of opportunity to do your homework and make your initial purchase both memorable and successful. There are three basic choices you need to consider to get you started in the right direction: Do you want a project car, a driver, or a museum piece? Figure this out and you'll be ahead of the game as you look for that perfect machine.

Project Cars

Project cars appeal to those of us with lots of time on our hands, plenty of skill at doing odd (or even common) jobs, and the desire to work on a car for long periods of time rather than just get in and head to the malt shop. There are many significant upsides to buying a project car, including the often dramatically lower price you will pay, the intimate knowledge you will have inside and out when you are done restoring it, and that all work will be done exactly to your standards (be they low or high).

The downsides are that you will have to commit to working rather than driving for some unknown—and in most cases, unforseeable—amount of time. Even with a running project car, much will be needed that will require you to take the car off the road for untold months. The big question before settling on a project car is to ask yourself if you have the skills needed to do the work and the discipline to really stay with the project. This last one is vital, as nothing sells more cheaply than a failed project. If you start it, you must either finish it or face long odds to come out even on the financial side.

The long and the short of your first acquisition

Drivers

Take a step up in the collector world from a project car and you have a driver, a car that runs well enough to use and not leave you stranded too often. This category comprises the vast majority of cars you will see for sale, well above project car status, yet still quite far below the concours or museum-quality level.

The great fun here is that you have a car to enjoy and drive, and within reason, you can improve bits and pieces as smaller projects along the way. If the carpets are tatty, or you always wanted those upgraded fancy alloy wheels, a wood steering wheel, or a better radio—all those things are well within reach. Maybe it's going back to the stock carburetor or upgrading to a better distributor? That's fine, as you can do that in a week-end or two and be back on the road where you want to be.

The downside of the driver is that you will not have a real "show car." If you want to do local "show-n-shine" events you may get lucky, but for regional shows, be prepared to be outgunned by those with deeper trophy lust. Even regional car shows in the middle of nowhere can attract some amazingly well-preserved and -restored old cars. If you want to win trophies, then you'll need to step to the next level.

Show Cars

Buying a show car is what many people first dream about when they think of buying their first collector car. It's kind of like dreaming about having your first date with Angelina Jolie. But buying a show car as your first collector car may really be a good idea. Do you really think you'll get anywhere with Angelina if it's your first time at bat?

For starters, if you have a true concours-winning car, don't plan on driving it much. Look around the parking lot of any serious car show—and some not-so-serious ones as well—and you'll see lots of trucks with covered trailers.

Show cars are too special, precious, and clean to drive to the show on their own power. The wildly competitive world of collector cars requires that your car be untouched by common road dirt, have no greasy fingerprints on the steering wheel, or, heaven forbid, show soot in the tailpipe!

You can drive the car, but realize that upon doing so, it will require many hours of cleaning. Most concours folks, even those with the best intentions to drive their cars, give up either on the driving part or the show part, as the punishment of cleaning is just too high a price to pay for using the car.

And I'm not talking about a wash job. True concours cars are as clean underneath as they are on top. The chassis and suspension parts have to be as immaculate as the interior. It's a tall order and not many cars exist at this level of cleanliness.

Why It Matters

You will find that the three different types of cars have three distinctly different owners, and you'll need a special aproach for each type. Those selling a project car will be the easiest to deal with. They will be out of space, out of money, out of time—or all three—and generally will have a realistic price on their machine. In most cases, they will be serious sellers and you will be able to negotiate from a powerful position.

Those with drivers for sale may be a bit tougher. If their car doesn't sell right away, they can continue to use and enjoy it—unlike the project car owner whose car beckons for more time and money each time the owner walks by it. Of course, the owner of a driver may want to move on to other cars and can certainly be a motivated seller. But because his car runs, he simply has more options.

The concours guys are usually the toughest sellers, partly because they are often the wealthiest, partly because they feel their car is very special, and partly because they can afford to wait for that special buyer who will pay their price. They don't really use their car much anyway, and it needs no work, so it's no big deal to let it sit around awhile longer.

Think carefully about what kind of car is really best for you and you'll be better prepared to find a good one. Then point yourself in that direction and have at it.◆

Eight Best Italian Sports Cars for the First-Time Collector

These cars were designed by and for people who wanted every minute behind the wheel to be a passionate experience

by Donald Osborne

Ferrari, Fiat, Maserati, OSCA, Lamborghini, Alfa Romeo. When people think of sports cars they often think Italian. After all, take a red Alfa Romeo Duetto Spider, a sunny day, a pair of wrap-around shades, and even the nebbish Dustin Hoffman looks like Marcello Mastroianni. The reputation Italian cars have for mechanical unreliability and expensive maintenance can argue against one as a choice for a first-time collector. But with the right car and a good mechanic, Italian sports cars can be a reasonable and certainly enjoyable choice.

One of the most important things to consider when buying an older Italian car is its history. Because many became rather inexpensive used cars before they became collectible, maintenance may have been deferred, or the car serviced by a ham-handed, shade-tree mechanic. If one is well serviced by an experienced and knowledgeable technician, it should prove to be as reliable as any car.

Parts should not be a problem for anything on our list. A large and active roster of suppliers (though certainly not in the league of those supplying British cars) supports vintage Alfas, Fiats, and Ferraris. Although smaller, a network of sources also exists to support pre-1975 Lancias as well. As with any collector car, owners clubs are a crucial source of information

about how to keep your Italian on the road.

The cars here are rather different in character, but they all share a uniquely Italian approach to driving, delivering the maximum involvement all the time. Whether being driven at nine-tenths on a track or at one-tenth on a leisurely Saturday evening cruise, the sounds they make, the way they handle, even the way you sit in them all tell you that they were designed by and for people who wanted every minute behind the wheel to be a passionate experience.

1964–66 Alfa Giulia Spider Veloce, $35,000–$45,000

The Giulia was introduced in 1963 as a successor to Alfa's first small sports car, the Giulietta. The differences were not great, but the engine was bumped up to 1,600 cc, making the car a more relaxed driver than its predecessor. "Veloce" denotes a higher state of tune for Alfas of the 1950s and 1960s. Twin-choke Weber carbs, hotter cams and 129 hp (rather than 108 in the Normale) were part of the package.

> **Pros:** Classic shape; great handling; SCCA racing heritage; good creature comforts for a '60s roadster
>
> **Cons:** Rusty floors; cars out of long storage will likely need brake and steering work; watch out for "Abnormales"—Normales with Weber carbs and Veloce badging stuck on
>
> **Bottom Line:** A true thoroughbred Italian sports car for the price of a new Mustang

1971–74 Alfa 1750/2000 Spider, $7,500–$10,500

The successor to the Giulia Spider was the iconic 1600-cc Duetto, or round-tail spider. The revised Kamm "square-tail" spider appeared in 1971 with a larger 1779-cc engine, and was given the more evocative name 1750 to tie it to the legendary Alfa six-cylinder of the 1930s. A 2-liter engine arrived in 1972. It remained in production, continuously evolving (not

1965 Alfa Giulia Spider Veloce

always for the better), until 1993. For a collector, the pre-1975 cars are the ones to have, offering a classic feel, svelte chrome bumpers, and modern drivability and comfort. The bad reputation of their SPICA mechanical fuel injection is mostly a result of ignorant mechanics. Properly set up, it works well.

Pros: Clean lines; handling; sweet, direct-action 5-speed gearbox; superbly engineered top; active club and great parts support

Cons: Rust; values do not support full restorations; weak second-gear synchro; valve jobs good for 45,000 miles; dashes crack easily

Bottom Line: A Pininfarina-designed classic, fun to drive, great exhaust sound, an Italian convertible experience at a reasonable cost

1974 Alfa Spider 2000

1974–79 Ferrari 308 GT4, $20,000–$29,000

If you're willing to ignore the old adage "four seats is two seats too many for a Ferrari," the Bertone-designed GT4 has many charms for the first-timer. They were conceived as "everyday" cars and will typically have higher mileages than most Ferraris. If you can give up the style of the 308 GTB/GTS that followed, Ferrari performance and road holding can be yours for Camry money. The usual cautions about service apply: Be sure it has been serviced regularly, not just with respect to mileage, but also age, as the cam belts have to be replaced every five years, to the tune of $2,500–$5,000.

Pros: Room for small kids or big grocery bags; near everyday usability and dependability; total parts availability

1975 Ferrari 308 GT4

Cons: Origami styling; four seats; parts and maintenance costs high relative to value; production volume (2,826) makes appreciation unlikely

Bottom Line: A great way to enter the Ferrari life at a reasonable price; above all else, buy only with documented history

1999–2004 Ferrari 360 Modena, $125,000–$150,000

When this successor to the 355 was introduced in 1999, it was hailed as a major step forward in the "basic" Ferrari. With its 400-hp engine, available paddle-shift F1 transmission, and clean lines, it was the ideal car to take Ferrari into the 21st century. Lessons were also learned from cars like the Acura NSX; it is agreed the 360 is the least idiosyncratic and easiest-to-live-with car ever to come from Maranello. Offering reasonable luggage space (room for the proverbial golf bag) and comfortable, yet supportive seats, it can be used far more often than you might think.

Pros: Easy to live with; factory support; modern conveniences; looks; performance

Cons: Still depreciating; fairly common; F1 transmission clutches can be short-lived

Bottom Line: Offers the Italian sports car experience with modern comfort and reliability

1969–72 Fiat Dino Spider, $25,000–$35,000

Ferrari's need to homologate a 2-liter V6 engine for Formula 2 competition resulted in two of the most interesting Fiats ever offered. The coupe, designed by Bertone, was attractive, but the Pininfarina-designed Spider was stunning. In spite of the superb engine and design, the car was a tough sell when it was new. Not many people (7,500 coupes and spiders made in six years) wanted to risk their *lire* on low Fiat prestige with high Ferrari running costs. The cars were rushed into production, so early ones had problems with engine reliability and build quality.

A 2.4-liter version was introduced in 1969, when assembly was moved to Ferrari to improve quality. Look for these later cars, as they have more horsepower, a better gearbox, and an independent rear suspension. As with every Ferrari-powered car, as complete a service history as possible will minimize unpleasant surprises.

Pros: Flexible, tuneful Ferrari V6; stunning looks

Cons: Major engine repairs can approach the value of the car; Fiat badge gets no respect; cars were born with rust; crappy Fiat switchgear

Bottom Line: A great buy if you can manage the risk and don't have a bad case of Prancing Horse envy

1967–72 Intermeccanica Italia, Coupe $20,000–$25,000 / Convertible $28,000–$38,000

This is a car in the hybrid tradition: Italian style with American horsepower. The story is convoluted, so suffice it to

1971 Fiat Dino Spider

say that the cars we're talking about here are the fifth iteration of the car, built from 1967–1972 and powered by a Ford 302 V8. Beautifully styled by Franco Scaglione, well-built and powerful, the cars found steady buyers until production was stopped by tightening U.S. emissions and safety standards in 1972.

Pros: Great performance; reliable, inexpensive-to-maintain mechanicals; rarity

Cons: Unobtainable trim; no "heritage"; thin market for resale

Bottom Line: Muscle car performance in a svelte Italian package

1965–76 Lancia Fulvia Coupe, $9,000–$17,000

The Lancia Fulvia was the successor to the Appia, the small-car offering of the innovative Italian firm. Introduced in 1965, the factory-designed coupe featured a narrow-angle, overhead-cam V4 engine, front-wheel drive, and a clean design. Beginning with 1.2 liters, the engine grew through 1.3 to 1.6 liters. The second-series cars, introduced in 1970 following Fiat's takeover of Lancia, added a five-speed gearbox to the mix. There was also a high-performance model called the HF, which formed the basis of the championship-winning Fulvia rally cars of the 1970s. The HF coupes will be at the higher end of the price range, with the

1972 Intermeccanica Italia

Lancia Fulvia Coupe

most expensive being the 1.6-liter HF model. Any Fulvia is a great handling, fun car to drive, and will set you apart from the crowd.

Pros: Superb design; racing history; rarity

Cons: Scarcity; parts availability; small resale market

Bottom Line: The individualist's choice, rewarding to own and to drive

1974 De Tomaso Pantera

1971–74 Pantera, $35,000–$65,000

Another Italo-American hybrid. Commissioned by the Ford Motor Company as a Corvette fighter for its Lincoln-Mercury dealers, the Pantera had all the right ingredients: a slick body designed by Tom Tjaarda for Ghia, the powerful Ford 351 Cleveland engine, and the backing of one of the world's largest automakers. The direct Ford connection lasted from the introduction in 1971 until 1974, though production continued until 1989 under the DeTomaso banner. Panteras offer ample interior room and amenities such as electric windows and air conditioning. Thanks to the tuneability of the high-performance Ford engines, many Panteras have been extensively customized. The best bets for a beginning collector would be one of the early (pre-'75) models, in stock or relatively stock form.

Pros: Creature comforts; performance; usual appeal; ease of service; club support **Cons:** Difficulty in finding stock cars; loud, "street-racer" image

Bottom Line: An Italian alternative to the Corvette◆

Favorite Ferraris Under $100k

A 365 Boxer is a rocketship, going through first, second, and third gears with amazing acceleration and soul-stirring sound

By Michael Sheehan

I get dozens of phone calls and emails from would-be first-time Ferrari buyers, and I always ask them the same questions: What's your "real" budget? Do you have any idea how much to expect for maintenance costs? Have you considered the pros and cons of old versus new? Are you prepared to pony up for the necessary pre-purchase inspection? What's your intended usage?

Most often, $100,000 tends to be the magic number for a first-timer, a sum that won't get you into too much trouble with your spouse but is still enough cash to buy a real Ferrari. What follows is a summary of the current market favorites in this price range, along with some considerations that can help identify which car might be right for you.

1962 Ferrari 250 GTE

problems you will find if you buy a perfect one. Add $25,000 for repairs if you buy one with a few needs.

Best of the '60S

The standard-bearer of the early V12 Ferrari is the 1960–63 250 GTE. Built at a time when a high performance sports car meant user-cruel, it was surprisingly easy to drive. Road & Track, in its August 1962 issue, wrote, "Anyone can drive one and enjoy the experience, the connoisseur who can afford one wouldn't have anything else—this car is (almost) every sports car owner's dream."

With 954 built, the 250 GTE was Ferrari's first high-volume model and a major commercial success. A good driver-quality car will bring at least $75,000 today, up from $50k–$60k two years ago. Be sure to tack on at least $10,000 for the

On to the '70S

While the 365 GTC/4 has its detractors, I feel the C/4 is *the* best buy under $100k. When new, these cars were more expensive than Daytonas, and with only 500 built they are rarer as well.

At $85,000 and climbing for an exceptional example, the C/4 can even be rationalized as "an investment." A major service starts at about $5,000, but the "while-you're-at-its" of new clutches, cam chains, water hoses, a/c reseals, new synchros, suspension bushings, and shock rebuilds can (and will) quickly double or triple that amount. At least the C/4 is simple enough that it can be worked on by anyone who is

1972 Ferrari 365 GTC/4

reasonably familiar with a Weber carburetor—and you don't need a laptop to check anything.

The Mid-'70S to Mid-'80S

First in the line of Ferrari's new mid-engined super-cars was the 365 GT4 BB, produced from 1973–76. With only 387 made, it remains the rarest of the Boxers, and the quickest, thanks to peaky cams and short transmission gearing. A good running 365 Boxer is a rocketship, going through first, second, and third gears with amazing acceleration and the wonderful sound of a very busy flat-12 with lots of carburetors sucking air. A good example can still be found for less than $100,000, but don't hesitate if the right car comes along at a bit more, as this one is soon moving into six-figure territory.

The 512 BB came next, from 1976–81. With only 921 cars produced, carbureted 512s are relatively rare compared to Ferrari's current production numbers. While not as quick as the 365 through the first three gears, the extra 600 cc certainly makes a difference on the top end, making the carbureted 512 the king-of-the-hill fastest of the Boxers. With ever-toughening emissions controls worldwide, Ferrari added fuel injection to the 512, creating the 512 BBi in 1981. Tuned for more low-end and mid-range performance, but a weaker top-end, the injected Boxers are more tractable in around-town driving. Through 1984, a total of 1,007 512 BBis were produced.

With room for the tallest driver, adequate air conditioning, light steering and excellent brakes, all Box-ers are a driver's delight. On the downside, while the balance and handling are good, once the limits are reached the car will swap ends without much warning on an over-exuberant or unwary driver.

The rather bland styling and concerns with certification (Boxers were never sold new in the U.S.) have kept values below those of the more attractive but less refined Daytona. But with Daytonas selling for $225,000-plus, a 512 BB or BBi at $85,000-plus is still a supercar bargain. Bear in mind that an engine-out service on these cars starts at about $6,000, with typical ancillary work easily doubling that amount.

Fewer Cylinders

The 1986–89 328 is relatively light and nimble to drive and beautiful to behold. Plus, it's instantly recognizable as a Ferrari, an important factor for most first-time buyers. A 328

1974 365 GT4 BB

1995 Ferrari F355

will give years of reasonably priced and entertaining driving, but as the final evolution of the 308, it is a 30-year-old design with only adequate performance, braking, and HVAC. Prices range from $35,000 for a high-miler GTB up to $70,000 for a 1989 GTS with ABS, convex wheels, and low mileage. As the last of the V8 models that don't require an engine-out service, $4,000 should pay for your 30,000-mile checkup (as opposed to $7,000-plus for later 348s, F355s, and 360s).

The 348 replaced the 328 in 1989, the first mass-produced Ferrari with a longitudinally-mounted engine and unitized body. Unfortunately, the 348 had more than its share of teething problems, but improved as it evolved, with viable electronics, great a/c and a user-friendly cockpit. When 348 shopping, run fast and far from any car that hints at deferred maintenance. Coupes sell for under $50,000 now, while a great 1995 Spyder can be found for less than $75,000.

The F355 was the first Ferrari to feature a Formula One-inspired shifter, a desirable unit that has proven to be relatively bulletproof and makes the car a great daily driver. F355s have only two major problem areas: faulty exhaust manifolds and valve guides that tend toward rapid wear. For those not used to the world of Ferrari prices, an exhaust manifold for a 355 is $2,500, not including the labor to install it, and an engine-out valve job can run $10,000-plus. Expect to pay $50,000 for a 1995 Berlinetta with over 30,000 miles, while a 1999 Fiorano Spyder with F1 transmission and under 5,000 miles

will take you outside this article's budget at $115k.

Enter the '90S

The 456 GT is a technological marvel and will provide a great ownership experience for the Ferrari buyer with small children and $75,000-plus to spend. With a 48-valve, 4-cam, 5.5-liter V12 putting out 442 hp, the 456 offers staggering performance, blasting through the quarter-mile in 13.4 seconds at 107 mph, and topping out at 186.

The quiet, user-friendly cockpit, luxurious seating, easy-to-read gauges and six-speed shifter make driving a pleasure, while the a/c and heater are more than adequate. While the 456 may lack the soulful exhaust sound of the C/4, its comfortable and quiet cockpit will make a 200-mile drive to your vacation spot a memorable experience, with no need to get out the aspirin or visit your chiropractor.

A major service on a 456 starts at about $5,000, but can go up if you add a new clutch, shocks, etc. These cars have now dropped from their new-in-1995 price of $225,000 to about $75k–$85k.

Overall, $100,000 should be plenty to get you a decent Ferrari, one that is a good first step on the ladder that ends up at $15,000,000 GTOs. If after you own one of the above cars, it turns out the Prancing Horse is not for you, you haven't risked much and can probably get most of your money back. If owning a 250 GTE makes you a 12-cylinder junkie, you've got the whole world of six- and seven-figure cars from Maranello just waiting for you to wave your wallet at them.◆

1999 Ferrari 456

Five Best Ferraris Over $1,000,000

The 512 hit 218 mph in fifth on the 3.5-mile Mulsanne Straight, the fastest piece of racing real estate on the planet

By Michael Sheehan

250 GTO: An investment better than stocks

Before attempting to delineate the best seven-figure Ferraris, I called multiple collectors, dealers, and historians for their feedback, and I must admit to being surprised at how varied the opinions were. Of course, I had my own ideas on the subject, but it was made clear from my conversations that when you've got deep, deep pockets, you've got many, many choices. While there was little overall consensus among those I surveyed, some favorites emerged.

Best Event Car

The 250 Testa Rossa (1956–61) is eligible for literally every event on the planet, from the Roman roadways of the Mille Miglia to the highways of the Colorado Grand to the lawn at Pebble Beach. When vintage-raced, TRs are reasonably competitive, running at the front in Ferrari-only races and near the front in multi-marque competitions.

The 250 TR perfectly captures the look of the late 1950s sports racer with its swoopy lines and sexy pontoon fenders. Even better, TRs are robust, don't break, and parts are available. A TR is a very forgiving car to drive, giving lots of feedback and helping to make a bad driver look good and a good driver look busy.

The price to be in the game? Over $10m.

Best Investment

While my crystal ball was recalled for defects around

250 Testa Rossa: From the track to the concours

mph on the way to a 218 mph top speed. Not for the timid or those with limited racing experience, when set up properly, a 512 is a joy to drive, with massive torque, a power curve that seems to go on forever, and tolerable brakes.

The price to win the Ferrari-Maserati Historic series? Under $2m.

Best First Ferrari Racer

In theory, the 250 Tour de France (1956–59) was available new to anyone with the ability to write a check to the local Ferrari dealer for $12,000. In fact, the best cars with the latest camshafts, pistons, and lightweight parts were reserved for the best-known, most talented, and well-connected drivers. Even so, a mildly tuned TdF was more than adequate to run away from virtually any competitor of its time, including Corvettes, 300SLs, and Jaguar XK 140s.

Nothing has changed in the last five decades, and the 250 TdF is still a great race car that rewards the skillful without punishing those of lesser talents. The soft suspension, skinny tires, live rear axle and light weight give great driver feedback and make for a great event car, race car, and even user-friendly weekend street car.

The price to get started? About $1.5m and up.

Best All-Around Buy

The 1966 275 GTB/C is one of the lesser known Ferraris, often overshadowed by its predecessors, the 250 GT SWB and 250 GTO. As Ferrari's last purpose-built GT racer, the 275 GTB/C is a true race car that is the rightful successor to the GTO. Faster and more technically advanced than the GTO, the 275 GTB/C is also rarer, with only 12 produced versus 36 GTOs.

Ferrari built these cars between the end of the 275 GTB

1991, I still opine that a 250 GTO (1962–64) is a pretty safe investment today. While they have now hit their former 1989 peak prices, these values are still low when you factor in inflation. If stock market and interest rate uncertainties continue, owning a GTO certainly seems prudent compared to owning several million shares of any number of publicly traded companies whose self-serving managers make used-car dealers look like philanthropists.

Ferrari GTO ownership also guarantees you an invitation to almost any event, competition, or concours. It means you are a top player in the world of collector cars, and have the trophy in your garage to prove it. Besides, GTOs rarely sit alone in a one-car garage, with virtually every owner's car serving as the centerpiece of a substantial Ferrari collection.

The price to park one in your garage? Don't expect any change from today's $12–$13m for a no-stories car.

Best Serious Vintage Racer

Okay, I'll admit it, my choice for the ultimate hot ride, combined with the ultimate sound, are the 1970 512 S and the 1971 512 M. They were built to run flat-out for 24 hours at Le Mans, and are very durable and almost never break in today's 30-minute vintage races. With a factory rating of 600 hp and weighing only 1,800 pounds, their performance is staggering.

Before today's chicanes were installed at Le Mans, the 3.5-mile Mulsanne Straight was the fastest piece of racing real estate in the world, and 512 drivers shifted from fourth to fifth at 195

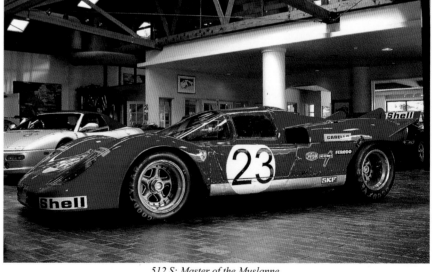

512 S: Master of the Muslanne

250 Tour de France: The $1.5m starter car

production run and the start of the 275 GTB/4 run, all of them fitted with a lightweight frame and body, powered by a three-carb, dry-sump 250 LM engine. The 275's *tipo* 213 engine was mistakenly homologated with three rather than six carbs, so this paperwork blunder was resolved by using three Weber 40 DF13 carburetors that gave over 300 hp at 7,500 rpm.

These were the last competition GT cars designed and built from the ground up by Forghieri and the racing department at Maranello.

The price for this durable vintage racer? A great bang-for-the-buck at about $1.5m.

Where Do We Go from Here?

All of these cars have now reached their 1989 high-water mark, but this is thankfully not because of a rush of speculators with too much money and too short a memory jumping on the bandwagon. Unlike the late 1980s, the Ferrari world of today is not one of Dutch tulip mania.

Vintage Ferraris are being bought by real people, with real money, and for real purposes. As this list shows, eligibility for events creates value, and there is a great deal of money out there willing to step up for personal satisfaction and entertainment. It's taken 15 years, but the Ferrari market is now strong across the board. As long as appreciation continues to be gradual and not led by greed, expect the market to remain strong and stable.◆

275 GTB/C

Ferrari Supercars Through the Ages

The price of dual-purpose excellence ranges from a bargain $250,000 to $3.5 million

By Mike Sheehan

The FXX is the latest Ferrari supercar, and in all ways but one trumps every Ferrari sold to the public before it. It's failing? It is a track-only car, and is not designed to be driven on the street (although you can bet enterprising enthusiasts everywhere will find a way to slap dealer or test ["provo"] plates on theirs for the run to Cavallino). However, once upon a time, the most memorable Ferraris were genuinely dual purpose, designed to be driven on both street and track. Which is where Ferrari's legend of performance all began. Let's examine some of the the key models, starting in 1949.

The 166 MM

As Italy returned to what passed for normalcy after WWII, Enzo Ferrari returned to racing. Because Italy hosted road races such as the Mille Miglia, the Targa Florio, and the Tour de Sicily, Ferrari built a series of dual-purpose cars able to dominate GT races and transport the wealthy in style.

Ferrari's first series-built supercar was the 166 Mille Miglia, introduced in 1949. Victories in the Targa Florio (S/N 0006M), at the Mille Miglia and Le Mans (S/N 0008M), and at the 24 Hours of Spa (S/N 0010M) told the world Ferrari had arrived.

Thirty-two 166 MMs were built. Twenty-six were bodied by Touring as Barchettas and four as Berlinettas. Zagato and Vignale each bodied one car as well. The 166 MM evolved into the 195 and the 212, and several cars were fitted with the larger Lampredi V12 to become the 275 and later 340. Racing success continued through 1952.

Prices start at about $1,500,00 and go up from there.

The 250 LWB "TdF"

As competition increased, Ferrari introduced the 250 LWB with S/N 0503 GT, delivered in April 1955. The car immediately won the GT class in the Tour de Sicily and the Mille Miglia. Shortly after, 250 LWB S/N 0557 won the Tour de France, earning the nickname TdF.

In 1956 Ferrari built only ten cars, with eight bodied by Scaglietti in a style similar to Pinin Farina's 250 and 375 Mille Miglias, and two by Zagato. For 1957 Scaglietti built ten cars with 14 louvers, there were two Zagato-bodied lightweights, and 15 cars with covered-headlights and three louvers. For 1958, 29 covered headlight cars were built, and for 1959, a mere eleven cars were built—nine with open headlights and two with covered headlights.

Prices vary from $1,500,000 for a good 1958 car up to $2,500,000-plus for a 14-louver 1957 TdF with great history.

The 250 SWB

The line between race and road cars widened when Ferrari introduced the 250 SWB in 1959 as a smaller, faster replacement for the 250 LWB.

The new 250 SWB won the Tour de France and GT class at Le Mans. Lightweight competition cars won races all over Europe, and more luxurious, or Lusso versions, defined Ferrari as the supercar for wealthy sporting gentlemen.

Prices range from $1,700,000 for a good steel road car to $3,500,000 and up for a 250 SWB "factory-built hot rod" SEFAC with significant history.

The 365 GTB/4 Daytona

While the 275 GTB and GTB/4 were sought-after road cars, they didn't have the overwhelming successes of their predecessors. The next supercar arrived with the 365 GTB/4 in 1968. Conceived as the ultimate Grand Touring car, the 365 GTB/4 Daytona was, to quote Road & Track, "the best sports car in the world. Or the best GT. Take your choice; it's both." Buyers agreed and bought 1,279 coupes, of which 122 were spyders.

With its abrupt tail, four menacing exhaust pipes, and aggressive "tail up-nose down" stance, the sleek Daytona represents the pinnacle of front-engined exotic car styling. Add 350 hp and a shrieking exhaust, and you have the ultimate '70s supercar. Daytonas dominated FIA GT classes, with class wins at Le Mans and the Tour de France.

The 365 GTB/4 Daytona remains the bargain of the supercar world, with drivers priced at $200,000 and great cars at $275,000.

The 288 GTO

The 288 GTO appeared in the mid-'80s. Aimed at the Group B rally series, the 288 GTO was also the top-of-the-line road car. In street trim, its twin-turbocharged V8 produces a massive 400 hp, with 365 ft-lbs of torque at 3,800 rpm. With 0–60 mph in under five seconds and top speed of 190 mph, it was the world's fastest production car in 1984. Even better, a 288 GTO is a tractable road car, with power windows and air conditioning. Only 272 were built, and it remains the first modern Ferrari supercar with performance beyond the capabilities of most owners.

Prices have been rising, and a great car will cost $450,000.

The F40

Introduced in June 1987, the F40 celebrated 40 years of Ferrari. It was derived from the 288 GTO Evoluzione and combined raw-edged styling with state-of-the-art engine, body, and chassis. Cost was no object—it featured a carbon fiber and Kevlar body with a steel space-frame and a 478-hp, intercooled, twin-turbo V8.

Formula One-sized wheels and a wind tunnel-tested body gave a 201-mph top speed and 0–60 times in the low 4 seconds. The F40 replaced the 288 GTO as fastest production car on the planet, and is equally tractable in town. Announced initially as being low production, 1,311 cars (more than the total number of Daytonas) were eventually built.

Ferrari re-entered GT racing with 19 ultra-high-performance F40 LMs for America's IMSA and Europe's GTC series. Designer Michelotto also built seven F40 GTs for the Italian Supercar Championship and another six F40 LM GTEs for the BPR GT series. The F40 LMs scored five podium finishes in eleven starts in the 1989–90 IMSA GTO Series, with Jean Alesi finishing third in S/N 79890.

F40 GT S/N 80742 won the Italian GT series in 1993, and F40 LM GTEs had four wins and 13 podium finishes in the BPR series. They might have done even better with factory support.

An F40 LM or F40 LM GTE goes out the door for about $750,000. F40s sell for $325,000–$400,000 for a 1992 with low mileage.

1950 Ferrari 166 MM

The F50

"Fifty years of racing, 50 years of winning, 50 years of hard work." With these words Luca di Montezemolo, head of Ferrari, introduced the F50 at the Auto Museum in Geneva, Switzerland, in 1995.

Ferrari announced that 349 F50s would be built, one less than supposed market demand. Only 56 U.S. F50s were built, making it the most exclusive Ferrari of its era.

Thanks to the rigid composite tub, the F50 is a spyder with staggering 200-mph performance. The normally aspirated V12, form-fitting composite seats in Connolly leather, and adjustable pedals make the F50 far more user-friendly than the F40. Only three F50 GTs were built but none ever raced.

A well-documented, low-mileage car will cost about $750,000.

The Enzo

Named after El Commendatore himself, Ferrari's latest bad boy combines Star Wars styling with F1 technology. Only 399 Enzos were sold to favored clients from 2002 to 2004. Thanks to input from the F1 program, the driving experience is a new world.

The carbon fiber tub is driven by a 660-hp, 5,998-cc Tipo L140 V12 engine that produces 650 hp at 7,800 rpm. It rockets the Enzo from 0–60 mph in 3.6 seconds, and top speed is almost 220 mph. Active aerodynamics, launch control, and myriad driver aids make the Enzo the most user-friendly supercar to date. And once again, Ferrari had the fastest production car in the world.

Expect to pay about $1,000,000–$1,300,000 for low-mileage example.

This brings us back to the FXX, which Ferrari introduced in December 2005. It's the ultimate test of "my wallet is bigger than yours." Only 29 were made for people able to spend an additional $1,827,000 over a basic Enzo—this for a car few of them can drive to any fraction of its capabilities.

If you've just retired from an oil company, be ready to write a check for $2,500,000.

The world of Ferrari owners and collectors has really split into two distinct groups. The first collects old cars—Daytona and earlier—and enjoys the limited (by today's standards) performance capabilities and the crude ergonomics.

The second group just wants to get into a supercar, turn the key, and become a track-day Schumacher. Part of the magic of Ferrari is that in this case, you can have the old or new performance any way you want. Just be prepared to write the check.◆

12-Cylinder Ferraris for the First-Timer

Drive the 550 after the reverse gear has bounced around in the transaxle, and the repair bill will climb to $7,500

By Mike Sheehan

Boxer—user-cruel or driver's delight?

The majority of first-time, 12-cylinder Ferrari buyers have $50,000–$100,000 to spend, and while that won't buy you much more than a keyfob for a collectible vintage Ferrari, it's plenty for a modern flat-12 or V12.

Ferraris in this price range are bought for looks, performance, and pride of ownership, not as investments. Here's a summary of later-model favorites, one of which might be just right for you.

The Boxer Still Remains

You've missed the bus for a 365 BB, but the 1976–81 512 BBs are still under $100,000. With only 921 cars produced, carbureted 512s are relatively rare compared to Ferrari's cur-

rent production numbers. Though the 365 trumps it through the first three gears, the 512's larger capacity certainly makes a difference on the top end, making the carbureted 512 the fastest of the Boxers.

To counter tougher emissions, Ferrari added fuel injection to the 512 in 1981, creating the 512 BBi. Tuned for more low-end and mid-range performance, the injected Boxers are more tractable around town. Through 1984, a total of 1,007 512 BBis were produced.

Some would argue that Boxers are user-cruel. I beg to differ. With room for the tallest driver, adequate air conditioning, light steering, and excellent brakes, I find Boxers to be a driver's delight. Just remember that while balance and handling are good, once the limits are reached the car will treat you to unexpected tail swapping. Due to certification issues because they were never sold new in the U.S., and because the styling is fairly bland by Ferrari standards, values have stayed below those of the more attractive but less refined Daytona. However, Daytonas now sell for more than $225,000, so a 512 BB or BBi at $85,000 to $95,000 is a bargain.

Bear in mind that Boxers are now 20 to 30 years old, so they can run up stratospheric repair bills. An engine-out service on these cars starts at about $6,000, with typical ancillary work such as a new multi-plate clutch, water pump, starter and alternator rebuilds, cooling system work, and a full hose replacement doubling that amount.

The good news is that Boxers are fully depreciated and gained about $10,000 to $20,000 in the last year. Further appreciation will cover future maintenance costs, at best. So buy a car with a recent service and it should be a joy for the next five years. When the 30,000-mile service is due, get out your checkbook or wave bye-bye.

Boss Testarossa

The 1986–89 Testarossa and 1992–94 512 TR, in my opinion, offer the biggest bang for the buck in the Ferrari world. Both are big cars, and they have heavy-feeling controls under 15 mph—but who drives a Ferrari under 15 mph? They have acres of torque, effortless performance, and a cruising speed that will put you in jail in all 50 states.

The bold but "Miami Vice" dated styling makes them instantly recognizable—always important to first-time Ferrari buyers—and they are user-friendly, with excellent air-conditioning and heater. A 1986–87 TR with 25,000 miles and all services done can be bought at $50,000 or so, a late 1988–89 with about 10,000–20,000 miles will bring $75,000–$85,000, and a 1992–94 can be found for $100,000 or less. If you're a big guy—over 6'3"—the Testarossa is for you.

The Testarossa flat-twelve is a Boxer engine with four valves, so the same deferred and future maintenance costs apply. With over 7,000 built, Testarossas were a great buy when new and—if maintained—can be a great buy today. They aren't long-term investments, but with exotic performance and looks at a Lexus price, they get my value vote.

Marnellos: Back to the Daytona

At the end of the TR series, Ferrari returned to front-engine technology and subdued styling with the 550 Maranello in 1996. The Maranello was the replacement for the 365

Dated "Miami Vice" styling, but supercar performance

550 Maranello: Engine contents under pressure

GTB/4. Like the Daytona, the 550 Maranello is aggressively styled with its cut-off tail and long-nosed good looks.

Fitted with a 5.5-liter, 48-valve V12 that pushes out 485 hp at 7,000 rpm, the 550 has a top speed of 199 mph and rips through a quarter-mile in 12.6 seconds. A total of 3,600 were built between 1996 and 2002. Today, a U.S.-legal European 1996 or 1997 Maranello is $85,000–$95,000, while mid–mileage 1997 or 1998 U.S. cars can be found for $95,000–$100,000.

As for pitfalls of ownership, early 550s run too much oil pressure and occasionally blow the oil filter apart, creating a major mess. Should the oil filter start to leak as an inattentive owner cruises down the freeway chatting on the cell phone, and he spins the bearings and scores the crank, the next stop is the dealer and a new engine for $75,000. If he stops in time, a rebuild is only $25,000. Preventing the problem is simple: Remove a few spacers in the oil system (one hour's labor), which drops the oil pressure.

The circlip holding reverse gear to the gear cluster sometimes fails on earlier 550s, resulting in major transaxle repair bills. If your 550 pops out of reverse, truck it to your local Ferrari service center and have the transaxle pulled and the circlip and reverse gear replaced at a cost of about $3,500. Drive the car with the transaxle making ominous sounds and, after the reverse gear has bounced around in the transaxle like a ball in a squash court, the repair bill will climb to about $7,500. Clutches, traditionally a weak spot with novice Ferrari drivers, don't seem to be a problem.

In the engines, it's not uncommon to do a compression leak-down check on a low-mileage 550 and find poor ring seating and leaky valve seats. If the compression on a car you are considering is weak, keep looking. Also, cam and front seals tend to start leaking after about 10,000 miles, so most owners skip the 15,000 mile service and simply go to straight to the 30,000-mile service. This includes cam seals, cam belts, tensioner bearings, and more for about $3,500. Check the records.

Life's Too Short to Drive Hondas

Don't think about "Ferrari" and "investment" in this price range. There is no upside to any of these cars, other than to fulfill the dream of Ferrari ownership. But life is too short to drive Hondas—at least on weekends. If you take your family on a Caribbean or skiing vacation and spend $10,000, you don't expect to sell those memories and make a profit, do you?

So enjoy your Ferrari for the pride of ownership, the thrill of seeing it when you open the garage door, and the chance to take your wife or buddy to Sunday brunch in Italian style, savoring the admiring looks you get from those accountant-types in their Camrys.

But remember: Buy the right car, commit to spending $5,000 a year in maintenance, and don't look back. Buy the wrong car, and you'll put your mechanic's kids through college; pre-purchase inspection is a must.◆

Ferrari Movers and Losers

Oddly, the jump in the market for 365 GTB/4 Daytonas and 365 GTC/4s has helped firm up prices of early 456s and 550s

By Michael Sheehan

I n today's Ferrari market, the winners far outnumber the losers. As you might expect, the only cars that are dropping in value are the newer cars like the 612 Scaglietti, 360 Modena, and the 550 Barchetta. Just like a Caddy or Accord, the minute you drive a new Ferrari off the lot, it becomes a used car.

Vintage Ferraris, on the other hand, are going gangbusters right now, with huge jumps in valuation for even such previously lukewarm models as the 365 GTC/4. On the bigger-money end of the spectrum, things are looking even brighter, especially for those cars that are eligible for vintage events and tours.

In fact, we've seen so many Ferrari values double in the last few years that some are asking whether the madness of the late 1980s is back. (Values went through the roof in 1989 before crashing, leaving many buyers stuck with cars that were worth just a fraction of what they paid.) But before we answer that question, let's take a look at which cars are moving the market.

Dropping Fast

The only direction the market for late-model Ferraris is moving is down. While the asking prices for these cars remain high, the selling prices are, of course, much lower. For instance, a six-month-old 612 now sells at $30k–$50k less than its window sticker of about $280,000.

Even a brand new F430 is soon going to be fair game for a hit on the secondary market. They are currently being flipped for a $60k–$70k premium over their just-under-$200,000 window sticker, but as supply increases and the richest and least patient kids on the block have fulfilled their desire, expect this number to drop to sticker and then lower over the next 24 months.

Hitting Bottom

The good news is that time cures all ills, meaning that ten-year-old 456s are now fully depreciated at about $75,000, while a first-year 1997 550 Maranello is also more or less fully depreciated at $110k–$125k. If you can live with a $5,000-plus service bill every year, both models offer state-of-the-art supercar performance and creature comforts for what is, in the Ferrari world, a pretty low price.

The "high volume" models—308s, 328s, Boxers, and Testarossas—are fully depreciated, and have little or no potential for appreciation. There are just too many of these cars for them to matter, and their costs of ownership are not really commensurate with their values.

Going Up

The big jump in the market for 365 GTB/4 Daytonas and 365 GTC/4s helped to firm up prices of the early 456s and 550s. A good Daytona coupe has risen from $115,000 a year ago to $150,000-plus today. A few years ago, a good 365 GTC/4 would struggle to break $50,000, but today the same car will bring $75k.

For example, 365 GTC/4 (S/N 15815) sold for $49,140 at Barrett-Jackson in January 2001. Just months later at the FCA National meet in Dallas it won the preservation award. In April of 2005, I sold it for $72,000.

F40s and F50s have been bumped up a bit, with a good U.S.-model F40 selling in the $325,000-plus range and $375,000 for an exceptionally low-mileage, no-stories example. A Euro F50 will bring about $650,000 and an under-500-mile, U.S.-spec car will bring $750k–$850k.

The standard-bearer "beginner" V12 Ferraris, the 250 GTE and 250 PF coupes, have also appreciated nicely. A good driver-quality 250 GTE should bring $75,000, and a similar 250 PF coupe $100k–$125k today. These are both up about 30% over last year's valuations.

Event Eligibility

The huge run-up in prices for "event friendly" Ferraris can be traced back to 1996, when Jean Sage and Jacques Swaters started the Shell Historic Ferrari Challenge in Europe, creating a factory-sanctioned event that showcased eligible historic Ferraris.

The prices for the best of the best immediately started climbing, with models like the 250 GTO, 250 TR, and 375 MM doubling within four years, re-doubling in the next four years, and then jumping again in 2005. Ultra-wealthy enthusiasts continue to seek out the most prestigious Ferraris in which to be seen on European circuits.

For instance, a 250 GTO (S/N 3909) was sold by Kato in Japan in September 1994 to John Collins of Talacrest in the U.K. for about $2.7m. It was then resold to David Morrison for about $3.5m, and sold again in January 1998 to the Mc-Caw brothers in a package, penciled at about $4.5m. Today this car is worth an easy $10m-plus.

A rising tide does indeed lift all boats, eventually. "Second level" Ferraris—the 250 TDFs, SWBs, and 500 TRCs—have followed along and have made big jumps in the last two years. I sold 500 TRC S/N 0708 MDTR and 857 Monza S/N 0578 for just $1m each in early 2003. Both are worth a one-phone-call $1.5m-plus today.

The third level of vintage Ferraris are those that are less pricey but still eligible for events like the Tour Auto and Tour de Espana, models like the 250 Lusso and 275 GTB. These have doubled and continued to climb even higher in the last year. I sold a short-nose 275 GTB (S/N 7333) for $275,000 less than a year ago; today the same car would make an easy $375,000.

What It All Means

The common denominator to almost all Ferrari sales today is that most cars are going to real end-users who are buying their dreams and plan on keeping their cars. Rarely are cars going from dealer to dealer without a real customer in sight. Today's buyers are far more patient and expect complete market-comparable surveys and evaluations before buying.

While older Ferraris have all gone up in value, in almost every case today's prices are far below the boom of 1989. A 365 GTC/4 is a bargain today at $75,000 compared to the $200,000 the same car would have brought then, just as a Daytona at $150k–$175k today is far cheaper than the $500,000 it would have cost to bring one home in '89.

It's taken 15 years, but the market is finally starting to show some strength across the board. The real question is, how long until outsiders with too much money and too few brains see the appreciation in prices, and decide they want some of this easy booty for themselves? When that happens, and happen it will, buckle your seatbelt and get ready for another wild ride.◆

Ferraris You're Guaranteed To Lose Money On

Practice standing in the corner of your garage tearing up stacks of $100 bills, just to get a sense of the ownership experience

by Michael Sheehan

Ferrari 456M

In my position as a purveyor of vintage exotic automobiles (that's a classy way to say used-car salesman), I find myself answering questions all too often that have the words "Ferrari" and "investment" in the same sentence.

Ferraris should be bought for fun and pleasure, with any possible financial upside as a secondary consideration. If you buy a Ferrari, drive it 10,000 miles and lose $20,000, I would hope that every one of those two-dollar miles was a great one.

Some Ferraris are good financial investments. The 250 GT Lusso has doubled in value, from $125,000 to $250,000 in the past two years, and F40s have gone from a low of $225,000 five years ago to a current $300,000-plus, which sure beats the stock market.

But most Ferraris are just used cars with a great exhaust

sound and a horrendous cost of repair. For the few offered here, you might want to practice standing in the corner of your garage tearing up stacks of $100 bills, just to get a sense of what a part of the ownership experience will be like.

At the top of the depreciation list are any of the recent production cars, with the exception of the Enzo. In 2004, a 456M GT or 456M GTA had a window sticker of $240,000. Today they are worth $145,000—even less for an automatic or a model in an off color. They are closely followed by the 575M. MSRP in 2004: $240,000. Value in 2006: $175,000 or less.

The 550 Maranellos are still dropping at the rate of about $15,000 a year, while the 1997 550s are close to fully depreciated.

In 2004, Modena 360 coupes were still sticker-plus items

1966 Ferrari 330 GT 2+2

on the dealer floor. With an MSRP of about $175,000, they still brought a small premium of $5,000–$15,000, but in 2006 these same cars are worth around $150,000.

Modena Spyders commanded a $35,000-plus premium above their $185,000 to $200,000 sticker when, but that was less by the end of 2005. In 2006, a low-miles 2004 Spyder sells in the $200,000 range, particularly becuase Ferrari introduced the 430.

Simply put, if you buy a brand new Ferrari, it will depreciate more in the first year than most people make in twelve months. But that's all part of the joy of having a *Cavallino Rampante* in your garage.

The Fiat-era cars—the flat-12 365 BB, 512 BB and BBi, the V12 365 2+2, 400, 400i and 412, along with the V8 308s, 328s, and Mondials—are fully depreciated. But many of these cars are now studies in deferred maintenance and can quickly garner stratospheric repair bills. All scream for a detailed pre-purchase inspection. Buy the right car, lose $5,000 a year and be happy. Buy the wrong car and put your mechanic's kids through college. There is no upside on any of these cars, save for being fun for the first-time Ferrari buyer.

The pre-Fiat era cars, from the Daytonas back to the 250 2+2s or 250 coupes and Cabriolets, range in value from $45,000 for a four-headlight 330 2+2 to $10 million for a GTO. As a rule of thumb, the higher the market value of the car, the harder it is

to go wrong. That's because the cost of doing a motor, say $35,000, is essentially the same in a nine-figure GTO as it is in a $50,000 250 GTE.

Blow the motor in your GTO, and you can adopt a "What, me worry?" attitude. Puke a rod through the block in your 250 GTE and your best bet is to prowl the junkyards for a 350 Chevy V8.

The worst V12 on the list, financially, is the aforementioned 330 GT. Its four-headlight front end is visually challenged, and values are in the $50,000 range for best-in-the-world examples. You can't buy a "barn find" for $20,000 and come out ahead, nor can you buy a beater that needs paint for $5,000 and end up a winner. In fact, if you buy one that needs a major service for $30,000, you'll still be a loser compared to buying a perfect one.

I also caution staying away from 365 GT 2+2s. Yes, Ferrari fanatics refer to them as elegant cruisers, but in fact they are heavy, almost ponderous cars with a bizarre, twin-alternator electrical system (on U.S. models) and a poorly designed load-leveling rear suspension that is best tossed out and replaced by Gabriel air shocks.

Asking prices are in the $50,000-plus range, so if you're worried about investment, frankly, you'd be much better off spending another $25,000 and getting a decent driver 330 GTC. That's a car that will always have a ready market.

The final car on my "don't go there" list is the 1990–92 348 GTS. The successor to the much-loved 328, it had pathetically bland styling (the ultimate sin in an Italian car) and a host of mechanical problems. Couple that with a $50,000 resale value at best, maintenance that never seems to end, and there's nowhere to go but down if you're thinking of buying one of these.

While some of the top-line pre-Fiat cars have appreciated tremendously over time, the only post-Fiat cars that have appreciated are the 288 GTO, the F40, the F50 and the Enzos, as these cars are very limited-production, top-of-the-line "artcars," The rest are just cars.◆

New Faces, New Tastes

While old-time collectors started with MGs and worked their way up to Ferraris, today's rich guys just start out at the top

by Mike Sheehan

Photos of Ron Tonkin collection courtesy of Ron Tonkin

A garage full of Italians is never a bad thing

Collectors are fetishists who keep like-kind things; stamps, bits of string, samples of different types of barbed wire—or vintage Ferraris. Recently, a new type of supercar collector has emerged who's broadening the boundaries of the hobby.

In the old days, a small Ferrari collection would include like-kind cars, such as a 275 GTS, a 275 GTB, and a 275 GTB/4, as the beginning of a 275 collection. Increase the budget, add a "Customer Cliente" 275 GTB/C, and a third series 1966 275 GTB/C, and you more or less completed the set.

Ferrari collections focused around 1950s, '60s, or early '70s coachbuilt or racing Ferraris, under the theory that Ferrari stopped building "real" Ferraris with the Daytona. Thanks to Fiat's influence in the early 1970s, the 512 BB, Testarossa, 400i, 412i, and V8-engined 308s, 328s, and 348s were often more user-friendly but lacked panache and raw performance, and their desirability faded. Die-hard collectors were often serious engineers—which often made them the best mechanics to work on their own cars.

Wanting to Be One Up

The new breed of younger, newly rich collectors all want to be one up on the next guy. They may not even be "car guys" but have a 288 GTO, an F40, an F50, and an Enzo, and they're interested in super exotica such as a 288 Evoluzione, an F40 LM or LM GTE, a 333 SP, an FXX, a Maserati MC12, or a McLaren F1. While the old-time collectors started with MGs and Jaguars and worked their way up to Ferraris, the new guys just start out at the top and buy whatever's fastest.

All of these supercars offer more raw power than most of the owners can use, so performance becomes subjective. While an Enzo is much faster than an F40, the F40 feels faster because of the sudden punch of the turbos, the wheel spin, and the feeling of running on the edge, thanks to a lack of traction control, active aerodynamics, launch control, and other driver aids standard on the Enzo.

As an example of how user-friendly the latest supercars have become, one of my American clients has an F40, an F50, an Enzo, and anything else he wants. He bought a new M-B SLR McLaren. After driving the 626-hp SLR and the 478-hp F40 back to back, he shipped the F40 to his local dealer because he felt the turbos were not kicking in. The dealer said the F40 was working well, he was just spoiled by the SLR.

The sophistication of new supercars makes Formula One speeds more accessible, and that thrill drives the new collectors. A few make time to compete in top-level GT or single-seater series and learn to drive close to their cars' performance levels. But most are too involved in business for that much focus, so they hire top-level drivers for track events and enjoy racing speeds from the passenger's seat of super exotica such as an F40 LM or a 333 SP.

The New Collectors

There are dozens of new collectors around the world, such as Tony Raftis in Australia, Rusty West in the U.S., Bernhard Dransmann in Germany, or Mehmet Rustu Basaran in Turkey. Virtually none has any interest in 1950s, '60s, or '70s Ferraris.

Raftis is an Australian computer guru who made millions importing IBM equipment. Besides his supercar stable, he can go even faster in his half-dozen WWII fighters.

West founded Market Scan, which allows dealerships to electronically qualify buyers while they're test-driving cars. The company delivered 83% of California lease cars last year—about $6 billion in business. He owns one of every-thing and attends numerous track days.

Dransmann made his fortune in real estate and the family furniture business. He has raced in various pro racing series in Germany, including the World Sports Racing Prototypes, driving a turbocharged Ford Escort in the early to mid-1980s. He owns a 288 GTO, F40, F40 LM, F50, Enzo, and FXX.

Mehmet Basaran is chairman and CEO of Anadolubank in Turkey. He's old money that's generated new money and owns a 288 GTO, F40, F50, Enzo, Superamerica, McLaren F1, Porsche Carrera GT—more than 80 newer supercars in all.

How long until the F50 becomes passé for the new collector?

Driven By Performance

The performance edge has always driven Ferrari collectors, even back to Carl Bross —perhaps the first serious Ferrari collector—who was convinced by Dick Merritt in 1965 that he should snap up old Ferrari race cars. Thanks to family money, Bross owned 340 Mexico S/N 0224AT, 375 MM spyder S/N 0370, 375 Berlinetta S/N 0416, 410 Sport S/N 0598, and multiple other 1950s super exotics. But while Bross had the best collection of significant Ferraris, he rarely used them.

Other early collectors included Norman Silver, Briggs Cunningham, Bill Harrah, and J. B. Nethercutt in the U.S., Pierre Bardinon in France, Anthony Bamford in England (who bought Bross's cars), and Albert Obrist in Switzerland. All these collectors bought old Ferraris because the cars were cheap and plentiful, and virtually all were purchased for less than $5,000—25% of the cost of a middle American home in 1970.

The age of the collection is a moving target. Cunningham, Harrah, Nethercutt, and Bamford were buying last year's, or at most, last decade's model. When I started collecting Ferraris, Comp Daytonas were still charging down the Mulsanne Straight and a 250 GTO was a ten-year-old racer.

My personal introduction to supercars was the 1970 24 Hours of Le Mans, when the 512 and the Porsche 917 were considered lethal weapons for use only by the most qualified drivers; yet in June 2005, at the Ferrari Challenge race at Mont Tremblant, the 360 Challenge cars lapped faster than well-driven 512Ms. That's progress, but the 512M will always be ultra-desirable when 360 Challenge cars are just used cars.

Tastes in cars change just like in other forms of art. While the dinosaurs of my generation think of many of these supercars as "new," everything is relative. In the view of some of today's new-age collectors, the F40 is just an underpowered 16-year-old car, and the 288 GTO is even more hopeless as it hits 22. All this is just proof that the bulge moves through the snake and life goes on, and excitement is where you personally find it.◆

Six Solid Roadsters

Are you looking for a classic sports car to drive to fun places, or for a car to have fun with when you want to drive?

By Gary Anderson

Dear SCM: I'm in the market for a British sports car. I would like to buy a very good, restored weekend driver. I've owned a Triumph TR4 and an MGA, but those were back in my college days. Now I'm just looking for something fun, something that will normally start and run, and something that may have some potential to keep its value.

I've been looking at Sunbeams, but I don't know much about them. I've thought about another Triumph or MGA, but I don't know if that is a good idea. Healeys are probably going to be more money than I want to spend. So I'm looking for suggestions on what model to buy, any special bits of information you could impart, and your thoughts on price and what to stay away from.—*J.P., via email*

I should start by noting that the phrase "a British car that will normally start and run" is considered an oxymoron in some circles.

However, if a British sports car is bought carefully, with advice from someone who knows the marque, then properly fettled by a specialist to make it safe and roadworthy, and after that given regular maintenance, it is certainly capable of dependable long-term use. British cars from the 1950s and 1960s routinely complete coast-to-coast journeys today with few or no problems.

I put your question to a group of my British car friends, who suggested that your choice should meet the following criteria:

1. Your car should be capable of modern highway speeds and be in good enough condition to be rugged and reliable.
2. It should be easy to work on, with repair and maintenance parts readily available.
3. It should have a good regional club network, on which you can rely for advice, technical assistance, and comradeship.
4. Good examples need to be generally available at reasonable prices.

1963 MGB

5. You will probably want to restrict your search to cars built before 1973, so you don't need to worry about smog restrictions in the most restrictive states.

But before you even get this far, there's another question to ask. Bob Kinderlehrer, the former president of my local Triumph club and a long-time owner of a TR3, suggests that you ask yourself whether you are looking for a classic sports car to drive to fun places, or for a car to have fun with when you want to drive. If you're interested in vintage sports car driving for its own sake, for the sheer thrill a classic car can bring when you take it out for a bit of exercise regardless of where you are actually heading, then any of the following British roadsters should fit the bill.

1963–67 MGB

You mention Sunbeams. While they are nice enough cars, there aren't many around, and good examples are difficult to find. Not so for the MGB. These roadsters are everywhere and as such, prices are more than reasonable. Good-to-excellent examples that don't require any major work can be found in most areas for $8,000 to $14,000, and in proper condition, they're almost trouble-free. No wonder a recent classic car

1971 Triumph TR6

1959 Triumph TR3

magazine poll voted the mid-'60s MGB as the best sports car of all time. The most desirable models are the "pull-handle" chrome bumper models from the mid-'60s, with piping-trimmed leather upholstery. While they built them through 1980, from 1968 on they became progressively less interesting due to smog and safety regulations.

1969–74 Triumph TR6

The six-cylinder Triumph, restyled from the TR250 by Karmann, is the most comfortable model of the Triumph line, far more so than the TR4. The clean lines and classic interior make a nice combination. In tests when it was new, magazines declared it the "last of the true sports cars." In terms of cost for condition and performance, the TR6 is probably the best bargain among British sports cars now. Look for one that has been restored to factory specs with relatively few upgrades, as many TR6s were ridden hard and put away wet. Good examples are pretty easy to find at $10,000–$15,000.

1962 MGA

1955–61 Triumph TR3

The TR3 is a sports car for the real purist, with the distinctive quirkiness of styling and handling that set sports cars apart from the herd in the '50s. They're far more interesting than the TR4, with knuckle-dragger low doors, limited weather protection, ox-cart suspension and heavy steering, making this car a true character builder. Still, they're in their element at highway speeds, especially if equipped with overdrive. These cars are treasured by their owners so they don't come on the open market very often, but excellent drivers can be bought for $15,000–$20,000.

1955–62 MGA

The MGA is attractive in an almost Italian way. Though limited in interior space, it is quite comfortable and very easy to work on. MGAs have built up their own strong support group, though they're not as common as Bs. Handling is exceptional, well beyond what would be required by the engine's unexceptional power. However, a well-done B engine swap is perfectly acceptable and makes the car into a great long-distance cruiser. MGAs are really beginning to come into their own and prices are starting to go up into Healey territory. Go for the plain vanilla 1500 or 1600, skipping the rare Deluxe and expensive, finicky Twin-Cam. Good drivers available for $18,000–$25,000.

1964–67 Austin-Healey 3000 Mk III (BJ8) Convertible

Yes, Austin-Healeys have recently been selling for record prices, but don't be deceived by the headlines. While pristine, just-restored cars from two or three top restorers get all the auction attention, there are always a reasonable number of good-looking, solid performers for sale in the club maga-

1967 Austin-Healey 3000 Mk III   *1970 Jaguar XKE*

zines for $30,000–$45,000. This is really everyone's ideal in sports cars, a great long-distance tourer capable of exceeding interstate speed limits for days on end, but still fun on back roads. And the exhaust note is without compare. The purists like the true roadsters with their pup-tent tops and sketchy side curtains, but your significant other will be happier with the convertibles. These were available in the last three years of production and have roll-up windows and more luxurious interiors.

1968–1971 Jaguar E-type SII

The Jaguar E-type (mistakenly called an "XK-E" by our Editor, but as he is now a Corvette owner, his judgment is suspect in any number of ways) is still the "ultimate crumpet-catcher." Sure, you can find examples selling in six digits, but if you want a driver instead of a collectible show piece, they're still affordable, more or less. Skip the numbers-matching trailer queens, and instead look for a good buy in a nice Series II. You'll give up the faired-in headlamps and dainty bumpers, but you'll get a solid 4.2-liter engine with all the

performance you can handle, and the improved cooling system is really a plus. With some patience, a good-looking roadster can be found for $35,000–$50,000.

As general advice, no matter how realistic your dream of finding happiness and recapturing your youth in a British sports car, you should take your time looking. Wait until you find a car that satisfies all your criteria. Don't buy a car with needs just because it seems cheap. Trust me, the emotional heartache and financial heartburn that go into making a bad car good are something you just don't want to go through.

Join the local club for the marque you think you want and get to know as much as you can about what you're looking for. Join a marque-specific chat forum on the Internet and don't be afraid to ask questions that might seem naïve—you'll be surprised at how helpful other enthusiasts will be. Drive as many examples as you can. When you do find a possible candidate, get the expert assistance of a specialist to help you check it out. There are lots of ways these cars can be bad even when they look good, so a no-excuses car is well worth waiting for.◆

Which XK to Buy?

Almost unintentionally, the XK 120 plunged Jaguar into the performance car business on a global scale

by Gary Anderson

1952 Jaguar XK 120 Roadster

The 1948 London Motor Show at Earls Court opened in an England scarred by bombsites and ration cards. The cars it offered were boring pre-war boxes—with six-year waiting lists. Simply put, they were built for an England that didn't exist anymore.

So the elegant Jaguar XK 120 roadster burst onto the scene like a spring breeze. It promised better days and set pulses racing among automobile buyers everywhere.

No matter that the car was just the setting for Jaguar's real jewel, the XK engine. Or that Jaguar expected to build only enough to fill dealers' windows in the United States, so they could bait-and-switch U.S. buyers into British sedans. Never mind that the 120 was uncomfortable and impractical, with a transmission and brakes that nowhere near matched the engine's performance.

None of that mattered. As the gambler said as he continued to play at a crooked roulette table, "It's the only wheel in town."

Almost unintentionally, the XK 120 plunged Jaguar into the performance car business on a global scale and held pride of place for enough years for Jaguar to correct the flaws and develop a full range of body styles.

As a result, today we can choose the original version, the upgraded second model, and an even more comfortable but less sporty third model, all of which can be had in a straight-forward two-seater, a hard top two-plus-two, or a posh convertible coupe.

The terminology used for these three body styles represents one of those strange little cul de sacs of automotive knowledge, used by those who employ their mastery of arcane trivia to one-up the newbies and wannabes. To protect you from those "experts," here is a primer on Jaguar pedantry. Consider it a bluffer's guide.

XK 120: OTS, Dontcha Know?

The confusion begins with what name one should give the original version of the XK 120. The program for the 1948 International Motor Show at Earls Court terms the XK 120 an "Open Two-Seater Super Sports." At the time, and to this day, that body style is often abbreviated OTS.

This model was a roadster in the truest sense, since the top folded down under the cowl behind the seats, and weather protection (such as it was) was supplied by vinyl side curtains clipped to the doors. There was no question that the top and side curtains were intended only as a last resort in the worst of weather, because visibility to the sides and back was almost nonexistent. And if they weren't brand new, the plastic windows were as clouded as a shower door. So every self-respecting OTS owner kept a hooded "car coat" and lap blankets in the boot.

In March 1951, a second body style was introduced, with the cockpit covered by a metal top and roll-up windows in the doors. Sales literature called this model the "Fixed-Head Coupé." In the same literature, the earlier model was now referred to as the "Roadster." If you want to play "gotcha" with the purists in your Jaguar club, insist that the term OTS can only be used to describe XK 120s made before the introduction of the fixed-head, as you adjust your monocle.

In the cockpit, the roadster was spartan, with the fascia and cockpit rails covered with vinyl colored to match the

1957 Jaguar XK140 MC Coupe

dominant upholstery color. In substantial contrast, the fixed-head had a polished wood fascia, matched with wood on the tops of the doors and at the bottom of the windscreen. There were even rudimentary occasional seats in the rear just big enough for two first-graders, or an ex-girlfriend having second thoughts about you.

Jaguar completed the XK 120 model line in 1953 with the introduction of the "Drophead Coupé." This offered the upscale cockpit of the fixed-head coupé with a lined cloth convertible top that echoed the lines of the fixed-head and looked elegant when erected. The top wasn't all that bad looking when folded—if you took the time to install the top boot. Otherwise, it looked like you were packing a mattress.

The XK 140, which replaced the XK 120 in early 1954, offered the same three body styles—roadster, fixed-head coupé, and drophead coupé—as did the XK 150, produced as the last of the XK line from late 1957 through 1961.

Make Your Choice

Of course, once you've got the body style language down, there's the small question of picking the model. The parameters here are pretty simple.

The XK 120 is perfect for the person who believes he or she must suffer to really appreciate classic cars. The steering wheel is too big, too close to the chest and knees for most drivers, and tipped with a scary point aimed directly at your sternum. The footwells are small, the steering less than predictable, the seats offer no lateral support, and the brakes are barely able to stop the powerful car in a reasonable distance. And you can bake a Yorkshire pudding in the footwell on a hot day. But the XK 120 is easily the most beautiful of the three, though the fender skirts and disc wheels of the original model may be an acquired taste.

In nice but not concours condition, a roadster/OTS will set you back $45k–$70k, a drophead coupé $45k–$65k, making the FHC a relative bargain at $28k–$45k. (Of course, if you must have one of the 240 alloy-bodied 120 roadsters, you'll be paying well over $100,000.)

The XK 140 corrected most of the ergonomic and driving flaws of the XK 120, and is quite comfortable and rewarding for both long-distance touring and spirited backroad driving. Unfortunately, the bumpers, though more practical than the tiny bars on the XK 120, are much too heavy for the lithe body.

The values of XK 140s are similar to those of the 120s, with the roadster at $45k–$70k, DHC at $40k–$65k, and FHC at $30k–$40k.

The XK 150 is far and away the best long-distance driver of the bunch, with the most powerful engine matched by excellent four-wheel disc brakes. The wider body finally offers enough room in the cockpit for those of more substantial girth, or what we might today call "fully sized" enthusiasts. Unfortunately, the width also gives the car a look that one respected Jaguar specialist called "podgy," a particularly apt choice of words.

Perhaps because they are somewhat visually challenged, 150s will dent your wallet a little less than the 140s, so if you're looking for a vintage Jaguar experience on a budget, one of these may be the ticket. Figure $35k–$50k for the roadster, ditto for the DHC, and $25k–$35k for the FHC. The high-performance S model, in both 3.4- and 3.8-liter versions, can add up to $30,000 to these numbers.

So, you pay your money and take your choice. Just keep in mind that, as Professor Higgins noted in *My Fair Lady*, the English don't much care what you say (when it comes to collector cars), so long as you pronounce it properly.◆

1958 Jaguar XK 150 DHC

Affordability and Collectibility Meet Here

A 911, if selected carefully, will have every bit as much resale potential as a 356 coupe

By Jim Schrager

1962 Porsche 356B

Twenty thousand bucks doesn't seem to go far today, especially in our hot vintage market. After all, with Healeys at $60,000 and even some MGBs hitting $30,000, how could you expect to buy an obviously superior car (at least in my opinion) for such a small amount? But you can. My picks balance the issues of appreciation potential, maintenance hassle, and ease of purchase. All the choices below offer excellent driving potential, as one of the great secrets of the vintage Porsche world is that these old cars, when you are behind the wheel, don't feel nearly as old as they really are.

The T-6 356B

My choice in a 356 for under $20,000 would be the best 1962–63 B coupe I could find. This model is the final body design for the 356 (the "T-6") and one of the better bargains. Values are quite stable, and a decent #2 car will just make our budget. It won't be perfect, but should have no big flaws, like significant rust, a noisy engine, or a clapped-out interior.

A 356 will provide the maximum "style points" for your money. They are old and rare enough to attract lots of attention, as well as an almost unending supply of smiles and friendly questions. However, 356s do require a reasonable level of mechanical attentiveness. This is not to say they are fussy, as when new they were very reliable and still can be. But many 356s have been bodged over the years, and the result is often a poor running and semi-reliable drivetrain. Unless you are highly knowledgeable, you'll need to find a wrench who knows 356s.

In the plus column for a 356 is one of the largest and most active model-specific clubs anywhere, the Porsche 356 Registry (for which I also write). They maintain a "talk list" that provides instant Internet access to a host of talented 356 folks. Visit their site at www.356registry. org; you don't need a 356 to join the club or the talk list. A good 356 is also an easy car to sell, with many people looking to enjoy its many virtues.

The Early 911s

An early 911 (1965–73) is the other option. These provide a different set of trade-offs from the 356 and considerably widen your choices. For starters, you can still get an open car, the Targa. This is no longer possible in a 356 where a drivable but lousy open 356 starts at about $35,000. In addition, the mechanical sophistication and substantial performance increase of the 911 make this a rather different breed than the charming but old-technology 356.

The early 911 world splits into two factions, the original, short wheelbase cars from 1965 to 1968 and the significantly improved long wheelbase 911s from 1969 to 1973. For a first 911, unless you find a very nice SWB car at an excellent price, I'd advise you to get a LWB. Porsche made numerous improvements in 1969 that make owning a used one a generally lower-cost and much happier event. Not only did the longer wheelbase improve the car's handling, the drivetrain, body and interior were improved in many large and small ways.

You might be able to locate a sunroof coupe for under $20,000, but Targas are much easier to find. You won't have quite the rock-solid integrity of the coupe, but the trade-off for open-air motoring is worth it to many owners. In general, Targas cost about the same as coupes (other than the rare soft-rear window Targas, built mostly on the early short wheelbase cars, which command a premium).

The good news is that any well-sorted 911 is a great car to drive, and most are quite easy to make right. The engineering on the 911 engine and transmission are so far advanced over the 356 (and the 356-engined 912) that 911s can exist as sunny day cars almost forever. On 1969 and later cars, the main mechanical upgrade is Carrera-style chain tensioners. If the car you are looking at has these, there is a good chance the car has had good care.

Values

A 911, if selected carefully, will have every bit as much resale potential as a 356 coupe. But you'll have to move quickly—while 356 coupe values are well established and quite stable, early 911 prices have moved sharply in the last few years, and seem destined to continue upward.

1973 Porsche 911

911 values are quite sensitive to model designation, unlike the 356s, where engine output has just a modest effect. A 911S can be worth twice what a 911T will bring, but most 911S cars will be out of your price range anyway. Don't despair, however, as the 911T or the mid-range 911E are great cars to drive, with their torquey engines and less-fussy specifications. You should find a decent 911T starting at about $15,000, with Es a few thousand more.

Style, Performance, and Options

For style points, the 911 is a much more familiar shape than the 356, although these early 911s have bright trim and quite different details than later cars. A good technician is always helpful for a 911, but the big difference, when compared to a 356, is the smaller chance that the 911 has been hacked together with non-original drivetrain pieces like Chinese-made pistons and cylinder sets, improper crankshafts, and incorrect carbs. The performance envelope of the 911 is a big step up from the 356, although those with both early 911 and 356 cars often report their 356s remain great fun to drive, within their own modest performance window. The 911 provides many more options as to road wheels (painted steel, chrome, Fuchs forged alloys in varying widths, Mahles and ATS cast wheels, just to name the stock offerings), modern radios, sports seats, and so on.

Under $20,000, you'll find a selection of 356 and 911 Porsches that will be fun to drive, reliable, and have good appreciation potential. You'll be entering an area of the Porsche hobby that is very active with plenty of fellow travelers. As far as fun for your dollar, these entry-level vintage Porsches can be one of the real sweet spots of the old-car hobby.◆

Five Porsches to Avoid at Any Cost

924 Turbos are truly one of Porsche's darkest moments, a car to avoid even if you're given one as a gift

By Jim Schrager

Excruciating tuition bills from the school of hard knocks have taught me that, no matter how fond I am of the cars from Stuttgart, some Porsches are best left unbought. Here's a rundown of those you should stay away from, lest you endanger your financial and mental health.

1. A 912 With a Bad Motor

I was recently called in to consult on the purchase of a 1967 912 that was for sale on eBay with a claimed "good" motor that just hadn't run in years. Of course, it was about as far from "good" as you can get; it was locked up solid. I wasn't surprised, as 912s far too often have major engine problems that are unable to be solved by simple tune-ups.

There are always those who have the "perfect" solution to this problem. Among the cars I've recently called on was a 1966 912 with a "funny noise" coming from the engine. It was a rust-free California car painted an incorrect color; the seller was asking $6,000. He was quick to volunteer that new big-bore kits were available for $300 and most any VW mechanic could easily rebuild the motor.

Longtime readers know where I stand on this sort of pseudo hot-rod modification. Not only do these cheapo rebuilds offend my sensibilities as a purist, but they usually result in a poorly performing engine that's impossible to keep in a correct state of tune. The result here is always the same: a largely undesirable

car that doesn't drive like a vintage Porsche should.

When new, 912s were great. They were a real bargain, giving their owners much of the 911 experience at a 35% discount. But today, rebuilding a 912 engine to original standards with no excuses is about an $8,000 affair. When the values for these cars are going to top out at $7,000 for a nice #2, you just don't have any room left to work.

2. A 911 With a Rusty Chassis

I'm not a big fan of 911s with any rust at all. But if it's isolated in the front suspension pan area, it can be repaired for about $2,000 and you can still have a solid car. Rust at the rear of a 911 is a different matter. This is anything but easy to repair—if it can be done at all—and is often the talisman of a chassis that's beyond hope.

While the aficionados will say that Stoddard Porsche (www.stoddard.com) now sells special repair panels for the

Porsche 944

rear chassis, I would still be wary of undertaking such major surgery. If the car is a 911S in good colors with its original MFI engine, it's probably worth doing. Even so, this will be a long and painful journey. Unless you know your stuff, it's best to keep looking.

Lest you not believe me, here's an example of what you can expect. A local Porsche friend bought a 1971 911E, in the great period color of Signal Orange, for the modest sum of $4,800. (And yes, it ran.) There was just one slight problem: The rear end had collapsed. Upon further inspection, it was clear that the rear torsion bar console had rusted through. Checkbook in hand, he started on his quest.

About $8,000 later, he had a $6,000 car on his hands. After he fixed the chassis, the rest of the car also needed work. After more than three tough years of trying to get the rust repair and chassis work correctly completed and the engine rebuilt due to its significant oil leaks, he cut his losses and sold the car for $6,000.

3. A 944 With a Blown Engine

Because 944 owners are often maintenance-averse, it's fairly common to find these cars with blown engines. This usually happens when their rubber-composite timing belts snap, unleashing an ugly cacophony of valves smashing into pistons.

Sure, these cars are dirt-cheap, and you can source another engine or even rebuild the one in the chassis. But resist the urge and buy a better car instead. The expense of getting and installing a new engine far outweighs the ease of simply buying a different 944. I recently saw a decent 1987 944 with good maintenance records

trade hands for $3,000. They are both plentiful and inexpensive enough that a project 944 is only a good idea if you're extremely bored or someone gives you a couple of free cars.

4. A Fakey-Doo 930

It's a Herculean task to sell a stock 930 once you've had your fun with it. Don't make an already tough job even harder by buying one with fake plastic bodywork. These cars just don't appeal to the hardcore Porsche folks, who tend to be more interested in finesse than flash, elegant engineering instead of raw horsepower.

A local dentist called me recently, desperately wanting to buy a 993 Turbo that was complete with Strosek bodywork, the full package that included tiny projector headlights. He was singing the praises of this machine, with its 600 hp and all the "fantastic" (his word) bodywork. At $125,000, he thought it was the bargain of a lifetime.

I took a look at the car and I think the only original panel was the roof. I advised the would-be buyer to put away his checkbook and wait awhile. Sure enough, six months later the car was still for sale, at the radically reduced price of $85,000. I still think that's too much.

My rule on these cars is take the same car in stock configuration and subtract 25% for all the body mods. That means I'd value this one at about $50,000.

5. All 924 Turbos

Turbo 924s don't rust, but that's cold comfort when it's parked at the end of your driveway, immobile. Any 924 is a troubled machine, but when you bolt a slapped-together turbocharger on that agricultural engine, you have a match made for masochists.

The truth is, these cars don't run for long. You may find a beautiful, low-mileage example, but I'll guess it's mostly because none of them racked up too many miles before trouble set in. This model is truly one of Porsche's darkest moments, a car to avoid even if you're given one as a gift.◆

Porsche 930   *924 Turbo*

Leading the Porsche Pack

I'm not sure what to call the Arizona buyers, but with their glorious ignorance of market prices, "enthusiast" doesn't come to mind

By Jim Schrager

1957 Porsche 356A Speedster   *1958 Porsche 356A Coupe*

After our wild ride in Arizona in January, there can be little doubt that these are high times in the Porsche market. Few people remember bigger prices, even including the dramatic and traumatic 1989–90 period. For some models, even vintage accessories have become unavailable, such as chrome horn rings for the 356B/C cars, Recaro Sport Seats for the 1967–73 911 cars, and the previously fairly common Les Leston wood steering wheels.

My favorite bit of nonsense I hear around the bar is that this time it's different because these are enthusiasts buying. Really? If it's an enthusiast who paid $135,000 for a decent but not special 356A Cabriolet, or $48,000 for an average 356B coupe, they have to be the most uninformed enthusiasts I've ever met.

I'm not sure what to call these trend-setters, but because of their glorious ignorance of market prices, something most dyed-in-the-wool collectors are acutely aware of, the term enthusiast doesn't readily come to mind. For sure they've never read a single copy of the 356 Registry Magazine or SCM.

Yet not every special Porsche is going to the moon, and even those moving up are doing so at differing rates. Here are a few bellwether examples in our wild market of 2006.

1956–58 356A Speedsters

No report on the Porsche market can be complete without an update on the 356 icon. These cars are doing well, with really special cars now topping $100,000, but they have slowed

down a bit. Pre-A Speedsters, 1954–56, tend to bring less money due to their more fragile and lower-performance drivetrains and less-than-modern handling.

Speedsters are not rare, with over 4,000 built, so the acceleration of prices speaks of a broad increase in demand. Decent drivers that were $50,000–$60,000 five years ago now can reach $90,000. But the air gets pretty thin for six-figure Speedsters, and such a car needs to be an awfully nice example. We have seen the heady increases of the past few years slowing down in step with the depreciation of the Euro, which appeared to be driving much of the buying power.

1956–59 356A Coupes

These went wild a few years ago and special cars topped $50,000, but they have not continued to accelerate. They are far more numerous than Speedsters, and while original-condition cars can still set records, more common nice examples have tailed off, although prices have not dropped. Call this one sideways.

1973–76 914 2.0 Roadsters

As we have reported, these have been moving up nicely, although from a very low starting point. It takes about $8,000 to buy a very nice car, defined as one without chassis or body rust, with good cosmetics and a decent interior. Subtract about $2,000 if the car has lost its fuel injection. 914s with carbs are

73 Porsche 914 2.0   *1973 Porsche 911T*

far easier to maintain, but rarely run as strong.

The biggest shocker when you drive a good 914 2.0 is how much fun they are. It's not a 911, but they feel light, peppy, and nimble, in the best tradition of the 356 and 912 cars.

1969–73 911T Coupes and Targas

Over the ten years we have been writing about 911T values, our target for a decent car has slowly risen, from about $10,000 to $12,000, and now we set the bar at $15,000, which still buys a "decent" 911T of this vintage. By decent I don't mean a car to drive across the county or a show winner. But I mean a solid used car that you can enjoy with no fatal flaws such as substantial rust, a smoky engine, or a trashed interior.

The bigger price movements have been in the low-mileage, original 911T cars. It was unusual to see one of these sell in the low $20,000s five years ago, but today asking prices can reach $30,000 and even higher. To qualify for this price level they must have proof of low mileage beyond the odometer reading and original carpets, seats, and paint.

1973 Carrera RS (Touring)

These were the first 911s to shoot up into the stratosphere above $100,000, and exceptional cars continue to bring well into six figures, which is quite amazing for a used 911. Although far rarer than a Speedster, with about 1,500 built, these aren't a 904 (with 120 built). Prices have slowed down this year, but have not fallen. This remains a seller's market not driven by the Euro, as most buyers are anxious U.S. enthusiasts.

Carrera GT

This is the highest performance street Porsche ever built. The car has powerful allure—many stars have one, and Jay Leno drove one to a new world record for a street-legal car. The design is breathtakingly beautiful and the finish quality, level of craftsmanship, and ultimate performance would make any 904 owner blush with envy. Yet Porsche had such difficulty selling the planned run of 1,500 that the production target has been lowered to 1,250.

Prices are soft on the exceptional supercar. How can this be, when 1,500 1973 Carrera RS cars were sold new without even trying? We tend to forget that everything, including exotic cars, has a price/volume relationship. The Carrera GT is the first production Porsche to sell at approximately five times the going rate for a standard 911. All earlier special Porsches sold at perhaps double production car prices.

Porsche discovered—as has Ford with the Ford GT—a car priced far above the standard price envelope for your marque makes demand very hard to estimate. If you're curious how strong the effect is, visit www.FordGTprices.com for a lively discussion of the effects of supply and demand on limited-production exotic GT cars.

And in the meantime, don't plan on making a killing with a quick flip on a Carrera GT.◆

1973 Porsche Carrera RS   *Porsche Carrera GT*

Best Bets in Cats and Snakes

Nobody will ever mistake a leaf-spring Cobra for a "kit car" and Tigers cost pennies on the dollar against anything else as interesting

by Colin Comer

CSX3127

As the rumble of Shelby auctions in Arizona and elsewhere fades away, it's time to look again at the Cobra market and include the underdog Sunbeam Tiger. The original CSX2000 leaf-spring 260-ci and 289-ci Cobras have shown enormous strength in the past five years. Prices seemingly vapor-locked in low six-figures are roughly $400,000 now.

With 515 "street" cars produced, these have always been desirable, but nowhere near as exclusive as a 250 GTO. However, few cars have captured the magic of the original wire-wheel, slab-sided Cobra.

Looking for Drivers

While an admittedly crude creation, Shelby managed to combine the automotive equivalent of oil and water. This reason—along with the recent trend of collectors wanting cars they can drive—has sent leaf-spring Cobra prices to their current level.

I love leaf-spring Cobras, and will never be without one. They are usable, beautiful, and dead simple to maintain—all with parts from your local NAPA outlet. But the best part is that nobody will ever mistake a leaf-spring Cobra for a "kit car." I think this contributes to the recent price surge.

Now for the big dog—the romping, stomping, CSX3000 427 Cobras—also known as the coil-spring cars. Always at the top of collectors' lists, they are far scarcer than the leaf-spring cars with just 260 "street" cars produced.

But while values have doubled from $300,000 five years ago to roughly $600,000 today, the 427 cars have not experienced the proportional increase of the earlier cars. A number of factors contribute to this; historically 427s have been twice as much as the leaf-spring cars, and buyers perhaps gravitated to the less-expensive car as an alternative.

While one cannot deny the pure automotive swagger of a 427, it has to contend with being the most replicated car of all time. The sheer number of 427 Cobra replicas—good, bad, and ugly—has weakened the market for original cars.

Shelby himself diluted the number of buyers by offering the new 4000 series Continuation cars, a very accurate replica of the originals. At roughly $100,000 for a Shelby-blessed CSX4000 car, I'm guessing many people opted to go this route even though they could buy the real deal. As an

original 427 Cobra owner, I contend there is no substitute and I'm sure other purists agree.

Shelby's Stepchild

The red-headed stepchild of the Shelby world is unquestionably the Sunbeam Tiger. It was produced by the Rootes Group in England when Ian Garrard hired Carroll Shelby to transform the anemic Sunbeam Alpine into a performance car.

The addition of the 260-ci Ford V8 (similar to the Cobra, but the two-barrel, 164-hp version) made a car worthy of being called "Tiger"—after the 1926 Sunbeam land-speed record holder.

Never intended to be a stark sports car like the Cobra, the Tiger is a highly competent touring car. Fitted with a standard 2.88:1 rear axle ratio and BorgWarner T-10 4-speed, it's a relaxed and capable high-speed machine with better than 125 mph on tap.

Tigers aren't particularly rare, with over 7,000 produced

Comer's Purple People Eater, the ultimate sleeper Shelby

from 1964 to 1967, but they've always had a loyal following. Production was split into three groups, consisting of 3,763 Mk I cars, 2,706 Mk IA cars, and 534 289-ci Mk II cars.

The problems with Tigers are modifications and abuse. Finding a stock Tiger that hasn't rusted out or been cobbled into an unrecognizable form is a challenge.

This makes it difficult to pin down an exact market value for an "SCM Approved" stock Tiger, as few of them change hands. I purchased a fantastic Mk IA example in the late 1990s for $11,000, and a one-owner Mk IA in similar condition in 2000 for $25,000, then a record price. The prevailing market today for a spectacular Mk I car is roughly $30,000 with a similar IA bringing $5,000–$10,000 over that.

The Mk II market is more difficult to peg. I've only seen six Mk II cars sell in the last ten years, and only one was spectacular. OK, I bought it, paying an out-of-the park record price of $59,000 on eBay Motors (item #4625301384).

I saw value in stepping up for a true 100% original, untouched, example of a Mk II—and I have since spent roughly $5,000 doing "might as well" maintenance and detailing. I don't regret it; these cars cost pennies on the dollar against anything else as interesting. I consider a great Tiger a solid buy.

What to Look For

Buy the best Cobra you can find. Thanks to the "Shelby American World Registry," details of every individual car's history are available. Production differences abound, so know what you are buying. Check for worm-and-sector or rack-and-pinion steering, and 260-ci or 289-ci engines. By the way, did you know 100 or so "427" Cobras left the factory with 428 engines?

Read and study the "Registry," and before buying a car join the club and contact Ned Scudder, Cobra Registrar, to ask if any new information is known about a particular car.

Many Cobras led difficult lives, but seem to have more than the average cat. New bodies, new frames—some new cars have been built around little more than a serial number plate. So do your homework.

What might seem insignificant in the red-mist, pre-purchase euphoria can be a huge issue after your check clears. Paying a world-record price may get you teased, but not as much as if you buy a pig in a poke.

Tiger buyers have a more tedious path. Many cars have been cloned using the Alpine shells, and the resulting "Algers" are not always easy to spot. Specific details can help authenticate a real car, beyond VIN tags and data plates. The International Registry of Sunbeam Tigers is available online, as is the Sunbeam Tigers Owners Association (STOA) and their current list of "TAC'ed" (Tiger Authentication Committee) verified cars.

A few hours using Google to track down Tiger details may avoid a red face later. Another resource is the out-of-print "Book of Norman" by Tiger guru Norman Miller. It contains the complete list of original Tiger VINs and production details.

Where Are They Heading?

Since my crystal ball fell off the bookshelf and broke, I look back to predict market trends. Historically, leaf-spring Cobras have traded at about one-half coil-spring Cobra values. Demand for the leaf-spring cars far outstrips supply, leading me to predict great examples will be $500,000 in the near future.

Following this, the 427 cars will be next. Tiger values have been on a steady upswing for some time, as educated buyers seek out great examples. I see no reason that a 20% annual appreciation won't continue.

The bottom line is find the right car, make sure it IS a right car, and buy it because you want it. Use it, enjoy it, and rest easy knowing that truly fine examples offer greater rewards to their owners than mere financial ones.◆

Buying Your First Collectible Muscle Car—The Second Time Around

What you want in your next muscle car is different from what you wanted back in the day

by Dave Kinney

1972 Dodge Dart Demon

For those of us who bought our first muscle car over 20 years ago (oh, hell, let's just admit we're old and it was really 35 years), a little reflection on what drove us then and what drives us now is in order.

We wanted fast. Fast is what a muscle car delivered, in spades. Smoky burnouts? You bet. Low ET's in the quarter mile? Absolutely. Six to eight miles per gallon? Who cares—gas was cheap. And disc brakes were exotic stuff, Polyglas tires were state of the art, and equipment and options were strictly of a go-fast nature. Air conditioning? That was for your mom's car, as were automatic transmissions and power steering. Spoilers, short throw shifters and bulging hoods—now that was more like it.

But that was then, in a world when cars were pretty primitive by today's standards. Just as your daily driver today does not have an 8-track unit installed under the dash, I'll bet what you want in your next muscle car is different from what you wanted back in the day. Face it, we are older, we are wiser, and most likely, we are wider too.

If your pals saw you in an automatic 'Cuda or GTO in

1969 Plymouth Barracuda Formula S

Chances are that doing smoking-tire 360s in your 442 just won't get your wife as excited today as it got your girlfriend back then.

That said, don't rush out and buy just any muscle car, even if you just sold your company and can't get your bulging wallet into your back pocket, even with those "relaxed fit" pants.

Make sure you buy what you really want, not something that was cheap but doesn't scratch your itch—you'll be happier in both the long and the short term. Forget about getting a deal on a clone, as even though they may cost less than the real deal now they will be worth much less later, and may prove a hard sell.

period, the laughter and derision might have been too much too handle. But no such peer pressure is lik ly to rear its ugly head today. Cars with four-speeds are still generally worth more, but a slushbox no longer carries the shame it once did, especially if you plan to drive in any of the traffic routinely found in major metropolitan areas.

Power steering has become something of a necessity, along with radial tires, as parking or low-speed maneuvering can be damn near impossible without it. The third part of the Holy Trinity of options—air conditioning—will make any muscle car more desirable, especially when you're sitting in traffic trying to get out of the parking lot of some car show on a 90-degree day in August.

Keep in mind, too, that you may find the overpowering acceleration of those beasts of the late 1960s a little underwhelming after spending the last decade behind the wheel of a modern, fuel-injected car. Your average V6 Accord can dust most muscle cars of yore—not to mention out-handle them. Of course, you're probably going to drive your new muscle car a bit more gingerly than you did when you were younger, and not just because you're going to pay a lot more for it.

Avoid cars with stories. Pass on ones with serious needs, unless you're the sort who wants to embark on a restoration and then know that you'll have little chance of getting your money back—so be sure to enjoy the restoration process as part of the ownership experience.

Overall, an inspection is the name of the game here. Consider it a kind of automotive pre-nuptial agreement, and those of you who wish you'd gotten one, of either flavor, will know exactly what I mean.

Make sure you budget for the hidden costs of ownership: insurance, maintenance, repairs, etc. But don't be too concerned with the single-digit gas mileage. For the few miles you're likely to drive your toy each year, some things don't change—even at two bucks per gallon, who cares?

And remember, you don't need big bucks to have a muscle car. Yes, it's too bad you traded your 1970 GTX Hemi convertible 4-speed for a Mustang II because you needed better gas mileage, but today there are still a few cars out there with plenty of grunt but that I still consider to be sleepers. Buy one, have some fun, and don't look back.◆

Nine Muscle Car Sleepers

You won't see your twin at every show, and you won't believe the performance of these jokers

By Colin Comer

1970 AMX 360

1972 AMC Javelin AMX

During the past couple of years, muscle car prices have accelerated as fast as the cars themselves. Boomers are flapping paddles (or waving 64-oz tubs of Coors) at six- and sometimes seven-figure amounts when choice pieces of Detroit Iron cross the block.

Rather than telling me (again) about how you'd like to have back the '69 Z/28 you sold for $1,500 in 1980 to finance your wedding reception at the Olive Garden, let's look at where the clever buys are in today's muscle-car market.

You can get style, power, nostalgia, and fun by venturing off the beaten path. These overlooked cars offer great value. They won't get you crowned King of Cruise Night at the local drive-in, but some are better packages than their expensive stablemates. Here are my picks under $40,000.

1970 AMX 360 ($24,000–$28,000)

From dearly departed American Motors, I have a few favorites. The two-seat 1968–70 AMX is finally gaining respect and value. Having the 390-ci 4-speed car with the factory "Go Pack" option puts you at the top of the (admittedly small) AMC pecking order, but lesser models could still be your admission ticket to the muscle-car world.

Early cars also came with 290 and 343 V8s, and in 1970

the new 360 was available. I'll take the 1970 Ram Air 360, with 4-speed, and dealer-installed Sidewinder side pipes. Ram Air was standard for 1970 and the front suspension was much improved. Be warned: the short-wheelbase AMX can be nearly as tricky as an early Porsche 930 Turbo in inexperienced hands. Each AMX has a numbered dash plaque, but in true AMC style, there are gaps in the sequence and cars with duplicate number plates are known to have been built by the factory.

1971–74 Javelin AMX ($18,000–$24,000)

The styling of the bulbous second-generation Javelin AMX continues to grow on me; as an added bonus, there's a back seat for kids, dogs, or spare parts. The optional 401-ci V8 was the ultimate AMC ground-pounder—and was even crammed into Pacer and Gremlin dragsters.

1971 Hornet SC/360 ($15,000–$20,000)

This is my top AMC choice. There were only 794 of these stodgy-looking two-door sedans built, but with a big factory hood scoop, stripe package, and Rally wheels put onto the Hornet, it looks macho. Well, a little macho, anyway. Don't take anything but a correct car with a 4-speed. You won't see

1971 SC/360 Hornet

1967 Buick Skylark GS400

your twin at every show, and the guys you race against at the vintage drags won't believe the performance of these little jokers. Plus, you can pick up parts cars for nothing.

1967 Buick Skylark GS400 ($17,000–$22,000)

This was the first year of the 400-ci engine with semi-wedge heads. It's a legendary torque monster. Contemporary road tests pegged these cars at six seconds for 0–60, not bad even by today's standards. Built on the convertible chassis with a boxed frame, heavy-duty suspension and brakes, and quick steering, this solid Buick ride combines great styling and respectable handling. This is a poor man's Chevelle Z16, for $200,000 less. The 1968–69 GS400 ($20,000–$25,000) is more of the same, with similar performance in a restyled body.

1966–67 Oldsmobile 442 ($20,000–$25,000)

In a similar vein, the 1966–67 Oldsmobile 442 is a great alternative to better-known later versions. A 350-hp, 400-ci

engine lives under the hood, and delivered high-14 second 1/4-mile times when new. Referred to as a "civilized supercar" at the time, it's very capable with a solid feel. Avoid the 1966 two-speed automatic. The 1967 is preferred by the 442 faithful as it had a Turbo 400 three-speed and was gussied up with a washboard hood and other details to separate it from a base Cutlass. Pick of the litter would be a 360-hp, Tri-Power '66, but you won't find a real one (clones, as with most muscle cars, are only a parts catalog away) in this price range unless you are really lucky.

1967 Plymouth Belvedere GTX/Dodge Coronet R/T ($30,000–$35,000)

Over at Camp Mopar, top picks are the 1967 Plymouth Belvedere GTX or her plain-Jane sister, the Dodge Coronet R/T. With a standard 375-hp 440-ci engine, great styling, more scoops than a box of Raisin Bran, competent Mopar torsion bar suspension, and non-offensive (i.e. bland) styling, both of these cars offer tremendous power and, when properly set up, great road manners.

1966 Oldsmobile Cutlass 442

1967 Plymouth Belvedere GTX

1969 Plymouth Barracuda Formula S

1969 Dodge Dart

1968–69 Dodge Dart GTS
($22,000–$28,000)

Next choice is the 1968–69 Dodge Dart GTS, the Nova Fighter. With clean styling penned by Elwood Engel, this is a potent 3,000-pound package with bulletproof 340-ci small block or available 383-ci big block motivation (but you'll have to add an extra $10,000 to the numbers above). As a car that can actually be fun to drive, I recommend a good 340 GTS with a 4-speed. In contrast, the 383- and 440-powered Darts are nose-heavy and braking-impaired (there was no room for power brakes in the crowded engine compartment).

1967–69 Plymouth Barracuda Formula S
($20,000–$25,000)

Plymouth smoothed out the Barracuda nicely for the second generation, and the 1967–69 Plymouth Barracuda Formula S is one of the most attractive muscle cars. Engine choices include 273-ci, 340-ci, and 383-ci V8s, and the same comments apply as with the Dart GTS. Both fastback and coupe body styles were available for Plymouth's fast fish. But a Barracuda isn't a 'Cuda; that was a late-1969 option package introduced with the 440-ci-equipped Barracuda and the high-performance package on the new-body 1970–74 Barracudas.

1963–65 Ford Falcon Sprint
($18,000–$22,000)

The 1963–65 Ford Falcon Sprint with 260 ci or 289 ci and a 4-speed is overlooked and under-appreciated. Ford relied heavily on these Falcon Sprints to fly the "Ford Total Performance" banner in 1960s international rallies, and they put on a great show in the Monte Carlo Rally. This chassis was the basis for the Mustang and 1965–66 Shelby GT 350 cars so you know it can be made to work well. Few domestic V8s are as free-revving or durable as a Ford small block. A 1965 289-ci 4-speed Falcon Sprint hard top with a set of MiniLite wheels is a performance package that looks better with each passing year. How cool is that?

With any car, I recommend buying the best you can find and making sure you get the real deal. Check the numbers, verify the tags, study the documentation. A great car is a solid investment, a shoddy one is a guaranteed disappointment.

Of course, if you've got the loose cash, go ahead and buy that '69 GTO Judge RA IV or '70 Chevelle LS6 454. However, by taking a slightly different approach and doing some homework, you can put a relatively rare muscle car in your own garage for a surprisingly small amount of money. And guess what—if you take proper care of it, it will never go down in value.◆

1964 Ford Falcon Futura Sprint

SPRING CARLISLE AUCTION

April 20-21, 2007 Carlisle Expo Center Carlisle, PA

REAL CARS. REAL PRICES.

1994 Dodge Viper
SOLD AT FALL AUCTION FOR $38,000

1987 Porsche 911
SOLD AT FALL AUCTION FOR $40,500

Consign your car today, or register to bid.

1936 Ford Street Rod
SOLD AT FALL AUCTION FOR $28,700

1957 Chevrolet Bel Air
SOLD AT FALL AUCTION FOR $78,000

For buying and selling information, call (717) 243-7855 or go online:

carlisleauctions.com

EXPERIENCE
CARLISLE Events

THE CARS. THE PEOPLE. THE EXCITEMENT.
Carlisle Events is the world's largest presenter of collector car, truck and motorcycle events for the entire family.

This high-line auction will feature hundreds of antique, collector and special interest cars, trucks and motorcycles.

Held during Spring Carlisle Collector Car Swap Meet and Car Corral (April 18-April 22)
Carlisle Expo Center is located just one block from the Carlisle PA Fairgrounds

Consignment Fee $250
Prime Hours $400
Bidder Registration Fee $100
Buyer Premium 5%
Seller Premium 5% no reserve
6% with reserve
Lic. #VB001027
Availability of vehicles subject to change.

ADDITIONAL AUCTION SERVICES PROVIDED BY OUR PARTNERS:

Preferred Insurance Company

Preferred Finance Company

Preferred Car Care Products

Preferred Transport Company

CORVETTE Z06 Call it what you will, but the Corvette® Z06® is the highest-performance productio
Lamborghini, and Aston Martin at Le Mans in 2006 for the fifth GT1 victory in six years. Its hand-built aluminum-bloc

The _____est.

car in Chevrolet® or GM® history. Codeveloped with the Corvette C6.R race car that beat Ferrari, V8 churns out 505 HP, 0–60 in 3.7 seconds, 198 mph on a test track, and 1.04g. Want more? chevy.com

Take a Different Road

Introducing the Simple Lease®

At Premier Financial Services, we believe that getting out of a lease

should be as easy as getting into one. Our Simple Lease® Program

affords you the flexibility of financing with the tax benefits of leasing,

allowing you the ability to change vehicles as often as you wish.

Mitch Katz, CEO

Experience the Premier Advantage • Call us today toll free at **877-973-7700**

Premier Financial Services

Vintage and Exotic Motorcar Leasing

www.premierfinancialservices.com

47 Sherman Hill Road, Woodbury, CT 06798

Buying Smart

There's no magic to buying a decent collector car. It takes thoughtfulness and a studied approach, one where you teach yourself about a marque before you buy, and where you carefully examine a car, with the help of experts when necessary, to determine what kind of shape it is really in.

Of course, few of us collect that way. I tend to prowl Internet classifieds looking for cars that are described as "perfectly restored" and at reasonable prices. Why should I spoil my fantasies by actually having a car examined, when I can pay for it, have it shipped thousands of miles to my door, and then discover it's a rusty pig that really would be happiest wallowing in iron oxide manure?

In short, car collecting starts and ends with passion, and we at Sports Car Market recognize that. However, at the same time, if we can help you interject just a bit of thoughtfulness and rationality into your collecting, we guarantee that you will be happier, much happier, with the types of cars you buy and the amounts you pay.

This section is required reading for anyone who would rather brag about what a great deal they got on a super car, than sit and cry in their 20-50 oil about the dumb car they paid too much for.—*Keith Martin*

Gee, What Do YOU Think It's Worth?

This seller was just shopping, kicking the financial tires to make sure he got all the money

by Jim Schrager

I recently got a call from a long-lost 356 enthusiast, a fellow with twenty-some desirable cars, a few dozen motors, countless boxes of parts and a sizable literature collection. Due to a major life change he will be moving to Europe, he said, and everything must go.

I made a few follow-up calls and it was always the same story: Whenever asked how much he wanted for any particular item, he'd say: "I don't have any idea. I've been out of this too long to know."

After some discussion, I made a fair offer for the car I was interested in, a 1959 356A Sunroof. He agreed it was all the money and promised that I had first shot. I urged him to act as I was ready to send a check, but he said, "Nah, don't worry. I promise it's yours."

This has happened to many of us. As I hung up the phone, I realized there were many things that didn't make sense about this guy. For starters, a fellow this deep into the hobby clearly has some ideas about what stuff is worth. Just one issue of Hemmings is all it takes to get some rough bearings; SCM if he really wants to learn a bunch.

Next, anyone who keeps that much stuff, most of it unused, is generally doing it for one reason: to make money. Most of his cars were undriven, the engines disassembled. Why have an extra few dozen motors? Can anyone use that many even in a lifetime of driving?

The Seller, Not the Car

Why give me, or anyone you don't know who hasn't even made a visit to your place, right of first refusal after just a phone call? This makes little sense.

So what gives? Well, the rest of the story is that this guy was just shopping, kicking the financial tires, and got out of my "right of first refusal" by simply changing his mind on what was for sale—for now. All in all, it was a total waste of time. How to avoid this in the future?

Look at the seller, not the car. That's really the secret to staying sane and having fun with the old car hobby. If the seller seems likely to make your life miserable, do your best to walk away.

Don't believe folks with big, deep experience who claim not to have the faintest idea of what their cars are worth. Serious sellers do their homework and come to the market with prices. Perhaps they need a call with a friendly buyer before revealing their price, but I have never yet found someone ready to sell who didn't have a number in mind.

I get worried when people tell too many non-car-related stories. Some people just need someone to talk to. A few off-topic sidebars are fine, but if you find that you, as a complete stranger, are being told someone's life story—repeatedly—be wary. By the end of these phone calls I heard what this guy's kids did for a living... more than once.

Try to observe the seller in other ways. This seller told me he had promised a project Speedster to a "good friend." Okay, fair enough. He then offered this same car for sale, on a "bring all offers" basis, on the Internet. Several people came to his house and he was able to coax ever-larger purchase offers. He then withdrew the car from all the buyers, and offered it to me as part of a package—unpriced, of course.

Get a Detailed List

Be wary if the seller won't provide a good, detailed list of what is for sale. I once did a deal for a large group of Porsche engines based on a pretty sketchy list. When the goods arrived, all were less than represented. Some "engines" were nothing more than cases; "roller cranks in excellent condition" were in fact suitable for use only as doorstops; "2-liter 911 engine being prepared for vintage racing" was a 1969 911T long block, dormant for dozens of years, that had apparently been prepared by storing it untouched in a damp environment. Needless to say, it wasn't a happy deal.

Our 356 seller got very specific when he was in the mood. For example, he asked how much disc brake conversions are going for. This is a desirable option, as it was provided only with the last two years of the 356 and can be used on almost any earlier A or B 356. He saw a set posted at $1,800 on a VW talk list. That's big money, but it's only an asking price. Of course it depends on condition, I told our secretive stash seller who claimed to know nothing. His response: "I've looked at the caliper bores in each of my seven sets and there are no rust pits. These parts are in excellent condition!" This is the same guy who refused to write a list of what he had for sale. Seems a bit inconsistent, doesn't it?

So what's the game here? It's a classic mismatch of minds. The seller is looking for big money due to his hours expended in accumulating his outstandingly wonderful worldly possessions. Think of all the early Saturday morning swap meets, the miles spent on the road, the haggling with owners. The seller

wants over retail to compensate for his Herculean efforts and the sheer majesty of his estate. He is looking for an emotional buyer who looks at the seemingly endless cache of parts and simply must possess them, damn the cost.

On the other hand, a thoughtful buyer is being forced to take lots of stuff he doesn't really want or need. To him, swap meets are fun, and he is glad to trade time for a lower price. He's looking for a discount to pay for his hassle in unloading what he doesn't want.

Most of the time, the twain never meet—or at least, not happily. Keep your checkbook in your pocket until you really know what you are getting. And be on the lookout for time-wasters masquerading as guys who "don't have a clue" what their merchandise is worth.◆

When There's $60,000 between #1 and #2

Price guides are never enough by themselves to accurately assess the value of a vintage Porsche

By Jim Schrager

Aetna Blue 356B Cabriolet

Dear Mr. Schrager: I am excited about a 1960 356B Roadster, repainted the original Aetna Blue (light, non-metallic blue/gray) with a gray interior and the 1600 Normal engine per the Kardex. Body panel gaps are very nice, although both doors are slightly out at their lower rear corners. No hard hits, pan has one section repaired properly, otherwise everything else is original and solid. All instruments rebuilt, Les Leston wood steering wheel, a jack and spare but no tool kit.

SCM says a current value of $40,000–$50,000, yet recent sales I can find seem quite a bit higher. Is the SCM guide behind the curve? What is your opinion of the range for cars in #1 condition? Some folks I have talked to are saying as high as $75,000. I am thinking the top end is about $65,000. Any input will be appreciated.—*Wray Brady, Pittsburgh, PA*

Price differences often involve condition. The SCM price

guide is for a #2 condition car, and is an "aggressive" buying target. This means the buyer has to work a bit to find a car at this price.

Don't expect to visit your local collector-car dealer and find cars right at our numbers. There is no organized wholesale market for vintage Porsches. Dealers, who buy from the same folks we all do, have costs that must be recouped. So their prices, in deference to their work at finding and presenting cars for sale, may be higher than our guide. Of course, you spend your money or your time when buying a vintage car, and for many of us, the margin a dealer makes is money well spent.

A #1 condition 356 can be twice the price of a #2, due to the tremendous expense—and hassle—involved. Strictly by our price guide, we call a #1 Roadster $80,000–$100,000 and have reported sales in that range.

Regarding the Roadster you are looking at, it sounds like it is between #1 and #2 condition, with a price range of $40,000–$100,000. Disappointed with that huge range? Welcome to the world of collecting, where price guides are never enough by themselves to accurately assess the value of a vintage Porsche.

Dear Mr. Schrager: I noticed Keith Martin commented on how hard his 911SC rode, and I have some thoughts and questions about my Porsches as well. I've disagreed with you for years, as I have always been a believer in getting the largest tires that will fit under the wheel wells of my various 911s. The more contact area I get on the ground, the higher the performance, in my mind. Plus it looks great with those big, fat meats in the wheel wells.

But now I have a 1974 911S Targa with stock six-inch wheels and original-type and -size tires and I can't believe how

Editor Martin's harsh-riding 911SC with 16-inch wheels

nice it feels. The steering isn't heavy and the ride isn't jarring anymore. I am now a believer in this idea that maybe Porsche does know more than I do about wheel and tire sizes.

But here are two technical talking points on which I can't agree with you:

1. You mention in your review of your 1976 912E (p.205) that the best tire for that car is a 185/65/15, as it is very close to the original 185/70/15 that was fitted to the six-inch wide wheels. I believe the better equivalent tire size is actually 195/65, as the diameter is essentially identical to the original 185/70 size.

2. I appreciate your affinity for the vintage look of steel wheels, but I believe that to lower the unsprung weight, a 911 really should have Fuchs alloys. In addition, with form following function and all that stuff, aren't the alloys more in keeping with the spirit of the original design?—***Philip Kahn, Denver, CO***

You are absolutely right that 195/65 tires approximate the rolling diameter of the original 185/70 size. But I am looking for more than just size—I am trying to rediscover that elusive "light yet connected" feel these cars had when new, the well-controlled ride without the harshness so often felt with high-performance tires. The same feeling you really like in your 1974 car is the feeling you will never have from a 911SC because of the wheel and tire sizes. Low-profile and high-per-

formance tires are fatter and stiffer than the set-up on the earlier cars, and both translate directly into harshness.

Those 185/65/15 tires also have another advantage, in that the final gear ratio is slightly raised (numerically), so the car feels just a bit faster through the gears. Many people like the friskier feel brought by slightly smaller diameter tires, especially in our world of 70-mph speed limits.

On the unsprung weight issue, you are correct. The lower the unsprung weight, the better the theoretical handling. I simply like the looks of the steel wheels, and unless on the race course, the difference in handling is exceptionally hard to notice.

I have done many head-to-head wheel swaps, noting differences in handling and road feel with dozens of different wheel and tire combinations, including the rare and ultra-lightweight Mahle "gas burner" 911T wheels. I could not, by the seat of my pants, detect a difference in ride or handling feel on the street based on different wheels. Yet I can immediately—within ten seconds on the road—feel the harshness of a 195/60 or 205/55 set of high-performance tires.

A long time ago I realized just how smart the guys at the Porsche factory actually were, and that for general street use, they almost always had the right idea. I'm glad you are thinking along the same lines.◆

Why Your Healey 3000 Isn't Worth $143,000

The buyer had a "Gone in 60 Seconds" list from his boss that included a big Healey—and he was out of time

by Gary Anderson

Build it for $75k, or buy it done for twice as much?

On Saturday evening at the Barrett-Jackson Auction in Scottsdale this year, a 1967 Austin-Healey 3000 BJ8 convertible painted "golden beige metallic," an original Healey color for the year—but not original to this particular car—with red leather interior, and absolutely no historical significance, sold for $143,100.

This is the most expensive public sale of a production Austin-Healey ever (exceeded only by the limited-production 100S and Works Healeys). It tops the previous high by more than $50,000. Only five years ago, the sale of a Healey for anything over $40,000 was big news.

The question is: Should observers attach any market significance to this sale? The short answer is no.

This sale didn't just border on irrationality; it crossed that border at somewhere around $80,000. But in terms of free-market economics, why should we call any auction sale irrational—as each transaction clearly represents what a willing buyer, along with a nearly-as-willing underbidder, agrees to pay for a certain item at a certain time.

You Could Build This Car For $75,000

Here's the biggest reason this sale falls outside of what I would call "reasonable": Anyone could go to the restorer who did the work on this car (or any of three or four other restorers with the same reputation for high-quality work) and ask him to create an identical car at a guaranteed price, and we suspect he wouldn't ask more than $75,000, tops. And that price would include the cost of the donor car. Would that be easy to do? Absolutely. There is no scarcity of 1967 Austin-Healey convertibles in restorable condition, and certainly no shortage of golden-beige metallic paint or red leather.

As an aside, golden beige metallic was a shade that was selected for a small number of big Healeys in what was expected to be the last year of their production. Until recently, original golden-beige Healeys were rare enough to have their own registry, but this car wasn't originally that color, so aside from its inherent attractiveness, there's no particular significance here.

It wasn't an unusual color even when Healeys were new; Jaguar used the same formulation on their Mk IIs and E-types during the period, calling it "opalescent golden sand." Healeys with that exterior color could be ordered with either a black or a red interior, but red is definitely the more attractive of the two choices with the golden-beige finish.

Tired of Resale Red

We don't know for sure, but it's possible that Kurt Tanner, the restorer of this car and a man who has managed to become a brand name in Healey restorations for auction sale, chose this color just because he was getting tired of building resale-red and bid-fetching-BRG convertibles.

Even considering the other Healeys that sold in January

in the superheated air of Scottsdale, this sale wasn't in any ballpark we know. The real news at this auction was that there were eight other sales of Healeys in the $50,000 to $85,000 range. Two sold at $50,000, four more sold for under $75,000, and two sold for about $85,000.

Even those are historically stupendous prices for Healeys, but they're basically what it would cost to buy a solid project car with all its parts and good body panels, then pay a shop to restore it to show condition. But that would take nine months or so, and there are many buyers coming into the market today who aren't prepared to wait for what they want. Time is a valuable commodity to the Boomers that bid at these auctions, and they're happy to pay extra for immediate gratification.

Certainly it's good for Healey owners that newly restored Healeys have been bid up over the past five years to the point where one might pay for a decent restoration without being underwater at the end of the process.

Rising auction prices don't necessarily mean the prices of average, everyday cars will rise, but they certainly call attention to a marque. Decent Healeys in the club driver category are now recognized for the value that they provide. They're fast enough to hold their own on the freeway, they're instantly recognizable, and they have earned iconic status.

Boomers Running Out of Time

More important, like '60s muscle cars, they fill the memory of Baby Boomers who have leisure time and discretionary income. We're now seeing decent drivers, which might have sold for a solid $25,000 five years ago, selling for $40,000.

As for the $140,000 sale, does it matter that a Healey has now sold for as much as an Aston-Martin DB5 or a Mulliner-bodied R-type Bentley? Is this sale likely to have any influence on the overall market value of Healeys?

We say no. If you can pay to have someone restore a Healey to your exact specifications for half what this buyer paid, even taking into account the time factor, then we must attribute that sale to something other than rationality.

If we had to invent a scenario to explain this transaction in any terms other than speed—or the Speed Channel-induced buyer's euphoria—here's one plausible story line.

Buyer Had a "Gone in 60 Seconds" Task

The buyer, who we know was buying cars on behalf of a wealthy car collector and museum developer, had perhaps a list of cars he was supposed to bring home—a "Gone in 60 Seconds" assignment—and at the end of the weekend, with only one Healey left to cross the block, he realized that a Healey was on that wish list and that he hadn't gotten one yet.

Whoops. Gotta have it. At any price. And with other bidders pretty much aware of his bidding style, there might even have been a game of chicken going on to push the bidding up.

Whatever the explanation, one golden beige metallic Austin-Healey went home for an incredible price, which made the restorer happy, and had many owners calling their insurance agents the following week to bump their agreed-value policies up another $5,000 or $10,000.

But if you're thinking of selling your Healey in the near future (even if it is golden beige with red upholstery), don't expect to have a buyer knocking at your door any time soon with $140,000 in his pocket. Buyers like that don't come along very often. And if you want one just like it, and can wait a few months, you will have saved yourself $65,000. Which will probably be just about enough to buy a perfect MGB at the next Barrett-Jackson.◆

Becoming a Muscle Car Detective

The best way to determine legitimacy is to understand how these cars were built

by Colin Comer

Technology has advanced to the point where almost any engine or VIN number can be recreated, and paperwork conjured up from thin air. Plus, as muscle cars continue to escalate in value, many now in the seven-figure range, the sharks in the business smell the blood of the rubes just waiting to be fleeced. We lived through it once before in 1989–91, but then it was vintage Ferraris and Jaguar C- and D-types that were growing like weeds. Today, it's Hemi 'Cudas and COPO Camaros.

Luckily, decoding a car and figuring out exactly what it was when it left the factory are relatively simple tasks.

What follows is a beginner's guide for a basic muscle car "scratch-and-sniff" test, or preliminary inspection. It is not a comprehensive how-to, but rather a guide to help you determine with relative ease just what you are looking at.

Let's start by examining "matching numbers," a common term that is widely abused. Matching numbers implies that a car is exactly as it left the factory, with its original factory-installed engine, transmission, and rear axle. However, to the unscrupulous few, matching numbers can mean that the number they stamped on the engine block five minutes ago matches the number that was on the original one.

First, original paperwork is invaluable in determining if a car is real: window stickers, build sheets, dealer invoices, warranty cards, registration cards, owner history. The more you have, the easier it will be to document the car. I always look at every slip of paper with a car; even the most insignificant receipt may hold valuable information, such as a tune-up that noted engine size, a gas receipt with mileage and date noted, etc.

The best way to determine the legitimacy of numbers is to understand how these cars were built. As mass-produced cars, foundries cast engine blocks and heads, body plants stamped out body shells, and eventually all components formed a finished car. Simple. Every part has a casting number and date, the body has a build date, and the completed car was assigned a date when finished. Obviously, all parts must predate the

Your car's birthmarks

completed car by a reasonable margin, usually one to three months.

Every Part Has a Number

These time frames vary depending on the plant at which the car was built (engine blocks cast in Detroit were shipped by rail to a plant in L.A., as opposed to being at the factory in Detroit the day of completion), and time of year (Christmas shutdown, for example, slows production and widens the window). This is basic detective work and I always look for consistency within dates on each car, rather than a set time frame. For example, if I find a block was cast in March 1969, I do not expect to find January 1968 cylinder heads. Remember, every part has a number and date on it, even window glass and bumper jacks.

Once you compile and compare all of the important date codes—for example, engine block, cylinder heads, intake manifold, body build date, and car completion date—it is time to look for the all-important "matching numbers."

Prior to 1968, many manufacturers did not have a VIN stamp on the block. This makes learning date codes and having concrete documentation that much more important. Certain high performance cars, such as Corvettes, 1965–67 289 "K code"-equipped Fords and Shelbys, did have the VIN on their engine blocks. Post-1968, all cars have at least the last six digits of their serial number somewhere on the engine block and transmission case.

With the proper research, you can determine how "numbers-matching" your recent find is.

Just Look It Up

Many books exist on decoding numbers, including what casting numbers are correct, where to find them, and how to decode every component on the car. A decent book on any make you are considering is money well spent. The Internet is also a powerful research tool. Google "Chevrolet casting numbers" for instance, and look at what comes up. Numerous online communities exist for most popular cars. More often than not, these discussion boards can be very helpful with specific questions.

If considering a Pontiac GTO, the best $35 you will ever spend is ordering a Pontiac Historic Services report. These reports are worth their weight in gold. From the original factory records, Jim Mattison of PHS will provide you with copies of the original factory invoice and build card when provided with a VIN number. If you are in a hurry, for $10 extra PHS will fax you a copy immediately. Even though a seller may have his own PHS documents, as copies of originals, they are easily altered and I do not deem them reliable unless I obtain them myself. Go to www.phs-online.com and follow the instructions to order your report.

For Shelby shoppers, go to www.saac.com and order a copy of the Shelby American World Registry. In this 1,400-page monster is every Shelby ever built, with known history listed for each individual car. There are sections on each year, production changes, part numbers, and hints and tips. Do not buy a Shelby without looking it up in the Registry.

I also recommend joining the club to gain access to the registrars who can help you with additional information on particular cars. These guys are the best and the club support offered by SAAC is second to none.

Ford buyers can contact Marti Auto Works for a complete report on any Ford car from 1967–73. Kevin Marti has Ford's entire production database for these years. Please note that these records also include all Shelby Mustangs produced from 1967–70 as well, and I highly recommend a Marti report in addition to checking the SAAC Registry. Marti Auto Works is on line at www.martiauto.com.

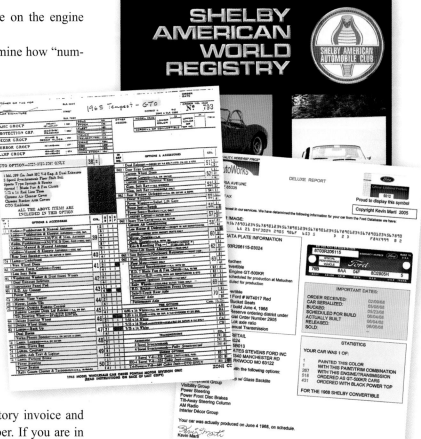

Protect your investment, do your homework

For Chrysler products, Galen V. Govier is the acknowledged authority. His company offers a wide range of services from basic decoding of cars over the phone to an on-site evaluation anywhere in the U.S. Govier also maintains The Chrysler Registry, which tracks all known examples of certain cars, at www.gvgovier.com

Above all, educate yourself on any car you are looking at and enlist the services of experts when needed. The time and expense of performing proper investigation is insignificant compared to the values of most cars. Chances are, you'll find that being a muscle car detective can have double rewards—first, in the knowledge you will gain, and second, by the sense of assurance you'll get knowing you've done your homework.

Of course, there are no guarantees, and even some of the world's top collectors are fooled by clones and air-cars now and then. But at least if you do your homework, you've got a running start on having the car you buy turn out to be what you thought it was, rather than a forger's delight.◆

Buying Classic Cars Online

While a vehicle transaction might be sight unseen, it need not be completely blind

by Steve Haas

The Internet has greatly changed many things in our lives. It is hard to imagine how we ever managed without being able to download detailed driving directions at a moment's notice or find instructions for setting up SU carburetors at 2:00 am. The Internet now enables us to purchase a steering wheel for an MG, or better yet, buy an actual MG from someone you have never met on the other side of the world; All that's left is to exchange funds and have it delivered to your home in a few days.

It wasn't that long ago that the idea of buying used cars over the Internet would have been met with derision. Since 2000, more than two million passenger vehicles (and millions of parts and accessories) have been sold on eBay Motors alone. In addition eBays other sites have also been a part of the Internet automotive experience.

Steve Haas

The basics of buying a collector car online are primarily the same as those for buying one down the street: Do your homework, learn what questions to ask, and stick to your budget. Most Internet sites aren't much different than the standard classified ads we grew up with. But eBay Motors is different, in both its geographic reach and its ability to help facilitate long-distance transactions.

The first reaction of those unfamiliar with eBay Motors is "How can anyone buy a used car sight unseen?". Keep in mind that 71% of vehicles sold on eBay Motors are interstate, and contrary to popular belief, plenty of information is available online to buy a car of your dreams.

For example, eBay's feedback system is an incredibly powerful tool. The number next to the seller's ID is a summary of feedback left by others with whom he or she has transacted on eBay. You can also view comments from past transactions and view details of recent sales. Don't underestimate the value of this information. Look for the type of items that this person has bought or sold and note if they are classic-car related. Don't necessarily discount new sellers (we all have to start somewhere), but you may seek additional information in this case.

The basic listing dool of eBay allows sellers to post up to 24 photos of a vehicle and gives them virtually unlimited space to describe a vehicle. There are other options that allow sellers to post even more photos or to host their own. So, unlike a classifieds ad, a good listing on eBay should give you a solid overview of a car's condition. If you don't see enough details, use the "Ask Seller a Question" link on the top of the listing to request additional information or photos.

As mentioned earlier, while a vehicle transaction might be sight unseen, it need not be completely blind, because eBay Motors offers links to professional services that can inspect a car for as little as $99. Granted, a $99 inspection isn't going to be able to tell you that the numbers match on that '63 Split-Window, but it will verify the overall condition. There are specialty inspection services out there for classic-specific needs, and prices vary according to the detail and expertise you need.

If you don't want to use an inspector or don't have time to arrange for one before the bidding ends, there are other options. For example, ask the seller to scan or photograph the front of the title and email or fax it to you. This will verify the vehicle ID number and the fact that the seller has the right to sell the car. If you know friends or fellow car club members who lives near the vehicle, ask if they can inspect it for you. If the seller refuses to allow this, it is probably a sign that you should look elsewhere.

Vehicle history reports are also available easily and inexpensively through eBay Motors. While services like CARFAX or Experian Auto Check only work for 1981 and newer vehicles, they do provide a valuable service that is only a click away. Qualifying vehicles on eBay Motors have a link on the VIN field that allows for an AutoCheck report at a substantial discount. For a small fee, one can verify the ownership history of a vehicle through public records like state registrations and inspections, insurance claims, reported accidents, and manufacturer recall records.

You should also pay close attention to the seller's terms and conditions. Notice what kind of deposit the seller wants and when he wants it, what forms of payment are acceptable, and if the deposit is refundable should the car fail to meet your expectations. You should clarify these terms and agree on contingencies before you bid. eBay recommends that one *never* use Western Union or other forms of untraceable methods for payment. Additionally, eBay Motors offers vehicle purchase protection for material misrepresentation for up to $20,000. This is of no additional cost to the seller or the buyer.

If you follow the steps above and use the same care you would buying a car offline, the Internet provides a way to find the car of your dreams in a manner that is convenient, transparent, fulfilling, and fun.◆

(Steve Haas is the Senior Manager of Autos for eBay Motors and drives a 1984 Porsche Carrera Cabriolet.)

Deferred Maintenance, Deal Killers, and Diminishing Returns

The repair list kicked the maintenance bill to $21,000, making our F40 seem like the Ferrari equivalent of a beater Camaro

by Michael Sheehan

All the needs of an abused Camaro, with stratospheric prices

Often when someone decides to part with a prized Ferrari, it may not have been started or driven for months or even years. Just as likely, chances are the new owner, excited by his new toy, wants to begin driving "now," and as often as he can. And that's where the problems can start.

A Visit From Father Time

Anyone buying a $4,500 1992 Chevy Camaro expects a worn suspension, flaccid shocks, minor engine leaks, a clunking differential, and a/c overdue for a recharge. The buyer gets basic transportation and accepts the shortcomings.

Ferraris also age. Someone buying a 1992 F40 will be spending about $335,000, yet their "new" F40 will have the same inherent, age-related problems as that Camaro. They will just cost much, much more to repair.

Virtually every 10-plus-year-old Ferrari needs the shocks rebuilt or replaced, suspension bushings replaced, brake hoses replaced, water pump rebuilt, water hoses replaced, an engine reseal because of oil leaks, and fuel cells replaced, if so equipped. All rubber or related components deteriorate with age—the key is to identify these issues and factor them into your sales negotiation.

Common sense and driver preservation dictate that safety-related items such as deteriorated brake lines or frozen shocks or brake calipers have to be repaired before the car can be used, and should be factored in at some percentage of the purchase price. While age-related problems are negotiable, other issues can be deal killers. These include major crash damage that has been poorly repaired, bent frames that have been badly fixed, or a sick engine that needs an expensive and mandatory engine rebuild.

Three Steps to a Happy Buyer

Any successful purchase of an older Ferrari involves three steps. First, a pre-purchase inspection that tells all involved exactly what potential problems are lurking. Secondly, an understanding on the buyer's part that these are "just used cars," ones that almost always need immediate post-purchase service work. And third, the acceptance that most of the money spent beyond the purchase price will never be recovered and becomes a diminishing return.

I usually recommend that buyers and sellers reach a percentage split agreement on the estimated cost of repairs. These agreements work well because buyers aren't nearly as eager to have every aging part on the car replaced if they are paying part of the bill, and sellers are (begrudgingly) paying for their own deferred maintenance.

Just One More Thing

The Ferrari caveat is that it is oh so easy to go into the "while you're at it" mode. While the brakes are off, let's have the calipers re-plated and re-sleeved. Isn't the moment while the suspension is apart for a bushing replacement the perfect time to powder coat or replate the suspension arms, like everyone else in the local Ferrari club has had done? And while the brake rotors are off being machined, how about powder coating the uprights and replacing the wheel bearings? Suddenly, a basic brake job and suspension bushing replacement has become a $20,000 restoration of both systems.

It is not, however, the seller's responsibility to provide the buyer with a suspension capable of winning a Ferrari Club of America National Meet Platinum Award under the guise of a routine service.

The $21,000 Lesson

As a quick example, in late 2004 I sold F40 S/N 90568, a car that had almost $100,000 in "go-fast" updates, such as F40 LM brakes, wheels, turbos, ECUs, throttle linkage, short shift kit, ad infinitum. This 1992 F40 had only 7,774 original miles and had seen less than 500 miles since it was last ser-

viced. On the test drive, it lit the tires up in third gear when the boost kicked in and was, simply put, scary fast.

Much to the surprise of all involved, the pre-purchase inspection found a long list of needed repairs, including a bent valve and a worn-out limited slip, so an engine-out service was mandatory. The starting estimate for the work was $15,000-plus, this on an unusually nice, supposedly "no stories" car.

The while-it's-apart list included the expected all new belts and hoses, brake pads, etc. A new clutch assembly, special brake work to fit an emergency brake to the LM racing brakes, and a radar detector kicked the final bill to $21,000-plus, making our "serviced only 500 miles ago" F40 suddenly seem like the Ferrari world's equivalent of that beater Camaro.

Fortunately, the buyer accepted that the majority of the problems were common to most 10-year-old Ferraris. After the usual negotiations, a compromise was reached, an equitable split for repairs was made, and a purchase agreement was signed. Both parties wound up satisfied.

Doing the Splits

The degree of compromise involved in any purchase is a matter of the seller's motivation to sell and willingness to accept less than was anticipated, factored against the buyer's desire to own the car and pay a little more for the privilege. Add in the broker's experience, his ability to explain the problems, and the negotiation skills that justify his commission, and the gap between expectation and reality in dealing with deferred maintenance can usually be resolved.

The buyer and seller here both had to accept that a 1992 F40 hot rod is worth about $325,000, and regardless of how much money is spent on recommissioning, it will remain a $325,000 car. The $21,000-plus for service will enhance the new owner's driving pleasure, safety and peace of mind, but that's it—no value add to the bottom line.

As I told the buyer, expect your used F40 to need the minimal maintenance of a Mercedes and you'll be disappointed. Expect it to need an infusion of love—and more than a few dollars to return it to its "as-new" condition—and you'll be rewarded with a terrific ride. Every hobby, from collecting stamps to racing in America's Cup, has a price attached. With Ferraris, expect the "pay to play" ticket to be a healthy one, and you won't be disappointed. At a local track day in your new F40, when you hit redline in third, crack a quick shift into fourth, and break the rear tires loose, I guarantee the amount you've spent to get there will be the furthest thing from your mind.◆

Everything Works, Just Don't Drive It

Once all the repairs were completed, I asked the seller to compensate me and showed him the receipts. He told me to get lost

By John Draneas

Dear SCM: Six months ago I purchased a 1965 Corvette 327/375 Fuelie convertible from a well-known Corvette specialist dealer for $85,000. The car was reported in writing to be numbers- matching and completely operational, condition #2+. But after driving the car on the highway at 60 mph for 30 minutes and in traffic for 15 minutes, I discovered a large number of problems.

From serious overheating to fuel-injection problems, fuel leaks, oil leaks, and an inoperative wiper motor, the total repair bill was about $8,000. I informed the dealer of the problems, which took the better part of three months to correct. During that time he said to save the receipts and we would work something out.

Once the repairs were completed, I asked him to compensate me and showed him the receipts, whereupon he basically told me to get lost. I reminded him that when he sold me the car he claimed that everything worked. He replied that the car worked for him every time he drove it around the block to get gas, and that the car was not supposed to be driven like I drive it.

I could not believe what I was hearing. "You mean to tell me that when you said 'everything works,' you meant only to start it, drive it a couple of blocks, then put it away?" To which he answered, "Yes," and said something about collector cars being just to look at.

So what do I do? When a car is claimed to be fully operational, does that not imply operational for common driving

Sure it "works", but what does that mean?

conditions? Do I have any legal recourse to be compensated for the work performed to get the car operational for normal driving?—**B.C., Florida**

At first glance, this seems like a pretty simple situation, with little doubt that our reader is entitled to compensation for his stack of repair bills. But during my 30 years of legal practice, I have learned three important things. The first is that your clients never really tell you everything the first time. The second is that there are always at least two sides to every story. And finally, that the truth in any legal dispute usually lies somewhere in between the first two points.

More to the Story

I asked the reader to send me a copy of the written report that he mentioned was a part of the sale. When he checked his sales documents, he found that the dealer had specified nothing in writing as to the condition of car. Nor was there a written warranty.

"I only have [the dealer's] verbal comments, with witnesses, that he said everything on the car works, and that it was a solid condition #2 car," the reader told me. "I believe the actual verbiage was, 'In complete working order.'" He went on to affirm that at no time, either verbally or in writing, did the dealer mention that there was anything wrong with the car.

The reader also told me that the dealer understood that he would probably rally the Corvette as well as take it to a race track.

A Potential Lawsuit

While this still looks like a pretty strong misrepresentation case, our reader has two problems, the most important being that he has nothing in writing.

The law does not require that representations or statements about the car be made in writing in order to be the basis of a claim. But it's a heck of lot easier to prove what was actually said if it's on paper, which is why my number-one mantra is to get everything in writing. While this usually means paying an attorney some money, it's cheap insurance against what in this case turned out to be an $8k disagreement.

Our reader states that he had witnesses present when the dealer described the condition of the Corvette, and this may be enough. Still, people hear and remember things differently, and the last thing you want at a trial is to get into a "Rashomon" retelling of the events.

Everything Works, Mostly

The second problem our reader faces in winning his case comes in what the law will interpret as the core of the contract. While the words the dealer used to describe the Corvette are simple enough, they are also capable of having more than one meaning. Just what does "everything works" mean?

"Working" does not necessarily mean working well, working perfectly, working under adverse conditions, or working for long. Nor does it mean not being in need of any repairs. Consider a motor that runs and drives but burns a quart of oil every 100 miles and needs a rebuild. Is it still "working?" Probably.

I don't think that the statement that the Corvette was a #2 car is a slam dunk, either. After all, SCM routinely rates auction cars as #2s without driving them. The 'Vette in question may have had a whole host of minor problems, but none of these were readily evident prior to the sale.

The Verdict

Although this case could go either way, I still like our reader's chances. The context for considering any misrepresentation claim should be based on what the purchaser would be reasonably expected to believe as a result of the seller's statements. With the way this car was represented and the dealer knowing of our reader's intended use, I would think that a judge or jury would conclude that the dealer misled our subscriber into believing that this car was better than it was, and would hold the dealer responsible for at least a portion of the repairs.

The moral here is to avoid this sort of situation by not just relying on the seller's descriptions of the collector car. Always get a thorough pre-purchase inspection and perform an extensive test drive. These are old cars, and they aren't perfect.

Get everything in a sales contract clearly stated, avoiding generalizations like "everything works" or "needs nothing." A checklist that rates each significant component of the car for condition on a sliding scale will make it a lot harder for the seller to change his story later.

Don't be reluctant to spend some money to draw up a written contract that spells out the specific condition and terms of a sale, as legal fees will always be a small percentage of the purchase price of a car. Do the math and it's usually far less than the tax and license costs. That's really pretty affordable protection and certainly much less expensive than a lawsuit after the fact.◆

Buying Techniques That Work

A flashlight is mandatory; use it to look for rust repair, panel replacement, and accident damage

by Colin Comer

Shelby American Automobile Club, www.saac.com

Have I got a deal for you

How do you keep a seller honest? Every seller has one goal in mind—getting your money—and even the most honest person can "forget" the truth. Over the years, I have developed a buying technique designed to catch Joe Isuzu, who wouldn't know the truth if it bit him. Herewith are some guidelines:

Read Between the Lines

Decipher what the seller's description really means. People have trouble putting a blatant lie in print for fear of getting caught or having it used against them. So what the description *doesn't* say is what you should worry about.

For example: "The 1969 Pontiac GTO Judge was equipped with a Ram Air III engine producing 366 hp." Guess what—I bet this Judge no longer has its original engine.

Previous owner said it ran and drove very well. Call a tow truck if you buy this baby.

"Completely original, with freshly done interior, respray, and new drivetrain." Be afraid, be very afraid.

Ask Tough Questions, Take Notes

Once you have studied the description, make your list. Ask questions that clarify what is written, as well as what is left out. Write down the seller's answers, especially if dealing face to face. An honest seller won't mind you taking notes; a dishonest one will squirm.

Research the car you are buying, and know important details, such as casting numbers on key components. Know what equipment was standard and what was optional.

Ask tough questions and keep asking until you are satisfied you get the truth. A "four-owner" car? Get the owners' names and ask if you may contact them. If the seller doesn't know the names, how does he know the car only had four owners? Such questions will help you decide if you should proceed.

Crawl All Over the Car

Check the seller's answers against the car. Have a flashlight and notepad, arm yourself with a book describing where the important numbers are located, and get dirty. Ever see buyers at auction wearing nice clean clothes, who never crack a hood or crawl under a car? They're asking for it. You'll see me in a T-shirt and jeans, with a pocket of greasy rags and a flashlight.

If you are not comfortable checking the numbers, get somebody who is—even if just to read them to you. Look for continuity among date codes and general appearance. If a 120,000-mile car has grease on everything except the serial number stamping and date-code casting on the engine block, look for a grinder and Home Depot stamp set under this seller's workbench.

How to Fing "Original" Sins

If the car appears to be real, start checking its condition. Your homework will have told you the trouble areas. For example, on early GTOs, the rear body mounts at the frame are the first place to look; these are the first place GTOs rust. It is also the last place anybody bothers to fix properly, and issues there are easy to spot.

If the car is reported to be unrestored, poke around for proof. Is the carpet original? Seat covers? Body panels? Paint? The desirability of unrestored cars has driven many to doll up tacky old dogs to look "unrestored".

Spend $300 and arm yourself with a digital paint-thickness gauge. This device, when held against paint, reports the thickness of the finish. Factory-applied paint is typically 2–5 mils; repaints will result in 8–10 mils or more.

At a recent auction, I was inspecting a car that proudly proclaimed "100% Original Factory Paint." Looking at it, I could see imperfections in the underlying prepwork—telling me the car had been repainted. Using my paint gauge, I walked around

the car and checked surface thickness at various points.

The seller spotted this and quite defensively came over and barked, "What is that THING you are aiming at my car?" My reply: "It's a lie detector." Seller: "What does it tell you?" Me: "You're guilty." 10–15 mils everywhere.

A flashlight is mandatory. Use it to look for rust repair, panel replacement, and accident damage. Look in the trunk, under the rear window area, then all the way down the quarter panels forward to the doors. Body filler and paint guns can reach nearly everywhere without much effort, except these areas. Look closely at panel seams and spot welds.

Study original cars and apply this knowledge to restored ones. Be thorough, be educated, and make sure the seller sees you making this kind of inspection. The guilty ones won't stop talking, and the honest ones will let you look to your heart's content.

Get All Claims in Writing

Here's a tip for auction buyers: If the car passes these tests to your satisfaction, ask the seller to put in writing any claims he has made to you verbally that are not on the printed auction description. If the auction announces a car as "documented with the original build sheet" but it is not on the window card, have the seller and the auction company note on the block ticket that the original build sheet will be delivered with the car.

Take it slow, inspect the car, and verify the seller's claims. If you are short of knowledge or confidence, the best money you can spend is to hire a specialist.

However, don't fall prey to one of the "nationwide vehicle inspection services" that have grown up lately. These firms subcontract their orders to local insurance adjusters. I guarantee they will know less than you do about the car in question.

Instead, call restoration shops or clubs in the area and ask for recommendations. Ask the inspector for multiple pictures and to follow a pre-determined checklist. Have these sent to you upon completion. These techniques should help you get the car you thought you were buying into your garage, rather than one that keeps giving you one bad surprise after another.♦

Choosing Performance Over Originality

After a quick blast down the highway in a highly modified Speedster, some buyers won't care about the lack of correctness

by Jim Schrager

1970 Porsche 914 "V8"

Dear Jim Schrager: After reading about your silver 1976 912E (p.205), into which someone had put a 2-liter 911 engine, I began to contemplate the reality of what was done—the bastardizing of a rare Porsche model. Although I'm primarily a purist, I thought back to some of the Porsches that I've owned, and wondered if the alterations I made to them were merely small changes or if I had really bastardized them. There was the '58 Speedster fitted with a Super 90 engine and later transaxle, the 914/6 that was modified via a 2.6-liter 911S and short gears, and the 1981 911SC coupe that I converted to an all-steel Turbo body with a bi-wing rear spoiler.

Back when I modified it, the Speedster was just a $2,500 car. The 914/6, although already rare when "improved" by me, maintained a technically correct appearance; I just gave it the ability to match a 289 Cobra on acceleration. The SC, well, they're a dime a dozen, and I went racing with that car.

Your article made me think about adaptation parameters; if there is such a thing, should there be? Of course, no one

in his right mind would stuff a 993 engine into a 1967 911R, or transplant a 914 1.7-liter engine into a lightweight 1973 RS. Although those are extreme examples, with your 912/911s you have used a semi-precious engine as a replacement heart for a car that was, from birth, a slug. Yes, the new engine solved the issue of why the '76 was a slug, but couldn't a case be made for the early engine being better used in a 1969–73 period 911?

Are there cars out there that should be preserved? Will there ever be a shortage of 911SCs that is significant enough that I should have preserved my coupe? Because of my Speedster's robust engine, did that beautiful, white, rust-free example survive the last 35 years, or did the extra power cause it to be wrapped around a tree?

Your 912E is a rather pretty car, so using the *SCM Price Guide,* as a 912E, it would be worth about $8k. If it had been born a 1976 911S and was in similar condition, it would be worth about $10k. After the surgical implant of the early 911S engine it has 180 DIN hp, compared to 165 DIN hp for a stock 2.7-liter 911S, and the modest 90 hp in its original four-cylinder form. What's it worth now? Or should a monetary result not be factored in?—*Pete Zimmermann, Bakersfield, CA*

Fire Up the Crystal Ball

At one level, you are right about the engine swap in my 912/911 and similar modifications to other Porsches—they can easily offend. But let's dig a few layers deeper. If what I am doing does not hurt the value—or maybe even helps it and at the same time makes the car a better performer, then I'm in favor, purists be hanged. This philosophy made modifications of my 250k-mile well-used 912E a no-brainer. With its original used-up four-cylinder running gear, the car was just plain worn out. I was lucky a previous owner had spent the time and money to fit a 2.0-liter 911 engine in there, and of course that was one of the big attractions for me. It meant that a lot of the hard work necessary for me to install a high-performance 2.2-liter 911S engine had already been done. Unless a stock 912E is a mint low-mileage example in great colors with original paint, I don't see any upside, no matter how long you wait.

But the values of our cars change over time, so to get things right requires a bit of crystal ball gazing. Since in general a car must be rare to be valuable, messing with cars with high production volumes is usually safe. However, in the Porsche world there are notable

1973 Porsche 914-errari

exceptions: Speedsters are not really that rare, with over 4,000 made, but are very valuable. Early 911S cars are not so rare, with a few thousand or so made each of seven years between 1967 and 1973, yet the values are very strong.

But 914-4 cars are not at all rare, with about 100,000 made, and neither are 911SCs, with production of over 60,000 units. I break this rule with the 912E, which is a rare car at just over 2,000 made. But like the "Notchback" 356B, any Sportomatic 911 (even an early 911S), the 911L, and the 912E, rarity does not always translate into value in the Porsche world.

There is another way to lose your shirt in this modification game, and that is to put too much in your upgrades. Examples include $50,000 914-4s made into fire-breathing 914-6 conversions, and 1973 911T cars made into near-perfect $75,000 Carrera RS clones. Keep an eye on what the market is for original vs. clone cars as you build your own ideal mongrel.

"Converted" Cars Newly Collectible

One recent trend is that some highly desirable "converted" Porsches can bring as much as their stock counterparts, although not from the same type of buyer. For example, consider a beautiful silver 356A Speedster, with a later 912 engine, smooth-shifting SC gearbox, and more recent powerful disc brakes. After a quick blast down the highway, some buyers

will be thrilled and not care about the lack of "correctness." They might not be interested in a Speedster with its original, more fragile running gear and modest performance, and might actually pay more for a "resto-mod" Speedster than for an original. Others will want nothing but the original parts, no matter how much they may interfere with the reliability or performance of the car and will only shell out the big bucks for the real thing. The same holds for converted 914-6 cars and 911T cars made into RS replicas. So you might end up with the same market value for a correct car and a modified one, but from two very different types of buyers.

As to my 912E, it was surely not worth $10k when I bought it at about half that on eBay, and I felt everything done to the car was pure upside. As to putting the 2.2S engine in an earlier chassis, you'd be amazed at how this big-bumper car drives with this engine. All that high-rpm power feels just like it does in an earlier chassis, and the wheels and tires work together to deliver the compliant yet responsive ride we all remember from the early S cars. As to what it's worth today, I'd say about $10k.

But I admit I wasn't worried about that, as this car was made for driving. And in that category, it's a real winner. So long as your modifications make driving and aesthetic sense, and are within the budget you set, I don't see any reason to be a slavish adherent to "originality at all costs." ◆

Five "Must-Checks" When Buying a Big Healey

If the doors don't open easily or close firmly, the chassis may be structurally unsound and repairs will be very expensive

By Gary Anderson

The Austin-Healey 100s and 3000s have continued to escalate in price over the past decade and now a recently restored example from a well-known restorer can cost up to $75,000. Nevertheless, big Healeys come on the market every month with asking prices less than half that amount. How do you tell whether you're getting good value for your money?

The basic principles to keep in mind are that chassis and body repair can be extremely expensive, but mechanical problems are relatively easy to fix and carpeting and basic running gear can be replaced easily. Following those principles, here are five things to check for when you're looking at one for sale.

1. Rust, rust, rust. Like location in real estate, rust is the major factor that separates a good buy from a monetary black hole. Almost anything else can be fixed within a predictable budget, but if extensive body repairs are necessary, costs can easily exceed any reasonable market value.

Unfortunately, if the Healey has just been given a fresh paint job, the rust worm may not be visible, but can still be doing its evil work. Fortunately, there's one pretty good test that will help avoid the bodge jobs. Check behind the "doglegs"—the sheet metal between the bottom of the door shut face and the rear fender opening. This area collects dirt and moisture from the rear wheel, and rust can easily start here and eventually chew into the frame rails and body panels.

If the car has really been a "no-rust, California car" all its life, or if previous body work has been properly done, you'll be able to see the end of the outer frame rail extending from beneath the door opening behind the outer fender panel. There will also be a triangular brace extending down from the door pillar to the frame rail directly behind the outer fender panel.

If either or both of these pieces are missing, it means that the car has been badly rusted and even more badly repaired.

Beware the dreaded tinworm

Don't bother to look any further. Walk away. If that area is intact, then check under the fender wells and along the underside of the rocker panels, as well as under the carpets, to further confirm that the body is in good shape.

2. Structural problems. The door gaps are another good indication of structural rust problems or badly done restoration. Basically, the Healey chassis consists of two complicated structures connected by two primary frame rails. If the frame is rusted under the passenger compartment, the car will bow in the middle, which will cause the door gaps to be uneven from top to bottom. If that's the case, or if the doors don't open easily and close firmly, the chassis may be structurally unsound and repairs will be very expensive.

Also, look under the car from front to rear to make sure the frame rails are straight and level. Crooked frame rails indicate a badly damaged or badly repaired chassis. This should also be a deal breaker for anyone but a masochistic body man.

3. Detail trim parts. Check to make sure that all the niggly little trim pieces are present, and in good shape or at least repairable. Finding a set of top bows, original gauges and instruments, side screens, or good chrome pieces can be difficult to impossible. No one currently makes a proper rear bumper for the 100, for example, or the correct rivet-secured trim rings for the headlamps.

Even before you begin your search, buy the books on Healey originality by Clausager, Robson, Piggot, and Anderson and Moment (check with the Healey clubs for these). Study them carefully to know what the Healey should look like.

4. Previous mechanical work. Read any Healey postings on the internet (www.team.net sponsors an excellent Healey mail list, as does the British Car Forum) and you'll often see the abbreviation "dpo" to explain a current problem with a Healey. This is shorthand for "dumb previous owner." Electrical problems, overheating, hot cockpits, and other challenges to pleasurable Healey ownership are too frequently blamed on British design or manufacturing quality. More likely, the problems actually developed during the period when these were just cheap old used cars, to be kept running at the lowest possible cost, frequently by folks who didn't know much about car repair.

Look for signs of previous poor maintenance, starting with the wiring harness. If there are any added wires visible outside the harness, if connections look rusty, or if the seller dismisses a problem of poor starting or accessories that don't work, as "well, it's just the Lucas electrics," you can guess that if you buy this car you're going to spend a lot of time chasing electrical problems or standing beside the road on a dark night when the car shuts down for no particular reason.

Other symptoms of "dpo" will be poorly fitted interior kits, old carpeting, a dirty, greasy engine compartment, or other obvious poor mechanical work. Sure, these can all be fixed, but if your intention is to drive and enjoy the car, rather than using it as the basis for an adult education course in British car maintenance, look for a better example to purchase.

5. Running condition. If, and only if, the car has survived this visual inspection—and if you spent less than an hour checking it out up to this point, you're letting emotion get the better of rationality—a road test will be in order. With the choke pulled out, the engine should turn over easily and enthusiastically, and start within a matter of seconds. Once the car is running, oil pressure should ramp up quickly to 60 pounds and then subside to around 40 pounds as the car warms up. Once the car is completely warmed up, oil pressure at idle shouldn't be below 20 pounds, and at cruising rpm of 2,500 or so, should be above 40 pounds.

Underway, the car should shift easily up through the gears, and overdrive should engage a second or so after the overdrive switch is flicked. Obviously the engine should sound smooth and sweet at idle, and respond quickly and eagerly to the throttle. As you drive, the steering should be responsive, with only an inch or so of free-play in the steering wheel; more than that could indicate worn steering gear. When you drive the car across a railroad grade crossing or on bumpy pavement, the car should track straight without a lot of vibration that would indicate kingpin problems, and rebound should be limited if the shocks are in good shape.

After about 15 to 20 minutes of driving, the engine temperature should be between 170 and 190 degrees; any lower and the thermostat may not be working, any higher and you may have a radiator problem or an engine that is badly clogged up. Don't be too concerned if temperature goes higher briefly when the engine is under load, like up a long grade on a hot day, but the temperature should drop back down into the correct range as soon as you're over the crest and coming down the other side.

If the car you're interested in survives all of this, then you may have a good buy that will give you a lot of pleasure and pride for some time to come. If it doesn't, then pass it up; Healeys may be rising in price, but they're not rare, and as the original hobby group ages, good, well-maintained cars are coming on the market more frequently. Just be patient, keep your antenna up, and a good example will find you.◆

Look for signs of bodywork, as well as important trim pieces

I'll Trade You My 'Cuda for Your Four-Cam

How to use 1031 exchanges to keep Uncle Sam from taxing the sale of your collector car

by John Draneas

1970 Plymouth Hemi 'Cuda

Let's say you were smart enough or just lucky enough to buy a Hemi 'Cuda coupe a few years ago for $75,000. Let's also suppose that you think that its current $500,000 value is the top of the muscle car market, and that it's the perfect time to sell it and buy a four-cam Ferrari 275 GTB. Before you do that, you might want to give a little thought to how your income taxes are going to affect the deal.

Many of us have never made any real money on a collector car and haven't had to worry about paying taxes on these profits. But when you finally hit the jackpot on a car that's appreciated like mad, know that the IRS will be there to remind you that it is your silent partner—and it gets a pretty big share of your booty, too.

Depending on the tax rates in your state, the government's cut on a sale like the 'Cuda I've described could run about $140,000. That's the equivalent of buying Uncle Sam a nice new convertible 911 Turbo, and leaves you that much short for your Ferrari.

Sidestepping the Taxman

So how do you avoid the tax collector, but still get to buy your Ferrari? By designing the transaction as what the tax law calls a "like-kind exchange." Under Section 1031 of the Federal Tax Code, you can exchange one asset for another of a like kind and not pay tax on the gain, as long as no cash goes into your pockets.

But chances are, the owner of the Ferrari you covet isn't going to want your 'Cuda, so you can't just trade even-up. Fortunately, the law allows you to do what's called a deferred exchange, using a qualified accommodator or middleman.

Doing this is pretty easy. You start by finding the buyer for your car. Once you have a contract with him, you transfer the title and the sales contract to the accommodator, who sells the car and holds on to the money. Then you locate your Ferrari and instruct the accommodator to buy it for you, which he does, in turn transferring ownership to you. That completes the transaction, and you've legally traded cars without any money from the deal coming into your possession, and thus you don't owe any tax.

The Fine Print

While all this sounds pretty simple, there are a lot of devils in the details. Here are a few of them:

1. You have to pick the right middleman. The accommodator cannot be anyone who has been your agent (employee, attorney, accountant, etc.) within the last two years, or someone related to any of those people, or a business entity you control. One experienced accommodator is Classic Automobile Reserve (www.car1031.com, 877.218.7800). Managing member Steve Drake, who serves as the CPA for Barrett-Jackson in his spare time, says, "Most collectors don't even realize that they owe taxes on the sale of their collector car." Drake says that his firm's fees vary with the nature of the transaction, but are usually below 3% of the value of the car.

2. Once the accommodator sells your car, you have 45 days to identify up to three potential replacement cars. Make sure you give careful attention to this requirement, because this period can fly by. You cannot extend it, and you can't add more cars to the list if the ones you pick don't pan out. So you must both be careful with the cars you select, as well as being sure to actually select three in the hopes of bettering your odds if your first deal goes south.

3. You have 180 days from the sale of your car to actually take title to the replacement car from the accommodator. This is usually the easier deadline to meet, because once the car has been identified, the purchase usually moves pretty quickly. But that might not be the case when the replacement is a new car that has to be ordered. Something like a Porsche Carrera GT or a McLaren SLR might incur a wait. But remember, the accommodator has to be the one to buy the car, then transfer it to you—the car can't be sold directly to you. You need to factor this second transfer into your timeline as well.

4. Although I won't go into the details, it is worth mentioning that it is possible to do a 1031 exchange with multiple cars, like replacing your 'Cuda with a Daytona and a Porsche Speedster.

Financing

Liabilities can complicate the equation a little bit. For instance, if we go back to our original example, any money you owe on the 'Cuda is compared against what you borrow to buy the 275 GTB. If the money owed on the 'Cuda is greater, the excess is treated as though it were cash received by you, and you pay tax on that amount. Simply stated, you can't pull any cash out of the deal.

But there can be a way around this, too. First, you make the exchange using all the cash available from the sale. Then, some time after all the dust has settled, you can take out a loan against the Ferarri. How long after? That's hard to say, as it has to be long enough for the transaction to be completely finished in all aspects, long enough for the loan to be a separate deal from the exchange, and long enough to demonstrate that this wasn't what you were planning to do all along. You weren't, were you?

Before you ask, leases just don't work with 1031 exchanges, as you have to own the replacement car when all is said and done.

Reverse Exchanges

Sometimes, the only reason you want to sell your car is because you found another one that you like better. What if the new car won't wait, it's a once-in-a-lifetime deal on that Ferrari, and you just have to buy it now and sell your Plymouth later? In these situations, it is possible to do a reverse exchange.

The way this works is you start by lending money to the accommodator to buy the Ferrari. The accommodator then stores the car until you find a buyer for your 'Cuda. (That's right, you can't drive the new car or keep it at your place during this time.) Then you transfer the 'Cuda and its sales contract to the accommodator, who sells it. You can then identify the Ferarri as the replacement car, which the accommodator will transfer to you, along with the cash from the 'Cuda sale that repays your original loan.

The IRS imposes similar timing rules on these reverse exchanges: You have 45 days from the purchase of the replacement car to sell the original one, and 180 days to finish the entire deal.

While 1031 exchanges can save you a lot of tax money, they do present lots of easy ways to go wrong, and any little missed detail can turn your deal into a taxable transaction. If you think you might be able to benefit from a 1031, it's best to get good advice, in advance, from a tax attorney or a competent CPA.◆

Two Words: Agreed Value

Take some time to educate yourself. Ask questions when you call for a quote

by McKeel Hagerty

Once a collector car is yours, whether you have it in your possession or it's just yours on paper, you must have it insured in your name. But that doesn't mean you should just add it to your standard auto policy. There are some big choices to be made, and you need to make sure you're protecting your collectible the right way.

There are many of things to consider with an insurance policy, but it all comes down to one question: "What do I get paid if something happens?" A standard auto policy may be fine for your standard auto. But a collectible car is a different animal. Simply put, if you have a special car that is appreciating in value, you need a special policy. There are two words to remember here: **Agreed Value**. With an Agreed Value policy, you and your agent have agreed upon the car's total value before the policy is issued, so any questions are answered in advance. You'll receive the full amount for which you have insured your vehicle if there's a covered total loss, with no depreciation. (If the car increases or decreases in value, the Agreed Value can be adjusted.)

The fact is, collector cars are not used like daily drivers. They aren't left in parking lots all day or used for running the kids to soccer practice on a regular basis. Since they are used in a limited way, they are less of a risk for the insurer. That means you can get better coverage at a lower price.

Where did I put that renewal form?

Approach insurance like you would any other resource for your collector car. Would you build a garage with a door that doesn't shut? Then don't get an insurance policy that leaves the door open. Take some time to educate yourself. Ask questions when you call for a quote. How can you use your car? Will the value be depreciated? Ask around for references. Do you know someone that's had a claim? What was his experience like? When you have a collector car policy, you'll get specialty service from people who understand collector cars. Then, you'll be able to relax and enjoy your car without worrying about everything that could happen to it.◆

(McKeel Hagerty is the CEO of Hagerty Insurance.)

Exotic Car Leasing: Have What You Want, Today

Leases can start for cars as inexpensive as $25,000 and go way past a million

by Paul Duchene

In your garage for under $8k/month

Perhaps, as the French say, it is better to travel hopefully than to arrive—but with a lease, it may be possible to do both. Exotic car leasing is booming, the billion-dollar bride of a re-energized collector car market.

And while most stare open-mouthed at the latest auction results—$3.2 million for the Oldsmobile F88 concept at Barrett-Jackson Scottsdale, $1.6 million for Howard Hughes' 1953 Buick Roadmaster at B-J Palm Beach, and $1.2 million for a Ferrari LWB California Spyder at Bonhams' sale in Switzerland last December—there are an increasing number of clever enthusiasts who are figuring out how to get behind the wheel of their dream car without plunking down boatloads full of long green.

Leasing companies report that their business rose 40%

between 2003 and 2004 as investors realized that classic and exotic cars can be as accessible as real estate.

"Many people we deal with do a lot of real estate investing. If you're one of those folks who has credit available to purchase real estate, you can use our credit line for a car instead of your own. The benefit of leasing is conservation of cash and credit lines," according to one principal in the business.

Mitchell Katz has been leasing collector cars through his Premier Financial Services (www.whynotlease.com) since the late 1970s, and says the business has changed dramatically in the last five to seven years.

"It's a combination of the strength of the market and general awareness of the industry," he says. "We sponsor auctions as well as vintage car rallies like the Colorado Grand, Copperstate 1000, and New England 1000, all to create more familiarity with our product."

Katz reckons they have thousands of leased cars stashed away in collectors' garages, and that the U.S. leasing business totals about $1 billion annually.

Customers usually find their car first, then contact a leasing company. "We don't get involved in buying and selling," says Katz. "Somebody locates a car at a price and comes to us to discuss financing. If we work out a deal, we purchase the car and lease it to them."

Twenty-Four and Out

Most leases run 60 months, but Katz says generally a client owns a car for 24 months, then moves on to something different. "We start around $25,000, but there's no limit on the high end. We just did a Mercedes 540K special roadster," he said—easily a million-dollar car.

Many collectors justify a purchase by saying, "this is the car I've always wanted, and I'm going to keep it forever." What they forget to add is, "Forever actually means, until I find something else I want even more"—which is one of the strengths of leasing. It allows you to swap cars often without having to come up with large amounts of cash.

Classic auto leasing varies from the typical view of a new-car lease as a three-year trap, says Katz. "Most people think, you pick out your car, drive it for three years and hand the keys back. We have a simple lease: simple in, simple out. People can pay off early without fees or penalties."

"Many people we deal with can afford to write a check for their car, but it's not a prudent way of doing business," he says. "We're giving people a way to make a monthly payment with a balloon at the end, as opposed to a check up-front and a larger payment."

The math on leasing is pretty simple, with interest typically in the 6% range. "In the type of lease we write, say for a $60,000 car over five years, you're looking at $1,000 a month in depreciation. But if there's a $30,000 balloon at the end of that time, the monthly depreciation goes from $1,000 to $500."

Buyers also avoid having to pay sales tax up-front in most states, merely paying tax on the monthly payment—though you'd want to check that in your state.

Horse Trading and Leasing

Ferrari is the poster child for leased exotics, and by one estimate, 60–65% of the leasing company's business involves Prancing Horses. "There are so few new Ferraris brought into the country each year, the average dealer gets maybe 35. So the secret to their success is to fortify their volume in used cars," according to one authority. "The market is so strong right now that a 2001 360 Spyder is still bringing what it sold for in 2001, or even more. A new-car buyer will put down a deposit and wait three years. But the guy who wants a car right now and is willing to buy one with 2,000 miles on it might pay $300,000—more than new."

Maintenance is the lessee's responsibility, though both Porsche and Ferrari have standard warranty procedures. "It's crucial that customers call us to check out a car they've found. If they do a deal, then take the car to a Ferrari dealer who checks the records and says the 15,000-mile service wasn't done—well, if it's out of warranty, that's a $7,000 service. For the guy on a shoestring, that's devastating," says our source.

Katz says insuring collector cars is not as expensive as people think. "The terms are the same, $100,000–$300,000 liability and $50,000 property damage. Insurance companies are flexible about deductions. Lots of times they write special policies because the drivers are putting so few miles on the cars."

But the question remains: Can you make money leasing collector cars?

Katz chuckles. "New Ferrari F430s and Enzos are selling over list, like the Bentley Continentals. If you had the foresight to get on the waiting list, you might lease it, drive it, buy it, and maybe make some money. But that's a rarity. People need to know it's going to cost them, and not look at leasing a car as a way to make money."

Instead, leasing is a way to have what you want, when you want it (now) and at a price you can afford. After all, isn't that the American way?◆

I Don't Want It Any More

The dealer will simply accept the buyer's cancellation of the contract and keep the $50,000 because the contract says he can

by John Draneas

Dear SCM: *I placed a $5,000 deposit on a Carrera GT a day after Porsche announced it was going to build the car. I signed an agreement which stated the deposit was refundable should I decide not to buy the car. Almost two years later, I was contacted and asked for an additional $45,000. At that time I signed a buyer's order that stated the deposit would be used as an installment payment on the car and was not refundable.*

In March 2004, I traveled to Leipzig, Germany, to test drive the Carrera GT at Porsche's Weissach facility. Upon returning, I called my dealer and said I no longer wanted the car. My reasons were many: a lack of daily driver capability due to the clutch design, a ride height that is too low to accommodate my driveway, a total lack of storage, and a weak resale market.

But the dealer said my deposit was nonrefundable and it was out of their hands. They told me to talk to Porsche in Germany about the matter. Having purchased two Porsches from this dealer in the past, I could not believe they were doing this to me. Now, I am left with no other option but to enlist an attorney to deal with the situation. Do you think I will get my money back?—SM, via e-mail.

This is an interesting and, I would think, somewhat common situation. Yet my research has yielded surprisingly little law defining deposits of this sort. So to analyze the situation, we have to fall back on applying general contract law principles and the Uniform Commercial Code.

Two-Way Street

Basic contract law tells us that unless so stated in the contract, it would seem doubtful that a buyer can change his mind

Now that I've driven it, I'm not excited

and get a refund of his deposit at any time. If that were the case, then he would not be legally obligated to perform under the contract, and that means the dealer probably wouldn't be either. You can't have a contract that is enforceable by only one party.

Most likely, a deposit on a new car would be viewed as an option contract. That would give the buyer the option to buy the car when it becomes available, and obligate the dealer to sell the car. If that is the case, then the deposit would be forfeited if the buyer decided not to take the car. However, if the buyer decides to buy the car, the dealer is obligated to sell it to him. This is a fair deal, and probably reflects what most people would expect under this sort of situation.

Still, it might be possible to get your deposit back if the terms of the deal are so imprecise that it does not add up to an enforceable contract. That is, before a court will hold up a contract as valid, there has to be a certain level of specificity on what the deal is all about.

Key terms that might be left open could include the specifics of the model to be purchased, the configuration of the vehicle, the purchase price, and the delivery time. But keep in mind that all of these points can be adequately dealt with in a contract, even if in a vague way, when the specifics are unknown at the time. For example, a deal to buy a "Carrera GT at MSRP once it becomes available," could be specific enough.

From Good to Bad

Our reader may have had a refund option at the start, but that likely changed when he converted his deposit to a firm order with the additional $45,000. At that point, he signed an agreement that stated that the entire $50,000 was non-refundable, and that the money had become the first installment payment on a purchase.

While that seems to be the last word, it is possible that the laws of the buyer's particular state provide some mechanism for getting out of the deal. For example, in New York, a deposit becomes refundable if the dealer is helping the buyer get financing for the purchase and the financing falls through. But, absent such a specific law, it would seem that the buyer is stuck. But he does have one last hope, and that's the Uniform Commercial Code.

Show Me the Money

In all likelihood, the dealer will simply try to accept the buyer's cancellation of the contract and keep the deposit because the contract says he can. But it might not be that simple. Under the Uniform Commercial Code (which may differ in some respects from state to state), the forfeited deposit may be viewed as liquidated damages. As such, this amount must be reasonable relative to the harm the buyer's default has inflicted upon the dealer. If the deposit is more than the amount of damage, the excess would be considered a penalty, and have to be repaid to the buyer.

The law would assume that the dealer can just resell the car and would be obligated to do so, to attempt to mitigate his damages. Still, the dealer would be able to recover monetary damages under two situations. One would be if he has to sell the car at a lower price. In that case, the damages are the difference in the sales prices. Given the waiting list for Carrera GTs, this isn't likely.

The other situation is where the car is resold at the same or higher price, but the dealer suffers a loss of volume. That is, the dealer could have sold another car just like this one to the next buyer, so the dealer winds up selling one less car than he otherwise could have. But given that Carrera GTs are all allocated, this isn't likely to be the case either.

So isn't $50,000 too much a price for our reader to pay? That's still hard to say. This dealer may have little trouble selling this Carrera GT, perhaps even at a higher price. On that basis, it might seem that any forfeiture would be excessive. But the question must be answered as of the time that the order was placed. At that time, the success of the car may not have been so predictable, and the forfeiture of the deposit may have been reasonable.

Get It in Writing and Read It

As I have written many times before, all of these matters should be specifically covered in a written contract. That way, nothing is left to chance, and provision can be made for the recovery of your legal fees if legal action becomes necessary to enforce the deal.

But our reader did have a written contract, which brings up another important point: Read the contract carefully and assume it will mean exactly what it says. He signed a contract that specified that his deposit was nonrefundable. Although we have identified a few ideas about how he might be able to get the deposit back, he is certainly going to have an uphill battle.

Remember, it is very dangerous to sign a contract that contains a provision you don't like. Don't fool yourself into thinking that the other party will not enforce it, either because of your relationship or because it would be unfair to do so. After all, if they weren't going to enforce it, why would they have made the effort to include it?◆

What To Do When It's Time to Pay

In an open-ended lease, you have the ability to end your lease early, allowing you to change vehicles as often as you wish

by Mitch Katz

"Tell me about your program." I hear this polite request each day from vintage, exotic, and collector car enthusiasts across the country. I enjoy responding because I know that behind that request is a desire to have a dream car make financial sense. It can, and it is always my pleasure to explain how.

There are many ways to purchase a collector car, including a variety of financing products. Leasing is one option that is extremely popular when buying a car for everyday use, but it is also one that is not often considered when acquiring a collector or vintage car. Of course, as with any purchase, it makes good sense to weigh the pros and cons of all of your financial options. Leasing will allow you to conserve your capital, drive more car than you would with financing, and offer you tax advantages that may not be available to you otherwise.

The lease you would use to obtain a collector car is not the same product offered by a dealer when buying a "daily driver." In the latter scenario, a dealer will provide a traditional, or closed-end, lease, which provides use of the car for a pre-determined period. Typically, after three or four years, you hand back the keys and hope to avoid charges for excess mileage and wear and tear.

An open-ended lease/purchase program is better suited for a collector car. This type of lease is more like a balloon note finance and allows you the flexibility of financing with the tax benefits of leasing. In this situation you make payments for a period of time and then are responsible for a fixed purchase option amount. At the end of the term, you have the following four options:

1. Purchase the vehicle outright and have the title transferred into your name
2. Refinance the balance with the leasing company and continue to make monthly payments
3. Trade in the car to a dealer and keep any difference above the purchase option
4. Sell the car to a private party and keep any difference above the purchase option

Easy to move on when you're done

Another significant difference between the two leases is the flexibility that the open-ended lease offers you for early termination. With a traditional lease, you are responsible for a stream of payments, and getting out early can be very costly. In an open-ended lease, you have the ability to end your lease early, allowing you to change vehicles as often as you wish. This can be vital for collectors who like to change cars frequently, and in my experience a significant number of them do.

Remember, as with any loan of this nature, it is important that you receive an amortization schedule at the inception of your lease. This will allow you to pay off your lease at any time.

The tax advantages of leasing vary, depending on where you are located. For example, sales tax in most states on a lease is paid monthly as a percentage of your payment. With traditional financing or outright purchase, you pay the tax in advance on the full purchase price of the vehicle. This difference can add up significantly.

Other benefits include taking a portion of your payment as a business expense, and using borrowed funds to free up your capital for other investments, like that 1963 Corvette you've had your eye on. Now that makes sense.◆

(Mitch Katz is the CEO of Premier Financial Services.)

Automobile Financing 101

It may be more feasible and financially attractive to purchase on a long-term loan rather than lease

by John J. Meldon

L ease or buy? That's a choice that buyers of collector cars face. Each has its advantages, and, especially with six- and seven-figure cars, it's a decision that should be made after consulting with your financial advisors.

If, after doing this, you decide financing a purchase is what you want, let me say what you should be looking for. Using my company, J.J. Best, as an example, we make it possible to obtain fast, low-cost, fixed low-rate loans starting at 6.99% simple interest, long-term lending with up to 15-year financing terms. Most loans can generally be considered and processed for approval within three to five minutes with next-day check availability. In essence, J.J.Best provides customers with a complete financial solution, start to finish.

Classic Car Financing Basics

Financial institutions our customers traditionally deal with would not lend on this automobile type. We understand the "precious collateral," and further understand the unique values underlying the classic car marketplace. Conventional lenders simply consider these types of vehicles as "used, worn-out cars." Frankly, your local credit union or bank most often just doesn't get that collector cars tend to rise in value rather than depreciate, and hence your 275 GTB/4 should be treated differently than a 2007 Escalade.

While interest rates have risen dramatically over the last five years and the Federal Funds Rate has escalated between 1% and 5% in the last two years, you should look for a company that has maintained stable fixed rates and offers 15-year long-term loan opportunities for potential classic car customers.

In many cases it may be more feasible and financially attractive to purchase on a long-term loan rather than lease, as many customers are accustomed to arranging on their new car financing. Bottom line, with purchasing, at the end of your term you actually own something.

How to Start

In general, new classic car customers considering their first purchase will need to have the following available to se-

Drive today, pay over 15 years

cure financing on their vehicle:
- Established credit history and good credit rating
- Satisfactory debt-to-income ratio
- Valid state or country driver license
- Proof of insurance
- Copy of seller's title (front and back)

My company will lend up to 98% of the purchase price of the vehicle, including tax and title fees incurred. If the customer needs insurance, we can arrange that.

Something extra we offer is that once a customer's loan is completed, we also offer that customer access to VISA and MasterCard accounts that allow him to place a photo of his newly purchased vehicle on the front of his credit card.

Please use the above features and benefits as a check list when you go shopping for classic car financing. Ask your friends where they have gotten their collector cars financed. At various auctions and shows, go to every finance company who has a booth—their very presence indicates that they are committed to the hobby.

And while we don't want to name names, you might ask the publisher of a well-known collector car magazine who helped him to arrange the financing of the silver 1963 Corvette from which he gets so much pleasure.◆

(John Meldon is the Chairman of J.J. Best Banc & Co., and a vintage car enthusiast.)

Will You Take $2,500 for Your Smashed MG?

Owners make the mistake of believing that adjusters are supposed to be "fair" when settling a claim

by John Draneas

Dear Legal Files: I own a 99,000-mile 1971 MGB-GT that was in excellent condition and drove like new when it was hit by a negligent driver, who was clearly at fault and was cited by the police. I don't want to get my insurance company involved, so I have been trying to settle my claim with the other driver's insurance company, but seem to be getting nowhere. They made me a ridiculous offer of $2,500 to total the car, which I rejected outright.

You say it's worth $7,000, but most insurance companies won't agree

Several months have passed, and I still get no contact from them. I wrote to the Ohio Insurance Board about a month ago. All I got back was a form letter, and still no contact from the insurance company. I hesitate to hire an attorney and start spending my own money when I am the victim entitled to due compensation. Can you suggest what I might be able to do?—**J.B., Canton, Ohio.**

Insurance claims seem to be the continuing bane of collector car owners. Part of the problem is that insurance claims adjusters are accustomed to dealing with damaged Dodge minivans, and often can't tell the difference between a collector car and just a very old used car. Their tendency is to assume that it's just an old used car, declare it totaled, write a small check, and move on to the next file.

Another part of the problem is that car owners make the mistake of believing that insurance adjusters are supposed to be fair when settling the claim. None of us expects a car dealer to be fair when selling us a car; why should we expect an adjuster to be fair when buying our wrecked car? The laws do require insurance companies to act in good faith, but "good faith" is quite a bit different from "fair." It leaves plenty of room for negotiation and difference of opinion about value, and also just plain ignorance.

It's not surprising that the state agency wasn't any help. They aren't consumer protection advocates who make sure you get full compensation. If they check into the situation and the insurance adjuster tells them that they are trying to settle the claim, but that you keep insisting on more money than your car is worth, it's usually enough for the agency to label it as a legitimate dispute and close their file.

Sorry, You Need a Lawyer

J.B.'s best course is to make an admittedly undeserved investment in an attorney. That will tilt the scale in several ways. It makes it clear that you are serious. It makes it clear that unwanted legal expense for the insurance company will likely follow if suit is filed. And, perhaps most important, it often brings the negotiations higher up the insurance company's ladder to a person who has broader authority to settle claims. But sometimes none of that happens until suit is filed. You have to be prepared for that, if it turns out to be the only way to get full compensation for your loss.

The SCM Price Guide indicates that J.B.'s MG is worth about $7,000. The difference between that and what the insurance company has already offered is $4,500. I hate to rub salt into the wound, but the attorney fees will easily become a significant erosion of the recovery, because one is legally unable to get reimbursement from the insurance company unless a specific state statute provides otherwise—which would be unusual.

But your attorney will know if there is any hope in this regard. For example, Oregon law allows the recovery of attorney fees for damage to personal property (cars fit that category) where the amount claimed is not more than $5,500. And you can be clever with that. Say your claim is $7,000. You might be better off suing for $5,500 and recover your legal fees than to sue for $7,000 and pay your own legal fees.

Call Your Insurer

J.B. may have made another mistake by not involving his own insurance company. He may be worried that his insurance premium might rise or his policy might get canceled if he made a claim against it, or perhaps he just feels that fairness dictates that the other driver's insurance pay the claim and he wants to assure that. But trying to do too much here might be working to his disadvantage.

Where the other driver is clearly at fault, there is no way that your insurance company is going to pay for the damage to your car. All they will do is negotiate the claim with you and the other company. Since they know that they are spending the other company's money, they will likely be more liberal about the value of the car. And they generally won't be able to penalize you for the claim when they didn't incur any loss.

Prevention is the Best Cure

Finally, J.B. is not dealing with a company that specializes in collectible cars, and would be better off if he were. The specialty companies offer two advantages. One is that they know collector cars and are more willing to recognize their true value. The other is that they offer the opportunity to establish an agreed value for your car. If it is totaled, the agreed value is paid without further debate. And if, as here, the damage was the other driver's fault, your insurance company will pay your claim at the agreed value and then take on the other driver's insurance company to get reimbursement. At that point, what can the other company possibly say about the value of the car? ◆

...we are your solution.

"THE EXPORT-IMPORT EXPERTS"

Martin E. Button, Inc. | Cosdel International Transportation | **415-777-2000** | info@cosdel.com | www.cosdel.com

Only the best for my baby.

Owning a Corvette is a bit like finding true love-you want the world to know just how you feel. Which is why we offer over 40,000 ways to keep the passion for your Corvette burning bright. Mid America Motorworks not only has quality parts and accessories for every model year Corvette, but also apparel and lifestyle products to show your delight in ownership. So go ahead and request a FREE Corvette Parts and Accessories catalog.

FREE CORVETTE PARTS AND ACCESSORIES CATALOG
Toll Free: 800.500.1500
Or visit www.mamotorworks.com/corvette

MID AMERICA MOTORWORKS™

Pursue your passion here.

Naturally, your favorite flavor changes from time to time.

With the Simple Lease™ from Premier Financial Services, you can switch cars as often as you like.

Combine that flexibility with incredible tax benefits you can't get with outright ownership or

traditional financing, and you've got a lease that's just your taste.

Premier
Financial Services
Vintage and Exotic Motorcar Leasing

Experience the Premier Advantage.

Visit www.premierfinancialservices.com or call 877.973.7700 for details.

Restoration Tips

The heartbreak of restoration is something every collector must come to grips with at one time or another. We buy a car that just needs "paint and upholstery," and three years and $125,000 later, we've got a completely restored car worth $75,000 on the best day of its life.

The articles in this section won't stop you from making irrational, emotion-driven decisions concerning the slightly decrepit car in the garage you're thinking of making into a concours prize winner, but hopefully they will slow you down a bit.

Go to restorers who know what they are doing. Don't let them go to school on your car. Be aware that doing anything to old cars is expensive, and if you don't want to pay, don't play in the first place.

Like a straight shot of single-malt whiskey, the advice in this chapter—all from experts who have been through the restoration process many times—will rock you back on your heels. And save you tens, if not hundreds of thousands, of dollars.

Before you start to restore any car, read this chapter. And then read it again. And then decide if you really want to pull the trigger. If you do, at least you can comfort yourself that you thought it all through before you began. You'll still have to take out a home equity loan to get the restoration finished, but at least this way you'll be planning on it from the start, rather than trying to explain to your significant other half way through why, instead of remodeling the kitchen, you're putting a new engine in the Ferrari.—*Keith Martin*

Restoration to the Highest Level

We asked Obry what it would cost to paint and put all the bits together to make a 90-point Dino

by Michael Sheehan

Chassis number: 08030

Everyone understands the difference between a driver and a show car. In general terms, one looks good from twenty feet away, and the other looks great up close.

But if you want to play in the real world, that of Pebble Beach or a Ferrari Club of America (FCA) concours, the road to a trophy gets long, complicated, and very, very expensive. To paraphrase the old racing adage, "Scoring well at Pebble costs money; how much do you want to spend?"

A Dino in need of paint and assembly that recently passed through my hands makes a perfect starting point for this discussion. Bruce Trenery, of Fantasy Junction, and I purchased a 1974 Dino 246 GTS, S/N 8030, a two-owner, late model, U.S.-delivered car with only 10,693 documented, original miles.

When we offered 246 GTS S/N 8030 for sale, we described it as "in primer after being stripped to bare metal as part of a potential platinum-level restoration, with a show-quality interior. Many parts reconditioned or new with new trim items, muffler, headers, and headlight covers and mount brackets. Everything boxed and labeled." The key word was "potential" platinum restoration.

The car had a great history. It was sold new to John Fergus of Westerville, Ohio. In 1997 S/N 8030 went to its second owner after covering just 8,100 miles. Fly Yellow with air conditioning, power windows, and Campagnolo wheels, it

S/N 8030, some assembly required

had the complete tool set, roll, jack, jack bag and lug wrench, tire chalk, and emergency triangle. It also had the original owner's manual, operations book and pouch with warranty card, radio card, Ferrari North America-supplied "How to Operate Your Dino" audio cassette, and the original key fob.

Additionally, 246 GTS S/N 8030 had just undergone an engine and transaxle reseal and detail by Patrick Ottis, which was ready to be reinstalled after paintwork. Great car, no stories.

The Cost to Get on the Road

Before marketing 246 GTS S/N 8030, we consulted various top shops regarding the work needed to finish the car and the expense of various levels of restoration. While the term "Pebble Beach restoration" is loosely tossed around, in fact very few cars even have a chance of being invited to Pebble, let alone to compete for a ribbon.

But while the chances of a serial-production Dino receiving a Pebble invite are non-existent due to the high number built (3,883 coupes and spyders), the FCA uses exactly the same stringent standards to judge Ferraris at Pebble as it does during the "Final Four" of Ferrari concours—Cavallino, the FCA National, Concorso Italiano, and Pebble. So what follows, which is an analysis of what it would cost to make a Dino into an FCA contender or show-winner, would apply whether the end destination was the Breakers in Palm Beach or the 18th fairway at Pebble Beach.

We went to Wayne Obry at Motion Products (www.motionproductsinc.net) in Wisconsin for estimates because he has a proven track record on the concours circuit and could commit to realistic completion dates.

We started by asking him what it would cost to finish this Dino to a 90-point level, essentially painting and assembling all the bits and turning these assemblies back into a car.

We got estimates of $12,000 to $15,000 and six to eight weeks to finish the body and paint, $12,000 to $15,000 and another six to eight weeks to re-assemble the car, $3,000 to $5,000 and another week or two to refit the engine, exhaust, a/c recharge, etc., and about $2,000 to rechrome the bare metal bumpers.

The ultimate selling price for S/N 8030 was $95,000, and the work needed added up to somewhere between $35,000–$40,000. So the new owner could conceivably have a very nice, concours-entry-level, 90-point car for $130,000 to $140,000.

And Then the Questions Began

After more than 30 years of selling Ferraris, I thought my advertisement was self-explanatory, but instead it brought a new group of eye-opening questions. One potential buyer asked "So if I buy it and get it painted and assembled, it's a 100-point car, right"? Another announced "I only buy 100-point cars, but like to drive my cars on the weekends." I knew I was back to explaining "Auto Restoration 101."

Let's look at where we started. 246 GTS S/N 8030 was shown at Concorso Italiano in 1998 and scored 85.5 points at the FCA concours there because of cracking original paint. S/N 8030 is unusually complete and original and has all the rare extras like a full set of books and tools; refinishing the paint and assembling the car with all locks, windows, and controls working almost assures 90 points.

What Platinum Entails

But what if we went for a "platinum-quality" restoration, an FCA term referring to a Ferrari that scores at least 95 points? Then we move to a much higher level of detailing,

fit, and finish. Note: All the costs below are in addition to the $35,000–$40,000 estimated above to reassemble the car to a 90-point standard.

Body & Mechanicals: Add another $3,000–$5,000 for the paintwork, an extra week or two to fit every body panel, inner door plate, and detail work inside the door jambs, under the three deck lids, and the inner edge of the engine compartment. Add $2,000 for a full body rubber kit, $3,000–$5,000 to fit the new rubber, and extra time to detail each part.

On the engine, every nut, bolt, and washer must be correct and new. Some get a black wash while others are cadmium plated. Repaint the air cleaner tank and carburetor air box and fit correct decals. Front and rear engine compartment bulkheads and fiberglass fender wells must be cleaned and painted. The exhaust, hangers, and tips must look like new. This and more all adds up to another $5,000–$7,000.

Interior: New mouse hair was supplied, so the dash must be removed, disassembled, and recovered—for about $3,000. Every interior screw and recessed washer must be new and aligned and items usually unseen—such as seat tracks—repainted. The steering column, brake pedal box, and hanging pedals must be painted, new pedal pads fitted, and more, at $5,000 to $7,000.

Underhood: The front underhood must be painted; the wiring, fuse boxes and relay box—all visible—cleaned and fuse box covers or fuse boxes replaced. The windshield washer bag, battery, and battery cables must be duplicates of the originals, the battery cover painted and hold-downs replaced. The foam pad that fits over the radiator has to be replaced. Total here, $5,000.

Total: To build a car that has a chance at a platinum trophy, we will have to spend another $25,000 to $35,000. That gives us somewhere between $160,000 and $175,000 invested. Or squandered, depending on your point of view. But if you want to chase a mythical 100-point car (rarer than a unicorn) you're going to have to open your wallet even deeper. Much, much deeper.

A Real Hundred-Pointer

Scoring 100 points with your 1988 Testarossa at the Sheboygan all-Italian concours and swap meet isn't really 100 points. The ultimate success is in the Ferrari classes at Pebble Beach, and only five Ferraris have ever scored 100 points at Pebble. According to Obry, here's what it will cost you to try to get to that level.

You approach the entire restoration completely differently from what was discussed above. You start by coordinating multiple mini-teams of specialists who disassemble, store, itemize, sublet, fabricate and metal finish, rebuild and repair, paint and polish, retrim and reassemble Ferraris. Our Dino now must come completely apart. The wiring, heater and a/c system, underdash components, and suspension will need to be completely disassembled, to the tune of $5,000 to $8,000.

Body & Mechanicals: Every part of the body must be test-fitted before and during the body and paint. Figure $25,000 to $35,000 for 100-point paint and $25,000 to $30,000 for 100-point assembly of the outer body. Add $5,000 to paint the frame, floors, and inner structures; $3,000 to powder-coat suspension arms, springs, and brackets, and $3,000 to cadmium plate mounting forks

Nice, but no trophy winner

and other parts. Add $5,000 for rebuilt shocks, new suspension bearings, bushings, and seals, and $7,000 to rebuild the brake calipers, master cylinders, and replace every hard metal line and soft rubber line on the car. Allow $5,000 to reassemble the suspension. Total so far—about $95,000.

Underhood: Rebuild heater boxes, heater valves, heater cables, clutch cable, wiring harness, and heater tubes. Another $10,000 should take care of parts, labor, and materials, except for the $5,000 wiring harness, relay panel, and fuse boxes from Italy. Allow $3,000 to fit the harness. Total: around $18,000.

Good as New Isn't Good Enough

Interior: Remember the "show-quality interior" our car was offered with? Toss it. Everything must be redone with perfect stitching, every trim panel laboriously fitted and up-holstered, with carpets to standards Scaglietti never dreamed of. Figure $15,000 for seats, door panels, dash, inner top, carpets, and trim pieces, and another $10,000 to pull the underdash components and reassemble the cockpit. The chrome trim must be redone to higher standards for $15,000 or so. If you recall, we estimated $3,000 to $7,000 to bring the engine compartment to 95-point platinum standards. Expect to spend $15,000–$20,000 if you are in search of 100 points.

At this point, we've spent $95,000 for our "builder," and another $155,000 to reassemble it to a prize-winning standard. It's not hard to see how this will end up north of $300,000, a price never achieved by a Dino, even in the late '80s.

And for your $300,000 investment, don't expect a guaranteed win, or even a car you can actually drive anywhere except onto and off of the concours lawn.◆

Restoration: Street, Show, or Race?

Sports car restorations can take one of three paths. Once you've headed in one direction, it's hard to change course

by Gary Anderson

Chuck Blakeslee in his daily-driver MGB

So you've found a classic British car—an MGB or Triumph TR4, perhaps—in someone's barn, or an old garage where it was parked many years ago. The rust is superficial, the body is in good shape, and all the parts are there. The price is good, in line with the price guide for "project cars." This could be your dream car after you restore it. But restore it to do what?

What kind of a dream do you have for that classic car? What you do with it when it's finished will make a major difference in what you'll spend to restore it, and the process you'll follow.

Three Key Questions

Let's break down the possibilities into three categories.

1. Fun daily driver: Take the car on club tours and out to meet friends on a Saturday morning.

2. Show car: Draw admiring glances from concours d'elegance judges and other club members.

3. Race car: You're sliding into the seat, pulling on your helmet, buckling the shoulder and lap belts, and heading onto the track in a vintage race.

In today's classic car hobby, those are three different ends to the journey, and the forks in the road come pretty quickly. Once you've headed in one direction, it's hard to change course and the cost differences are dramatic.

To illuminate the road map, we talked to Kent Prather, six-time SCCA national champion in MGAs and one of the most respected builders of racing MGs in the country. Then we spoke with Jim Perell, an organizer of concours events in the Sacramento area and the proud builder and owner of an MGB show car that's been featured in several national magazines. Finally we asked our buddy Chuck Blakeslee, who owns an attractive MGB that he drives two or three days a week and takes on tours with local car buddies.

Prather reckons a nice MGB, or similar British roadster of the '50s and '60s, will cost $10,000 to $15,000 to take from "ran-when-parked" to a fun driver. If you want to show the car in judged events, plan on spending $25,000 to $40,000. And if you want to go racing, pony up $35,000 to $60,000.

Baby, You Can Drive Your Car

For a daily driver, plan a basic rebuild on the engine and transmission, and while the engine is out redo the brakes and shocks, replace the interior upholstery with a ready-made kit, and get a reasonable paint job at a local shop without dismantling the car and after doing the prep work yourself. If you're lucky and don't need pricey parts for the engine or any major bodywork, you should get by with $5,000 for mechanicals and $5,000 for paint and trim. Your money will be pretty safe. If you build a good driver, somebody else will appreciate that too.

However, if the car is going to be shown at local concours

for a season or two before you start to drive and enjoy it, then take it down to the frame. Every part needs to be stripped, cleaned, refurbished, and refinished. It's got to look better than original.

Since you're putting serious money into the cosmetics, have a good engine shop do the engine. Jim Perell rebuilt his engine to exact original specs (called "blueprinting"), and went through the mechanicals. The cost sheets for his MGB show he has $17,000 into drivetrain, suspension, and electrics.

Paint and bodywork costs real money in a show car. Be very clear with your body shop about what you want and how much you can spend. It takes hours to smooth a surface so that it will reflect straight lines, and each hour can add $50 to $75 to the bill. Perell invested over $20,000 in his paint and bodywork. A good (but not great) job might have cost half that; on the other hand, if he had been after a "best-in-the-country" paint job, he could easily have spent another $10,000.

Why Concours is Costly

Interiors are another issue. Upholstery kits are fine for a driver, but on a show car the pleats have to be exactly equal and straight, the welts smooth, and the stitches exact. Perell spent over $8,000 having a correct-style interior custom-made for his MGB and a good top hand-fitted.

Then there's the question of replacement parts. A lot of catalog stuff will fit fine and work dependably. But anyone who knows what the original part looks like can spot the difference in finish, shape, logo, or color between a new-old-stock (NOS) part and a reproduction.

Patience and the miracle of eBay can unearth good original parts, but always at a price more expensive than "repops." Perrell figures he spent about $5,000 to find the right replacement trim and other cosmetic components. He's got an MGB on which he's spent over $50,000, but he's won several shows, and feels he's getting good value from his investment.

However, he will frankly admit it takes a real effort to drive it down to the ice cream parlor or park it on the street while running an errand. He can't help thinking about all the effort he's invested and how easy it would be to get a scratch or a dent.

Do You Want to Race—Or Win?

Perhaps you'd prefer hot laps to hot wax, and your idea of a parade is a pace lap, not Main Street. Maybe you're dreaming of racing.

1962 Sebring MGB race restored by Butch Gilbert

Here Kent Prather is very clear. Before you go down that road, be sure you're going to enjoy racing, because a car prepared to be safe in current vintage racing—not only for the driver but for other drivers around him—is undriveable on the street. And it's the most expensive alternative of the restoration options we are examining here.

Speed costs money; how fast do you want to go? You can install a roll bar, safety belts, catch tanks, and a fuel cell in your street car, replace the wheels with safe racing wheels and tires, and buy a suit, shoes, and helmet for about $3,000 to $5,000. That gets you into track schools, where you can drive at speed but can't actually race.

But at this level of preparation, your car won't be competitive, even though it might get through the technical and safety inspection. You won't be as fast, nor will your car be as responsive and predictable, as your competition. You'll be a moving chicane.

If you really want to race—even at the polite vintage level—you'll strip the interior for weight and safety and install a racing seat for support. You'll need to completely rebuild the engine and transmission with racing-quality components and replace the entire suspension with new or excellent original components.

And if you want to be competitive, you're easily in Prather's estimate of $35,000 to $60,000. At the lower price, you'll be safe, have a car that will challenge your ability, and teach you to race. But if you want to be at the front of the grid, count on the top of the range. And the car will be noisy, uncomfortable, difficult to drive at low speeds, and probably illegal on the highway.◆

Restoring Your High School Sweetheart

Although bias-ply tires look great, they'll make your car wander like a drunken hound on the scent of fifty rabbits

by Colin Comer

So you just bought your high school dream car at auction—that Plum Crazy 1970 Hemi Road Runner with a four-speed.

Now it's time to drive it and—holy smoke! The belted tires follow every crack in the road; it doesn't want to turn or stop; the engine's spinning at 4,500 rpm at 70 mph; and you can't hear yourself think.

Maybe Thomas Wolfe was right—you can't go home again. And if you do, you'll find Peggy Sue isn't your 100-pound high school sweetheart any more. But maybe she moved out to California and had herself nipped and tucked? That's what you need to do with your dream car: Upgrade it and give it a chance to fulfill your high school fantasies.

There have been huge technological advances in the 40 years since the first muscle cars rolled out of Detroit. They've raised our expectations of how a car should drive. Perhaps it's time to make that perfectly restored muscle car behave as good as it looks.

Having four-wheeled garage art is only half the fun. Weather permitting (I do live in Wisconsin), I drive an old car every day.

Unless you are satisfied with a trailer queen or a limited-use concours car, improvements can peel away the years from that old Detroit iron.

First make sure the car will actually get from point A to point B. Although British car owners know driving shoes must also be comfortable walking shoes, there is no need for that here.

Don't be afraid to sacrifice strict originality for everyday usability

Concentrate on basics: spark, fuel, cooling, starting, and charging.

1. Ignition: Conversion kits exist to rid your distributor of its breaker points and replace them with reliable solid-state electronics. It's completely hidden; I like the PerTronix brand. For under $100, you can't go wrong.

2. Fuel: Make sure everything is absolutely perfect from the fuel tank forward, including having factory-specified fuel line diameters. I have seen lots of big blocks with small block line sets and sending units. Get the car on a chassis dyno with an exhaust gas analyzer to make sure the carburetor jetting, timing, and distributor advance curve are spot-on. I've seen increases of over 50 hp from a proper "super tune." A properly set-up, carbureted V8 will run nearly as well as a fuel-injected one. At this point we have a car that really runs and still looks bone-stock. Be thorough, though, and inspect, calibrate, and change everything from the ignition wires to the idle jets—the devil is truly in the details.

3. Cooling System: Put the original date-coded radiator in storage and buy a stock-appearing, high-performance version—either brass or aluminum painted black. Install the right thermostat and make sure the cooling fan is correct and the shroud is in place. If equipped with a fan clutch, check that it works.

4. Starting System: Buy a modern sealed battery with more juice than stock, and no more acid leaks. Have the starter rebuilt correctly, and make sure all cables are tight and insulated properly. Invest in a high-output rebuild of your stock alternator, and if equipped, hide a solid-state external regulator under the cover of an original points-style version.

5. Transmission: Now that we have this baby humming, let's make her dance. Steep gears and four speeds sound great on paper, but in reality, nobody wants to be spinning 4,500 rpm at 70 mph. Bolt-in five-speed conversions are readily available for all domestic cars—and if that doesn't appeal to you, calculate your overall tire diameter and what rear axle ratio you'll need to put your engine around 3,000 rpm at 70 mph. For automatic transmission cars, four-speed automatic overdrive transmission conversions are available—again, bolt in and swap back to stock if you ever need to. Have the driveshaft balanced. Measure and correct the rear differential pinion angle to minimize vibration, if needed. A car that can go down the freeway effortlessly is more useful than one that is a half-second faster in the quarter mile, but makes you feel like you're stuck in a Mixmaster when you're on a cruise.

6. Tires: Although correct bias-ply tires look great, they'll make your car wander like a drunken hound on the scent of fifty rabbits. Calculate the overall diameter and width of the OEM tire and find a suitable radial replacement. For suspension, install improved bushings, establish proper ride height using good aftermarket springs painted and detailed to look stock, and add a good set of gas shocks painted the OE color. Blueprinted and quick-ratio steering boxes rival the best rack-and-pinions. Research aftermarket companies to learn correct alignment settings or your suspension won't work properly. Most suspensions were fairly well engineered when new, and only become ineffective after many years of Joe Bob Cooter deciding he "knows better than all them fancy engineering types in Deetroit."

7. Brakes: Bolt-on disc brake kits are available and the change is easily reversible. Updated lining material is available for both factory and aftermarket systems. On cars prior to 1967, it's a good idea to incorporate a dual-circuit master cylinder in place of the stock single-circuit. Make sure all rubber parts and hoses are new, and that the lines and hoses are properly routed where they won't be cut by other components or melted by the exhaust. Brake upgrades such as vented rotors, bigger calipers, and even bigger rear drums are available, but they're not necessary for the street if the stock system is fresh. Remember to use a high quality DOT 4 fluid and change it every year.

8. Gremlins: Lastly, have a competent mechanic chase out the "bugs." If your lights or wipers don't work, you surely won't find out until 10:00 pm about 300 miles from home on a deserted country road. Your car functioned reliably when new and should do so now. There is no excuse for a car that doesn't work.

Following this program, I've built some super-reliable and thoroughly enjoyable old muscle cars. There's nothing like a thousand-mile road rally or showing your 40-year-old taillights to a Honda festooned with more wings than a Wright Brothers experiment.◆

The Ins and Outs of Odometer Replacement

If the odometer is replaced, and the replacement does indicate the actual mileage of the car, then no further disclosure is required

by John Draneas

Dear SCM: I enjoy and appreciate your "Legal Files" column, but any SCMer who has been on the wrong end of an odometer discrepancy should be offended by your March 2005 article on replacement odometers. You went to great lengths to portray the situation as a minor legal inconvenience for the seller, with no mention of a moral dilemma. Would you feel the same if it was the dealer doing the misrepresenting?

You also stated that you wouldn't be inclined to accept the proposition that the odometer repair requires the dealer to represent the vehicle as "True Mileage Unknown." Please look a little more closely at the federal laws concerning odometers—if the car rolls into the repair facility with the odometer not turning, by law it is TMU and must be disclosed as such. Failure to do so by a dealer can cost him his license and earn him prison time.

The question that was asked of the Ferrari 348 owner was, "Has the odometer ever been tampered with, rolled back or disconnected?" You say that the owner's answer of "no" was technically correct. Really? Is it actually possible to replace an odometer without disconnecting it?

The owner made a moral judgment when he stated that the odometer reading on his car was correct. The fact that you speak not of right or wrong but simply of liability is troubling to anyone who has been a victim of odometer fraud, either by a dealer or a private party.—*M.B., Laguna Beach, CA*

First, a quick refresher. My March column dealt with a reader who owned a 348 that had had its defective odometer replaced. The work was done by his local Ferrari dealer, which reset the new unit to reflect the actual miles on the car. The owner had all the paperwork to back this up, which he gave to the guys at a different Ferrari dealership, along with

Turning back the clock can land you in prison

all the other service records, when he traded in his car on a 360 Modena.

While completing the transaction, one of the documents he filled out asked him if the odometer on his car had ever been tampered with. He replied "no." A couple of days later, the dealer called him, reduced the trade-in allowance for the 348, and demanded more money to make the deal work, as the 348 had been misrepresented and the dealer was now going to have to list the car as TMU.

Curbing Fraud

The actual law in question here is the Federal Odometer Act (FOA), which was enacted to curb odometer fraud, and to a great extent it has. Of interest to us is that it makes two specific things illegal. The first is driving a vehicle when you know the odometer is disconnected or inoperable, with the intent to defraud. The second is altering or tampering with the odometer with the intent of changing the actual mileage shown.

The FOA also imposes the now familiar disclosure requirements on everyone who transfers a title on a car that is less than 10 years old. You must state one of the following:

1. The indicated mileage is the actual mileage.

2. The indicated mileage is the actual mileage over the odometer's mechanical limit. (For example, 13,000 indicated miles is actually 113,000 when you have a five-digit odometer.)

3. That the indicated mileage is not the actual mileage.

Repairs are Covered, Too

Odometer repairs are also covered by this statute. If an odometer is repaired and it is impossible to register the actual mileage of the car, the odometer must be reset to zero and a sticker explaining the discrepancy must be attached to the left front door frame of the car. Thereafter, the inaccuracy of the odometer reading must be disclosed when transferring title.

However, if the odometer is replaced and the replacement odometer *does* indicate the actual mileage of the car, then no sticker or further disclosure is required. In this case, the owner is able to certify the mileage as actual when he transfers the title.

This is precisely what our reader did, and thus his answering "no" to the dealer's disclosure form is not a misrepresentation. He stated the odometer reading reflected the actual mileage of his car, which it did. As the reader described the situation to me, the defective odometer was replaced with a new one that had been adjusted to reflect the actual mileage of the car. There is nothing in the FOA that treats the odometer being physically disconnected for repair as any sort of violation, at least not unless the car is driven while it is disconnected. The reader had the old odometer and the signed docu-

ments to prove it—what more could he be expected to do?

Similarly, I do not see how the dealer has a problem with this Ferrari. The indicated mileage is the actual mileage of the car, and can be represented as such.

Fraud Abounds

I don't mean to minimize odometer fraud by any means. The National Highway Traffic Safety Administration recently published a study that determined odometer fraud occurs in as many as 3.47% of cars less than 10 years old, and costs consumers over $1 billion per year, or about $2,336 per case. These are pretty big numbers.

Odometer fraud is a hot topic. An Internet search readily linked me to numerous Web sites maintained by lawyers who handle these types of cases, and to many state-sponsored sites that alerted people to the problem and gave tips about how to detect it.

Odo Resetting, Just Sign Here

But I found the most interesting sites were the ones that offered digital odometer reprogramming services. These operations all offer legal disclaimers to advise that tampering with the mileage is illegal, and that they will do their work only on the basis of your promise that you aren't going to do anything illegal with the odometer after its displayed mileage is adjusted. I saw one shop that even requires an agreement to reimburse it for any liability it might incur for having adjusted your odometer.

Which brings us to a point we have made time and time again in SCM. The best way to have confidence in an odometer reading is for the seller to provide service bills that stretch back several years, with each representing an odometer reading that is in sync with the use the car is represented to have had. Anything else is really just wishing on an odometer and hoping for the best.◆

Leaning Into the Punch of Deferred Maintenance

The inner carburetor bodies, jets and floats were covered by a thick coat of rock-hard asphalt-like fuel sediment

by Mike Sheehan

Beauty was only skin deep

In May of 1985 I purchased an unusually nice 365 GTC/4, S/N 14965, finished in black lacquer with black leather, and resold it immediately to a client in San Francisco. In October of 1985 I re-purchased 365 GTC/4 S/N 14965, then resold it in November to a client in Hawaii. Between these two sales, my service department replaced the clutch, rebuilt the transmission, aligned the suspension, replaced the a/c hoses and adjusted the Webers. Mileage on delivery to Hawaii was 40,055. A great looking, great driving C/4 with no stories.

Over the years I kept in touch with the Hawaiian owner, and on my vacations to Hawaii he offered to let me use the 365 GTC/4 as my driver, as he rarely used the car. While I didn't take his offer to use the 365 GTC/4 while in Hawaii, a mutual friend did and in late 2000 reported, "It needs a bare-metal repaint, and the a/c went away years ago." But at the time "it ran fine," and had only 44,618 miles when he dropped it off, just 4,563 miles more than were on this 365 GTC/4 when I sold it to Hawaii years earlier.

Early this year, the owner offered to sell me his little-used 365 GTC/4. All six carbs were frozen solid in the closed position, and he didn't want to deal with coordinating the work or the logistics of shipping a non-running car from Hawaii. The affordable shipping rates are all roll-on, roll-off, which presumes a running car. So any work needed would have to be done in Hawaii prior to shipment.

The price was very attractive, but, after decades of writing on the perils and pitfalls of deferred maintenance and having used the 365 GTC/4 and carbureted 400 Ferraris as the poster children for deferred maintenance, I knew all too well the potentially deep money pit I was being offered. Attractive price or not, it screamed caveat emptor, and so some serious forethought was in order.

Mr. Smarty Builds a Budget

This C/4 was long past time for a full 30,000-mile major service, and a few calls to the best California shops confirmed that the recommended service included rebuilding all six carbs, adjusting the long cam chain and all 24 valves, degreeing the cams, overhauling the distributors and changing all the fluids. Labor estimate times ranged from the Ferrari factories very optimistic 32 hours to 46–60 hours by the best California independents.

Cam cover studs complicated the head scraping process

Always the optimist, I assumed about 46 hours at $90 or so per hour would do the job, so about $4,400 plus $500 or so in parts for a total of $4,600. Add in another 20 hours—or $1,800—to rebuild the brake calipers and replace the rubber brake lines, as they deteriorate from the inside-out, and another $800 in brake parts, so $2,600. Add another $1,000 to replace the fossilized rubber water hoses and another $1,000 for the hardened water pump seals and gaskets, so about $9,000 should more than cover the needed work if done by a California shop. Even better, the shop in Hawaii was quoting a friendly $60 per hour, not California's $90–100 per hour, so the bill should be well under $8,000.

I've got thirty years experience dealing with every possible aspect of older Ferraris and so should have seen virtually every possible complication by now. I had also sold this car twice before and felt I knew it well; it was a "no-stories" car and, to quote the last driver, "it ran well." I didn't see what could go wrong; the final bill should be under $8,000, so FedEx soon had my check for payment in full.

From Princess to Pig

A few weeks later, I was in Hawaii to buy several other Ferraris and stopped to inspect my recent purchase, throwing open the proverbial Pandora's money-box. I was shown that the aged fuel inside the six Webers had turned to asphalt,

and the inner carburetor bodies, the jets, the floats and every internal part of the carbs had a thick coat of rock-hard fuel sediment. The carbs had to be carefully heated to soften the fuel-turned-to-asphalt enough to allow the choke and accelerator pump's pistons to be pulled free from the quagmire in the carb bodies. Once apart, the asphalt-coated internals were immune to today's environmentally-friendly but impotent carburetor and parts cleaners. After several days in the carb cleaner, every part had to carefully excavated, layer by layer, with scrapers, taking care to not damage the delicate parts, and then finally cleaned with soft wire brushes and wire probes. A two-hour disassembly and cleaning had become a ten-hour heat-and-scrape exercise followed by a 26-hour wire brush-and-clean job. Say goodbye to a non-budgeted 36 hours at $60 per hour, or $2,160.

But wait, there's more. The dual aluminum gas tanks each had old fuel that had turned into half an inch of molasses. Each tank had to be cleaned by pouring a few gallons of watery carburetor and parts cleaner into them, sealing the openings, then allowing the solvent to sit for days while occasionally sloshing the cleaner back and forth, then straining the semi-solids from the goop and recycling the cleaner. As for the brass screen fuel filter, it was a throw-away. Non-budgeted time to drain the fossilized fuel and detoxify the fuel tanks and strainer system: 14 hours, or $840.

Once out and apart to be cleaned, the fuel tanks and trunk

floor became a while-you're-at-it-why-don't-you-paint-it, and so were repainted before reinstallation, adding in another non-budgeted four hours, or $240. Adding to the fuel system nightmares, the ossified fuel had plugged the fuel pumps and the insides of the flexible and metal fuel hoses, so all had to be disassembled and cleaned, adding another 6 hours, or $360.

Most amazing was the 27.5 hours of mind-numbing labor needed to scrape 33 years of carbon from the cam cover gaskets, in slow and careful 1/32" increments. They were permanently glued to the aluminum heads with the Italian version of hardening Permatex. Making the job more difficult was that the gasket surfaces were well hidden in a forest of cam cover studs, so a wood chisel was used to avoid gouging the aluminum surfaces. Each short and careful stroke of the chisel had to be prefaced by packing paper towels inside the cylinder head to prevent the carbonized gasket fragments from falling into the open engine, and each stoke was taken with a vacuum hose in hand, to suck up the carbonized gasket fragments before they could fall into the engine's internals.

Just as the fuel had fossilized, the brake fluid had turned to rusty Jell-O and the brake calipers had to be cleaned with the same mind-numbing detail work as the fuel system, so add another non-budgeted $480. This same gelatinous brake fluid also meant the master cylinder had to be rebuilt, another three hours, or $180. Additionally, the brake vacuum pump uses a wire-wrapped rubber suction hose, covered in a cotton based material that had reverted to dust over the years, and so had to be replaced, adding in another non-budgeted $200 in parts and $180 in labor.

The next surprise was extra time needed to cut free fos-

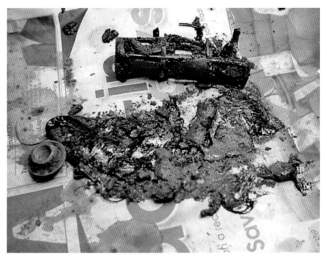

Fuel strainers

silized water and heater hoses, scrape the aluminum surfaces of the now-exposed crystallized powder on the aluminum water pipes and overhaul all the frozen heater valves—another non-budgeted bill of eight hours at $60, or $480. Needless to say, the water pump seals were beyond redemption, and so another $500 in parts and labor were quickly added in. Of course, the grease used in the distributor advance mechanism had long ago gone to its maker, so another $480 in cleaning labor was needed. As for the a/c compressor and drier, a mere $600 in parts and labor cured their ailments. Last but not least, the original air injection tubes had simply been crudely folded over and had to be carefully heated to be removed and then properly capped, at another $360. The list of frozen nuts and stripped threads that had to be repaired was part of a voluminous list of other minor one- and two- hour add-ons that went on for pages.

Was there any good news? Yes, the valve assembly was serviced without surprises, the valve adjustments all came within specifications and the cam chain was tensioned without complications. The cams had to be re-degreed, but within the time I had allotted.

Even better, the car itself was solid; the original leather had a nice patina; the body was straight; the decent black paint actually enhanced the 365 GTC/4 fish-mouth; the Borrani wire wheels were serviceable and, oh, happy days, the rising market should make up for my unexpected expenses!

Earth to Mike? Hello?

Even the experts need the occasional wake-up call—and this was certainly a big one. As an expert, I should have expected the worst, and more. Indeed, the very experienced Hawaiian Ferrari specialist doing the work was surprised that I was surprised. Looking back, if I had a detailed pre-purchase inspection done, my offer would have been less, but my lower offer would not have bought the car. If I wanted the car, the price was the price and I simply had to accept the long list of problems that would unfold.

Had the owner put in fresh gas and circled the island twice a year, few of these problems would exist. The bottom line—I now owned the car and had to live with an extra 200 hours of excavating and exorcising fossilized fluids, frozen parts and deferred maintenance. Even with the friendly Hawaiian price of $60 per hour, the final bill was about $15,000, $7,000 above my budget, and the true price of very long-term deferred maintenance. While every 365 GTC/4 will need this maintenance over its lifetime, I simply hadn't budgeted to do it all at once.◆

My 6-Cylinder FrankenPorsche

The 16" x 6" wheels looked wrong, were not stock on this car or any Porsche in 1976, and made it ride like a truck

by Jim Schrager

It's what's in the back that counts

We constantly stress that when it comes to market value, original is best. But from time to time a car comes along where the factory just got it wrong, the basic model has no collectible appeal, and upgrades that drastically improve its performance are something to consider.

I purchased a 1976 912E sunroof coupe on eBay, with about 250,000 miles on the clock, for $5,450. A full service folder accompanied the car, verifying the mileage. I have driven the car several thousand miles myself, and what is right and wrong with this machine gives a thorough picture of what happens after the new wears off.

For starters, as regular readers may recall, I am not a fan of the one-year-only 912E. By the time it was for sale on eBay, this one had blissfully lost its original VW four-cylinder motor and there was a trusty 911 engine in its place. For those of you looking for a collectible, this car would be a severe disappointment. But since I believe that the 912E is absolutely not

collectible, for me the installation of a far better engine was a pure upgrade.

Bye-Bye to the Four

The original VW engine first puked at 118k miles, was rebuilt, and then thoroughly destroyed itself at 221k by launching a rod through the case, at which time it was far cheaper—and better—to install a decent used 911 engine.

The engine installed was a 1969 911T, the lowest-horsepower 911 engine ever built, at 110 DIN. These are quite easy to source and can be had in running condition for about $2,000. It is still a very nice engine, fitted with trusty, if expensive, Weber carbs. The conversion from 912E to 911 was well done, with a proper 911 dry-sump oil tank and all OE sheet metal on the engine. The car ran and drove quite well, although I was interested in installing a higher-horsepower 911 engine.

The car arrived with original seats hiding under cheap

seat covers. They had to go. A decent pair of used seats from our collection made an immediate improvement. The steering wheel was aftermarket junk, about two inches smaller than the original, and it was swapped for an excellent original purchased at a swap meet for $27. The carpets had been replaced and were not OE material, but were acceptable. The radio was broken and we installed a period Sony AM/FM/cassette. The door pockets and plastic attaching the hardware were ratty; all this was rebuilt with about $15 worth of small parts.

No Rust, No Way

The wheels were zooty 16" x 6" later Fuchs alloys, fully polished. They looked wrong, were not stock on this car or any Porsche in 1976, and made the car ride like a truck. It was, no doubt, surefooted at 120 mph, but I don't often find myself at 120 mph. I swapped them for a painted set of steel wheels, standard issue on 912Es, as shown in the 1976 brochure.

The car was still in its original silver with black interior. The paint was a modest-quality respray, showing some age. As always, I attacked the mechanical and interior issues first, then moved on to the paint only when I was sure the rest of the car was sound. The chassis was solid, "no rust," as they say. Of course, all 1976 911s chassis should be sound, as this is the first year of full chassis rustproofing. However, the battery pans can still rust and the front fenders were not galvanized until model year 1981.

The transmission, brakes, steering, and suspension were stock and worked well—the result of the consistent and thorough maintenance. Stock steel wheels, 6" x 15", and a set of 185/65/15 Pirelli P400 tires transformed the car for street use. It retains all the handling and response built into every 911 chassis and rides like a car instead of a buckboard.

Now Let's Get Some Horses

All that was left was the engine, and here I put in one of my favorite early 911 set-ups, a 1971 2.2S, complete with mechanical fuel injection (MFI) and 180 DIN hp. This engine was purchased through a Porsche Internet talk list and had been rebuilt a few years ago. It was cheap at $3,500 because most racers want more displacement. I like the feel of small-bore, high-compression, short-stroke, vintage power, and this is the last 911 engine of its type. We sold the 1969 911T engine and carbs for $2,000 to a needy 1969 Targa. Going to a 2.2S and MFI from a 2.0T for just $1,500 was a real bargain.

Projects yet to do? The paint looks good from 30 feet; someday I may want to make that three feet. I'd like to put in a set of genuine OE carpets, but since I drive this car in the winter, I'm not sure that's the best use of my limited funds.

When I total up everything I've spent, it's around $7,500, not counting my personal time. And my best guess is this car would bring around $10,000 if offered on eBay. So the question is, am I deriving enough pleasure out of my FrankenPorsche to justify my expenditures? Especially in this case, as the 912E was so pathetic, the answer is yes.

And don't think about trying this with your garden variety MG or Triumph or Alfa. They simply don't have the underlying engineering that allows them to go this many miles, or to take this kind of performance upgrade.

With good care, 911s can run almost forever—consider our Editor's 911SC, with 177,000 miles, and the bottom end has never been apart. It's this kind of basic strength in construction that makes this whole project possible.◆

2.2S fits nicely

Swap-meet steering wheel

Restoration Escalation

A restoration is like a war-planning exercise, coordinating multiple teams of specialists working at insanely expensive prices

by Michael Sheehan

Expect to pay handsomely for every point you hope to score at concours

Over the years, the term "restoration" has had evolving meaning in the Ferrari world. Back in the 1970s, it meant new paint, clean leather, maybe a valve job or an engine rebuild, some non-original chrome work and a great detail. Today, however, it implies much more.

The assumption now is that a restored Ferrari is one worthy of a place on the lawn at Cavallino, Concorso Italiano or even Pebble Beach. As this standard and the times have changed, so have the costs, which have escalated dramatically.

More Work

In the 1980s and early 1990s, a "Pebble Beach-quality" restoration was usually estimated at about 2,000–2,500 hours labor, plus parts, machining, sublet and materials. Today, the same car would be subjected to 3,000–3,500 hours, and a whole new world of peripheral expenditures would be tacked onto the bill for things like research, logistics, and presentation.

This is because when a restored Ferrari is finally ready to show, a full support staff is needed. These people cover detailing upon delivery, show setup, and most importantly, prepping the owner for presentation. The car's owner must be briefed such that he can understand the entire restoration and become familiar with every aspect of the work. Hopefully he can convince the judges of the veracity of the work, not only by knowing the answers to their questions, but by anticipating potential questionable areas before being asked.

A restoration is like a war-planning exercise, coordinating multiple teams of specialists who disassemble, store and itemize, sublet, fabricate and finish, rebuild and repair, paint and polish, retrim and reassemble insanely expensive and usually unique pieces at a price and with a firm deadline. In the small world of concours entrants, miss your target date for Cavallino or Pebble Beach, and you lose your client.

The Shops

Today, I believe there are only four large total-service restoration shops with ten or more employees in the U.S. These are Motion Products in Wisconsin, Bobby Smith in Texas, Dennison Motor Sport in Washington, and Paul Russell and Co. in Massachusetts. All are located in the suburbs or farther removed from the expenses of the big cities.

There are several smaller shops such as CAROBU Engineering and F.A.I. in Southern California, and Patrick Ottis and Perfect Reflections in the San Francisco area, or David Carte in Virginia. All have had Ferraris at Concorso Italiano or Pebble Beach in August.

Sadly, there are no large restoration-only shops left in California. While California may be car-crazy, it is also one of the most litigious places on the planet and a large, high-profile shop filled with top-end Ferraris is simply a target for every lawyer fresh out of law school who believes a law degree guarantees a house at the beach and a paid-for BMW.

Overhead and Regulations

It costs a lot of money to keep the doors open at a restoration shop. There are many costs, such as hazardous material disposal, that have gone sky-high in the past 20 years. From painting, plating, and powder coating to machining and sand blasting, all of these processes have become increasingly regulated due to the environmental implications of the materials involved. The effect on the cost of a restoration has been huge. While it once cost $10k to do the chrome on a 275 GTB, the same job is $35k today.

For a further example, in 1989 I outfitted my expanding restoration shop with a brand-new, industry-standard paint booth and the latest piston-type compressor and air drier. It cost me $30k for the booth and $15k for the compressor, installed and ready to go.

When I re-leased the same building in 1998, the new tenant had to install a new downdraft paint booth and a new rotary air compressor with a dryer system. Cost? About $225k for the booth and $50k for the rest, all to comply with newer regulations. Undoubtedly today you're looking at an even bigger bill.

Labor costs are another factor. In the mid-1980s, a top mechanic or painter might make $50k a year, while today the same top-level technicians can expect a healthy six figures. I know some shop managers that could literally name their salary.

Think this run-up in costs is crazy? Consider the cost of insurance. All restoration shops now insist their customers carry their own insurance, as the cost to insure a facility filled with a dozen or more Ferraris, all valued at over $1m, is simply unobtanium.

The Ever-Rising Bar

There are no more barn-find 375 MMs or 250 GTOs, so today's restoration is almost always the recycling of last decade's Pebble Beach contender, but to an ever-higher standard. The factors driving this start with the general competitiveness of the Ferrari industry.

In the 1970s, restoring old cars, even Ferraris, usually meant hot-rodding them and chroming everything in sight. But not anymore. Today it is not enough to complete a world-class restoration, but the result must be documented, in voluminous photo albums that are used to convince skeptical judges that every detail is absolutely correct. The wrong trim, the wrong fasteners, the lack of a photo to show how something was done and you just dropped a point further away from the podium.

There are many anal-retentive trainspotters, including most of the top judges in the hobby, who take this stuff very seriously. Some judges are professional restorers themselves. These guys dedicate massive hours of research and documentation to their craft, scanning in old photos and linking up online to more clearly define the standards for concours excellence.

Cuteness Doesn't Count

Cars are usually judged at concours by starting at 100 points and then subtracting points for flaws. Only Motion Products has scored 100 points at Pebble Beach, and it has done so five different times, making it the standard bearer for both top quality and research in the world of restorations.

The paradox of restoration is that the big collectors, those with multiple best-of-the-best Ferraris who can hire the very best shop and can afford the best presentation, expect to win. So the reality is such that a lesser car requires even more work and higher standards to beat the big guys at their game and bring home a trophy.

While I was able to do a quality restoration on a four-cylinder 1930 BMW cabriolet for about $35,000, and my eleven-year-old twins brought home a third-place podium finish in a mini-car class based more on "cuteness" than presentation, the highly competitive Ferrari world is a bit different.

Just as speed costs money in racing, the same applies to restoration. To gain that extra point, that extra edge, it is always extra-expensive. When you're up against the most desirable and unique Ferraris in the world, competing against the best shops and some of the wealthiest men in the world, winning is an expensive art form.◆

Sending the Prince of Darkness on His Way

Original starters were heavy, drained the power supply when they turned the engine, and had a bad habit of burning out bearings

by Gary Anderson

Let's face it, our beloved British cars aren't perfect. Perhaps by standards of the period they were pretty good, but when compared to modern cars, they're really not very safe, certainly not as reliable, and you're not going to find one that has the 100,000-mile service intervals we've come to expect from new cars.

Yet despite these shortcomings, we specifically buy these old cars today to take on 1,000-mile tours and other fun-time events. So in the spirit of tweaking for comfort and safety without changing the character of your old car or detracting from its value, here are seven changes for you to consider (of course, most of these apply to all old cars, not just those from England). Where applicable, we have included a representative Web site. But this is a situation where Google is truly your friend.

Spin-on Oil Filter

Most older British cars came equipped with an elaborate cartridge system that makes changing the oil filter a challenge. The original filters had bolts, washers, spacers, gaskets, and O-rings. Leave any part off, install it crooked or backwards, and you can easily wind up with oil all over your garage floor.

Adapters are readily available from British car parts suppliers that allow you to use a standard modern spin-on oil filter from the nearest Pep Boys. Better, this change is simple to reverse. $150 (www.mossmotors.com)

Multi-bladed fans help to keep temperatures—and repair bills—down

Lightweight Multi-Blade Fan

Overheating is a standard problem with British cars. If you look at the rudimentary and crudely made two-blade or four-blade fans that were original equipment, this isn't surprising. Also, these old cast or pressed fan blades occasionally break free and spin into the radiator or body work. An easy solution is to replace the original fan with a modern lightweight plastic six-blade fan. You can usually find a suitable one in an auto parts store or through car clubs. $45–$75 (www.ntahc.org for Healey version, others at www.napaonline.com)

Alternator

The original generators were just about adequate to power the headlights, taillights, and heater while recharging the battery, and they were big and heavy to boot. Your best bet is to replace it with a modern alternator. They're small, lightweight, and produce two or three times the power of the original generator. A bonus is that an alternator will power everything you could want to mount on the car, including those neat rally lights, your discretely installed audio system, and a power point for your cell phone and computer. $100–$150 (Installation info can be found at www.mgaguru.com/mgtech/electric/ac101.htm)

High-Ratio Starter

Original starters were exceptionally heavy, put a huge drain on the power supply when they turned over the engine, and had a bad habit of burning out bearings. They also use a Rube Goldberg arrangement of springs and gears to engage the ring gear, another typical source of starter problems.

Fortunately, the Japanese have come up with small, lightweight gear-reduction starters that draw much less power to spin up the engine, will spin it faster, and are a bolt-in replacement. $269 (www.aptfast.com), or buy a rebuilt 1988–91 Isuzu Trooper starter for your MGA/MGB and similar models for $85. (www.autoexpress.safeshopper.com)

12-Volt Battery

Many British cars came with two six-volt batteries mounted on the frame behind the seats that were only accessible after you'd removed the dog, the luggage, the carpet, and the access door.

Though you're probably still stuck with the original location, at least you can pull out the two old six-volt batteries, and replace them with one good deep-cycle, low-maintenance 12-volt battery the same size as one of the old six-volt jobs. $65–$85 at any auto parts supplier.

Modern Fuse Panel

Nearly all British cars came with two fuses. Typically one fused the horn and the other fused most of the other electrical circuits. This setup has led to long, learned treatises on what happens when the smoke escapes from the electrical circuit of a British car.

A good idea is to add some inline fuses—for example, to the rear light circuit and the front light circuit—so that a short doesn't result in total loss of lights or complete incineration of the entire electrical system.

A better idea is to install a modern fuse panel in some discrete but accessible place in the interior or engine compartment, and run each of the separate circuits through its own fuse. This change isn't easily reversible, but it costs less than $25, improves the car's reliability and in many cases enhances its value. (A good list of instructions that apply to almost every British Car can be found at www.mgaguru.com/mgtech/electric/et201b.htm)

Five-Speed Transmission

Though this improvement is expensive, substitution of a five-speed transmission from a Japanese junker or English Ford for the original transmission, using one of the readily available conversion kits on the market, is a good thing in most British marques.

A modern five-speed will provide smoother shifting, generally better intermediate gearing, and a nice top gear for 70-mph cruising. You won't be able to accelerate any faster, but at least you won't be terminally uncomfortable at cruising speed. $2,500–$3,000 (www.quantummechanics.com)◆

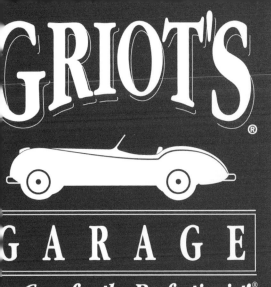

Built to run 'til the road wears out!

Does a swirl in your paint ruin your whole day?

Only From Meguiar's
SERIOUS CAR CARE FOR CAR CRAZY PEOPLE™

If this is you, you're Car Crazy. And that means you'll really love Meguiar's NXT Generation® Tech Wax™...its the most technologically advanced synthetic wax for today's modern finishes and clear coats. Our breakthrough formulation goes on and comes off easy without a powdery residue to visually eliminate fine swirls, protect against UV damage, and leave your finish "amped up" with a deep, wet-look shine that is unbelievably intense. ESP technology creates a tough polymer bond for xtreme durable protection. For more information visit

Selling

Selling one of your collector cars can be the best day of your life. Or the worst, depending on how you handle it. In this section, you'll find pithy advice on how to minimize the tax implications of selling a car, what your options are if the high bidder at an auction refuses to pay up, and the legalities you'll encounter when you bid on your own car.

In the end, our goal is to help you get the most for your car, with the least grief. That way you'll have that much more to spend on your next one.—*Keith Martin*

Is It Legal to Bid on Your Own Car?

In a "no reserve" auction, chandelier bids are misrepresentations and fraud

by John Draneas

I hadn't even made it to the Phoenix airport on my way home when my cell phone started ringing with Arizona auction rumors. When I did get home, there were emails waiting for me with the same stories—cars sold to chandeliers, sellers buying their own cars back, buyers refusing to perform, you name it. The phony or chandelier bidding stories got my curiosity going. Several people asked me what the law says about this, so I decided to find out.

We are going to address only two issues here. One is the proverbial "chandelier bid," where the auctioneer calls out and recognizes a bid that no one seems to have made. The other is bidding on behalf of the seller on his own car, either by the seller himself, by a friend or agent of the seller, or by the auctioneer.

Bidders should read their agreements so they know their rights—and those of the auction company

The Law

Auctions are firmly covered in the Uniform Commercial Code, which is a commercial law adopted in all the states, although each state is free to make modifications to its version. Of interest to us is Section 2-328, which sets out the rules on auctions. Since individual states can modify the uniform rule if they chose to, I looked at Arizona's version as the most relevant to our situation. Arizona adopted UCC Section 2-328 without modification, likely the same law as in your state.

The Meaning of the Reserve

Under the law, auctions are considered to be "with re-serve" unless it is made clear that the sale is being made without reserve. The reserve is the minimum price that the seller will accept for the car. For the seller's benefit, it is kept secret between the seller and auctioneer. A reserve auction carries one additional legal difference: The seller may withdraw the car from the auction at any time before the gavel falls. In a "no reserve" auction, once the first bid is made, the seller can no longer withdraw the car from the auction, and it sells to the highest bidder.

There are two schools of thought on reserves. The traditional view is that the seller is always better off with a reserve because it affords obvious protection against a horrible result if the high bid is woefully below the real value of the car.

The more modern view is that "no reserve" auctions work better because the bidders know the car is going to sell, and they are more motivated to bid. Proponents of this view point out that in a reserve sale, bidding frequently jumps once the auctioneer announces that the seller's reserve has been met. In a "no reserve" sale, this bidding heat begins as soon as the car is driven onto the block.

Whether or not the "no reserve" theory really brings higher sales prices is open for debate. But when things don't go as planned for proponents of the theory, there is plenty of incentive to "help" the real bidders reach the "right" price on the car; in other words, to protect the buyer against his car selling for far less than expected.

Chandelier Bids

Chandelier (or phantom) bids are a well-recognized fact of auction life. In fact, at our SCM Insider's Seminars, we strive to teach attendees how to tell if there is "real money" on a car. But as common as the practice is, is it legal?

The answer is: No. Chandelier bids are misrepresentations and fraud. But you won't find any court cases on it. Not only is it hard to know when a chandelier is bidding, proving it in court is even tougher.

Chandelier bidding is often justified in reserve auctions on the "no harm no foul" theory. That is, there won't be a deal struck until the reserve is met anyway, so no one is damaged when the auctioneer helps things along. But that misses one key point. As a seasoned negotiator, I like being the high bidder in a no-sale auction. That gives me the leverage to find the seller afterward and try to negotiate a deal off the block (but still with the auction company involved, obviously).

Seller Bidding

The UCC is quite clear on the issue of sellers bidding on their own cars. It's generally illegal. The courts have cut some slack for sellers in reserve auctions, on the basis that no real bid was going to take the car as long as the reserve had not been met. But "no reserve" auctions are an entirely different story.

In a "no reserve" auction, seller bids are illegal unless the real bidders have been given notice that the auctioneer will allow sellers to bid on their own cars. If notice is given, there is no legal problem, and "buyer beware" prevails. But if notice is not given and the seller buys the car, the legal situation gets very interesting. The UCC clearly states that the highest real bidder has the right to either cancel the purchase or to buy the car at the highest real bid made. And, in one court case involving intentional bid rigging, the highest real bidder was awarded punitive damages to boot.

What sort of notice is sufficient to validate seller bids? Obviously, an announcement made on the block by the auctioneer will do the trick, but no auctioneer really wants to do that. Curious, I checked my bidder's agreement from one of the recent Arizona auctions. There it was: The auction house reserved the right to accept bids from sellers, and even to make the bids for them. I had been warned in black and white, in unmistakable language. Is it legally sufficient? I would imagine that it is, since it has my signature on the bottom. Funny, though, it took me five years of registering as a bidder at this auction to notice that little sentence.

All of these rules apply equally to Internet-based auctions. The UCC is not limited to bricks-and-mortar auction houses. Oddly enough, Internet auctions may make it easier to prove phony bidding, even though the opposite may seem to be the case. The advantage is that Internet bids are made in writing, and there is a discoverable record of who made which bids.

Buyer Beware

As illegal as many of these tactics are, bear in mind that they are common. Learn to know how to "read" the bidding, and how to know if there is real money on a car. Decide how much you are willing to pay before you even start to bid, and stop bidding when you get there. Not all auction houses bend the rules, and even the best ones have a hard time keeping the sellers from engaging in these practices. Read your bidder's agreement carefully, and see what the rules really are at that particular auction.◆

Tax Consequences of Selling Your Car

In some cases, waiting a few weeks, or even a single day, to sell your car can result in substantial tax savings

by John Draneas

Collector car values are skyrocketing, and many of us have substantial gains in our collections. More and more collectors are wondering if the market is peaking, and whether they should sell. If they do sell, what are the tax consequences? Although many of us want to stay in denial about this, gains on collector cars are fully taxable, and failing to report them runs the risk of a tax fraud charge.

On the other hand, collectors who are new to the game are buying cars at today's rather feisty prices. Of course, if the market keeps going up, they will accrue substantial gains. But if the bubble bursts, as some expect, these investors could suffer losses. Are there any tax advantages to soften the blow?

Start With the Right Pigeonhole

You should begin by identifying the tax character of your collector car, which depends on the purpose behind your ownership and the way in which you use it. The various classifications, and their general tax characteristics, are as follows:

Personal use: This is the car that you drive for personal purposes; that is, your regular driver, not used in your business. You cannot depreciate the car. If you make money on it, the gain is taxable as a capital gain. If you lose money on it, there is no tax benefit afforded.

Investment: This is the car that you buy to make money on when it appreciates. It can be driven only in a limited manner, otherwise it becomes a personal-use automobile. It can be a blue-chip collectible, but doesn't have to be. You cannot depreciate it. If you make money on it, the gain is taxable as a capital gain. If you lose money on it, the loss is a capital loss.

Business use: This car is driven as part of your business and you can depreciate it. If you make money on it, the gain is taxable as ordinary income to the extent of the depreciation that you have previously claimed on the car, and capital gain thereafter. If you lose money on it, the loss is deductible as an ordinary loss.

Inventory: This is the car that you own to sell to your customers in the ordinary course of your business. You cannot depreciate it. If you make money on it, the gain is taxable as ordinary income. If you lose money on it, the loss is deductible as an ordinary loss.

Which is Better?

If you have a gain, it's best if it's a long-term capital gain. Long-term means you owned the car for at least a year. The result is that the profit is taxed at a maximum 28% federal

1958 Porsche Speedster Tax Recap

ESTIMATED CAPITAL GAINS TAX IF PURCHASED AS AN INVESTMENT		
Length of Ownership	Under 1 Year	Over 1 Year
Purchase Price	$100,000	$100,000
Sold Price	$150,000	$150,000
Income	$50,000	$50,000
Tax	$17,500 (35%)	$14,000 (28%)
Net Profit	$32,500	$36,000

tax rate (collector cars do not qualify for the 15% rate). A short-term capital gain is taxed the same as ordinary income, at your regular income tax rates up to 35%. Which means that in some cases, waiting a few weeks, or even a day, to sell your car can result in substantial tax savings (see sidebar).

If you have a loss, an ordinary loss is best because it can be deducted against your ordinary income. Subject to various limitations, that can yield up to a 35% benefit. A capital loss can be offset against other capital gains, yielding a 15% or 28% benefit, or deducted against ordinary income at the rate of $3,000 per year. Any unused loss will carry forward.

State income taxation is generally the same as the federal treatment, although that differs in some respects in some states, and the tax rates vary widely.

A popular tax deferral technique for real estate is a "like kind" exchange. The same can be done with collector cars. If you meet the various rules that apply to the economics of the exchange, you can exchange one collector car for another without paying tax. This technique is available for collector cars held for investment and business use. It is not available for cars held for personal use or as inventory.

The IRS Doesn't Play Fair

These distinctions were highlighted in a U.S. Tax Court case decided last year. This case dealt with the tax consequences of losses on the sale of collector cars by David Taylor Enterprises, Inc. after the death of its sole shareholder.

Taylor was a successful car dealer in the Houston area and one of the largest Cadillac dealers in the world. Taylor had a passion for classic cars and established an impressive inventory at his Galveston, Texas, facility. This effort began in 1979 with the purchase of a 1931 Cadillac Roadster for $40,000, and resulted in 80 car sales over 12 years.

All the classic cars were impeccably restored. They were stored in a temperature-controlled facility known as the David Taylor Classic Car Museum. The public was allowed to pay admission and tour the museum. All cars were available for sale at all times. They were kept on jack stands to protect the tires from leakage and flat spots, they were started every six weeks, and the oil was changed every six months.

In the years prior to Taylor's death, the corporation sold eleven cars, at gains of up to $143,000 on one car. It reported all gains as ordinary income from the sale of its inventory. After Taylor's death, it became necessary to raise cash to pay estate taxes, and 69 cars were quickly sold through a broker, not uncommon in this type of situation. The sales produced substantial losses, which the corporation deducted as ordinary losses, logical because the cars had always been treated as inventory.

The IRS challenged the deduction of the losses. They seized upon the storage of the cars in the museum, separate from the new car inventory, the admission fees charged to the public, the collector license plates on the cars, and the relative infrequency of sales (eleven) before Taylor's death. They also claimed the relatively long times the cars were owned (typically seven to ten years) and the lower level of marketing as compared to the new cars was proof that the cars were not held as inventory.

Rather, the IRS claimed, the cars were held for exhibition as museum pieces. As such, they were investment assets, and the losses were required to be treated as capital losses. With no capital gains against which to offset the capital losses, that produced a tax increase of about $545,000. Although not directly stated in the court's opinion, my estimate is that the sale of the 69 cars after Taylor's death generated a loss of over $1.5million.

The Tax Court was not persuaded by the IRS. The judge couldn't understand the museum piece argument: "We question whether the dealership would expend effort to acquire, rebuild, and maintain the classic cars if the purpose was merely to display them, stationary, at a museum." Obviously, and luckily for the estate, the judge was not a car guy.

The Court also criticized the IRS's lack of consistency. The IRS never objected when the corporation paid income tax at the higher ordinary rates on its profits when it sold the eleven cars in the years prior to Taylor's death. It reported the profit from those sales as ordinary income, and paid taxes at ordinary rates. But now that the pendulum had swung and the cars were being sold at losses and generating ordinary deductions, the IRS wanted to raise questions. That is true, but that's what they do.

Near-Total Victory

The taxpayer won. Yet even though it seemed like the IRS didn't have much of a case, a contested audit was required, along with an appeal within the IRS and litigation in the U.S. Tax Court. I would guess that this entire exercise probably cost the corporation at least $100,000 in legal fees. But at least the legal fees are deductible as ordinary expenses, reducing their net cost by 30%–45%. Admittedly, that seems like little consolation, but when dealing with the IRS, you take any prizes you can, no matter how small.◆

When the High Bidder Won't Pay Up

Even though the Porsche was "sold" when the hammer fell, it was never "sold" for purposes of the seller's contract

by John Draneas

Bidders may be qualified to buy, but that doesn't mean they'll go through with the deal

Our firm recently represented an SCM subscriber who had the seemingly impossible happen. He consigned his 1960 Porsche 356B Roadster to a very well-known auction company. At the end of spirited bidding, the hammer fell on a high bid of $95,000, and our client started buying champagne for all his friends. The bid seemed very high for a single-grille 356 Roadster, but this one had been expertly restored to all-original condition, carefully driven and maintained, and extremely well presented at the auction.

The next day, our client's jubilation turned to utter disbelief. The auction company informed him that the buyer came that morning to apologize about having a change of heart. He no longer wanted the car and refused to pay for it.

Faced with no better alternative, the auction company placed the Porsche in secure storage, engaged its attorneys to make the buyer fulfill his obligation, and assured the seller that all would be worked out. After many weeks of getting nowhere, the seller contacted our firm to sort out the mess.

Exactly What is Guaranteed

"After all," our client asked, "the auction company pre-qualifies all bidders, and they all have provided proof of financial ability, haven't they?" Yes, but there is a practical limit to what they can do.

Auction companies routinely qualify their bidders in four ways: cash or cashier's check deposit; bank letter of credit; bank letter of guarantee; and authorized credit card. This situation would not have happened if either of the first two methods had been employed, but cash or cashier check deposits are very awkward at this level. So is the formal bank letter of credit: The issuing bank imposes a fee whether the letter of credit is used or not, and it is quite complicated to create. Thus, both these methods are uncommon.

The more common methods are the bank letter of guarantee, where the bank irrevocably commits to honoring a check written by its customer up to a specified amount, and the credit card. But both of these methods suffer from one very significant flaw—the buyer must write a check or sign a credit card charge slip. And if he or she just refuses to do so, there is nothing the auction company can do to force a signature.

Sold Means Sold—Sometimes

Our client insisted, "Shouldn't that be the auction company's problem? Shouldn't they have to pay me because they approved this guy?" The first place to look for answers is the seller's contract with the auction company. This one seemed pretty good for our client; it did obligate the auction company to pay him once the car was sold. But in another section, the contract defined "sold" as when the auction company has received payment from the buyer. That left us at a dead end. Even though the Porsche was "sold" when the hammer fell, it was never "sold" for purposes of the seller's contract.

We next checked the bidder's contract with the auction company. It made it quite clear that the buyer was in default, but what was the recourse? Could the auction company force the buyer to complete the sale?

That is what the law describes as "specific performance"—forcing the buyer to do specifically what he agreed to do. But there are hoops to jump through before you can get this remedy. It will be allowed if the item is unique (this is where the "every piece of real property is unique" concept comes from), but this car was not unique. Otherwise, you have to show "irreparable harm," meaning that money damages cannot adequately compensate for your loss. But that doesn't work either, because we could simply sell the Porsche to someone else and sue the buyer for the sales price difference and any added sales expenses.

And there is yet another shortcoming with the bidder's contract—the seller is not a party to it, and doesn't have the legal ability to enforce it. Only the auction company can enforce it, and its damages would seem to be limited to its lost sales commissions.

When the Hammer falls

So we look to a third contract, the one between the seller and the buyer. It was created the moment that the hammer fell. With the auctioneer acting as the agent for the seller, a meeting of the minds occurred, and a contract arose between the seller and the buyer, which the seller can enforce. But this contract has three practical shortcomings:

1. The court is unlikely to force the buyer to actually buy the car (see "specific performance" above), so to determine his actual losses, the seller will have to sell the car to someone else and then sue the buyer for his losses.
2. Say the seller lives in Seattle, the buyer lives in Atlanta, and the auction was held in Scottsdale.
   The seller can sue the buyer the buyer in Atlanta or Scottsdale, but not Seattle. That makes the seller's legal effort more expensive.
3. It is highly unlikely that the seller will be able to recover his attorney fees. That usually requires a specific contractual provision, and we don't have that. That makes the process expensive.

Making Lemons Out of Lemonade

Faced with these contractual limitations, we worked with the auction company to minimize our client's losses as best we could. The second bidder on the car, at $90,000, was unwilling to buy the car, but said he would bid on it again if it ran through the next auction. The third bidder, at $85,000, wanted the car but thought that $75,000 was plenty under the circumstances.

Ultimately, I was able to convince the auction company to refund the seller's $1,500 in auction entry and transport expenses, agree to handle the seller's next sale at no commission, and just buy the car for $81,000.

That was actually a very fair deal for the seller. At the $95,000 high bid, the seller's net cash would have been $86,850. But if you give the auction company a little benefit of the doubt and dismiss the high bidder as a flake, the seller's net at the $90,000 underbid would have been only $82,200. The seller has a number of other collector cars, some more valuable than the Porsche, and the promised commission-free sale can even put him ahead of the game.

Protecting Yourself

Clearly, this situation was a fluke. It is hard to believe that a qualified high bidder would refuse to write the check. But I doubt this was the first time it has happened. For instance, consider a high bidder who believes that he was snookered by auction or chandelier bidding, or one who simply had been hitting the bidder's bar a little too hard and got his zeros mixed up, deciding the next morning he just won't pay.

This auction company acted very responsibly, and with a little creativity the situation was resolved with minor losses for the seller. But you can't always count on that happening, and it makes sense to consider this situation before you consign your collector car to an auction. Much of your protection comes from the reputation and practices of the auction company. But if enough money is involved, it wouldn't hurt to have your attorney take a close look ahead of time at the auction company's bidder's contract, as well as its consignment contract, and advise what kind of legal situation you might end up in if the unexpected happens again.◆

"This page is too expensive for modesty,
so let's be brief:"

www.bartholland.com

Restoration Company Bart Holland - Plankier 22-26 – NL-2771 XL Boskoop
Tel 0031-172-211344 - Fax 0031-172-218321 - Email info@bartholland.com

Fine Historic Automobiles

Resources

It's not what you know, it's who you know.

And in this chapter, you'll be able to find out just who you need to know, whether it's for your Abarth or tires for your Zimmer that you need.

The experts at Sports Car Market have pulled together a massive listing of resources, from restoration shops to car clubs to vintage racing groups to web sites. Whatever your vintage automotive needs, the chances are good you'll find a path, or at least help moving along your path, here.—*Keith Martin*

Car Clubs

There's no better source of information than talking with another owner of the same type of car that you have, or are thinking of buying.

Club Name	Location	Web
20th Century Chevy, Inc.	PO Box 371 Washington, IN, 47501	www.20thcenturychevy.com
356 Registry, Inc.	27244 Ryan Rd. Warren, MI, 48092	www.356registry.org
912 Registry	PO Box 1299 Blue Jay, CA, 92317-1299	www.912registry.org
AACC-UK—Association of American Car Clubs UK	PO Box 2222 Braintree, Essex CM7 9TW ENG	www.motorvatinusa.org.uk
Adirondack Corvettes, Inc.	2 Third Ave. Whitehall, NY, 12887	www.adirondackcorvettes.com
Alaska Sports Car Club	411 West Tudor Rd. Anchorage, AK, 99503	www.aksportscarclub.org
Alfa Romeo Owners Club—USA	PO Box 12340 Kansas City, MO, 64116	www.aroc-usa.org
All American Corvette Club	PO Box 306 Cliffside Park, NJ, 07010	www.a-a-c-c-.com
Allante Owners Association	140 Vintage Way #456 Novato, CA, 94945	www.allante.com
Aloha Mustang & Shelby Club of Hawaii	PO Box 6216 Honolulu, HI, 96818	www.aloha.net/~djhamma/mustcal.htm
Altoona Corvette Club	PO Box 2346 Altoona, PA, 16601	www.altoocorvetteclub.com

Club Name	Location	Web
AMC Rambler Club	2645 Ashton Rd. Cleveland Heights, OH, 44118	www.amcrc.com
AMC World Clubs	7963 Depew St. Arvada, CO, 80003-2527	www.amcwc.com
AMCA— American Motors Club of Alberta	10823 Shamrock Place SW Calgary, AB, T2W 0R2 CAN	www.geocities.com/motorcity/pit/1710/
American Bugatti Club	600 Lakeview Terrace Glen Ellyn, IL, 60137	www.americanbugatticlub.org
American Chevelle Enthusiasts Society —ACES	4636 Lebanon Pike, Suite 195 Nashville, TN, 37076-1316	www.chevelles.com
American MGB Association	PO Box 11401 Chicago, IL, 60611-0401	www.mgclub.org
American Motors Owners Association, Inc.	6756 Cornell St. Portage, MI, 49024-3412	www.amotiol.com
Antique Automobile Club of America—AACA	501 Governor Rd. PO Box 417 Hershey, PA, 17033	www.aaca.org
Appalachian British Car Society	143 Stonewall Heights Abingdon, VA, 24210	www.britcars.net
Aston Martin Owners Club	Freeman and Co. 1301 Ave of the Americas, 30th Floor, New York, NY, 10019	www.amoc.org
Belgium Federation of Old Vehicles	De Bruynlaan 38 Begijnendijk, 3130	www.bfov.be
Bentley Drivers Club	16 Chearsley Rd. Long CrendonAylesbury Bucks, HP18 9AW ENG	www.bdcl.co.uk
Bloomington Gold Corvettes USA	705 E Lincoln Suite 201 Normal, IL, 60152	www.bloomingtongold.com
Bloomington/Normal Corvette Enthusiasts Club	PO Box 1552 Bloomington, IL, 61702-1552	www.blnlcorvetteenthusiasts.homestead.com
Blue Gray Chapter Oldsmobile Club of America	6 Arwin Dr. Hummelstown, PA, 17036	www.innernet.net/jcdell/bluegray/index.html
Blue Ridge Chapter ACBS	8702 Lake Forest Dr. Jonesboro, GA, 30236	www.coolwoodies.com
Blue Ridge Corvette Club	PO Box 1 Stuarts Draft, VA, 24477	www.citymotors/net/brcc
Blue Ridge Land Rover Club	Rt. 3, PO Box 55G3 Davisville, WV, 26142-9762	www.brlrc.org
Bluebonnet Region #6 VCCA	720 Falling Leaves Dr. Adkins, TX, 78101	www.geocities.com/funstarz/
BMW Car Club of America	640 South Main St. Suite 201 Greenville, SC, 29601	www.bmwcca.org
BMW CCA Club Racing	4726 Belfield Dr. Dublin, OH, 43017-2593	www.bmwccaclubracing.com
Boss 429 Owners Directory	1744 Holly Springs Rd. Mount Airy, NC, 27030	www.bossperformance.com
Brampton Corvette Club	45 Franklin Ct. Brampton, ON, L6T 3Z1 CAN	www.globalserve.net/~vgg/
Bridgehampton Historical Society	PO Box 977 Bridgehampton, NY, 11932	www.hamptons.com/bhhs/road2001.htm
California Association of Sunbeam Tiger Owners	18771 Paseo Picasso, Irvine, CA 92603	www.catmbr.org
Chevrolet Nomad Association	2367 E Yaqui St. Sierra Vista, AZ, 85650	www.chevynomadclub.com/

Club Name	Location	Web
Chrysler 300 Club, Inc.	PO Box 1336 Hereford, AZ, 85615-1336	www.chrysler300clubinc.com
Chrysler 300 Club International	PO Box 56088 Sherman Oaks, CA, 91413-6988	www.chrysler300club.com
Citroen Car Club, Inc.	PO Box 743 Hollywood, CA, 90078	www.citroens.org
Classic AMX Club	PO Box 948069 Maitland, FL, 32751	www.amcwc.com
Classic Car Club of America—CCCA	1645 Des Plaines River Rd. Suite 7 Des Plaines, IL, 60018	www.classiccarclub.org
Classic Car Club of Southern California, Inc.	30 Hackamore Ln. Suite 1, Bell Canyon, CA, 91307-1065	www.socalccca.org
Classic Corvette Club	PO Box 682 Moorestown, NJ, 8054	www.classiccorvetteclub.com
Classic Corvette Club UK	18 Palmerston Rd Westcliff, Essex, SS0 7TB ENG	www.btinternet.com/~a.s.greenfield
Classic Jaguar Association	2860 N Victoria D.r Alpine, CA, 91901	www.classicjag.org
Club Cobra	414 Lybarger St. NE Olympia, WA, 98506	www.clubcobra.com
Continental Mark II Association	5225 Canyon Crest Dr. Ste. 71-217cma Riverside, CA, 92507	www.markii.com/markii/cma
Cooper Car Club Ltd.	17 Waterlaide Rd. Hartlebury, Worchestershire, DY11 7TP ENG	www.coopercars.org
Corvette Club of America	PO Box 9879 Bowling Green, KY, 42102	www.corvetteclubofamerica.com
Corvette Club of America—NCCC	PO Box 3355 Gaithersburg, MD, 20885-3355	www.corvetteclubofamerica.org
Corvette Club of Delaware Valley	PO Box 397 Willow Grove, PA, 19090	www.ccdv.com
Corvette Club of Illinois NCCC	1415 Mayfair Rd. Champaign, IL, 31821-5021	www.ccofi.org
Corvette Club of Manitoba, Inc.	PO Box 42032 RPO Ferry Rd. Winnipeg, MB, R3J 3X7 CAN	www.airwire.com/~gilej/corvette_club.html
Corvette Club of Michigan NCCC	PO Box 510330 Livonia, MI, 48151	www.corvetteclubmi.com
Corvette Club of Northeast Pennsylvania	1040 N Washington Ave. Scranton, PA, 18509	www.ernccc.org/ccnepa
Corvette Club of Northern Delaware	PO Box 10103 Wilmington, DE, 19850-0103	www.vetteclub.org
Corvette Club of Nova Scotia	12828 Hwy. 4 RR 2 Wentworth, NS, B0M 1Z0 CAN	www.geocities.comm/motorcity/track/1629
Corvette Club of Ontario	PO Box 1065 Adelaide St Station, Toronto, ON, M5C 2K4 CAN	www.ontariovettes.com
Corvette Club of the Palm Beaches	132 VanGogh Way Royal Palm Beach, FL, 33411	www.corvetteclubpalmbeach.com
Corvette Marque Club of Seattle	PO Box 534 Kirkland, WA, 98083	www.corvettemarqueclub.com
Corvette Owners Club of San Diego	8130 La Mesa Blvd #184 La Mesa, CA, 91941	www.cocsd.com

RESOURCES

Club Name	Location	Web
Crosley Automobile Club, Inc.	80 Beech Dr. Edgewood, KY, 41017	www.ggw.org/cac
Cross Flags Corvettes	2710 Dellworth St. Columbus, OH, 43232	www.crossflagscorvettes.com
Cruisin Buddies Rod Custom Classic	7 Kress St. Binghamton, NY, 13903	www.cruisinbuddies.com
Cruisin' Tigers GTO Club	230 S Hudson St. Westmont, IL, 60559	www.cruisintigersgto.com
Cruzin' Few Unique Vehicle Club	#54 Mansell Trailer Park New Brighton, PA, 15066	www.geocities.com/cruzinfew
Crystal Coast Mopar Club	509 Rosemary Dr. Newport, NC, 28570	www2.coastalnet.com/~u4d6r6mh
CSRA Canadian Street Rod Association	PO Box 308 STN "U" Toronto, ON, M8Z 5P7 CAN	www.csra.on.ca
DeLorean Owners Association	879 Randoph Rd. Santa Barbara, CA, 93111	www.deloreanowners.org
Dino Register	77150 Calle Arroba La Quinta, CA, 92253	www.angelfire.com/ca2/dinoregister/
Early Mustang Club of Colorado	PO Box 21706 Denver, CO, 80221	www.earlymustang.com
ELVA Owners Club	8 Liverpool Terrace Worthing, West Sussex BN11 1TA ENG	www.elva.com
Facel Enthusiasts USA	PO Box 2531 Palos Verdes, CA, 90274	www.geocities.com/motorcity/show/2564/facel-vega.html
Fairlane Club of America	340 Clicktown Rd. Church Hill, TN, 37642	www.fairlaneclubofamerica.com
Falls City Mustang Club	2005 Poppy Pl. Jeffersonville, IN, 47131	www.fallscitymustangclub.com
Fastiques Rod & Custom of Southern Ohio, Inc.	PO Box 745 Owensville, OH, 45160	www.pumpkinruntiols.com
F-Body Association of St. Louis (F.A.S.T.)	208 Oak Park Village Dr. Wildwood, MO, 63040	www.fastlouis.com
Ferrari Club Argentino	3 de Febrero 312 Rosario Sta Fe, 2000 ARG	www.ferrariclub.com.ar
Ferrari Club of America, Inc.	PO Box 720597 Atlanta, GA, 30358	www.ferrariclubofamerica.org
Florida West Coast Region AACA	14968 Imperial Point Dr. N Largo, FL, 33774	www.aaca.org/fwcr
Flywheels Car Club	404 S Second St. Silverton, OR, 97381	www.theflywheels.com
Ford Fairlane Torino Ranchero Registry 1968–1969	2585 S Taylor Rd. Cleveland, OH, 44118	www.fordfairlane.com
Ford Galaxie Club of America	4583 Wilburn Dr. Everton, AR, 72633	www.galaxieclub.com
Ford Mercury Restorers Club of America	PO Box 2938 Dearborn, MI, 48123	www.fmrcoa.org
Ford Motorsports Enthusiasts	PO Box 1331 Dearborn, MI, 48120-1331	www.teamfme.com
Gateway Z Club	PO Box 3694 Ballwin, MO, 63022-3694	www.gatewayzclub.com
Golden Gate Chapter Austin-Healey Club, Inc.	1160 LaRochelle Terr B Sunnyvale, CA, 94089-1754	www.jtpr-inc.com/ggahc

Club Name	Location	Web
Golden Gate Chapter of Vintage Volkswagen Club of America	13771 Harding Ave. San Martin, CA, 95046	www.ggcvvwca.org/
Golden Gate Lotus Club	PO Box 117303 Burlingame, CA, 94011	www.gglotus.org
Intermeccanica Enthusiasts Club	PO Box 1868 West Chester, PA, 19380	www.intermeccanica.org
International 100,000 mile/KM Plus Club	12600 Rockside Rd. Cleveland, OH, 44125	www.highmile.com
International Amphicar Club	PO Box 760 Burlington, KY, 41005	www.amphicar.com
International Ford Retractable Club	PO Box 289 Brockport, NY, 14420	www.skyliner.org
International Mercury Owners Association	6445 W Grand Ave. Chicago, IL, 60707-3410	www.mercuryclub.com
Jaguar Clubs of North America	234 Buckland Trace Louisville, KY 40245	www.jcna.com
Kustoms of America	2812 Lebanon Rd. Nashville, TN, 37214	www.kustomsofamerica.com/
L.A. Roadsters	PO Box 11357 Burbank, CA, 91510-1357	www.laroadsters.com
Lincoln & Continental Owners Club	PO Box 570709 Dallas, TX, 75357-0709	www.lcoc.org
Lotus Ltd.	PO Box L College Park, MD, 20741	www.lotuscarclub.org
Manx Dune Buggy Club	PO Box 1491 Valley Center, CA, 92082	www.manxclub.com
Mazda Club	PO Box 11238 Chicago, IL, 60611	www.mazdaclub.com
MB 300 Adenauer International Club	6464 S Nelson Way Littleton, CO, 80127	www.adenauer300.com
Mercedes-Benz Club of America	1907 Leraray St. Colorado Springs, CO, 80909-2872	www.mbca.org
Mercedes-Benz Owners' Association	Langton Road Langton Green TN3 0EG	www.mercedesclub.org.uk
Mercedes-Benz Veteranen Club Deutschland (MVC)	Flurrstr. 76, 44145 Dortmund, 44145	www.mvconline.de
MG Drivers Club of North America	18 George's Pl Clinton, NJ, 08809-1334	www.mgdriversclub.com
MG Octagon Car Club	Unit 1/2 Porchfields Enterprise ParkColton Rd. Trent Valley, Rugeley, Staffs, WS15 3HB ENG	www.mgoctagoncarclub.com
MG Owners Club	Octagon House1 Over Road, Swavesey, Cambridge, CB4 5QZ ENG	www.mgownersclub.co.uk
MGCC of Toronto	PO Box 64Station R Toronto, ON, M4G 3Z3 CAN	www.geocities.com/motorcity/shop/6055/index.htm
MGs of Baltimore	5237 Glen Arm Rd. Glen Arm, MD, 20157	www.qis.net/~socs/mgob.html
Miata Club of America	6850 Shiloh Rd. E, Suite D Alpharetta, GA, 30023	www.miataclub.org
Music City Mustang Club	PO Box 780 Fairview, TN, 37062	www.musiccitymustangclub.org

Car Clubs

Club Name	Location	Web
Mustang 428 Cobra Jet Registry	PO Box 247 Burke, VA, 22009-0247	www.428cobrajet.org
Mustang Club of America	3588 Hwy. 138, PMB 365 Stockbridge, GA, 30281	www.mustang.org/
Nash Car Club of America	1 N 274 Prairie Glen Ellyn, IL, 60137	www.shcarclub.org
Nash Car Club of America/PNW Region	17839 Wallingford Ave. N Shoreline, WA, 98133	www162.pair.com/shram/sh
Nashville British Car Club	120 40th Ave. N Nashville, TN, 37209	www.shvilletn.org/nbcc/
National American Motors Drivers & Racers Association	PO Box 987 Twin Lakes, WI, 53181-0987	www.mdra.org
National Association of (94–96) Impala SS Owners	1565 E Highway 100 #6 Bunnell, FL, 32110	www.impalaclub.com
National Association of Antique Automobile Clubs of Canada Corporation	3512 Marine Ave. Belcarra, BC, V3H 4R8 CAN	www.aaccc.ca
National Auto Sport Association, LA Chapter	662 Longfellow Ave. Hermosa Beach, CA, 90254	www.open-track.com
National Capital Mustang Association	PO Box 311078 Wellington St, Ottawa, ON, K1Y 2Y3 CAN	www.ncma.cc
National Capital Region Mustang Club	4886 Tobacco Way Woodbridge, VA, 22193	www.ncrmc.org
National Chevelle Owners Association	7343-J W Friendly Ave. Greensboro, NC, 27410	www.chevellereport.com
National Chevy Association	947 Arcade St. Paul, MN, 55106	www.tiolchevyassoc.com
National Chevy/GMC Truck Association	PO Box 607458 Orlando, FL, 32860	www.chevygmctrucks.com
National Corvette Museum	350 Corvette Dr. Bowling Green, KY, 42101	www.corvettemuseum.com
National Corvette Owners Association	900 S Washington St. #G-13 Falls Church, VA, 22046	www.ncoa-vettes.com
National Corvette Restorers Society	6291 Day Rd. Cincinnati, OH, 45252-1334	www.ncrs.org
National Council of Corvette Clubs	3701 S 92nd St. Milwaukee, WI, 53228-1611	www.corvettesnccc.org
National Firebird and Trans Am Club	PO Box 11238 Chicago, IL, 60611	www.firebirdtaclub.com
National Historic Route 66 Federation	PO Box 423 Tujunga, CA, 91043-0423	www.tiol66.com
National Impala Association	2928 4th Ave. PO Box 968 Spearfish, SD, 57783-0968	www.nationalimpala.com
National Monte Carlo Owner's Association, Inc.	PMB 214 38 S Blue Angel Pkwy. Pensacola, FL, 32506	www.montecarloclub.com
National Motorists Association	402 W 2nd St. Waunakee, WI, 53597-1342	www.motorists.org
National Nostalgic Nova	PO Box 2344 York, PA, 17405	www.nnnova.com
New England MG T Register Ltd.	PO Drawer 220 Oneonta, NY, 13820-0220	www.nemgt.org
Packard Club	420 S Ludlow St Dayton, OH, 45402	www.packardclub.org

Club Name	Location	Web
Packards of Chicagoland	PO Box 1031 Elmhurst, IL, 60126-9998	www.geocities.com/chicagopackard
Pantera International	18586 Main St Suite 100, Huntington Beach, CA, 92648	www.panteracars.com
Pantera Owner's Club of America	PO Box 459 Hadlyme, CT, 6439	www.panteraclub.com
Panther Enthusiasts Club UK	91 Fleet Rd, Cove Farnborough, Hampshire, GU14 9RE ENG	www.pantherclub.fsnet.co.uk
Pierce-Arrow Society, Inc.	2014 S Timbers Hill Rd. Richmond, VA, 23235	www.pierce-arrow.org
Pontiac Owner's Association	1202 Cork Ave. Papillion, NE, 68046	www.geocities.com/poay2k/poa.html
Porsche 356 Club	23738 Barona Mesa Rd. Ramona, CA, 92065	www.porsche356club.org
Porsche 914 Club	4300 Sandmound Blvd. Oakley, CA, 94561	www.dgi.net/914/
Porsche Club of America	PCA Executive Office PO Box 30100 Alexandria, VA, 22310-8100	www.pca.org
Renault Alpine Club International	Carnation Rd. 15 Therwil, 4106 SUI	www.renault-alpine.com
Renault Owners Club of North America	7418 Collett Ave. Van Nuys, CA, 91406	www.renaultownersclub.org
Rolls-Royce Enthusiasts' Club	The Hunt House Paulerspury Northhamptonshire, NN12 7NA ENG	www.rrec.co.uk
Rolls-Royce Owners Club	191 Hempt Road. Mechanicsburg, PA, 17055	www.rroc.org
Roskilde American Bil Club	Kamstrupsti 2 Roskilde, 4000 DEN	www.roskilde-abc.dk
Route 66 Association of Illinois	#166 2743 Veterans Pkwy. Springfield, IL, 62704	www.il66assoc.org
Route 66 Auto Club	PO Box 3266 Quail Valley, CA, 92587	www.route66autoclub.com

Club Name	Location	Web
Saab Club of North America	7675 Bear Trap Jct. Saginaw, MI, 55779	www.saabclub.com
Sacramento Jaguar Club	3211 Kincade Dr. Placerville, CA, 95667	www.jc.com/clubs/sw06.htm
Saddleback Mustang Association	PO Box 3765 Mission Viejo, CA, 92690	www.saddlebackmustang.org
Saints Car Club	PO Box 1632 Port Orchard, WA, 98366	www.saintscarclub.org
San Antonio Jaguar Club	9823 Strathaven San Antonio, TX, 78240	www.sajaguarclub.org
San Diego Jaguar Club	5338 Soledad Rancho Ct. San Diego, CA, 92109	www.sdjag.com
San Diego Pontiac Club	6778 Cibola Rd. San Diego, CA, 92120	www.sdpoci.com
San Diego Region Porsche Club of America	2537 Honey Springs Rd. Jamul, CA, 91935	www.pcasdr.org/
San Diego Saab Owner's Group	10559 Lansford Ln. San Diego, CA, 92126-5902	www.annexus.com/sdsog
Shelby American Automobile Club SAAC	PO Box 788 Sharon, CT, 6069	www.saac.com
Studebaker Drivers Club, Inc.	PO Box 1743 Maple Grove, MN, 55311	www.studebakerdriversclub.com/
Studebaker.org	715 Frierson Ln. Kingstree, SC, 29556	www.studebaker.org
Subaru Club of America	PO Box 84 Camden, DE, 19934	www.subaruclub.com
Sunbeam Alpine Owners Club of America	1125 Winsail Cove Loveland, OH, 45140	www.sunbeamalpine.org
Swallow Doretti Register	93 Mount Pleasant Road Davenham Northwich, CW9 8JH ENG	www.doretti.co.uk
The Maserati Club	PO Box 5300 Somerset, NJ, 08875-5300	www.themaseraticlub.com
The Milestone Car Society	626 N Park Indianapolis, IN, 46204	www.milestonecarsociety.org
The Saab Club of North America	PO Box 683 Middletown, OH, 45044	www.saabclub.com
The Skyscrapers International Car Club	4552 Camellia Ave. Studio City, CA, 91602	www.cadillacworld.tv
The Spyder Club	70 Angelica Dr. Framingham, MA, 1701	www.spyderclub.com
The Super Stock AMX Registry	30115 Hwy 281 N Suite 126 Bulverde, TX, 78163	www.southtexasamc.bigstep.com
Tigers East - Alpines East	7807 Charlotte Dr. Huntsville, AL, 35802-2805	www.teae.org
Toyota Land Cruiser Association	PO Box 210 Windsor, CA, 95492	www.tlca.org
Toyota MR2 Mk1 Club	301 Park Road Loughborough, LE11 2HF ENG	www.mr2mk1club.com
TR8 Car Club of America	266 Linden St. Rochester, NY, 14620	www.team.net/tr8/tr8cca/index.html
Trabant USA	1200 West Walnut Springfield, MO, 65806	www.geocities.com/trabantusa

Club Name	Location	Web
Triumph Roadster Club	59 Cowdray Park Rd. Little Common, Bexhill on Sea East Sussex, TN39 4EZ ENG	www.triumphroadsterclub.fsnet.co.uk
Triumph Standard Motor Club	4610 Cloverlawn Dr. Tampa, FL, 33624	www.triumphstandardmotorclub.com
Tucker Automobile Club of America	9509 Hinton Dr. Santee, CA, 92071-2760	www.tuckerclub.org
Tucson Region AACA	3770 E 27th St. Tucson, AZ, 85713	www.aaca.org/tucson
United Council of Corvette Clubs	59 Shiawassee Ave. Akron, OH, 44333	www.unitedcouncil.com
United Kingdom Buick Club	PO Box 2222 Braintree, Essex, CM7 9TW ENG	www.motorvatinusa.org.uk
United Kingdom Chapter National Corvette Restorers Society	71 Green Ln St Albans, Hertfordshire, AL3 6HE ENG	www.ncrs.co.uk
Vintage Car Club of Canada	PO Box 2312 Princeton, BC, V0X 1W0 CAN	www.vccc.com
Vintage Chevy Van Club	PO Box 50905 New Orleans, LA, 70150	www.vcvc.org
Vintage Modified Racing Association	17414 Bothell Way SE Suite 673, Mill Creek, WA, 98012	www.vmraracing.com
Vintage Mustang Club of Kansas City	PO Box 40082 Overland Park, KS, 66204	www.vintagemustangofkc.com
Vintage Mustang Owners Association	PO Box 5772 San Jose, CA, 95150	www.vntg-mustang.com/
Vintage Rallies	80 Jackson Hill Rd. Sharon, CT, 06069	www.vintagerallies.com
Vintage Sports Car Club of America VSCCA	116 Sawyer Hill Rd New Milford, CT, 6776	www.vscca.org
Vintage Sports Car Drivers Association	3160 Thorn Apple River Drive, Grand Rapids, MI, 49546	www.vscda.org
Vintage Triumph Register	PO Box 655 Howell, MI 48844	www.vtr.org
Vintage Thunderbird Club International	1304 Greenwood Schertz, TX, 78154	www.vintagethunderbirdclub.org
Voitures Anciennes Du Quebec, Inc.	445 Rue Comtois Otterburn Park, QC, J3H 3Z8 CAN	www.vaq.qc.ca
Voitures Anciennes et Classiques de Montreal	13,760 Forsyth Montreal, QC, H1A 3S6 CAN	www.geocities.com/clubvacm/
Volkswagen Type 181 Thing Registry	700 SE Crescent Dr. Shelton, WA, 98584-8665	www.type181registry.com
Western New York Centre MGCC	1286 Mill Creek Run Webster, NY, 14580	www.mgcarclub.com
Western Pennsylvania Region AACA	123 Fosterville Rd. Greensburg, PA, 15601	www.aaca.org/westernpa/
Willowa Chapter—Mighty Mississippi Mopars	11027 Mound View Dubuque, IA, 52003	www.chicagolandmopar.com
Willys-Overland Jeepster Club	167 Worcester St. Taunton, MA, 02780-2088	www.jeepsterclub.com
Yenko Sportscar Club	PO Box 375 Alton, MO, 65606	www.yenko.net ◆

Taking It Apart and Putting It Back Together

In today's world, you are far better off taking your car to a shop that specializes in your marque. Otherwise, you're paying for a mechanic's education, and not everyone will get an "A" the first time out.

Alabama

Automotive Restoration Co.
Rockford
256.377.1226

Arizona

Arizona Street Rods
Phoenix
602.233.2178

Rick Dore Kustoms
Phoenix
602.547.3512

Tenth Street Auto Body Specialists
Phoenix
310.542.5824

Arkansas

Twin Lakes Auto Body
Mountain Home
870.425.9590

California

Alan Taylor Co., Inc
Escondido
760.489.0657

Alfa Romeo Specialist
San Carlos
650.508.8187

Antique Auto Restoration
Monterey Peninsula
831.393.9411

Randy Ema
Auburn, Cord, Duesenberg
Orange
714.633.3883

Custom Auto Service
Santa Ana
714.543.2980

Gran Turismo Motors
Glendale
818.546.2971

Moal Coachbuilders
Oakland
510.834.9066

RESOURCES

Willhoit Auto Restoration
Long Beach
937.526.3655

Colorado

Clayton Restorations Ltd.
Castle Rock
303.688.4035

MotoGraphix
Colorado Springs
800-7HOGART

Connecticut

Automotive Restorations Rolls-Royce
Stratford
203.377.6745

Enfield Auto Restoration
Enfield
800.749.7917

Everything Muscle
Middlefield
860.349.4570

Manchester Motor Car
Manchester
860.643.5874

Delaware

Muscle Car Enterprises
Townsend
302.659.6390

Sports Car Service, Inc.
Wilmington
302.764.7222

Florida

Greg Donahue Collector Car Restoration
Florida City
352.344.4319

Harbor Auto Restorations
Rockledge
321.633.3227

Proper Motor Cars, Inc.
St. Petersburg
727.821.8883

Realistic Auto Restoration
St. Petersburg
727.327.5162

Georgia

Atlanta Auto Restoration
Hampton
770.946.8946

Jen Jacs Restorations
Garden City
912.966.601

Ron's Restorations
Sharpsburg
888.416.1057

Route 66 Restorations
Suwanee
678.714.6606

Then and Now Auto Restoration
Marietta
770.592.4411

Traywick Automotive
Columbus
706.565.4990

Idaho

Classics by Jaggers
Boise
208.323.4733

Glenn Vaughn Restoration
Post Falls
208.773.3525

Illinois

Custom Cars Unlimited
La Grange
708.354.7888

Custom Classics
Island Lakes
847.487.2222

Old Coach Works Restoration, Inc.
Yorkville
603.553.0414

Indiana

Lavine Restorations, Inc.
Nappanee
219.773.7561

Nationwide Auto Restoration
Jefferson
812.280.0165

Precision Coachworks
Jasper
812.482.4313

Iowa

Anderson Restoration LLC
Kanawha
641.762.3528

Healey Werks
Lawton
712.944.4900

Kansas

Affordable Street Rods
Great Bend
620.792.2836

Auburn Parts Co.
Wellington
620.326.7751

Classic Auto Restoration
Abilene
785.479.2060

Stouffer's Classic Auto Restoration
Hays
785.628.3000

Kentucky

Antique Auto Shop
Elsmere
859.342.8363

RESOURCES

239

RESOURCES

Darryl Lampert
Louisville
502.459.2639

Louisiana

Gwen Banquer Design
Norco
985.764.8401

Maine

Autolab Ltd.
Portland
207.878.2105

Maryland

Corvette Specialties of MD
Eldersburg
410.795.3180

Flemings Ultimate Garage
Annapolis
877.283.5987

Vintage Restorations Ltd.
Mount Airy
301.831.5300

Massachusetts

2nd Generation Automotive Restoration
Walpole
508.364.5442

N.E. Carriage Shop
Plymouth
781.582.1388

Rensport
Framington
508.385.8911

Sports Leicht Restorations
Topsfield
987.887.1900

Michigan

Classic & Exotic service
Troy
248.362.0113

Classic Metal Restoration
Brighton
810.225.2490

Hyde Auto Body
Auburn Hills
248.852.7832

Randy Hall Specialty Cars
Iron Mountain
906.774.5897

Randy Church Restorations
St. Charles
989.865.8171

Weirs Body Werks
Grand Blanc
810.695.9189

Minnesota

Classic Iron Ranch
Cambridge
763.689.6710

Odyssey Restoration
Spring Lake Park
763.786.1518

Mississippi

J. Coreys Customs
662.841.2226

Custom Auto Engineering
Flora
601.879.3313

Missouri

Fred's Fabrication
Cuba
573.885.4055

Montana

Golden Beetle Car Co. of Montana
Billings
406.245.2100

Kelly's Kustoms
Billings
406.373.5997

Nebraska

Custom Image Motorsports
Omaha
402.330.4148

Flying "A" Restoration
Omaha
402.593.1090

Nevada

Restoration Station
Las Vegas
702.269.9751

Mustangs of Las Vegas
Las Vegas
702.236.1770

New Hampshire

RMR Restoration
Hollis
603.465.7270

New Jersey

Bob Platz' Precision
Camden
856.966.0080

Grey Hills Auto Restoration, Inc.
Blairstown
908.362.8232

Hibernia Auto Restoration
Hibernia
973.627.1881

Palmer Automotive
Audubon
908.637.4444

Steve Babinsky
Bernardsville
908.766.6688

Stone Barn, Inc.
Vienna
908.637.4444

New Mexico

Corrales Classic Farms
Albuquerque
505.898.5788

Euro Motor Sports
Sante Fe
505.424.6767

New York

Classic Restorations
Stony Point
845.429.4942

European Foreign Classics
Great Neck
516.826.6200

Nichols Restoration
Branchport
315.595.2576

RJ Cars Mopar Specialist
Arkport
608.739.4242

Stonebridge Motor Co
Corning
607.936.2227

North Carolina

Classic Automotive Restoration
Belews Creek
336.595.3900

The Winning Collection
Asheville
828.658.9090

North Dakota

Dales Auto Restoration
Bismark
701.258.5336

Odens Rod Shop
Fargo
701.298.0749

Ohio

A1 Auto Restoration
Russia
937.526.3655

D&D Classic
Covington
937.473.2229

Hills Automotive
Racine
740.949.2217

L&N Old Car Co.
Newberry
440.564.7204

Murphy's Classic Restorations
Dover
330.343.8778

Oklahoma

OK Classics
Shawnee
405.273.6699

Zack's Classics
Hobart
580.726.2280

Oregon

Cool Change Classic
Gold Hill
541.855.1642

Custom Auto Restoration
Portland
503.230.7970

Steve's Auto Restoration
Portland
503.665.2222

Pennsylvania

Older Car Restoration
Mont Alo
717.749.3383

Precision Auto Restoration
Havertown
610.789.2271

Sussex Motor & Coach
Jim Cox
Matamoras

Rhode Island

Grundy Engineering
West Greenwich
401.392.3334

Sacchetti Classic Auto
Warwick
401.461.0900

South Carolina

Low Country Auto Restoration
Olar
803.368.3024

South Dakota

AA Restoration
Rapid City
605.343.9452

Cliff's Auto Restoration
Sioux Falls
605.335.6066

Tennessee

Alloway's Hot Rod Shop
Louisville

Texas

Hatfield's Restorations
Canton
866.635.9699

Jeff Lilly Restoration
San Antonio
216.695.5151

Wade's Rod & Custom
Wylie
972.442.1430

Utah

**Customs & Classics
Restorations Etc.**
Salt Lake City
801.288.1863

Vermont

Perfection Performance Motors
Vergennes
802.877.2645

Virginia

Expectation Restoration
Royal Front
540.635.6467

Northside Automotive and Custom
Madison
540.948.5511

White Post Restorations
White Post
540.837.1140

WW Motor Cars
Broadway
526.896.8243

Washington

Buffalo Restorations
Puyallup
253.535.2142

Murray Motor Car
Monroe
425.487.1902

Quality Restorations
Port Orchard
360.371.2165

Sabin Restorations
Auburn
253.876.7763

West Coast Restorations
Snohomish
360.568.8948

West Virginia

Vintage Motor Car Co.
Harpers Ferry
304.728.1990

Wisconsin

Auto Restoration Shop
Spooner
715.635.8818

Fellion Auto Restoration
Burlington
262.534.6166

Kens Classics
Muscoda
608.739.4242

Newtons Auto Restoration
Spring Green
608.3588.2422

Valenti Classics
Caledonia
262.835.2070

Wilson Classic Car
Burlington
888.763.1903

Wyoming

Frontier Rod & Restoration
Cheyenne
307.634.0496

Rick's Rod Shop
Casper
307.237.7668

S & L Classics
Casper
307.237.5170

Canada

British Columbia

Rudi & Company
Victoria
250.727.6020

RX Autoworks
North Vancouver
604.986.0102

Ontario

The Guild of Automotive Restorers
Bradford
905.775.0499

RM Restorations
Blenheim
519.352.4575 ◆

Automobilia Websites

www.pogogas.com
Reproduction gas globes

www.fingerlakemetalcraft.com
Custom signs and accessories

www.vintageAutoPosters.com
Original automotive posters

www.redlineracing.com
Automotive posters

www.fill-er-up.com
Gas pumps, signs, air meters

www.autoshopsigns.com
Reproduction signs

www.thegaspumpstore.com
Gas pumps parts

www.oilsign.com
Reproduction signs

www.carcover.com
Reproduction signs and diecast models

www.nostaligamerchants,com
Vintage bicycle parts

www.fillingstation.com
Gas pump parts

www.bluediamondclassics.com
Pedal cars and parts

www.genuinehotrod.com
Diecast engine replicas, signs, metal wall art, etc.

www.aaronfosterdesigns.com
Vintage license plate art

www.campbellchevydesigns.com
Custom crankshaft lamps

www.jonathankendall.com
Automotive inspired gifts and accessories

www.kirkfwhite.com
European tinplate toys, tether cars

www.RPMAutobooks.com
Automotive books

www.oilcanbook.com
Oil can identification book

www.gaspump.com
Electric gas pump faces, oil bottle spouts

www.crspub.com
Petroleum literature

www.cooksclassics.com
Vintage gas pumps and diner decor

www.automobiliausa.com
Repops and originals—gas pumps, etc

www.automobiliamonterey.com
Dealer show info

www.arteauto.com
Posters, brochures, programs, and art

www.bobsautomobilia.com
1919–1956 Buick Restoration Parts and Accessories

www.automobilia.no
Scandinavian

www.lmgauto.com
Books, art, prints, and posters

www.carhobby.com
Promotional cars and info

www.automotive-links.com/ent/col/col.htm
Collectibles, petroliana, pedal cars

www.vintage-automobilia.com
Art, posters, magazines, parts

www.arteauto.com
Art and prints

www.nostalgiaonline.com/clocks.php
Repop neon clocks

www.cocacolacoolers.com/automobilia.htm
Memorabilia and collectibles

www.trafficlights.com/svader.htm
Gas pumps, globes, traffic lights

www.pumaperiodpumps.com
Pumps, signs, memorabilia

www.schifferbooks.com/automobilia.html
Books

www.aqgarage.com
Clothing, gifts, collectibles

www.efindparts.com/automobilia.htm
Subscription service for finding stuff

www.motorsportsclub.com/automobilia.html
Vintage speed accessories

www.nostalgia-unlimited.com/coke.html
Motobilia from the 1950s

www.the-forum.com/auto/index.htm
Online mall

www.classicpreservation.com/oldstuff14.html
Collectibles and repops

www.blastfromthepastautomobilia.co.uk
UK auto literature

www.motor-web.com/classic/mca-automobilia-memora-bilia.htm
Dealer list in UK for vintage and classic automobilia

www.steveaustinsautomobilia.com
Racing art

www.the-forum.com/AUTO/autoref.htm
Collectors books

www.arniebrown.com
Badges and patches

www.motorlit.com/index.html
Rare and out-of-print automotive books

www.bonhams.com
auction house

www.monacoauctions.com
Pre- and post-war collectibiles

www.larrykay.com/automobilia.html
Cars and automobilia

www.jmjauto.com
Racing memorabilia

www.vintagecars.about.com/od/automobilia
Resource links to collectors, etc.

www.carhobby.com
Cars and brochures

www.locomobilia.com
Transportation memorabilia

www.antiquemystique.com/automobilia.htm
Old license plates, parts, and collectibles

www.oldgas.com/search/Automotive_Automobilia.html
French site for memorabilia

www.carbooksautomobilia.it/index.html
Books

www.jimpike.co.uk
UK site for automobilia and literature

www.roaring-twenties.com/antiques
Antique auto collectibles

www.rubylane.com/collectibles/,id=1.39.html
Auto collectibles

www.cultureandthrills.com/Category.asp?c=36
Brochures and press kits

www.autosinfo.com/dir/Collectibles
Collection of auto related websites

www.classicpreservation.com/oldstuff.html
Collectibles ◆

Vintage Racing Websites

by Thor Thorson

I was asked to come up with a list of Vintage Racing web sites for this guide, which is easy enough. The problem is figuring out how to present them so they make any sense. I decided to break the question into categories.

Clubs

The truism "all politics are local" applies in spades to Vintage Racing. There are at least 27 different organizations scattered around the country that put on events. Fortunately, most if not all of these belong to a single umbrella organization, the Vintage Motorsports Council. If you want to find a U.S. vintage racing club, go to

http://www.v-m-c.org/members

There you will find links to everybody's websites, and you can find the club close to you. The one serious group not listed there is General Racing, Steve Earle's Monterey/Wine Country/Lime Rock organization.

http://www.generalracing.com/

Schedules

With 28 groups running events around the U.S., figuring out who is putting on what when can be a challenge. Each of the clubs posts its own schedule on their web site. The best online resource to find the general national picture is Vintage Motorsport Magazine's website, **http://www.vintagemotorsport.com/race_calendar.asp**

International

If you have dreams of driving internationally or are simply curious about what they're doing across the pond, the following are some of the more obvious sites:

• The Monaco Historic Grand Prix—**www.acm.mc**

• Classic Le Mans—**www.lemansclassic.com/fr/index.html**

• The Goodwood Revival—**www.goodwood.co.uk/revival/**

In Europe there are a number of organizers for series:

•Thoroughbred Grand Prix—**www.tgpf1.com/** (serious F1 racing)

• More relaxed and genteel racing series for both F1 and various sports racing cars are run by The Masters Series—

http://www.themastersseries.com

• Under 2-liter sedans can go play in Carol Spagg's new series—

www.historicmotorracingnews.com

• If you fancy long distance vintage racing, try Classic Endurance Racing—

http://www.classicenduranceracing.com/uk/index.asp ◆

Model Car Websites

1:8 scale model of the 1967 Eagle-Gurney Weslake V12 from Real Art Replicas, www.realartreplicas.com

CAR MODELS

www.carmodels.com
Latest model cars online

www.hobbylinc.com
Over 20 manufacturers at discounted prices

www.hobbytron.com
3,000 models to choose from at low prices

www.miniwerks.com

www.motormedia.co.uk
Scale models including road cars, rally cars, and 1/43 scale.

www.rocousa.com
Model cars from Tamiya, RC Glow engines, and static models

www.alpimodel.com
BBR, MR, Minichamps

www.policecarmodels.com
1:18 scale model police cars

www.showrods.com
Road and rally models

www.marshmodels.com
Resin models

www.megahobby.com
Model cars & trucks

www.arteauto.com
Large selection of car models

www.slot-cars.com.uk/

www.maybach.ru/en/diecast.htm
Maybach models

www.collectorsnetUSA.com
Slot car models

www.ProlineModels.com

www.Extremecustomtoys.com

www.fg.modelsports-gmph.de
RC car models

www.depotland.com
All car models currently produced

www.HobbyShop.monsterMarketplace.com

www.aj-modelworks.co.uk
1:24 scale models

www.lowridershop.de
Low rider models

www.pitlanemodels.com

www.minichamps.de

www.bbrmodels.it
Racing models

www.overstock.com
40%–80% off on replica cars

www.gearheadsindy.com
Minichamps

www.scaleautoworks.com
1:18 scale high quality models

www.ugofadini.com
Land speed record model cars

www.scaleautoworks.com
1:8 scale Pocher models

www.santapod.co.uk/m
NHRA, Funny car

www.sell-it-easy.de/shop
Pocher, Bburgejo, Revell

www.abcmodelsport.com
Minicraft car models

www.valleymall.com/bluemountainhobbies
Kits and accessories

www.realartreplicas.com
Limited edition, large scale replicas

DIECAST AUTOMOBILES

www.gmpdiecast.com
Diecast replicas

www.milestonemodelcars.com
1:18 scale diecast

www.dominionmodels.com
1:43 scale American diecast cars

www.collectiblediecast.com
1:18 or 1:24 die cast cars and trucks

www.ewacars.com
ewa diecast

www.Ediecast.com
Meet the model of your dreams—huge selection

www.iDcow.com
Die cast models

www.DanburyMint.com
Danbury Mint models

www.FranklinMint.com
Franklin Mint models

www.toseaka.com
Diecast models

www.allthebrands.com
Franklin Mint

www.diecastauto.com
Franklin Mint at discount

www.bestprice.com/toy-vehicle
Diecast

www.Porsche.com
Porsche diecast

www.toysrus.com
Diecast toys

www.bizrate.com
Bargains on diecast

www.diecasts.com
Diecast cars

www.collectiblediecast.com
1:18, 1:24 Dub city, Ertyl, Jadatoys, Autoart, etc.

www.toyconnection.com
Small-sized toy diecast cars

www.dealtime.com
Deals on diecast cars and other toys

www.sailingusintl.com
Diecast cars and other novelty items

www.hobbytron.com
Diecast model cars etc.

www.pedalcarsofyesterday.com
Diecast models and retro-style pedal cars

www.toysandhobbies.com
Diecast car models, many scales at low prices

www.diecaststation.com
High quality models cars. Large selection low prices.

www.diecastlegends.com
Latest releases from the world of models.

www.unitedtrucks.com
Diecast trucks

www.AngeleenTshirts.com
1:18 Mini Cooper diecast

www.diecastblast.com
Diecast cars

www.internethobbies.com
Tamiya diecast car models

www.legacydiecast.com
Official store of die cast zone

www.kremlingifts.com
1:43 scale Russian diecast model cars

www.sportscraftcars.com
Diecast collectible cars

www.babez.de/carmodel.php
Diecast car models

www.motormint.com
Classic diecast cars

www.wellsmodels.com
Diecast cars

www.abcmodelsport.com
Revell diecast

www.3000toys.com
Ertyl, First Gear

www.hot-trucks.com
Diecast trucks

www.shopzilla.com
1:18 scale diecast

www.prestigediecast.com
Diecast racing collectibles

www.allcarmodels.com
Diecast models

Corgi Diecast

www.sierratoysoldier.com
Collectible Gorgi diecast models

www.corgi-toys.com
Corgi collectibles

www.gohobbies.com
4,000 diecast cars at discount

www.pacprod.com
Corgi diecast

NASCAR Diecast

www.checkeredflagdiecast.com
Current and classic NASCAR diecast

www.pitstopdiecast.com
NASCAR and NHRA diecast

www.sactruckracing.com
NASCAR, stock cars, dirt cars, funny cars, dragsters, and more

www.racingusa.com
NASCAR Superstore

www.diecastnow.com
Action NASACAR Diecast

www.store.tgcgifts.com
NASCAR die cast

www.dealtime.com
Deals on NAASCAR diecast cars

www.1lap2go.com
Tony Stewart diecast

www.whateversports.com
NASCAR diecast

www.fansedge.com
NASCAR diecast

www.prosportsmemorbilia.com
NASCAR diecast

www.store.nascar.com
NASCAR diecast

www.nextag.com
NASCAR diecast

www.chipganassiracing.com
Ganassi diecast

www.yournascar.com
NASCAR diecast

www.collectiblestoday.com
NASCAR diecast

www.dealtime.com
NASCAR diecast

www.blueflameauthentics.com
Rusty Wallace diecast

www.cheapdiecast.com
2006 Jeff Gordon designed by Chip Foose

www.goHobbies.com
NASCAR diecast

FORMULA 1 MODELS

www.oneracing.com
1:18 Scale F1 models

www.curbstonemodels.com
Saen scale F1

www.tomotorsports.com

www.f1miniatures.com

www.f1.com

www.bigboystoyz.com
RC F1 models

www.tameokits.com
1:43 metal kits

www.formula1-rc.com
RC racing models

www.f1specialties.com

www.beverlyhillsmotorsport.com

www.gpma.org

www.f1modeler.com
World of F1 in scale

www.dodads.com.au

www.f1worldshop.com

www.f1models.biz

www.robertocave.it
1:43 scale F1

www.exclusivescale.com
Ferrari

www.shockmodel.com

www.geocities.com
1:43 scale F1 diaramas

www.littlebolide.com
Ferrari and F1

HOT WHEELS

www.hotwheels.com

www.monstermarket.com

www.dealtime.com

www.speedgear.com

MISC. SITES

www.ewoss.info

www.mimniadec.fr
500 online references

www.clearwaterdisplays.com
Diecast display cases

www.micromark.com
Car modeling tools

www.displaycaseoutlet.com
Hot Wheels display cases ◆

RESOURCES

Glossary of Car Terms

Gearheads have a language all their own, and most of it is printable. Here is an automotive Rosetta Stone to help you on your way.

Barn Find	A car found in long-term storage in highly original although not necessarily orderly or complete condition.
Base Coat/ Clear Coat	A paint system that consists of several coats of a "base" color and several coats of hardened "clear." It is the clear coat that produces the depth and gloss.
Bias Ply Tires	Tires in which the cords or plies are wrapped around the tire in a diagonal overlapping manner. Produces higher rolling resistance and more heat than a radial design.
Big Block	Any large displacement optional engine. Usually over 400 ci.
Black Plate Car	A car still registered with its original black and yellow California plate issued in the 1960s. Indicative of a car that has always been in California.
Blue Plate Car	A car still registered with its original blue and yellow California plate issued in the 1970s. Indicative of a car that has always been in California.
Body-Off Restoration	A comprehensive restoration during which the body is actually removed from the chassis and every component is either replaced or renewed. Chassis and undercarriage should show to a high standard in a proper body-off restoration.
Bored	Method of increasing the displacement of an engine by enlarging the cylinder bores.
Brightwork	Shiny metal on the exterior of a car. Either chrome, polished stainless stee,l or polished aluminum.
Chandelier Bid	An auctioneer tactic used to advance bidding that has not reached the reserve in the absence of activity on the part of an actual bidder. Not used by reputable auction houses.
Classic	A trademarked term of the Antique Automobile Club of America. Refers to a limited number of significant pre-war (and several post-war) cars designated as "Full Classics."
Clone	A car that has been altered to appear as though it is a more desirable model than it actually is. A clone can easily become a counterfeit depending on the seller's representations. Also called replica, tribute, or recreation.
Coachbuilder	Firm that was commissioned to build bodies for bare chassis. *Karrosserie* in German, *Carrozzeria* in Italian and *Carrosserie* in French.
Concours	Short for Concours d'Elegance, a judged showing of finely restored cars. Also a statement of condition. "Concours" condition is synonymous with a car in show-worthy condition.
Continuation car	A type of replica usually very accurate and involving some of the original parts and constructors. Often serial numbered consecutively with the originals.
Convertible	Any open car with roll-up windows.
Convertible Coupe	An open two-door bodystyle with a well finished and lined convertible top. Europeans refer to it as a "drophead coupe."
Convertible Sedan	An open four-door bodystyle with a well finished and lined convertible top. Europeans refer to it as a "drophead sedan."
COPO	Acronym for Central Office Purchase Order. Most commonly applied to 427-ci Camaros ordered "straight from the assembly line."
Detailing	The process of cleaning and light refurbishing of an automobile often in preparation for show or sale.
Displacement	Total of the volume of each cylinder of an internal combustion piston engine. Denoted as cubic inches (ci), cubic centimeters (cc), or liters, (L).
DOHC	Double overhead cams. A cylinder head design where the cams are located in the head and actuate the valvegear directly rather than by pushrods. Driven by chains or a belt.

Driver Quality	A car that is a deteriorated older restoration or a cosmetically freshened but not restored car. Not showorthy, but suitable to be driven and enjoyed without worry. Also referred to simply as "a driver" or "everyday driver."
Electronic Fuel Injection	Fuel injection system where fuel is metered by means of an electronic "computer."
Enamel	Generally an acrylic-based paint that produces a durable high-gloss finish with minimal rubbing. Two-stage or "base coat/clear coat" enamels produce an even glossier, more durable finish. Extremely toxic when mixed with catalyzed hardeners.
Etceterini	Originally a term describing Italian cars other than Fiat, Ferrari, and Maserati. Now shorthand for any oddball make or model.
Flat Six or Flat Four	Denotes engine architecture where the cylinders are horizontally opposed and separated by a centrally located crank shaft. "Boxer" or "Pancake" are synonyms. Porsche is the most frequent proponent of this design.
Fright Pig	A car that is in unusually poor condition. Implies a certain level of dishonesty to the condition, as if an attempt has been made to make the car appear better than it actually is or includes poorly executed modifications or "upgrades."
Hard Top	Body style that does not use a B-pillar, creating a continuous open area when both side windows are rolled down
Kardex	The certificate of authenticity issued by the Porsche factory to the owner of a Porsche. States the original colors and options.
Lacquer	A cellulose-based automotive paint favored by manufacturers until the late 1950s. Multiple coats and hand or machine rubbing produces a high gloss. Lacquer finishes are fragile and crack and check with age.
Matching Numbers	A matching-numbers car is one that has all of its original numbered components intact so that they match precisely those numbers recorded by the factory in its records.
MB Tex	Or "Tex." Trade name of a high quality leatherette used by Mercedes-Benz.
Mechanical Fuel Injection	Early type of fuel injection where mixture was determined and fuel metered by means of mechanical pump rather than electronics. Common makers were SPICA, Bosch, Bendix, and Kugelfischer
Muscle Car	Intermediate-sized vehicle with a large-displacement, large-horsepower engine. Pontiac GTO created by John Z. DeLorean was among the first muscle cars. Popular in U.S. and Australia in the 1960s and '70s.
NART	Acronym for North American Racing Team, applied to Ferraris campaigned by American distributor Luigi Chinetti. The "NART" Spyder was shorthand for a very limited run of 275 GTB street cars specially commissioned by Chinetti as open cars.
Nut and Bolt Restoration	A comprehensive restoration in which every component is either replaced or renewed, whether "body-off" or "rotisserie," in the case of a unibody car.
Original	In the strictest sense of the word, all mechanical components and surfaces of the car are unaltered from the way the car left the factory, as opposed to "restored as original," in which factory finishes and surfaces are replicated as part of the restoration process.
Overhead Cam	Cylinder head design where the valve gear is actuated by chain- or belt-driven cams located in the top of the cylinder head rather than by pushrods. Design generally allows higher maximum revs.
Panel Fit	Refers to the quality of evenness in the gaps on the opening surfaces of an automobile body, ie. doors, hood, trunk lid, etc.
Phaeton	Open four-door body style that lacks roll-up side windows. Dual cowl phaetons have two windshields.
Provenance	An automobile's documentable history or pedigree. Always refers to a specific example rather than a marque or a model.
Radial tires	Tires in which the cords or plies are wrapped around the tire at a ninety degree angle.
Redline	Maximum safe revolutions per minute recommended by the manufacturer. Usually indicated by a red marking on the tachometer.
Replicar	An amalgam of the words "replica" and "car." A modern recreation or simulation of any historic or collectible car. Most replicars are sold as what they are with no attempt to deceive.
Roadster	An open two-seater generally with side curtains instead of roll-up windows.

RESOURCES

Rotisserie Restoration	Restoration usually undertaken on a unibody car in which the bare tub is attached to a rotating "rotisserie" so that the underside can be refurbished to the same standard as the upper sufaces of the car.
RPM	Revolutions per minute. A measure of engine crankshaft speed.
Shill Bid	A bid procured by a seller at an auction solely to increase the price paid by the sucessful bidder. Strictly illegal.
Side Curtains	Weather protection on an open car in lieu of roll-up windows that consists of removable plastic sliding windows attached via sockets in the tops of doors.
SOHC	Single overhead cam.
Speedster	Open car body style that usually has a rudimentary top, low windshield, and limited weather protection.
Stroked	Method of increasing the displacement of an engine by increasing the stroke of the piston.
Trailer Queen	A car usually restored to a very high standard that is seldom driven and most often trailered to shows.
Turbo	Short for "turbosupercharger" or simply "turbocharger." An exhaust gas-driven forced-induction system designed to increase horsepower without increasing displacement or fuel consumption.
Unibody	A car constructed in a manner where the body and floorpan form a single structural unit as opposed to a separate body and frame car.
Whale Tail	Aerodynamic device appended to the engine lid of a Porsche 911 Turbo. Also called a rear spoiler.
Wire Wheels	Road wheels that consist of a rim and center hub laced with wire spokes. Ususally secured by a single center lock nut or "knockoff."
Yenko	Don Yenko, a legendary Pennsylvania Chevrolet tuner famous for his Camaro and Chevelle Specials.

British to American

Bonnet	Hood
Boot	Trunk
Cellulose	Lacquer
Fender	Bumper
Five Star Petrol	Leaded Premium Gasoline
Hood	Convertible Top
Hood Sticks	Convertible Top Frame
MoT	Safety Inspection
Punter	Bidder or Buyer (connotes one who is somewhat uninformed)
Scuttle	Cowl
Shunt	An accident, usually racing related
Spanner	Wrench
Tappets	Valves
Two-pack Paint	Base Coat/Clear Coat Paint
Windscreen	Windshield
Wing	Fender ◆

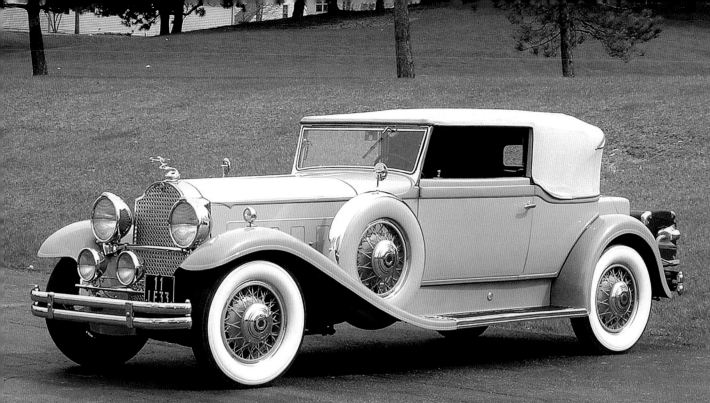

FedEx, for Your Packard®, Not Just Your Packages

FedEx Custom Critical Passport Auto Transport is the FedEx choice for car people.

We think about overhead cams more than overnight letters. Our specialized equipment includes air-ride suspension and liftgates for safe, horizontal loading. We're the originator of fully enclosed transport for fine vehicles, combined with the reliability you expect from FedEx.

passport.fedex.com 1.800.736.0575

The name, "Packard", is the registered trademark of The Packard Club (PAC) (www.PackardClub.org) and is used with permission.

Custom Critical

Relax, it's FedEx.®

© 2006 FedEx

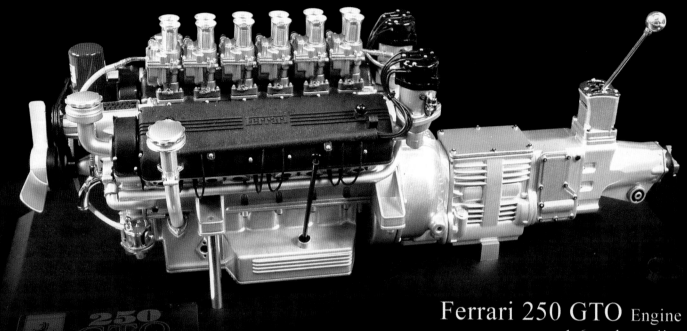

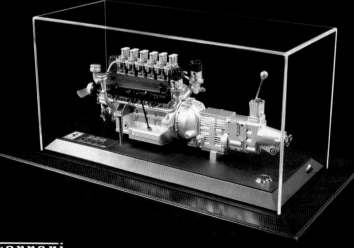

DURABLE, MODULAR, FUNCTIONAL

The Ultimate Metal Garage Cabinets

Baldhead can change the way you think about your garage. With our versatile and durable metal garage cabinet system, you can now create the ultimate showpiece with the ability to be totally functional.

Baldhead garage workbench and storage cabinet systems are made of a durable steel construction, and finished with an easy-to-maintain textured powder coat finish that will last for years. Enhanced with heavy duty drawer slides for smooth operation, and European-style door hinges for complete adjustability, these garage cabinets are the best there is.

BALDHEAD CABINETS • 20522 Builders Street • Bend, OR 97701 • Telephone: 877.966.2253

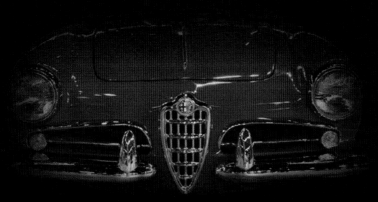

Price Guide & Ratings

In the end, it's all about money. Sort of. One of the first questions asked about a collector car is, "What's it worth?"

In this section, we address that question head on, telling you what over 2,000 models of collector cars are worth in today's market.

You'll find two numbers by each car, which represent a buy-sell range. The first number is what we are comfortable telling you to pay, and the second is what we think you should ask when you go to sell. You may find some cars for less, and sell others for more, but overall we think the range is representative of the market.

In addition, we have a ratings of long and short term collectibility, plus a treat—our recommendation of the Best 100 Cars Under $50k.

By the time you finish this chapter, you'll know how much you'll have to spend to get what you want, and even better, on the budget side, we give you one hundred to pick from that are all really quite affordable.

So within two weeks of finishing Keith Martin's Guide to Car Collecting, we expect that you will have gone out and hunted down the car of your dreams, paid the right price for it, and hauled it home to your garage.—*Keith Martin*

Price Guide

The SCM Price Guide represents our estimates of the buy-sell range in #2 condition. **As condition and history are the ultimate determinants of value,** a specific car must be evaluated according to its own merits. An automobile priced above our guide is not necessarily overpriced, nor is one priced below it a bargain.

KEY

Investment Grade

Note: This is not a value appreciation guide. Rather, it is an overall ranking of the desirability of the car, regardless of current market conditions.

A Cars that will always have a following and will always bring strong money when they are offered for sale. They embody the attributes of style, performance, historical significance, rarity, and competition history that often typify first-rank collectibles. Examples are the Ferrari SWB, the Mercedes-Benz 300Sc Roadster and the Alfa Romeo 8C 2300 Monza.

B Cars that have something special about them, often technical innovation, style, or competition provenance—but normally not all three. They were generally produced in far larger numbers than the A-tier cars. Examples are the Austin-Healey 100/4, the Ferrari 512 BB, and the Lotus 7.

C Cars that have some inherent interest, but had few special or desirable characteristics. Examples are the Porsche 914, the Saab Sonett II, and the Triumph TR4.

D Cars that had the potential to be interesting but failed to be successful in the collector car marketplace, often due to design, engineering or styling flaws. Examples include the Ferrari 400 2+2, the Acura NSX, and the Alfa 2600 Sprint.

F Cars with few if any redeeming characteristics, that are consequently hopeless in nearly every way. Examples include the Alfa Romeo Alfetta sedan, the Iso Lele, and the Lotus Eclat.

Appreciation Ratings

★★★★★ Value likely to increase much more than the market at large, perhaps as much as 25% in the next 36 months.

★★★★ Will outperform the market at large; perhaps 10% gain in 36 months.

★★★ Fully priced at the current time. Will appreciate along with the market at large.

★★ Somewhat overpriced today, or a car that is slightly out of favor. May represent a good buying opportunity if you think the market's opinion of the car will change.

★ Often a recent production car that is still depreciating heavily, or a vintage car whose maintenance costs far outweigh its market value and appeal. These collector cars are only good buys if you can do work yourself and love orphans.

	Years Built	No. Made	Buy-Sell Price Range Low	High	Grade	Rating
ABARTH						
207A Boano Spider	57	12	$110,000	$160,000	B	★★★
Zagato 750 Double Bubble	58–61	n/a	$21,000	$36,000	C	★★★
Record Monza	59–62	n/a	$32,000	$47,000	B	★★★
(Add $15k for correct twin-cam engine; $38k–$60k for 850-cc twin-cam; $70k–$90k for 1000-cc twin-cam Bialbero.)						
850 TC 2+2	62–66	n/a	$12,000	$15,000	C	★★
AC						
Ace roadster	53–63	226	$80,000	$110,000	B	★★★★
Aceca coupe	54–63	319	$40,000	$70,000	C	★★★
Ace Bristol roadster	56–63	466	$100,000	$150,000	B	★★★★
(28 cars, all RHD, were fitted with Ford Zephyr 6-cylinder engine, Rudd alloy head, and triple Webers. Add 25%)						
428 coupe	67–73	58*	$35,000	$50,000	C	★★★
428 convertible	68–73	28*	$60,000	$100,000	B	★★★★
ACURA						
NSX coupe	91–99	n/a	$25,000	$45,000	D	★
NSX coupe	00–05	n/a	$50,000	$70,000	D	★
(Add 5% for T-top. Deduct 15% for automatic.)						
ALFA ROMEO						
RL Normale/Turismo	22–25	1,702	$60,000	$80,000	C	★★

Price Guide

	Years Built	No. Made	Buy-Sell Price Range		Grade	Rating
			Low	High		
RL Sport/Super Sport	25–26	929	$80,000	$100,000	C	★★★★
RL Targa Florio	23–24	4	$350,000	$500,000	A	★★★★
6C 1500 Normale	27–29	1,058	$60,000	$80,000	D	★★
6C 1500 Sport	28	inc.	$95,000	$125,000	C	★★★
6C 1500 SS Supercharged	28	inc.	$260,000	$350,000	B	★★★
6C 1750 Turismo	29–33	2,259	$75,000	$95,000	C	★★
6C 1750 Gran Touring	30–32	inc.	$90,000	$130,000	C	★★
6C 1750 GS SC 2+2	30–33	inc.	$200,000	$250,000	B	★★★
6C 1750 GS SC Zagato	30–33	inc.	$500,000	$650,000	A	★★★★
6C 1750 GS Touring	30–33	inc.	$500,000	$650,000	A	★★★★
(For previous two models, deduct up to $100k for non-matching engines.)						
8C 2300 long chassis	31–34	130	$1,500,000	$2,200,000	A	★★★
"Le Mans" Team Cars	31–34	12	$2,500,000	$3,000,000	A	★★★★
8C 2300 short chassis "MM"	31–34	20*	$4,000,000	$5,000,000	A	★★★★
8C 2300 "Monza"	31–34	26	$4,000,000	$5,000,000	A	★★★★
Tipo B Monoposto (P3)	32–34	15	$2,300,000	$2,600,000	A	★★★★
Tipo C Monoposto (8C-35)	35–36	6	$3,000,000	$3,500,000	A	★★★★
6C 2300 saloon coachwork	34–39	1,606	$50,000	$65,000	D	★★
6C 2300 special coachwork	34–39	inc.	$100,000	$200,000	B	★★★
6C 2300 Mille Miglia	38–39	inc.	$300,000	$325,000	A	★★★★
8C 2900 short chassis	36–38	17	$8,000,000	$10,000,000	A	★★★★
8C 2900 long chassis	36–38	27	$6,000,000	$7,000,000	A	★★★★
(2,594 6C 2500 chassis of all types were built. Numbers below are included in that figure.)						
6C 2500 SS (coachbuilt)	39–43	50–100	$200,000	$275,000	B	★★★
6C 2500 SS Corsa	39–40	10*	$300,000	$500,000	B	★★★
6C 2500 cabriolet (coachbuilt)	39–53	50*	$200,000	$350,000	B	★★★
6C 2500 SS (coachbuilt)	46–53	383	$230,000	$335,000	B	★★★
6C 2500 Frec. D'Oro	46–50	680	$50,000	$75,000	C	★★
6C 2500 Villa D'Este	49–53	25	$280,000	$350,000	B	★★★
1900 5-window coupe	51–54	949	$60,000	$85,000	B	★★★
1900M 4WD	51–53	1,949	$10,000	$15,000	D	★
1900 3-window coupe	55–58	854	$70,000	$90,000	B	★★★
1900 cabriolet	52	91	$50,000	$75,000	B	★★
1900 Zagato (SSZ)	55–57	28*	$300,000	$385,000	A	★★★★
2000 Spider	58–62	3,443	$28,000	$35,000	C	★★
2600 Spider	62–65	2,255	$35,000	$45,000	C	★★★
2600 Sprint	62–66	6,999	$12,000	$20,000	D	★
2600 Sprint Zagato	65–67	105	$70,000	$100,000	B	★★★
750 Sprint Normale	54–59	7,000*	$20,000	$30,000	C	★★★
750 Spider Normale	55–59	7,000*	$25,000	$33,000	C	★★★
750 Spider Veloce	56–59	2,300*	$30,000	$45,000	B	★★★★
(For '56–'57 Veloces, add 50% for event eligibility.)						
750 Sprint Veloce	56–59	1,100*	$40,000	$45,000	B	★★★★
750 Sprint (Lightweight)	56–57	100*	$80,000	$120,000	A	★★★★
750 SS (low-nose)	57–58	100*	$35,000	$50,000	B	★★★★
101 1300 Spider Normale	59–62	7,800*	$18,000	$26,000	C	★★★
101 1300 Spider Veloce	59–62	500*	$30,000	$60,000	B	★★★★
101 1300 Sprint Normale	59–62	17,000*	$15,000	$30,000	C	★★★
101 1300 Sprint Veloce	59–62	1,900*	$35,000	$45,000	B	★★★★
101 1300 Sprint Speciale	58–62	1,366	$35,000	$45,000	B	★★★★
SZ-1	60–61	169	$120,000	$150,000	B	★★★
SZ-2	61–62	44	$135,000	$160,000	A	★★★★
TZ-1	63–64	101	$325,000	$470,000	A	★★★★
TZ-2	64–65	12	$1,200,000	$1,400,000	A	★★★
(Note: TZs and SZs are easy to fake. Prices are for authentic cars with paperwork.)						
101 1600 Spider Normale	62–65	9,250	$20,000	$30,000	C	★★★
101 1600 Spider Veloce	64–66	1,091	$35,000	$45,000	B	★★★★
101 1600 Sprint Normale	62–64	7,107	$15,000	$25,000	C	★★★
101 1600 Sprint Speciale	63–66	1,400	$40,000	$55,000	B	★★★★
Giulia Sprint GT	63–66	21,542	$10,000	$20,000	C	★★★

	Years Built	No. Made	Buy-Sell Price Range		Grade	Rating
			Low	High		
Giulia Sprint GT Veloce	66–68	14,240	$15,000	$25,000	B	★★★
Giulia GTC	64–66	1,000	$16,000	$25,000	B	★★
Giulia TI Super	63–64	501	$19,500	$25,000	B	★★★
Giulia Super	65–72	124,590	$9,000	$15,000	B	★★★
4R Zagato	66–68	92	$30,000	$50,000	B	★★★
1600 GTA Stradale	65–67	560	$90,000	$110,000	B	★★★
1600 GTA Corsa	65–67	inc.	$110,000	$130,000	A	★★★
1300 GTA Jr. Stradale	68–71	447	$80,000	$100,000	B	★★★
1300 GTA Jr. Corse	68–71	inc.	$90,000	$115,000	A	★★★
1750 GTAM	68–72	40	$110,000	$125,000	A	★★★
(Note: GTA prices are especially affected by originality, completeness, and history.)						
TT 33/2 Stradale	67–69	18	$1,000,000	$1,200,000	A	★★★★
TT 33/2 (2-liter)	67–69	30	$500,000	$650,000	A	★★★★
TT 33/3 (3-liter)	69–72	20	$450,000	$575,000	A	★★★★
TT 33 12 cylinder	75	12	$350,000	$500,000	B	★★★
TT 33 SC 12 (Supercharged)	77	2	$375,000	$450,000	B	★★★
Duetto	66–67	15,047	$15,000	$25,000	B	★★★
Spider 1750 (Roundtail)	68–69	inc.	$15,000	$20,000	B	★★
GTV 1750	69	44,265	$10,000	$20,000	B	★★★
1300 Junior Zagato	68–72	1,108	$18,000	$25,000	B	★★★
1600 Junior Zagato	72–75	402	$25,000	$30,000	B	★★★
Montreal	72–75	3,925	$16,000	$22,000	C	★
(Deduct $2,500 if not properly state- and federal-certified.)						
Berlina 1750/2000	69–74		$2,000	$3,500	D	★★
GTV 1750/2000	70–74	37,459	$10,000	$20,000	C	★★★
Spider 1750/2000	70–74	n/a	$5,500	$9,000	C	★★★
Spider 2000	75–81	n/a	$5,000	$8,000	D	★★
Alfetta sedan	75–79	n/a	$2,000	$3,000	F	★
(Deduct $500 for automatic.)						
Alfetta GT (U.S.)	75–79	13,715	$2,500	$4,000	F	★
Spider 2000	82–84	n/a	$4,000	$5,500	D	★
GTV-6 coupe	81–83	n/a	$3,000	$5,000	D	★★
GTV-6 Balocco coupe	82	350	$4,500	$5,500	C	★★
GTV-6 coupe	84–86	n/a	$4,500	$7,000	C	★★
GTV-6 Maratona coupe	84	n/a	$5,000	$7,000	C	★★
GTV-6 Twin Turbo coupe	85	n/a	$10,500	$13,000	B	★★★
Spider 2000	85–86	n/a	$3,500	$6,000	D	★
Milano sedan	87–89	n/a	$2,500	$4,000	D	★
(Deduct $1,000 for automatic.)						
Milano Verde sedan	87–89	n/a	$3,000	$6,000	C	★★
Spider 2000	87–90	n/a	$4,500	$7,000	D	★
Zagato ES-30	90–92	1,020	$20,000	$26,000	C	★★
164/164L sedan	91–95	n/a	$3,500	$6,500	F	★
164S sedan	91–95	n/a	$6,000	$8,000	C	★★
(For '94–'95 164, add $3,000 for 4-cam on "L" and "LS" models. For '95 164Q, add $2,000.)						
Spider 2000	91–92	n/a	$6,000	$11,000	D	★★
Spider 2000 (Commemorative Edition)	93	n/a	$8,500	$14,000	D	★★
(Deduct $1,500 for automatic.)						
ALLARD						
K2	51–52	119	$43,000	$60,000	B	★★★
K3	52–54	62	$40,000	$60,000	B	★★★
J2X	52–54	83	$130,000	$175,000	B	★★★
AMC						
SC/Rambler	69	1,512	$19,000	$35,000	C	★★★
Rebel "Machine"	70	2,362	$15,000	$24,000	C	★★★
AMX	68–70	20187	$19,000	$32,000	C	★★★★
(Add 30% for 390 engine; 10% for Go Pack, Big Bad colors, or Shadow Mask paint. Deduct: 20% for automatic; 20% for 1968 models.)						
Javelin SST	68–70	69,027	$10,000	$15,000	C	★★
(Add 20% for 390 engine; 10% for Big Bad colors.)						
Javelin "Mark Donohue"	70	2501 (inc)	$17,500	$27,500	C	★★★

Price Guide

	Years Built	No. Made	Buy-Sell Price Range		Grade	Rating
			Low	High		
Javelin "Trans Am"	70	100 (inc.)	$26,000	$37,500	B	★★★★
Javelin AMX	71–74	16,961	$12,000	$17,000	C	★★
(Add 25% for 401 engine.)						
AMPHICAR						
770 convertible	61–68	n/a	$35,000	$60,000	C	★★★
ARNOLT-BRISTOL						
Bolide roadster	54–59	142	$45,000	$60,000	C	★★★
DeLuxe roadster	54–59	inc.	$50,000	$73,000	C	★★★
Mk II coupe	54–59	3	$125,000	$200,000	B	★★★
ASTON MARTIN						
(For all Aston serial production cars through current, deduct 25% for RHD in U.S. only.)						
DB2 coupe	50–53	302	$55,000	$105,000	C	★★★
DB2 DHC	50–53	102	$75,000	$125,000	B	★★★
DB3 coupe	51–53	10	$450,000	$600,000	A	★★★
DB2/4 coupe	53–55	492	$45,000	$80,000	C	★★★
DB2/4 DHC	53–55	73	$80,000	$140,000	B	★★★
DB2/4 Bertone Spyder	53–55	3	$500,000	$750,000	A	★★★★
DB3S Team car	53–56	n/a	$2,500,000	$3,000,000	A	★★★★
DB3S Customer car	53–56	3	$1,200,000	$2,000,000	A	★★★★
DB2/4 Mk II coupe	55–57	199	$65,000	$85,000	C	★★★
DB2/4 Mk III coupe	55–57	551	$75,000	$125,000	C	★★★
DB2/4 Mk III DHC	55–57	inc.	$135,000	$240,000	B	★★★★
DB2/4 Mk III Notchback	55–57	inc.	$65,000	$105,000	B	★★★
DBR1	56–60	5	$3,000,000	$4,500,000	A	★★★★
DB4 Series I–IV coupe	58–63	925	$105,000	$155,000	B	★★★★
DB4 Series V coupe	61–62	185	$155,000	$230,000	B	★★★★
DB4 DHC (I–V)	58–63	inc.	$225,000	$395,000	B	★★★★
(For Series IV–V SS triple-carb engine, add $5,000; Series V covered headlights, add $5,000.)						
DB4GT	59–63	75	$750,000	$1,100,000	A	★★★★
DB4GT Zagato	60–63	19	$2,500,000	$3,000,000	A	★★★★
(For factory team race cars—1VEV and 2VEV—add 25%.)						
DB5 coupe	63–65	886	$160,000	$225,000	B	★★★★
DB5 coupe Vantage	63–65	inc.	$185,000	$240,000	B	★★★★
DB5 DHC	64–65	123	$250,000	$350,000	A	★★★★★
DB5 Shooting Brake	64–65	12	$200,000	$250,000	C	★★★
DB6 Volante (short chassis)	65–66	37	$280,000	$425,000	B	★★★★★
DB6 coupe	65–69	1,321	$115,000	$175,000	B	★★★★
DB6 Vantage coupe	65–69	inc.	$130,000	$190,000	B	★★★★
DB6 Shooting Brake	65–69	6	$180,000	$225,000	C	★★★
DB6 Volante (long chassis)	66–69	140	$205,000	$280,000	B	★★★
DBS (6 cyl.)	67–72	857	$35,000	$55,000	D	★★★
DB6 Mk II coupe	69–70	240	$150,000	$185,000	B	★★★
DB6 Mk II Volante	69–70	38	$250,000	$400,000	B	★★★
(Add $5,000 for Vantage.)						
DBSV8	70–72	399	$35,000	$55,000	C	★★★
AM Vantage	72–73	70	$35,000	$55,000	C	★★★
AMV8 SII/III	74–79	1,259	$35,000	$60,000	C	★★★
(AMV8 SII/III pre-"Oscar India" V8s have leather dashes. Production for SIII Vantages was 43.)						
AMV8 Volante	79–82	350	$45,000	$75,000	C	★★★
(All Volantes had "Oscar India" wood dashes.)						
AMV8 SIV (carb.)	79–85	299	$60,000	$105,000	C	★★★
("Oscar India" SIVs can be identified by their wood dashes.)						
AMV8 S. 4 (inj.)	86–89	4	$85,000	$125,000	C	★★★
Lagonda saloon	83–85	645	$25,000	$40,000	D	★★
Volante	83–86	inc.	$55,000	$85,000	C	★★
(Injection became standard in late '86.)						
Vantage Volante	87–89	58	$75,000	$120,000	B	★★★
Lagonda saloon	85–87	n/a	$20,000	$45,000	D	★★
Volante (inj.)	86–89	n/a	$55,000	$85,000	C	★★★
Lagonda saloon	88–89	n/a	$35,000	$60,000	D	★★

	Years Built	No. Made	Buy-Sell Price Range		Grade	Rating
			Low	High		
Virage coupe	91–92	n/a	$30,000	$60,000	C	★★
Virage Volante	92–93	n/a	$70,000	$100,000	C	★★
Virage Volante (Widebody)	93	13	$100,000	$150,000		★★
DB7 coupe	97–03	n/a	$35,000	$95,000	C	★★
DB7 Volante	97–03	n/a	$40,000	$100,000	C	★★
DB9 coupe	04–		$135,000	$160,000		★★
DB9 Volante	04–		$150,000	$175,000		★★
V12 Vanquish coupe	02–		$220,000	$234,000		★★
V12 Vanquish S coupe	05–		est. MSRP	$255,000		★★
AUBURN						
Custom/Standard Eight						
Boattail Speedster	31–34	est. 56,000	$145,000	$195,000	B	★★★★
Phaeton	31–34	inc	$90,000	$150,000	B	★★★★
Cabriolet	31–34	inc	$100,000	$175,000	C	★★★
Sedan	31–34	inc	$27,000	$40,000	C	★★
Coupe	31–34	inc	$32,000	$50,000	C	★★★
Custom/Salon Twelve						
Boattail Speedster	32–34	est. 2,000	$160,000	$230,000	B	★★★★
Phaeton	32–34	inc	$130,000	$185,000	B	★★★★
Cabriolet	32–34	inc	$100,000	$140,000	B	★★★
Sedan	32–34	inc	$30,000	$45,000	C	★★
Coupe	32–34	inc	$35,000	$50,000	C	★★★
851/852 Supercharged						
Boattail Speedster	35–36	est. 500	$225,000	$340,000	A	★★★★
Phaeton	35–36	inc	$100,000	$155,000	B	★★★
Cabriolet	35–36	inc	$90,000	$120,000	B	★★★
Sedan/Coupe	35–36	inc	$45,000	$95,000	C	★★
AUDI						
Quattro coupe	90–91	n/a	$3,500	$5,000	D	★★
TT coupe	00–05	n/a	$15,000	$30,000	C	★
TT convertible	00–05	n/a	$20,000	$30,000	C	★
AUSTIN/MORRIS						
Mini Cooper	62–64	30,000*	$13,000	$24,000	C	★★★
Mini Cooper S	64–66	13,922	$18,000	$30,000	B	★★★
(Model years and non-S production numbers for U.S. models only.)						
AUSTIN-HEALEY						
100-4 (BN1, 3-sp)	53–55	10,010	$28,000	$45,000	B	★★★
100-4 (BN2, 4-sp)	55–56	4,604	$28,000	$50,000	B	★★★
100S	55	50	$200,000	$300,000	A	★★★★
100M	55–56	640	$50,000	$75,000	B	★★★★
100 w/ Le Mans kit	55–56	n/a	$35,000	$50,000	C	★★★
100-6 BN4 (2+2)	56–59	11,294	$25,000	$40,000	C	★★★
(BN6 2-seat, add $5,000)		4,150				
3000 Mk I (BT7) 2+2	59–61	10,825	$28,000	$45,000	B	★★★★
(For BN7 2-seat, add $5,000)		2,825				
3000 Mk II BT7 (2+2) tri-carb	61–62	5,096	$35,000	$55,000	B	★★★
(For BN7 2-seat, tri-carb, add $10,000)		355				
(For 100-6/3000, add $2,000 for factory 2-seat hard top; $1,000 for 4-seat hard top. Deduct $2,000 for disc wheels.)						
3000 Mk II BJ7 (roll-up windows)	62–63	6,113	$35,000	$55,000	B	★★★
3000 Mk III (BJ8)	63–67	17,712	$50,000	$100,000	B	★★★★
BJ8 factory-built rally cars	63–67	7	$100,000	$200,000	B	★★★
Bugeye Sprite	58–61	48,987	$11,000	$24,000	B	★★★★
Sprite	61–71	80,360	$5,000	$10,000	C	★★
BENTLEY						
3-Liter (saloon or bitsa) short std.	22–25	1,622	$75,000	$125,000	C	★
*Open, matching #'s/original		inc.	$100,000	$200,000	B	★★★
3-Liter TT Replica	22–24	inc.	$120,000	$200,000	C	★★★
3-Liter Speed Model Red Badge (bitsa)	23–29	inc.	$120,000	$160,000	B	★★
* Matching #'s/original		inc.	$160,000	$275,000	A	★★★
6-1/2-Liter	25–30	545	$300,000	$500,000	B	★★

Price Guide

	Years Built	No. Made	Buy-Sell Price Range		Grade	Rating
			Low	High		
*Matching #'s/original		inc.	$400,000	$650,000	A	★★★★
4 1/2-Liter (bitsa)	27–31	665	$175,000	$300,000	B	★★
*Matching #'s/original			$350,000	$1,000,000	A	★★★
6-1/2-Liter Speed Six (bitsa)	28–30	inc.	$500,000	$1,000,000	B	★★
*Matching #'s/original			$500,000	$15,000,000	A	★★★★
4 1/2-Liter Supercharged	29–31	55	$600,000	$1,750,000	A	★★★★
8-Liter	29–31	100	$400,000	$1,000,000	A	★★★
4-Liter	31–32	50	$100,000	$150,000	B	★★★
3 1/2-Liter saloon	33–36	1,177	$40,000	$60,000	C	★
*Rare/attractive/open		inc.	$100,000	$300,000	B	★★★
4 1/4-Liter saloon	36–40	1,234	$60,000	$95,000	C	★
*Rare/attractive/open		inc.	$150,000	$350,000	B	★★★
(38–39 MR/MX series, add 15%.)						
Mk V	39–40	35	$75,000	$150,000		★
Mk VI standard steel saloon	46–52	5,368	$25,000	$50,000	D	★
(Add 40% for 4.6-Liter engine.)						
Mk VI coupe	47–52	inc.	$45,000	$75,000	D	★
Mk VI Drophead	47–52	inc.	$75,000	$125,000	C	★★★
R-type standard steel saloon	52–55	2,486	$25,000	$50,000	D	★
R Continental/Fastback/HJM	52–55	208	$250,000	$400,000	B	★★★★
S1 standard steel saloon	55–59	3,107	$22,000	$40,000	D	★
S1 Continental/Fastback/HJM	55–58	431	$100,000	$250,000	B	★★
(LHD cars will likely bring a 25% premium in the U.S.)						
S1 Continental (PW)	55–58	inc.	$70,000	$110,000	B	★★★
S1 Continental DHC/LHD	55–59	inc.	$275,000	$350,000	A	★★★★
S1 Continental DHC/RHD	55–59	inc.	$130,000	$160,000	B	★★★
S1 Continental Flying Spur	58–59	inc.	$75,000	$130,000	B	★★
S2 Continental (MPW)	59–62	388	$35,000	$55,000	B	★★★
S2 Continental DHC	59–62	inc.	$60,000	$100,000	A	★★★★
S2 standard steel saloon	60–62	1,922	$18,000	$30,000	D	★
S3 standard steel saloon (LHD)	62–65	1,318	$40,000	$60,000	D	★
S3 Continental Harlequin Headlights	62–66	312	$50,000	$80,000	D	★★
S3 DHC Harlequin Headlights	62–66	inc.	$90,000	$150,000	C	★★★
S3 Continental Flying Spur	63–66	inc.	$80,000	$150,000	B	★★
T standard steel saloon	65–76	1,721	$10,000	$20,000	D	★★
T1 MPW saloon	66–70	98	$18,000	$32,000	D	★★
T1 MPW convertible	66–70	77	$35,000	$47,000	B	★★
Continental Flying Spur	77–81	433	$27,000	$40,000	C	★★
Continental Turbo	81	8	$40,000	$60,000	C	★★
T2 standard steel saloon	77–81	n/a	$15,000	$30,000	C	★★
Corniche saloon	77–80	n/a	$27,000	$40,000	D	★
Corniche convertible	77–84	n/a	$40,000	$75,000	C	★
Mulsanne standard steel saloon	80–87	531	$18,000	$27,000	B	★★
Mulsanne Turbo	82–85	519	$20,000	$30,000	C	★
Continental convertible	85–89	n/a	$45,000	$75,000	C	★
Continental convertible	90–92	n/a	$55,000	$110,000	B	★
Continental convertible	93–95	n/a	$90,000	$125,000	B	★★
Turbo R	85–98	n/a	$25,000	$70,000	B	★
Turbo R	92–95	n/a	$35,000	$67,000	C	★
Continental coupe	85–87	n/a	$30,000	$50,000	C	★
Eight	84–92	1,734	$18,000	$40,000	C	★★
Mulsanne S sedan	87–92	966	$18,000	$32,000	C	★
Turbo RT LWB	97–98	216	$37,000	$65,000	C	★
Continental R	91–02	n/a	$68,000	$92,000	C	★
Brooklands	92–98	1,619	$28,000	$48,000	C	★
Brooklands R	97–98	100	$32,000	$62,000	C	★
Turbo S	94–96	60	$30,000	$50,000	C	★
Azure	98–06	n/a	$88,000	$160,000	B	★★
Continental T	97–02	n/a	$90,000	$135,000	C	★
Arnage RL	97–	n/a	$90,000	$160,000	C	★

	Years Built	No. Made	Buy-Sell Price Range		Grade	Rating
			Low	High		
Arnage R	02–	n/a	$85,000	$150,000	C	★
Continental Flying Spur	04–	n/a	$150,000	$175,000	C	★
Continental GT	04–	n/a	$135,000	$150,000	C	★★
Continental GTC	05–	n/a	$140,000	$155,000	B	★★★
BITTER						
SC coupe	83–84	n/a	$8,000	$12,000	F	★
SC coupe	85	n/a	$10,000	$16,000	F	★
BIZZARRINI						
5300 GT and Strada	65–69	100*	$200,000	$275,000	B	★★★
BMW						
328	37–39	465	$195,000	$250,000	A	★★★
Isetta 250/300	55–62	158,728	$15,000	$30,000	C	★★★
Isetta 600 2+2	57–59	34,813	$10,000	$14,000	D	★★
507 roadster	56–59	253	$300,000	$400,000	A	★★★★
(Add $10k for Rudge knock-offs; $10k for factory hard top. Deduct $15k if car has sedan replacement block.)						
(Most serial production BMWs should be regarded as "used cars." Condition is the prime determinant of value.)						
2800CS	68–71	9,399	$7,800	$11,500	C	★★
Bavaria 4-dr.	71–74	39,056	$3,500	$5,500	D	★
3.0CSL	71–72	1,039	$19,500	$29,000	C	★★★
3.0CS	72–74	11,063	$8,500	$14,500	C	★★★
1600 coupe	67–70	277,320	$5,000	$7,000	C	★★★
2002 coupe	68–71	339,084	$6,500	$9,000	C	★★★
2002 coupe	72–74	inc.	$6,600	$8,900	C	★★
2002 tii coupe	71–75	38,701	$10,500	$16,500	B	★★★
2002 Turbo	73–75	1,672	$12,000	$17,000	B	★★★
2002 coupe	75–76	inc. 2002	$4,200	$6,600	C	★
320i coupe	77–80	n/a	$2,200	$3,600	F	★
320i coupe	81–83	n/a	$2,600	$3,800	F	★
318i coupe	84–85	n/a	$2,000	$3,500	F	★
325e coupe	84–87	17,756	$2,000	$4,000	F	★
325i coupe	87–88	n/a	$3,250	$5,700	F	★
325i convertible	87–89	n/a	$4,250	$6,250	D	★
325i convertible	90–91	n/a	$4,250	$7,000	D	★
630 CSi coupe	77	*	$4,800	$6,400	D	★★
633 CSi coupe	78–82	*	$5,000	$6,500	D	★★
(*6-series sales for 78–82 were 32,292. U.S. sales of B21 for 77–83 were 8,785.)						
633 CSi coupe	83–84	5,332	$5,200	$6,800	D	★★
635 CSi coupe	85–87	17,354	$6,500	$8,500	D	★★
635 CSi coupe	88–89	4,241	$7,500	$10,500	D	★★
750iL 4-door	88–89	23,721	$3,900	$6,500	F	★
750iL 4-door	90–91	15,318	$5,800	$8,500	F	★
850i coupe	91–92	11,932	$13,000	$19,000	D	★
840i coupe	94–97	5,808	$16,000	$28,000	D	★
M1 coupe	79–80	450	$68,000	$88,000	B	★★
(M1 production numbers include Group 4 & 5 competition models.)						
M3 coupe	88–91	n/a	$10,000	$13,000	C	★★
M5 4-dr. (Euro)	85–90	2,000*	$8,500	$12,000	D	★
M5 4-dr.	91–92	n/a	$10,000	$14,000	D	★
M6 coupe	87–88	n/a	$14,000	$18,000	D	★
L7 4-dr.	86–87	n/a	$5,000	$6,500	D	★
L6 coupe	87	n/a	$6,500	$9,000	D	★
M3 coupe	95–97	22,597	$10,000	$16,000	C	★★
Z3 roadster (4-cyl.)	96–97	n/a	$9,000	$12,000	D	★
Z3 roadster (6-cyl.)	97–02	n/a	$11,500	$22,000	C	★★
(Add $4,000 for M coupe/roadster.)						
Z8	00–03	5,703	$75,000	$105,000	C	★★
BRICKLIN						
SV1 coupe	74–75	2,897	$15,000	$25,000	D	★
BUGATTI						
Type 37A Grand Prix	25–29	291	$195,000	$350,000	A	★★★

Price Guide

	Years Built	No. Made	Buy-Sell Price Range		Grade	Rating
			Low	High		
Type 43/43A	27–31	160	$350,000	$1,000,000	B	★★★
Type 44 cabriolet	27–30	1,250	$120,000	$200,000	A	★★★
Type 50 coupe surprofilee	30–34	10	$1,000,000	$2,500,000	B	★★★
Type 50 Tourer	30–34	65	$500,000	$1,200,000	B	★★★
Type 57 Atalante coupe	35–38	40	$450,000	$700,000	A	★★★
Type 57/57C Stelvio cabriolet	34–39	100	$300,000	$550,000	A	★★★
Type 57SC Atalante coupe	36–38	16	$1,600,000	$3,000,000	A	★★★
EB110	92–95	139	$180,000	$300,000	B	★★
Veyron	06	300	est. MSRP	$1,200,000	B	★★
BUICK						
Skylark GS 400	65–67	23,442*	$14,000	$19,000	C	★★★
Convertible	65–67	6,122	$19,500	$25,000	C	★★★★
Skylark GS 400	68–69	17,009*	$18,000	$23,000	C	★★★
Convertible	68–69	4,230	$24,500	$30,500	C	★★★★
(Add 20% for 4-sp. Deduct 20% for 1968 models.)						
Skylark GS 400 Stage 1	69	1,256	$31,500	$42,000	B	★★★★
Convertible	69	212	$52,500	$68,000	B	★★★★
Skylark GS 455	70	8,732	$26,000	$32,000	B	★★★★
Convertible	70	1,416	$35,000	$45,000	A	★★★★
Skylark GS 455 Stage 1	70	8,732	$50,000	$60,000	B	★★★★
Convertible	70	1,416	$75,000	$100,000	A	★★★★
Skylark GSX 455	70	678	$55,000	$65,000	A	★★★★
(Add 20% for 4-sp; 30% for Stage 1.)						
Skylark GS 455	71–72	15,991*	$22,500	$28,000	B	★★★★
Convertible	71–72	1,754	$30,000	$40,000	B	★★★★
Skylark GS 455 Stage 1	71–72	1,529	$32,000	$41,000	B	★★★★
Convertible	71–72	162	$65,000	$80,000	A	★★★★
CHEVROLET						
Camaro						
SS 350	67–68	36,469	$23,000	$35,000	C	★★★★
Convertible	67–68	inc.	$25,000	$40,000	C	★★★★
SS 396	67–68	23,068	$31,000	$55,000	B	★★★★
Convertible	67–68	inc.	$30,000	$65,000	A	★★★★
Z/28	67	602	$60,000	$90,000	A	★★★★
Yenko Camaro	67	107*	$250,000	$300,000	A	★★★★
Z/28	68	7,199	$40,000	$60,000	B	★★★★
(Add 20% to '67–69 Z/28 for R/S option.)						
Yenko Camaro	68	64*	$225,000	$275,000	A	★★★★
SS 350 Pace Car	69	3,675	$28,000	$55,000	C	★★★★
Convertible	69	inc.	$35,000	$60,000	C	★★★★
SS 396 Pace Car Convertible	69	n/a	$38,000	$75,000	B	★★★★
Yenko Camaro	69	200*	$250,000	$300,000	A	★★★★
Z/28	69	20,302	$50,000	$100,000	B	★★★
Z/28	70–73	27,744	$22,000	$35,000	B	★★★★
(Add 10% to '70–'73 Z/28 for RS option.)						
SS 396	70–72	27,415	$25,000	$40,000	C	★★★
Z/28	74	n/a	$16,000	$25,000	D	★★★
Z/28	77–78	69,256	$7,000	$13,000	D	★★
Z/28	79–81	173,286	$7,000	$15,000	D	★★
Pace Car	82	6,360	$7,000	$11,500	D	★
Pace Car	93	633	$12,000	$19,000	D	★
Chevelle						
SS 396 (360-hp)	65	n/a	$25,000	$35,000	B	★★★★
SS 396	66–67	n/a	$25,000	$55,000	B	★★★★
Convertible	66–67	n/a	$35,000	$65,000	B	★★★★
SS 396	68–69	n/a	$25,000	$55,000	B	★★★★
Convertible	68–69	n/a	$35,000	$65,000	B	★★★★
Yenko Chevelle	69	99*	$250,000	$300,000	A	★★★★
SS 396 (402/454)	70	62,372	$30,000	$60,000	B	★★★★
Convertible	70	inc.	$35,000	$65,000	B	★★★★

	Years Built	No. Made	Buy-Sell Price Range		Grade	Rating
			Low	High		
SS 454 LS5 (360-hp)	70	4,298	$45,000	$55,000	B	★★★★
Convertible	70	inc.	$43,000	$75,000	B	★★★★
SS 454 LS6 (450-hp)	70	4,475	$70,000	$110,000	A	★★★★
Convertible	70	inc.	$275,000	$375,000	A	★★★★
(Add 25% for 4-sp.)						
SS 396	71–72	82,000	$20,000	$35,000	C	★★★
Convertible	71–72	inc.	$25,000	$40,000	C	★★★★
SS 454 LS5	71–72	n/a	$30,000	$55,000	C	★★★
Convertible	71–72	n/a	$35,000	$65,000	C	★★★
Corvette						
Corvette prices are based on CPI Black Book values. Copyright 2006, Hearst Business Media Corporation ALL RIGHTS RESERVED.						
Roadster	53	300	$125,000	$200,000	A	★★★★
Roadster	54	3,640	$70,000	$100,000	B	★★★★
Roadster	55	700	$66,000	$120,000	A	★★★★
Convertible	56	3,467	$47,000	$81,000	B	★★★★
Convertible	57	6,339	$47,000	$82,000	B	★★★★
Convertible	58	9,168	$43,000	$76,000	B	★★★★
Convertible	59	9,670	$42,000	$73,000	B	★★★★
Convertible	60	10,261	$43,000	$75,000	B	★★★★
Convertible	61	10,939	$43,000	$74,000	B	★★★★
Convertible	62	14,531	$44,000	$77,000	B	★★★★
Add for the following (1956–62):						
265/225-hp (1956)		3,080	$6,000	$8,500		
283/245-hp (1957–61)		8,284	$4,000	$9,000		
283/250-hp (1957–60) FI		961	$10,000	$17,000		
283/270-hp (1957–61)		9,636	$7,500	$12,000		
283/275-hp (1961) FI		118	$13,000	$21,000		
283/283-hp (1957) FI		43	$23,500	$41,000		
283/290-hp (1958–60) FI		2,511	$24,000	$41,000		
283/315-hp (1961) FI		1,462	$24,000	$42,000		
327/340-hp (1962)		4,412	$5,100	$11,200		
327/360-hp (1962) FI		1,918	$30,000	$53,000		
Auxiliary hard top		36,120	$2,000	$2,700		
Coupe split-window	63	10,594	$41,000	$72,000	A	★★★★
Convertible	63	10,919	$36,000	$63,000	A	★★★★
Coupe	64	8,304	$33,000	$56,000	B	★★★★
Convertible	64	19,925	$35,000	$60,000	A	★★★★
Coupe	65	8,816	$39,000	$67,000	B	★★★★
Convertible	65	15,376	$40,000	$70,000	A	★★★★
Coupe	66	9,958	$41,000	$72,000	B	★★★★
Convertible	66	17,762	$44,000	$76,000	A	★★★★
Coupe	67	8,504	$45,000	$79,000	A	★★★★
Convertible	67	14,436	$50,000	$88,000	A	★★★★
Add for the following (1963–67):						
327/340-hp (1963)		6,978	$4,400	$7,000		
327/350-hp (1965–67)		18,682	$2,400	$3,500		
327/360-hp (1963) FI		2,610	$30,000	$51,000		
327/365-hp (1964–65)		12,182	$4,000	$7,000		
327/375-hp (1964–65) FI		2,096	$20,000	$35,000		
396/425-hp (1965)		2,157	$27,300	$48,000		
427/390-hp (1966–67)		8,948	$16,000	$28,000		
427/400-hp (1967)		2,101	$27,500	$47,300		
427/425-hp (1966)		5,258	$27,500	$48,000		
427/435-hp (1967)		3,754	$52,500	$90,000		
Auxiliary hard top		23,130	$1,400	$2,000		
Air conditioning		11,997	$3,600	$5,000		
Knock-off wheels		n/a	$4,700	$6,700		
Aluminum wheels (1967)		720	$5,600	$8,100		
Side exhaust		8,585	$1,300	$1,700		

	Years Built	No. Made	Buy-Sell Price Range		Grade	Rating
			Low	High		
Coupe	68	9,936	$18,000	$36,000	C	★★★★
Convertible	68	18,630	$23,750	$47,500	B	★★★★
Coupe	69	22,129	$18,800	$38,000	C	★★★★
Convertible	69	16,633	$24,300	$48,500	B	★★★★
Coupe	70	10,668	$19,000	$38,000	C	★★★★
Convertible	70	6,648	$24,500	$49,000	C	★★★★
Coupe	71	14,680	$17,900	$35,700	C	★★★★
Convertible	71	7,121	$24,300	$48,500	C	★★★★
Coupe	72	20,496	$19,400	$38,750	C	★★★★
Convertible	72	6,508	$25,300	$50,000	C	★★★★
Add for the following (1968–72):						
327/350-hp (1968) L79		9,440	$2,300	$4,000		
427/390-hp (1968–69) L36		18,248	$7,200	$13,000		
427/400-hp (1968–69) L68		4,004	$11,000	$20,000		
427/435-hp (1968–69) L71		5,620	$20,000	$30,000		
427/435-hp (1968–69) L89		1,014	$33,000	$52,500		
350/350-hp (1969–70) L46		17,756	$2,000	$4,000		
350/370-hp (1970) LT1		1,287	$8,000	$16,000		
454/390-hp (1970) LS5		4,473	$8,000	$17,000		
350/330-hp (1971) LT1		1,949	$7,100	$14,100		
454/365-hp (1971) LS5		5,097	$7,700	$15,100		
454/425-hp (1971) LS6		188	$44,000	$75,000		
454/270-hp (1972) LS5		3,913	$6,800	$13,000		
350/255-hp (1972) LT1		1,741	$6,900	$12,000		
Auxiliary hard top		24,434	$1,200	$1,600		
Air conditioning		52,674	$1,800	$2,600		
Coupe	73	25,521	$13,500	$23,500	C	★★★★
Convertible	73	4,943	$19,000	$33,000	C	★★★★
Coupe	74	32,028	$12,000	$21,000	C	★★★★
Convertible	74	5,474	$18,000	$31,000	C	★★★★
Coupe	75	33,836	$10,000	$18,000	C	★★★★
Convertible	75	4,629	$18,000	$31,500	C	★★★★
Coupe	76	46,558	$9,500	$16,500	C	★★★★
Coupe	77	49,213	$9,800	$17,000	C	★★★★
Coupe	78	24,991	$10,300	$18,000	C	★★★★
Silver Anniversary	78	15,283	$13,000	$22,750	C	★★★★
Pace Car	78	6,502	$19,000	$33,500	C	★★★★
Coupe	79	53,807	$10,600	$18,500	C	★★★★
Coupe	80	40,614	$11,000	$19,300	C	★★★★
Coupe	81	40,606	$11,600	$20,300	C	★★★★
Coupe	82	18,648	$12,400	$21,700	C	★★★★
Collector Edition	82	6,759	$16,750	$29,300	C	★★★★
Add for the following (1973–82):						
454 (1973–74) LS4		11,400	$3,500	$7,000		
350 L82		64,033	$2,400	$4,300		
Glass roof (1978–82)		79,005	$550	$800		
Aluminum wheels		168,109	$600	$950		
Auxiliary hard top		8,754	$1,100	$1,600		
Coupe	84	51,547	$6,700	$10,600	D	★★
Coupe	85	39,729	$7,100	$11,100	D	★★
Coupe	86	27,794	$7,500	$11,500	D	★★
Convertible	86	7,315	$10,400	$16,000	D	★★
Coupe	87	20,007	$7,900	$12,000	D	★★
Convertible	87	10,625	$10,800	$16,400	D	★★
Coupe	88	15,382	$8,500	$12,700	D	★★
Convertible	88	5,357	$11,200	$16,900	D	★★
35th Anniversary coupe	88	2,050	$13,500	$21,500	D	★★
Challenge Racer	88	56	$26,500	$39,200	D	★★
Coupe	89	16,663	$8,900	$13,200	D	★★

	Years Built	No. Made	Buy-Sell Price Range		Grade	Rating
			Low	High		
Convertible	89	9,749	$11,800	$17,400	D	★★
Challenge Racer	89	60	$26,500	$39,200	D	★★
Coupe	90	12,967	$9,300	$13,600	D	★★
ZR1 coupe	90	3,049	$23,500	$34,300	C	★★
Convertible	90	7,630	$12,500	$18,300	D	★★
Coupe	91	12,923	$9,700	$13,900	D	★★
ZR1 coupe	91	2,044	$24,000	$34,600	C	★★
Convertible	91	5,672	$13,000	$18,700	D	★★
Coupe	92	14,604	$10,300	$14,500	D	★★
ZR1 coupe	92	502 (inc.)	$24,500	$34,800	C	★★
Convertible	92	5,875	$13,800	$19,600	D	★★
Coupe	93	15,898	$11,200	$15,700	D	★★
ZR1 coupe	93	448 (inc.)	$31,000	$43,400	C	★★
Convertible	93	5,692	$14,700	$20,500	D	★★
40th Anniversary coupe	93	6,749 (inc.)	$16,700	$23,300	D	★★
40th Anniversary convertible	93	inc.	$20,000	$28,000	C	★★
40th Anniversary ZR1 coupe	93	inc.	$34,500	$48,300	C	★★
Coupe	94	17,984	$12,100	$16,700	D	★★
ZR1 coupe	94	448 (inc.)	$32,500	$44,900	C	★★
Convertible	94	5,346	$15,600	$21,500	D	★★
Coupe	95	15,771	$13,300	$18,000	D	★★
ZR1 coupe	95	448 (inc.)	$34,000	$46,300	C	★★
Convertible	95	4,971	$16,400	$22,300	D	★★
Pace Car convertible	95	527 (inc.)	$27,100	$36,900	D	★★
Coupe	96	17,167	$14,700	$19,600	D	★★
Convertible	96	4,369	$17,300	$23,100	D	★★
Collector Edition coupe	96	4,031	$17,000	$22,800	D	★★
Collector Edition convertible	96	1,381	$19,500	$26,100	D	★★
Grand Sport coupe	96	810	$24,500	$32,900	D	★★
Grand Sport convertible	96	190	$29,000	$38,900	D	★★
Add for the following (1984-96):						
Auxiliary hard top		n/a	$1,200	$1,800		
6-sp.		n/a	$550	$750		
Callaway Twin Turbo		497 (inc.)	$13,000	$19,750		
LT4 engine (1996)—std. on GS		n/a	$2,500	$3,700		
Coupe	97	9,092	$16,500	$21,800	D	★★
Coupe	98	19,235	$17,500	$22,800	D	★★
Convertible	98	11,849	$21,500	$28,000	D	★★
Pace Car convertible	98	1,163 (inc.)	$29,500	$38,400	D	★★
Hard top	99	4,031	$19,000	$24,400	D	★★
Coupe	99	18,078	$19,600	$25,000	D	★★
Convertible	99	11,161	$22,900	$29,300	D	★★
Hard top	00	2,090	$20,900	$26,300	D	★★
Coupe	00	18,113	$21,500	$27,000	D	★★
Convertible	00	13,479	$24,300	$30,600	D	★★
Coupe	01	15,681	$24,300	$30,000	D	★★
Z06 hard top	01	5,773	$29,000	$36,000	C	★★
Convertible	01	14,173	$27,000	$33,500	D	★★
Coupe	02	14,760	$26,800	$32,700	D	★★
Convertible	02	12,710	$30,000	$36,600	D	★★
Z06 hard top	02	8,297	$32,000	$39,000	C	★★
Coupe	03	12,812	$29,600	$35,500	D	★★
Convertible	03	14,022	$33,400	$40,000	D	★★
Z06 hard top	03	8,635	$33,000	$39,600	C	★★
50th Anniversary coupe	03	4,085	$33,500	$40,200	D	★★
50th Anniversary convertible	03	7,547	$37,400	$44,900	D	★★
Coupe	04	16,165	$32,200	$38,000	D	★★
Convertible	04	12,216	$37,000	$43,700	D	★★
Z06 hard top	04	5,683	$37,000	$43,700	C	★★

Price Guide

	Years Built	No. Made	Buy-Sell Price Range		Grade	Rating
			Low	High		
Commemorative coupe	04	2,215	$35,400	$41,800	D	★★
Commemorative convertible	04	2,659	$40,700	$48,000	D	★★
Z06 Commemorative hard top	04	2,025	$40,700	$48,000	C	★★
C6 coupe	05	26,278	$40,900	$47,500	D	★
C6 convertible	05	10,644	$48,900	$56,700	D	★
Coupe	06	n/a	$46,000	$51,500	D	★
Convertible	06	n/a	$54,000	$60,500	D	★
Z06 coupe	06	n/a	MSRP:	$64,890	C	★★
Impala						
Impala SS	94	n/a	$9,000	$12,000	F	★
Impala SS	95	n/a	$9,500	$13,500	F	★
Impala SS	96	n/a	$10,500	$14,500	F	★
Nova						
Nova SS	62–65	n/a	$13,000	$25,000	C	★★★
Nova SS	66–67	20,200	$20,000	$45,000	C	★★★
Nova SS 327 L79	66–67	n/a	$30,000	$55,000	B	★★★★
Nova SS 396 L78 (375-hp)	68–70	n/a	$36,000	$50,000	B	★★★★
(Add 25% for 4-sp—must have original paperwork.)						
Nova SS 350	68–72	n/a	$16,000	$23,000	C	★★★
Yenko Nova 427	69	23*	$400,000	$500,000	A	★★★★
Yenko Nova Deuce	70	120*	$80,000	$100,000	B	★★★★
Nova SS 350	71–72	n/a	$11,500	$15,250	C	★★★
Nova SS 350	73	n/a	$7,000	$11,500	D	★★★
CHRYSLER						
300 coupe	55	1,725	$30,000	$60,000	C	★★★
300B coupe	56	1,102	$30,000	$60,000	C	★★★
300C coupe	57	1,918	$30,000	$40,000	C	★★★
Convertible	57	484	$60,000	$80,000	B	★★★
300D coupe	58	618	$35,000	$45,000	C	★★★
Convertible	58	191	$95,000	$110,000	B	★★★
300E coupe	59	550	$55,000	$65,000	C	★★★
Convertible	59	140	$90,000	$100,000	B	★★★
300F coupe	60	964	$42,000	$50,000	C	★★★
Convertible	60	248	$80,000	$90,000	B	★★★
300G coupe	61	1,280	$40,000	$50,000	C	★★★
Convertible	61	337	$80,000	$95,000	B	★★★
(Add 25% for 4-sp.)						
300H coupe	62	435	$19,000	$25,000	C	★★★
Convertible	62	123	$50,000	$70,000	C	★★★
300J coupe	63	400	$25,000	$30,000	C	★★★
300K coupe	64	3,022	$13,500	$19,000	C	★★★
Convertible	64	625	$25,500	$34,000	C	★★★
300L coupe	65	2,405	$13,000	$16,000	C	★★★
Convertible	65	440	$25,000	$30,000	C	★★★
CISITALIA						
D46	46–48	36	$60,000	$100,000	A	★★★
202MM (Spider Nuvolari)	47–51	30	$200,000	$300,000	A	★★★
(For incorrect engine, deduct 25%. Beware, as Cisitalias are currently the fake du jour. The replicas never used Cisitalia chassis numbers. They generally have a Simca engine, look brand new—because they are—and have no paperwork or history.)						
202 coupe	47–54	153	$100,000	$200,000	A	★★★
202 cabriolet	47–54	17	$115,000	$190,000	A	★★★
CITROËN						
DS21 Decapotable	64–71	n/a	$60,000	$85,000	C	★★
SM	70–75	12,920	$10,000	$25,000	C	★★
CORD						
L–29						
Sedan	29–32	5,010	$63,000	$91,000	B	★★★
Brougham	29–32	inc.	$75,000	$97,000	B	★★★
Convertible sedan	29–32	inc.	$145,000	$196,000	B	★★★
Cabriolet	29–32	inc.	$150,000	$200,000	B	★★★

	Years Built	No. Made	Buy-Sell Price Range		Grade	Rating
			Low	High		
810						
Sedan	36	1,764	$45,000	$66,000	B	★★★★
Phaeton	36	inc.	$112,000	$160,000	A	★★★★
"Sportsman" convertible	36	inc.	$140,000	$200,000	A	★★★★
812						
Sedan	37	1,066	$44,000	$68,000	B	★★★★
Phaeton	37	inc.	$110,000	$160,000	A	★★★★
"Sportsman" convertible	37	inc.	$110,000	$175,000	A	★★★★
SC "Sportsman"	37	inc.	$150,000	$200,000	A	★★★★
SC Phaeton	37	inc.	$175,000	$275,000	A	★★★★
DAIMLER						
SP250	59–64	2,650	$15,000	$25,000	C	★★
DATSUN						
1600 convertible	66–70	n/a	$6,500	$16,000	C	★★★
2000 convertible	68–79	n/a	$8,000	$18,000	C	★★★
240Z	70	n/a	$10,000	$20,000	C	★★★
240Z	71–73	n/a	$9,000	$15,000	D	★★★
260Z	74–75	n/a	$5,000	$9,000	D	★★
280Z	75–78	n/a	$4,500	$10,000	D	★★
280ZX	79–83	n/a	$4,200	$10,000	D	★★
DELAGE						
D-6 65 cabriolet	34–35	est. 250	$60,000	$130,000	B	★★★
D-6 70 coupe	37–39	inc.	$70,000	$165,000	B	★★★
D-6 70 cabriolet	38–39	inc.	$90,000	$205,000	B	★★★
D-6 75 coupe	38–39	inc.	$75,000	$125,000	B	★★★
D-6 75 cabriolet	38–39	inc.	$75,000	$155,000	B	★★★
D-6 (3-liter) coupe	46–49	inc.	$55,000	$100,000	B	★★★
D-8 Torpedo	29–31	est. 2000	$175,000	$450,000	A	★★★
D-8C coupe	29–33	inc.	$110,000	$175,000	A	★★★
D-8S cabriolet	30–33	inc.	$175,000	$300,000	A	★★★
D-8 15 coupe	32–34	inc.	$100,000	$205,000	A	★★★
D-8 85 cabriolet	34–35	inc.	$95,000	$200,000	A	★★★
D-8 105 cabriolet	34–35	inc.	$150,000	$250,000	A	★★★
D-8 120 cabriolet	36–39	inc.	$250,000	$600,000	A	★★★
D-8 120 Aerosport	36–39	inc.	$350,000	$1,200,000	A	★★★

(Prices are for factory coachwork. Cars with unusual and/or exceptional coachwork may be worth multiples of these amounts.)

	Years Built	No. Made	Low	High	Grade	Rating
DE TOMASO						
Vallelunga	67	50*	$75,000	$85,000	B	★★★
Mangusta	67–71	400*	$42,000	$83,000	B	★★★
Pantera	71–74	5,629	$40,000	$65,000	B	★★★
Pantera GT/L, GTS	75–89	3,500*	$40,000	$65,000	B	★★★★

(For true GT5, add $3,500.)

	Years Built	No. Made	Low	High	Grade	Rating
DELAHAYE						
135MS coupe	35–39	n/a	$100,000	$450,000	B	★★★
135MS cabriolet	35–39	n/a	$150,000	$375,000	A	★★★★
135M coupe	46–53	n/a	$90,000	$180,000	B	★★★
135M cabriolet	46–53	n/a	$100,000	$250,000	A	★★★
135MS cabriolet	46–53	n/a	$115,000	$195,000	A	★★★★

(Prices can vary greatly depending on coachwork and history.)

	Years Built	No. Made	Low	High	Grade	Rating
DELOREAN						
DMC-12	81–83	8,583*	$20,000	$32,000	C	★★★

(Includes 3 gold-plated cars.)

	Years Built	No. Made	Low	High	Grade	Rating
DODGE						
Challenger						
Coupe (340 or 383)	70–71	83,009	$25,000	$35,000	C	★★★
Convertible	70–71	5,388	$35,000	$50,000	C	★★★
T/A	70	2,399	$55,000	$90,000	B	★★★
R/T	70–71	36,505	$35,000	$45,000	C	★★★
w/Six Pack (440)	70–71	1,890	$70,000	$90,000	B	★★★
w/Hemi	70–71	418	$175,000	$250,000	A	★★★

Price Guide

	Years Built	No. Made	Buy-Sell Price Range Low	Buy-Sell Price Range High	Grade	Rating
R/T Convertible	70	2,737	$75,000	$100,000	B	★★★
w/Six Pack (440)	70	90	$225,000	$375,000	B	★★★
w/Hemi	70	9	$750,000	$1,000,000	A	★★★
(Add 25% for R/T 440. Add 40% for factory Shaker hood.)						
Rallye (340)	72	6,902	$20,000	$25,000	C	★★★
Rallye (340)	73–74	n/a	$18,000	$25,000	C	★★★
(Add 25% for 4-sp.)						
Charger						
Charger (440)	66–67	53,088	$20,000	$28,000	C	★★★
w/Hemi	66–67	586	$60,000	$80,000	B	★★★
R/T	68–70	n/a	$40,000	$50,000	C	★★★
w/Six Pack (440)	70	n/a	$60,000	$90,000	B	★★★
w/Hemi	68–70	116	$150,000	$275,000	A	★★★
Charger 500	69–70	500	$65,000	$80,000	C	★★★
w/Hemi	69	52	$175,000	$250,000	B	★★★
Daytona (440)	69	433	$175,000	$225,000	B	★★★
w/Hemi	69	70	$600,000	$800,000	A	★★★
R/T	71	3,118	$30,000	$65,000	C	★★★
w/Six Pack	71	178	$75,000	$90,000	B	★★★
w/Hemi	71	63	$100,000	$175,000	A	★★★
(Add 25% for 4-sp.)						
Coronet						
Coronet Hemi	66	714	$60,000	$85,000	B	★★★
Convertible Hemi	66	27	$150,000	$225,000	B	★★★
Coronet R/T	67	9,553	$22,000	$35,000	C	★★★
Convertible	67	628	$35,000	$45,000	C	★★★
R/T w/Hemi	67	283	$175,000	$250,000	B	★★★
R/T (440)	68–70	n/a	$40,000	$55,000	B	★★★
w/Six Pack	70	194	$65,000	$85,000	B	★★★
w/Hemi	70	330	$100,000	$145,000	B	★★★
R/T Convertible w/Hemi	68–70	20	$275,000	$350,000	A	★★★
w/Six Pack	70	16	$100,000	$130,000	A	★★★
(Add 25% for 4-sp.)						
Super Bee						
Super Bee	68–70	n/a	$35,000	$45,000	B	★★★
w/Six Pack	69–70	3,175	$55,000	$75,000	B	★★★
(Add 50% for 1969.5 M code; 25% for 4-sp.)						
w/Hemi	68–70	383	$110,000	$145,000	A	★★★
Super Bee	71	n/a	$25,000	$40,000	C	★★★
w/Six Pack	71	99	$75,000	$105,000	C	★★★
w/Hemi	71	22	$200,000	$275,000	B	★★★
(Add 25% for 4-sp.)						
Dart						
GTS 340	68–69	n/a	$20,000	$26,000	C	★★
GTS 383	68–69	n/a	$35,000	$65,000	C	★★
GTS 440	69	n/a	$55,000	$65,000	C	★★
Convertible 340	69	760	$25,000	$40,000	C	★★
(Add: 30% for 383.)						
Demon						
Demon 340	71–72	10,798	$20,000	$75,000	C	★★
Other						
Super Stock Hemi	68	80	$250,000	$350,000	B	★★
DUAL-GHIA						
Convertible	56–58	n/a	$93,000	$200,000	C	★★★
Coupe	61–63	n/a	$58,000	$100,000	C	★★★
DUESENBERG						
Model J						
Convertible Sedan	29–37	est. 480	$650,000	$700,000	A	★★★★
Tourster	30–35	inc.	$700,000	$825,000	A	★★★★
Phaeton	29–37	inc.	$600,000	$800,000	A	★★★★

	Years Built	No. Made	Buy-Sell Price Range		Grade	Rating
			Low	High		
Murphy open sedan	29–32	inc.	$650,000	$900,000	A	★★★★
Murphy convertible coupe	29–34	inc.	$750,000	$850,000	A	★★★★
Murphy torpedo convertible	30–34	inc.	$750,000	$950,000	A	★★★★
Murphy sedan	29–34	inc.	$450,000	$510,000	A	★★★★
Murphy town car	29–34	inc.	$500,000	$750,000	A	★★★★
Rollston town car	30–37	10	$450,000	$600,000	A	★★★★
(Add 25% for original supercharger. Exceptional or rare coachwork can command higher prices.)						
FACEL VEGA						
HK500	59–61	500	$37,000	$75,000	B	★★★
Facel II	62–64	184	$76,000	$93,000	C	★★★
Facel III	62–64	1,500	$15,000	$23,000	C	★★
FERRARI						
166 Spyder Corsa	47–48	8	$800,000	$1,100,000	A	★★★
166 MM Berlinetta	48–50	12	$1,100,000	$1,800,000	A	★★★
166 MM Barchetta	48–50	25	$1,400,000	$1,700,000	A	★★★
166 Inter	48–51	38	$600,000	$750,000	B	★★★★
195 Inter	50–52	19	$400,000	$600,000	B	★★★★
340 America Closed	51	12	$600,000	$2,000,000	A	★★★★★
340 America Open	51	13	$1,000,000	$3,000,000	A	★★★★★
340 Mexico	52	4	$2,000,000	$2,900,000	A	★★★★
342 America Berlinetta	52–53	3	$500,000	$600,000	A	★★★★
342 America cabriolet	52–53	3	$700,000	$2,000,000	A	★★★★
212 Export (closed)	51–52	9	$600,000	$1,100,000	B	★★★★★
212 Export (open)	51–52	8	$1,300,000	$1,700,000	B	★★★★
212 Touring Barchetta	51–52	7	$700,000	$1,200,000	A	★★★
212 Inter	51–52	84	$450,000	$800,000	B	★★★★
225 Sport	52	22	$750,000	$1,400,000	A	★★★
166 MM Berlinetta S2	52–53	4	$1,100,000	$1,400,000	A	★★★
166 MM Spyder S2	52–53	9	$1,300,000	$1,500,000	A	★★★
250 MM	52–53	13	$1,200,000	$1,800,000	A	★★★
250 MM Berlinetta	52–53	16	$1,200,000	$1,800,000	A	★★★
340 MM	53	9	$2,500,000	$3,400,000	A	★★★
500 Mondial	53–54	33	$1,000,000	$1,600,000	A	★★★
375 MM	53–54	16	$3,250,000	$4,000,000	A	★★★
375 MM Berlinetta	53–54	7	$3,750,000	$4,500,000	A	★★★
250 Europa Series I	53–54	18	$450,000	$600,000	B	★★★★
375 America	53–54	12	$450,000	$1,100,000	A	★★★
375 MM+	54	6	$4,000,000	$5,000,000	A	★★★
250 Monza	54	4	$2,700,000	$3,400,000	A	★★★★
750 Monza	54–55	33	$1,000,000	$1,300,000	A	★★★
250 Europa Series II	54–55	34	$500,000	$750,000	B	★★★
410 Sport Spyder/coupe	55	4	$4,200,000	$6,500,000	A	★★★
860 Monza	55–56	2	$2,000,000	$2,400,000	A	★★★
500 TR	56	17	$1,000,000	$1,400,000	A	★★★★★
410 Superamerica	56–59	37	$750,000	$950,000	A	★★★★
250 GT Boano/Ellena	56–58	130	$200,000	$400,000	B	★★★★
250 GT Tour de France	56–59	77	$1,400,000	$1,800,000	A	★★★
(Early Pininfarina-bodied "roundtail" TdFs ('56) will command a premium.)						
*14 louver competition car		8 (inc.)	$1,800,000	$2,400,000	A	★★★
*Zagato-bodied		5 (inc.)	$1,750,000	$2,500,000	A	★★★
500 TRC	57	19	$2,000,000	$2,100,000	A	★★★
250 Testa Rossa (all)	56–61	34	$7,000,000	$14,000,000	A	★★★★★
250 GT PF cabriolet Series I	57–59	40	$800,000	$1,500,000	A	★★★
250 GT PF cabriolet Series II	59–62	200	$300,000	$400,000	B	★★★★
250 GT California Spyder LWB	57–60	42	$1,500,000	$2,000,000	A	★★★
*Alloy-bodied		9	$2,500,000	$3,500,000	A	★★★
250 GT California Spyder SWB	60–63	51	$2,900,000	$3,500,000	A	★★★★
*Alloy-bodied		3	$3,000,000	$5,000,000	A	★★★★
250 GT Interim Berlinetta	59	7	$1,000,000	$1,500,000	A	★★★★
250 Pininfarina coupe	59–62	350	$125,000	$175,000	B	★★★★

Price Guide

	Years Built	No. Made	Buy-Sell Price Range		Grade	Rating
			Low	High		
250 GT SWB (steel)	60–62	122	$1,500,000	$1,800,000	A	★★★★
*Alloy-bodied w/no stories		inc.	$3,500,000	$4,500,000	A	★★★★
*SEFAC variant	61	23	$4,500,000	$5,000,000	A	★★★★
400 Superamerica	60–64	45	$600,000	$1,200,000	A	★★★★
250 GTE 2+2	60–63	955	$75,000	$145,000	C	★★★
250 GTO	62–64	39	$10,000,000	$14,000,000	A	★★★★
250 GTL Lusso	62–64	350	$400,000	$500,000	B	★★★★
330 LM Berlinetta	63	4	$5,000,000	$7,000,000	A	★★★
330 America	63	50	$75,000	$150,000	B	★★★★
330 GT 2+2 (4-headlight)	63–65	1,080	$50,000	$90,000	C	★★★
330 GT 2+2 (SII 2-headlight)	65–68	inc.	$50,000	$110,000	C	★★★
250 LM (no stories)	64–65	32	$4,500,000	$6,000,000	A	★★★★
500 Superfast	64–66	36	$500,000	$650,000	A	★★★
275 GTB/2 shortnose	64–66	450	$425,000	$550,000	A	★★★★
(Add $25k for longnose; $25k for 6 carbs; $25k for alloy body; $5,000 for outside filler cap.)						
275 GTB/C shortnose	65	11	$1,800,000	$2,200,000	A	★★★★★
275 GTB/C Le Mans	65	3	$4,500,000	$7,500,000	A	★★★★
275 GTS	65–66	200	$300,000	$400,000	B	★★★★
275 GTB/C	66	12	$1,800,000	$2,200,000	A	★★★★★
275 GTB/4	66–68	280	$650,000	$800,000	A	★★★★
(Add $500k for alloy body.)						
275 GTB/4 NART Spyder	67–68	10	$4,500,000	$5,000,000	A	★★★★★
330 GTC	66–68	600	$175,000	$225,000	B	★★★
330 GTS	66–68	100	$400,000	$550,000	B	★★★
365 California Spyder	66–67	14	$750,000	$900,000	A	★★★
206 GT Dino	67–68	144	$95,000	$125,000	B	★★★
365 GTC	68–70	168	$175,000	$250,000	B	★★★
365 GT 2+2	68–71	800	$75,000	$120,000	C	★★★
365 GTB/4 Daytona coupe	68–73	1,273	$200,000	$225,000	B	★★★
365 GTS	69	20	$500,000	$600,000	B	★★★
365 GTB/4C (Factory Daytona Comp.)	71–73	15 (inc)	$2,000,000	$2,500,000	A	★★★
Non-factory Daytona Comp.	71–73	5 (inc)	$1,000,000	$1,500,000	B	★★★
365 GTS/4 Daytona Spyder	72–73	124	$600,000	$800,000	A	★★★★
365 GTC/4	71–72	500	$65,000	$95,000	C	★★
246 GT "Dino" coupe	69–74	2,609	$85,000	$120,000	B	★★★
246 GTS Spyder	72–74	1,274	$100,000	$175,000	B	★★★
(Add $7,500 for "chairs and flares.")						
365 GT4 2+2	72–76	470	$15,000	$40,000	D	★★
365 GT4 BB	74–76	387	$100,000	$160,000	B	★★★
308 GT4 2+2	74–79	2,826	$19,000	$40,000	C	★★
308 GTB (fiberglass)	75–77	712	$35,000	$55,000	C	★★★
(Add $5,000 for dry sump.)						
308 GTB (steel)	75–79	2,089	$20,000	$30,000	C	★★
308 GTS	77–79	3,218	$22,000	$32,500	C	★★
512 BB	76–81	929	$75,000	$95,000	B	★★
400 2+2 carbureted	76–80	502	$17,000	$24,000	D	★★
(Add $2,500 for 400/400i with manual shift.)						
512 BB LM	79–80	25	$700,000	$900,000	B	★★★
308 GTBi	80–82	494	$20,000	$27,000	D	★★
308 GTSi	80–82	1,743	$20,000	$27,000	D	★★
400i	80–84	1,308	$18,000	$28,000	D	★★
Mondial 8 coupe	81–82	708	$15,000	$25,000	D	★★
512 BBi	82–84	1,007	$65,000	$85,000	B	★★★
308 GTBi QV	83–85	748	$28,000	$35,000	C	★★★
308 GTSi QV	83–85	3,042	$28,000	$45,000	C	★★★
Mondial coupe QV	83–85	1,848	$20,000	$27,000	D	★★
Mondial cabriolet QV	83–85	629	$21,000	$30,000	C	★★★
288 GTO	84–85	272	$400,000	$500,000	B	★★
Testarossa	85–87.5	7,200	$40,000	$60,000	C	★★

	Years Built	No. Made	Buy-Sell Price Range		Grade	Rating
			Low	**High**		
Testarossa	87.5–91	inc.	$50,000	$70,000	C	★★
412	85–89	576	$25,000	$35,000	D	★★
Mondial 3.2 coupe	86–88	987	$24,000	$32,000	D	★★
Mondial 3.2 cabriolet	86–88	810	$25,000	$35,000	C	★★
328 GTB	86–89	1,345	$35,000	$52,000	B	★★★
328 GTS	86–88	6,068	$35,000	$50,000	B	★★★
328 GTS	89	inc.	$40,000	$80,000	B	★★★
F40	88–91	1,315	$325,000	$395,000	A	★★★
Mondial 't' coupe	89	840	$30,000	$40,000	C	★★★
Mondial 't' cabriolet	89–91	1,010	$35,000	$50,000	D	★★
348 tb	90	2,895	$45,000	$55,000	C	★★★
348 ts	90–92	4,230	$45,000	$55,000	C	★★★
512 TR	91–95	2,280	$95,000	$105,000	C	★★
456 GT	92–03	1,548	$55,000	$75,000	C	★★
456 GTA	95–03	inc.	$55,000	$85,000	C	★★
456M GT/GTA	98–03	403	$60,000	$145,000	C	★★
348 Spider	93–95	1,090	$55,000	$70,000	B	★★
F512 M	94–96	500	$115,000	$150,000	C	★★
F355 Berlinetta	94–99	3,938	$50,000	$85,000	B	★★
F355 GTS	96–99	2,048	$65,000	$85,000	B	★★
F355 Spider	95–99	2,663	$75,000	$95,000	B	★★
F50	95–97	349	$675,000	$775,000	A	★★★
550 Maranello	96–03	1,600	$100,000	$135,000	B	★★
355 Serie Fiorano	99	100*	$75,000	$110,000	B	★★
360 Modena	99–05	n/a	$120,000	$165,000	B	★★
360 Modena Spyder	00–05	n/a	$170,000	$225,000	B	★★★
360 Modena Challenge	00–05	n/a	$95,000	$125,000	B	★★
430	05–	n/a	$225,000	$245,000	B	★★
430 Spyder	05–	n/a	$300,000	$325,000	B	★★
550 Barchetta	01	448	$220,000	$265,000	B	★★
Enzo	03–04	400	$850,000	$950,000	B	★★★
575M Maranello	03–	n/a	$145,000	$195,000	B	★★
575 Superamerica	04–	n/a	est. MSRP	$290,000	B	★★
612 Scaglietti	05–	n/a	est. MSRP	$255,000	B	★★

*Concerning "cut-cars": non-factory, non-NART Spyder conversions are valued primarily by the quality of workmanship. In today's market, rarely is a cut car valued more than the coupe from which it is derived.

Formula One Cars

	Years Built	No. Made	Low	High	Grade	Rating
312 "Spaghetti Exhaust"	'60s	12	$800,000	$1,000,000	A	★★★
70–80 312 B & T series	68–70	40*	$450,000	$600,000	A	★★★
Turbocharged	81–88	36*	$225,000	$275,000	A	★★

Ferrari Sports Prototype Racers

	Years Built	No. Made	Low	High	Grade	Rating
Front-engined V6 (Dinos)	57–60	6*	$2,750,000	3,750,000	A	★★★
(Includes 196, 206, 246, 296 S without stories.)						
Rear-engined V6 & V8 Dino racers	61–67	25*	$1,450,000	$1,850,000	A	★★★
(Includes 166, 196, 246, 286, 268 SPs without stories.)						
Rear-engined V12 racers	63–67	22*	$4,000,000	$9,500,000	A	★★★
(Includes 250P, 275P, 330P, 330P2, 275P2, 365P, 330P3, 365P2/3, 330 P4, 330 P3/4 (412P) without stories.)						

FIAT

	Years Built	No. Made	Low	High	Grade	Rating
8V (body by Rapi)	53–55	114 total	$245,000	350,000	B	★★★
Body by Zagato (28)		inc.	$275,000	$450,000	A	★★★
Show Cars/Other Coachwork		inc.	$50,000	$175,000	B	★★★
(Correct 8V engines are difficult to find. Deduct 40% for incorrect type or no engine. Add 25% for significant, documented history.)						
1100/1200 TV roadster	57–58	n/a	$9,000	$15,000	C	★★
1200/1500 roadster	59–67	n/a	$7,500	$9,000	D	★★
Fiat Dino Spider	66–72	n/a	$22,500	$35,000	B	★★
Fiat Dino coupe	66–72	n/a	$11,000	$18,000	D	★★
850 Spider	67–74	n/a	$4,000	$6,500	D	★★
124/2000 Spider	68–85	n/a	$4,000	$6,000	C	★★
X1/9	74–90	n/a	$2,000	$4,000	F	★

Price Guide

	Years Built	No. Made	Buy-Sell Price Range		Grade	Rating
			Low	High		
FORD						
Fairlane and Torino						
Fairlane GT/GTA	66–67	51,685	$14,000	$22,000	C	★★★
Convertible	66–67	6,444	$20,000	$32,000	C	★★★
(For 390 engine, add $7,500.)						
Talladega 428	69	n/a	$24,000	$34,000	C	★★★
Torino Cobra 428	68–69	n/a	$18,000	$27,000	C	★★★
Torino GT 429 CJ	70–71	88,560	$18,000	$27,000	B	★★★
Convertible GT CJ	70–71	5,552	$26,000	$34,000	B	★★★
Torino Cobra 429	70–71	10,749	$17,000	$26,000	C	★★★
Mustang						
V8 convertible	65–66	15,000**	$29,500	$40,000	B	★★★★
GT convertible	65–66	inc.	$35,000	$45,000	B	★★★★
(Add 40% for K code; 20% for 4-sp.)						
Coupe	65–66	909,011**	$15,500	$22,000	B	★★★★
2+2 fastback	65–66	145,231**	$22,000	$32,000	B	★★★★
(Add 40% for K code; 20% for 4-sp.)						
V8 convertible	67–68	n/a	$20,000	$26,000	C	★★★★
GT convertible	67–68	n/a	$23,000	$30,500	C	★★★★
GT fastback	67–68	113,367	$28,000	$32,000	C	★★★★
GTA fastback	67–68	inc.	$28,500	$32,500	C	★★★★
(Add 20% for 390 engine; 40% for 428 CJ in 1968.)						
Mach 1 351	69–70	113,428	$24,000	$35,000	C	★★★★
Mach 1 428 Q code	69–70	15,864	$40,000	$55,000	B	★★★★
428 CJ convertible	69–70	inc.	$60,000	$80,000	B	★★★★
(Add: 20% for 4-sp.)						
Boss 302	69–70	8,252	$36,000	$55,000	A	★★★★
(Add 20% for 1969 model.)						
V8 convertible	69–70	inc.	$24,000	$32,000	C	★★★★
(Add 15% for SCJ; 25% for SJC code with Drag Pak; $2,000 for Shaker hood on 428 CJ and Boss 302.)						
Boss 351	71	1,806	$45,000	$55,000	C	★★★★
Mach 1	71–73	99,564	$20,000	$28,000	C	★★★★
Mach 1 429 CJ	71	1,255	$36,000	$50,000	B	★★★★
V8 convertible	71–73	n/a	$18,000	$26,000	C	★★★
Mustang II Cobra	75–78	n/a	$5,500	$8,500	D	★★
Boss 429	69–70	1,359	$175,000	$225,000	B	★★★★
(Add 10% for 1969 model.)						
SVO	84–86	9,502	$4,000	$7,000	D	★★
Saleen	85–86	341	$6,000	$8,500	D	★★
Saleen	87–88	988	$7,500	$12,000	D	★★
Saleen	89–90	977	$9,000	$15,000	D	★★
Saleen	91–92	109	$10,000	$15,000	D	★★
(** Denotes number made and includes all models.)						
GT						
GT	05–	n/a	$150,000	$170,000	C	★
Shelby						
Cobra 260	62–65	n/a	$325,000	$475,000	A	★★★★
Cobra 289	63–65	n/a	$350,000	$500,000	A	★★★★
(Deduct $15k for worm-and-sector steering.)						
Cobra 427	65–67	260	$550,000	$650,000	A	★★★★
(Deduct $20k for 428)						
Daytona coupe	64–65	6	$4,000,000	$6,000,000	A	★★★★
GT350	65	521	$250,000	$325,000	A	★★★★
GT350 R	65	34	$700,000	$800,000	A	★★★★
GT350	66	1,368	$125,000	$135,000	A	★★★★
GT350 H	66	999	$125,000	$150,000	A	★★★★
(Deduct 10% for automatic.)						
GT350	67	1,175	$90,000	$105,000	A	★★★★
GT500	67	2,048	$150,000	$185,000	A	★★★★
(Deduct 10% for automatic.)						
GT350	68	803	$70,000	$90,000	A	★★★★

	Years Built	No. Made	Buy-Sell Price Range		Grade	Rating
			Low	High		
Convertible	68	404	$90,000	$125,000	A	★★★★
GT350 H	68	224	$65,000	$85,000	A	★★★★
GT500	68	1,044	$75,000	$100,000	A	★★★★
Convertible	68	402	$115,000	$155,000	A	★★★★
GT500 KR	68	1,053	$100,000	$135,000	A	★★★★
Convertible	68	517	$185,000	$220,000	A	★★★★
GT350	69–70	935	$55,000	$70,000	B	★★★★
Convertible	69–70	194	$85,000	$97,500	B	★★★★
GT500	69–70	1,534	$80,000	$100,000	B	★★★★
Convertible	69–70	335	$135,000	$160,000	B	★★★★
(Add 25% for Drag Pak. Deduct 10% for automatic.)						
Thunderbird						
Convertible	55–57	53,166	$26,000	$45,000	C	★★★
E code Convertible	57	inc.	$42,000	$60,000	C	★★★
F code Convertible	57	194	$80,000	$130,000	B	★★★
(Deduct $1,000 for only one top.)						
Coupe	58–60	173,891	$14,000	$21,500	C	★★★
Convertible	58–60	24,255	$25,000	$39,500	C	★★★
(Add 25% for J code.)						
Coupe	61–63	173,468	$12,000	$17,000	C	★★★
Convertible	61–63	26,273	$23,500	$34,500	C	★★★
(Add $1,000 for M code.)						
Sports Roadster	62–63	1,882	$30,000	$40,000	C	★★★
(Add $5,000 for M code.)						
GT40						
Mk I–IV	64–69	102*	$800,000	$1,200,000	A	★★★★
(Includes road and race cars from original phases of production. Prices will vary greatly for cars with significant history.)						
FRAZER NASH						
Le Mans Replica	48–56	n/a	$80,000	$115,000	B	★★★
GORDON-KEEBLE						
Coupe	64–68	99	$20,000	$40,000	D	★★
GRIFFITH						
Series 400 coupe	65–66	36	$30,000	$50,000	C	★★
HISPANO SUIZA						
H6 cabriolet	19–24	n/a	$180,000	$260,000	A	★★★
H6 phaeton	19–24	n/a	$180,000	$240,000	A	★★★
H6B cabriolet	24–28	n/a	$175,000	$250,000	A	★★★
H6B convertible sedan	24–28	n/a	$155,000	$220,000	B	★★★
H6C phaeton	28–31	n/a	$550,000	$700,000	B	★★★
J12 Type 68 cabriolet	31–38	n/a	$320,000	$450,000	A	★★★
K6 cabriolet	33–39	n/a	$170,000	$220,000	B	★★★
(Prices can vary greatly depending on coachwork and history.)						
HONDA						
S800	67–70	n/a	$7,500	$16,000	D	★★★
INTERMECCANICA						
Italia coupe	67–72	500*	$20,000	$34,000	C	★★★
Italia convertible	67–72	inc.	$32,000	$54,000	B	★★★
ISO						
Rivolta coupe	63–70	799	$25,000	$45,000	C	★★
Grifo	65–74	412	$70,000	$120,000	B	★★★★
(Add $7,000 for 427 V8; $2,500 for longnose model. Deduct $2,500 for 351 V8.)						
Lele	69–74	317	$15,000	$30,000	F	★★
ISOTTA FRASCHINI						
Tipo 8 Touring	19–24	n/a	$450,000	$675,000	A	★★★
Tipo 8A cabriolet	30–32	n/a	$580,000	$780,000	A	★★★
Tipo 8A convertible coupe	25–32	n/a	$560,000	$765,000	A	★★★
Tipo 8A S cabriolet roadster	25–32	n/a	$620,000	$820,000	A	★★★
Tipo 8A SS dual cowl phaeton	25–32	n/a	$735,000	$945,000	A	★★★
Tipo 8A SS roadster cabriolet	25–33	n/a	$800,000	$1,100,000	A	★★★
(Prices can vary greatly depending on coachwork. For Castagna coachwork, add 15%.)						

PRICE GUIDE & RATINGS

	Years Built	No. Made	Buy-Sell Price Range		Grade	Rating
			Low	High		
JAGUAR						
SS I coupe	31–36	n/a	$35,000	$45,000	C	★★
SS II coupe	31–34	n/a	$33,000	$43,000	C	★★
SS 90	35–36	n/a	$100,000	$150,000	B	★★
SS 100 2 1/2-Liter	36–40	190	$130,000	$175,000	B	★★★
SS 100 3 1/2-Liter	38–40	118	$180,000	$230,000	A	★★★
SS saloon	35–40	n/a	$20,000	$30,000	D	★★
SS DHC	38–40	n/a	$43,000	$50,000	B	★★
Mk IV saloon	45–49	n/a	$22,000	$30,000	D	★★
Mk IV DHC	47–49	n/a	$45,000	$65,000	B	★★
Mk V saloon	49–51	n/a	$16,000	$25,000	D	★★
Mk V DHC	49–51	n/a	$45,000	$60,000	B	★★
XK 120 roadster (Alloy)	49–50	240	$150,000	$220,000	A	★★★★
XK 120 roadster	51–54	7,391	$60,000	$95,000	B	★★★★
XK 120 coupe	51–54	2,678	$40,000	$80,000	C	★★★
XK 120 DHC	53–54	1,769	$60,000	$85,000	D	★★★
(Add $5,000 for SE option—dual exhausts, spoke wheels, cams, etc.)						
XK 140 roadster	54–57	3,347	$55,000	$95,000	B	★★★★
XK 140 DHC	54–57	2,740	$50,000	$75,000	B	★★★
XK 140 coupe	54–57	2,797	$40,000	$78,000	C	★★
(Add $5,000 for MC option—C-type head, cams, suspension, and spoked wheels.)						
XK 150 3.4 roadster	58–61	1,339	$50,000	$90,000	B	★★★
XK 150 3.4 DHC	58–61	2,489	$45,000	$75,000	B	★★
XK 150 3.4 FHC	58–61	4,101	$40,000	$65,000	C	★★
(Add $5,000 for 3.8L engine.)						
XK 150S 3.4 roadster	59–61	1,466	$80,000	$135,000	A	★★★★
XK 150S 3.4 DHC	59–61	inc.	$65,000	$90,000	B	★★★
XK 150S 3.4 FHC	59–61	inc.	$45,000	$60,000	B	★★★
(Add $15k for 3.8L 150S FHC & DHC; $50k for 3.8L 150S roadster.)						
Mk VII saloon	51–56	n/a	$13,000	$18,500	F	★★
Mk VIII saloon	57–58	n/a	$13,000	$20,000	F	★★
Mk IX saloon	59–69	n/a	$16,000	$22,000	F	★★
Mk X/420G	62–64	n/a	$9,000	$15,000	F	★★
Mk II saloon 2.4	56–59	83,000	$8,500	$12,000	D	★★
Mk II saloon 3.4	60–66	inc. 2.4	$15,000	$18,000	D	★★
Mk II saloon 3.8	60–67	inc. 2.4	$25,000	$40,000	B	★★★★
(Deduct $2,000 for disc wheels; $2,000 for automatic; $1,500 for no overdrive.)						
XK C-type	50–53	54	$900,000	$1,400,000	A	★★★
XK D-type	53–55	77	$1,000,000	$2,500,000	A	★★★
XK-SS	56–57	18	$1,000,000	$1,500,000	A	★★★
(Price ranges for XK C, D, and SS Jaguars are determined by provenance, completeness and originality. A car with all of its original parts and no stories will bring three to four times that of a "bitsa" with only a few authentic parts.)						
XKE Factory Lightweight (SI)	61–62	16	$1,000,000	$1,300,000	A	★★★
XKE 3.8 convertible (flat floor) (SI)	61–62	7,827	$60,000	$90,000	B	★★★★
XKE 3.8 coupe (flat floor) (SI)	61–62	7,669	$40,000	$60,000	B	★★★
XKE 3.8 convertible (SI)	62–64	inc.	$50,000	$80,000	B	★★★★
XKE 3.8 coupe (SI)	62–64	inc.	$35,000	$45,000	B	★★★
XKE 4.2 convertible (SI)	64–67	9,548	$50,000	$100,000	B	★★★★
XKE 4.2 coupe (SI)	64–67	7,770	$35,000	$60,000	B	★★★
XKE 2+2 coupe	66–67	4,220	$20,000	$35,000	D	★★
(Deduct $3,000 for automatic.)						
XKE 4.2 convertible (SII)	68–71	8,627	$45,000	$70,000	B	★★★
XKE 4.2 coupe (SII)	68–71	4,855	$25,000	$35,000	C	★★★
XKE 2+2 coupe (SII)	68–71	5,326	$19,000	$35,000	D	★★
(Add $1,000 for a/c. Deduct $3,000 for automatic.)						
XKE V12 convertible (SIII)	71–74	7,990	$40,000	$75,000	C	★★★
XKE V12 coupe (SIII)	71–74	7,297	$30,000	$45,000	B	★★
(For SIII, deduct: $3,000 for automatic; $2,000 for disc wheels; $1,000 for no a/c. Add $3,000 for factory hard top.)						
XJ 220	91–93	300	$150,000	$190,000	B	★★
(Due to changes in U.S. DOT laws, XJ 220s can now be brought into the U.S.)						

	Years Built	No. Made	Buy-Sell Price Range		Grade	Rating
			Low	High		
XK8 coupe	97–04	n/a	$19,000	$55,000	D	★
XK8 convertible	97–04	n/a	$20,000	$60,000	D	★
XKR coupe	97–04	n/a	$30,000	$70,000	D	★
XKR convertible	97–04	n/a	$30,000	$70,000	D	★
JENSEN						
Interceptor II/III FHC	66–76	6,387	$12,000	$24,000	D	★★
Interceptor FF coupe	67–71	inc.	$14,000	$24,000	C	★★
Interceptor III DHC	74–76	inc.	$20,000	$30,000	C	★★
JENSEN-HEALEY						
Convertible	72–76	10,453	$5,400	$11,000	D	★★
GT	76	inc.	$5,700	$9,000	F	★★
LAGONDA						
M45 saloon	34–35	70	$80,000	$105,000	B	★★
M45 Tourer	34–35	inc.	$90,000	$110,000	A	★★★
LG6 DHC	36–40	n/a	$62,000	$125,000	B	★★★
LG6 Tourer	36–40	n/a	$85,000	$100,000	B	★★★
V12 Rapide roadster	38–40	n/a	$160,000	$200,000	A	★★★
V12 Touring	38–40	n/a	$65,000	$90,000	A	★★★
2.6-Liter DHC	48–53	n/a	$22,000	$35,000	C	★★
3.0-Liter DHC	53–58	n/a	$24,000	$40,000	C	★★
LAMBORGHINI						
350 GT	64–66	143	$80,000	$140,000	B	★★★
400 GT 2+2	66–68	244	$55,000	$90,000	B	★★
Miura P400	66–69	465	$100,000	$200,000	B	★★★
400S	69–71	138	$150,000	$250,000	B	★★★
400SV	71–72	148	$350,000	$450,000	A	★★★
Espada	68–78	1,223	$25,000	$45,000	C	★★
Islero (400 GT version)	68–69	129	$30,000	$55,000	D	★★
"S" version	68	102	$40,000	$60,000	D	★★
Jarama (both versions)	70–76	327	$20,000	$35,000	D	★★
(Add $7,500 for "S.")						
Urraco P 250	72–76	525	$15,000	$25,000	D	★★
P200	75–77	66	$12,000	$20,000	D	★★
P300	75–79	198	$25,000	$35,000	D	★★
Countach LP400	74–76	149	$80,000	$115,000	B	★★★★
LP 400 S	76–82	235	$75,000	$90,000	B	★★★
LP 500 S	82–85	323	$75,000	$90,000	B	★★★
LP 5000 QV	85–88	610	$65,000	$90,000	B	★★★★
25th Anniversary	1989	657	$75,000	$90,000	B	★★★★
Silhouette	76–78	52	$25,000	$40,000	C	★★
Jalpa P 350	82–88	410	$20,000	$47,000	D	★★
LM002	87–90	300	$50,000	$67,000	C	★★
(For American version, add $15k.)						
Diablo	90–93	n/a	$82,000	$100,000	D	★★
Diablo VT	94–99	n/a	$100,000	$130,000	D	★★
Diablo	96–01	n/a	$105,000	$130,000	D	★★
Diablo VT roadster	96–99	n/a	$130,000	$160,000	D	★★
Murcielago	02–	n/a	$195,000	$245,000	D	★
Murcielago roadster	05–	n/a	$290,000	$315,000	D	★
Gallardo	04–	n/a	$140,000	$175,000	D	★
Gallardo Spyder	06–	n/a	$225,000	$250,000	D	
LANCIA						
B20GT coupe S1–6	51–58	3,121	$45,000	$60,000	B	★★★
(Note: S1, 2, & 3 were all RHD, and are valued higher in Europe than S4, 5, & 6 due to racing history. In the U.S., add: $1,000 for Nardi steering wheel; $1,500 for Nardi floor shift; $5,000 for Nardi carb kit; $2,500 for period Webasto sunroof; $7,500 for Borrani wires.)						
B24 Spider America	54–55	240*	$150,000	$250,000	A	★★★★
(*Factory number, but probably optimistic.)						
B24 convertible	55–59	521	$100,000	$150,000	B	★★★★
(Add: $5,000 for Nardi carb kit; $2,500 for factory hard top; $5,000 for Borrani wires.)						
Flaminia GT Touring	59–68	1,718	$15,000	$28,000	C	★★

	Years Built	No. Made	Buy-Sell Price Range		Grade	Rating
			Low	High		
GTL 2+2 Touring coupe	62–65	300	$11,000	$14,000	D	★★
Flaminia convertible	59–68	848	$20,000	$30,000	C	★★
Flaminia Sport (Zagato)	59–63	593	$55,000	$90,000	B	★★★
(Four variations: Covered headlight 2.5L; open headlight 2.5L; double bubble sport with 2.8L; super sport with chopped tail. Add for all Flaminias: $5,000 for added triple Weber carbs; $4,000 for original 2.8L, 3C model.)						
Fulvia coupe	65–73	104,769	$7,000	$15,000	C	★★
Fulvia 1.2/1.3 HF coupe	65–68	1,317	$12,000	$16,000	B	★★★
Fulvia 1.6 HF coupe	69–76	4,948	$16,000	$19,000	D	★★
Fulvia Sport (Zagato) alloy	65–67	909	$15,000	$20,000	C	★★
Fulvia Sport (Zagato) steel	67–76	6,193	$13,000	$19,000	C	★★
Stratos	74–76	500	$55,000	$70,000	B	★★★
LOTUS						
Six	53–58	110	$30,000	$40,000	C	★★
Seven S1	57–60	242	$28,000	$35,000	B	★★★
Seven S2	60–68	1,350	$30,000	$37,000	B	★★★
Seven S3	68–70	350	$20,000	$25,000	B	★★★
Seven S4	70–73	625	$11,000	$14,500	B	★★★
Caterham 7	74–82	n/a	$12,000	$17,000	D	★★
Lotus XI (S1 & S2)	56–60	270	$52,000	$77,000	A	★★★★
Elite S1 & 2 (Climax eng.)	58–63	1,076	$35,000	$50,000	B	★★★★
(This number represents "complete body units" finished or not. Actual production number runs from 1,029 to 1,076.)						
Elan S1 convertible	62–64	9,053	$18,500	$26,000	B	★★★
Elan S2 convertible	64–66	inc. S1	$21,500	$26,500	B	★★★
Elan S3 convertible	65–68	inc. S1	$17,000	$22,000	B	★★★
Elan S3 coupe	66–68	inc. cvt.	$13,000	$18,000	B	★★★
Elan Plus 2	67–74	4,798	$9,000	$12,500	D	★★★
Elan S4 convertible	68–74	inc. S1	$19,000	$25,000	B	★★★
Elan S4 coupe	68–74	inc. cvt.	$11,000	$16,000	C	★★★
Europa S1	67–68	8,969	$4,500	$7,700	C	★★★
Europa S2	69–72	inc.	$7,000	$11,000	C	★★★
Europa TC/Special	72–74	inc.	$12,000	$15,000	B	★★★
(217 TC/Specials were numbered; the rest were decaled and stickered.)						
Elan 26R (S1 & S2)	65–66	97	$95,000	$125,000	A	★★★
Europa 47	68–70	55	$65,000	$85,000	A	★★★
Cortina MkI	62–66	2,894	$14,000	$21,000	C	★★
Cortina Mk2	67–70	4,032	$6,000	$10,000	D	★★
Elite S1	74–80	2,225	$5,500	$9,000	F	★★
Eclat S1 Sprint	75–80	1,302	$6,500	$10,000	F	★★
Esprit S1	78–80	718	$6,500	$10,000	D	★★
Esprit S2	78–80	1,045	$10,000	$14,500	D	★★
E. Turbo/Carbs (Giugiaro)	80–82	378	$8,250	$12,000	D	★★
E. Turbo	83–85	1,023	$12,500	$19,000	D	★★
E. Turbo/Inj. (Giugiaro)	85–87	506	$13,000	$19,000	C	★★
E. Turbo (new style/220-hp)	88	495	$16,000	$21,000	C	★★
E. Turbo (SE gearbox, 230-hp)	89	121	$15,000	$23,000	C	★★
E. Turbo SE (intercooled, 264-hp)	89–93	1,608	$15,000	$30,000	C	★★★
E. Turbo S4 (264-hp)	94–95	385	$24,000	$35,000	B	★★
E. Turbo S4 (300-hp)	95	64	$25,000	$36,500	B	★★★
Elan M100	90–91	3,855	$12,000	$17,000	D	★★★
Elan S2	94	800	$12,000	$15,000	D	★★
Elan S2s were built for U.K. and R.o.W. only.)						
Esprit V8	97–03		$30,000	$65,000	C	★
Elise (U.S. model)	05–		$39,000	$44,000	D	★
MASERATI						
A61500	46–50	61	$100,000	$300,000	B	★★★★
(60 PF coupes, 1 Zagato)						
A6GCS/A6GCM	47–53	16	$600,000	$700,000	A	★★★★
A6GCS/53	51–53	52	$600,000	$850,000	A	★★★★
A6G54/A6G2000 Allemano coupe	54–57	21	$175,000	$215,000	B	★★★★
A6G54/A6G2000 Frua Spyder	54–57	12	$400,000	$500,000	B	★★★★

	Years Built	No. Made	Buy-Sell Price Range		Grade	Rating
			Low	High		
A6G54/A6G2000 Zagato coupe	54–57	20	$550,000	$800,000	A	★★★★
(Also 6 Frua coupes, 1 Zagato Spider built.)						
150S	55–57	24	$600,000	$900,000	A	★★★★
200S, Si	55–58	30*	$1,200,000	$1,700,000	A	★★★★
300S	55–58	28	$2,750,000	$4,000,000	A	★★★★
450S	56–58	10	$3,500,000	$4,500,000	A	★★★★
3500 GT, GTi	57–65	1,991	$50,000	$70,000	C	★★★
3500 GT Vignale Spyder	59–64	227	$100,000	$175,000	B	★★★★
(Add $5,000 for wires, $3,500 for 5-sp.)						
5000 GT Allemano coupe	59–64	32	$225,000	$350,000	A	★★★★
5000 GT Special Bodies	59–64	inc.	$200,000	$500,000	A	★★★★
(Coachwork by Touring, Michelotti, Frua, Pininfarina, Ghia, Bertone.)						
Birdcage Tipo T 60/61 front engine	59–61	22	$1,700,000	$2,800,000	A	★★★★
Birdcage Tipo 63/64 rear engine	60–61	6	$650,000	$900,000	B	★★★
Sebring coupe SI	62–65	346	$45,000	$75,000	C	★★
Sebring coupe SII	65–66	98	$40,000	$70,000	C	★★
Quattroporte I	63–69	776	$12,000	$17,000	D	★★
Mistral coupe	64–70	828	$35,000	$60,000	C	★★
Mistral Spider	64–69	120	$75,000	$120,000	B	★★★
Mexico 4.2	65–68	250	$16,000	$21,000	D	★★
(Add $2,000 for 4.7 version.)						
Ghibli 4.7L coupe	67–70	1,149	$45,000	$65,000	B	★★★
Ghibli SS 4.9L coupe	70–73	inc.	$50,000	$80,000	B	★★★
Ghibli Spider 4.7L	69–71	100	$125,000	$155,000	B	★★★
Ghibli SS Spider 4.9L	71–72	25	$145,000	$190,000	B	★★★
Indy	69–74	1,136	$16,000	$24,000	C	★★
(Add $2,000 for 4.7L or 4.9L engine.)						
Bora	71–80	571	$33,000	$45,000	B	★★★
Merak	72–76	1,832	$15,000	$23,000	D	★★
Khamsin	74–80	421	$18,500	$30,000	C	★★
Merak SS	76–80	277	$18,000	$25,000	C	★★
Kyalami	77–82	150	$16,000	$26,000	C	★★
Quattroporte II	73–75	13	$7,500	$11,000	C	★★
Quattroporte III	78–87	2,155	$15,000	$20,000	D	★
Biturbo coupe	84–87	n/a	$7,500	$14,000	F	★★
Biturbo Spider	86–88	n/a	$3,000	$6,000	F	★★
Biturbo Spider (Inj.)	89	n/a	$6,500	$10,000	F	★★
(For all Biturbos, deduct $2,000 for automatic.)						
228	89–90	n/a	$6,500	$10,000	D	★★
430	89–90	n/a	$6,500	$10,000	D	★★
Spyder	02–04	n/a	$55,000	$70,000	C	★★
Coupe	02–04	n/a	$60,000	$75,000	C	★★
Quattroporte V	05–	n/a	$90,000	$100,000		
MAZDA						
RX-7	79	n/a	$3,000	$5,000	D	★★
RX-7	80–85	n/a	$2,500	$4,500	D	★★
RX-7	93–95	n/a	$9,500	$14,500	D	★
MCLAREN						
F1	94–98	106	$900,000	$1,200,000	A	★★★★
MERCEDES-BENZ						
K Sedan Custom	26–30	150	$200,000	$300,000	B	★★★
K Tourer	26–30	inc.	$350,000	$525,000	A	★★★
S Sportwagen	27–30	146	$425,000	$625,000	A	★★★★
S Tourer	27–30	n/a	$375,000	$600,000	A	★★★
SS cabriolet	28–35	107	$650,000	$1,000,000	A	★★★
SS roadster	28–35	n/a	$750,000	$1,200,000	A	★★★★
SSK roadster	28–32	33	$6,000,000	$8,000,000	A	★★★
290 cabriolet	34–36	n/a	$125,000	$250,000	B	★★
380 cabriolet	33–34	154	$325,000	$460,000	A	★★★
500K Tourer	34–36	325	$1,300,000	$1,900,000	A	★★★★

Price Guide

	Years Built	No. Made	Buy-Sell Price Range Low	Buy-Sell Price Range High	Grade	Rating
500K cabriolet B	34–36	inc.	$375,000	$560,000	A	★★★★
500K Special roadster	34–36	29	$2,500,000	$4,000,000	A	★★★
540K coupe	36–39	419	$160,000	$215,000	A	★★★★
540K cabriolet	36–39	inc.	$500,000	$1,000,000	A	★★★★
540K Special roadster	36–39	inc.	$2,500,000	$4,500,000	A	★★★★
190SL/300SL						
190SL convertible	54–64	25,881	$40,000	$65,000	B	★★★
(Add $1,500 for factory hard top.)						
300SL Gullwing (Steel body, Type 198.040)	54–57	1,371	$350,000	$480,000	A	★★★★
300SL Gullwing (Alloy body, Type 198.043)	55–56	29	$700,000	$850,000	A	★★★★
(Add $20k for Rudge wheels; $5,000 for factory luggage. Deduct $8,000 for no belly pans.)						
300SL Roadster (drum brake, T. 198.042)	57–61	1,377	$265,000	$340,000	A	★★★★
300SL Roadster (disc brake)	61–62	269	$290,000	$365,000	A	★★★★
300SL Roadster (disc brake, alloy engine)	62–63	210	$375,000	$450,000	A	★★★★
(Disc brakes from S/N 2780 on, alloy engine block from S/N 3049 on. Add: $20k for Rudge wheels; 5,000 for factory luggage; $5,000 for factory hard top.)						
230/250/280SL						
230SL	63–67	19,831	$25,000	$45,000	C	★★★
250SL	67–68	5,196	$28,000	$50,000	C	★★★
280SL	68–71	23,885	$40,000	$60,000	C	★★★
(Add $1,500 for 4-sp; $5,000 for ZF 5-sp. Deduct $2,500 for no hard top.)						
(Note: '72 and later SLs and SLCs should be regarded as "used cars" with little collectible potential. Condition is the prime determinant of value.)						
350SL roadster	71–72	15,304	$14,000	$19,000	D	★★
450SLC coupe	73–77	66,298	$8,500	$12,000	F	★★
(Add $3,000 for 1973 450SLC.)						
450SL convertible	74–77	inc.	$10,000	$15,000	D	★★
450SLC coupe	78–80	inc.	$8,000	$11,000	F	★★
450SL convertible	78–80	inc.	$12,000	$20,000	D	★★
380SLC coupe	81	45,056	$7,500	$11,000	F	★★
380SL convertible	80–83	inc.	$9,000	$14,000	D	★★
380SL convertible	84–85	inc.	$12,000	$20,000	D	★★
560SL	86–87	49,347	$13,000	$20,000	D	★★
560SL	88–89	inc.	$15,000	$24,000	D	★★
300SL	90–92	n/a	$14,000	$21,000	D	★★
500SL	90–92	n/a	$17,000	$24,000	D	★★
SLK roadster	97–04	n/a	$18,000	$35,000	C	★★
SLR McLaren	04–05	n/a	$400,000	$520,000	D	★
Other Collectible Mercedes-Benz						
170S cabriolet A	49–51	2,394	$28,000	$35,000	C	★★★
220 cabriolet A	51–55	1,167	$60,000	$85,000	B	★★★
220 cabriolet B	51–55	950	$35,000	$85,000	B	★★★
220 coupe	54	83	$40,000	$50,000	B	★★★
(13 hard top coupes w/sunroof, 70 w/o.)						
300 cabriolet D (4-dr. convertible)	51–53	642	$90,000	$140,000	B	★★★★
(Production number includes A,B,C models.)						
300 4-dr sedan	51–53	n/a	$18,000	$25,000	D	★★
300S (2-dr) cabriolet	52–53	203	$190,000	$210,000	B	★★★
300S coupe	52–53	216	$85,000	$125,000	B	★★
300S roadster	52–53	141	$200,000	$275,000	B	★★★
300b 4-dr sedan	52–53	6,214	$15,000	$20,000	D	★★
300b 4-dr cabriolet D	54–55	91	$100,000	$140,000	B	★★
300c 4-dr cabriolet D	56–67	n/a	$100,000	$140,000	B	★★
300c sedan	55–58	n/a	$15,000	$20,000	D	★★
300Sc coupe	55–58	98	$150,000	$195,000	B	★★★
300Sc cabriolet A	55–58	49	$350,000	$450,000	A	★★★★
300Sc roadster	55–58	53	$350,000	$450,000	A	★★★★
220S cabriolet	56–59	3,290	$70,000	$110,000	C	★★★
220S coupe	57–60	2,081	$21,000	$31,000	D	★★
300d cabriolet D (Adenauer)	58–62	65	$135,000	$185,000	B	★★★
300d 4-dr sedan	58–62	3,077	$25,000	$45,000	D	★★

	Years Built	No. Made	Buy-Sell Price Range		Grade	Rating
			Low	High		
220SE coupe	58–60	n/a	$25,000	$35,000	C	★★
220SE cabriolet	58–60	n/a	$80,000	$135,000	B	★★★★
220SEb coupe 2-dr.	60–65	16,902	$15,000	$25,000	C	★★
220SEb cabriolet	60–65	inc.	$50,000	$65,000	B	★★★
300SE cabriolet	62–67	3,127	$45,000	$65,000	B	★★★
250SE coupe	66–68	6,213	$25,000	$30,000	C	★★
250SE cabriolet	66–68	inc.	$35,000	$50,000	B	★★★
300/450SEL 6.3/6.9	68–78	6,525	$15,000	$32,000	C	★★
280SE cabriolet (high grille)	68–69	5,187	$60,000	$135,000	B	★★★
280SE cabriolet (low grille)	1970	inc.	$60,000	$140,000	B	★★★★
280SE 3.5 coupe	70–71	4,502	$30,000	$40,000	C	★★
(Add $1,500 for factory sunroof. Deduct $1,500 for no a/c.)						
280SE 3.5 cabriolet	70–71	inc.	$110,000	$150,000	B	★★★
(Add $1,000 for console shift automatic. Deduct $1,500 for no a/c.)						
190E 16-valve	86–87	n/a	$10,000	$15,000	F	★★
C36 Sedan	95–97	n/a	$8,000	$12,000	F	★
MERCURY						
Cougar						
Coupe	67–70	320,496	$15,000	$20,000	C	★★★
XR-7	67–68	59,933	$15,000	$20,000	C	★★★
XR-7G (Gurney)	67	37	$30,000	$40,000	C	★★★
GT 390	67–68	n/a	$22,000	$30,000	C	★★★
GT-E	68	602	$25,000	$30,000	C	★★★
Eliminator	69–70	4,611	$15,000	$25,000	C	★★★
Convertible	69–70	8,118	$15,000	$20,000	C	★★★
XR-7 convertible	69–70	6,001	$18,000	$25,000	C	★★★
Cougar convertible	71–73	4,247	$9,500	$15,000	D	★★★
XR-7 convertible	71–73	6,811	$14,500	$21,000	D	★★★
(For Eliminator, add: $4,000 for Boss 302 engine; $6,000 for 428 CJ.)						
Cyclone						
Cyclone GT	66–67	n/a	$12,000	$19,000	C	★★★
Convertible	66–67	n/a	$18,000	$27,500	C	★★★
(Add $7,500 for 390 engine.)						
Cyclone CJ	69	3,261	$18,000	$25,000	C	★★★
Spoiler II	69	n/a	$15,000	$25,000	C	★★★
Cyclone GT	70–71	12,457	$13,000	$20,000	C	★★★
Spoiler	70–71	1,984	$13,500	$21,000	C	★★★
(Add 50% for 429 CJ or SCJ.)						
MG						
NA Magnette roadster	34–36	n/a	$35,000	$45,000	C	★★★
PA Midget roadster	34–35	1,900	$30,000	$43,000	C	★★★
PB Midget roadster	34–36	526	$42,000	$80,000	C	★★★
NB Magnette roadster	35–36	98	$37,000	$52,000	C	★★★
SA drophead coupe	36–39	n/a	$36,000	$50,000	C	★★★
TA drophead coupe	36–39	n/a	$25,000	$40,000	C	★★★
VA drophead coupe	37–39	576	$34,000	$62,000	C	★★★
WA drophead coupe	38–39	n/a	$30,000	$40,000	C	★★★
TB roadster	39–40	n/a	$20,000	$40,000	C	★★★
MG TC	45–49	10,000	$30,000	$40,000	B	★★★
MG TD	49–53	29,664	$27,000	$35,000	B	★★★
MG TF 1250	53–54	6,200	$25,000	$35,000	B	★★★
MG TF 1500	55	3,400	$28,000	$40,000	B	★★★
MGA 1500 roadster	55–59	58,750	$20,000	$30,000	B	★★★★
MGA 1500 coupe	55–59	inc. rdstr.	$18,000	$23,000	C	★★
MGA Twin-Cam roadster	58–60	2,111	$30,000	$40,000	B	★★★★
MGA Twin-Cam coupe	58–60	inc. rdstr.	$23,000	$28,000	C	★★★
MGA 1600 roadster	59–61	31,501	$29,000	$35,000	B	★★★★
MGA 1600 coupe	59–61	inc. rdstr.	$20,000	$24,000	C	★★
MGA DeLuxe roadster	60–61	82	$28,000	$40,000	B	★★★★
MGA 1600 Mk II roadster	61–62	8,719	$20,000	$35,000	B	★★★★

	Years Built	No. Made	Buy-Sell Price Range		Grade	Rating
			Low	High		
MGA 1600 Mk II coupe	61–62	inc. rdstr.	$20,000	$24,000	C	★★
MGA Mk II DeLuxe roadster	61–62	313	$28,000	$35,000	B	★★★★
MGB convertible Mk I	62–67	387,675	$14,000	$20,000	B	★★★★
MGB (chrome bumper)	68–74	inc.	$11,000	$16,000	B	★★★
MGB (rubber bumper)	75–80	inc.	$6,000	$9,500	C	★★
(For MGB, add: $1,000 for factory hard top; $500 for overdrive. For MGA/B, deduct $2,000 for disc wheels, except on Twin-Cam and DeLuxe.)						
MGB-GT	65–67	125,597	$7,500	$11,000	B	★★★
MGB-GT	68–74	inc.	$6,000	$11,000	C	★★
MGB-GT V8	73–76	2,591	$13,000	$16,000	B	★★★
MGC convertible	67–69	4,552	$12,000	$24,000	B	★★★
MGC-GT	67–69	4,457	$10,000	$20,000	C	★★
(Deduct $1,000 for automatic.)						
Midget	61–64	16,080	$6,000	$10,000	D	★★★
Midget	64–66	22,601	$5,000	$7,500	D	★★★
Midget	66–74	99,896	$5,000	$7,500	D	★★
(1967 model is the highest valued, at up to $1,000 more)						
Midget	74–79	73,899	$4,800	$7,500	D	★★
MORETTI						
GS Bialbero (750 cc)	54–56	96	$150,000	$175,000	B	★★★
Barchetta Bialbero (750 cc)	63–69	n/a	$175,000	$275,000	B	★★★
(Spare engines are non-existent. Cars w/o engines have marginal value at best. Add 25% for documented, significant history.)						
MORGAN						
Flat radiator models	45–53	750*	$25,000	$30,000	B	★★★
Plus 4 (Triumph powered)	54–68	3,390	$24,000	$38,000	B	★★★
4/4 (Ford powered)	54–90	n/a	$20,000	$30,000	B	★★★
(Prices are for 4-seat models. For 2-seat and DHC models, add $4,000. For SS, add $4,000.)						
SS	60–69	102	$75,000	$100,000	A	★★★★
(Factory-built only, matching numbers.)						
Plus 8	68–90	2,500	$25,000	$45,000	C	★★
MUNTZ						
Jet	51–54	394	$50,000	$85,000	C	★★
NISSAN						
300ZX	84–87	n/a	$2,500	$4,250	F	★★
300ZX Turbo	84–87	n/a	$2,750	$4,500	F	★★
300ZX Twin Turbo	88–90	n/a	$3,000	$6,000	F	★★
300ZX Twin Turbo	91–93	n/a	$5,000	$9,000	F	★★
300ZX Twin Turbo	94–96	n/a	$6,000	$13,000	F	★★
(Deduct $1,000 for 2+2 body style.)						
OLDSMOBILE						
442	64	2,999	$15,000	$24,000	C	★★★
442	65	25,003	$14,000	$22,500	C	★★★
442	66–67	46,826*	$16,000	$25,500	C	★★★
442 convertible	66–67	5,933	$22,000	$32,000	C	★★★★
442	68–69	36,642	$15,000	$25,000	C	★★★
442 convertible	68–69	9,437	$22,000	$35,000	C	★★★★
W-30	68–69	2,300	$35,000	$45,000	B	★★★★
(Add 25% for 4-sp.)						
Hurst 442	68–69	1,421	$50,000	$60,000	C	★★★★
442	70–71	27,189	$25,000	$34,000	C	★★★
442 convertible	70–71	4,237	$30,500	$42,000	B	★★★★
W-30	70–71	4,020	$60,000	$70,000	B	★★★★
W-30 convertible	70–71	374	$175,000	$350,000	B	★★★★
(For '70-'71 442 and W-30. add 25% for 4-sp.)						
Rallye 350	70	3,547	$25,000	$35,000	C	★★★
SX 455	70–71	n/a	$20,000	$28,000	C	★★★
SX 455 convertible	70–71	n/a	$30,000	$38,000	C	★★★
442	72	9,845	$14,500	$22,500	C	★★★
442 convertible	72	1,171	$20,000	$28,000	C	★★★
W-30	72	772	$32,500	$40,000	C	★★★★
W-30 convertible	72	113	$60,000	$70,000	B	★★★★
Hurst	72	499	$22,000	$32,000	C	★★★

	Years Built	No. Made	Buy-Sell Price Range		Grade	Rating
			Low	High		
Pace Car convertible	72	130	$30,000	$44,000	C	★★★
OPEL						
GT	69–73	n/a	$3,500	$7,000	D	★★
OSCA						
MT4	48–56	72	$400,000	$500,000	A	★★★★
750	56–60	18	$225,000	$350,000	A	★★★
1600 GT	58–61	128	$150,000	$175,000	B	★★
(1600 GT price is for Zagato Berlinetta. Deduct: $30k for Fissore body; $40–$60k for Boneschi body.)						
PEGASO						
ENASA coupe	50–52	14	$240,000	$280,000	A	★★★
Saoutchik coupe	52–55	14	$200,000	$300,000	A	★★★★
Saoutchik cabriolet	52–54	4	$300,000	$400,000	A	★★★★
Touring coupe (flat windshield)	53–57	30	$250,000	$300,000	A	★★★★
Touring coupe Panoramica	55–57	8	$325,000	$425,000	A	★★★★
Serra roadster	55–56	3	$180,000	$250,000	A	★★★★
PLYMOUTH						
Barracuda						
Barracuda	64–65	n/a	$9,500	$13,000	C	★★★★
Formula S	65–66	n/a	$14,000	$19,250	C	★★★★
Barracuda	67–69	n/a	$9,500	$13,000	C	★★★★
Formula S	67–69	n/a	$20,000	$27,000	C	★★★★
Convertible	67–69	8,510	$17,000	$25,000	C	★★★★
Formula S 383	67–69	n/a	$35,000	$40,000	C	★★★★
'Cuda 440	69	n/a	$55,000	$75,000	C	★★★★
Super Stock Hemi	68	n/a	$250,000	$300,000	B	★★★★
Gran Coupe	70–71	9,798	$20,000	$25,000	C	★★★★
Convertible	70–71	2,568	$35,000	$45,000	C	★★★★
'Cuda 340/383	70–71	n/a	$50,000	$60,000	C	★★★★
'Cuda 440	70–71	n/a	$45,000	$65,000	C	★★★★
'Cuda 440 Six Pack	70–71	1,992	$75,000	$100,000	B	★★★★
'Cuda convertible	70–71	1,009	$60,000	$80,000	C	★★★★
'Cuda Six Pack convertible	70	n/a	$250,000	$275,000	B	★★★★
'Cuda Six Pack convertible	71	n/a	$300,000	$325,000	B	★★★★
(For previous four models, add 25% for 4-sp; 10% for Track Pak, 25% for Shaker hood; additional 40% for 1971 model year.)						
AAR 'Cuda	70	2,724	$60,000	$100,000	B	★★★★
Hemi 'Cuda	70	652	$250,000	$325,000	A	★★★★
Hemi 'Cuda convertible	70	14	$1,500,000	$2,000,000	A	★★★★
(Add 25% for 4-sp; 10% for Track Pak.)						
Hemi 'Cuda	71	107	$555,000	$650,000	A	★★★★
Hemi 'Cuda convertible	71	7	$2,000,000	$2,500,000	A	★★★★
(Add 25% for 4-sp.)						
Belvedere						
Hemi Belvedere	66–67	64*	$70,000	$95,000	B	★★★★
GTX						
GTX	67	686	$25,000	$35,000	C	★★★
Convertible	67	inc.	$30,000	$50,000	C	★★★★
Hemi	67	108	$90,000	$105,000	B	★★★
Hemi convertible	67	17	$275,000	$350,000	B	★★★★
GTX	68–70	1,651	$35,000	$65,000	C	★★★
Convertible	68–70	inc.	$55,000	$65,000	C	★★★
Hemi	68–70	680	$100,000	$140,000	B	★★★
Hemi convertible	68–70	47	$275,000	$350,000	B	★★★★
Six Pack	70	678	$65,000	$80,000	C	★★★★
GTX	71	n/a	$35,000	$45,000	C	★★★
Six Pack	71	n/a	$70,000	$90,000	C	★★★
Hemi	71	30	$190,000	$215,000	B	★★★★
Road Runner						
Road Runner	68–70	2,952	$30,000	$45,000	C	★★★★
Convertible	69–70	inc. above	$60,000	$70,000	C	★★★★
Six Pack	69–70	3,929	$60,000	$75,000	B	★★★★

Price Guide

	Years Built	No. Made	Buy-Sell Price Range		Grade	Rating
			Low	High		
Hemi	68–70	1,938	$125,000	$160,000	B	★★★★
(Add 50% for 1969.5 Six Pack M code; add 25% for Hemi 4-sp. Deduct 20% for 1968 model.)						
Road Runner	71	n/a	$30,000	$40,000	C	★★★★
Six Pack	71	246	$80,000	$100,000	C	★★★★
Hemi	71	55	$200,000	$225,000	B	★★★★
Road Runner/GTX	72–74	38,239*	$20,000	$22,000	C	★★★★
(*indicates Road Runner only)						
Satellite						
Hemi	66–67	817	$75,000	$95,000	C	★★★
Convertible	66–67	27	$175,000	$200,000	B	★★★
Superbird						
Superbird (440)	70	1,069	$100,000	$140,000	B	★★★★
Six Pack	70	716	$150,000	$225,000	B	★★★★
Hemi	70	135	$295,000	$325,000	B	★★★★
(Add 25% for 4-sp.)						
PONTIAC						
Firebird						
V8 coupe	67–69	n/a	$14,000	$18,000	C	★★★★
Convertible	67–69	n/a	$20,000	$24,000	C	★★★★
400 coupe	67–69	n/a	$22,000	$28,000	C	★★★★
Convertible	67–69	n/a	$28,000	$38,000	C	★★★★
Trans Am (Ram Air IV add 75%)	69	697	$70,000	$105,000	B	★★★★
Formula	70–73	30,926	$16,000	$23,000	C	★★★
Trans Am	70–73	11,400	$21,000	$32,000	C	★★★
Trans Am SD-455 ('73 add 50%)	73–74	1,155	$45,000	$55,000	B	★★★
Formula SD-455 ('73 add 50%)	73–74	101	$42,000	$50,000	B	★★★
(For all 1967–74, add 25% for 4-sp.)						
(Add $4,000 for Ram Air III on 400 engine; $1,000 for Formula; $1,000 for 455 engine.)						
Trans Am	74–76	84,230	$9,000	$16,000	D	★★★
Trans Am 455	75–76	73,975	$9,400	$16,500	D	★★★
Trans Am	77–78	162,086	$8,500	$15,000	D	★★★
Trans Am 10th Anniversary	79	7,500	$14,000	$22,000	D	★★★
Trans Am	79–81	201,497	$8,000	$14,500	D	★★
Turbo Pace Car	81	2,000	$13,000	$20,000	D	★★
Trans Am 15th Anniversary	84	55,374	$8,000	$12,000	F	★★
GTO						
GTO	64	24,806	$24,000	$34,000	C	★★★★
Convertible	64	6,644	$30,000	$42,000	B	★★★★
GTO	65	64,041	$32,000	$42,000	C	★★★★
Convertible	65	11,311	$45,000	$55,000	B	★★★★
GTO	66	84,148	$25,000	$31,000	C	★★★★
Convertible	66	12,798	$40,000	$45,000	B	★★★★
GTO	67	72,205	$30,000	$35,000	C	★★★★
Convertible	67	9,517	$45,000	$55,000	B	★★★★
GTO	68	77,704	$22,000	$27,000	C	★★★★
Convertible	68	9,980	$27,000	$35,000	B	★★★★
GTO	69	58,126	$26,000	$32,000	C	★★★★
Convertible	69	7,328	$30,000	$38,000	C	★★★★
Judge	69	6,725	$65,000	$80,000	B	★★★★
Judge convertible	69	108	$150,000	$175,000	B	★★★★
GTO	70	32,737	$26,000	$32,000	C	★★★★
Convertible	70	3,615	$32,500	$40,000	C	★★★★
Judge	70	3,629	$60,000	$75,000	C	★★★★
Judge convertible	70	168	$145,000	$160,000	C	★★★★
GTO	71	9,497	$20,000	$24,000	C	★★★★
Convertible	71	357	$27,000	$34,000	C	★★★★
Judge	71	661	$80,000	$100,000	C	★★★★
Judge convertible	71	17	$250,000	$275,000	C	★★★★
GTO	72	5,807	$14,000	$18,000	C	★★★

	Years Built	No. Made	Buy-Sell Price Range		Grade	Rating
			Low	High		
GTO	73	4,806	$8,000	$12,000	C	★★★
(For all GTOs, add 20% for 4-sp.)						
(For 1964–66, add 35% for Tri-Power. For 1967–69, add 40% for Ram-Air III; 75% for Ram-Air IV.)						
(For 1970–72, add 15% for 455 V8; 50% for 455 HO V8.)						
PORSCHE						
356						
356 Coupe "pre-A"	50–55	7,627	$45,000	$55,000	B	★★★★
(Two-piece windshield until April, '52. One-piece "bent" window until Oct. '55. Standard one-piece curved from then on.)						
356 Roadster	50–55	1,685	$55,000	$65,000	B	★★★
356 Speedster	54–55	1,233	$65,000	$85,000	B	★★★★
356A Coupe	56–59	13,010	$40,000	$45,000	B	★★★
356A Roadster	56–59	3,367	$55,000	$65,000	B	★★★
356A Speedster	56–58	2,911	$75,000	$90,000	B	★★★★
356A convertible D	59	1,330	$65,000	$75,000	B	★★★★
(For 356 and 356A, add $2,000 for Super engine.)						
356A Carrera GS coupe	56–59	541	$110,000	$130,000	A	★★★★
(This is total production for all GS and GT cars. Numbers below included.)						
356A Carrera GS cabriolet	56–59	140	$110,000	$130,000	A	★★★
356A Carrera Speedster	56–59	75	$160,000	$190,000	A	★★★★
356A Carrera GT coupe	56–59	541	$150,000	$175,000	A	★★★★
356A Carrera GT Speedster	56–59	72	$190,000	$250,000	A	★★★★
(There were 7 pushrod GT Speedsters built.)						
356B coupe (T-5 body)	60–61	8,556	$20,000	$25,000	C	★★
365B cabriolet (T-5)	60–61	3,091	$40,000	$45,000	B	★★★
356B roadster (T-5)	60–61	2,649	$65,000	$75,000	B	★★★
356B Notchback (T-5)	60–61	1,048	$15,000	$20,000	D	★★
(Spotter's Note: T-5 body has gas filler cap inside trunk; T-6 has external gas filler cap.)						
(For 356B, add: $2,000 for Super engine; $3,000 for Super-90.)						
356B coupe (T-6)	62–63	6,289	$24,000	$35,000	C	★★
356B cabriolet (T-6)	62–63	3,096	$45,000	$55,000	B	★★★
356B "twin-grille" roadster (T-6)	1962	248	$90,000	$110,000	B	★★★★
356B Notchback (T-6)	1962	697	$20,000	$28,000	D	★★
Carrera 2 GS	62–65	360	$145,000	$185,000	A	★★★★
Carrera 2 cabriolet	62–64	88	$175,000	$225,000	A	★★★★
356C coupe	63–65	13,507	$25,000	$40,000	B	★★★
356C cabriolet	63–65	3,174	$50,000	$70,000	B	★★★★
356 SC coupe	63–65	inc. coupe	$27,000	$45,000	B	★★★
356 SC cabriolet	63–65	inc. cab	$60,000	$75,000	B	★★★★
(For all 356, add: sunroof, $3,000; Rudge wheels, $10k; cabriolet hard top, $1,000; Speedster hard top, $4,000. Deduct: 15% of value for wrong engine per Kardex; 25% of value for improper exterior color for model year.)						
911: Small Bumper, Short Wheelbase						
911 2.0 coupe	65	235	$20,000	$30,000	B	★★★★
911 2.0 coupe	66–68	10,399	$20,000	$35,000	B	★★★★
911 2.0 Targa	67–68	1,427	$20,000	$38,000	B	★★★★
911S 2.0 coupe	67–68	4,689	$30,000	$40,000	A	★★★★
911S 2.0 Targa	67–68	1,160	$30,000	$40,000	A	★★★★
911L 2.0 coupe	68	1,169	$20,000	$35,000	B	★★★
911L 2.0 Targa	68	307	$20,000	$35,000	B	★★★
911: Small Bumper, Long Wheelbase						
911T 2.2 coupe	69–71	13,019	$20,000	$35,000	B	★★★
911T 2.2 Targa	69–71	7,303	$20,000	$35,000	B	★★★
911E 2.2 coupe	69–71	5,027	$22,000	$37,000	B	★★★★
911E 2.2 Targa	69–71	935	$22,000	$37,000	B	★★★★
911S 2.2 coupe	69–71	1,430	$25,000	$40,000	B	★★★★
911S 2.2 Targa	69–71	2,131	$25,000	$40,000	A	★★★★★
(Deduct 15% for 1969 2.0L cars.)						
911T 2.4 coupe	72–73	9,964	$20,000	$30,000	B	★★★
911T 2.4 Targa	72–73	7,968	$20,000	$30,000	B	★★★
(Add $2,000 for 1973.5 911T w/ CIS injection.)						
911E 2.4 coupe	72–73	2,490	$20,000	$30,000	B	★★★★
911E 2.4 Targa	72–73	1,916	$20,000	$30,000	B	★★★★

Price Guide

	Years Built	No. Made	Buy-Sell Price Range		Grade	Rating
			Low	High		
911S 2.4 coupe	72–73	3,180	$30,000	$40,000	B	★★★
911S 2.4 Targa	72–73	1,914	$30,000	$40,000	A	★★★★
(Add $1,000 for sunroof; $3,000 for soft-window Targa. Deduct $1,000 for 4-speed transmission.)						
Carrera RSL "Touring"	73	1,360	$100,000	$150,000	A	★★★
Carrera RS "Lightweight"	73	200	$200,000	$300,000	A	★★★★
911: Federalized Bumper						
Carrera 2.7 Euro coupe	74–75	16,977	$30,000	$35,000	B	★★★
911S 2.7 coupe	74–77	inc. abv.	$8,000	$13,000	D	★★★
911S 2.7 Targa	74–77	inc. abv.	$8,000	$13,000	D	★★★
Carrera 2.7 coupe (U.S.)	74–77	inc. abv.	$10,000	$15,000	C	★★★
Carrera 2.7 Targa (U.S.)	74–77	inc. abv.	$10,000	$15,000	C	★★★
Carrera 3.0 coupe (Euro)	76–77	inc. abv.	$15,000	$17,000	C	★★★
Carrera 3.0 Targa (Euro)	76–77	inc. abv.	$15,000	$17,000	C	★★★
911SC: Federalized Bumper, Wide Body						
911SC coupe	78–83	35,607	$13,000	$17,000	C	★★
911SC Targa	78–83	27,678	$13,000	$17,000	C	★★
911 "Weissach" Edition	80	408	$14,000	$18,000	B	★★
911 Ferry Porsche Edition	82	200	$14,000	$18,000	B	★★
911SC cabriolet	83	4,187	$14,000	$18,000	B	★★
930 Turbo						
930 Turbo 3.0 coupe	75	284	$16,000	$22,000	B	★★
930 Turbo 3.0 coupe	76–77	2,596	$18,000	$23,000	B	★★
930 Turbo 3.3 coupe	78–85	10,004	$19,000	$27,000	B	★★
(2,918 U.S. legal production. All '75, '80–'85 930s are gray-market. Deduct 35% for gray market, 50% if no EPA/DOT papers.)						
Carrera and Speedster						
Carrera	84–86	36,834	$16,000	$18,000	C	★★
Carrera Targa	84–86	19,502	$16,000	$18,000	C	★★
Carrera cabriolet	84–86	22,283	$17,000	$19,000	C	★★
Carrera	87–89	inc.	$19,000	$23,000	C	★★
Carrera Targa	87–89	inc.	$19,000	$23,000	C	★★
Carrera cabriolet	87–89	inc.	$21,000	$25,000	C	★★
(Add factory wide-body appearance group, $4,000; factory turbo-look, $4,000.)						
911 Turbo 3.3	86–89	4,363	$22,000	$26,000	C	★★
911 Turbo 3.3 cabriolet	87–89	2,002	$28,000	$35,000	C	★★
911 Turbo 3.3 slantnose	87–89	675	$25,000	$32,000	C	★★
911 Turbo 3.3 Targa	87–89	657	$25,000	$32,000	C	★★
Carrera Club Sport	88	340	$25,000	$29,000	C	★★★
25th Anniversary coupe	89	875	$21,000	$25,000	C	★★
25th Anniversary cabriolet	89	inc. above	$23,000	$27,000	C	★★
(For U.S., 120 coupes, 100 cabs, 80 Targas.)						
Speedster	89	2,065	$45,000	$55,000	C	★★★
964						
Carrera 2	90–94	n/a	$22,000	$24,000	C	★★
Carrera 2 Targa	90–94	n/a	$22,000	$24,000	C	★★
Carrera 2 cabriolet	90–91	n/a	$22,000	$24,000	C	★★
Carrera 4	89–94	n/a	$22,000	$24,000	C	★★
Carrera 4 Targa	90–94	n/a	$22,000	$24,000	C	★★
Carrera 4 cabriolet	90–91	n/a	$22,000	$24,000	C	★★
C2 Turbo coupe	91–93	5,125	$35,000	$43,000	C	★★
(Add 20% for 1992 380-hp S models; 80 built.)						
America Roadster	92–93	n/a	$40,000	$45,000	B	★★★
Carrera 2 Speedster	93–94	925	$42,000	$47,000	B	★★
993						
Carrera	95–97	46,919	$28,000	$45,000	C	★
Carrera 4	95–96	inc.	$28,000	$45,000	C	★
Carrera cabriolet	95–98	inc.	$28,000	$45,000	C	★
Carrera 4 cabriolet	95–98	inc.	$28,000	$45,000	C	★
Carrera Targa	96–98	inc.	$28,000	$45,000	C	★
Carrera 4S	96–98	inc.	$34,000	$49,000	C	★
Carrera S	97–98	inc.	$34,000	$49,000	C	★

	Years Built	No. Made	Buy-Sell Price Range		Grade	Rating
			Low	High		
993 Twin Turbo	96–97	n/a	$75,000	$85,000	B	★★
(Deduct 25% for gray market.)						
993 Turbo S	97	180	$90,000	$125,000	B	★★
996						
Carrera	99–04	n/a	$30,000	$60,000	C	★★
Carrera 4	99–04	n/a	$30,000	$60,000	C	★★
Carrera cabriolet	99–04	n/a	$30,000	$60,000	C	★★
Carrera 4 cabriolet	99–04	n/a	$30,000	$60,000	C	★★
Carrera Turbo	02–04	n/a	$65,000	$100,000	C	★★
Carrera Targa	02–04	n/a	$45,000	$70,000	C	★★
GT3	99–01	n/a	$70,000	$95,000	B	★★
GT2	02–04	n/a	$165,000	$185,000	B	★★★
997						
Carrera	05	n/a	est. MSRP	$75,000	C	★
Carrera 4	05	n/a	est. MSRP	$80,000	C	★
912						
912 coupe (1.6L)	66–69	29,212	$6,500	$10,000	D	★★
(Add $500 for Targa.)						
912E coupe (2.0L)	76	2,099	$6,500	$10,000	D	★★
914						
914-4 (1.7L)	70–73	114,479	$5,000	$8,000	C	★★★
914-6	70–72	3,351	$12,000	$16,000	B	★★★
914-6 GT	71	11	$75,000	$150,000	A	★★★★
914 R	72	4	$75,000	$125,000	A	★★★★
916 (2.7 RS spec engine)	72	20	$75,000	$125,000	A	★★★★
914S (aka 914-8)*	72	2	$100,000	$150,000	A	★★★★
(*Custom built for Porsche family members.)						
914-4 (2.0L)	73–76	inc. abv.	$6,000	$9,000	B	★★★★
914-4 (1.8L)	74–76	inc. abv.	$5,000	$7,500	C	★★★
924						
924	77–82	122,304	$3,200	$4,500	F	★★
924 Turbo	78–83	12,356	$3,300	$5,500	D	★★
924 S	87–88	n/a	$4,500	$6,000	D	★★
928						
928	78–82	n/a	$6,000	$8,000	D	★★
928 S	83–86	n/a	$9,000	$12,000	D	★★
928 S-4	87–88	n/a	$11,500	$13,500	D	★★
928 S-4	89–90	n/a	$17,500	$22,500	D	★★
928 S-4	91–92	n/a	$21,000	$27,000	D	★★
(Add $1,500 for 928 GT.)						
928 GTS	93–95	n/a	$30,000	$46,000	D	★★
944						
944 coupe	83–85	n/a	$4,000	$6,500	F	★★
944 coupe	86–87	n/a	$5,000	$7,000	F	★★
944 coupe	88–89	n/a	$5,700	$8,200	D	★★
(Add $750 for "S"; $2,000 for Turbo; $2,500 for "S" Turbo.)						
944 S2 coupe	89–91	n/a	$9,000	$13,000	D	★★
944 S2 cabriolet	90–91	n/a	$13,000	$19,000	D	★★
968 coupe	92–93	n/a	$13,000	$18,500	D	★★
968 cabriolet	92–93	n/a	$16,500	$23,000	D	★★
Boxster						
Boxster roadster	97–04	n/a	$20,000	$38,000	C	★
Boxster S roadster	00–04	n/a	$22,000	$44,000	C	★
Carrera GT	04–05	n/a	$350,000	$400,000	B	★★
Competition Cars						
(Price ranges for competition Porsches are determined by provenance, completeness, and originality. A car with all of its original parts and no stories will bring three to four times that of a "bitsa.")						
550	54–55	90	$500,000	$600,000	A	★★★★★
550A	56–57	39	$550,000	$650,000	A	★★★★★

(Includes Le Mans coupes. Most 550As were sold in the U.S. and have only SCCA history. Add at least 25% for documented international provenance. Factory team FIA cars add 60%.)

PRICE GUIDE & RATINGS

Price Guide

	Years Built	No. Made	Buy-Sell Price Range		Grade	Rating
			Low	High		
RSK	58–59	34	$750,000	$850,000	A	★★★★★
695GS Abarth Carrera	59–62	21	$750,000	$850,000	A	★★★★★
RS 60/RS 61	60–61	35	$750,000	$850,000	A	★★★★★
904 GTS	63–64	122	$500,000	$600,000	A	★★★★★
(Production includes 104 four-cylinder 904s, 12 six-cylinder 904s, 6 eight-cylinder 904s.)						
906 Carrera 6	1966	65	$450,000	$600,000	A	★★★★★
910	67–68	34	$475,000	$650,000	A	★★★★★
908-01/908-02/908-03	68–69	62	$650,000	$1,300,000	A	★★★★★
917 LH/K/10/20/30	69–71	70	$1,000,000	$2,000,000	A	★★★★★
(25 FIA non-turbo endurance cars, 20 Can-Am type open cars.)						
Carrera 3.0 RSR	73–74	60	$350,000	$450,000	A	★★★★★
(15 3.0 RSRs were built in 1973 for IROC.)						
Carrera 2.8 RSR	73	43	$350,000	$450,000	A	★★★★★
959 "Komfort"	86–88	200*	$200,000	$235,000	A	★★★
(Some 959s were built up from parts, and VIN numbers higher than 290 have been observed. "Komfort" street models were equipped with power leather seats, a/c, p/w, etc.)						
907	67–68	n/a	$650,000	$800,000	A	★★★★★
RENAULT						
R5 Turbo	83–86	3,576	$15,000	$20,000	D	★★
ROLLS-ROYCE						
Silver Ghost (British)	07–25	6,173	$75,000	$800,000	B	★★★
Silver Ghost (Springfield)	21–26	1,703	$75,000	$800,000	B	★★★
Phantom I (British)	25–29	2,258	$100,000	$400,000	B	★★★
Phantom I (Springfield)	26–31	1,241	$100,000	$400,000	B	★★★
P II closed/formal	29–35	1,681 (incl. 281 Cont.)	$50,000	$125,000	C	★
*Rare/open coachwork		inc.	$125,000	$225,000	B	★★★
P II Continental saloon	31–35	inc.	$60,000	$150,000	C	★
*Rare/open coachwork		inc.	$200,000	$400,000	B	★★★
Phantom III closed/formal	36–39	719 (incl. 4	$35,000	$80,000	C	★
*Rare/open coachwork		inc.	$100,000	$200,000	B	★★★
Twenty hp	22–29	2,940	$22,000	$45,000	C	★
*Other coachwork		inc.	$45,000	$75,000	B	★★★
20/25hp saloon	29–36	3,827	$25,000	$45,000	C	★
*Other coachwork		inc.	$45,000	$85,000	B	★★★
25/30hp saloon	36–38	1,201	$20,000	$40,000	C	★
*Other coachwork		inc.	$40,000	$70,000	B	★★★
Wraith	38–39	491	$25,000	$75,000	C	★★★
Silver Wraith	46–58	1,244 std. WB, 639 LWB	$30,000	$60,000	C	★★
Silver Wraith "S"	56–59	inc.	$60,000	$120,000	B	★★
(Includes 4.9L engine and power steering.)						
Phantom IV	50–56	18	$500,000	$1,000,000	B	★★★★
Silver Dawn standard steel saloon	49–55	761	$35,000	$65,000	C	★★
Silver Cloud I standard steel saloon	55–59	2,238 std. WB, 122 LWB	$30,000	$50,000	D	★★
Silver Cloud I HJM DHC (LHD)	55–59	inc.	$250,000	$350,000	B	★★★★
Silver Cloud II standard steel saloon	59–62	2,418 std. WB, 299 LWB	$20,000	$35,000	D	★★
Silver Cloud II HJM DHC (LHD)	55–59	inc.	$225,000	$325,000	B	★★★★
Silver Cloud II DHC	60–62	inc.	$135,000	$175,000	B	★★★★
Phantom V	59–68	832	$60,000	$90,000	C	★★
Silver Cloud III standard steel saloon	62–65	2,555 std. WB, 254 LWB	$50,000	$80,000	D	★★
SCIII HJM DHC (LHD)	62–65	*50	$275,000	$375,000	B	★★★★
(Deduct $100k for RHD or non-factory conversions. Factory-built DHCs are properly termed "adaptations.")						
Silver Shadow standard steel saloon	66–76	16,717	$10,000	$20,000	D	★★
Silver Shadow MPW coupe	67–70	571	$18,000	$25,000	D	★★
Silver Shadow MPW DHC	67–70	505	$30,000	$45,000	B	★★★★
(Rebadged as Corniches in 1971, with 6.75-liter engine.)						
Corniche S1 coupe	71–76	780	$22,000	$27,000	D	★★
Corniche S1 convertible	71–76	1,233	$35,000	$45,000	B	★★★★

	Years Built	No. Made	Buy-Sell Price Range		Grade	Rating
			Low	High		
Camargue	75–86	514	$25,000	$45,000	C	★★
Corniche S2 coupe	77–81	310	$25,000	$35,000	D	★★
Corniche S2 convertible	71–76	1,595	$35,000	$50,000	B	★★★
Silver Shadow II	77–80	8,980	$15,000	$25,000	D	★★
(Production number includes Bentley T2.)						
Silver Wraith II	77–80	2,154	$25,000	$45,000	D	★★
Corniche convertible	78–85	n/a	$30,000	$55,000	C	★★
Silver Spirit	81–82	n/a	$15,000	$25,000	D	★
Silver Spur	81–90	n/a	$20,000	$40,000	D	★
Corniche II convertible	86–89	n/a	$40,000	$70,000	C	★★
Corniche III convertible	90–91	n/a	$75,000	$95,000	C	★★
Silver Spirit II	91–92	n/a	$30,000	$45,000	D	★
Silver Spur II	91–93	n/a	$32,000	$50,000	D	★
Corniche IV convertible	92–95	n/a	$87,500	$125,000	C	★★
Silver Spur III	94–98	n/a	$35,000	$55,000	D	★★
Silver Dawn	95–97	n/a	$35,000	$55,000	D	★★
Flying Spur	95	n/a	$60,000	$75,000	C	★★★
Phantom	03–	1000/yr	$225,000	$300,000	C	★★
SAAB						
GT-750	58–62	app. 400	$8,000	$14,000	C	★★★
GT-850	63–65	n/a	$8,000	$12,000	C	★★★
Monte Carlo 850	65–67	n/a	$9,000	$13,000	C	★★
Sonett II (2-stroke)	67	258	$6,000	$10,000	C	★★
Sonett II V4	67–69	1610	$5,500	$8,500	C	★★
Sonett III	70–74	8351	$3,000	$5,500	C	★★
SIATA						
300BC	49–52	70	$50,000	$75,000	C	★★★
(Deduct $5,000 for Fiat 1100 engine.)						
Daina cabriolet	51–55	80	$35,000	$65,000	C	★★★
(Add $5,000 for Grand Sport (twin Webers); $7,500 for alloy body.)						
208 coupe (Farina & Balboa)	52–55	25*	$200,000	$350,000	B	★★★★
208S America roadster	52–55	36*	$200,000	$300,000	A	★★★
(Correct 8V engines are difficult to find. Significant deduction for incorrect type or no engine. Examples with exceptional and fully documented history can command exceptional prices.)						
STANGUELLINI						
1100	47–56	60	$110,000	$210,000	B	★★★
(Price for OHC or DOHC engines. Deduct: $10k for pushrod engine; $10k for 750 engine.)						
Formula Junior	59	120	$35,000	$45,000	B	★★★
STUDEBAKER						
Avanti R1 Coupe	63–64	4647	$16,000	$28,000	C	★★
Avanti R2 Supercharged Coupe	63–64	inc.	$20,000	$32,000	C	★★
Avanti II	65–83	2241*	$12,000	$16,000	C	★★
(The Avanti II was not built by Studebaker, but by former dealer Nathan Altman.)						
SUNBEAM						
Alpine roadster (early style)	53–55	3,000	$11,000	$20,000	C	★★
Alpine roadster	60–67	69,251	$7,500	$11,000	C	★★★
Tiger Mk I/IA (260-ci)	64–67	6,498	$25,000	$34,000	B	★★★★
Tiger Mk II (289-ci)	67	571	$29,000	$49,000	B	★★★★★
TALBOT-LAGO						
T150C coupe	34–39	n/a	$100,000	$250,000	B	★★★
T150SS teardrop coupe	36–39	n/a	$2,500,000	$4,000,000	A	★★★
T150C-SS Figoni cabriolet	36–39	n/a	$750,000	$2,000,000	A	★★★
T150C convertible	34–39	n/a	$150,000	$350,000	A	★★★★
Record sedan	47–56	n/a	$65,000	$150,000	B	★★★
Record cabriolet	47–56	n/a	$65,000	$225,000	A	★★★★
Grand Sport coupe	53–54	n/a	$175,000	$550,000	B	★★★
Grand Sport cabriolet	53–54	n/a	$200,000	$550,000	A	★★★★
(Examples with exceptional coachwork and fully documented history can command exceptional prices.)						
TOYOTA						
2000GT	67–70	351	$175,000	$225,000	B	★★★
MR2	85–87	166,104	$1,800	$3,000	F	★★

Price Guide

	Years Built	No. Made	Buy-Sell Price Range		Grade	Rating
			Low	High		
MR2	88–89	inc.	$2,200	$3,500	F	★★
(Add $1,500 for Supercharger)						
MR2	91–95	19,082	$3,000	$5,000	F	★
(Add $2,000 for Turbo)						
TRIUMPH						
1800/2000 roadster	46–49	4,501	$19,000	$28,000	C	★★
(TR2/3 add $750 for overdrive; $1,000 for factory hard top.Deduct $2,000 for disc wheels,)						
TR2 (long door)	53–54	8,628	$26,000	$35,000	B	★★★
TR2 (short door)	54–55	inc.	$23,000	$35,000	B	★★★★
TR3 (small mouth)	55–57	13,378	$21,000	$32,000	B	★★★★
TR3A (large mouth)	57–61	58,236	$19,000	$32,000	B	★★★
TR3B	62–63	3,331	$21,000	$35,000	B	★★★
TR4	61–64	40,253	$15,000	$20,000	C	★★★
TR4A	64–68	28,465	$16,000	$22,000	C	★★★
(Add $500 for IRS; $1,000 for surrey top (TR4/TR250); $750 for overdrive. Deduct $1,000 for disc wheels.)						
TR250	68	8,484	$17,500	$22,000	B	★★★★
TR6 (small bumpers)	69–74	94,619	$15,000	$22,000	B	★★★
TR6 (rubber bumpers)	75–76	inc.	$13,000	$18,000	C	★★
TR7	76–81	112,368	$4,000	$6,000	F	★★
TR7 convertible	79–80	inc.	$4,000	$6,000	D	★★
TR8 coupe	80–81	2,497	$5,000	$8,000	D	★★
TR8 convertible	80–81	inc.	$7,500	$11,000	C	★★
Stag	70–77	25,877	$9,000	$12,500	D	★★
Spitfire Mk I/II	62–67	82,982	$5,500	$8,000	C	★★★
Spitfire Mk III	68–70	65,320	$5,500	$7,500	C	★★★
Spitfire Mk IV	70–74	70,021	$4,500	$7,000	D	★★
Spitfire 1500	75–80	95,829	$4,500	$7,000	D	★★
GT6 coupe (Mk I)	67–68	15,818	$5,500	$7,500	C	★★
GT6+ coupe (Mk II)	69–70	12,066	$5,500	$7,500	C	★★
GT6 coupe (Mk III)	70–74	13,042	$5,000	$7,000	C	★★
TUCKER						
48 Torpedo	48	51	$320,000	$480,000	A	★★★★
TVR						
Griffith	63–66	300	$30,000	$40,000	B	★★★
Tuscan	67–71	n/a	$32,000	$46,000	B	★★★
(For Griffith and Tuscan, add $2,000 for 271-hp V8.)						
2500 coupe	71–73	n/a	$7,500	$10,500	C	★★
2500M coupe	72–77	n/a	$6,500	$10,000	C	★★
Taimar	76–79	395	$6,500	$10,000	C	★★
Taimar roadster	78–79	258	$10,000	$15,000	C	★★
Tasmin	83	n/a	$6,500	$10,000	C	★★
280i	84–87	n/a	$7,000	$10,500	C	★★
VECTOR						
W8	85–92	18	$100,000	$130,000	D	★★
VOLVO						
P1800	61–63	6,000	$7,500	$12,000	C	★★
1800S	63–69	23,993	$6,000	$12,000	C	★★
1800E	70–72	9,414	$7,500	$12,500	C	★★
1800ES	72–73	8,078	$7,500	$12,500	C	★★
1800ESi	74	n/a	$7,500	$13,000	C	★★ ◆

How Does Your Car Rate?

W hat makes a car collectible? And what makes one car more desirable than another? At SCM, we have long felt there was a need for an evaluation and rating system for collectible cars that considered more than just transaction prices.

After all, market value can fluctuate wildly. Consider the Maserati Ghibli. Its value has gyrated from $150,000 in 1990 to $35,000 in 2000. Yet the underlying characteristics that make it collectible haven't changed.

To help understand what sets the Ghibli and other special interest cars apart, we are creating the Martin Guide to Collectible Cars. A dedicated group of experts, enthusiasts and collectors have been hard at work for some time on this. Here, 98 models are evaluated according to five factors of collectibility and assigned a Martin Rating. A perfect score will be 100.

Criteria used will include rarity, physical beauty, historical significance, performance, and "fun factor." The algorithms used to determine these ratings are complicated, and combine objectivity and subjectivity. (Are the lines of the Ferrari 308 GT4 striking and modernistic, or does it resemble a cheese-wedge-shaped doorstop?)

While most guides evaluate cars solely on financial terms, the Martin Guide will go beyond the bottom line and delve into intrinsic, significant, and definitive characteristics. Our goal is to provide a convenient tool for hobbyists and collectors to use to help them evaluate the relative desirability and usability of a car.

The Guide will provide a quick way to find out which models of a marque are the most desirable. The Martin Guide applies to models only, not to specific cars. With the Martin Guide we are setting out to provide the first-ever industry-wide tool that can be used to evaluate nearly every model of collectible car ever built. These 98 are just the beginning.

Rating Key (100 Points Total)

R = Rarity (20 Points)
B = Physical Beauty (20)
P = Performance in Its Era (20)
H = Historical and Technological Significance (10 Each)
F = The Fun Factor: Drivability, Spares, Ease of Maintenance, Event Eligibility (5 Each)
MR = Martin Rating
IG = Investment Grade

Year	Marque	Model	R	B	P	H	F	MR	IG	Low	High	Comments
62	Ferrari	250 GTO	19	20	20	20	19	98	A	$10,000,000	$14,000,000	The ultimate front-engined Ferrari sports/racer and the ne plus ultra of homologation specials.
36–39	Mercedes-Benz	540K Special roadster	19	20	19	20	20	98	A	$2,000,000	$2,650,000	The most glamorous car of the 1930s. Phenomenal performance for the era. Just cross your fingers that the original owner's name didn't include "The Butcher of..."
56–57	Jaguar	XKSS	19	20	20	19	19	97	A	$925,000	$1,300,000	Oozes charisma. It's a thinly disguised Le Mans winner for the road. Factory fire assured immortality.
67–68	Ferrari	275 GTB/4 NART Spyder	19	20	19	20	18	96	A	$3,500,000	$4,000,000	Let's see, Chinetti, McQueen, the ultra-rare open-top version of what is already one of the most desirable post-war sports cars—it's the bluest of blue chips.
60–63	Aston Martin	DB4 GT Zagato	19	19	19	18	19	94	A	$2,500,000	$3,000,000	Aggressive and charasmatic sports/racer. Although not a success on the track in its day, it is now viewed as Aston's 250 SWB.
50–53	Jaguar	XK C-type	18	19	19	19	19	94	A	$800,000	$1,000,000	Beautiful, unfussy for what it is, and a Le Mans winner. From the days when you could drive a contender to the circuit.
60–62	Ferrari	250 SWB	18	19	18	19	19	93	A	$1,400,000	$1,600,000	Awesome dual-purpose GT truly at home on the road or in competition.
65	Ford	GT40 MkII	19	18	20	19	17	93	A	$500,000	$800,000	Ford's sharp stick in the Ray-Bans of Enzo Ferrari is the stuff of legends.
54–57	Maserati	A6G54/A6G2000Z	19	19	19	17	19	93	A	$500,000	$700,000	Brutish sports/racer from the period when Maserati was a credible competitor to Ferrari.
54–57	Mercedes-Benz	300SL Gullwing	16	19	18	19	20	92	A	$300,000	$350,000	The post-war Mercedes. Style, speed, handling—and those doors.
73	Porsche	Carrera RSR	17	18	20	19	18	92	A	$350,000	$450,000	The ultimate 911. Ducktail, Carrera graphics, and lightweight accoutrements all add to the mystique.

Year	Marque	Model	R	B	P	H	F	MR	IG	Low	High	Comments
37	Cord	812 SC Sportsman	17	19	18	20	17	91	A	$150,000	$200,000	Supercharged FWD stunner. Puts some competent post-war cars to shame in the performance and handling department. Shame about the tricky gearbox.
70	Plymouth	Superbird Hemi	19	17	18	19	18	91	A	$175,000	$205,000	Legendary over-the-top nose and wing were homologation items. Hemi is the MOPAR holy grail.
64	Porsche	904 GTS	18	19	19	18	17	91	A	$500,000	$600,000	Almost as lovely as a Ferrari 250 LM, it's one of the most attractive mid-engined racers ever.
63–65	Shelby	Cobra	16	19	19	19	18	91	A	$300,000	$375,000	The AC Ace, prettiest British sports car of the '50s, plus the verve of a small block Ford and the star power of a certain Texan, equals an all-time great.
65	Shelby	GT350	17	18	18	19	19	91	A	$175,000	$200,000	The Texas chicken farmer's first Mustang special is the most visceral of the "production" Shelby Mustangs.
35–36	Auburn	Boattail Speedster SC	17	20	18	18	17	90	A	$175,000	$250,000	Simply a masterpiece of art deco flamboyance, with excellent performance for the period.
56–59	BMW	507	17	20	17	18	18	90	A	$300,000	$400,000	Hands down, the most attractive post-war BMW. Lithe, charismatic, and rare.
47–54	Cisitalia	202	17	20	16	20	17	90	A	$100,000	$150,000	The single car that defined the new post-war style of an envelope body with fender crowns higher than the hood. Scant performance from a tiny motor, but that's not the point.
71–72	Lamborghini	Miura 400SV	18	20	20	18	14	90	A	$350,000	$450,000	Still (and likely forever) the most beautiful mid-engined sports car. An outrageous performer but fragile and impractical.
54–55	Lancia	Aurelia B24 SA	17	19	17	18	19	90	A	$125,000	$200,000	A rare combination of Italian style plus an almost Teutonic obsession with engineering and quality.
53–57	Pegaso	Touring coupe (flat windshield)	19	19	18	19	15	90	A	$250,000	$300,000	A backward military dictatorship of a country with no car-producing heritage builds a Ferrari-like GT. Commitment required, as parts are as common as a passenger pigeon.
67–68	Porsche	911S Targa	17	18	18	19	18	90	A	$22,000	$28,000	Arguably the prettiest 911, the rare, short wheelbase "S" is peaky and tricky fun.
48	Tucker	48 Torpedo	19	17	19	19	16	90	A	$300,000	$400,000	A sad glimpse of what might have been had Preston Tucker's advanced sedan been mass-produced and developed.
53	Chevrolet	Corvette	17	17	16	20	19	89	B	$100,000	$140,000	Rare first edition of an American institution.
62–64	Ferrari	250 GTL Lusso	17	20	16	18	18	89	B	$300,000	$400,000	More beauty than beast, a comparatively sedate performer that is nonetheless the most beautiful closed Ferrari road car.
68–73	Ferrari	365 GTB/4 Daytona	16	18	19	18	18	89	B	$150,000	$250,000	The last "classic" two-seat, front-engined, V12 Ferrari, and to many, the last Ferrari of consequence.
53–55	Fiat	8V Zagato	18	19	18	19	15	89	B	$245,000	$350,000	The only Fiat so undeniably great that it overcomes the stigma associated with the badge. Fiat Dino owners will wait in vain for this recognition.
51–54	Jaguar	XK 120 roadster	14	19	19	19	18	89	B	$55,000	$80,000	The first true post-war sports car. Incredible perfomance for the era and the beginning of an incredible decade for Jaguar.
52–54	Allard	J2X	18	16	19	16	19	88	B	$95,000	$140,000	Sydney Allard's cycle-fendered, Cadillac powered-weapon was the Cobra of the '50s.
62–67	Jaguar	E-type Series I OTS	13	20	19	20	16	88	B	$45,000	$70,000	Aerodynamicist Malcolm Sayer penned one of the most iconic shapes of all time. Sheer numbers keep it out of the top tier.

Year	Marque	Model	R	B	P	H	F	MR	IG	Low	High	Comments
56–63	AC	Ace Bristol roadster	17	19	17	17	17	87	B	$70,000	$90,000	Rarity, fine handling, and a gorgeous, Italianate lightweight body.
55	Chevrolet	Bel Air convertible	13	18	17	20	19	87	B	$60,000	$90,000	Iconic piece of Americana and 1950s swagger. First to sport the greatest small-block V8 of all time.
56	Chevrolet	Corvette 265/225-hp	15	18	18	17	19	87	B	$55,000	$77,500	Prettiest of the solid axle Corvettes with the first iteration of Chevy's sweet small-block V8.
64–66	Lamborghini	350 GT	18	17	19	18	15	87	B	$80,000	$140,000	First running of the Bull. A terrific first effort preferred by many contemporary testers to Ferrari's offerings.
56–59	Alfa Romeo	750 Spider Veloce	16	18	17	16	19	86	B	$30,000	$45,000	Maybe the prettiest volume-produced, small displacement sports car ever. Jewel-like in every respect from masterful detailing to multiple alloy castings.
63–65	Aston Martin	DB5	16	18	17	18	17	86	B	$160,000	$225,000	Forever linked with Ian Fleming's suave spy 007, the DB5 is a beautiful GT in the classic sense.
72–74	Ferrari	246 GTS Dino	16	19	17	17	17	86	B	$75,000	$125,000	A close second to the Miura in the looks department. The only collectible production Ferrari with fewer than 12 cylinders.
74–76	Lamborghini	Countach LP 400	18	17	20	17	14	86	B	$80,000	$115,000	Gandini's arresting original design before the descent into self-parody. Brutal performer like the Miura. Just as impractical.
56–58	Porsche	356A Speedster	16	16	17	18	19	86	B	$65,000	$70,000	Max Hoffman's idea of a stripped-down loss leader became the 356 to have.
67–70	Toyota	2000GT	17	18	16	18	17	86	B	$135,000	$160,000	The most collectible car ever to come from Japan. Relatively modest performance and inability to accommodate those of typical Western stature hurt.
63	Chevrolet	Corvette coupe (340-hp 4-sp.)	14	18	17	18	18	85	B	$40,400	$62,000	Bill Mitchell's and Zora Arkus-Duntov's dream car come alive. Split-Window coupe is the iconic mid-year 'Vette.
65–74	Iso	Grifo	17	19	18	15	16	85	B	$50,000	$90,000	Another Giugiaro masterpiece. The eyeball of a 275 GTB without the heartache. Chevy lump will never be mistaken for a Latin V12, but it is the sweetest small block ever.
58–63	Lotus	Elite	16	19	17	17	16	85	B	$28,000	$35,000	Amateur Peter Kirwan-Taylor responsible for one of the most beautiful small bore sports/racers ever. Revolutionary fiberglass monocoque construction.
64–67	Pontiac	GTO	13	17	18	19	18	85	B	$22,000	$35,000	The original muscle car and the only one to have inspired a more than tolerable song.
64–67	Austin-Healey	3000 MkIII (BJ8)	13	18	17	18	18	84	B	$32,000	$50,000	The last Big Healey is the most user-friendly and the best performer.
62–64	Facel Vega	Facel II	18	18	17	15	16	84	B	$50,000	$85,000	Glamorous gallic grand routier, a favorite of celebrities. Brawny Chrysler power and easy to live with, but punitively expensive to restore.
60–63	Ferrari	250 GTE 2+2	16	17	17	17	17	84	B	$75,000	$125,000	Ferrari's first mass-produced road car is a pleasantly-styled if slightly ponderous GT.
60–68	Lotus	Seven S2	16	15	18	18	17	84	B	$22,000	$27,000	Chapman paid more attention to the Seven's weight than the most binge/purge-obsessed supermodels. Payoff was race car handling and excellent perfomance.
63–65	Porsche	356 SC coupe	14	16	17	19	18	84	B	$25,000	$30,000	The ultimate development of the 356. From an Austrian sawmill to this finely developed piece of industrial design in 15 years.
64–66	Austin	Mini Cooper S	14	15	18	20	16	83	B	$15,000	$22,500	Sir Alec's giant-killer. A shockingly competent handler even today. Makes even the most ham-fisted driver look ready to take on the Monte Carlo Rally.

Year	Marque	Model	R	B	P	H	F	MR	IG	Low	High	Comments
64–66	Lotus	Elan S2 convertible	14	17	18	18	16	83	B	$21,500	$26,500	Drivers still swear that even on tires that today wouldn't be suitable for Segways, the handling is otherworldly.
67–73	Maserati	Ghibli coupe	16	20	17	15	15	83	B	$35,000	$60,000	Achingly beautiful Giugiaro design saddled with a pedestrian rear suspension and a V8 instead of a high-revving V12.
66–67	Alfa Romeo	Duetto	13	17	17	18	17	82	B	$15,000	$20,000	Immortalized as the graduation gift to Dustin Hoffman in the 1967 film, "The Graduate," it has all of the typical Alfa attributes.
64–66	Ford	Mustang convertible	13	17	15	19	18	82	B	$29,500	$40,000	A Falcon in a sport jacket, but what a jacket. Possibly the most instantly recognizable American car ever.
55–57	Ford	Thunderbird	13	17	16	18	18	82	B	$25,000	$42,000	Ford's softer answer to the Corvette. It's a pleasant sunny-day cruiser.
55–62	MG	A roadster	13	18	16	18	17	82	B	$15,000	$30,000	Lovely to look at, delightful to drive, and cheap to keep. An ideal first collector car.
45–49	MG	TC	14	17	14	20	17	82	B	$22,000	$32,000	The sports car America loved first as long as they weren't in a hurry. Spindly and fragile-appearing, it would corner rings around the average post-war American hippo.
55	MG	TF 1500	15	17	14	18	18	82	B	$20,000	$30,000	The last traditional separate fender MG was arguably the most graceful and certainly the best performer.
67	Sunbeam	Tiger MkII	16	17	17	16	16	82	B	$23,000	$30,000	Rootes commisioned Carroll Shelby and Ken Miles to turn its boulevardier Alpine into the king of the mid-priced sports car jungle. 289 Mk IIs are rare and fast.
62–63	Triumph	TR3B	15	16	16	17	18	82	B	$20,000	$27,000	Tough-as-nails end of the line for the side-curtain TR benefits from all-synchro box and larger engine.
72–74	BMW	2002 tii	13	15	17	19	17	81	B	$10,500	$16,500	Another Max Hoffman home run. The category-defining sports sedan.
71–74	DeTomaso	Pantera	14	18	18	16	15	81	B	$30,000	$45,000	Handsome Ghia-bodied middie is a more practical alternative to a Bora or a 308.
67–69	Pontiac	Firebird 400 coupe	15	17	16	16	16	81	B	$20,000	$25,000	Prettier twin to the Camaro suffers from the "not a Chevy" syndrome.
62–63	Studebaker	Avanti R2	16	16	17	16	16	81	B	$18,000	$28,000	Raymond Lowey's controversial fiberglass GT with love-it-or-hate-it looks failed to save Studebaker.
70–73	Datsun	240Z	13	17	16	18	16	80	B	$9,000	$17,000	Style, reliability, and performance. Huge production numbers and national origin will always hold it back.
66–72	Fiat	Dino Spider	16	17	17	16	14	80	B	$22,500	$35,000	Relatively handsome, appealing roadster that is unfortunately not quite handsome or appealing enough to overcome the stigma of its pedestrian badge.
54–64	Mercedes-Benz	190SL	13	17	15	16	19	80	B	$35,000	$50,000	A German T-Bird. A pleasant boulevardier, harmless unless you try to restore one.
73–76	Porsche	914/4 2.0L	13	16	17	17	17	80	B	$6,000	$9,000	Shunned back in the day as neither Porsche nor VW, revisionists now see it as a cheeky proto-Boxter. The first mid-engined production Porsche.
68–70	AMC	AMX 390	15	17	17	15	15	79	C	$18,000	$30,000	The short-wheelbase Javelin has looks and performance let down by typical Kenosha quality and hard-to-find parts.
62–67	MG	B roadster	13	16	15	18	17	79	C	$12,000	$17,000	Pretty, sturdy, and accessible. Doesn't excel in any one category, but the whole is undeniably greater than the sum of its parts.
72–74	Alfa Romeo	GTV 2000	13	18	16	16	15	78	C	$9,500	$15,000	Giugiaro again pens another for the ages, this time with Bertone. A wonderful small GT.

Year	Marque	Model	R	B	P	H	F	MR	IG	Low	High	Comments
68–71	Jaguar	E-type Series II OTS	13	17	16	17	15	78	C	$40,000	$55,000	Idiotic "safety" and emissions regs took the edge off the Series I's style. Still a nice driver, as worthwhile improvements were made to cooling and brakes.
72–76	Maserati	Khamsin	17	17	17	16	11	78	C	$18,500	$30,000	Striking Bertone design; among the few wedges that has held up well. Euro version much prettier. Citroen hydraulics and parts prices make it suspect.
66–67	Oldsmobile	Toronado	13	18	17	18	12	78	C	$7,000	$12,000	Stunning looks and a technical milestone. Size, poor brakes, and expense of restoration work against it.
69–76	Triumph	TR6	13	17	15	17	16	78	C	$12,000	$18,000	Rugged good looks, smooth six-cylinder power make this last vintage Triumph a sports car everyone should own once.
72–74	BMW	3.0CS	14	18	16	16	13	77	C	$8,000	$14,000	Very handsome pillarless coupe for the descriminating is unbelievably rust-prone and expensive to restore.
71–74	Jaguar	E-type Series III OTS	13	16	17	17	14	77	C	$38,000	$55,000	Turbine-smooth V12 returned the pace at the expense of grace. The last E-type was more a grand tourer than a sports car. Notoriously unreliable.
68–71	Mercedes-Benz	280SL	13	17	15	16	16	77	C	$33,000	$45,000	Neither terribly sporty nor light, they are comfortable, well-made and a more capable boulevardier than a 190SL.
65–66	Griffith	Series 400	19	13	16	12	16	76	C	$26,000	$37,000	What to do with some spare TVR bodies and chassis designed to cope with a hundred or so horsepower? Double it? Triple it? A diabolical, homemade little beast.
68–78	Lamborghini	Espada	16	17	17	15	11	76	C	$25,000	$45,000	Polarizing Bertone design is broad and low, a real V12 four-seater—but so's the more conventional Ferrari 412 with added cachet of the Prancing Horse.
78–83	Porsche	911SC	13	15	18	15	15	76	C	$13,000	$17,000	The nearly perfected air-cooled 911, it lacks only the purity and vintage charm of the 1965–73 cars and the chain tensioner upgrades of the 1984–89 series.
67–68	Mercury	Cougar XR7	13	17	15	15	15	75	C	$14,000	$17,000	A stretched and sophisticated Mustang, the original XR7 had one of the nicest interiors of any American car of the era.
65–67	Triumph	TR4A	13	16	15	15	16	75	C	$16,000	$21,500	The zenith of the four-cylinder Triumph sports car. Agricultural motor but independent rear suspension, neat Michelotti styling and decent poke.
78	Chevrolet	Corvette coupe Silver Anniversary	13	16	16	14	15	74	C	$12,700	$21,000	From the era when Chevy had no idea what to do with the 'Vette. Wankle? Mid-engine? Keep the same stale model for another five years? Silver leather is repulsive.
59–64	Daimler	SP250	16	13	16	14	15	74	C	$20,000	$28,000	A great little hemi V8 stuck in a body only Bela Lugosi could love. Great brakes, crude chassis. A car of multiple paradoxes.
62–73	Volvo	P1800	13	16	15	14	15	73	C	$8,500	$12,500	Rugged Swede with decent performance for the sporting pipe-smoker.
61–68	Amphicar	770	16	13	13	19	11	72	C	$25,000	$35,000	It's a car. No, it's a boat. It's not a good example of either, really.
81–83	DeLorean	DMC-12	14	14	15	17	12	72	C	$12,000	$22,000	Ill-conceived, underpowered, and constructed by a largely unskilled workforce with no car-producing heritage and a finish more at home on a high-end range.
66–69	Porsche	912	13	17	14	14	14	72	C	$6,500	$8,500	The charm of an early 911 (especially early SWB cars); unfortunately no economy over the 911 and a huge performance deficit.

Martin Rating

Year	Marque	Model	R	B	P	H	F	MR	IG	Low	High	Comments
70–75	Citroën	SM	14	17	16	16	8	71	C	$10,000	$15,000	SM doesn't stand for "sadomasochist;" however, anybody who buys a less-than-perfect SM qualifies as one. Stunning, but a Franco-Italian joint-venture? Scary.
74–75	Bricklin	Coupe	16	14	15	15	9	69	D	$11,500	$19,500	Appallingly made stab at a category-defining "safety sports car," it was a kit car-esque answer to a question nobody asked.
78–80	Lotus	Esprit S1	16	17	15	16	5	69	D	$6,500	$10,000	The entry-level Bond ride is a stylish but typically underdeveloped underacheiving '70s Lotus product.
70–74	Saab	Sonnett III	14	15	15	13	12	69	D	$3,000	$6,500	The III was a great improvement style-wise over previous models. Modest performance and still no compelling reason to own unless FWD and plastic body appeal to you.
84	Chevrolet	Corvette	13	16	16	14	9	68	D	$6,700	$10,750	Chevy skipped the 1983 model year—they probably should have gone for two in a row. Horrible quality, bone-jarring ride, and arcade instrument panel are the lows.
68–73	Opel	GT	13	17	14	12	12	68	D	$3,000	$5,500	2/3 scale Corvette that didn't have 2/3 Corvette performance. Surprising that it lasted as long as it did against the 240Z.
76	Porsche	912E	16	15	13	12	12	68	D	$6,500	$8,000	A placeholder until the reprehensible 924 was ready. That in and of itself has to tell you something. Only a 911 deisel could have been less exciting than this VW-powered slug.
74–77	Porsche	911S 2.7	13	15	15	15	9	67	D	$8,000	$10,000	A rare flop for Porsche. Hot-running and alloy problems in the engines make these 911s to avoid. ◆

100 Cars Under $50k

ere's the collector car question of the day. Using the Martin Rating system, how do cars that most people can actually afford—those under $50,000—stack up?

We think you'll be surprised; we were. As we added the numbers up, we took a new, fresh look at some cars, like first-generation RX-7s, and Volvo P1800ES sport wagons, that both rate fairly high and won't bust your bank account.

Use the ratings below as a kind of "collector car dowsing rod," where a fairly high numerical evaluation, coupled with a low price, might lead to a car that can offer a great deal of driving pleasure in relation to the number of dollars spent.

After all, at SCM we maintain that the most important part of enjoying a car is not how much it costs, or whether your friends will give you a high-five when you show up, but instead just how much fun you have when you are behind the wheel. And the Martin Ratings can give you a head start on ferreting out not just the fun cars, but the budget-friendly ones as well.

Rating Key (100 Points Total)
R = Rarity (20 Points)
B = Physical Beauty (20)
P = Performance in Its Era (20)
H = Historical and Technological Significance (10 Each)
F = The Fun Factor: Drivability, Spares, Ease of Maintenance, Event Eligibility (5 Each)
MR = Martin Rating
IG = Investment Grade

PRICE GUIDE & RATINGS

Year	Marque	Model	R	B	P	H	F	MR	IG	Low	High	Comments
54–63	AC	Aceca	17	19	14	15	14	79	C	$40,000	$70,000	Thoroughly lovely coupe version of the Ace lacks the performance and parts support of comparable Astons.
62–65	Alfa Romeo	2600 Spider	16	17	14	15	14	76	C	$28,000	$35,000	Attractive, large open Alfa is clumsy and doesn't enjoy the sparkling performance that its looks and heritage suggest.
72–75	Alfa Romeo	Montreal	15	18	16	15	10	74	C	$16,000	$22,000	Striking concept car looks let down by unsophisticated chassis. T33 racer-derived engine complex and pricey to fix.
81–86	Alfa Romeo	GTV6	13	16	15	12	9	65	D	$4,500	$7,500	BI and Bertone effort; a decent performer hobbled by a miserable shift linkage and usual Alfa rust and reliability issues.
67–72	Aston Martin	DBS	16	15	15	11	12	69	D	$35,000	$55,000	Understated big Aston is a relatively sedate performer. No surprise as it was designed for an eight but powered by a six.
74–79	Aston Martin	AM V8 SII/III	16	16	17	14	15	78	C	$35,000	$60,000	William Towns-styled V8 comes off as a Brutish British Mustang. A fine '70s GT.
55–56	Austin-Healey	100-4 BN2	16	19	15	19	16	85	B	$28,000	$50,000	The first big Healey is the prettiest, with luscious curves and a folding windshield. Agricultural engine and gearbox are the lows.
58–61	Austin-Healey	Bugeye Sprite	13	16	14	19	18	80	B	$11,000	$24,000	Any time any car anywhere is referred to as cute, Donald Healey should get a royalty check. An SCCA fixture for over 40 years.
83–84	Bitter	SC coupe	14	15	13	8	9	59	F	$8,000	$12,000	A coachbuilt Opel that looks like a Ferrari 400i but unfortunately goes like a 450SL.
71–72	BMW	3.0CSL	16	19	17	15	12	79	C	$19,500	$29,000	Supporters say it's BMW's 2.7 Carerra RS. Detractors note that this supposed lightweight wasn't much faster than a 3.0CSi.
68–70	Datsun	2000 roadster	13	15	15	15	13	71	C	$8,000	$18,000	Nondescript looks hide a really decent performer. Ghastly rust issues and indifferent parts support hurt. Forgotten by all but a few.
67–71	De Tomaso	Mangusta	17	19	18	16	11	81	B	$42,000	$83,000	Makes a Miura look user-friendly. Does its best to reinforce every low-production exotic stereotype. But oh, so pretty.

PRICE GUIDE & RATINGS

Year	Marque	Model	R	B	P	H	F	MR	IG	Low	High	Comments
59–61	Facel Vega	HK500	17	17	16	15	16	81	B	$37,000	$75,000	Beautifully built Chrysler-powered French GT. Stirling Moss spent his own coin to own one. Underrated but likely to stay that way.
65–68	Ferrari	330 GT 2+2 SII	16	16	17	14	16	79	B	$50,000	$110,000	Single headlight car is a handsome large GT; however, Ferrari 2+2s will never be top-tier collectibles.
80–84	Ferrari	400i	16	15	15	12	11	69	D	$18,000	$28,000	Understated looks that some perceive as bland plus high running costs will forever make these the entry-level V12 Ferraris.
64–68	Gordon-Keeble	GK-1 coupe	18	15	17	9	10	69	D	$20,000	$40,000	Plain looks (although a Giugiaro design) and total obscurity outside U.K. doom a pleasant GT in spite of sparkling performance.
67–70	Honda	S800	14	15	14	15	11	69	D	$7,500	$16,000	Technically interesting 800-cc rev-monster is too tiny for all but denizens of the Yellow Brick Road. Spares nearly extinct.
67–72	Intermeccanica	Italia convertible	17	18	17	12	16	80	B	$32,000	$54,000	Beautiful Ford-powered Italian-American hybrid will forever suffer because of a lack of pedigree.
63–70	Iso	Rivolta	16	15	17	12	14	74	C	$25,000	$45,000	An Italian Gordon-Keeble. Slightly more handsome, slightly less obsure, and slightly more desirable. Also Corvette-powered.
58–61	Jaguar	XK 150 FHC (3.4)	14	17	16	15	15	77	C	$40,000	$65,000	End of the line for the series that began with the brilliant XK 120. Portly and past its prime but still pleasant and reasonably reliable.
74–76	Jensen	Interceptor III DHC	16	17	15	12	11	71	C	$20,000	$30,000	A credible Aston V8 Volante alternative. Lack of pedigree will deny it the upside of an Aston; however, Mopar power ensures serviceability.
72–76	Jensen-Healey	Convertible	14	15	16	11	9	65	D	$5,400	$11,000	Should have been a world-beater. Relatively modern British sports car let down by nondescript looks and poor quality.
67–70	Lamborghini	Islero 400GT	18	16	18	8	9	69	D	$30,000	$55,000	A cleaned-up 350GT, the Islero was completely overshadowed by the spectacular Miura.
72–74	Lotus	Europa TC	14	15	18	19	14	80	B	$12,000	$15,000	A brilliant handler with bizarre looks. First middie for the masses. Typical Lotus fragility.
65–73	Lancia	Fulvia	13	17	16	17	14	77	C	$7,000	$15,000	A jewel-like little GT. Pre-Fiat cars put together the best. Never officially imported into the U.S. and therefore less recognized than they should be.
64–70	Maserati	Mistral coupe	16	17	17	13	14	77	C	$35,000	$60,000	Pretty Frua body and a decent performer in spite of rev-adverse long-stroke six. Parts prices are punishing.
65–66	Maserati	Sebring SII	16	16	16	13	14	75	C	$30,000	$40,000	Slightly less lovely and potent than a Mistral. Suffers from the same lazy powerplant and parts issues as a Mistral.
72–76	Maserati	Merak	16	16	15	14	8	69	D	$15,000	$23,000	Lackluster first-generation middie. Modest performance, high upkeep. Citroen cars a real headache.
79	Mazda	RX-7	13	16	15	17	8	69	D	$3,000	$5,000	First production Wankel sports car suffers from derivative styling and short-lived rotary apex seals.
71–72	Mercedes	350SL	13	16	13	12	13	67	D	$14,000	$19,000	Quintessential trophy wife's trophy car. Little to interest drivers.
70–71	Mercedes	280SE 3.5	15	18	13	12	13	71	C	$30,000	$40,000	Relatively modest performer, expensive to restore but truly lovely to look at.
58–60	MG	A Twin-Cam roadster	16	18	17	18	16	85	B	$30,000	$40,000	As pretty as almost any '50s sports car, could have been the British Alfa Giulietta but reliability issues (since solved) killed it.

Year	Marque	Model	R	B	P	H	F	MR	IG	Low	High	Comments
68–90	Morgan	Plus 8	16	17	17	15	12	77	C	$25,000	$45,000	A rolling archeological find that is nonetheless great (albeit demanding) fun. Early narrow-body Moss-box cars the most pure.
69–71	Porsche	911T	14	17	16	17	16	80	B	$20,000	$35,000	Among the most practical early 911s. Lowest horsepower but tractable and lacking trouble-some mechanical fuel injection of later cars.
73.5	Porsche	911T cpe. CIS	14	17	17	18	18	84	B	$22,000	$37,000	Arguably the best all-around pre-1974 911. A grown-up 911 in nearly all respects. Lacks only a fully galvanized shell and reliable chain tensioners.
70–72	Porsche	914-6	15	16	17	17	18	83	B	$12,000	$16,000	Proto-Boxster with the heart of a 911T. Difficult to understand for some, but the market values this all-Porsche middie the same as a 911T.
58–62	Saab	GT-750	17	14	13	15	14	73	C	$8,000	$14,000	The zenith of Saab two-sroke performance with some genuine period rally provenance. Still, too slow and too homely to generate much excitement.
60–67	Sunbeam	Alpine	13	17	14	13	13	70	C	$7,500	$11,000	Stylish well-made MGB alternative. Leisurely performance, a bit soft, and Rootes parts more of a challenge than BMC parts.
53–54	Triumph	TR2 long door	14	16	16	18	18	82	C	$26,000	$35,000	First real post-war Triumph sports car. Miles better than its T-series MG competition.
80–81	Triumph	TR8 convertible	16	16	17	18	10	77	C	$7,500	$11,000	Usual British quality issues aside, it's a decent car. In open top form looks have aged well. The last Triumph sports car.
71–73	Triumph	Stag	13	16	15	10	9	63	C	$9,000	$12,500	Could have been a better 450SL. Typical poor British execution, and Triumph's insistence on using their own suspect V8 sank it.
62–67	Triumph	Spitfire Mk I/II	13	18	14	15	13	73	C	$5,500	$8,000	Michelotti-styled Spit is nearly as pretty as an MGA. Modest performance and tricky swing-axle handling are the downside.
72–77	TVR	2500M	16	16	16	10	12	70	C	$6,500	$10,000	2500M is less homemade than earlier TVRs and is almost attractive. No better performer than a TR6, from which mechanicals come.
84–87	TVR	280i	16	15	15	8	8	62	D	$7,000	$10,500	Passé dart-like plastic body over a capable tube chassis. TVR hitched its wagon to the wedge look ten years late.
72–74	Volvo	1800ES	14	17	15	12	14	72	C	$7,500	$12,500	Geneuinely pretty sport-wagon is tough and practical.
68–70	AMC	Javelin SST	13	18	16	15	12	74	C	$10,000	$15,000	AMC's answer to the Mustang is a clean and very handsome design. Parts much more problematic than Big Three muscle cars.
54–59	Arnolt-Bristol	DeLuxe Roadster	18	17	17	15	15	82	B	$50,000	$73,000	You have to love any car built by someone named "Wacky." Great performer, interesting story. Bertone looks polarizing, though.
65–67	Buick	Skylark GS 400	13	16	16	14	16	75	C	$14,000	$19,000	Hard to imagine today, but Buick was involved in the muscle-car craze. Skylark GS 400 a first and fairly average effort.
68	Chevrolet	Corvette coupe 327/300	14	18	17	17	13	79	C	$18,000	$36,000	First year a bit of a lemon. Would be repeated in 1984. Still, significant as the first of the long-lived C3 series and gets progressively more handsome every year.
65–83	Avanti	II	16	17	15	14	12	74	C	$12,000	$16,000	A unique story of the passion of a few refusing to accept a car's demise. Doesn't translate into passion by the market. Newman-Altman cars the best.

Martin Rating

Year	Marque	Model	R	B	P	H	F	MR	IG	Low	High	Comments
68	Triumph	TR250	15	16	15	17	17	80	B	$17,500	$22,000	One-year-sonly model combines vintage Michelotti style with the smooth Triumph straight six. The real alternative to a big Healey.
75–86	Rolls-Royce	Camargue	17	14	13	15	12	71	C	$25,000	$45,000	A rare stylistic flop from Pininfarina. Few compelling reasons to seek out one of the few good ones out there.
71–76	Rolls-Royce	Corniche S2 convertible	16	17	13	18	16	80	B	$35,000	$50,000	The quintessential rich-guy ride. Always in style, from Beverly Hills to San Tropez.
78–82	Porsche	928	13	14	18	16	8	69	D	$6,000	$8,000	Porsche's flagship. Bucked the air-cooled rear engine paradigm. A German Corvette to the cynics. Parts and service now difficult and expensive.
62–65	Alfa Romeo	2600 coupe	14	16	14	13	11	68	D	$12,000	$20,000	Editor Martin still maintains these to be Alfa's finest entry into the light-truck segment. Unwieldy, not especially pretty, and a parts hassle.
67–73	AC	428 coupe.	18	17	19	9	11	74	D	$35,000	$50,000	Handsome Frua Maserati Mistral clone has blistering big-block Ford performance. Body spares extinct and nearly forgotten even when still in production.
61–71	Austin-Healey	Sprite	13	16	14	15	14	72	C	$5,000	$10,000	Along with the Midget, was the inexpensive sports car for a generation. One of the most popular entry-level vintage racers.
77–80	Bentley	Corniche coupe	16	15	13	15	13	72	C	$27,000	$40,000	Big coupe is less ostentatious than a Roller. Little to compel ownership.
75–78	Datsun	280Z	13	16	16	13	11	69	D	$4,500	$10,000	Many survivors out of a huge production run, national origin, and massive unattractive bumpers weigh against collectibility.
76–81	Triumph	TR7 coupe	13	12	14	13	7	59	F	$4,000	$6,000	The doorstop look is jarring with the coupe's notchback. Abysmal quality and reliability are part of the reason why storied marque is no more.
77–82	Porsche	924	13	15	14	11	6	59	F	$3,200	$4,500	Miserable ride, suspect Audi build quality, expensive parts, indifferent performance—the list goes on.
76–77	Porsche	930	16	17	18	19	14	84	B	$18,000	$32,000	An icon. Diabolical handling part of the mystique. May hold the record for killing the most professional athletes. Unsatisfying to drive around town.
72–73	Porsche	911S 2.4	15	18	18	17	18	86	B	$30,000	$40,000	Road & Track put it best: "Performance on the order of an American supercar without the stigma of low cost." Or non-existent braking, handling, or build quality.
67–69	MG	C convertible	15	16	16	16	17	80	B	$12,000	$24,000	Unfairly maligned when new as clumsy, the C shaves two seconds off the B's 0-60 time and is a pleasant tourer.
84–87	Maserati	Biturbo	14	14	17	8	5	58	F	$7,500	$15,000	Difficult to know where to begin. Plain looks, appalling quality, a grenade waiting for the pin to fall out. Best forgotten.
69–74	Maserati	Indy	16	17	17	14	10	74	C	$16,000	$24,000	A much more attractive 2+2 than an Espada. Suffers from long-stroke V8 and scarce and expensive parts.
71–80	Maserati	Bora	16	18	18	17	13	82	B	$33,000	$45,000	Maserati's first mid-engined production car. It's no Miura in looks but it is handsome and a credible performer even with a V8 rather than a V12.
51–58	Lancia	Aurelia B20 coupe	15	20	17	20	16	88	B	$45,000	$60,000	The category-defining GT. Advanced engineering and peerless good looks.

Year	Marque	Model	R	B	P	H	F	MR	IG	Low	High	Comments
70-76	Lamborghini	Jarama	17	14	18	10	8	67	D	$20,000	$35,000	Slightly less controversial looks than an Espada, still overshadowed even by the Islero. Too big and too heavy. Punishing upkeep expenses.
69-74	Iso	Lele	17	13	17	5	7	59	F	$15,000	$30,000	A Bertone misfire. Bizarre looks. Unpopular models from obscure manufacturers rarely appreciate. Reasonable go courtesy of Ford or Chevy V8.
76	Chevrolet	Corvette coupe	13	16	16	14	14	73	C	$9,500	$16,500	Nothing offensive; emission controls meant a generally mediocre year for the Corvette. Already past its prime in '76 , it would be around another seven years.
64-65	Plymouth	Barracuda	13	14	16	16	14	73	C	$9,500	$13,000	The Mopar boys' first attempt at a Mustang-style pony car. Really not a bad effort; its worst sin is that it's homely.
49-53	MG	TD	13	16	13	18	18	78	B	$27,000	$35,000	A slightly updated TC now available in LHD. Always charming, simple, and popular.
79-86	Maserati	Quattroporte II	16	15	16	15	8	70	C	$7,500	$11,000	Potent sedan was a symbol of '80s excess. Sly Stallone and Mike Tyson owned one. Enough said. Usual crippling Maserati parts issues.
74-79	Ferrari	308 GT4 2+2	16	15	16	13	12	72	C	$19,000	$40,000	The realities of fuel costs, taxes, safety, and emissions issues were not kind to exotics. Cars like this and the Maserati Merak were the result.
74-90	Fiat	X/19	13	15	13	12	6	59	F	$2,000	$4,000	Clever repackaging of the Fiat 128 drivetrain. Nimble and modern. Modest performance and typical Fiat reliability and rust issues shout "run away."
68-85	Fiat	124/2000 Spider	13	17	15	15	11	71	C	$4,000	$6,000	Italian MGB is better in many ways but lacks the robustness of the MG and the inexpensive and accessible parts.
81-82	Ferrari	Mondial 8	16	14	16	10	8	64	D	$15,000	$25,000	Silly squashed-cheese-grater looks, a pain to maintain, and no reward for your suffering.
62-64	Facel Vega	Facel III	16	17	15	11	11	70	C	$15,000	$23,000	Alfa 2600 competitor significant as the car that sank Facel. Warranty claims from miserable Facel engines did the deed. Volvo- and BMC-powered cars quite nice.
55-62	BMW	Isetta	13	12	10	19	18	72	C	$15,000	$30,000	Isetta saved BMW from bankruptcy and put a generation of war-weary Germans back on the road. A historical curio or just plain cute.
58-62	Alfa Romeo	101 1300 Sprint Speciale	16	18	16	18	17	85	B	$35,000	$45,000	Arresting looks; one of the first production cars to give serious thought to aerodynamics. A bit too heavy to be a serious competition device. Body spares gone.
66-67	Jaguar	XKE SI 2+2	15	16	17	15	13	76	C	$20,000	$35,000	The addition of space sacrifices the grace. Still, the covered headlights make up somewhat for the hunchback.
65-68	Maserati	Mexico	17	15	17	12	11	72	C	$16,000	$21,000	Bland big Maser totally overshadowed by its own stablemates. The usual Maserati parts and expense issues.
72-76	Lamborghini	Urraco P250	17	17	15	12	8	69	D	$15,000	$25,000	Appealing looks but disappointing performance and crippling maintenance costs.
62-64	Jaguar	Mk X/420G	13	13	15	10	8	59	F	$9,000	$15,000	Cartoonlike proportions; this ponderous pachyderm runs counter to everything Jag stood for in the '60s.
66-74	MG	Midget	13	16	14	15	14	72	C	$5,000	$7,500	Appealing entry-level sports car. The '72–74 "round-arch" cars are actually quite pretty.
70-73	Pontiac	Firebird Formula	13	18	17	14	15	77	C	$16,000	$23,000	The market will always find the T/A more desirable. A pity. The twin-hood scoop Formula is the real looker.

Year	Marque	Model	R	B	P	H	F	MR	IG	Low	High	Comments
75–81	Alfa Romeo	Spider 2000	13	16	15	13	11	68	D	$5,000	$8,000	Pleasant sunny-day car let down by diabolical Spica injection, lack of rarity, and rust.
75–79	Alfa Romeo	Alfetta GT	13	15	15	10	6	59	F	$2,500	$4,000	2000 GTV a tough act to follow. Alfa did themselves no favors here. Still SPICA-injected.
72–82	Maserati	Kyalami	18	16	16	10	10	70	C	$16,000	$26,000	A Latin Mercedes 450SL that you can't get parts for. Little reason to seek out one of the 150 built.
79–83	Datsun	280ZX	13	15	15	10	10	63	D	$4,200	$10,000	The first of many insults to the Z. A bloated two-tone disco-mobile compared to the original 240.
83–85	Ferrari	308 GTSi QV	15	17	17	18	12	79	C	$28,000	$45,000	Forever associated with a popular TV show and a pretty decent car by the time of the four-valve injected models.
90–92	Ferrari	348 ts	15	15	17	13	10	70	C	$45,000	$55,000	Dated styling and reliability issues make this one of the least popular Ferraris of recent years.
74–80	Lotus	Elite S1	16	11	15	9	6	57	F	$5,500	$9,000	Inexcusable looks, miserable quality. General Manager David Slama can attest that free may be too expensive.
54–68	Morgan	Plus Four	16	17	15	17	17	82	B	$24,000	$38,000	Prettier, rarer, better performing than an MG TF 1500. Lacks only the name recognition of the MG.
77–80	Rolls-Royce	Silver Shadow II	15	15	13	14	12	69	D	$15,000	$25,000	These stately upper-crust sedans are a maintenance black hole.
83–86	Renault	R5 Turbo	15	14	18	16	6	69	D	$15,000	$20,000	Enormously entertaining. The hottest of '80s hot hatches. Comes at a price. Le Hand Grenade.
88–91	BMW	M3	13	16	18	17	12	76	C	$10,000	$13,000	The first applicaton of Motorsport magic to the 3-series. An edgy, rough performer with real street cred. Revered by many.
77	BMW	630CSi	13	17	16	14	9	69	D	$4,800	$6,400	Lovely Paul Bracq-designed coupe is for the time being just a used car.
77–80	BMW	320i	13	15	14	18	9	69	D	$2,200	$3,600	Hated by many just because it replaced the 2002. Hated by more because with this model BMWs became a fashion accessory.◆